FENG SHUI FLOWERS

"The Tao is called the Great
Mother:
Empty but inexhaustible,
it gives birth to infinite worlds.
It is always present within you.
You can use it any way you want."

Lao Tzu

FENG SHUI FLOWERS

Bringing health, wealth and happiness into your home

Jo Russell

vega

To Chloe and my family

A heart-felt thank you to all those involved in this book: Jamie of the Oriental Garden for his inspiration and warm hospitality; Lisa Betts, our feature florist for her understanding and interpretation of the feng shui criteria; Wayne Riley and Tim Meakin for their designs; Malcolm Watson and Keno Payne for their scholarly help; Jane Alexander for her patience; Andrew Sutterby for his design and art direction; and Derek St. Romaine for his flair with the camera.

© Vega 2002
Text © Jo Russell 2002

ISBN 1-84333-561-1

A catalogue record for this book is available from the British Library

First published in 2002 by
Vega
64 Brewery Road
London, N7 9NT

A member of **Chrysalis** Books plc

Visit our website at www.chrysalisbooks.co.uk

Printed and bound in Slovenia

Acknowledgements

The publisher would like to thank Derek St Romaine for the original photography and for the library photographs used in this book, Paddy Mounter for the artworks, and Chris Bernstein for the index.

The photographs on the pages below are from the Chrysalis library:
Pages 1, 12, 16, 21, 22, 25 (top), 28, 32, 33, 38, 40, 55 (left), 60 (left), 61, 63 (top), 70, 71, 76, 77, 80, 84, 85, 166, 167, 168, 169

Design & Art Direction: Andrew Sutterby
Production: Susan Sutterby
Project management: Jane Alexander

CONTENTS

CHAPTER ONE

FENG SHUI IN CONTEXT

"Nature's richness lies in its power to nourish all living things; its greatness lies in its power to give them beauty and splendour. Thus it prospers all that lives."

Lao Tzu

The Tao

The Feng Shui rules and guidelines in this book are based on the insight and observations of the Tao, or the Way, the wisdom of Ancient China. By fine tuning the natural vibrations of your environment you can create powerful, energizing displays of positive chi, or energy. Through flowers, you can focus this energy on an aspiration, a desire or a dream you have that otherwise may have remained unconscious. Balancing the energies of yin and yang will bring harmony to your environment, clearing the harmful energy that drains concentration and blocks natural vibrations.

The Origin of the Tao

Approximately fifteen billion years ago there was nothingness, a vast emptiness, known as the 'primeval atom' – until the Big Bang occurred. Then a light-creating energy appeared and fused with the vast darkness, which exploded, sending out waves of powerful energy, creating the universe. The vast emptiness divided into two forms of energy capable of generating power. These energies continually rise and decline, one gains power over the other, until, at its zenith, it can only give in to its opposite. These two opposing yet mutually complementary energies are known as yin and yang. They compete for strength but are equal; their efforts cause tension, which inspires change. Together they are unified and through their expressions everything within our world and universe is created and maintained. These concepts were recognized by the Ancient Chinese over five thousand years ago and have remained intact in the age of scientific analysis and nuclear physics.

Above The energy stored through winter in seeds and bulbs is released in a surge of growth in spring.

What is the Tao?

The Tao is the name given to the ultimate force of energy, which encompasses the universe and everything contained within it. The natural vibrations of combined matter and spirit evolve through cycles: this gives form and substance to life as we know it.

The Tao is described as the Way. By following the energy of the Tao we are following the path of least resistance, just as bamboo yields to the wind and water flows around obstacles in its course. To go against the natural vibrations of energy would be to swim against the tide and could lead to premature exhaustion.

The Tao is unbiased; it is both the energy that creates life and the energy that welcomes its destruction. For the Tao allows the process of change and through its practice it is possible to live in harmony with benevolent and prosperous energy, while being mindful of potentially harmful energy.

According to the Tao, spirit and matter are entwined. Taoism is not a religion, rather it is a way of living in harmony with nature. In nature we see

Above *Gentle curves in the landscape generate favourable chi. Here chi will follow the river and meander among the trees.*

birth followed by rapid growth, stability in maturity and then a gradual decline until death and disintegration. This process occurs not only to humans but to all life, including plants. We are part of a universe where everything consists of pure energy holding together atomic matter suspended in space. Galileo discovered that all motion and attempts to prevent motion were a result of force. Energy is an electromagnetic force. It is involved in the interaction of matter: on a macrocosmic scale we see the movement of the planets in the universe and on a microcosmic scale we see atoms vibrate.

All matter is composed of atoms, which are themselves made of electrical particles that vibrate with energy. The vibrations vary in frequency and length depending on the make-up of the object. We can measure these waves, such as radio waves, light waves, x-rays, gamma rays and so on. Though we are aware of the huge spectrum of variable wavelengths that surround us, we cannot physically touch, see, or smell extremely high or extremely low frequencies, but they can influence us profoundly.

Most people can perceive light wavelengths between 0.00007 cm (red light) and 0.0004 cm (ultraviolet). This is just a small percentage of the existing wavelengths. Insects are sensitive to higher frequencies and so are able to read messages from flowers that we are unable to perceive. The ultraviolet markings on a petal, called beelines, are flight paths that help insects collect nectar and cross-pollinate plants. Sadly, the majority of this amazing work is invisible to the naked eye. Yet we are still sensitive enough to respond to the vibrations – just as we cannot see heat but can feel the infrared rays on our skin.

Yin and Yang

The Tao is ultimate energy. It made possible the creation of yin and yang, opposing yet reflecting forms of energy. Everything is composed of yin and yang energy in varying combinations, which are open to change. The dynamics of these two energies are best represented by the well-known tai chi symbol.

Traditionally the black energy represents the receptive and feminine quality of yin, whereas the white is associated with the active and masculine yang energy. The symbol shows that at the most excessive part of either energy there still remains a small amount of the opposite. This maintains balance and harmony, as even in the most extreme periods of yin or yang energy, there still remains another perspective, represented by the dot found in each of the two fishes of the tai chi symbol. It is impossible to have one hundred percent yang or yin energy, as there will always be a percentage of the opposite energy contained within. Equally it is impossible to have one hundred percent perfect feng shui – it simply doesn't exist, which is why balance is so highly respected. With equilibrium, it is possible to act deliberately from a place of calmness; this is much preferred to sudden impulses or reactions made under extreme conditions.

"Everything flows on and on like a river, without pause, day and night."

Confucius

Opposites

It is through the logic of opposites that we are able to differentiate between high and low, fast and slow, hot and cold and so on. This concept is the basis of understanding life. Everything is composed of yin and yang energy, which is never static but constantly evolving. Every day we see clear examples of yin and yang, such as in the pattern of day and night. Dawn represents the beginnings of yang light-giving energy that increases to bring daylight. It peaks at midday and then naturally begins to decline, yielding to the yin energy of night.

Yin and yang energy is not static: even objects that appear unchanging are affected by the motion of opposites. For example, the side of a mountain in

Above right *Sunflowers follow the sun and typify yang chi.*
Left *The snowdrop appears in winter, and is able to flourish despite the powerful yin energy of this season.*

Yin Rooms
Toilet
Cloakroom
Storeroom
Bedroom
Bathroom
Cupboard
Dark room

Yang Rooms
Kitchen
Lounge
Playroom
Study
Reception
Office
Bright room

Tangible and Intangible

The fusion of yin and yang energy can be witnessed in the wonderful variety of nature. Nature provides valuable lessons to inspire us. Every time a seed germinates or a bud bursts open it is following its spiritual potential. Thinking is a yang energetic activity, acting on that thought in the physical realm is a yin activity.

YIN AND YANG ATTRIBUTES

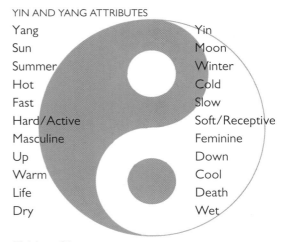

Yang	Yin
Sun	Moon
Summer	Winter
Hot	Cold
Fast	Slow
Hard/Active	Soft/Receptive
Masculine	Feminine
Up	Down
Warm	Cool
Life	Death
Dry	Wet

full sun has more yang energy than the side that is cast in shadow. It is the same mountain, but its ambience differs depending on the position of the sun.

Physical and Spiritual Manifestation

Yin energy relates to the physical world: it lends form to the slowest vibrations. Yang energy is energy in its purest form: it is spirit yet to develop into matter. Thought is a form of yang energy, as are emotions. The most powerful expression of emotional energy is love.

Spirit vibrates at a higher frequency than matter. People are a mixture of yin and yang, so we have a physical body and are empowered with thought and emotions. Feelings are a manifestation of spiritual energy. When we are happy our hearts open and we are able to receive and conduct powerful universal energy. We feel elated when we are happy because we are vibrating at a higher frequency than when we are feeling heavy or down.

Buildings and rooms respond similarly: some rooms contain more yang energy than the quieter yin rooms. Typically the yin and yang rooms are:

Taking Charge

With discipline, we can change the frequency of our internal and external surrounding wavelengths through meditation or focused thought. However, with simple feng shui principles you can enhance the levels of energy within your home and workplace. You can learn to recognize the areas that could be usefully activated and create beautiful feng shui flower cures or enhancers to improve the chi in your environment.

The Three Trinities of Luck

The Tao is One; it gives birth to two forms of energy, yin and yang. Yang is pure energy or spirit and yin is the receptive matter that houses the yang energy, giving it form and substance. From these comes a third form of chi: conscious thought. These three manifestations of chi are known as the Three Trinities of Luck or the Three Great Treasures and they are responsible for the journey that our lives take.

Yin and yang represent earth and the heavens. These two powerful forms of energy constitute two thirds of our luck and destiny. The other force is free will: our actions shape our potential destiny into fate.

Tien Chai: Astrology

Tien chai, or Heaven's Luck, is extremely powerful spiritual energy caused by the motion of the stars in their magnetic fields of energy. Our map of destiny is determined by the position of the stars and planets at the time of birth. A Chinese astrologer can read your map of destiny and establish your levels of good and bad luck and auspicious and inauspicious dates. Tien Chai cannot be altered, as you cannot change your time of birth, but feng shui can help you take advantage of your good luck and ameliorate your bad luck.

Ti Chai: Feng Shui

Ti chai, or Earth Luck, is energy that emanates from the earth and is caused by physical manifestations. It is altered by changes within the landscape and by natural phenomenon. Your perception of life is influenced by the environment you grow up in. Locations with high levels of yang chi are stimulating and active, whereas yin areas are quieter and subdued. You can move or adapt the feng shui of your environment to increase benevolent chi and disperse negative chi.

Ren Chai: Free Will

Ren chai, or Man Luck, is a direct result of thought and action. We all have the ability to make choices, to focus our minds, act with determination and fulfil our ambitions. Opportunities may present themselves, but it is up to us to turn them into tangible results. We can be our own undoing: irrespective of the wealth or poverty of our background, if we do not apply ourselves eventually our creative spirit will wither away. Without spirit the body will cease to survive.

The Symbolism of Money

Chinese coins represent two powerful forces of chi, heaven and earth. The circular shape of the coin, associated with heaven, surrounds and encompasses the central square hole, a shape that symbolizes the reliable earth. When a person uses the coins as currency, the Three Trinities of Luck trilogy is completed. A person's luck is to a certain extent determined by choices made from free will, yet is also influenced by patterns of energy that emanate from nature. The coins represent heaven and earth, but it is up to us to decide on their use.

Above and right *Fresh, moving water and an abundance of plants create auspicious energy in this feng shui garden.*
Left *Coins are powerful symbols of the metal element and prosperity and can be used in flower arrangements as feng shui activators for wealth.*

Wu Hsing: The Five Elements

The Ancient Chinese were acute observers of the natural world. They determined that there are subtle forms of chi other than yin and yang. Based on five elements – wood, fire, earth, metal and water – these forms of energy behave with some predictable characteristics.

The Five Elements

The elemental forces are held in tension, similar to the cycle of yin and yang, that allows change. Each element has strengths and weaknesses: as they interact with each other they create powerful vibrations that have either a positive or negative effect on us and our surroundings. Everything in the universe is composed of energy: yin and yang and the five elements. Their interaction with each other gives life its abundance and diversity. The theory of the five elements is used extensively in feng shui. A simple example of the elements is the comparison between the seasons. Spring, a time of rapid growth, has the elemental chi of wood, whereas the hot sunny climate of summer is associated with fire. At the end of summer we enter a season of harvest, autumn, governed by the metal element. In winter yin energy, governed by the water element, increases. The qualities associated with water are cold, dark and wet. Earth is the transitional element, and governs the time between the seasons.

Below *Chaenomeles flourishes in cool yin conditions.*
Top right *Young leaves typify the rapid growth of spring.*
Right *These arum lilies exhibit all the confidence of summer.*
Below right *Autumn is influenced by the metal element.*

Seasonal Cycles

By living in accordance with the natural order of yin and yang and the five elements we can tap into the universal energy that helps shape our lives. We can predict the peaks and troughs, enhancing the highs and minimizing the lows. Favourable energy becomes auspicious and negative energy is dispersed.

WOOD

The wood element is associated with plants, flowers and trees: without wood we could not produce food or medicine. Wood is associated with the arousing energy of thunder, announcing the oncoming spring.

FIRE

The fire of summer produces the energy that warms the soil and stimulates growth, that allows plants to photosynthesize. The element that is associated with spirit, fire also gives us strength and courage.

EARTH

The earth element is the late-summer energy of ripening crops. The stability of the earth element lends shape and form. The earth element is the transitional element between the other seasons. Earth is the mother: receptive and nurturing, it sustains life.

METAL

The metal element is associated with organization and efficiency; without it crops would not be harvested or properly stored, leading to premature decay. The simplicity of metal encourages harmony.

WATER

The element of water is associated with the cold, dark receptive months of winter, when nature replenishes its depleted energy. Associated with changes occurring beneath the surface, it is the life-giving element: without water the wood element would wilt and die.

WOOD

Known as the growing element, wood represents rapid growth, new beginnings, expansion and expression. It is the element that fuels the fire, nourishing and supporting the spirit. It is a compassionate, caring element and is associated with health and healing, travel and increasing creativity, wealth and prosperity. It vibrates at a frequency that accompanies healing, expression, inspiration and development.

Flowers with Wood Energy

Wood energy is represented by lush foliage, leaves, stems, branches, bark and fruits as well as by flowers. Traditionally the colour most associated with this element is green. Wood flowers are effective when used in the southeast for wealth and prosperity and in the east for addressing health matters and to encourage travel. Place these flowers in the south to increase the chi supporting fame and recognition. Placed in the north they will act as an outlet for chi that has become stagnant or blocked in business. In the west and northwest they have a stimulating effect on relationships.

Wood Attributes

The energy of the yang aspect of this element can be compared to the energy of an established mature tree. It is strong and dominant; on the negative side it can exhibit stubborn behaviour. The yin aspect is more flexible and moderate: it can easily adjust to its environment and has a gentler persona.

Happy wood behaviour is creative, expansive, inspiring, caring and expressive. Unhappy or extreme wood can become jumpy and, if left unbalanced, can accumulate into angry outbursts, or periods of tension. For example, a person who becomes frustrated because of perfectionism is likely to be suffering from an imbalance of wood energy. If the wood energy of your environment is unbalanced, rectifying the problem using feng shui will harmonize the chi of the building or landscape. It will increase the inhabitants' sense of well-being and improve their energy levels.

Wood Associations
Plants and flowers.
Supported by water.
Body: Eyes, liver and limbs.
Colour: Green.
Numbers: 3, 4.
Shape: Rectangle (column/tree trunk).
Directions: East, southeast.
Enhance wood energy: November, December, February, March, June and July.
Most auspicious: November and March.
Avoid excess wood: September and January.

Right *The beautiful peeling bark of the Betula Costa is its most stunning feature and represents yang wood chi.*
Below left *Lush green foliage and dainty flowers radiate the yin aspect of wood energy. This arrangement of herbs also brings healing energy into your home.*
Below *A formal green garden makes full use of wood energy and provides a tranquil setting for contemplation and inspiration. The yew hedge encloses the garden, and contains favourable energy.*

FIRE

Known as the spiritual element, fire represents warmth, joy and happiness and gives us strength and courage. It is the most active, energetic and yang of the five elements, encouraging spontaneity. Associated with the sun, its energy is illuminating; opening the heart is an expression of the fire element. Identified with love, vitality, passion, warmth, courage and determination, too much fire can spark hot tempers, especially during the summer.

Flowers with Fire Energy

Red flowers and exotic flowers from a hot climate have fire energy and are useful in rooms that carry predominately yin energy. The flowers immediately become a focal point and an icebreaker in a cool atmosphere. Red accessories can be used to activate other flower aspirations.

In the south and southwest, these flowers bring chi associated with action, fame, love, relationships and marriage. Fire elemental flowers bring warmth and can melt the hardened metal element – useful if you are having problems expressing yourself or if you have overwhelming chi in the west or northwest.

Fire Attributes

The yang aspect of this element is associated with heat and spirit. Open-minded and straightforward, yang fire makes a powerful public statement. Yin fire energy is gentler; it is sensitive to emotions and represents the caring-sharing aspect of fire. The spontaneous element, fire is useful for drawing attention and for increasing confidence and power.

Happy fire behaviour is romantic, passionate, sexy, spontaneous, warm and energizing. Unhappy fire can become irritable or vulnerable. Left unbalanced it can lead to short temper, vulnerability or nervous disorders.

Fire Associations

Supported by wood.

Body: Blood, brain, heart and nervous system.

Colours: Pink, red and purple.

Number: 9.

Shape: triangular.

Directions: South.

Enhance fire energy: February, March, June, July and May.

Auspicious: February, June and October.

Avoid excess fire: April, August and December.

Weakened: September and January.

Above *A soft, romantic yin fire arrangement of nerines.*
Right *The upward pointing pink ginger flower has all the attributes of yang fire chi.*

EARTH

The element that provides stability, earth provides the boundaries necessary for a contented life. For example, the earth element represents the vase that prevents the water from spilling over the table.

The element that makes possible the union of plant to water, earth grounds and supports us and encourages comfort and relaxation. Supported by fire energy, it gives shape and form to ideas.

Flowers with Earth Energy

Earthy flowers include those in shades of gold and yellow, vibrant orange and indulgent chocolate. The earth element follows naturally from the fire element. Orange and sunny yellow represent happiness, vitality and spontaneity – great for welcoming guests or lifting chi in the entrance. Browns and chocolate nourish the senses and nurture the soul. Earth flowers are compact and encourage grounding and support. Edible flowers are influenced by this element.

Use these flowers in a reception as a focal point to encourage people to feel at ease. In a lounge or conference room they regulate communication and discussion. Earth flowers and accessories are effective activators in the southwest and northeast. They support the chi for concentration, staying power and security. They bring stability to chi in the west and northwest, supporting relationships.

Earth is an effective feng shui cure in the south, where it can tame unfavourable fire chi. To ground unstable energy in business use earth flowers in the north, particularly if the levels of either yin or yang are excessive. These flowers are beneficial if your chi is being drained or if you are feeling low or depressed. In earth arrangements, your accessories can include ceramics, pebbles, crystals, sand and soil.

Earth Attributes

Earth energy nurtures and protects; this element is typically associated with the mother. Earth vibrates at the lower frequencies and gives form and substance to pure energy. It is involved in the processes of digesting information and in bodily digestion.

A transitional element, earth is involved in the processes of death and rebirth. Earth is the receptive element to all matter at the point of death: everything decomposes back into the earth, enriching it. Earth is important for focusing and letting go. It supports the metal element by lending weight to decisions.

Earth Associations

Supported by fire.

Body: Flesh, cells, stomach, spleen and digestive organs.

Colours: Yellow, beige and brown.

Numbers: 2, 5 and 8.

Shape: Square.

Directions: Southwest, centre, northeast.

Enhance earth energy: May, June, July, September, October and January.

Auspicious: January, April, July, October.

Avoid excess earth: February, March, November and December.

Yang earth chi can be compared to the majesty of a mountain: it stands quiet and still, yet commands enough power to dominate the landscape. Hills and mountains were thought to have celestial dragon chi: favourable dragon chi could provide security, protection, wisdom and purity of spirit. Like the nurturing soil, yin earth has a gentle energy. Contented earth energy is happy and settled; it can be centred and wise, receptive and sympathetic. Linked to nourishment, it can be comforting but it can lead to overeating or disorders. Weak earth energy can be supported by increasing the fire or by balancing the earth chi. Excess earth energy results in laziness and requires an outlet such as an increase in the metal element.

Left *A contemporary arrangement of stones adds weight to the design and brings yang earth energy to a garden.*

Above *Yellow flowers in a compact design emphasize the warm, receptive qualities of yin earth energy.*

METAL

Metal represents structure and efficiency. It can be analytical and decisive, is clear and simple and can eliminate the illusions that can cloud our perceptions of reality. Removing misunderstandings, this element inspires harmony.

Metal is associated with mechanical objects such as the workings of a clock, where each part is aware of and works in harmony with its neighbour. Efficient teamwork is ascribed to the metal element.

Flowers with Metal Energy

Representing purity and harmony without hidden surprises, flowers with metal chi encourage clarity and order. These flowers can be arranged simply and should never be fussy. Metal is represented by the colour white: these flowers will enhance the *other* colours in a room and can create a calming presence in an otherwise dominating fiery room. Related to the chi of the heavens, white is reflective and pure.

Metal flowers have overlapping layers of petals, round shapes or curves. They are unparalleled in a classic or elegant situation such as a wedding. Metal flowers can be dramatic: arrange white flowers with a little black to create a strong contemporary image.

Place these flowers in the west or northwest to protect the family, aid networking and promote communication in relationships. To support the career, place these flowers in the north. Calm an overactive fire energy by placing metal flowers in the south. To control spending place a small arrangement in the southeast; in the southwest it will relieve jealousy.

Metal Attributes

The practical element used in networking, accounting and transportation, metal can be clear and precise and is therefore useful in boardrooms and offices. The yang aspect of metal is related to structure and organization. The yin aspect is more concerned with communication, networking, stimulation and finer details. Yin metal is highly attractive, with simple and graceful curving lines, compared to the straight and strong contrast encouraged by the yang metal.

Balanced metal behaviour can be calm, quiet, meditative, clear and precise. When extreme it can become cold, hard, expressionless, and judgmental. A person with weak metal will be full of doubts and indecision and may have difficulties in self-expression.

Above *Flowers with metal chi suit formal and classic designs.*
Top right *The metallic container, white flowers and circular shape all typify yin metal energy and aid communication.*
Right *This arrangement emphasizes straight lines and uses large white flowers for a more yang metal energy.*

Metal Associations

Supported by earth.

Body: Skeleton, skin, hair, teeth and nails.

Colours: White, cream and metallic.

Numbers: 6 and 7.

Shape: Circle.

Directions: West and northwest.

Enhance metal energy: April, May, August, September, December and January.

Auspicious: January, May and September.

Avoid excess metal: February, March, June, and July.

WATER

This element possesses mystical and reflective energy. It can appear very still and settled but, unlike the earth energy of the mountain, it can have deep currents underneath. Water is the element most associated with wisdom, intellect and magic. It is the source element.

The element of water is used in rituals such as cleansing and purification ceremonies. It is symbolic of life: it is absorbed by plants and animals to replenish lost fluids and it transports minerals and nutrients. Water is often associated with communication; it is linked to the magical, intuitive and feminine qualities of the moon and the planet Mercury.

Flowers with Water Energy

Water flowers are cool and quiet as they have more yin than yang energy. Water element flowers are associated with peace and tranquillity and are useful when you want to allow your mind to drift aimlessly, trouble free. Water has the ability to dissolve blocks; when all else fails it moves around them – water follows the flow. It increases communication and replenishes scorched or barren lifeless energy with its hydrating life force. It also promotes prosperity.

Represented by shades of blue, violet, purple and black, these flowers can be dramatic but mostly they are pacifying. They can have intuitive and deeply mysterious associations due to protective and spiritual energy and they promote calm and relaxation.

Placed in the east they are highly beneficial during ill health as they promote rejuvenation and convalescence. They assist prosperity if placed in the southeast. These flowers can be useful cures in the west or northwest if there are tensions building in relationships, particularly family arguments, as they encourage people to talk about their grievances.

Water Attributes

Water is a transitional element – it has no fixed shape or structure and conforms to the boundaries and limitations it finds within its environment. This is very useful when engaged in meaningful conversation. It supports the energy for transporting ideas onto paper; it can release suppressed energy and dissolve blocked chi. It replenishes life and prevents dehydration. Dried flowers are not really recommended as feng shui cures or activators as the communicative energy of water is missing. Without the element of water the arrangement becomes a magnet for dust; the brittle, fragile flowers will attract shar (negative) chi.

The yang aspect of the water element can be described as having the forceful nature of the ocean: vast and powerful, it has deep resources and can be purposeful. In extreme conditions yang water can become unfavourable, such as suddenly becoming impulsive or destructive. Yin water is more gentle and tolerant, with an energy characterized by a drop of dew on a blade of grass or a soft fall of rain.

Water energy can be deep and wise: it represents the intellect and the intuition. It can easily become too deep and lead to overwhelming displays of emotions or even depression. When it is happy it is communicative and free, flowing along with ideas and the system without a care – like a stream it simply moves around potentially destructive obstacles.

Top right *A standard arrangement of cornflowers embraces the energy of yin water, especially with their black centres. Yin water is more sensitive and humble than yang water and encourages us to go with the flow.*
Right *The lotus growing in the blue container, along with the water lilies, carry yang water chi, associated with wisdom.*

Water Associations

Supported by metal.

Body: Kidneys, bladder, fluids and reproductive organs.

Colours: Blue and black.

Number: 1

Shape: Irregular.

Direction: North.

Enhance water energy: February, March, April, May, July, August, September, November, December and January.

Auspicious: April, August and December.

Avoid excess water: June

Feng Shui Time Keeping

Chi generated by the natural formations of the earth is susceptible to change, as it is influenced by the dimensions of time. Feng Shui time keeping is described by the term 'Heavenly Stems and Earthly Branches'.

The stems and branches are an elemental system for marking the influences of the different months of the calendar. There are twenty-two characters altogether, each with a different attribute. The five elemental energies (wood, fire, earth, metal and water) are infused with yin and yang and so create ten subtle characteristics of pure spiritual energy. These are the heavenly stems and represent energy in its purest form. There

are twelve earthly branches, one for each month of the year. The earthly branches can have stored elemental energies trapped inside, which are only exposed during exceptional times, such as a clash or combination from another earthly branch. When the stored elements are released they can provide sudden and unpredictable opportunities or obstacles.

As every year can be marked by an influence of the heavenly stems and earthly branches so too can the months and days of the year. It will take a cycle of sixty years before the same stems and branches are in exactly the same combination again.

Heavenly Stems	Earthly Branches
Yang wood	Rat, yang water, December
Yin wood	Ox, yin earth, January
Yang Fire	Tiger, yang wood, February
Yin fire	Rabbit, yin wood, March
Yang earth	Dragon, yang earth, April
Yin earth	Snake, yin fire, May
Yang metal	Horse, yang fire, June
Yin metal	Goat, yin earth, July
Yang water	Monkey, yang metal, August
Yin water	Rooster, yin metal, September
	Dog, yang earth, October
	Pig, yin water, November

This table is useful when considering which elements are suitable for an occasion such as a birthday surprise, wedding, auspicious day, or ceremony. Choosing the suitable elements for the date in mind will support the earthly branches of that date, which will encourage favourable associations and support sheng (positive) chi.

Left *Bring blossom into the home to celebrate the onset of spring and welcome in the new year. The Chinese favour peach, plum and cherry blossom.*

Above Golden chrysanthemums are considered auspicious as they flower profusely during the autumn, when many other flowers are out of season. Their golden colour symbolizes both the sun and wealth.

The Ancient Chinese devised a feng shui flower calendar thousands of years ago. It is said these blooms are chosen for their harmonious relationship with the chi of a specific month.

February	Peach blossom
March	Peony
April	Cherry blossom
May	Magnolia
June	Wisteria
July	Lotus
August	Pear blossom
September	Mallow
October	Chrysanthemum
November	Winter Gardenia
December	Poppy seed heads
January	Plum blossom

Auspicious Days

According to feng shui, there are auspicious places as well as auspicious times. It is possible to align flower arrangements to specific months of the year and corresponding compass direction, bridging the heaven's luck to the feng shui through deliberate action – this is known as a Three Harmony Combination and is an extremely effective way of encouraging auspicious energy into your environment.

During the auspicious times of the wood element, arrange flowers with this element in mind and use seasonal flowers. For this element choose a selection of foliage and woody stems. Contrast and texture can enhance the yang aspect of this element. Green flowers and petals emphasize the yin aspect of this element, or use plants that are flexible with pliable stems to represent the yin-wood aspect.

The wood element influences the east and the southeast directions. If your entrance or most active (yang) room is found in these sectors it will be sensitive to the wood elemental energy, particularly during November, March and July, when this chi is most auspicious.

An auspicious star for romance is found in the east sector that will respond well to and be activated by a simple vase of pink flowers such as tulips, peonies, calla lilies or roses (with thorns removed to avoid negative chi). The influence of this star is heightened during March.

The fire element rises in energy during February, June and October. If possible, arrange flowers in the southern sector of your home or business to harmonize with this energy. The fire chi can be enhanced with the colours red through to purple. Incorporate candles and atmospheric lighting into the design to further increase the fire chi.

The south sector has a star that is auspicious for success and change and is associated with wild romance and passion. Use flowers that embrace the fire element to enhance this chi and to create a bold display. Creating a focal point during June will be beneficial, as this star is very closely associated with joy and celebrations.

The earth element is receptive to all seasons and periods of the year but it is more powerful during January, April, July and October.

The metal element becomes influential during the autumn and is auspicious during January, May and September. Flowers that are designed with this element in mind will be favourable when placed in the metal sectors (west and northwest). An auspicious star in the west influences romance, harmony and communication. The influence of this star is heightened during September.

To attract chi for knowledge you can choose between the northeast sector governed by the earth

Above *This arrangement encourages family harmony, with the elders symbolized by the lotus seed heads, the children by the lisianthus buds, and the adults by the open blooms.*

element or choose to activate the water element. The water element helps the flow of information.

Placing flowers that emphasize the water element in the north will activate the most auspicious direction to promote careers or business. Placed in the southeast, water element flowers will attract energy associated with wealth and prosperity. This element increases in power during the winter and there is a harmony combination during the months of April, August and December.

An auspicious star in the north sector for the element of water is powerful during December.

Above Bring in a simple vase of lilac from the garden to disperse the heavy chi of winter. Its fresh fragrance will cleanse the atmosphere and lift the spirits.

The Three Harmony Combinations

Auspicious months to use specific elements.

Wood	Mar – Jul – Nov
Fire	Feb – June – Oct
Metal	Jan – May – Sept
Water	Apr –Aug – Dec

There are periods of the year when certain flowers and elements should be avoided, as they will disrupt rather than support the energy waves. There is no cause for alarm as unexpected behaviour can be liberating and stimulating; however, an unexpected surprise or opportunity is one thing, a big shock can be distressing. To eliminate potential problems, it is best to avoid excessive use of certain elements during the Three Shars Period. The table below shows when the elemental chi of the flowers should be limited against the universal chi of the heavens.

THE THREE SHARS

Wood Element Avoid excessive use of the yang aspect of this element during August. Limit the use of the yin wood energy during September. Avoid excessive use of the wood element generally during January.

Fire Element Avoid excessive use of the yin aspect of this element during November. Limit the use of the yang aspect during December. Avoid excessive use of the fire element during April.

Metal Element Avoid excessive use of the yang aspect of this element during February. Limit the use of the yin aspect during March. Avoid excessive use of the metal element during July.

Water Element Avoid excessive use of the yin aspect of this element during May. Limit the use of the yang aspect during June. Avoid excessive use of the water element during October.

An in-depth study of the stems and branches system reveals layers of personality traits and behaviour patterns. Formulas relating to the stems and branches are used not only in advanced levels of feng shui but also when drawing up birth charts in Chinese astrology. Stems and branches relate to time and space and can be used to harmonize relationships with man and his environment. The stems and branches are found within the 24 mountains on a lo-pan feng shui compass.

Celebration Flowers

The flower arrangements and aspirations in this book are examples of the interplay between man and nature, yin and yang energy, the five elements and, where applicable, time, as indicated by the stems and branches. Here we look at some important dates that generate specific chi as well as personal days for remembrance (yin) and days for celebrations (yang) in the Far East and the West.

CHINESE CELEBRATIONS
Chinese New Year

This is one of the most important celebrations of the year in the Chinese calendar and celebrations often last three days. Chinese New Year is exciting! Dragons and dancing lions chase away the doom and gloom of winter with firecrackers and music. Celebrate new

Above *Stems of blossom are often given as gifts at Chinese New Year to bring good fortune throughout the coming year.*

opportunities for the New Year in the house with sprigs of tree blossom. Avoid bringing apple blossom into the house, as this has negative associations according to traditional wisdom in the West. The Chinese favour the ethereal pink and white blossom of the plum or cherry tree.

Ch'ing Ming Festival

Known as the Festival of the Dead, Ch'ing Ming normally falls on 5 April in the solar calendar. It literally means pure and bright and on this day the Chinese sweep and clean the burial tombs of their ancestors. In the northern plains of China it is easy to spot the ancestors' tombs, as they are the only places where trees are not cut down for timber. The willow tree is important to this festival and women and children wrap small pieces of it into their hair. Branches of willow are placed by the side of the tomb to ward off evil spirits and to attract good luck. An auspicious tree, willow is said to attract rain and is used in prayers during droughts.

Duan Wu Jie Festival or Dragon Boat Festival

This festival is celebrated on the fifth day of the fifth month in the lunar calendar, a day traditionally associated with inauspicious energy and so the dragons chase away evil spirits. The day is also associated with the story of Qu Yuan, who served in the court of Emperor Huai (475–221) BCE. He despaired of the continuing wars and threw himself into the Miluo River. Legend states that the people who witnessed his death were so horrified they threw *zongzi* (a special dumpling wrapped in fresh bamboo leaves), eggs and other food into the river to feed the fish while they tried to salvage his body. Ever since, people have remembered the hero Qu Yuan by eating *zongzi*.

Above A dragon sits on a bed of bamboo and orchids, with pussy willow in vases to protect the home from negative chi.

The Moon Festival – Mid-Autumn Festival

This romantic and happy festival is celebrated on the fifteenth day of the eighth month. Legend says that Chang Er flew to the moon, where she remains today. Families celebrate by watching the full moon rise, eating moon cakes and singing moon poems. The moon festival is also for lovers and brings romance and happiness. Celebrate this auspicious time with plants that are sensitive to the rhythms of the moon, such as almond, lotus, mandrake and water lily.

Chong Yang Festival

The Chinese Chong Yang Festival is a happy and joyous celebration, held on the ninth day of the ninth month, which is an auspicious day in an auspicious month. The people often gather for a party, pin leaves of cornus to their clothes and celebrate with chrysanthemum flowers. It is a day to honour and remember

a young man called Heng Jing, who fought with a demon of death and plague and won. First, he made the demon dizzy with the scent of chrysanthemum liquor and cornus leaf and then he fought and finally killed the demon with his sword.

WESTERN CELEBRATIONS
New Year

New Year's Day is observed all over the world. People gather to celebrate the ending of one year and to welcome the chi of a New Year. Flowers can help to maximize auspicious energy. Choose flowers that are bright and bold, or ones that will be impressive and exciting. Suitable flower aspirations with powerful yang chi are Fame and Recognition (page 108), Abundance (page 104) and Congratulations (page 124).

St Valentine's Day

Whether you are giving or receiving flowers on Valentine's Day you are experiencing romance. Traditionally, Valentine's Day is associated with red

Above This bouquet balances the yin and yang aspects of fire energy to suggest passionate love.

roses. Yet imagine how much more exciting it would be to express an individual declaration of love. Choose your Valentine's flowers from the heart, embodying the softness and feminine qualities of yin fire. Choose flowers that encapsulate tenderness and affection – perhaps peonies or roses. Always remove thorns as they encourage the chi for conflict.

Mother's Day & Father's Day

Perhaps there is greater emphasis on flowers with Mother's Day than there is with Father's Day, but it needn't be so. Many traditional designs are available, yet little thought has gone into the energy emanating from the flowers. For both occasions choose flowers that increase the energy for appreciation and love — suitable aspiration designs for this purpose are Thank You (see page 128), Congratulations (suitable for new mothers, see page 124) and adaptations of the Family Harmony bouquet (see page 140).

Easter

In spring the chi of the natural world is stimulated and activated. The sun warms the earth and triggers the growth hormones of plants. Children respond to this energy and enjoy the excuse to dress up and explore the countryside looking for treasure. Nowadays Easter treasure consists of chocolate eggs, but Easter still evokes images of pretty girls in bonnets chasing clues left by the Easter Bunny among the daffodils. Bring the spring energy into the home with cherry blossom, daffodils, tulips and hyacinths.

Memorial Day

This US holiday marks the beginning of the summer season and is often celebrated outside with a barbecue. As summer approaches, daisies erupt over the lawn. Wrap daisy chains around the stems of glasses or napkins for outside parties, or sprinkle this edible flower onto desserts for a fun topping.

Independence Day

Independence Day is an important holiday in America. For a patriotic display, use red, white and blue flowers. Or convey a simple message by using a perfect calla lily or lotus, symbolic of peace. Alternatively, create a bold design that suggests flower fireworks. Suitable flower aspirations for this holiday include Fame and Recognition (see page 108), Congratulations (see page 124) and Abundance (see page 104).

Halloween

Gourds, pumpkins and vines are all bewitching accessories for Halloween. Grinning jack-o-lanterns can be combined with clusters of multicoloured

Above *An arrangement for Halloween uses seasonal flowers to complement the traditional carved pumpkin.*
Above right *Fruit can be added to Thanksgiving displays.*

gourds and cobs of corn. Charm ghosts and ghouls with flowers arranged around the entrance and on window sills. Chinese lanterns make wonderful accessories for a Halloween-themed bouquet.

Thanksgiving

An important American holiday, Thanksgiving is a time to give thanks and to share in the abundance of nature. Elaborate arrangements of gourds and multi-coloured corncobs are used for table decorations and overflowing bowls of fruit are set upon tables laden with food. Set them off with attractive foliage and flowers that enhance the energy of this appreciative time. Suitable arrangements for this holiday are the Abundance (see page 104) and Congratulations (see page 124) aspirations. Incorporate fruit into your design: oranges are especially favoured in feng shui and are believed to draw money into the house.

Christmas

The winter festive season can be commemorated with flowers. Aromas such as pine, clove, orange and cinnamon are traditional Christmas scents and pine cones, dried oranges and bunches of cinnamon can be incorporated into Christmas wreaths of evergreen leaves. Keep holly leaves away from a table display or a feng shui flower arrangement, as the sharp points of the leaves are not harmonious to family gatherings.

Understanding Feng Shui

Feng shui is the term given to the harnessing of natural energy emanating from the land. Natural energy or chi can be benevolent or malevolent. It can strike without warning, like a sudden spring thunderstorm; equally it is the gentle breeze that wafts the scent of summer blossoms in from the garden.

Our environment has an enormous influence on our health and well-being. We can choose to change the way we live, but we may be unaware of how our homes and working environments are affecting us.

Feng shui is the practice of living in harmony with nature. It recognizes pockets of energy that exist in the landscape and within buildings. It strives for balance between yin and yang and the five elements. Feng shui can also be used to enhance certain aspects of our lives, to enrich the chi that may be missing or weakened by other external factors. The wisdom of feng shui and the Tao applies to each and every situation and environment: a home on a mountain, the twist of a leaf or the smoothness of a stone – each can be described in terms of yin and yang and the five elements.

Encouraging positive energy into the home will increase benevolent energy, encourage opportunities, benefit your health and promote harmonious relationships. It will also reduce the risk of malevolent energy attacking the self, family, friends and colleagues.

Just as nature expresses itself by combining yin and yang and the five elements in an infinite variety, so we express ourselves through our behaviour and emotions. Feng shui allows us to recognize and then balance the chi in our environment. We can apply cures and enhancers with flowers, activating chi to encourage happiness and well-being. Flowers are one of the most beautiful expressions of nature: the sheer diversity of colour, scent and texture is dazzling.

Feng Shui and Flowers

Flowers have long been an accepted medium to raise the spirits or ambience of a room. Normally, bouquets of flowers are arranged to be aesthetically pleasing, yet little emphasis is given to the meaning behind the action – that is saved for the tiny card accompanying the bouquet. Most of us send and receive multi-purpose bouquets suitable for any occasion. Yet compare a bouquet put together without thought to an artistic concoction of scent, colour, texture and heart-felt meaning that will capture the imagination and show the sincerity of the person behind each curling petal and twisted leaf. Imagine how much stronger the influence would be if each flower in the bouquet was carefully chosen for a particular intention or aspiration.

"The scientist's religious feeling takes the form of a rapturous amazement at the harmony of natural law."

Einstein

When creating feng shui flowers, the intention is to cultivate precious fields of energy, to condense and focus the chi for activating an aspiration or achieving balance. The flowers become an expression of our wants and desires. Once created, the arrangement can be placed in a favourable direction according to the chi of the environment. The auspicious energy will accumulate and gather momentum. By spending time in the room with the arrangement, we naturally absorb these positive vibrations, thus increasing favourable energy and reducing the possibility of responding to the negative aspects of our lives.

Right *A contemporary display uses Chinese paper lanterns as colourful containers to brighten a stagnant sector.*

CHAPTER TWO

COMMUNICATION THROUGH FLOWERS

*"Yet through the gentle use of the senses
we can experience joy on the earth plane,
encounter beauty, develop sensitivity and
discrimination. With right use of the senses
we know the immanence of spirit in matter."*

Henrich S Ripszam

The Benefit of Flowers

Nature has the ability to reach deep into our subconscious in ways that remain mysterious. One way of unravelling these secrets is to apply natural resources with feng shui principles.

Feng shui has been portrayed as a complicated and lengthy process, yet it needn't be. Levels of positive energy can be increased immediately by using fresh and inspiring flowers. What other manifestations of nature have such variety, expression and benefit? The unfurling of each petal is an individual expression of beauty. The seductions of a candid lily bud, releasing heady scent from fragrant stamens, can stir memories of summer afternoons just as powerfully as the scent of cinnamon bark can conjure images of Christmas.

Flowers respond to universal energy seemingly without the complications that beset humankind. Their life cycles are in accord with the seasons and the natural resources around them. Spring is a mark of their courage and strength as daffodils, crocus, snow-drops and hyacinths push away the debris of winter. Their message is clear – wake up! Plants and flowers mark the seasons, following their silent potential, and provide us with commodities crucial for our survival. Offering themselves freely for food, medicine and communication, flowers ask for nothing in return.

Flowers are as essential to healthy living and well-being as vegetables: we just absorb the energy in a different way. With such an abundance of flowers you can change the atmosphere of a room purely by harnessing their subtle but potent energy.

Flower Personalities

Have you ever wondered at the personality of spring tulips? Initially they command attention as they stand upright with their heads poised proudly; later you find them sprawling, drenched in shafts of sunlight, the stems twisting to catch the final drops of sun. They are in harmony with the surrounding energy: at first active and alert, as the day passes and the chi changes they respond by yielding, softening and relaxing.

The happy, sun-seeking sunflower also has a strong personality. As its head stretches up to follow the movements of the sun this flower communicates joy. Mistletoe and roses are entwined in legends of love, and the poppy has a reputation for magic and helps us remember those who have passed on.

Flowers aren't static, they're an operative force and respond to atmospheric changes. They interact and play with levels of light and temperature, moving

Left and right *Ikebana make excellent feng shui activators, and bring the vibrant energy of plants into your living space.*

and swaying either way. They can glow or they can cast shadows; at times they can be translucent and luminous, at others they can appear robust and hearty. The mood of your flowers can vary as much as the spectrum of colours. Strong stems combined with compact flowers make a dramatic impact, whereas sweeping lines suggest a feminine elegance. Trailing flowers, especially in whispers of powder blue and lilac, soften edges and calm strenuous chi.

Ikebana

Ikebana is a Zen style of flower arrangement that strives for simplicity and naturalness. Ikebana strives to represent heaven, earth and consciousness, otherwise known as Lao Tzu's Three Great Treasures, or the Three Great Trinities. The flowers are chosen and arranged in a state of concentrated awareness, acting in the here and now.

Space is an important criteria in any flower arrangement – ikebana, feng shui or otherwise. Space is an ingredient as much as flowers; it allows the arrangement to breathe and simplifies the message of the flowers, making the final arrangement uncomplicated and harmonious. Flowers packed tightly together run the risk of clutter and overcrowding.

Choosing flowers can be approached as a meditation; carefully consider each stem, petal and flow of line. Go slowly, for rushing is not a Zen quality: it suggests your mind is distracted. Meditate on each aspect of the plant, create structure and shape and allow the chi to flow and the eye to follow. Once picked, treat flowers with the special care you would give to a friend. Though no longer connected to the ground they are still very much alive and willing to fulfil their potential – to radiate the atmosphere with their charm and beauty. Careless handling is surely neglectful.

"Man by nature inherits the love of flowers."
Maund

Healing Flowers

Plants and flowers provide us with food and clothing and the medicinal value of plants is recognized in every country of the world. Flowers are used in pharmaceutical drugs: for instance, digitalis, a derivative of foxglove, is used to treat heart conditions. A cut, burn or sting can be immediately treated with the gluey sap from a leaf of aloe vera, while plants such as tea tree have powerful antiseptic properties. Plants promote the healing process of just about every kind of ailment you can think of, from snake bite to depression.

Chinese doctors treat the source of the problem and not the symptoms by looking at the overall balance of the body and emotions. They use herbs as a quick and effective way of restoring balance.

Flowers express beauty, wisdom and power and in the past flowers were seen as symbols for these attributes. Flowers were associated with the stars and planets and with deities, indicating what an important place flowers held in our history. People who knew the properties of plants were held in the highest regard. Indeed, herbal medicine forms the foundation of the medicine we receive today.

Edible Herbs

In Europe herbalism established a reputation as an effective method of healing. Herbalists understood the natural secrets of holistic healing and knowledge of the properties of herbs would often be passed down through the generations by word of mouth. Unfortunately this approach encouraged a level of distrust and fear in the community. Many herbalists were women who seemingly possessed great healing powers, and some people felt threatened. In 1484 the *Malleus Maleficarum* was published, which detailed ways of identifying a witch and during the subsequent witch hunts some precious information regarding the healing properties of herbs and plants was lost.

Thankfully, herbs were regarded highly for their flavour and the herb garden became a valuable part of the kitchen garden. Gradually, plants were disassociated with magic and instead studied scientifically, eventually leading to medicinal breakthroughs and advancements.

Not all the knowledge of the spiritual value of plants has been erased. Flowers are still highly valued in aromatherapy and homeopathy and are used to make flower remedies and herbal tinctures. Together they can treat a wide variety of physical and psychological ailments.

Herbs can usefully be grown on window ledges, and as well as being unsurpassed in the kitchen they can provide valuable assistance as insect repellents. The most popular herbs to discourage insects are garlic, chives, fennel and basil. Plant these herbs

Above *St John's wort, called the 'herbal prozac', is also a valuable homeopathic remedy for the nervous system.*
Right *The common Viola Odorata is a useful herb.*
Below right Pulsatilla vulgaris, *a useful homeopathic remedy.*
Below left *A pretty arrangement of edible and healing herbs.*

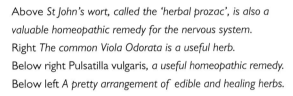

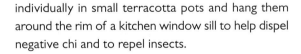

individually in small terracotta pots and hang them around the rim of a kitchen window sill to help dispel negative chi and to repel insects.

Homeopathy

Homeopathy is one of the most popular forms of alternative medicine. Some of the most common homeopathic remedies are derived from flowers. Pulsatilla, the meadow anemone, is used to treat colds and boosts the immune system. Aconite or monkshood provides a valuable remedy for fever and shock. *Hypericum perforatum* (St John's wort) is a homeopathic treatment for jangling nerves and is well-known herbally as an anti-depressant. Many plants used in homeopathy are extremely poisonous: never pick a plant without identifying whether it is harmful.

Left *Lavender essential oil is soothing and relaxing.*
Above *Digitalis, a valuable pharmaceutical medicine for the heart, was originally extracted from the common foxglove.*
Right *Herbs thrive in pots: even a window box can provide herbs for the kitchen and to include in feng shui aspirations.*

Aromatherapy

Aromatherapy uses essential oils to heal the body, mind and spirit. Essential oils are extracted from flowers, herbs and resins, their energies concentrated into a tiny bottle. Essential oils should never be applied directly to the skin; dilute them in a carrier oil before using for massage or adding to a warm bath. Undiluted oils can be vaporized in a burner.

The oils can change the mood of a room just as easily as they influence the spirit of a person. Your favourite essential oils can be incorporated into your feng shui flower arrangements or used on their own. Clary Sage (*Salvia sclarea*) is a powerful antidepressant and promotes a feeling of well-being. It can be a tonic and has balancing and restorative properties. Clary sage is yang and can induce calmness and sedation. It blends well with rosemary and ylang ylang oils.

Another favourite essential oil used for its uplifting and rejuvenating qualities is Rosewood (*Aniba rosaeodora*). When blended with base oil and rubbed into the skin it acts as anti-ageing oil, stimulating the cells and regulating the tissues. This oil is said to have aphrodisiac properties and clears the mind and calms the nerves. Rosewood blends well with geranium, tangerine and ylang ylang.

Flower Remedies

Dr Edward Bach believed that illness on the physical plane was a manifestation of a profound illness of the emotional or mental plane. After twenty years of research he pioneered flower remedies as a means of treatment. His 38 remedies have been widely used to improve the well-being of the mind and body. Perhaps his best known essence is Rescue Remedy, a combination of cherry plum, clematis, Star of Bethlehem, impatiens and rock rose. It is an excellent remedy for anxiety, stress and shock.

Spiritual Associations of Flowers

Flowers are enshrined with meaning in our folk tales and in our religious customs. Using flowers with specific symbolism in your feng shui arrangements can add depth of meaning.

Some flowers have powerful historical associations with birth, death, marriage and ceremonies. Other flowers are said to possess magical powers – many cultures believe that specific flowers are gifts from the gods and should be treated as such.

The Symbolism of Flowers

Flowers such as bamboo, lilac and gardenia are associated with strength and virility and are believed to increase personal power. Other flowers, such as plum blossom, are believed to bestow their gifts only during auspicious times.

Jasmine is frequently used in Hindu shrine offerings and a mixture of marigold petals and rose petals are thrown at the feet of Hindu couples during wedding ceremonies to ensure their happiness and prosperity.

For the Chinese, the peony is a symbol for good fortune, wealth and happiness and is associated with the goddess of love. The chrysanthemum is said to possess magical properties that promote health and longevity. In China it is said that wise men pick the flower of the chrysanthemum. Chrysanthemums clean toxins from the atmosphere: they effectively absorb pollutants and synthetic fumes emitted by carpets and soft furnishings as well as reducing the electromagnetic fields from electrical equipment.

The marigold has an unusual history. In parts of Mexico it is associated with death; it is said that marigolds grew where the blood of Indians killed by Spanish invaders touched the earth. The marigold is also used as an offering to the Aztec goddess of the land of the dead, Xochiquetzal. She was the goddess of all aspects of love, including marriage, of change and magic, fun and dance – she is symbolized with a dove and a marigold.

Rosemary was sacred to the Ancient Greeks and Romans, who considered it a symbol of rejuvenation. It was believed that a sprig of rosemary kept behind the ear would stimulate the brain and would increase levels of concentration and memory. In the past sprigs of rosemary were carried by mourners during a funeral and thrown onto the coffin to prevent the spread of disease. It is said that a rosemary tonic can be used to treat hair loss and baldness.

Sandalwood has powerful spiritual associations. Growing as an evergreen tree in India, it is still used to make incense and furniture and in temple buildings. Sandalwood is often burnt at funerals and during Indian weddings to bless the union. Used as an offering to shrines, it is believed to encourage acceptance, self-expression, and peace. The Ancient Egyptians used sandalwood during the embalming process.

Ylang ylang is a seductive flower with strong emotional and sexual connections. In Indonesia ylang ylang petals are scattered across the beds of newlyweds. It is an antidepressant and an aphrodisiac.

Traditionally, camomile is an auspicious flower, with powerful abilities for attracting and sustaining love. In the past, young maidens would wash their hair in water infused with camomile flowers and would sprinkle camomile tea onto the sheets of their beloved to encourage passion! It is said that a sprig of camomile hung on a baby's crib will ward-away evil spirits. Camomile tea soothes the nerves and makes a wonderfully relaxing bedtime drink.

Above right Flowers can honour your path, whatever spiritual tradition you follow.

The Lotus

The lotus is sacred to Buddhists and Buddha is often depicted sitting on a lotus. The lotus flower symbolizes the beauty and courage of energy that begins life in dark and murky depths, engulfed in water. As the plant matures, its buds break the surface of the water and gently open in the presence of light, providing beautiful sculptured flowers. Since it closes its flower at sunset and reopens it at dawn, it is an ancient symbol of light. The lotus was also sacred to the Ancient Egyptians, associated with the creation of life and appearing often in temple architecture. In Hinduism the lotus is the symbol of Lakshmi, goddess of beauty, wealth and happiness. Confucius remarked that the purity of the lotus rising from the muck and muddy water was symbolic of the 'superior man'. Lotus flowers or seed heads are said to promote good fortune in the home or business.

CHAPTER THREE

APPLYING THE PRINCIPLES

*"Open yourself to the Tao,
then trust your natural responses
and everything will fall into place."*

Lao Tzu

The Thought Behind the Action

The art of living happily is a responsible one. It is not idleness or succumbing to desires that will make us happy, nor will isolation from the material world give instant enlightenment. However, we can become more aware of our relationship to our surroundings, and as our levels of perception and understanding expand we can take greater control of our own destiny.

Before embarking on a life-altering exercise, give yourself plenty of time and space for thought. Applying feng shui to flowers is quick and effective, achieving maximum results with minimum effort – providing the thought behind the action is sincere. When considering which aspiration you would like to activate or when addressing the overall quality of chi in your environment, start by consciously removing distractions from your mind. Recognizing and improving sectors of energy in your life is serious business, and it is advisable to give each aspiration or room as much attention as possible. The more love, care and focus you generate, the greater your rewards will be.

Be practical with size and shape, and do not be inclined to activate too many aspirations all at once, as sudden and dramatic changes will be disruptive initially – it is better to make gradual improvements that grow over time. When sending feng shui flowers as gifts for others, consider their character. Personalize the flowers by choosing an appropriate aspiration, or use the stems and branches table (see page 26) to choose flowers that are sensitive to their birthdays.

Clear Intentions

Often we are disappointed when a situation doesn't meet our expectations. There could be a number of reasons behind our disappointment, yet we should always be aware of thought, action and consequences.

A percentage of the responsibility for an outcome is always ours; perhaps we were distracted or our intentions were unclear. When experimenting with feng shui flowers, begin with a clear intention, never rush or force anything as it only serves to cloud your judgement. Keep your intention focused as you choose the flowers, and allow that energy to flow into the arrangement as you place each stem. Complete your intention by placing the flowers in their designated sector, thereby activating the aspiration and the process of accumulating sheng (positive) chi.

Aspirations and Intentions

We all have ambitions, goals and desires. We all want to improve our love life, get rich, achieve harmony in the home, be more assertive/successful at work, or lose weight. This book has been written to help you identify and *achieve* your aspirations.

Activating aspirations (yang) is as much a part of Taoism as yielding to force (yin). Both are part of the same rhythm of nature. To begin with, there is a yin aspect, which requires a period of quiet stillness and real honesty. Look deep inside to determine which aspect of your life you would most like to change. This process can be greatly enhanced with deep breathing or with exercises such as yoga or tai chi, which gather chi, aid concentration and open the chakras (energy centres of the body). The spirit will settle and the mind clear as distractions gradually melt away. The final acts of designing and arranging the flowers provide an outlet for chi, and represent a bridge between the spiritual realm and physical reality.

Feng shui techniques are tried and tested formulas that have been used by the Chinese for thousands of years. They help you to achieve an aspiration by activating the corresponding areas of your contained

Above *This simple arrangement would bring yin metal chi to a room, encouraging a sense of peace and harmony.*

space, according to the elemental directions found on the bagua. Chi is able to grow and gather momentum. The high frequency of radiating energy will be absorbed into your body and into the room during the life span of the flowers. The positively charged atmosphere connects to pure universal energy, ultimately connecting you to your dreams and desires and re-creating them in a physical form. This process can be speeded up considerably by opening your chakras. Just be careful what you wish for – it might just happen!

Thought and Emotion

Every time you spend time with an arrangement of feng shui flowers, or even pass by, you are reminding yourself of your aspiration and that you are ready to accept the changes necessary to enable you to achieve your desire. This prompting is enough. Then let go and act only when the opportunity presents itself and never with excessive force – this discipline is known as wu-wei.

We spend most of our time and energy pursuing security, maintaining reputations or just coping with daily demands. Often we try to squeeze as much as possible into our busy schedules, and often become frustrated and demoralized. Frequently we are over-stimulated; our energetic patterns are constantly disrupted. If we push ourselves beyond reason, eventually we become strained and vulnerable to exhaustion and disease. We squander the important yin pursuits, such as resting and relaxing, which are vital if we are to remain alert and function fully.

Living under harsh conditions will affect our lives as we harden our attitudes. Conversely, if we are indul-gent we will eventually become spoiled. Ideally we should live in an area that suits our personality. A home or workplace should provide ample but not extreme levels of yang chi, balanced with calming yin energy to aid rest and rejuvenation. By slowing down and opening our awareness to the bountiful world that surrounds us, we are able to unify the yin and yang of our professional and personal worlds.

We can learn to cultivate our internal energy or spirit and increase our well-being by following simple Taoist disciplines such as abdominal breathing,

"A journey of a thousand miles begins with a single step."
Taoist proverb

on the lungs. Pulling chi into the abdominal area is known as breathing into the *dan tian*, an important energy centre known as the furnace. The very act of breathing is a portrayal of the relationship between yin and yang energy. The rising and descending of the breath is like a bellows that sustains the fire chi of the spirit.

The body is an energy field and the meridians (energy channels) transport chi, connecting the energy centres of the body (chakras). When energy is able to flow freely, we fulfil our potential but when energy lines are blocked and chi stagnates, our vitality decreases and we may eventually become sick. Practising deep breathing, meditation, tai chi or yoga increases our strength and sensitivity and allows us to experience the movements of universal chi within the body. True awareness of the body, the environment and the relationships we have with the outside world opens us to the Tao. Living in harmony with these forms of energy will strengthen and cultivate vital fields of energy, increasing our good fortune.

wu–wei and exercises such as tai chi or yoga. These techniques will increase your awareness of energy, both in your body and in your surroundings.

Feng Shui for the Body

Tai chi and yoga are tried and tested methods for balancing the yin (body) and yang (mind). Both incorporate deep breathing. These exercises dissolve distractions, gather and cultivate chi, calm the mind and energize the body. There are many other forms of exercise and meditation that can also help, but tai chi and yoga are both suitable for a modern lifestyle.

All spiritual exercises and meditations stress the importance of the breath. Deep breathing, or abdominal breathing, uses the diaphragm to draw slow deep breaths into the body while shallow breathing focuses

Wu-Wei

The Taoists call the process of cultivating chi and vital essences wu–wei. It literally means non–being or non–doing. This term really should not be taken out of context, as the true meaning is to remain calm, centred and still among the chaotic and disrupted external world. Practising wu–wei means to concentrate your potential until the right time for action. When this time presents itself, and it always will, you are prepared, nurtured and ready for action. Like a bulb under the ground in winter, you cultivate your energy and wait for the natural season to arrive before opening into your full glory.

The Ancient Chinese embraced the importance of the right action at the right time. They saw limitations as useful vessels to contain potential and cultivate precious energy. Their ambition was to remain centred in spite of the highs and lows of daily life.

Realism and Disillusionment

When preparing to change the energy inside your room or building you should be mindful of realistic expectations. We can overindulge our imagination, undermining an aspiration with quite unrealistic expectations. If we are unable to distinguish between fantasy and reality we cannot gather our scattered chi and take advantage of the opportunities that come our way. Should we press on regardless, we may eventually obtain the desired results through sheer force, oblivious to how we got there and worried about maintaining our position.

We have become accustomed to a competitive and hostile world. With our hectic lifestyles we often find ourselves bombarded with deadlines, distractions and anxieties. Our recreational time can be stressful: we may counteract stress with competitive sports and for entertainment we watch violent television programmes. This distracts us from the natural rhythms of life and blocks access to universal chi. It is overstimulating and we waste precious time, miss opportunities and do not reach our true potential.

Macro–Scaling

Throughout recorded history we see the rise and fall of ancient civilizations; their power rises to a peak and then we see a downward spiral that leads to their eventual downfall. A chaotic world is not unique to the twenty-first century. Throughout humankind's existence on earth, he has been hindered by the events caused by the dynamic reactions of yin and yang. The peaks and troughs of events are a part of us, just as much as the air we breathe and the water we drink. We are unable to prevent the interplay of yin and yang, however hard we may try.

Micro–Scaling

Changing our attitude from denigrating nature to embracing its harmony is a very real and positive step towards a brighter future. Applying Tao to flowers is

Left A single black parrot tulip prevents negative yin chi from accumulating in a stagnant corner.

an initial, positive and active way of enjoying the benefits of nature. Flowers can enhance the feng shui of your home or business. Act with deliberate firmness and treat your aspirations seriously. Construct the bouquet with care, mindful of each flower, focusing your energy with purpose.

"Successful people are economical in their actions and careful about time. Time is hard to come by and easy to lose."

The Masters of Huainan

Increasing your Luck

This book shows you how to clear energy lines of harsh or negative chi; to identify and refresh stagnant areas of your life and environment with living and creative energy and to recognize those periods that require action and those that require stillness. This is the Way of the Tao, of living in harmony with our surroundings and with the natural order of the world.

For example, imagine that your mind and thoughts are a flowerbed. Should the soil (conscious thought) be littered with toxins, waste, stones and rubbish, we can safely assume that not much will grow – not helpful if we need to provide food to feed ourselves and our families. However, even if we were challenged with a barren land in which to plant our ideas, we can, through careful thought and deliberate care and attention, prepare and nurture the soil in which to plant the seeds of potential ideas.

We can nurture our ideas daily, to check their development. Have they germinated or are they already prospering and growing healthily? Perhaps we neglected them in favour of something else, only to find that, starved of care during the precious early stages of development, they have suffered from wilt,

Above *A gold-sprayed pot transforms a simple arrangement into a potent feng shui activator to encourage wealth.*

or even lost the heart to survive. Equally, if we were to force our seedlings into rapid growth and then transplant them into a hostile environment before they were strong enough to cope, it wouldn't be a big surprise to see them flounder and fail.

It is possible to act from a space that enables us to apply ourselves with a focused intention, applying just the right amount of energy at just the right time without the need of excessive force or violence. Then we are able to achieve our desired results with a minimum of effort.

Feng Shui Principles

Success with feng shui depends on following rules that have evolved over thousands of years. These guidelines are tried and tested methods of maximizing benevolent energy.

There are many feng shui schools and formulas and many more are guarded in secret. Some of the schools conflict with one another but this book reduces confusion by highlighting the basic ground rules. These simple rules, plus clear intentions and sincerity, are all that is necessary to reap results from feng shui flowers.

The Elemental Relationships

One of the most important formulas for harnessing and utilizing energy is the formula of elemental cycles. Through careful observation through the ages, the Ancient Chinese recognized two energetic patterns that occur time and time again. These two dynamic movements, known as the Cycles of Elemental Birth and Destruction, affect the five elements directly.

Constructive Cycle

The constructive cycle shows the birthing or supportive cycle, where each element has the ability to give birth to its neighbouring element, beginning with the energetic pattern of fire. The diagram shows that the earth element naturally follows the fire element, as once fire has exhausted its supply of fuel (wood) it turns into ash (earth). When the earth is compacted and put under pressure it condenses minerals into metal ore (metal). When a metallic substance is placed under intense pressure, such as high heat (yang), it becomes a liquid. Equally, in extreme cold (yin) metal will attract condensation (water). Water has the ability to nourish life (wood) – without water we would quickly die. Wood has the ability to fuel the fire, just as food replenishes flagging energy levels.

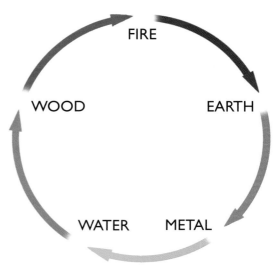

Destructive Cycle

Just as there is a birthing cycle or constructive cycle of the elements, so is there an opposite cycle. Instead of supporting, increasing and giving birth to an element, the destructive cycle of elements reduces, suppresses and eventually destroys the chi of another element. For instance, fire will cause a rigid metal

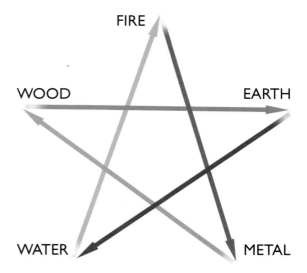

Above A vase of garden flowers on a window sill helps prevent an external poison arrow from disrupting the home. Right A single red anthurium represents yang fire chi and could raise the frequency of an otherwise yin room.

object to weaken. Metal has the power to cut into wood and wood has the strength to break up and absorb the nutrients from the earth. Earth can spoil clean water, and water can quickly extinguish a fire.

Applying the Cycles

We need to understand both elemental cycles to improve the chi in any given area. For example, if your house is facing south, it is influenced by the elemental fire energy. You could enhance this energy with the constructive cycle by supporting the fire energy with red accessories, red plants and lighting. An effective and natural way of creating harmony would be to add plants and flowers as this would support wood, the element that gives birth to fire.

If you live in a south-facing building where the yang energy is overwhelming, such as in a busy street, you would instead consider using the destructive cycle of elements, to ground the impulsive and exhausting fire

chi. The earth element is useful here – containers of low-growing yellow flowers set amongst a cluster of stones will draw negative chi away from the entrance and down towards the receptive earth, neutralizing potential harm. The metal element is also useful to calm excitable or uncontrolled fire chi. Use gentle flowing curves and white, cream and silvery colours to reflect away the intensity of fire, preventing it from harming the home.

These principles can be applied to every element, direction, building, room and even, on a smaller scale, to a bouquet of flowers. The bagua identifies the elemental energy that applies to each sector of your home.

Bagua & Lo–Shu

The bagua or pa–kua literally means eight sides or eight numbers; it derived its magical associations through the arrangement of trigrams.

Discovering the Trigrams

Around 3000 BCE the great sage Fu Hsi invented the concept of the trigrams. The trigrams represent his interpretation of how yin and yang and the five elements interrelate with man and natural phenomena. A trigram consists of three layers of lines that are combinations of yin and yang.

A broken line represents yin energy, an unbroken line represents yang energy. Altogether there are eight possible trigrams. Each trigram is a representation of natural phenomena. Fu Hsi arranged the trigrams into a sequence known as the Early Heaven Arrangement, an arrangement that is said to generate protective power as a talisman in feng shui cures and rituals. Much later, King Wen rearranged the trigrams to apply the logic of man's existence on the earth. This sequence of trigrams created the bagua, which means eight diagrams or sectors.

TRIGRAMS AND NATURAL PHENOMENON

Heaven
Three yang
lines

Water
Yin bottom line,
middle yang line and top yin line

Earth
Three yin lines

Fire
Yang bottom line with yin line
in centre and yang line on top

Wind
Yin line on bottom with
two yang lines on top

Thunder
Bottom yang line with
two yin lines on top

Mountain
Yang line on top with two
yin lines on bottom

Lake
Two yang lines on bottom
with one yin line on top

Left In the tai chi symbol, black represents feminine yin
energy and white represents masculine yang energy.
Yin always contains an element of yang and yang always
contains an element of yin, represented by the dots.

Bagua and Associations

The bagua recognizes patterns of energy and their corresponding relationships and associations; these appear around the tai chi symbol, and include the trigrams, numbers, directions and many more associations. Each side of the bagua will have an element and corresponding aspiration. Using the eight sectors of the bagua as a guide it is possible to place beautiful arrangements of flowers in the appropriate parts of your home or business to enhance the elemental chi found there. In addition, by combining careful thought and planning with intention, we realize opportunities as and when they appear.

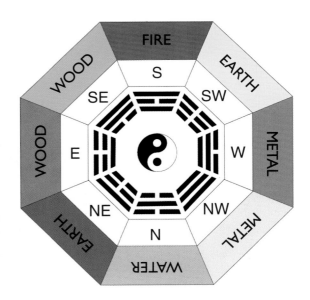

"Tao is like the ocean.
All rivers run to the ocean without
filling it up.
All water comes from it without ever
emptying it."
Zhun Mang

Aspiration Sections of the Bagua

An understanding of the bagua is essential to comprehend feng shui. Each sector or side of the bagua is associated with a direction, an element, a trigram and an aspiration. These aspirations form the basis for the feng shui flower arrangements in this book.

The sectors of the bagua can be used as a template over the floor plan of your house, or over your room if you decide to energize one room only. Use the bagua to decide your feng shui requirements when wishing to energize a part of your home, activate an aspiration or for choosing the relevant colours, shapes and textures for a feng shui bouquet.

South: Fame and Recognition

The south is the most yang and dynamic of all the directions and is represented by the fire element. It requires nourishment from the wood element to function continually, so incorporate lush foliage into designs for favourable results. The number nine represents this sector – an auspicious number. Red, pink and purple flowers are most associated with this element, but coral, terracotta and burgundy all carry fire chi, as does vibrant orange. The flowers should be bold, striking and angular. Avoid spikes, thorns or sharp edges, as they are associated with poison arrows. Incorporating atmospheric lighting and candles into your flower arrangements is auspicious in the south.

Southwest: Romance and Marriage Harmony

This sector is represented by the earth element and provides powerful nurturing and receptive energy, symbolizing the devotion of the great mother or mother nature. This is the sector most associated with love and so will be nourished by the chi of yin fire, a soft and romantic energy. Flowers that can support this sector

will range from earthy colours such as gentle yellows and browns to shades of pink. Incorporate crystals into your arrangements, especially rose quartz or golden topaz, to increase the positive vibrations. If you do use

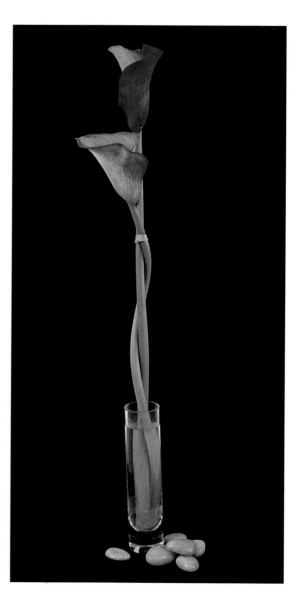

crystals, avoid yang wood (branches) in the bouquet. Ceramic containers also will benefit the chi of this direction. Keep the design simple and balanced. This sector is associated with the number two, so you could use two small arrangements side by side, one concentrating on female qualities (soft colours and trailing

Below left *The yin earth/fire chi of the calla lilies entwined together encourage intimacy when placed in the southwest. The stones represent the earth element and add weight.* Below *The clean lines of this yin metal arrangement support networking skills and open communication. The flowers are connected to each other to emphasize this.*

flowers) and the other on yang energy (bold and showy flowers). Keep the pair in harmony by using the same vases and use at least one flower common to both.

Above *This soft white and green arrangement supports harmonious relationships, suited to the west or northwest.* Below right *A simple career enhancer emphasizes the water element and supports it with single white metal chi flowers.*

West: Children and Projects

Represented by the metal element, this sector governs aspects of our lives concerning order, efficiency and discipline. It is most associated with communication, children and initiating projects. The metal element can be cool and rigid; it is the element that encourages harmony and the chi to make simple but firm decisions. Earth and other metal elements support the west. Flowers that contain the chi associated with the metal element tend to have smooth and graceful lines and textures and are elegant and sophisticated. A white calla lily is a perfect example of a flower with metal chi. Other than white, earth shades of yellow, terracotta and brown support the west.

Incorporating stones, crystals and wires will support the flowers for this sector, providing they are kept in proportion to the arrangement of flowers. Number seven represents this sector. Children would benefit by studying or completing homework in this sector.

Northwest: Networking and the Ancestors

This sector is also influenced by metal energy. It has stronger masculine energy than the west and so order and structure are more predominant here. This chi will support all members of the family and encourage harmony between relationships. Photos of friends and family next to the flowers will be auspicious here. This sector is associated with the number six. Choose flowers that represent the metal element: concentrate upon curves and swirls within the design for harmony. Metal containers and white, silver and cream plants are auspicious in this sector.

North: Career

Represented by the water element, this sector is enhanced by the most mystical, intellectual and mysterious of all the five elements. The north affects the energy associated with business, career developments and promotion. It is supported by the metal and water elements. Unusually shaped flowers, and blue and purple flowers emphasize the water element; cool

creams and whites will enhance the metal element. To activate the aspiration, stimulate, or move, the water: introduce bubbles, lights (floating candles can be used) or a mister. The number one influences this sector, so one sculptured bloom floating in a pool of water would be auspicious here.

Northeast: Education and Spirituality

This sector is best for those seeking quiet and solitude as it enables the chi to settle and collect. Influenced by earth energy, it is an ideal sector for meditation, studying or for activities that require periods of deep concentration. The number eight represents the northeast, which is an auspicious number. The flowers for the northeast should incorporate the earth element, with compact shapes and earthy textures. An arrangement of stones at the base of a shallow dish around a central display of yellow chrysanthemums set low on a table will symbolize the grounding energy available in this direction. Earth energy is supported by the fire element so incorporate candles into the arrangement or position the flowers near to candles.

East: Health and Travel

Represented by the wood element, this sector is responsible for change, expression, ideas and healing. Plants are renowned for their healing properties and this direction enhances that value. To encourage the health aspect, use softer and more feminine yin flowers. The more robust and active yang wood energy is more suitable to the energy associated with movement and adventure. This sector is associated with the number three. A wood sector, the east is supported by the water element. Wood and water energies are supported by bright blues and a variety of greens.

Southeast: Wealth and Prosperity

This sector is influenced by the elemental energy of wood. Wood energy is able to grow and express

Above Cheerful yellow flowers represent the earth element and can be used in the northeast to increase receptivity and concentration levels or as an outlet for extreme fire energy.

itself. Collecting the chi that gathers in this sector will improve the energy that supports opportunities for wealth and prosperity. The flowers that best support this aspiration are bold and energizing: use layers of foliage and bright, eye-catching flowers. Four is the number associated with this sector. Colours can include reds, orange and yellow for floral statements; the shape and texture of the leaves and petals should sway towards the yang aspect. Fruit can be auspicious in this design to represent the fruit received after one's labours. The wood element is supported by the water element. In this sector it is beneficial to emphasize the water element, to nourish the wood.

Accurate Bagua Alignment

By identifying the power pockets in your environment and finding out which sector of the bagua they correspond to, you can energize the chi at its full potential. By placing flowers in that area with an intention in mind you will be focusing the chi and helping your dreams become tangible reality.

The Black Hat School of Feng Shui, which was invented in 1984, arranges the bagua by aligning the northwest, north and northeast of the bagua template over the main entrance of the floor plan regardless of the actual compass directions. Traditional feng shui schools arrange the bagua template to correspond with the actual compass directions. This book and the advice it gives are based upon the ancient wisdom of traditional feng shui.

Lo–Shu Grid

It is possible to identify the power points of your home through the sectors of the bagua and with the lo–shu grid. The aspirations, elements, directions and associations for the nine boxes on the grid are the same for the lo–shu as they are for the bagua.

SE	S	SW
4	9	2
E 3	5	7 W
8	1	6
NE	N	NW

The Ancient Chinese believed that numbers and geometry hold the keys to the secrets of the universe. Indeed, the language of mathematics can describe the binary code of yin and yang and is fundamental to the operation of high-tech computers. The Ancient Chinese had great respect for sequences of numbers. The most powerful sequence of numbers is the Lo Shu Magic Square, which is a powerful feng shui formula with magical properties. The grid is a magic square: the lines of numbers add up to fifteen, whatever direction you try.

The only difference between the bagua and the lo–shu is the format in which they divide the floor plan into sectors, affecting the placement of the flowers. Buildings and rooms are variable, their shape and directions reflect their personalities. Some buildings are easier to divide into boxes such as the lo–shu whereas others respond better to the bagua sectors. The only real way to decide which formula works best for you is it to try them both.

The formulas of the lo-shu and the bagua evolved over approximately five thousand years and are entwined with feng shui, Chinese medicine and tai chi, among other things. When these formulas are used in conjunction with an accurate scaled floor plan and corresponding directions, they are extremely potent for feng shui purposes.

The lo-shu grid gives the bagua its numerical values. Numerology can be incorporated into your bouquets by using various numbers of flowers depending on which section of the bagua you are activating.

Bottom Eight red yang roses represent the eight directions of the bagua; the one darker yin rose represents the centre. Below Flowers emphasize the calligraphy on this vase. Bottom left A Buddha statue provides a focus for meditation.

Drawing a Floor Plan

It is imperative that you have a reasonably accurate floor plan complete with corresponding compass directions for successful feng shui analysis. If possible, include the furniture on your plans for a clear idea of the movements of chi. Draw your plan onto graph paper to check that the dimensions are correct. Try to keep everything in scale.

Chi is able to pass through glass, such as windows; it will be softened and hindered somewhat by soft fabrics, but it will still be able to pass. Therefore it is important to mark the windows on your floor plan as possible areas to activate or suppress.

When you feel comfortable identifying the yin and yang and the five elements chi that is swirling around the building or room, compare this to the compass directions affecting that area. To do this, take your compass readings, mark them on your floor plan, and compare this to the bagua template on page 65.

Using a Compass

Include the entrances and openings to your home on the floor plan and add their compass directions to identify the relating chi influence. For example, should the main entrance to your building open in the south, it will face the direction associated with fame and recognition. If it faces north, the direction of intellect, it would enhance the chi necessary for a successful career or for good communication. Each direction has its related associations.

Some feng shui consultants have an extremely valuable compass known as a lo-pan. These are inscribed with ornate markings that revolve on a disk until the direction is aligned with the compass needle. From this simple measurement comes a wealth of information relating to the energy of the landscape and its corresponding influence. However, for the purpose of improving the atmosphere with feng shui flowers, a simple compass will give good results.

When taking compass measurements for the first time, choose a compass that is simple and easy to read, or buy an electronic compass, which will give you accurate readings at a push of a button. Remember the needle will always point to magnetic north.

Stand facing the direction to be measured. For example, to discover which direction your house faces, stand with your back to the property. The compass needle will spin as it searches for magnetic north. Once it settles, you can mark due north onto your floor plan. It is now possible to enter the other cardinal directions, south, east and west. These represent the celestial feng shui animals: the turtle, the phoenix, the dragon and the tiger. Find where these directions are in relation to the room or the building floor plan, and then draw in the sub–directions: southeast, northeast, northwest and southwest.

It is important to mark the direction of the main entrance. This may be different to the direction the front of the building is facing, but because the main entrance is the main point of access for people and energy, it must be considered. The same rule applies *internally*: if you are living in an apartment, mark onto your plan the main entrance for the building and the main entrance to your own private space, as the energy will be affected accordingly.

Creating a Floor Plan with Feng Shui Sectors

Once you have a floor plan complete with accurate dimensions and compass directions, it is time to draw in the aspiration sectors. There are two methods: one uses a nine-square grid template based upon the lo–shu design, the other uses eight triangular sectors based upon the bagua design. Whichever style you decide to use is fine, as the directions of the aspirations will remain the same. However the bagua template does allow for greater accuracy. The bagua or lo–shu template can be applied to the whole floor plan or to a single room.

Once you are satisfied with the dimensions of your floor plan, it is important to find the centre of your home. On the plan, draw a faint line from the top right corner of the property to the diagonally opposite corner, and another from the top left to the diagonally opposite corner. The point where the lines cross is the 'tai chi centre' of your property and should be

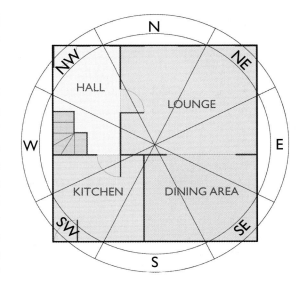

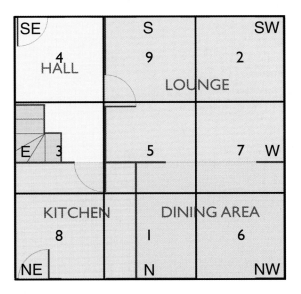

treated with respect. Never allow this area to become congested or overstimulated, as it will affect the general ambience of the remainder of the property. This is the area where chi will head for and metamorphose. This area should be left empty if possible and it is not an auspicious area for storing food or medicines.

From the centre point, take a pencil and compass and draw a circle whose circumference encases the building to identify the correct alignment of the bagua sectors. Draw in the bagua sectors.

The completed floor plan should be handled with care; you could even laminate it as you are likely to be handling it frequently while applying feng shui techniques to your environment. The same is true for a bagua template: it proves its worth time and time again. Advanced feng shui schools use a template of the Twenty-four Mountains, which gives an even deeper knowledge and understanding of the chi emanating from the landscape.

The final floor plan should include a detailed drawing of the building (furniture placement optional) with accurate measured dimensions, complete with corresponding compass directions and bagua sectors.

CHAPTER FOUR

THE ART OF PLACEMENT

"The destinies of men are subject to immutable laws that must fulfil themselves. But man has it in his power to shape his fate, depending on whether his behaviour exposes him to the influence of benevolent or of destructive forces."

Lao Tzu

Understanding Placement

Our moods, emotions and energy levels are greatly affected by our surroundings. People who live in busy cities adopt lifestyles that are in harmony with a mass population and are influenced by many different customs, some of which can clash at times, causing disturbances to the harmony of our environment. Many factors affect our lives but feng shui can help us gain greater control over the outcome of events.

Placement

Before deciding upon the design and ingredients of your feng shui flowers you must consider their placement to realize the full potential of your aspirations. You need to identify potentially harmful factors in your environment, which could render your feng shui flowers ineffective. Or you may be fortunate enough to have ample space and an auspicious entrance with free-flowing elemental chi that will make your environment auspicious. By identifying and preparing your environment you can encourage favourable chi to accumulate.

Accumulating Favourable Energy

The chi that affects us the most is the energy that accumulates wherever we spend our time. If we are balancing our time between professional and personal commitments we will be influenced by energy emanating from the workplace and the home.

Where possible we should choose colours and furnishings that have a pleasing effect on the eye and atmosphere. In the workplace this will not only increase staff harmony and productivity, but also it will improve business relations with customers. A vase of fresh flowers in the reception area or entrance has the same effect. Within the home it is important to refresh areas that have become tired or unbalanced. Some flowers have a calming effect, some are fun, others are welcoming – all will have a message. Placing them in their corresponding directions will unite them to their favoured elements, attracting harmony and benevolent energy.

Favourable energy can lift and inspire, encouraging a flow of harmonious energy that connects to a universal supply of pure chi. Unfavourable energy can deplete the spirit and cause sickness, tension and conflict. It can undermine your resources and affect your finances and the future opportunities of your offspring. We may be sleeping, eating and relaxing in areas that are immersed in unfavourable energy. The ideal placement for feng shui cures is crucial: you do not want to encourage the wrong form of energy as it will encourage unfavourable chi to accumulate.

Right Flowers can slow chi that runs along flat surfaces. Below Agapanthus encourages the metal element and prevents a build up of unfavourable chi from the computers.

Identifying Chi in your Environment

Before beginning to identify the chi in your home, it is advisable to walk around each room and note how much light is available, describe the size and shape of the room, outline the colours used in the furnishings and the activity of the room – is it more yin or yang, or a balance between the two? Remember yang rooms are brighter and more active than yin rooms, which inspire peace and tranquillity.

Chi will be a combination of yin and yang energies; these are transitional energies that continually change, just as a day is divided into daytime and nighttime.

Above Sriped parrot tulips complement the interior design and supply cheerful yin wood and fire chi.

On a subtler level chi can be identified by the five elements. An area that is situated underground, such as a basement, will be heavily influenced by the earth element. A room with a lot of electrical equipment will contain more metal energy than any other element, as will simple Zen designs.

The water element becomes more influential when a property is situated near water. Ideally the view of water should be at the front of the property, not behind, as traditionally water represents a flow of opportunities and it is better to have this chi in front of you. Water behind you indicates past opportunities or, even worse, insecurity.

The fire energy is energetic and busy; this element would apply to a room which encourages this type of activity, such as a fast-food restaurant. A room painted bright red will encourage a forceful, yang type of energy compared to a room that has been painted a calming yin blue or lilac.

Evaluating the levels of yin and yang and the five elements emanating from the colours and materials used on the walls, floors and soft furnishings will take a little practice initially. Then you should decide whether the overall effect is pleasing, balanced or distressing, and then take steps to either enhance or disperse the relevant energy. Some areas will naturally attract positive energy just as there are areas that will generate negative energy, such as bathrooms and long narrow corridors.

Identifying Sheng and Shar Chi

Sheng chi is positive energy and shar chi is negative energy. As yin and yang applies to absolutely everything, so we must accept that energy can be either positive or negative. Chi is always moving; it enters through windows and doors and around objects. It will follow the lines and contours of each and every object

Left *This cheerful, compact arrangement provides a boost of creative yang energy to a yin interior.*
Below *This imposing arrangement will prevent any stagnant chi accumulating in the corner.*

become tainted and spoiled. Chi that follows long, sharp and narrow lines (such as a narrow corridor) will pick up speed until it is too fast to be of any constructive use. Shar chi is caused by sharp edges, broken and dirty surfaces and stale atmospheres – it will respond by collecting malevolent energy. The chi will gather momentum until it hits an obstacle, which could be you or a member of your family. Chi that is fast or furious will be difficult to harness; instead of being useful it is harmful, and should be avoided. Shar chi is associated with sharp or jagged lines and is linked to poison arrows (see page 72).

it encounters, influencing and energizing along the way. As it moves it is depositing and collecting chi. Encountering an object with curved or soft edges, such as a petal or leaf, it will flow gently, weaving in and around the flowers, collecting positive energy.

Sheng chi is positive energy that lends itself to benevolent opportunities; it is easily harnessed and favourable. Slow moving and meandering, it is encouraged to flow, preferably in curves. Living flowers maintain sheng chi, particularly if they are beautiful and full of expression.

Shar chi, on the other hand, is hostile, unfavourable energy that has the potential to harm or inflict injury upon us. Normally it is too fast or too slow to be of any benefit and instead encourages fresh energy to

Poison Arrows

Poison arrows are created by objects that generate unfavourable energy. They are at their most harmful when positioned opposite an entrance or window as they have the ability to slice the chi entering the building.

Over time poison arrows can cause hostile energy that induces conflicts and if left to accumulate this energy can be the direct cause of illness and emotional dramas. Hostile energy can be responsible for laziness, exhaustion, insomnia, sickness, conflicts, arguments and poverty. The degree of potential harm is relative to the proportion of the poison arrow at the point of impact. Poison arrows can be created by external objects opposite the entrance and openings of the building and, importantly, internally will follow the lines of sharp corners such as a desk or cupboard. As the effects of poison arrows are unfavourable, it is advisable to avoid sitting, sleeping, eating, working and living in their line.

Exterior Poison Arrows

Offensive poison arrows are caused by anything that has an aggressive or threatening appearance. Chi that gathers speed by following straight lines becomes harmful. Objects that can cause chi to move in this way include tall tree trunks, poles, towers, corners, sharp edges, roofs, electricity pylons, and roads directed straight towards your front door. Spiky or thorny plants can also stimulate aggression.

For a poison arrow to be effective, it must be directly opposite your entrance or window and at a close distance; a poison arrow in the distance will not be as harmful as one close by. The larger, sharper and more threatening the poison arrow, the more damaging the chi. The period of time spent in the vicinity of the poison arrow is also important: the more time spent the greater the potential harm. If you have identified a poison arrow affecting your environment, you can reduce the harmful effects. Dealing with poison arrows will automatically improve the overall quality of chi in the building, thereby improving the effectiveness of the feng shui flowers cures and enhancers. For help combating exterior poison arrows it is advisable to seek a professional feng shui consultant.

Interior Poison Arrows

Interior poison arrows are caused by overhead beams, corners from cabinets, long corridors, pillars and any other objects that cause sharp angles to be directed at you while sleeping, eating, sitting or working.

Interior poison arrows are easier to take care of than exterior poison arrows, as it is possible to disguise them or move away from their offending effects without constructional changes to the building. If you are suffering from interior poison arrows, you can:

Move your seating or sleeping position away from the offending poison arrow.

Place an object in front of the poison arrow, such as a plant or bouquet of flowers.

Naturally slow chi by keeping lights switched on near or under the offending poison arrow.

Drapes and soft fabric can hide a multitude of sins, as will large plants with plenty of foliage. Choose large-leafed varieties with an emphasis upon yin chi rather than yang energy, as the intention is to absorb harmful chi and transform it into benevolent energy.

Right An earthy display of warm-toned tulips and roses creates a receptive and welcoming atmosphere and encourages chi to move around the arrangement instead of rushing past.

Difficult Areas

Long, narrow corridors encourage chi to move quickly, and may lead to a poison arrow. The position of the corridor is critical for determining the effect that it will have on the property. If the corridor leads on from the main entrance, it will affect the whole house; if it is on the upstairs landing, it will only affect that floor.

The direction of the energy moving along the corridor is another consideration. For example, should the chi be moving in long straight lines from east to west it will cause a disturbance or weakness to the energy that is circulating in the north and south sectors of your environment. Ideally treat the problem areas and corridors to high levels of positive yang energy, thereby reducing the possibility of shar chi from accumulating. Suitable cures and enhancers include lights and plants. Atmospheric lighting will slow chi, while displays of flowers or plants along the corridor will break up the straight lines.

The Main Entrance

One of the most important feng shui considerations for the home and business is the main entrance. The main door is the most frequent point of access to the majority of buildings, yet sometimes the 'main door' may be a side door. Every time people cross the threshold of this area, energy is activated and transferred. The very action of opening and closing a door affects the chi. Energy is transported from the exterior into the interior and vice versa. Should this area be ugly and unloved, negative or neglected chi will accumulate. These unfavourable influences will be stirred every time a person crosses their path.

Imagine the impression created when a person visits you for the first time. Should the main access to your space be littered with obstacles or overgrown and obstructed, the person may assume that you are uncaring or difficult. It may not be an accurate description but it will nevertheless place you at a disadvantage.

To encourage auspicious energy to enter and transport its benefits to the remaining building it is advisable

to address the landscape surrounding your property and the overall impression of the main entrance, hall or foyer. Never allow your entrance to give an impression of mess or waste. Broken objects, clutter and dead or dying plants should be removed, especially from the path leading to the main entrance. Healthy plants, stones and an abundance of flowers will attract wildlife and harmony: this is the energy that you want to encourage into the home or office.

If the front of your home or office is spacious and bright, it will encourage a warm and friendly welcome. A light left on above the entrance will slow chi before

Above *Abundant planting softens the edges of an otherwise hostile environment and will slow down unfavourable chi.*
Left *A profusion of wisteria complements the front of the house, drawing attention to the yin fire energy. The main entrance to your home should be as positive as possible.*

it enters the building, which is favourable. The entrance should be as large and as uncluttered as possible to maximize positive energy. If your door opens to a poison arrow, it is important that you take steps to reduce the negative influence as much as possible.

Blast from the Door

Chi that enters a room via a doorway may often be strong and purposeful; it is advisable that this chi is directed away from people, to prevent a phenomenon known as Blast from the Door. As the name suggests, this chi can be hostile, especially if it is

moving too quickly to be useful. Chi enters a room through the windows and doors, therefore it is important not to expose your back to an open door or window. Nor should you be the first obstacle that the blast from the door encounters.

The blast from the door may cause you to become anxious and unsettled. Concentration will be disrupted every time there is a distraction at the door; if your back is exposed to the door it will mean having to look over your shoulder to determine the cause of the activity. Ideally, you should sit in a comfortable position with a solid wall behind your back to give support and with an open space in front of you.

Three Door Effect

To capture as much sheng chi as possible and to reduce the risk of chi escaping or leaking, the back of your property needs to provide support, otherwise chi will be squandered before it has had a chance to be utilized properly.

The most common problem for weak or lost chi is known as the Three Door Effect. This is where the front door and back door are in alignment – there may even be a third opening along the same alignment. Chi will follow the alignment and quickly rush from the entrance, straight through the building, and out through the back, without being able to replenish the depleted energy levels of the building. If chi has not been given the chance to circulate through the rest of the property it will not be useful for activating aspirations. Even worse, if chi is moving too quickly it will create chaotic situations. Activators, cures and enhancers will be wasted during periods of chaos and disturbance.

To reduce the possibility of this effect, keep at least one of the doors closed to slow the chi or prevent it from escaping. Encourage chi to circulate into other areas of your building by introducing flowers, especially near the windows and doors.

Geopathic Stress

Geopathic stress can be caused by underground streams or fissures, by intense pressure or by natural energy lines (ley lines). The causes of geopathic stress may vary but the implications for your environment do not.

Geopathic stress will disturb the feng shui of your home or business. Plants are effective tools to assess the extent of changeable energy in your surroundings. Plants placed in an area with energy stress will suffer from premature wilt or death; when moved away from the problem area they thrive. Dowsing is another method of identifying geopathic stress.

If you suffer from geopathic stress, where possible move the furniture to reduce the possibilities of working, relaxing, eating and sleeping over the stress fault.

Declining Support
Quiet chi will collect in corners; if left unattended for long periods it will become stagnant and negative. Placing a living object, such as a bouquet of flowers, into a corner will transform negative into positive chi. However, if the flowers are left to wilt and die, the chi will become harmful once more. Never allow flowers used in aspirations to remain once they have passed their best – this would symbolize the opposite of your intentions and could devalue the aspiration.

Missing Corners: Cures with Mirrors
The best configuration for a building is a regular shape, such as a square or rectangle. Irregularly shaped buildings are more difficult to balance as they suffer from missing corners or sectors. Missing corners or sectors will dramatically alter the energy patterns of your environment. If this is a problem with your house, see which elemental energy is lacking by cross-checking with the floor plan and bagua template.

You can re-create the impression of a missing corner with the clever use of mirrors. Their reflective properties make mirrors exceptionally valuable feng shui cures and enhancers. They can be used to reflect positive images, doubling the auspicious energy. They can be positioned to bounce light into and around a room and they are useful for creating an illusion of space.

Above *A mirror reflects a positive image and fills in a missing outside corner. The arch and white and silver planting represent metal energy which is auspicious in the west.*
Right *Flowers can reduce the ill effects of geopathic stress.*

Never position a mirror opposite the entrance, as it will reflect fresh chi straight out again. You should always check that the reflection in the mirror is positive, do not allow negative images access to mirrors as you will only increase unfavourable energy. Use large mirrors rather than small mirrors, to reduce the possibility of fractured images. Glass that has joints, such as mirrored tiles or mirror mosaics, will split the image into different pieces, causing confused chi. When hanging a mirror to reflect your own body, use a mirror that is as large as possible and try to reflect the whole body. Never position a mirror that only reflects part of the head. Mirrors in the bedroom are not recommended, especially if they reflect the body while in bed: these disturb sleep patterns as chi bounces from the body to the mirror and back again.

Symbolic Stars

The lo-pan compass illustrates a selection of symbolic stars in the 24 Mountains. These power pockets have an extra twist of auspicious chi. Once activated, they can increase the chi relating to romance, travel and good fortune.

The four cardinal directions – north (rat), south (horse), east (rabbit) and west (cockerel) – each contain a symbolic star. Affectionately known as Prosper Stars, they are favourable for love and relationships and encourage happy and joyful occasions. Keep these areas clean and trouble free and display fresh flowers here to generate auspicious energy.

Travelling Horses are stars that promote change, travel or movement. Once harnessed, these areas will offer some protection while travelling, though it is worth noting that the effectiveness of these stars is based upon the time spent with them and not away

from them! The four stars that support this energy are found in the northeast (tiger), southeast (snake), southwest (monkey) and the northwest (pig). Tapping into the auspicious stars is similar to activating the bagua sectors. Once you have identified the sector of the building and the elemental direction you can prepare to activate your chosen star with flowers.

Trouble Shooting

As well as identifying areas that can be enhanced with flowers you should also note those areas of your environment that manifest unfavourable energy.

The cycle of elements can be used in reverse, to deactivate potentially harmful chi in your home or business. If you are repeatedly suffering from the same problem or obstacle, the cause could be negative chi in your environment. Negative energy can disrupt relationships, health and finances, and if the negative aspects of any of the elements accumulate they will eventually affect the physical plane. Luckily, using the destructive cycle of elements we can reduce or suppress negative chi to regulate the energy around us. For example, if the water energy is extreme or excessive it could result in turbulent chi and become malevolent. Only the earth element has the power to contain and tame the water element in extreme situations – earth can absorb the excess water chi, reducing the risk of emotional outbursts.

We can also use the destructive cycle in a situation where the sector we wish to activate is found in a negative area such as a toilet or bathroom, kitchen, garage or storeroom. For example, if we wish to activate the chi associated with fame and recognition we would look at the south sector of our building. If a toilet is positioned in the south sector it will reduce our chances of increasing positive energy, as a toilet is associated with waste. We could

The Symbolic Stars

Above Peonies are renowned for their association with love and prosperity. Place this arrangement in one of the cardinal directions to activate the symbolic stars for happiness.

reduce the negative shar chi emanating from the toilet by increasing the earth element. Earth has the ability to reduce the intensity of the fire element and settle the chi of active water (toilets). We could achieve the desired result by absorbing the negative energy through flowers, such as placing a low mound of compact yellow flowers in a ceramic pot inside the offending room. Chrysanthemums are invaluable for their miraculous ability to clean the atmosphere of toxins and harmful energies and would make a suitable choice of flower for this purpose. To support this cure, use smooth stones, sand or compost in the base of the container to represent earth chi.

Settings, Containers and Atmosphere

Every room and building has a personality that is dependent on its relationships with other buildings or rooms, the surrounding landscape, the colour, shape and texture of the hard and soft furnishings, and the degree of available light.

When planning a feng shui flower arrangement, give the same consideration to the container and flowers as you would to the furniture. The container must enhance the design of the flowers and be in tune with the overall concept of the aspiration and the room.

Some containers have a unique beauty of their own and only require a single stem to complete the whole; any more would be too much. Others are simple and serve a purpose to suit the flowers. The container must be chosen carefully as both flowers and vase activate an aspiration. As a general rule, long, straight flower arrangements will require tall straight containers and curved, compact displays will prefer a rounded, squat container. Balance is the key.

Ceramic bowls, vases and shallow dishes are available in a huge variety of colours and shapes. Glass, chrome, bronze and galvanized zinc containers all offer their unique advantages.

Final Placement

Before embarking upon your aspiration, check which would be the most suitable location for its final placement. Then decide which elemental energy needs to be encouraged: this will affect your choice of container. The container should work in harmony with the room and with the direction of the placement area.

Once the setting and proportion are finalized, the flowers can be arranged. At this stage focus your chi inward: take deep breaths, using the diaphragm to pull the breath down to the dan tian (just beneath the navel). This will condense chi and balance the chakras in the body. You should arrange the flowers when you are emotionally balanced, happy, relaxed and peaceful; arranging flowers when you are angry, hurt or upset will reverberate this energy back into the room. Carefully consider your setting and proportions for the most auspicious feng shui placement.

Once you have identified the areas in your home or workplace that would benefit from a boost of healthy, living chi, match it to the corresponding aspiration. You may decide on a bouquet that is not connected to an aspiration but rather one that brings balance and harmony to a sector or element. For example, a missing corner in the southwest will suffer from weakened earth energy. A fresh vase of daffodils will support this sector.

Above *Here the fire energy of the cornus and the pot is grounded by the yellow sunflowers.*
Right *A hot yang arrangement of flowers is suitable for an area that needs a dramatic boost of energy.*

Space Clearing

There is some confusion as to whether space clearing and feng shui are one and the same thing. The answer is that they are not; they are, however, mutually beneficial.

Space-clearing techniques have attracted a lot of attention recently for their therapeutic and energizing effects. Space clearing and removing clutter can be liberating, clearing a room of negative chi that may have been stagnant for years. Chi can become unfavourable when it is trapped or ignored – like dirt, it will build in layers, slowly disrupting and spoiling the fresh energy entering your space. Space clearing is invaluable for removing this stuck energy and preparing a new space for feng shui aspirations, cures or enhancers. If you do not clean the space before you apply the wisdom of feng shui it is as if you have prepared a lavish banquet only to eat from dirty plates.

Keeping your home and environment clean and clutter free reduces the risk of negative chi collecting along with dust and debris. Dealing with household chores as and when they arrive prevents them from becoming a burden and should be encouraged. Chi influences everything it encounters. Ensure that the chi that you are attracting is as positive as possible. Space clearing can refresh a new home or office, particularly if the atmosphere is heavy or dull.

Most properties are made of bricks and mortar, substances governed by the earth element. The earth element is receptive and is able to absorb and retain energy. It will store the powerful wavelengths erupting from an argument, shock or trauma. We receive these vibrations subconsciously and will be influenced by them. This negative energy can cling to buildings; sticky waves of shar chi will collect and poison the surrounding atmosphere. In these circumstances, clearing the space of negative energy is highly recommended.

Simple Space-Clearing Techniques

Open two windows in the room to be cleared to create an airflow and allow fresh chi to enter.

Be firm with clutter: remove and recycle or dispose of everything you don't want or need.

Remove all trace of dust, cobwebs and debris from corners and dark spaces.

Use either candles or lamps to increase the light in corners and dark areas for a minimum of three hours.

Cleanse the room with incense or aromatherapy oils such as lavender, wafting the aromas in rooms that have experienced unhappy or stagnant energy, especially in the corners. Sage is an excellent herb for dispelling negative chi and can be bought as smudge sticks.

Music and sound can cleanse and energize space. The pure sound of a tuned bell or singing bowl is perfect for space clearing, otherwise use a favourite piece of classical or sacred music, or rhythmic clapping.

Active movement such as dance or simply waving the arms while chanting or singing will remove stale chi.

A salty solution made from tepid water and sea salt can be sprinkled at the entrances to your space to purify the chi entering and leaving your premises.

A vase containing lemon balm, burdock, Solomon's seal or cress will calm hostile environments.

Do any or all of the exercises when you are feeling happy, grounded and focused – you do not want to remove one level of anxiety and replace it with another.

Space clearing prepares the building for later feng shui cures and enhancers. Feng shui works at a deeper level, taking into account the setting of the building, personal details of the inhabitants, the surrounding shape of the landscape, the source and directions of waterways, roads, drains and the interior of the buildings.

Right This vase of bluebells and rosemary combined with incense will effectively cleanse a room of negative chi.

Choosing Flowers

When choosing flowers, be as fresh and as exciting as your imagination will allow. The more thought you put into the design, the quicker you will achieve noticeable results.

Making the arrangements should be fun, as an expression from the heart is a free flow of universal energy. If we are truly enjoying ourselves as we work, rest or play we are capable of generating enough energy to manifest great changes in our lives.

Remember to keep the flowers in proportion with the room and aspiration as you will be generating chi. If your south sector is dark, restricted or narrow (yin), it will not respond well to a dominant display of flowers that become an obstruction. Equally a small vase of a few casual red flowers placed in the corner of a bright and busy spacious room will not generate enough impact to be effective. Proportion is relative.

When arranging a bouquet of flowers it is always worth considering seasonal flowers, as these are in harmony with nature – they will also be cheaper than the more exotic varieties. For a more personal touch, choose flowers that you have grown yourself in your garden. Many flowers are now commercially available all year round; these may be useful for particular aspirations.

Nature has provided us with a huge range of shapes and colours of flowers. Should you go shopping without a clear idea of what you want you the sheer range and diversity of the flowers may be confusing. Before spending your money, take your time and remember a few basic rules:

Be clear about the aspiration that you would like to focus on in your life and check the corresponding bagua direction and elemental requirements.

Find the best location according to the bagua and aspiration direction.

Make a list of the yin/yang and five element requirements, such as colour, shape and texture.

Make sure you use fresh flowers.

Check that the flowers and container possess the correct balance of yin/yang qualities to represent the aspiration requirements (see Part 2 for examples).

Check that the display provides the correct feng shui requirements and suits the area for placement.

Activating Aspirations

Living in harmony with the Tao and using feng shui brings balance and equanimity to your life. The first step is preparation. In the past, Chinese scholars approaching the *I Ching* would prepare by ritually bathing to purify the mind, then cleanse the room to obtain the most auspicious flow of chi. Thoroughly prepare your room, calm yourself and collect your thoughts before embarking on an aspiration.

Above *The heady scent of lilies adds another dimension to this feminine summer arrangement.*

Right *This bright, sunny display in its natural setting is a celebration of the informality of summer.*

CHAPTER FIVE

FLORAL ASPIRATIONS

*"Know the masculine
But keep to the feminine
Become a river
To all under Heaven
As a river flows,
Move in constant virtue;
Return to the infant state."*

Lao Tzu

Health and Healing

This arrangement promotes healing and helps create a therapeutic atmosphere. A balanced and harmonious wood elemental energy is essential for good health. The Three Harmony combination enhances the chi most beneficial for healing: it combines flowers with balanced wood chi with other natural ingredients that emphasize yin water and yin earth.

The three-harmony combination is best achieved by emphasizing soft, feminine shapes, shades and textures. Suitable colours include pale greens, soft blues and gentle pinks or yellows. The Three Harmony formula encourages rejuvenation and provides benevolent chi for anyone who is convalescing or is in poor health. Add some perfumed flowers, as scent can soothe the emotions and refresh the room. Incorporate some pink flowers to symbolize love and to make a thoughtful gift for someone who is ill or in hospital.

To support the energy for health, place the flowers in the east. As this is a wood sector you can afford to use more foliage, emphasizing the yin aspect of this element. Buds will be auspicious and will energize the room as they open. Placed in the east during spring, these flowers will chase away the winter blues.

As this design is intended to restore health and provide a soothing atmosphere, replace the flowers as soon as they begin to wilt.

Feng Shui Attributes

This aspiration attracts positive energy into your environment by using foliage that encourages the gentle recuperating energy of wood. Fleshy leaves inspire an abundance of health. Use rounded rather than spiky leaves, as angular shapes would be overly stimulating. The fresh powder-blue hyacinths nestling alongside blue hydrangea lift the spirits. Blue flowers represent yin water chi. Renowned for its ability to cleanse and purify, the water element nourishes the healing process of the wood energy.

The sprigs of mimosa stretching upwards incorporate the yang energy of wood and provide valuable yin earth energy with the splashes of yellow. Yin earth energy can be enhanced by placing these flowers in a square vase or container and by making the arrangement compact. Green flowers and plenty of foliage support the wood element. Only a touch of yin earth chi is required, so either use a square container or represent this element by using yellow and pink flowers.

"If I keep a green bough in my heart, the singing bird will come."

Traditional Chinese proverb

When you are ready to construct your arrangement focus on the curative properties of the plants. Each flower has the ability to restore flagging energy levels. Spring flowers are one of the first indications of a new surge of energizing universal chi and are useful to restore low winter energy levels.

Where possible, incorporate fragrant blooms into your bouquet. Herbs could be incorporated into a small arrangement for a bedside table. Herbs that are especially associated with healing include lavender,

1 Gather your raw materials together. Select only strong and healthy blooms; you do not want weak or delicate flowers that will incur frail chi. Trim the ends and plunge them into water for at least one hour to allow them to replenish any flagging water reserves.

2 Prepare the flowers by stripping all foliage from the parts of the stems that will be beneath the water line, as leaves or flowers kept under water will very quickly spoil the water. Cut long stems to their required length. Bend the aspidistra leaves over and fasten them with a discreet staple. Alternatively, you could use fine florist wire to secure the tip of the leaf to the stem.

rosemary, basil, lemon balm and St John's wort. Sprigs of herbs can be included in an arrangement or tied to the vase. Plaited lavender stems could be wrapped around the base of the container.

Placement

The chi associated with rejuvenation and well-being is the caring wood element, found in the east sector of the bagua. If your entrance is in the east, this aspiration is emphasized. This arrangement is also favourable in the southeast and in the north sector will promote well-being in a professional setting. If placed in the south it will lift the spirits and restore strength. It is not supported in the west and northwest.

Choosing your Container

Three elements support good health: wood, water and earth. To represent the wood element, choose a container in the shape of a column or rectangle or cover your container with leaves. To portray the water element, use a blue glass vase or add blue food colouring to the water. A square or cubic ceramic container would be characteristic of yin earth.

Alternative Flowers

In winter it may be difficult to buy flowers that suggest abundant health, but throughout the year you can buy green, yellow and pink orchids, which look wonderful against lush foliage and last for at least six weeks.

3 Foliage provides the basic shape and structure and harmonizes the wood element. Distribute the ruscus evenly to provide clean sweeping lines that promote unhindered energy as a backdrop for the flowers. Then position the mimosa evenly to soften the lines.

4 Continue building the arrangement by adding the hydrangea. Position the hyacinths between the hydrangea. Finally place the aspidistra leaves into the base of the arrangement to strengthen the overall design.

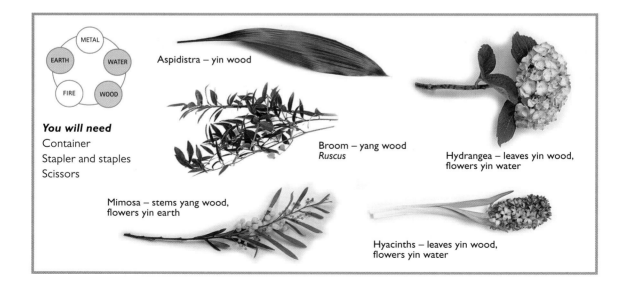

Aspidistra – yin wood

You will need
Container
Stapler and staples
Scissors

Broom – yang wood
Ruscus

Hydrangea – leaves yin wood, flowers yin water

Mimosa – stems yang wood, flowers yin earth

Hyacinths – leaves yin wood, flowers yin water

Travel

This stimulating design invites change and encourages us to get up and go! It has powerful energy, especially when placed in the east. The yang flowers from hot climates suggest far-away locations and the bright, bold, vibrant colours represent active yang energy.

While constructing the arrangement, focus on far-away destinations or changes to your routine. You can increase the potential of this chi by visualizing yourself at your destination or in a new situation. Allow the flowers to remind you of your aspiration every moment you are able to spend time with them. Keep personal items relating to travel, such as holiday photos, near to the flowers to enhance this aspiration even further.

This arrangement allows for true freedom of expression – the more creative and inspired you make it, the better. The flowers can be dramatic and the overall design should be striking. Allow them to become a focal point and a conversation piece, for the more attention they generate the stronger the chi for attracting change. Choose bold yang colours such as oranges, reds and deep yellows, balanced with lots of foliage and large, glossy green leaves.

Feng Shui Attributes

Flowers to support the chi for this aspiration will always be available, as exotic flowers can be bought all year round. Flowers with unusual shapes and interesting textures, such as the bird of paradise (strelitzia), provide an exotic image and, combined with the rich foliage, they will attract positive chi. The palm leaves inspire images of faraway golden beaches and their long fronds balance the larger flowers and create sweeping lines in the arrangement. They provide valuable yang wood chi, influencing the chi for travel and change. This is supported by the yin wood chi of the aspidistra leaves.

The sunflowers provide yang earth chi and the brilliant gerbera act as a fire elemental activator. The abundant supply of wood energy from the lush foliage provides plenty of fuel for the fire energy.

"Each time the wind blows the butterfly finds a new home on the willow."

Basho

To eliminate the possibility of negative shar chi gathering, always replace the flowers as soon as they are past their best. This arrangement has a strong influence during spring and summer but it will be hindered during autumn and winter.

Placement

The chi associated with change and travel is found in the east sector. If your entrance is in the east the aspiration for change is emphasized. This is also the sector for healing, so flowers in the east sector will stimulate the chi for health: an ill person will be sensitive to activated yang energy in the east. Yin flowers are used in the health aspiration (page 88) whereas the travel aspiration uses active yang wood ingredients.

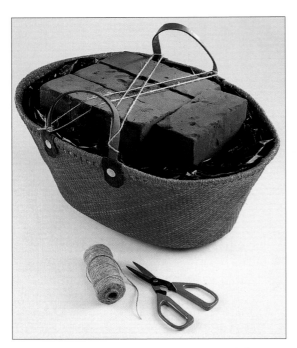

1 Soak the florist foam by laying it on water and allowing it to sink. Line the beach bag with plastic lining and fill with the soaked florist foam. Secure the foam with string to help prevent moisture loss. Leave $1/2$-inch (4 cm) of foam above the line of the bag to support your flowers. Tuck in the plastic so it doesn't show.

2 Make a five-pointed star shape with the large palm leaves to provide a basic structure. Place the leaves from the centre, so they cover the florist foam and the edge of the bag and give the impression that the leaves are bursting outwards. Fill in with the aspidistra and bird of paradise leaves. Position the salal and eucalyptus between the spaces of the larger leaves.

The east sector is associated with rapid growth, health, ideas and inspiration and responds to change, travel and movement. A stunning display of flowers in this area generates yang energy: as this accumulates it inspires change. You can increase the fire chi by incorporating candles or lights into the design. The east is governed by wood and so responds harmoniously to the fire element, just as wood fuels a fire.

Wood energy is expansive, full of opportunity and expression. Yang wood can be adventurous and optimistic: when it is positive it brings possibilities for adventure, when it is negative it can result in sudden explosive outbursts. In the southeast sector flowers with yang wood energy support the chi for prosperity. In the north they encourage change to career or business, so be careful! They support the chi for fame and recognition in the fiery south sector. Avoid them in the west and northwest.

Choosing your Container
The wood element is supported by water, so choose a container that is able to store a wide expanse of water. An ample reserve of water can be achieved with a large piece of florist foam neatly hidden inside a large container.

Alternative Flowers
Flowers to provide the activating fire chi needed for this aspiration include red or pink ginger flowers, pink or orange protea, or red anthuriums.

3 Cover some florist's wire with green florist's tape. Push one end of the wire firmly into a gerbera head, and carefully bend the wire round the stem. This will support the head and prevent the gerbera suffering from premature wilt.

4 Place the sunflowers and the bird of paradise flowers into the arrangement one at a time. Push the flowers firmly into the foam, following the theme of chi bursting from the centre of the arrangement. Then carefully place the gerberas into the available spaces. The final arrangement should appear full and expansive.

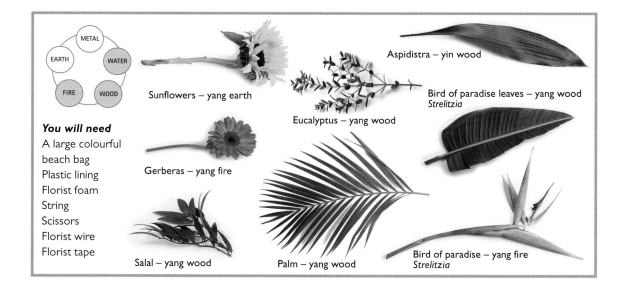

You will need
A large colourful beach bag
Plastic lining
Florist foam
String
Scissors
Florist wire
Florist tape

Sunflowers – yang earth

Gerberas – yang fire

Salal – yang wood

Eucalyptus – yang wood

Palm – yang wood

Aspidistra – yin wood

Bird of paradise leaves – yang wood
Strelitzia

Bird of paradise – yang fire
Strelitzia

Children: Fun and Funky

It is said that the natural state of a baby is happiness. Once his or her needs have been met the baby reverts back to a state of inner contentment. Children have a zest for life: they explore and marvel at the treasures they find. Enhance this inquisitive chi with an arrangement that is fun, captures the imagination of young children and stimulates the senses.

A flower arrangement that sparks the interest of children is not only a valuable introduction to the wonderful world of nature but also an excuse to have fun together. Children will respond happily to bright colours, especially bold and vibrant reds and yellows. To encourage an atmosphere of fun that is in accord with the natural energy of children, choose flowers that are interesting and unusual. Bright colours with shiny luminous surfaces coupled with silky leaves or furry catkins encourage the desire to touch and explore. Use energetic yang colours such as red, orange and yellow for a playroom or activity centre or choose cooler colours to encourage calm.

Feng Shui Attributes

The striped parrot tulips are fun and unusual with their alternate strips or red and yellow fire energy. Their bendy stems are relaxed, encouraging the flexible and understanding nature of yin wood. The tulips are eye-catching and will generate stimulating fire energy; this chi is supported with the bold red gerberas complete with yellow eyes. Giant buttercups are provided by the yellow ranunculus.

Within the structure of foliage are loops of steel grass secured with string. These encourage the eye to return to the centre of the arrangement. The base of the arrangement is deep-green glossy leaves of palm, aspidistra, fatsia and ruscus, providing both yin and yang wood energy. This protective foundation to the arrangement provides the powerful and creative expression of wood elemental energy.

Placement

To support the energy of children, place the final arrangement in the west, which is most associated with children and the family. Alternatively you can place them in the east sector, which is the sector responsible for growth and expression.

"The tiny child shown a flower opens its mouth."

Seifu-jo

Both sectors are favourable for children, though choose which sector you are going to place the flowers in before you embark on the design as the east sector is governed by the wood element and the west is governed by the metal element. Placing a wood elemental arrangement into a metal sector will have a stimulating and liberating effect, not advisable in the company of wayward teenagers, as the chi is likely to cause an unexpected outburst!

This bouquet has been arranged specifically for the east sector. To stimulate quieter children, place it in the southeast, south (though be aware of over

I Place the smaller vase inside the larger vase and fill the gap in between with your selection of candies to give the impression that the flowers are growing out from the candies. Make sure the smaller vase reaches up to the lip of the outer vase, as a vase that is too tall or too small will expose the stems and give away the trick.

2 Bend the steel grass into loops and secure with string. Trim the stems and unwanted leaves of the ingredients. Place the palm and fatsia leaves opposite one another for balance, creating long sweeping lines up and out. Add the steel grass, ruscus and aspidistra, giving height and texture. The arrangement should be open and showy.

stimulus) or north. It will have an active effect when placed in the west and northwest, though it is not recommended for long periods. These flowers are best avoided in the northeast and southwest sectors.

Choosing your Container

As bright colours intensify this aspiration, you can afford to be as wild and inspirational as you like. Follow the guidance of the children, allowing them to express themselves freely. Have on hand an assortment of accessories such as stones, ribbon, sequins, paint and glue. You could incorporate favourite sweets into the design. You will need two vases (one inside the other) and lots of sweets or candies to fill the gap in between the vases.

Alternative Flowers

Whatever the season, there will always be flowers available to support the chi for this aspiration. Consider flowers whose colours, shapes and textures will stir curious imaginations. Choose fresh, bright greens, yellows and reds.

Small flowers are magnets for little fingers; tiny arrangements can be made from daisies and violets or threaded together as a chain. Alternatively buy miniature fruit and vegetables and encourage children to design these into an exciting arrangement.

Bluebells are reputed to attract fairies and combine wonderfully with unusual peachy hyacinths. The heady perfume of the hyacinths provides another valuable feng shui activator.

3 Wire the heads of the gerbera (see page 168), continuing the spiral of wire down to the water level so the gerberas can retain their shape or be bent into curves. Arrange the gerberas in a group for maximum impact. Tie the parrot tulips into bunches of three with florist string (not wire, which can cut into the stems).

4 Carefully arrange the tied parrot tulips into the design to provide extra height and depth. The long stems of the tulips are naturally bendy; tying them together in groups of three will provide stronger lines and make a bigger impact. To finish, position the ranunculus to give added height and depth to the overall arrangement.

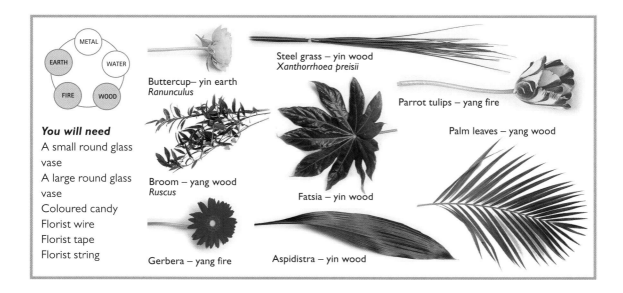

Buttercup– yin earth
Ranunculus

Steel grass – yin wood
Xanthorrhoea preisii

Parrot tulips – yang fire

Palm leaves – yang wood

Broom – yang wood
Ruscus

Fatsia – yin wood

Gerbera – yang fire

Aspidistra – yin wood

You will need
A small round glass vase
A large round glass vase
Coloured candy
Florist wire
Florist tape
Florist string

美好将来

Wealth and Prosperity

To attract energy for encouraging prosperity you need to make a strong and purposeful statement. The arrangement should generate powerful yang energy, increasing the chi for opportunities to increase wealth.

An energetic arrangement creates drama and power; necessary fuel for an aspiration that is associated with gain. Dramatic flowers combined with contemporary shapes and textures are invaluable for stimulating the senses and generating positive chi.

Wealth can take many forms, not necessarily limited to opportunities to increase money. However, to draw just money towards you, incorporate a little of the metal element into the design. Coins are auspicious metal accessories. In this arrangement Chinese coins are tied to red string and attached to the container. Alternatively, scatter a few coins into the bottom of the containers to energize the water with money-making energy. Don't be greedy though, as too much metal energy will destroy the wood chi.

The sector for wealth and prosperity is governed by the wood element, so use flowers and foliage that emphasize exuberant wood chi. Fruits could be incorporated into this aspiration, or a bowl of fruit could be placed near the flowers: pomegranates are associated with treasure and bananas and coconuts are sacred to Ganesh, the Hindu god of prosperity.

Feng Shui Attributes

The flowers are clearly arranged in four layers for maximum impact and to correspond with the bagua numerology of the southeast sector. The bottom layer of flowers is central to the overall display and should have the most concentrated yang energy; this is achieved with a layer of red amaryllis. The next

two layers contain two contrasting textures. Both the bells of Ireland and lime-green cultivated millet reinforce the wood element. The top layer is represented by the clear blues of the delphiniums, providing supportive water elemental energy.

The sequence in which the layers of flowers are arranged promotes the natural flow of energy. The delphiniums represent the chi of water. Water will naturally move downwards, where it will encounter the receptive layer of the bells of Ireland and the cultivated millet. The water energy will combine with the chi of the wood energy, nourishing it with supportive energy. The bottom layer of amaryllis represents the upward strive of the fire energy. This powerful energy is associated with ambition and drive.

"Perfect nobility does not need a title; perfect wealth does not need possessions."

The Masters of Huainan

Wood is replenished by the water element. The water element can be emphasized when water chi may be naturally low, such as during the summer. Wood chi is expressive and has courage and strength. It can grow rapidly, like mint loose in the garden, or it can be encouraged to grow and mature slowly over time. Wood energy naturally bears fruit, and fruit can be symbolic of financial rewards.

1 Soak the florist foam by letting it sink into water. Stick two pieces of double-sided sticky tape to the aspidistra leaves. Place the leaves vertically around the vase, slightly overlapping them, to cover the vase. Tuck the tops of the leaves over the edge of the vase. Push the soaked florist foam into the base of your container.

2 Position the showy amaryllis in a low line, to create the first layer of the arrangement. Leave the width of a stem between each stem. Handle them carefully as they bruise easily. Do not overcrowd as this would restrict free-flowing chi, which will eventually manifest into chi that restricts the flow of finances.

Placement

Flowers to encourage wealth and prosperity should be placed in the southeast sector, where they generate the chi associated with growth, ideas and inspiration. If your entrance falls in this direction, this aspiration is emphasized. Wood chi is exhausted by the fire element and too much will deactivate the aspiration. Bear this in mind if placing the flowers in the south. The earth element is grounding, and this arrangement will be useful for investments in the southwest and northeast. The metal element is associated with money, though use only small amounts, as too much metal will exhaust the wood chi. These flowers have a stimulating effect in the west and northwest, but are not recommended for long-term use.

Choosing your Container

You will need a long circular vase to represent the wood element, which can be covered in attractive foliage or pieces of bark.

Alternative Flowers

In Eastern cultures gold is the symbol of prosperity. Emphasize gold with a dazzling display of golden flowers, or spray a terracotta pot gold and fill daffodils and purple irises. Yellow is associated with happiness: yellow blooms encourage positive chi and adding purple will activate a feng shui combination said to draw the chi for prosperity. During early spring, use witch hazel or forsythia instead of daffodils. Avoid spikes or thorns, which stimulate arguments over money.

3 Arrange the second layer of millet, which, along with the bells of Ireland in the next layer, represents the wood element. Finish with a layer of delphiniums to represent water, which nourishes the wood. Push the flowers firmly into the florist foam. This should be a strong and purposeful arrangement, encouraging yang masculine chi for striving forward and reaching goals.

4 To finish, tie three Chinese coins around the base of the flowers and the top of the container to activate the arrangement for wealth and prosperity. Fire is the element which will best activate this aspiration. Arrange the coins with two yang sides either side of the central yin side of the coin to make the trigram for fire.

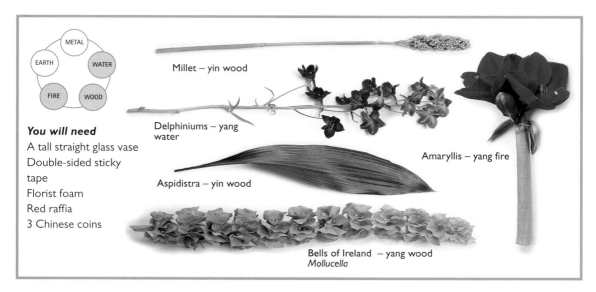

Millet – yin wood

Delphiniums – yang water

You will need
A tall straight glass vase
Double-sided sticky tape
Florist foam
Red raffia
3 Chinese coins

Aspidistra – yin wood

Amaryllis – yang fire

Bells of Ireland – yang wood
Mollucella

Abundance

The word abundance suggests contentment and satisfaction. When you have everything in abundance, there is cause for celebration. This aspiration should incorporate the chi of the heavens, with flowers that represent the joy and illumination of the sun, creating an expansive and open impression.

This is an opportunity to be daring and inventive with your flowers. The final result should be strong and striking: vibrant colours will ensure a vivid impact, while showy flowers will draw attention. This aspiration can be used for expressing love, from an open gesture of friendship to passionate attraction.

These flowers are exceptionally useful in professional circumstances and make a wonderful display with which to greet the public. As these flowers are bright and showy they demand recognition and appreciation: choose flowers in yang colours such as reds, oranges and yellows and put them with flowers in contrasting colours. Set them off with plenty of dark green foliage to give support and foundation.

Feng Shui Attributes

The elements that best represent the aspiration for abundance are yin and yang aspects of wood chi for expression and creativity, yin fire for sensitivity and love and yang fire for spirit and vitality. Water chi is important for depth and to replenish energy. The wood and fire elements should be strong; the water chi is for support. The combination of yang water and yin fire chi is favourable, resulting in a boost of auspicious energy to the wood element.

The open and flat flowers, the anthurium and open lily, represent the open nature of abundance. The flowers and foliage give favourable yang energy to support positive energetic patterns. The stems are strong and upright, the flowers full and fresh. Bright colours are vibrant and energizing. They are supported with plenty of rich foliage for interest and to support the wood element. Palm, Swiss cheese plant and aspidistra leaves were chosen for this aspiration. Stems of hellebore provide valuable interest.

"Before enlightenment, chop wood and carry water; after enlightenment, chop wood and carry water."

Zen proverb

This is an arrangement that wants to be noticed. The flowers are strong and alert, full of confidence and spirit. This is not an aspiration for fragile or delicate flowers and foliage.

The yin aspect is incorporated with plenty of foliage. Yin wood chi is crucial for absorbing the potentially threatening or aggressive yang energy emanating from the yang flowers. Yin wood is flexible and inspirational, qualities included in this bouquet to balance the sheer power of such an abundant statement.

Placement

The flowers are best situated in a yang room or entrance, where they are able to influence the chi for opportunities and gain. However, flowers that have been arranged to create abundant energy can be

1 Trim the ends of the stems and plunge them into deep water at least an hour before you begin the arrangement. Clean and prepare your container. Wrap your decorative bark sheet around the circumference of the vase and either secure to the vase with double-sided sticky tape or fasten the ends of the sheet together with wire.

2 Begin to arrange the foliage to provide the basic shape and structure of the design. Start with the larger leaves, the palm, dracaena, aspidistra and Swiss cheese plant leaves. These leaves dictate the final height and spread of the design, so discard leaves that are too small or too large.

used in several sectors and for a variety of situations: this arrangement can increase the chi for wealth, health and harmonious relationships. Use this aspiration sparingly or for a specific goal. Used for special occasions the flowers will achieve the maximum results; used on a daily basis they suggest greed, which can stimulate the chi for worries.

To bring abundant energy to finances, place the arrangement in the southeast sector and concentrate upon the wood and water elements, with a little red or pink to represent yin fire. Or use it to restore the yang chi of a room previously infected with sickness. The south is associated with joyful activities and this aspiration makes a celebratory entrance. Avoid these flowers in the west, north and northwest.

Choosing your Container

Choose a tall, circular container to represent the wood element and enhance the wood chi by covering the vase in leaves, foliage, or bark. Wood supports and gives birth to the fire, the element responsible for activating wood, thereby energizing the aspiration.

Alternative Flowers

In spring masses of daffodils, hyacinths, crocus and iris or a simple mound of clustered tulips can replace the exotic species used in this abundance aspiration. In summer use lilies for scent and gladioli for structure. The autumn brings fruits, chrysanthemums, golden corn and autumn foliage. In winter use sprigs of juniper and cypress with bold red poinsettias.

3 Add the smaller of the palm leaves. Place the showy hellebores, guelder rose and anthuriums between the foliage, developing the shape. The soft lines of the hellebores and guelder rose soften the lines and the green flowers all add wood chi to the arrangement.

4 Impart yang fire to the arrangement by adding the colourful flowers and open blooms. The bright and attractive colours of the ranunculus, lily, arum, kangaroo paws and orchid trigger this stimulating energy. The flowers should be in an upright, thrusting position.

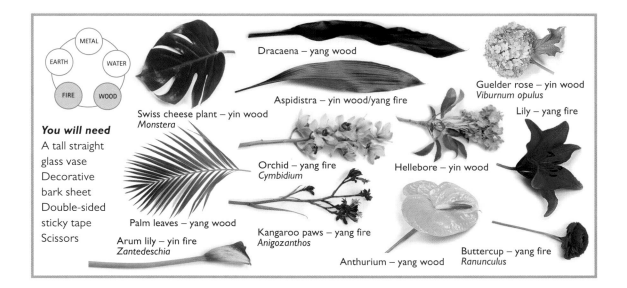

You will need
A tall straight glass vase
Decorative bark sheet
Double-sided sticky tape
Scissors

METAL
EARTH
WATER
FIRE
WOOD

Dracaena – yang wood

Guelder rose – yin wood
Viburnum opulus

Aspidistra – yin wood/yang fire

Lily – yang fire

Swiss cheese plant – yin wood
Monstera

Orchid – yang fire
Cymbidium

Hellebore – yin wood

Palm leaves – yang wood

Kangaroo paws – yang fire
Anigozanthos

Arum lily – yin fire
Zantedeschia

Anthurium – yang wood

Buttercup – yang fire
Ranunculus

Fame and Recognition

This arrangement lifts and inspires the spirits, illuminates and enhances a goal, draws attention to a focal point and makes a positive statement. The aspiration could also be arranged as a hand-tied bouquet as a gift for those celebrating an achievement or auspicious occasion.

The main objective of this aspiration is to create a powerful and positive yang activator that can be placed in the south sector of your home or business, the sector traditionally associated with the chi for fame and recognition. The aspiration should represent intense levels of fire energy – positive, yang chi.

The arrangement includes flowers with notable wood characteristics, denoting determination, maturity and ambition. The wood chi has been combined with strong fiery chi, which generates energy for clarity and illumination. The combined energy provides weight and stability. Use stones to activate the Three Harmony combination.

Creating and displaying this aspiration will stimulate the chi for recognition, important for receiving a positive response to ideas and for appreciation of hard work, time and effort. An energetic arrangement creates a dramatic atmosphere; the fire chi stimulates the atmosphere and the senses. A bright, eye-catching, vibrant display of reds and oranges with a splash of yellow, it mimics the flames and feathers of the celestial animal, the phoenix, which attracts good fortune. The overall impression is of an explosion of energy and a burst of light.

Feng Shui Attributes

This arrangement has more yang chi than the more receptive yin chi. Like the heliconia (lobster claws), flowers for this aspiration should have strong, upright and even angular features. The gladiola and protea are invaluable for presenting different aspects of fire chi; the gladiola represents flames shooting upwards and the protea resembles exploding embers. The phormium leaves look like flames and the amaryllis is bursting forth from the centre.

"The true perfection of man lies not in what man has, but in what man is."

Oscar Wilde

Leaves and stems make a vibrant, bold statement. The phormium leaves are used in the exterior and interior of this arrangement, suggesting fire chi moving from the ground up. Fire requires wood as fuel and incorporating both yin and yang aspects of the wood element ensures the aspiration will remain active as long as the flowers are fresh. The wood element also stimulates the chi for inspiration and rapid growth.

Placement

Fire chi is associated with excitement, illumination and opportunities to celebrate. Fire can warm the skin, inspire passion, lift the spirits and illuminate mind and body. This energy is found in the south sector of the bagua. If your entrance falls in this direction this aspiration is emphasized.

1 Wrap three layers of double-sided sticky tape around the vase. Peel off the backing tape and firmly press the red dracaena leaves vertically around the vase, slightly overlapping them to cover the glass. Twist together several strands of red dogwood and secure the ends with wire or tape to make two rings. Slip these over the top and the bottom of the vase.

2 Carefully slide phormium leaves under the dogwood rings to lie on top of the dracaena leaves. The prominent strips of red and green over the deep burgundy create interest, drawing chi up from the base and pushing it up and out, mimicking the action of fire.

Fire energy can be overwhelmed by too much earth or metal chi and an uncontrolled water element can extinguish fire chi completely, which should be considered if placing these flowers in the north, west, northwest, northeast and southwest.

The arrangement is designed for the south sector but can be extremely effective in an entrance, especially in the southeast and east. These flowers bring supporting energy to the southwest and northeast.

Choosing your Container

Make sure your container can accommodate the long stems of the heliconia and other large flowers. Choose a long straight vase to represent wood, which supports fire for this arrangement. The vase could

also be decorated with decorative bark. You could plait other pliable twigs, such as pussy willow, and wind them around the container.

Alternative Flowers

Where possible, include flowers that originate from a hot or dry climate, such as ginger and orchids. These flowers are grown in yang climates and will emphasize the yang conditions. In the winter use three long stems of amaryllis to suggest warmth. In spring, simple red tulips can make a low-budget fame arrangement. In autumn incorporate red foliage blended with bright balls of allium or strips of crocosmia. A single stem of pink orchid combined with ginger stems against ferns can support this aspiration.

3 Strip unwanted leaves from the foliage and flowers and trim the stems. Arrange the phormium leaves to establish the basic structure. Place the bird of paradise leaves towards the back, fanning outwards, to support and balance the flowers. Position the grevillea further forward, filling the gaps with fiery red foliage. Place a stem of dracaena in the front and add the the cordyline.

4 Position the heliconia evenly across the sides and centre of the arrangement. Add the vibrant amaryllis, which intensifies the strong colours and powerful presence of the heliconia. Position the gladioli alongside the heliconia. Finally, place the protea close to the amaryllis for maximum impact.

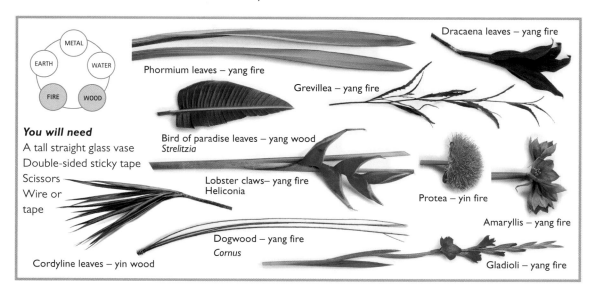

METAL
EARTH   WATER
FIRE   WOOD

Dracaena leaves – yang fire

Phormium leaves – yang fire

Grevillea – yang fire

You will need
A tall straight glass vase
Double-sided sticky tape
Scissors
Wire or
tape

Bird of paradise leaves – yang wood
Strelitzia

Lobster claws– yang fire
Heliconia

Protea – yin fire

Amaryllis – yang fire

Cordyline leaves – yin wood

Dogwood – yang fire
Cornus

Gladioli – yang fire

性 感

Passionate Love

The passionate aspect of love is more yang than yin: it is sexy and exciting, bold and positive. A flower arrangement with this chi is infused with passion; the bouquet is designed to turn heads and state a purpose, causing a stir with its boldness.

To achieve this aspiration a dramatic effect is needed. Contrasting colours and textures are used, mixing glossy leaves with velvety tactile rose petals. Colour has the greatest impact; shades of red are imperative for activating powerful yang energy. Demanding attention and energizing the atmosphere, red is associated with the fire element and corresponds with the base or root chakra, which is the energy centre for boosting sensuality and desire. Encouraging favourable fire chi into the environment will stimulate this form of energy, raising the temperature and arousing passion.

The aspiration for this arrangement must be bold, with dynamic intentions! The final result should be powerful, to rekindle flagging romances, generate passion or to initiate new relationships.

Feng Shui Attributes

Fire energy is bold and passionate and generates heat and light. Flowers with this elemental energy make a simple but strong message of love and desire. Although this aspiration emphasizes the yang fire elemental chi, there should be a balance between the yin and yang aspect of the flowers.

This is achieved by combining the glossy red anthurium, representing deliberate male chi, and the softer texture of the female rose. The rose's deep, intense colour still invokes the passion of the fire chi, though the message is yielding compared to the thrusting chi of the anthurium.

Roses have long been associated with love. Darker red roses are now readily available in colours from burgundy through to almost black. Their overlapping petals are sultry and seductive, longing to be touched. The round and open bowl is host to two varieties of roses, their heads peeking through the strands of bear grass, again inviting a closer inspection or offering themselves to be touched.

"Let the beauty we love be what we do."

Rumi

The energy of fire requires fuel; otherwise the flames of passion will slowly become exhausted. To prevent the arrangement suffering a shortage of replenishing chi, the wood element is represented by dark-green leaves that whip around the inside of the glass and are concentrated at the base of the arrangement. The lily grass used throughout the bouquet sustains and supports the fire element. As soon as the flowers have passed their best, replace them, otherwise negative shar chi will creep into the relationship.

The colours of the flowers are strong and vibrant. Pastel shades do not have the same impact – they enhance a softer, more romantic love. Scented roses are more auspicious than the non-scented. Whatever the season, you will find fiery, bold and striking flowers to support the chi for this aspiration.

1 Let the florist foam fill with water by laying both pieces onto a large bowl of water. Trim and strip the flowers of thorns and unwanted foliage. Cover the largest piece of florist foam with dracaena leaves, fastened into position with staples, and place in the centre of the large bowl. Place the smaller piece of florist foam in the side dish next to the main bowl.

2 Line the large glass bowl with long whips of bear grass. The grass is naturally springy and will support itself. Use long pieces at random heights for maximum interest and alternate with wispy, feminine fern for contrast. Push the short-stemmed rose heads into the dracaena-covered florist foam in the large bowl so they peek cheekily through the layers of bear grass and fern.

Placement

Fire energy, associated with love, excitement and spontaneity, is best represented in the south. This aspiration can also be placed in the southwest to support romance and loving relationships. The south calls for recognition, useful for drawing the attention of a potential new love; traditionally the southwest is associated with marriage and established relationships, so activate the chi in the southwest to improve existing relationships. This aspiration can be arranged as a hand-tied bouquet to indicate your open heart and passionate intentions to a new love.

In the east or southeast these flowers will be auspicious for passion. Avoid placing these flowers in the north, west, northwest and northeast.

Choosing your Container

You will need two containers. One should be a large and open glass bowl; the second should be a small side dish large enough to hold a section of florist foam, but discreet enough not to dominate the main container.

Alternative Flowers

This aspiration can be adapted into a hand-tied display, perfect for a passion-inducing Valentine's Day gift or for a special anniversary. Roses are a traditional symbol of passionate love, but dark-red peonies and burgundy gladioli could also be used to represent the passion of love and the fire of romance. The flowers must be red to represent the element of fire, and adding some foliage will fuel the fire energy.

3 Continue adding the rose heads to the larger bowl. Position the anthuriums so they lead the eye from the centre of the arrangement. Trail the ivy and lily grass out in a protective arm to the second arrangement, linking them up in a gesture of companionship and love.

4 Position the foliage in the smaller bowl, then the roses, to define the overall shape and atmosphere of the arrangement. Add the hebe to provide a wonderful contrasting texture to the roses and anthurium. Position the lily grass, ivy and anthurium and entwine them in a sweeping curve to represent love and protection.

Dracaena – yang fire

Rose – yin and yang fire

Anthurium – yang fire

Ivy – yin wood

You will need

A round wide-based glass vase
A small side dish
Large piece of florist foam
Small piece of florist foam
Stapler and staples
Scissors

Hebe – yin wood

Lily grass – yang wood

Tree fern – yin wood

Bear grass – yang wood
Dasylirion

Romantic Love

**This aspiration incorporates three elemental energies that
combine favourably to provide auspicious energy relating to
peace, harmony and well-being. Flowers are often associated with
romance and symbolize love. This arrangement, in its
heart-shaped vase, would make a perfect gift for Valentine's Day.**

A bouquet of flowers with the energy of romance will emanate a compelling message, inspiring intimate chi and an exchange of trust and respect. Yin fire chi is especially associated with romance and sensitivity; it is indulgent and designed to be deliciously savoured; yang fire chi encourages wild passion, spontaneity and excitement.

To open your heart wide enough to trust and love another displays great courage and strength. To give love unconditionally automatically generates more love. To give and receive wholeheartedly is to be in harmony with the Tao; it is freedom unhindered by thoughts of self.

Feng Shui Attributes

The soft shades used here encourage yin romantic fire energy – bright, vibrant or bold colours would activate energizing yang chi. Roses are typically associated with romance, and rosebuds symbolize new love about to unfold. Make sure that the roses have their thorns removed for the bouquet. Flowers that imply luxury and velvety softness are indulgent and enticing – perfect for this aspiration. Even the soft chi of yin fire will need support from the wood element: choose dark foliage or moss to offset the pale sugar pinks of the rose buds.

Candles can be incorporated into the design or placed next to the flowers to generate auspicious fire chi; the positive energy will activate the sector gently and romantically. Use two candles to represent the two people in the relationship.

Construct the arrangement with loving thoughts and an openness of the heart. Do not be tempted to rush through this arrangement and avoid arranging these flowers if you are tired or distracted as you will lose much of the powerful intention that truly enhances the flowers.

Lovers and poets alike favour the perfume of roses. Experiment with different varieties to find the one that lifts your heart. If the roses you choose are unscented, sprinkle a drop of rose absolute essential oil on the base of the bouquet, taking care not to stain the petals, buds or furniture.

Placement

Flowers signify romantic love, especially when they are placed in the corresponding sector of the bagua. If you want to draw favourable energy that develops commitment and brings opportunities for a successful marriage, activate the southwest direction, which is associated with marriage and romantic happiness. This sector of the bagua is influenced by earth chi, so flowers with the earth elemental influence will be auspicious here. Earth is supported by the fire element, so use fiery colours like reds, pinks and purples to support this aspiration further.

According the 24 Mountains School formula there are four Stars of Romance, auspicious areas for

1 Ensure you have no torn or bruised petals as these will go brown and could taint the harmony of the chi that is being activated. Strip the leaves and thorns of the roses and trim the stems. Leave approximately 1 inch (3 cm) of the foliage close to the heads of the roses on the stem, which should remain above the water line. Place the prepared roses into tepid water and plant feed overnight.

2 Float your florist foam onto fresh water and leave it to gradually collect water. Carefully line your container with fresh moss, leaving room in the centre to position the soaked florist foam.

activating love, which can be attuned with the seasonal energy of the year. The east sector has an auspicious star for romance during March, in June the south becomes auspicious, in September the romantic star in the west is heightened and in December the romantic star can be found in the north. In the north sector you may unintentionally attract a romantic relationship in a professional environment, so be careful!

Choosing your Container

Ideally, use a heart-shaped glass container, which can be lined in fresh moss. Alternatively, use a large plate with a circumference large enough to hold a piece of florist foam that has been cut to the shape of a heart, a universal symbol of love.

Alternative Flowers

Fresh peonies loosely spilling from a ceramic bowl will activate the chi of this aspiration just as favourably as roses, as the peony is said to be a most auspicious flower. Both peony and rose are highly regarded for their beauty and mystical properties. Peonies are said to be able to attract wealth and have the ability to ward off negative shar chi. Other flowers that have loving energy and are said to encourage feelings of love are lavender, mint, basil, rosemary and violets.

Another excellent choice is the chocolate flower (*Cosmos astrosanguineus*), which has a delicious chocolate scent, combined with deep maroon to brown velvety petals. Mix them with burgundy roses for a stunning effect.

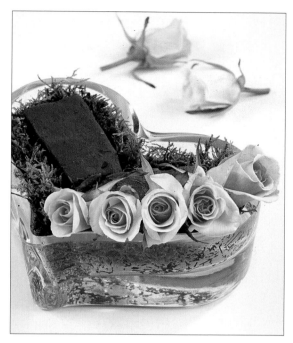

3 Cut the rose heads and foliage from the stems one at a time and carefully place each rose head into the florist foam. Begin to outline the shape of the vase, which will define the heart shape even further, reinforcing the aspiration. Take your time: every movement should be a deliberate action.

4 Keep adding roses and foliage until the heart shape is full and the arrangement is complete.

Red Peonies

Such radiance of green,
So casual and composed;
The tint of her dress
Blends crimson with pink.
The heart of a flower
Is nearly torn with grief:
Will spring's brilliance
Ever know her heart?

Wang Wei

You will need
A heart-shaped vase
Scissors
Moss
Florist foam

Delicate pale pink
roses – yin fire

A Wedding Bouquet

9

Flowers have long been associated with declarations of love and wedding ceremonies. Flowers can express grace, purity and harmony: positive qualities to attract during an auspicious occasion such as a wedding. A wedding ceremony would be incomplete and joyless without flowers. This aspiration is infused with auspicious chi and follows the Three Harmony formula, which encourages the chi for elegance and harmony.

For this aspiration, the design should be simple, serene and elegant. These qualities are associated with the metal element, as are cream or white flowers with gentle curves or overlapping petals. The cooler chi of the metal element can be warmed with romantic yin fire chi by introducing touches of pink to the arrangement. The Three Harmony combination is activated with floral ingredients that combine the metal element with flowers that possess touches of yin fire and yin earth.

The flowers used for the wedding bouquet should also be used for the bridesmaids' flowers, the buttonholes, the garlands and the table displays.

Feng Shui Attributes

Soft feminine lines, curved petals and curling leaves all symbolize the pure harmonious chi necessary for this aspiration. The flowers should allude to affection and romance, and so the receptive qualities of yin chi are recommended, with clean sweeping lines. Sharp, angular or vibrant-coloured flowers are too yang for a traditional Western wedding (the Chinese prefer to attract yang energy at a wedding: the bride wears a red dress and red flowers are thrown at the couple).

For this aspiration yin metal is preferred to yang metal; yin metal inspires the qualities of simple harmony. It is associated with communication and

respect, qualities necessary in any marriage. Yang metal has a harder and more structured approach and may draw disciplinarian chi to the relationship!

"Nurture your true nature.
Only talk the truth.
Make love your gift to others."

Lao Tzu

Orchids are perfect for this aspiration: not only are they stunningly beautiful but they also have a strong presence. This flower in fact represents the underlying influence for the bouquet: too many contrasting ingredients would spoil the overall appearance. The other flowers complement the main flower influence, and should encourage curves and circular motions. The gentle overlapping petals of the lisianthus imply softness and sensitivity and their tiny buds symbolize love yet to open and unfold. Receptive chi is found nestling amongst the foliage. The ivy is chosen to bind love together.

Dominant, extreme yang flowers are avoided. Bold or vibrant colours are not useful to this aspiration in large quantities, though can be used in tiny amounts to draw attention to the more important creams, white and soft shades of pink.

Placement

This aspiration has been designed to be mobile, but it can be used as a feng shui activator too. If your intention is to accumulate auspicious energy which will eventually lead to marriage, then you must nurture the identified sector and keep it free from hostile forces including loud or aggressive music, noise or activities. As this is an aspiration for human harmony it shouldn't be overwhelmed with activity; a busy entrance in this direction will disturb the chi from gathering and so will reduce the possibility of marriage.

Two sectors support this aspiration: the west sector, which is governed by the metal element, and the southwest sector, which is governed by the earth element. When placing flowers in the west choose flowers that have a calming and endearing quality. Cream or white blooms with variegated or silver foliage are auspicious here and soft pinks will add warmth to the arrangement.

The southwest sector thrives on warmer tones than the west sector. Choose flowers in shades of pink and complement them with some creamy yellow tones. Again the emphasis is on a low and solid arrangement, encouraging the chi to settle and gather, growing in strength and support. Curves capture the attention of the eye and encourage chi to revolve in and around the flowers.

Choosing your Container

For this bridal bouquet you will need to arrange the flowers into a bridal holder, which is available from most professional florists. As a feng shui activator, choose a ceramic container that is fairly shallow and wide to house accessories such as stones, crystals and pebbles that add weight and are grounding. Candles can be incorporated into the design: using a candle to represent both people in the relationship is auspicious and complements the bagua association with number two in the southwest sector.

1 Choose blooms that have the purest colours and the most graceful curves. Select a combination of full open flowers expressing chi that has nothing to hide; buds with petals about to open representing the chi influencing the near future; and tight buds symbolizing the distant future and a growing family. Soak the bridal holder. Lay out the flowers ready to be arranged.

Alternative Flowers

Roses and peonies are perhaps the most auspicious flowers to use to express unconditional love because of their ancient mystical associations. However love comes in many shapes and forms and for a spring wedding sugar-pink tulips would be gorgeous and cream arum lilies would make an elegant bouquet.

Honeysuckle, believed to inspire commitment and devotion, could replace the ivy. Add fragrant lilies and roses to your design; their perfume will inflame the coldest of hearts. You could incorporate rosemary in the bouquet for its traditional protective qualities. An almond tree in the southwest corner of your garden will ensure a long and happy marriage!

2 Position the bridal holder into a large upside-down flower pot at a 45-degree angle, visualizing the natural angle the bride would use during the day. Position the orchid in the centre as the main focal point. With clipped pieces of ivy and lily grass, mark out the outline of the design, concentrating on clean sweeping curves, and fan out the overall height and width.

3 Strengthen the central focal point with the rose heads. The delicate pink of the rose will push the crisp white of the orchid to the forefront and draw attention to colour in the orchid throats, activating the yin fire and earth chi. The roses should trail from the centre, linking the lily grass and ivy to the composition. Trail the lisianthus by roses and fan them either side of the orchid for balance.

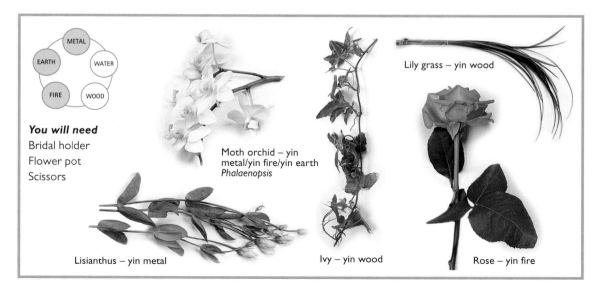

You will need
Bridal holder
Flower pot
Scissors

Moth orchid – yin metal/yin fire/yin earth *Phalaenopsis*

Lily grass – yin wood

Lisianthus – yin metal

Ivy – yin wood

Rose – yin fire

Congratulations

This energetic and cheery bouquet conveys feelings of happiness. Any joyous situation can be expressed in flowers; the flowers can honour a celebration, be given as a gift for a birth or engagement, symbolize pleasure and prosperity, or mark a job well done.

Bigger arrangements are useful for important ceremonies such as the opening of new businesses, to draw in auspicious energy from the beginning. New homes respond well to flowers that entice celebrations into the environment.

The flowers in this aspiration act as a focal point to celebrate achievement. The flowers should be bright and bold, with contrasting colours, as these demand more attention than single-colour bouquets.

Vibrant yellow lifts the spirits, whereas the earthy colours add weight and density. Choose flowers that are wide and open to represent the opening of the heart and exchange of elated energy. Open blooms are preferable to closed buds as they indicate sincerity and emotional openness.

Feng shui Attributes

The flowers that form the basic structure of the bouquet should thrust out and upwards, supporting the flowers in the forefront. The flowers have strong but not overwhelming yang energy to stimulate positive energetic wavelengths. The aspiration uses yang fire, yin and yang earth and yin and yang wood. Balance is important to this aspiration: to maintain the supportive qualities wrap the base of the arrangement in assorted layers of foliage.

Flowers such as sunflowers are invaluable owing to their close association with the sun; their large smiling heads will lift and follow the motion of the sun as it stretches across the horizon. The chi they are most associated with is happiness and exuberance. The anthurium in the unusual shade of coffee enhances the yang aspect of the arrangement and adds interest.

The colour, shape and texture of the flowers inspires a bubbly and happy attitude. Yellow is the colour associated with gold and the sun and encourages confidence and centring; this is further emphasized by the anthurium and stimulated by the burst of orange protea.

"Because happiness is not an ideal of reason but of imagination."

Immanuel Kant

Placement

Place the flowers where they command attention; opposite the entrance of a room so they will create a vibrant first impression. Placed near to a window, they will capture the chi of sunlight and create a cheerful atmosphere.

The southern sector of the bagua describes the energy linked with fame and recognition and flowers placed here will amplify the vibrations of festivity and achievement. Placed in the west, they connect to the energy of the family, and in the northwest they are associated with the chi of friends and colleagues. When placing bold yang flowers in metal sectors, increase the earth element by using yellow and brown flowers and tone down the intensity of the fire

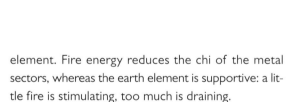

1 Leave the flowers overnight in deep water to fully recharge the stems with water. Trim the stems and remove any leaves that will be below the water line.

2 Hold a sunflower in one hand and surround it with foliage, turning the bouquet as you go. Add the foliage, anthurium, protea and sunflowers, alternating one stem at a time. When the bouquet outgrows your hand span, tie the string to a central sunflower stem and wrap it firmly around the stems, turning the bouquet. Add the rest of the flowers, wrapping the stems tightly in string.

element. Fire energy reduces the chi of the metal sectors, whereas the earth element is supportive: a little fire is stimulating, too much is draining.

Placing this aspiration in the north will stimulate the chi for success in your work. However, do not activate this sector with earth energy, as water is ultimately hindered by too much earth energy.

Choosing your Container

This aspiration is designed as a hand-tied arrangement to give as a gift. To attract energy that will bring opportunities for you to celebrate, choose a vase with fire and earth chi, such as terracotta. A ceramic vase brings grounding energy, useful when placing these flowers in the south, west and northwest.

Alternative Flowers

This is a strong and impressive aspiration, with yang chi, which is maximized by compacting the flowers. The same effect can be achieved with other flowers. In spring use tulips or daffodils, with forsythia for height and yellow variegated foliage for balance.

Summer arrangements could use bright gerberas or burgundy gladioli with sunflowers, or unusual brown flowers, including brown banksia, chrysanthemum, freesia, gerbera and rose. Autumn bestows the gift of rich-coloured foliage which can be combined with dazzling dahlia, rudbeckia, nerine and chrysanthemum. In winter, when fire chi is naturally weak, use hotter colours. To convey joy during the winter, use bright-red poinsettias and amaryllis.

3 Make sure the string is tied firmly to the stems, otherwise your arrangement will become untidy. Once all the flowers are in position, trim the ends of the stems to make a neat shape.

4 Make two sandwiches, each with a sheet of coloured paper in between two sheets of cellophane. Lay one sandwich on top of the other at 90-degrees and place the flowers in the centre. Gather up the corners, and draw them towards the bouquet until they are pulled underneath the flowers. Secure with string. Finish the bouquet by disguising the string with attractive raffia.

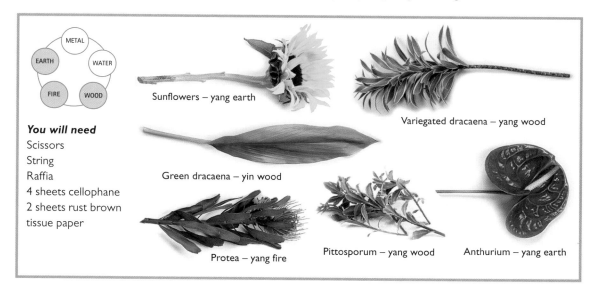

You will need
Scissors
String
Raffia
4 sheets cellophane
2 sheets rust brown
tissue paper

Sunflowers – yang earth

Variegated dracaena – yang wood

Green dracaena – yin wood

Protea – yang fire

Pittosporum – yang wood

Anthurium – yang earth

Thank you

Friendship cannot be measured yet it certainly can be appreciated. Sometimes we are in need, at others we are able to give help or support to those around us, creating an exchange of favourable energy. This feng shui aspiration allows you to express your appreciation and exchange loving energy.

The situations may vary but the feeling of elation that accompanies a thank you never differs. A gift of flowers is always an acceptable means to convey a thank you, but sometimes the true meaning of flowers becomes diluted. To accentuate heart-felt appreciation with flowers, choose flowers that are uplifting and that have happy, cheerful personalities.

Positive energy is created by combining two bold contrasting colours, such as purple and orange. A softer, more caring message is conveyed by using contrasting shades of pink and yellow, although the chi still combines the strengths and characteristics of yin fire and yin earth.

As well as making a beautiful hand-tied bouquet that expresses gratitude, this arrangement can be placed in the home to accumulate chi for appreciation of hard work, time and effort.

Feng Shui Attributes

The combination of flower ingredients determines the chi that you wish to extend. Soft pastel shades generate energy that is far more sensitive and receptive than the energy created by vibrant tones; bright colours have yang chi, which is more masculine than the amenable yin energy.

This arrangement concentrates on the sensitive and considerate qualities of yin fire and earth energies. The zesty lemon complements the warmer tones of the pink yin fire tulip, while the bear grass jutting upwards causes a yang chi reaction, imperative to balance the composition and for feng shui activity. Tulips are wonderful conductors of chi, as they happily contain an even balance of yin and yang energy and can achieve positive energy patterns on their own or by supporting other flowers.

"The only true gift is a portion of oneself."

Immanuel Kant

Choose flowers that are still in bud to increase the longevity of the arrangement and to allow the full potential of the flowers to remain intact until they are given to the recipient.

Placement

This aspiration is designed as a gift, but should you receive flowers like these, place them where their chi will combine favourably with the energy of the room and direction. This bouquet concentrates on yin fire and earth energies, so is suited to the southwest, where it can add support to the relationships sector. Remember, a little thanks goes a long way! They will also thrive in the east, where they will encourage appreciation of your efforts; they may also stimulate change if you've been feeling taken for granted. In the southeast they can be given as a gesture of

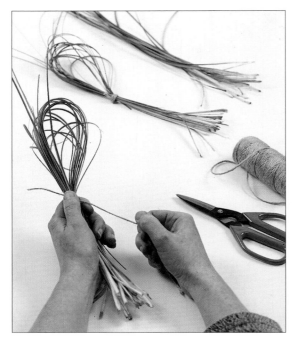

1 Bunch together twenty strips of bear grass and secure with florist wire or a strip of florist tape around the stem ends. Bend the bunched bear grass over and fasten the top to the centre with string, creating a top loop. Prepare several bunches of looped bear grass in this way but leave some bunches straight, as both styles will be used to enhance the energy of the tulips.

2 Strip away the bottom leaf of each tulip and trim the stems to remove the plug. Soak them for an hour to recharge their stems with water. Lay them out neatly on your work surface. Trim the ends of the bear grass and treat it to a decent wash to remove dirt and mud from the leaves.

appreciation for support. They are even auspicious in the south, where they will generate favourable chi so that people will appreciate you! In the north they draw attention from superiors – useful if you're looking for promotion. In the metal sectors of the west and northwest they are auspicious for sharing thanks with friends, family and colleagues.

Choosing your Container

The container should complement the flowers as much as possible – do not be tempted by a large or elaborate jug or container that will dwarf the flowers. A simple round glass vase or ceramic pot will push the chi of the flowers forwards and keep the eye concentrating on the colour, shape and texture of the flowers. Proportion and balance are imperative for this design, as a thank you is acceptance of an exchange of favourable chi. A thank you that is unbalanced suggests unfairness; a gift should never suggest mild manipulation or be given with the intention of gain.

This arrangement has been designed as a hand-tied bouquet, complete with a transportable water reserve. Once these flowers have reached their destination, the cellophane and tissue paper should be discarded and the flowers should be placed, as they are, into a simple container.

3 Take a looped bunch of bear grass and hold it in one hand. Add your flowers in coloured groups of three for a stronger impact. Position the tulips into the holding hand around the looped bear grass, turning the bouquet regularly to ensure an even distribution. Tie the end of the string to a central stem and wrap it around the stems firmly enough to hold the flowers in position but not so tight as to restrict the water flow. Wind the string around the stems until the arrangement is complete.

4 Trim the stem ends with scissors. Cut a hole in the base of the decorative paper to expose the stems. Lay the cellophane and tissue paper down and wrap the arrangement. To create a water reserve for your flowers, take two sheets of cellophane and stick them together with waterproof florist tape. Place your arrangement in the centre of the cellophane and draw up the corners. Tie around the base of the arrangement with string to create a reservoir and then hide the string with decorative ribbon. Carefully fill the reservoir.

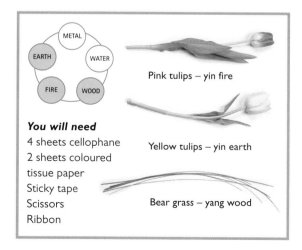

Pink tulips – yin fire

Yellow tulips – yin earth

Bear grass – yang wood

You will need

4 sheets cellophane
2 sheets coloured
tissue paper
Sticky tape
Scissors
Ribbon

Alternative Flowers

Many flowers could replace the tulips used in this aspiration. To create an energizing bouquet to convey heartfelt thanks you need to increase the chi that accompanies relationships based on trust and respect. The chi that best supports a relationship of this kind is yin fire for sensitivity and thoughtfulness and yin earth for receptivity and response. This is provided by softly coloured pink and yellow flowers. Green flowers could be used, providing you incorporate a representation of yin fire energy, for spirit, and that the final effect is feminine. Avoid architectural plants, which could be overwhelming.

欢迎

A Warm Reception

Flowers can greet the visitor with a brilliant display of powerful and positive energy, providing a warm and welcoming introduction that will spread throughout the rest of the building. First impressions are lasting impressions: create a focal point that will generate positive energy for the entrance.

This arrangement can be used both personally and professionally, as both the home and the business will prosper from a feng shui enhancer that boosts chi as it enters the building. The display should be exuberant enough to draw attention but in keeping with the proportions of the room: do not be tempted to place a huge arrangement in a hall or next to the main door that cannot afford the space, as the flowers then risk becoming a nuisance.

Locations that can afford a generous and creative arrangement include hotel lobbies, restaurants and bars, and sports, health and leisure clubs. Any industry that serves the public and would like to make a warm and positive welcome for their customers would benefit from this aspiration.

Flowers are so diverse, ranging in size, shape and texture and are available in a kaleidoscope of colours. Their presence subtly alters the mood of a room. Scented flowers make a good first impression as they stimulate the senses without a visual prompt, occasioning a pleasing welcome or a memorable entrance.

Feng Shui Attributes

A formal arrangement needn't be a dull arrangement. The flowers in this aspiration make a stunning impact, visible even from a distance owing to the precision of each stem and flower. Ample spacing is important to allow the chi freedom to flow. This arrangement requires weight and purpose, which is provided by the heavy ceramic container. For balance the flowers should be chosen for their strong visual impact and be placed deliberately into florist foam in strong modern lines. The combination of the container, the flowers and their positioning will influence the energy entering the building, positively charging the atmosphere with favourable chi.

Choose flowers that have predominantly strong yang energy to support active and positive energetic patterns. In this aspiration the yang energy is achieved and maintained by the glorious reds of the gingers and anthurium flowers.

"When your reception is small, your perception is shallow: When your reception is great your awareness is broad."

The Masters of Huainan

Fire requires fuel so it is advisable to incorporate the wood element to provide replenishing chi. The deep green of the large aspidistra and cordyline leaves provides an excellent backdrop for the alliums, proteas and anthuriums. The yang chi is accentuated by the thrusting red leaves of the dracaena. These push the central flowers to the forefront and provide a further focus of interest.

Placement

Ideally this arrangement should be placed near to or opposite the main entrance; otherwise place it where it can create the most impact as a focal point. This arrangement is intended to draw favourable attention and to welcome new guests and old friends.

The chi that most demands attention, gives warmth and is illuminating is the fire element, which is represented by the south sector of the bagua: placing the flowers in this sector will be auspicious and will harmonize with the chi of this direction.

Should you place the flowers in the east or southeast, you will still be supporting the fire element as both these sectors are governed by the wood element and will act as fuel to replenish flagging fire levels.

If you place these flowers in the north, northeast, west or northwest you will need to be a little more patient as these sectors will drain and exhaust the energy of the flower display. The chi of a warm welcome will not be ignored, but these sectors do not support fire chi and the flowers may spoil earlier than flowers in supportive directions. If you do use these directions, enhance the fire chi with additional lighting, such as candles or spotlights.

Choosing your Container

Both the shape and materials of the container should enhance the yang earth energy: use a large and impressive square ceramic container. The container should be large enough to accommodate the flowers but not dominate them. The impressive arrangement should create a sumptuous welcome and the container should not draw attention away from the flowers.

Alternative Flowers

Choose flowers that are large and impressive; yang chi is recommended for its positive qualities, but for balance it is important to include flowers and foliage that will represent the receptive and sensitive yin

1 Remove unwanted foliage from the flowers and leaves and trim the ends of the stems before soaking them in clean water. Allow the florist foam to fill with water. If your container is for garden use and is not waterproof, line the inside with a waterproof fabric. Position an upturned flower pot in the container and stand the florist tray on top. Sit the soaked florist foam on top of the tray, with a minimum of 3 inches (8 cm) florist foam above the rim of the container. Fasten the florist foam securely to the container with florist tape. The florist foam should be large enough to support the weight and angle of the heavier flowers.

energy. Sunflowers have a wonderfully positive attitude and are infused with yang earth chi, whereas the birds of paradise make a dramatic statement and boost the arrangement with yang fire chi.

Use fragrant flowers if possible, as scent makes a strong impact. You could trickle a few drops of an appropriate essential oil, such as geranium, onto the raffia that is tied to the vase, but be careful the perfume does not clash with the flowers and become confusing. Some oils stain or even remove varnish from furniture, so administer them with care.

2 Place three dracaena leaves at the back to represent yang fire chi and add the ginger flowers. Position aspidistra leaves at the base and add the protea. Make another line with the dracaena leaves and anthurium to provide a firm foundation to the arrangement. Introduce folded aspidistra leaves around the base together with rhododendron and cordyline leaves.

3 Once the basic shape and structure is established, add the smaller flowers, the allium and carnations. Position these flowers strategically to encourage the eye to roam throughout the arrangement. Position the alliums so they encourage the eye to return to the centre. Angle the carnations to balance the spread of the ginger flowers and anthurium.

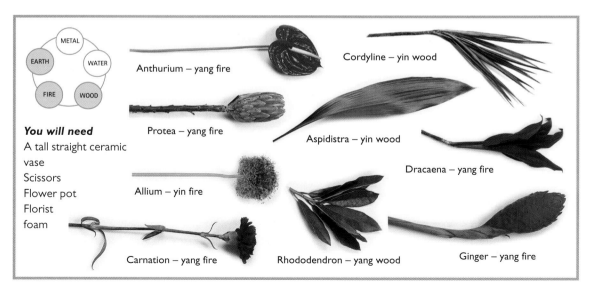

METAL
EARTH
WATER
FIRE
WOOD

Anthurium – yang fire

Cordyline – yin wood

You will need

A tall straight ceramic vase

Scissors

Flower pot

Florist foam

Protea – yang fire

Aspidistra – yin wood

Dracaena – yang fire

Allium – yin fire

Carnation – yang fire

Rhododendron – yang wood

Ginger – yang fire

Inspiring Projects

We can all benefit from an aspiration that is designed to give a little inspiration and provide a creative boost to sluggish systems! Occasionally our chi becomes depleted and our internal reserves run almost empty. Turn this negative situation into a positive application of creation and expression – be daring and adventurous, expand the limits of your imagination, and dissolve creative blocks.

The design of this arrangement can be as daring and contemporary as you wish, to reflect your mood and décor. Perhaps this aspiration will enable you to channel your frustrated chi into a work of art. Incorporate buds into the arrangement to suggest unfolding creativity. Let this arrangement prompt you to free your inner spirit and imagination and let go of stress and tension with flowers that vibrate with favourable chi and help release pent-up stress.

Incorporating the masculine aspect of the wood energy installs determination, maturity and ambition. A yang-inspired arrangement creates a powerful presence and activates energy for activity and ideas; a more yin bouquet reduces tension and induces calm.

Feng Shui Attributes

This aspiration stimulates the mind and helps prevent stagnant or unfavourable chi from accumulating. The shapes, shadows and textures of the design and thought-provoking flowers arouse curiosity and the use of simple and uncluttered plants clears the mind.

Both yin and yang wood energies are represented. The strong upright stems of curly bamboo provide yang wood chi, while the monstera leaves represent the receptive and caring yin wood chi.

Steel grass is bent into loops to match the contours of the phormium leaves. The loops encourage the eye to roam, yet always return to the centre, similar to returning to an original focus after a distraction. The contrasting lime petals of the anthurium have a similar effect, drawing attention to the centre, encouraging the accumulation of chi.

"I do not know whether I was then a man dreaming I was a butterfly, or whether I am now a butterfly dreaming I am a man."

Chuang Tzu

Finally the requirement of yin metal chi is met with the three cream Tokyo chrysanthemums. This keeps the chi calm and collected. Do not overwhelm the display with metal energy, which would exhaust the creativity of the wood chi.

Placement

Place this arrangement in the west, which is governed by the metal element, to fully stimulate the chi for clarity and harmony. The west sector is also responsible for structure, organization, communication and efficiency – powerful qualities that can make progress and ensure discipline. Inspiration is provided as the

1 Soak the florist foam, flowers and foliage. Curve several Swiss cheese plant leaves inside the container. Position a fatsia leaf in the front. Dribble a little water in the base of the glass container to keep the leaves moist. Sit the florist foam comfortably on top of the container in a florist tray and secure with the florist tape. The florist foam should be large enough to support the height and weight of the arranged flowers (the bamboo is the heaviest). The bamboo stems need to be inserted into a minimum 3 inches (8 cm) of supportive material.

2 Position the curly bamboo stems in strategic places, turning the stems until the desired impression is achieved. Take your time as the bamboo supports the other flowers; it will be difficult to alter their position once the other flowers have been included. Stagger the stems so that they are at different heights, representing different levels of consciousness.

wood element stimulates the cooler metal sector. Alternatively, place this arrangement in the east, and use flowers that incorporate the metal element to stimulate ideas and imagination from the wood chi.

Place these flowers in the north or south sector to draw attention to your ideas. Avoid placing them in the northeast, southwest and northwest.

Choosing your Container

Lining the large glass vase with the monstera leaves arouses initial interest, especially if there is a source of light behind the container casting shadows. The container needs to be large enough to be in proportion to the tall bamboo stems. The openness of the vase will allow chi to circulate freely.

Alternative Flowers

In winter, when the chi for inspiration is weakest, plant a selection of early-flowering spring bulbs such as snowdrop or grape hyacinth. Add some witch hazel flowers to activate the earliest glimpses of yang energy. Cover the soil with moss or rounded pebbles or even crushed crystals. The burst of energy as the bulbs emerge will cheer and inspire.

3 Take a series of phormium leaves and steel grass, bend them into appealing loops, secure with staples or florist wire and place them into the base of the bouquet. Balance the phormium leaves with two loops of steel grass, creating a powerful contemporary image.

4 Disguise the florist foam with a fatsia leaf and the shiny palettes of the lime-green anthurium flowers. Trim the ends of the chrysanthemums and remove unwanted foliage. Finally, position the chrysanthemums into the curves of the staggered bamboo stems. Position the flowers at different heights, reinforcing the idea of different levels of consciousness.

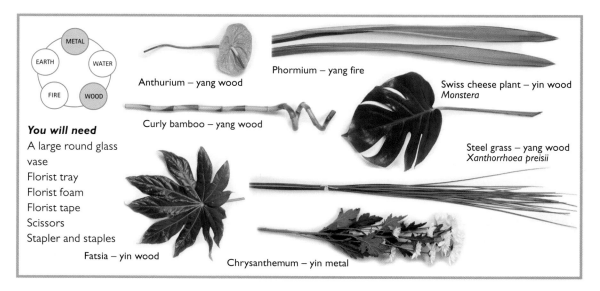

METAL

EARTH   WATER

FIRE   WOOD

Anthurium — yang wood

Phormium — yang fire

Swiss cheese plant — yin wood
Monstera

Curly bamboo — yang wood

Steel grass — yang wood
Xanthorrhoea preisii

You will need
A large round glass vase
Florist tray
Florist foam
Florist tape
Scissors
Stapler and staples

Fatsia — yin wood

Chrysanthemum — yin metal

Family Harmony

Every relationship will respond positively to an atmosphere of harmony. Chi that is able to meander softly around a room will gently nourish everyone it encounters. Enhance relationships by consciously designing a bouquet for the sector in the bagua that represents family harmony.

This one bouquet is designed to represent the whole family. Children, young adults, parents and grandparents: each generation can be included in the arrangement. Use tiny buds for very small children and babies, mature open flowers to represent adults and seed heads to represent the elders.

Metal is the element most associated with family harmony and also provides structure and discipline. It encourages self-expression and easy communication without emotional dramas, as the chi of the metal element is simple and decisive. Associated with the father, metal is represented by the heaven trigram.

Extreme metal can be cold and hard: qualities which could fuel resentment. To counteract negative chi, the Three Harmony combination formula is introduced, bringing auspicious chi to the home.

Feng Shui Attributes

The Three Harmony combination uses flowers that incorporate the nurturing yin earth element with the warm and compassionate yin fire chi and the harmony and communication of yin metal chi. The most favourable colours to use include creams, pinks and soft yellows, supported by the caring and flexible greens of wood chi. The soft pink lisianthus combines favourably with the deep pink of the rose.

There is a careful emphasis on soft and yielding shapes, colours and textures to provide a yin aspect to the metal element and add essential balance.

Curves and circular shapes strengthen the favourable aspect of the metal energy, encouraging the chi to revolve and circulate, which will then spiral out into the room. Chi that moves in curves is auspicious for smooth communication; chi that moves suddenly or in short bursts encourages loud or sudden outbursts.

"Tao is the father-mother of each being, which it creates, dissipates and re-creates as another being."
Chuang Tzu

The soft, delicate pinks of the rose and lisianthus represent the yin fire energy of the unconditional love of the mother. This is surrounded by pussy willow buds and small flowers in different stages of opening, representing the children. The grandparents are symbolized by the branches of the delicate catkins.

The guelder rose provides a splash of cheery green, a colour that promotes growing and healing energy. Its clusters of tiny petals huddle together to form a round dome. This complements the open, creamy peony, representing communication and gentle protection. The white snapdragon stretches yin energy outwards, releasing potential and inspiration with each opening bud. The pussy willow provides balance and represents the upward growth of yang wood chi and the abundant foliage represents yin wood chi.

1 Soak the florist foam and the flowers. Place the soaked florist foam into the container and secure it with florist tape. Prepare your foliage and lay each variety out separately.

2 Begin to arrange the foliage, alternating the various leaves while designing the basic shape and structure. Start from the centre and move outwards in a circular clockwise movement to increase yang positive energy. Clip the foliage to the height necessary for the proportions of the container, creating a round mound of foliage that will balance the depth of the container.

Placement

Place these flowers in the west to enhance relationship harmony and unhindered communication. To encourage the chi for order and discipline, position the flowers to the northwest, where there is a greater emphasis upon the yang energies. If your entrance falls in this direction this aspiration is emphasized.

In the north these flowers will enhance business, especially structure and networking. Communication, efficiency and streamlining will improve. In the northeast the quiet earth chi of the mountain will have an outlet and can help draw out a shy person.

Avoid placing the flowers in the east, southeast and south. In the southwest, this bouquet supports harmony and communication between couples.

Choosing your Container

Use a short round vase with floral foam to represent supportive earth energy and provide stability. This arrangement is also well suited to a metal container to support the chi of the west.

Alternative Flowers

Try lotus seed heads to represent the wisdom of the grandparents, for their architectural beauty and for their spiritual associations. The green shamrock chrysanthemum is a favourable flower to use in this arrangement as the petals curve inwards, inspiring an air of gentle protection, and the foxtail lily could replace the energy of the antirrhinum. Use scented lilies, rose and jasmine to further enhance this aspiration.

3 Introduce the larger flowers, the peony, the rose and the white snapdragon, considering balance and proportion. Allow enough space between the flowers to allow the chi to flow favourably. The florist foam and the rim of the vase should be completely covered but the arrangement should not be overcrowded.

4 Fill the larger spaces with the guelder rose and the double lisianthus. Start adding small bunches of upright and looped bear grass. Finish the arrangement with the slender stems of pussy willow and the catkins. The fuzzy buds of pussy willow stems represent the energy of children about to burst with potential.

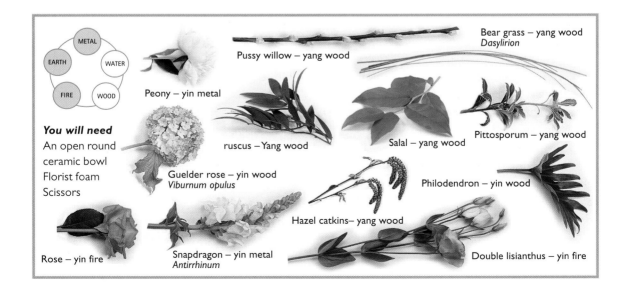

Bear grass – yang wood
Dasylirion

Pussy willow – yang wood

Peony – yin metal

ruscus – Yang wood

Salal – yang wood

Pittosporum – yang wood

You will need
An open round ceramic bowl
Florist foam
Scissors

Guelder rose – yin wood
Viburnum opulus

Philodendron – yin wood

Hazel catkins– yang wood

Rose – yin fire

Snapdragon – yin metal
Antirrhinum

Double lisianthus – yin fire

Networking and Socializing

To encourage energy that will influence networking favourably you need to address metal elemental chi, for this is the connecting energy that encourages integrity and inspires harmony. Communication that is infused with metal energy will take discussion to a higher level and will encourage everyone to respond favourably.

The metal element influences order and structure in social circles. Extreme metal chi is unfavourable, resulting in situations where rules act as controlling agents rather than as benevolent forces that serve the members of the society. This aspiration can be used as an effective cure in these situations, encouraging openness and effective decision making. Extreme metal energy can become cold and hard, without room for flexibility. This arrangement will inspire a return to communication and harmony; the never-ending circles push the chi along, reducing stagnation and establishing connections.

The flowers should not dominate the room or the sector they are placed in, as the intention is to promote balance and harmony. In a conference room or board meeting these flowers will be auspicious when placed discreetly along the wall, breaking up possible poison arrows and energizing chi in corners.

Feng Shui Attributes

This arrangement emphasizes circles and curves. The main circular shapes are created by florist foam. The shape of the foam is enhanced with flowers chosen for their openness and compact texture, to suppress aggressive behaviour, which would be stimulated by sharp flowers. The colours and textures of the flowers contrast strongly, stressing yin and yang.

The wire emphasizes the metal element and looks like a figure of eight – a continuous, never-ending loop. The balls of flowers act as reserves of replenishing energy. The chi will follow the lines and shapes created by the flowers and the contours of the wire and will reinvest energy generated by the flowers. The central ball is the largest and strongest focal point. Making a statement with rings of black and gold, it is supported on either side by two smaller balls filled with white chrysanthemums.

"The enlightened no longer have an 'I' for they have united all parts in ecstatic contemplation of the One."

Chuang Tzu

The design of three balls of flowers with yin and yang characteristics emphasizes the trigram for water, which represents the unhindered flow of positive chi. This trigram is created by the dark central ball flanked on either side by the white balls; the black ball represents receptive yin energy and the two white balls represent supportive yang energy. The balls are attached to each other with loops of wire to accent the metal element and to emphasize the need to establish a connection to communicate effectively.

1 Soak the floral foam balls by allowing them to sink into water. Remove unwanted foliage from the flowers and trim the stems, then soak them in clean water for an hour. Remove the petals from the gerbera heads. Cut the heads away from the stems, leaving at least 1 inch (3 cm) of stem beneath the flower heads.

2 Put the soaked balls into the container, with the largest one in the middle. Carefully mould several lengths of thick wire into smooth arcs to make a continuous-looking loop. Make sure the lengths of wire are in proportion to the overall arrangement and then firmly push them into the balls.

The tiny inner petals of the gerbera centres create bands of gold, representing circles within circles; as they interlock and support each other, they mimic the behaviour of the metal element. The arrangement uses simple shapes and fluid harmony – dazzling or adventurous displays of flower chi would serve as a distraction and could disturb concentration.

Placement

The sector most associated with order, networking and socializing is the northwest sector, ruled by the metal element. Metal also rules the storage of powerful energy that forms the basis for structure and discipline – valuable ingredients to provide the foundations for any successful organization.

This aspiration will add drama to social occasions without being flamboyant. It will help business prosper, increasing productivity by encouraging people to share their ideas and act as a team. In the west, these flowers are auspicious: here the emphasis is more on discussion than on meeting new associates or building confidence. The arrangement will act as an outlet for the earth energies of the northeast and the southwest, reducing heaviness or lethargy. These sectors will support the metal energy of the flowers. These flowers are supportive in the north and influence the energy directed at business and careers.

Avoid placing these flowers in the south sector as the intensity of the fire elemental energy will melt the chi of structure and discipline and will weaken

3 Begin to insert the gerbera heads into the central ball. Start from the top and carefully arrange the flower centres closely together, following simple lines. Do not push them into the foam at random intervals, as this will not support the metal energy as favourably.

4 Push the chrysanthemum heads into the two smaller balls. Again the emphasis is on order and structure. The flowers should touch, to eliminate ugly spaces, but avoid overcrowding, as this will spoil the flow of energy, creating periods of intensity. Finally, dribble a little water into the container to prolong the life of the aspiration.

your results. However, if there is an extreme level of yang energy in the south these flowers will effectively reduce negative shar chi.

Choosing your Container

Use an oval, elongated or round shallow dish, preferably metal. Or choose a ceramic container, as the earth element best supports the metal element.

Alternative Flowers

True black flowers to represent the chi of yin water are difficult to find but the centres of cream gerbera and the black viola are both very dark. Black parrot tulips and the true black grass, *Ophiopogon planiscapus* 'Nigrescens' are also suitable if arranged in a vase.

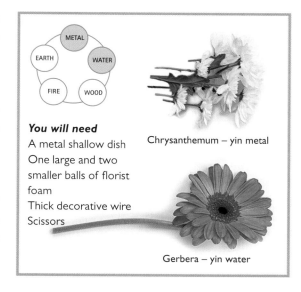

You will need
A metal shallow dish
One large and two smaller balls of florist foam
Thick decorative wire
Scissors

Chrysanthemum – yin metal

Gerbera – yin water

Dinner Parties

This arrangement uses flowers as a feng shui activator to ensure a successful dinner party. The combination of the colours and textures of the flowers and their personalities will enhance the atmosphere and encourage fluid conversation.

16

This formal arrangement adds a touch of elegance and sophistication to the table, without obstructing the view of the person opposite you. The cooler colours are warmed and activated by the chi of the candles. The flowers should complement the occasion and the décor of the room holding the function. A bold and energetic arrangement inspires a dramatic atmosphere, a perfect accompaniment for a glamorous dinner party. The flowers can be unusual or atmospheric, with trailing blooms or upright stems depending upon the mood you wish to create.

"The more creatively you live your life, the more you will experience your essential nature."

Lao Tzu

Keep the theme of the flowers consistent with the main floral feature if decorating napkins or laying a single bloom on a plate as a floral finishing touch. For a strong impact, choose flowers that contrast with each other, although they should never direct the eye totally away from the table or the guests. The flowers should not conflict with each other, nor should the arrangement be so huge and impressive that it is literally in the way. Never arrange flowers so that they obscure the view across the table. A picnic in the garden, a barbecue or an *al fresco* supper will be enhanced by a simple arrangement of flowers.

Alternatively use flowers in the meal itself: many fresh flowers and plants are edible and have wonderful zesty flavours (see page 169).

Feng Shui Attributes

These flowers were chosen for their pleasing ability to quietly enhance the atmosphere without being aggressive or obvious. The colours, shapes and texture of the flowers will encourage the yin metal and water elements, with a touch of the receptive yin earth energy for support.

The clean, crisp, overlapping white petals of the ranunculus and the white lily represent the yin metal element. The perfume of the lily releases positive sheng chi and its soft creamy yellow strip along the inside of its petals provides earth energy.

The flow of communication is aided by the chi of yin water, which is generated by the vivid-blue flowers of the hyacinth and delphinium.

Placement

To increase favourable energy in the dining room, identify the sector of bagua that affects that room. Ideally the chi will have a favourable influence from the metal energy, the chi associated with communication and harmony. Place the flowers in the northwest or west sector to stimulate this elemental energy.

There should also be a substantial influence from the east energy, which is responsible for growth, abundance and creativity. Placing the flowers in the

1 Soak the posy pad and trim the flower stems. As soon as the posy pad has absorbed enough water, insert the candles into the candleholders and place them in a central position in the florist posy pad.

2 Build the initial shape and structure with the foliage. Slightly angle the stems so that they gently curve up and outwards. Keep your scissors close to hand and trim any stray leaves to keep the shape uniform and consistent.

east or southeast directions, which are governed by the wood element, will encourage varied topics of conversation and will help everyone to express themselves freely.

In the south, the flowers will stimulate fire energy, which will generate chi that is less formal and more suitable for a celebration. Flowers for a party would benefit from warmer tones and flowers that are less formal than this arrangement.

Avoid placing these flowers in the north, where they will encourage conversation to revolve around business. In the northeast the flowers will encourage a more philosophical direction or conversation will become broken or fragmented as the chi encourages a quieter, meditative atmosphere.

Choosing your Container

An arrangement for a dinner party should not become an obstruction, so use a low or shallow container with added florist foam, or even a professional florist posy pad especially developed for such a purpose.

Alternative Flowers

Alternative blue flowers include allium, hydrangea and lavender and can be combined with cream roses, hyacinths, carnations and amaryllis.

Use flowers from your garden for informal arrangements, which will harmonize with their natural environment. Choose bright cheerful colours in fun containers, such as beaded pots, or containers hidden inside summer baskets.

3 Arrange the larger flowers, the lilies and the hyacinths. Position them next to the candles and close together for maximum effect. This arrangement will not respond favourably to overcrowding: use the spaces between the foliage as guides and position the flowers so they expose their full petals without crushing one another.

4 Finish the arrangement with the small flowers. Place the ranunculus and delphiniums evenly throughout the arrangement, filling ugly gaps and complementing the larger flowers. To complete, punctuate the arrangement with the tips of plain and variegated foliage.

You will need
A florist posy pad
Candle holders
Cream candles
Scissors

Lily – yin metal (stripe yin earth)

Salal – yang wood

Pittosporum – yang wood

Buttercup – yin metal
Ranunculus

Broad ivy – yin wood

Hyacinth – yin water

Delphinium – yin water

Career Enhancer

There are times when we need to ready ourselves for action or face situations that require confidence or assertiveness. This aspiration will enhance the chi for your career. You could use it to help you focus on getting a promotion or a new job.

Sadly, it is often difficult to maintain a happy and balanced equilibrium. We all suffer from demands and have to meet deadlines and may become frustrated. During periods of intense dehydration and stress our internal energies may become blocked and our ability to concentrate fragmented. The chi that is responsible for our intelligence, our careers, and the way we apply ourselves to everyday situations could become weakened.

The water element governs intelligence and the intellect. Water chi is the energy that maintains life in all living things; it is the chi that controls fluids, regulating the flow of life. It is found in the north sector of the bagua. When this energy is clear, strong and purposeful all areas of our lives are enriched with the life-giving force of water. This aspiration enhances this energy and is a positive statement that may affect your outlook in life.

Ideally, energy gathering in this area of our lives should be fresh and meandering, and move with a fluid grace. Under stressful situations this chi can become blocked or turbulent, unhappy and rocky. Negative shar chi could be triggered, stirring up unhappy memories, phobias and feelings of fear or despair. We may become unsure and lose precious spontaneity. Even worse, this chi could become spoiled through neglect or self-denial.

To enhance this element, supporting the chi of the north, an 'active' water arrangement is called for. Water can be enhanced with flowers, lights, bubbles, fish and water misters. For this aspiration to be fully effective, ensure the water is clean and fresh at all times and never allow it to become dirty or stagnant. Use ionized water to help prevent a build up of limescale and the development of algae.

Feng Shui Attributes

The north sector of your room or building brings a chi that acts as an outlet for our intelligence and creativity. These qualities are used both professionally and within the home and family. If we can apply ourselves fully to everyday tasks, without distraction, we can find peace and harmony.

*"Flow with whatever may happen and let your mind be free:
Stay centred by accepting whatever you are doing. This is the ultimate."*

Chuang Tzu

The career sector of the bagua is associated with the number one, so this aspiration uses a single flower. This also encourages the association of setting yourself one task at a time and concentrating on that one task. As the positive chi gradually increases, so too will your attention span and you will find that you are able to apply yourself to any enterprise that you set your mind upon. The metal element best

1 Clean your container thoroughly to remove any traces of plant residue or lime-scale. Check the working parts of the electronic misting equipment and clean if necessary. Add the water and a few drops of blue colouring agent to make the water a rich blue.

2 Choose your one flower with deliberate care and attention. It should be as perfect as possible, for that single flower will represent the chi you wish to encourage. An open bloom is preferred to a closed one. Trim the stem to allow the plant to drink as much water as possible.

supports the water element, so this aspiration uses a single white peony. Peonies have spiritual associations and increase the chi for happiness, wealth and prosperity, and successful relationships.

Placement

To enhance career or business opportunities, place this arrangement in the north sector of your home or office. These flowers will act as an outlet for strong metal energy; this is useful if chi is overwhelming and rigid. The water element will increase fluid communication and lubricate the wheels of any organization.

Avoid placing this aspiration in the south, where it will clash and encourage conflict or, at the very least, it will dampen the spirits. This aspiration is also ineffective in the earth sectors of the northeast and the southwest, as earth has the ability to absorb water, reducing the potency of the water chi. It will support the chi of the wood and will replenish the wood chi reserves, increasing the energy for wealth and prosperity, travel and inspiration. However, in these directions the chi will be too weakened and exhausted to be an effective feng shui activator for career opportunities or promotion.

Choosing your Container

This aspiration requires a large expanse of water, therefore choose a shallow dish with a wide circumference. Otherwise use a vase that complements a single bloom and displays a large water reservoir to

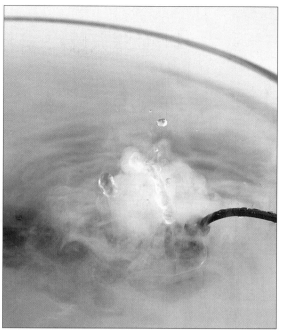

3 Following the manufacturer's instructions, place the mister into the water, then switch it on. Do not switch the mister on without water, as the vibrating membrane will quickly burn out. Cut the stem of your chosen flower to just $\frac{1}{2}$ inch (1 cm) and carefully position the bloom in the water.

3 The mister will gradually produce enough mist to cover the entire surface of the bowl and activate the aspiration with positive chi.

emphasize water chi. The water can be coloured with a few drops of black ink or blue food colouring to support the water chi even further.

The water element is associated with irregular shapes and so an asymmetric or unusual container would be suitable for this aspiration, especially if it were made from a metal material.

Alternative Flowers

Always use the most perfect single flower you can find. If possible it should be fully open, white and be able to float. The lotus flower, although difficult to find, would be perfect for this aspiration. Otherwise camellia, amaryllis and, of course, the water lily would all be suitable candidates.

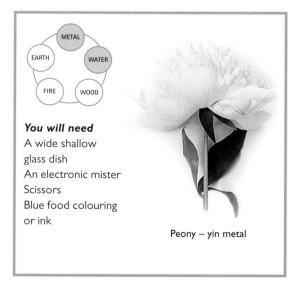

You will need
A wide shallow
glass dish
An electronic mister
Scissors
Blue food colouring
or ink

Peony – yin metal

Inner Spirit Meditation

The ingredients for this aspiration are chosen to de-stress and rejuvenate the soul, to bring inner peace and calm, and to encourage detachment from the hectic external world. Place them in a quiet area of the house and allow yourself to spend time in quiet contemplation.

Sometimes the world around us is moving so fast that our heads begin to spin and our thoughts spiral. We are bombarded by thousands of images, advertisements, and sound waves that upset our ability to focus and concentrate until it becomes difficult to make rational judgements. When prolonged, extreme stress can cause ill health.

This is a useful arrangement for situations that require a tranquil and composed atmosphere. Nurturing the inner spirit is just as important to the body as a well-balanced meal. We need to listen to the body and treat it with the care and respect it deserves. Balance is the key to happiness and longevity. We should encourage objects into our home that promote relaxation or act as aids to meditation as a positive step towards taking control of our destinies.

Earth and metal elemental energy encourages chi to settle and become grounding. The earth element provides the receptive and nurturing energy of the Great Mother, the metal chi provides grace and purity, here represented by one perfect bloom.

Feng Shui Attributes

While considering which flowers you should use for this aspiration, look carefully at every aspect of the flower. Check for imperfections such as staining or brown edges. Discard flowers or leaves that have been bent or scored. Take as much time as you can allow, as this is also part of the meditative process.

This aspiration uses an orchid plant complete with a root system, symbolizing the connection nature has to both the earth and the spirit realms. The roots are covered with layers of stones and sand, their contrasting textures add receptive yin earth energy to the arrangement.

"Tao is not far away from where you are. Those who go looking elsewhere always return to here and now."

Lao Tzu

Choose a cream, white or golden orchid, as these colours are associated with metal elemental chi, which supports this arrangement. Dark-green foliage at the base of the plant balances the slender elongated stem of the orchid. Equilibrium is the key to this aspiration; the energy of the earth generates valuable yin chi, balancing the yang energy of the determined yet humble orchid, which reaches upwards.

Metal energy thrives in conditions with clean lines, here provided by the orchid. Metal is the element that can cut through misconceptions or illusions, such as our unreasonable fears and desires. It is also the element that discards clutter in favour of discipline and harmony. By encouraging this element into your environment you will help to transform chaos into tranquillity. The earthy ingredients – the sands, soil and

stones – support the metal chi of the orchid. The container has the solid, regular shape of a cube, representing yang earth energy.

Placement

The best placement area for this aspiration is in the northeast sector of the bagua, which is home to the trigram of the mountain, symbolic of peace, inner spirit and meditation.

If the northeast sector of your home is an active or busy area, it is unlikely that the chi will settle enough to become influenced by this arrangement. The same is true for an entrance or main door in this sector; it will be difficult to encourage chi to become quiet, as chi will move every time the entrance is used.

To make the most of this aspiration, place it in an area where chi circulates slowly and softly. A quiet room such as a study, small office, treatment room or even a bedroom will contain chi that is settled and thus useful for this aspiration. Place the flowers in the northeast sector of this room to tap into and retain the chi suitable for meditation. Make sure you spend time in quiet contemplation with the aspiration.

"Be simple and true to your own nature. Be selfless and at peace with the way things are."

Lao Tzu

This arrangement would be useful in the southwest to bring peace, respect and stability to relationships, or in the west and northwest to support the strength of the business and family communication. Placed in the north, this aspiration will support the career, providing that the metal chi influence is greater than the energy of the earth. The south, southeast and east direction do not support the elemental requirements and will hinder this aspiration.

1 Take the broken pieces of ceramic or crocks and place them into the container, adjusting them in conjunction with the orchid pot to gauge the final height of the orchid. The orchid pot should be just beneath the rim of the square glass vase.

Choosing your Container

Choose a clear, square glass vase to represent the earth element. Otherwise use a ceramic or china container. A plain or glazed ceramic vase will support the earth element; a white or metal container will support the metal element. A simple vase can present a single bloom elegantly and provide a beautiful focus for meditation.

Alternative Flowers

This aspiration can be achieved with a single perfect flower held in a simple slender vase or container. The concept here is to provide a simple yet stunning impression without the use of force or fuss. Pushing oneself too hard or using force in a situation is

2 Position the orchid onto the crocks and carefully pour in the first layer of sand. Continue adding the assorted layers of sand until the container is full and the plant pot hidden. Use brown, white, green and red sand and blue glass nuggets to represent the colour associations of the five elements.

3 Finally add the coloured glass to the top of the sand to completely cover the surface. This will help to conserve the moisture in the vase.

detrimental to your spirit and ultimately could even affect your health. The same rule applies to the flowers chosen for this aspiration – too many flowers crammed together will send out more energetic information into the atmosphere, stimulating the mind rather than encouraging it to let go and ready itself for contemplation.

Single classic blooms, such as a poppy head in bud or a budding peony, hold potential energy yet to unfold. The bulbous heads are full of chi that has yet to develop and fully express itself. A single rose or stately calla lily would also be a suitable choice. To make the most of this design choose simple but complementary containers than enhance the slender and sophisticated lines of the flower on show.

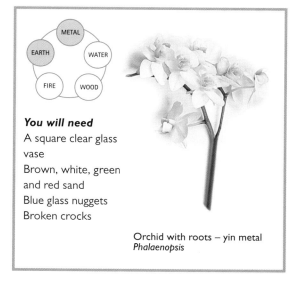

You will need
A square clear glass vase
Brown, white, green and red sand
Blue glass nuggets
Broken crocks

Orchid with roots – yin metal
Phalaenopsis

知识

Education and Knowledge

19

**The flowers and materials chosen for this arrangement
are designed to calm the spirit and focus the mind. Appealing
to children as well as adults, this aspiration will aid
concentration and support the chi for retaining knowledge,
imperative during revision or exams.**

The chi that best absorbs information is the earth element – just think of the receptive quality of the soil when it absorbs rainfall. Earth is protective and reliable and will bring stability to every situation. This aspiration encourages you to take gentle steps, one at a time, and to make gains softly, moving forward in stages. Biting off more than you can chew will cause stress levels to rise and becoming overwhelmed will fracture concentration and could block internal energy flows, causing frustration and scattering chi.

To increase our awareness and improve our concentration we must find an area where we are free to relax. Calming the mind and the spirit enables the brain to prepare for new information. It is impossible to learn new information with a mind full of distractions or insecurities. Wisdom is enhanced by slow and deliberate actions, like constructing a building one block at a time. The plants used in this design have been chosen with these concepts in mind.

Feng Shui Attributes

The bamboo steps are symbolic of the different stages of knowledge. The five steps of this aspiration represent the five elements and fifteen stems of bamboo are used because fifteen is a powerful number. Bamboo is an auspicious plant, highly valued for its flexibility, durability and strength. Bamboo is renowned for its longevity; with just a little fresh water and room to breathe it can live for up to seventy-five years.

Either side of the bamboo are bright-yellow chrysanthemum heads. These compact flowers represent the receptive energy of the earth and support the bamboo stems, securing them in place. Chrysanthemum is one of the sacred flowers of the Ancient Chinese; according to the formulas of feng shui it is auspicious and traditionally is said to possess magical properties and enhance wisdom.

"Trying to understand is like straining to see through muddy water. Be still and allow the mud to settle."

Lao Tzu

Chrysanthemums can remove pollutants from the atmosphere, encouraging positive chi that feeds the brain and enriches the blood. Chrysanthemum petals are edible and can be added to salads or used as an unusual garnish. The compact flowers are arranged to support the bamboo, which is arranged in steps leading upwards, symbolizing the steps to a higher education. Alternatively, the steps could be viewed as different levels of awareness.

Golden chrysanthemums are a good choice for this arrangement as this colour is closely associated with gold and prosperity. The deep blue of the container represents the chi of yang water, associated with intellect and wisdom.

1 Trim the chrysanthemum stems and remove unwanted foliage. Lay the florist foam on top of fresh water and allow it to soak. As soon as the foam has absorbed enough water place it into the container.

2 Cut the stems of bamboo to their required lengths. They should make five steps. The first step is one short stem, the second two longer stems, the third three longer still and so on.

Placement

This aspiration should be placed in the northeast direction, which symbolizes the energy of the mountain trigram. This chi encourages contentment, peace and stillness – not to be mistaken with inactivity.

For this aspiration to be as effective as possible, it should be placed on a desk or table close to the person who is studying. The combination of the shape, texture and flowers will reassure and act as a reminder to take things slowly. Spending time close to this arrangement will open the energy channels in the body and help the mind receive new information.

Avoid placing this arrangement in an area that is regularly disturbed, such as a lounge or playroom, as the activity of the room will prevent receptive chi from accumulating. This will also apply to rooms that have their entrance in the northeast sector; a busy entrance will generate yang active energy, which could be stimulating but will also be disturbing.

Placing this arrangement in the southwest sector of a building will support the chi affecting relationships. When this arrangement is placed in the south it will reduce the intensity of the fire energy and so can calm overactive chi – useful for hyperactive children.

Avoid these flowers in the east and southeast, where the directional chi will break up and disturb the chi you are trying to create. In the north, governed by the water element, this arrangement is restricted, as earth has the ability to disturb water and water can exhaust and undermine earth chi.

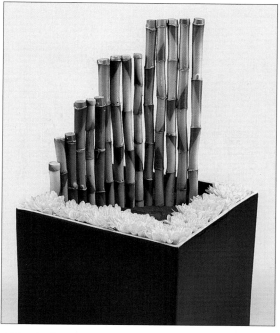

3 Gently mark an arc on top of the florist foam with a pen or pencil as a guide for the bamboo. Carefully place the smallest stem of bamboo into the florist foam along the guided path. One by one, place the bamboo in order, gradually gaining height and following the mapped arc until all the stems are in their final position.

4 Cut the flowers stems to approximately 1 inch (3 cm), just enough to hold their position in the florist foam. To complete this aspiration, cover the remaining florist foam with the golden chrysanthemum heads.

Choosing your Container

As this aspiration requires the influence of the earth elemental chi, choose a square container that represents this chi. Use a ceramic or terracotta container rather than clear glass otherwise you will see the unsightly florist foam. A ceramic shallow dish or plate can be used, providing the chrysanthemums and bamboo steps successfully disguise the floral foam.

Alternative Flowers

You can position the bamboo steps growing out from clipped eucalyptus and purple smokebush (cotinus) foliage as an alternative to the chrysanthemums, as both eucalyptus and smokebush are associated with education and wisdom.

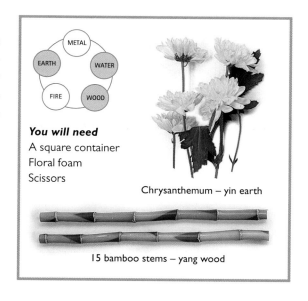

You will need
A square container
Floral foam
Scissors

Chrysanthemum – yin earth

15 bamboo stems – yang wood

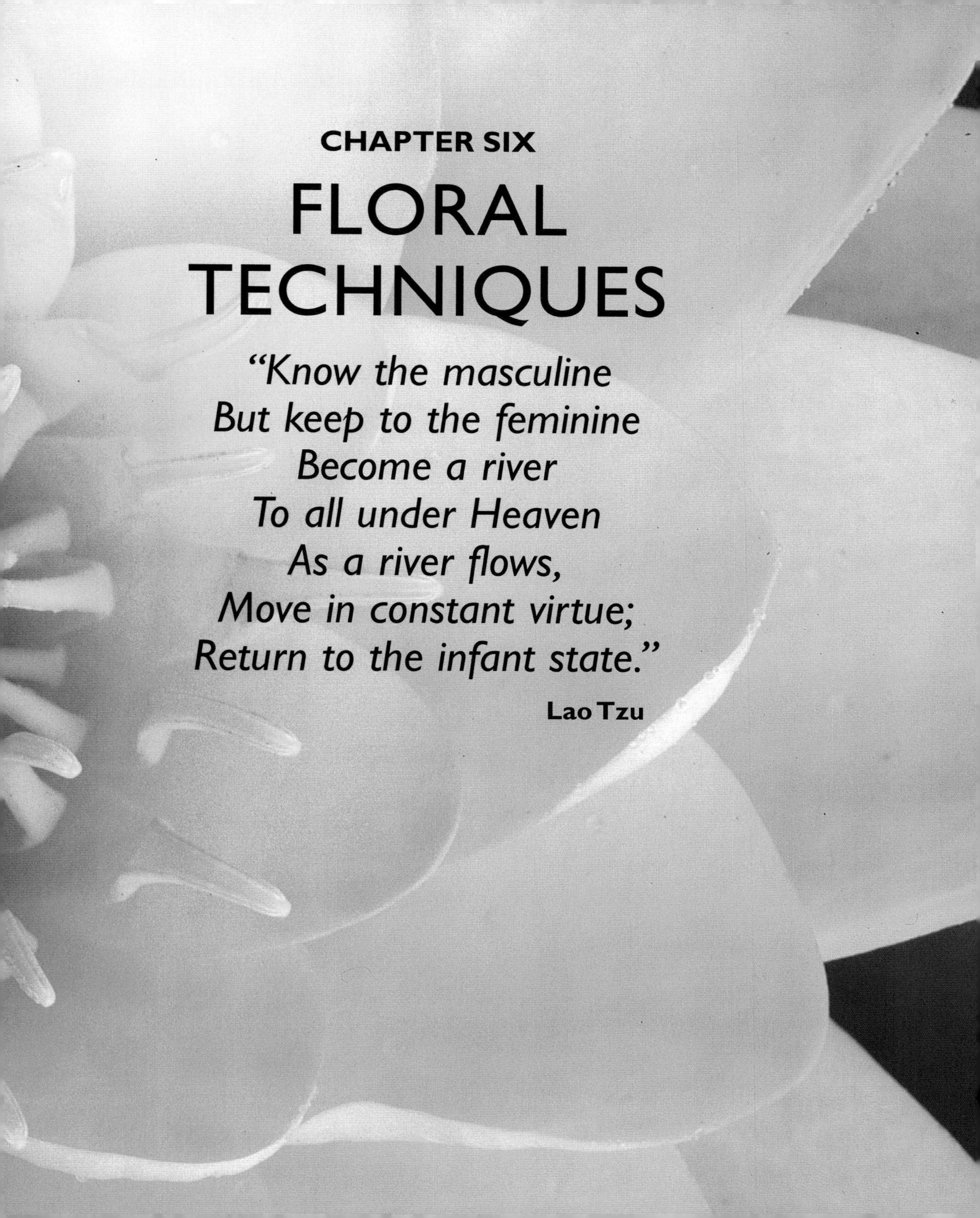

CHAPTER SIX

FLORAL TECHNIQUES

"Know the masculine
But keep to the feminine
Become a river
To all under Heaven
As a river flows,
Move in constant virtue;
Return to the infant state."

Lao Tzu

To bring out the full potential of your aspirations, pay attention to the practical requirements of your flowers. The scope of your intentions and depth of your imagination will be wasted if the flowers are unable to breathe or draw up water adequately. Flowers will last much longer once they have been prepared and treated professionally. Though they have been cut and removed from the life-sustaining soil, they are still very much alive and in need of care. Flowers that are wilting or past their best will not support an aspiration; instead they will emanate negative shar chi and hinder your aspiration.

FLORAL TECHNIQUES
Practical Preparation
Once you have bought your flowers home, treat them with the same care and attention as would a professional florist. Simple techniques will not only encourage strong chi but will also prolong the life of your arrangement.

Trimming
Always trim the ends of the stems of flowers as, once cut, flowers naturally form a plug to prevent further water and nutrient loss. Remove an inch or two from the bottom to reopen the stems for transporting water to the rest of the flower. Drooping flower heads are a telling sign of blocked stems; once this happens the flower will quickly wilt.

Exotic flowers tend to last longer than some other varieties; even so their lives can be prolonged by trimming their stems weekly. Cut the end of the stem just above any brown staining; this is caused by bacteria and will prevent the plant from drawing water.

Flowers will continue to expel their sticky residue, gradually poisoning the water in the vase. Refresh the water weekly by standing the vase under running water to flush away toxins or bacteria that have built up.

Some plant residues clash with others and decrease the life expectancy of your arrangement. Keep tulips and daffodils apart from other flowers.

Container Care
Make sure that your container is scrupulously clean. Even traces of plant residue will dissolve into water and can be drawn up by the flower; if too many particles are left in the water the lines of communication become blocked. Once this happens the flower is unable to draw fluids and the life span of the flower is rapidly reduced. In between arrangements always clean your container thoroughly with bleach (traces of bleach will not harm flowers and could even extend the life of some blooms).

Help Your Flowers Last Longer
Always buy flowers that are fresh and, if possible, before they are fully mature. Buy from a florist that smells fresh and clean. To prevent your flowers

Trimming the stems.

Splitting the stems.

out. After they have drawn water, hollow-stemmed plants can be plugged with a little piece of cotton wool to prevent further water loss.

Split the ends of roses and flowers with woody stems vertically before placing them in deep warm water. Leaves and foliage can be soaked for an hour, although no longer, or they will lose their texture. Do not soak furry or silky haired leaves.

Large, shiny or glossy foliage can be treated to an occasional wipe from a damp cloth with a few drops of oil or with a special leaf spray to encourage leaf shine.

Charcoal tablets in water help to keep the water pure. Flowers last longer in cooler temperatures, so keep them away from direct sources of heat and out of direct sunlight. In hot weather spray your flower arrangement with a fine mist of cool water.

Feed your flowers with suitable food; most florists supply a sachet of flower food with the flowers, which not only provides replacement sugars to promote flowering but also agents that reduce bacteria.

Reviving

Some flowers are susceptible to early dropping or sudden wilt owing to water loss; roses and gerberas are particularly prone to early dropping. To bring them back to life, perform this emergency revival procedure. Unwrap the flowers, trim the end from the stem and cut a small vertical nip into the cut end of roses. Remove the lower foliage and trim the thorns from rose stems. Carefully wrap each stem in paper to support the flower head and to keep it straight (use paper rather than plastic, which would encourage the plant to sweat). Plunge the stems into deep lukewarm water, up to just below the base of the flower heads, and leave overnight, if possible. In the morning the flowers should be upright and fully charged with water. If this technique fails, return the flowers to the florist, who can then pass on the complaint to the supplier.

suffering quickly from wilt, you need to fill the stems with water. Water loss is at its lowest during the evening as plants lose water during the day through evaporation and transpiration, therefore if using blooms from the garden, pick them at night or early in the morning.

Encourage water into the stems by cutting the ends of all bought flowers and standing them up to their necks in a large container of tepid water for several hours. A teaspoon of sugar added to the water will help condition the flowers and foliage. Remember to strip the foliage from the stems that are to be submerged under water, as they will rot in the water and poison the flower.

Cut the ends from the flowers at an angle to prevent an airlock in the stem, which will stop water from being absorbed. Cutting the stem at an angle will also increase the surface area of the stem that is able to draw water. Remove a minimum of $1/_2$-inch (2 cm) off the end of the stem, which will have dried

FLOWER ARRANGING TECHNIQUES

Wiring

Wiring flowers is a useful technique for securing the flowers in place, necessary for arrangements that are slightly different, such as head-dresses, bridal bouquets and garlands. It is important that the wires remain invisible in the final display, which can take some practice. However, with the right technique and suitable wire it is entirely possible to wire a leaf or a flower and keep the appearance natural and fluid. Choose a wire that is a suitable weight for its task. For example a tiny leaf will require a fine wire fastened to its spine, while a bud or flower head will require a heavier wire.

To wire a leaf, turn the leaf face down and insert the wire two-thirds up, either side of the spine of the leaf. Pull one end of the wire through the holes

Wiring a flower stem and leaf.

and make a loop, fastening the end to the bottom of the leaf and to a part of the other wire. Remember to leave a few centimetres of plain wire at the base of the leaf free to enable you to wire it to other flowers. The leaf can now be bent into shape.

When wiring soft and bendy stems or delicate flowers, use as fine a wire as possible – wire as fine as thread is still supportive. Carefully wrap the wire around the stem, working up the plant. Once completed, the stems can be manipulated into shape without distressing the plant.

Heavier wire can be used for heavier items, such as fruit, or as support by pushing the wire through the stem. For the heaviest objects, twist two wires together and distribute the weight evenly.

Candle Holders

Many arrangements come alive when candles are added to the display. To secure the candles in place, use a specialized candleholder, available from most florists. These are useful for long, slender candles. Heavier candles, or candles with a broad base, can be self-supportive.

Pin-holders

Some florists use a floral pincushion to secure flowers in place. These vary in size and are mostly useful for formal designs or low containers. Pincushions can be used in conjunction with wires and other floral materials.

Floral Foam

As with pincushions, floral foam is used for securing flowers and is a valuable sponge-like material which stores moisture for the flowers. A coarse foam is available for dry-flower arranging but in feng shui we use fresh flowers as they still contain the vital life force that is able to conduct energy. Dried or silk arrangements are aesthetically pleasing but lifeless.

Before using the foam, place it onto a deep bowl of water and just leave it to absorb water. Do not push it into the water as this often leads to an airlock, and the centre of the foam will remain dry. Floral foam is inexpensive and available in a variety of shapes and sizes. It can be cut into shape and is re-usable.

Preserving Flowers

Occasionally it is worth treating your flowers and foliage to a preserving technique. Probably the most popular method is drying, however for feng shui purposes avoid using dried flowers. Dried flowers do not create negative energy, indeed, like any *object d'art* they generate favourable energy, but they do not last. Dried flowers tend to be brittle and delicate and can quickly become bruised, attracting dust and shar chi. It is far better to use fresh flowers for their wonderful stimulus upon the senses.

Preserving with Glycerine

It is possible to prolong the life of some flowers and leaves by feeding them a water and glycerine solution. Stand the plants in a solution of one part glycerine to two parts water and leave until they change colour, topping up the mixture as necessary. Submerge large leaves such as aspidistra and fatsia in one part glycerine to one part water until they change colour. Beech that has been preserved in this way turns a beautiful black and can provide valuable contrast with other colours.

"Fallen blossoms aren't by nature without feeling:
Changed into mud in spring, they still nurture flower's growth."

Lao Tzu

THE FIVE ELEMENTS AND THEIR ASSOCIATED COLOURS

Earth	Metal	Water	Wood	Fire
Yellow Brown Beige	White Gold/Silver Metallic colours	Black Navy	Shades of Green	Red Pink Purple

Colours as Cures

One of the quickest and most effective methods of changing an energetic wavelength is to change the colour of your surroundings. It needn't be on a grand scale; flowers are versatile and colourful and they are unique feng shui activators and enhancers.

The wavelengths that create colour are absorbed and analyzed by the mind, body and spirit. Using colour with its corresponding elemental associations will stimulate the energy stored in the home and the body. Thought patterns will change in the presence of auspicious energy. As benevolent feng shui energy increases, the chi eventually manifests into physical opportunities. In their correct placement, flowers will draw attention to your aspirations, preparing mind and body for action.

The table below shows each of the elements and their relationship with one another, with their corresponding colours. This table will help you match your feng shui flowers with the colour of your décor.

	Earth	Metal	Water	Wood	Fire
Supported by Colours to use	fire red/pink/purple	earth yellow/brown	metal white/metallic colours	water black/navy blue	wood greens/pale blue
Controlling Colours to use	water black/navy blue	wood greens/pale blue	fire red/pink/purple	earth yellow/brown	metal white/metallic colours
Exhausted by Colours to use	metal white/metallic colours	water black/navy blue	wood greens/pale blue	fire red/pink/purple	earth yellow/brown
Destroyed by Colours to use	wood greens/pale blue	fire red/pink/purple	earth yellow/brown	metal white/metallic colours	water black/navy blue

Choosing the Right Colour

Here are some suggestions for flowers in various colours which can be used in your own aspirations.

Lime Green

Popular lime green flowers include *Euphorbia palustris* and *E. polychroma*, shamrock chrysanthemums and hacquetia. Other green flowers include *Helleborus foetidus* and *H. argutifolius*, Moluccella (bells of Ireland), *Alchemilla mollis* (lady's mantle), *Amaranthus caudatus* 'Viridis' (love lies bleeding) and the lime-green variety of nicotiana (tobacco plant) and zinnia.

Yellow to Orange

Look for yellow to orange varieties of fritillary, doronicum, iris, narcissus and primula, achillea, alstroemeria, dahlia and lily. Later in the season try verbascum (mullein), gladioli, zinnia, rudbeckia (coneflower) and crocosmia. Otherwise there are knipholia (red-hot pokers), or the papery physalis alkekengi (Chinese lantern). Finally try golden varieties of chrysanthemum and solidago (golden rod).

Pinks to Red

Flowers that are shades of pink to red will carry fire energy. Primulas, stocks and tulips of this colour are available in spring and summer. Dicentra and pyrethrum, allium, aster, astilbe and iberis are all available in fire colours. Roses, dahlia, kniphofia (red hot poker), salvia, lilies, gladioli and nerine are other valuable flowers. Also consider dianthus (carnation), sweet peas and pelargoniums.

Purple to Blue

To bring the cool tranquil shades of the water element into the home or business use anemone, blue iris, allium and aster. There are tiny blue campanula, cornflowers and purple clematis. Or choose delphiniums, lupins, veronica or agapanthus among many others.

Black

Some varieties of flowers have been bred to look almost black. Look for black tulips, viola and roses to add drama and impact to your arrangements.

Silver to White

White flowers and silver foliage supply metal chi, which supports the water element. Use white stocks, narcissus, chrysanthemums, tulips, dahlia, gladioli, phlox and asters. Lilies, peonies and orchids add drama.

Edible Flowers

These edible flowers are also useful for feng shui flower arrangements.

Alpine Pink *Dianthus alpinus*
Anchusa *Anchusa azurea*
Apple Mint *Mentha suaveolens*
Arugula (Salad Rocket) *Eruca vescaria ssp. Sativa*
Basil *Ocimum basilicum*
Bergamot *Monarda didyma*
Borage *Borago officinalis*
Chamomile *Chamaemelum nobile*
Chives *Allium schoenoprasum*
Citrus *Citrus sinensis* and *Citrus limon*
Courgette *Cucurbita pepo var. Courgette*
Cowslip *Primula veris*
Daisy *Bellis perennis*
Dandelion *Taraxacum officinale*
Day Lily *Hemerocallis*
Dill *Anethum graveolens*
Evening Primrose *Oenothera biennis*
Fennel *Foeniculum vulgare*
Geraniums (scented) *Pelargonium*
Hibiscus *Hibiscus rosa-sinensis*
Hollyhocks *Alcea rosea*
Hyssop *Hyssopus officinalis*
Lavender *Lavandula angustifolia*
Lemon Balm *Melissa officinalis 'Auera'*

Lemon Verbena *Aloysia triphylla*
Marigold *Calendula officinalis*
Nasturtium *Tropaeolum majus*
Primrose *Primula vulgaris*
Rose *Rosa*
Rosemary *Rosmarinus officinalis*
Saffron *Crocus sativus*
Sage *Salvia officinalis*
Sunflower *Helianthus annuus*
Sweet Cicely *Myrrhis odorata*
Sweet Rocket *Hesperis matronalis*
Sweet Woodruff *Galium odoratum*
Tiger Lily *Lilium lancifolium*
Thyme *Thymus vulgaris*
Wild Marjoram/Oregano *Origanum vulgare*

Seasonal Flowers

Where possible buy seasonal flowers for your designs, to be in harmony with the rhythms of the seasons. The flowers will also be cheaper and easily available.

Scented Flowers

Fragrant flowers are auspicious because their perfume can transform the atmosphere. In Ancient China many flowers were included as feng shui tools because of their scent. Honeysuckle, jasmine, lilac, lilies, lotus, roses and wisteria generate positive sheng chi.

Spiritual Flowers

Some flowers are traditionally associated with the the planets. Flowers said to contain the masculine and magical properties of the sun include marigolds, sunflowers, St John's wort, chamomile and heliotrope. Almond flowers, lily of the valley, lotus, mandrake,

Right Gerberas tend to wilt so they are packed with their heads supported. Wiring them will provide support at home.

water lily and peony express the feminine and receptive qualities of the moon. Flowers blessed with the chi from the planet Mars include broom, hops, lilies, nettles, thistles, tobacco, woodruff and wormwood. The planet Mercury governs cinquefoil, fern, honeysuckle, valerian and vervain. Trees with this energy include hazel and pine.

Jupiter governs the chi relating to money, honour, authority and knowledge. Plants that carry this chi include agrimony, clover, dandelion, fir, meadowsweet, betony, shamrock and verbena. The ash, cedar, oak and poplar are associated with this planet.

Venus is associated with love, beauty, children and friends. To tune into this planet with flowers use blackberries (remove sharp thorns), briar, catnip, coltsfoot, rose, sandalwood and yarrow. The birch, elder and myrtle trees are linked to Venus.

Saturn has a close affinity with comfrey, cypress, ferns, horsetails, ivies, mullein, reeds and vines. The alder, elm, holly and yew trees are associated with Saturn, the planet of drama, studies, groups, the elderly and striving for success.

Moon Planting

The moon governs the tides and moisture levels in plants. Growing plants and flowers in tune with the cycles of the moon will greatly enhance their potential. Pick flowers for feng shui aspirations either late in the evening or first thing in the morning, while the sap is still strong inside the plant. Avoid picking flowers at midday as they will quickly wilt.

"A Ch'an initiate is naturally timorous at the shadow of flowers: Awakened from a dream, I offer my gatherings to thank Ling-hsiao."

Translated by Irving Y. Lo

INDEX

THE DINNER DOCTOR IS IN

Looking for new ways to streamline dinner? Try doctoring what the supermarket has to offer. Here's a colorful selection of the tasty dishes you'll turn out with this book by your side, starting on this page with some ideas for a package of ground beef.

MEXICAN "LASAGNA"   PAGE 243

MEATY ZITI   PAGE 292

CUBAN PICADILLO   PAGE 205

FAMILY-STYLE VEGETABLE SOUP   PAGE 99

8 DISHES TO MAKE WITH A DELI CHICKEN

A crisp roast chicken from the supermarket is the taking-off point for these fast, no-fuss dishes—for busy weeknights or even last-minute entertaining.

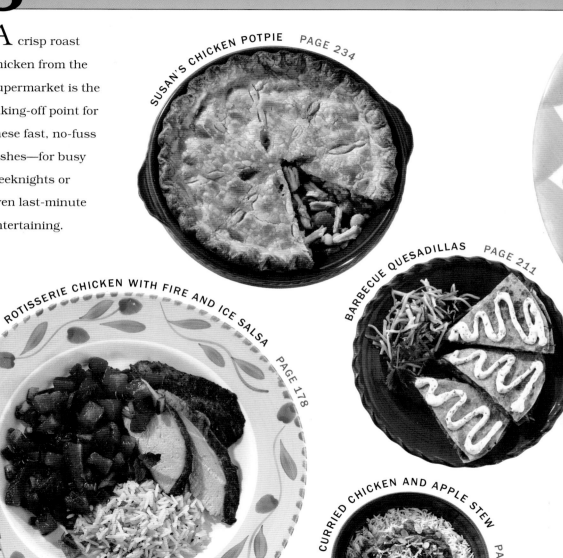

SUSAN'S CHICKEN POTPIE PAGE 234

BARBECUE QUESADILLAS PAGE 211

ROTISSERIE CHICKEN WITH FIRE AND ICE SALSA PAGE 178

CURRIED CHICKEN AND APPLE STEW PAGE 168

TUSCAN CHICKEN   PAGE 180

CARIBBEAN CHICKEN CHILI   PAGE 110

SANTA FE POLENTA   PAGE 310

CURRIED CHICKEN AND ARTICHOKE CASSEROLE   PAGE 222

AND MORE . . .

- **Asian Chicken Salad** *page 154*
- **Poppy Seed Chicken Casserole** *page 231*
- **Parmesan Chicken and Biscuit Pie** *page 232*
- **Chicken Laredo** *page 227*

4 DISHES TO MAKE WITH PASTA

Keep a variety of choices in your cupboard. Then, use your noodle (!) and make a sauce while the water comes to a boil and the pasta cooks. Dinner is ready to toss and serve in practically no time.

PASTA SHELLS WITH TUNA PAGE 287

SATURDAY NIGHT FEVER PASTA PAGE 274

ROTINI WITH PROSCIUTTO PAGE 284

PENNE WITH BLUE CHEESE PESTO PAGE 300

5 DISHES FROM REFRIGERATED DOUGH

Keep a can of crescent roll dough in the refrigerator and you're on your way to turning out stellar appetizers, breads, and desserts.

AROMATIC MUSHROOM GALETTE   PAGE 43

LITTLE CINNAMON SWEET ROLLS   PAGE 432

CHERRY TOMATO AND BASIL TART   PAGE 390

APRICOT-ALMOND COFFEE CAKE   PAGE 434

SPICED PLUM PASTRIES   PAGE 511

These fabulous, fresh side-dish or main-dish salads might begin with a bag of greens, but in minutes they turn into much, much more.

BLUE CHEESE, WALNUT, AND APPLE SLAW PAGE 127

STRAWBERRY FIELD SALAD PAGE 118

PAGE 139

TEX-MEX LAYERED SALAD

AND MORE . . .

- **John's Summertime Slaw** page 129

- **Fast Asian Slaw** page 131

- **Warm Arugula Salad with Roasted Asparagus** page 135

ASIAN CHICKEN SALAD PAGE 154

SUSAN'S PENNE AND TOMATO SALAD PAGE 152

SPINACH AND ORANGE SALAD PAGE 122

SOUTHWESTERN SLAW WITH AVOCADO PAGE 130

BLACK-EYED PEA AND SPINACH SALAD PAGE 143

- **New Year's Layered Spinach Salad** *page 141*
- **Spinach Salad with Fresh Peaches, Pecans, and Popcorn Chicken** *page 156*

4 DISHES FROM MUSHROOM SOUP

Y ou can't beat the creaminess of canned mushroom soup—or the way it makes casseroles so velvety and delicious.

MOM'S BROCCOLI AND RICE CASSEROLE PAGE 355

SPAGHETTI CASSEROLE PAGE 241

CHICKEN TETRAZZINI PAGE 224

SO EASY TUNA NOODLE CASSEROLE PAGE 260

4 QUICK PANTRY DISHES

CREAMY POTATO SOUP PAGE 83

SWIRLY DOGS PAGE 217

NACHO CHEESE SOUP PAGE 97

DUN-BUTTERED MUFFINS PAGE 419

It couldn't be simpler: One package of hot dogs plus a package of corn bread twist dough, or any of dozens of other fast pantry combos, equals dinner or dinner go-withs.

8 DISHES THE KIDS WILL LOVE

Who cares if the cheese is pre-shredded, the muffins begin with a mix, or you start with a can of soup? Your children will adore these shortcut dishes—and you for making them.

LEMON BLUEBERRY MUFFINS   PAGE 425

PAT'S MINI HAM BISCUITS   PAGE 55

HOME-STYLE MACARONI AND CHEESE   PAGE 263

COCONUT-AND-CURRY-SCENTED PEAS AND RICE   PAGE 374

BLENDER CHEESE SOUFFLÉS   PAGE 268

NANCY'S POPCORN SOUP   PAGE 86

SCHOOL MORNING WAFFLES   PAGE 444

SOUR CREAM CINNAMON LOAF   PAGE 438

AND MORE . . .

- **New-Fashioned Pimento Cheese** *page 24*

- **Mini Cheese Calzones with Hot Marinara Sauce** *page 41*

- **Chicken Fajita Wraps** *page 61*

- **Let the Kids Make Broccoli Cheese Soup** *page 81*

- **Barbecue Quesadillas** *page 211*

- **Not-So-Impossible Moussaka Pie** *page 245*

8 MEALS FROM A SLOW COOKER

Dinner can simmer in your slow cooker or Dutch oven while you're away, providing you with terrific hands-off dishes like these.

SWEET-AND-SOUR BRISKET OF BEEF PAGE 337

ALL-DAY BEEF BOURGUIGNON PAGE 333

SAVORY PORK CARNITAS PAGE 341

STEAK AND GRAVY FOR THE KIDS PAGE 328

HEARTY LENTIL AND SAUSAGE STEW · PAGE 346

MOM'S POT ROAST · PAGE 335

SLOW-COOKER WHITE CHILI · PAGE 326

ROAST TURKEY BREAST IN A BAG · PAGE 318

Only eight? That's all that would fit on this spread! There are myriad ways to doctor an ordinary cake mix to make it extraordinary.

ORANGE DREAMSICLE LAYER CAKE PAGE 465

CHOCOLATE FUDGE RIBBON CAKE PAGE 471

THE BEST POUND CAKE PAGE 473

TRIPLE-DECKER PEANUT BUTTER CAKE PAGE 461

EASY ITALIAN CREAM CAKE   PAGE 458

BUTTERNUT SQUASH LAYER CAKE   PAGE 456

LEMON POPPY SEED LAYER CAKE   PAGE 450

BLACKBERRY WINE CAKE   PAGE 469

AND MORE . . .

- **Farmhouse Chocolate Potato Cake** *page 454*
- **Lula's Coconut Tarts** *page 483*
- **Banana Bread Pie** *page 490*
- **Butterscotch Pecan Focaccia** *page 508*
- **Brownie Drops** *page 516*

Turn to page 448 for a full selection of cakes, pies, and cookies that begin with a box of mix.

4 DISHES TO MAKE WITH PUFF PASTRY

Here are four ways to turn versatile frozen puff pastry into showstopping appetizers or desserts.

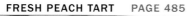

PUFFY CHEESE TWISTS   PAGE 40

ARTICHOKE AND FETA PIZZA   PAGE 46

FRESH PEACH TART   PAGE 485

PAGE 509

CINNAMON PALMIERS

the Dinner Doctor

by ANNE BYRN

Photographs by Mike Rutherford Studios

WORKMAN PUBLISHING · NEW YORK

WITH LOVE TO MY CHILDREN—
KATHLEEN, LITTON, AND JOHN

▼ ▼ ▼

Library of Congress Cataloging-in-Publication Data
Byrn, Anne.
The dinner doctor/by Anne Byrn.
p. cm.
Includes index.
ISBN 0-7611-2680-5 (alk. paper)—ISBN 0-7611-3070-5
1. Dinners and dining. 2. Quick and easy cookery. I. Title.

TX737.B97 2003
641.5'4—dc21   2003043070

Cover design by Paul Hanson
Book design by Lisa Hollander with Sophia Stravropoulos and Miyoung Lee
Photography: Mike Rutherford Studios
Food stylist: Teresa B. Blackburn
Cover photograph of author: Anthony Loew

Workman books are available at special discounts when purchased in bulk for premiums and
sales promotions as well as for fund-raising or educational use. Special editions or book excerpts
can be created to specification. For details, contact the Special Sales Director at the address below.

Workman Publishing Company, Inc.
708 Broadway
New York, NY 10003-9555
www.workman.com

Printed in the U.S.A.
First printing, October 2003

10 9 8 7 6 5

ACKNOWLEDGMENTS

▼ ▼ ▼

As I finish this book the world feels a lot more harried than it used to, but home cooking continues to be a tie that binds. No matter how short the recipes have become, at least we are cooking, baking, and sitting down together to share a meal. And for that, I am thankful. For all of you who have written to me over the years and shared recipes, I am thankful. I appreciate your kind notes and questions.

For Martha Bowden and Mindy Merrell, my creative food friends in Nashville, and for Lucille Osborn, a caring and talented chef who lives outside Philadelphia and bakes my cakes for QVC, I am ever so thankful.

For Suzanne Rafer, my editor, and for Jim Eber, my publicist, I am thankful; their wisdom and energy has been unflagging. To Jenny Mandel, who arranges appearances on QVC, thank you for your enthusiasm and persistence; and to Pat Upton, Amy Hayworth, Justin Nesbit, the Web site folks, thank you for making it all look so simple. I know it is not. Thanks to Martha Crow for patiently copy editing this text. And to Beth Doty and Robyn Schwartz for helping to move things along. Thanks to Peter Workman, for believing in this book and having the vision once again, and to Paul Hanson and Lisa Hollander, who design things so well. To every enthusiastic Workman employee in the office and in the field who talks up my books and cooks by them, thank you.

To Nancy Crossman, my agent, who handles those things I don't have the time or the organizational skills to tackle, thank you.

To Mike Rutherford and Teresa Blackburn, thanks for the beautiful photos and the fun week cooking in your studio.

On the home front, this book and both *Cake Mix Doctor* books would never have been possible without the love and support of my family. For my sisters Ginger and Susan, and Susan's family, and for my sweet aunts, I am especially thankful. To my children, Kathleen, Litton, and John, thank you for your candid critique. For my friend Beth Meador, who let me cook in her kitchen when mine was torn up during remodeling, I am thankful. For Dorothy and Diane, I am always thankful. To Flowerree O., Janet, and Flowerree G., thanks for being my out-of-town cheerleaders.

And for my generous and loving husband, John, I give you a big hug and kiss. This book was not all about cake, and for that I know *you* were thankful! Now, let's get cooking!

CONTENTS

▼ ▼ ▼

Strawberry Field Salad, Southwestern Slaw, Susan's Penne and Tomato Salad, and crunchy, crouton-filled Ripe Tomato Panzanella.

THE MAIN DISH

PAGE 160

A fresh and different take on some favorite entrées, using those delicious store-bought rotisseried chickens, pre-cleaned shrimp, and quick-cooking cuts of meat to get dinner on the table in no time flat. Wait until you try One-Bowl Chicken Souvlaki, Thai Shrimp and Asparagus, and Barbecue Quesadillas.

ONE-DISH COMFORT FOOD

PAGE 220

The casseroles and pot pies that comfort and soothe are easy to prepare. In 30 minutes you can have a Parmesan Chicken and Biscuit Pie, and a So Easy Tuna Noodle Casserole in less than 25, and a Mexican "Lasagna" in under 40.

PASTA PRESTO

PAGE 270

A pantry that includes plenty of pasta and a few jars of sauce to doctor means dinnertime relief. Mushroom and Ham Linguine, Monday Night Penne Marinara, and Fast Four-Step Lasagna are sure to be family favorites. And don't overlook the recipes here for those packages of pre-cooked polenta—Blue Cheese Polenta with Wilted Spinach and Toasted Pine Nuts is pure heaven.

HANDS-OFF COOKING

PAGE 316

The slow cooker makes those meltingly tender roasts and braised beef dishes real possibilities for midweek meals. Sweet-and-Sour Brisket of Beef preps in 10 minutes and so does Mom's Pot Roast with Vidalia Onion Gravy. Don't overlook the oven, either. No-fuss preparations and no-bother cooking make Roast Turkey Breast in a Bag a good choice, too.

VEGGIE HEAVEN

PAGE 350

One-Bowl Ratatouille, Mediterranean Roast Potatoes and Asparagus, and Down Home Corn are just a few of the great vegetable side and main dishes gathered in this chapter. Plus 15 Ways to Doctor Frozen Spinach.

SAVORY & SWEET LIGHTNING FAST BREADS

PAGE 404

A basket of fragrant warm bread turns soup or salad into dinner. Fresh Angel Biscuits, Provençal Olive Bread, or Scallion and Cheddar Supper Bread bake up in the time it takes to put the finishing touches on the main dish.

DESSERTS FROM THE DOCTOR

PAGE 448

Dinner without dessert? Not in my house. Here are some new

favorites from the Cake Mix Doctor. Triple-Decker Peanut Butter Cake, Chocolate Fudge Ribbon Cake, Orange Crumble Pumpkin Pie, plus quick Weekday Wonders—Banana Bread Pie, Spiced Plum Pastries, Lula's Coconut Tarts, and much, much more.

THE DINNER DOCTOR PANTRY

PAGE 522

Beyond the milk, butter, and eggs— what needs to be in the fridge, freezer, and pantry to earn you your degree in dinner doctoring.

A PRESCRIPTION FOR DINNER

I t wasn't long after the first *Cake Mix Doctor* cookbook was published that many of the readers who were pleased with the recipes for great easy-to-make desserts started asking me what I cooked for the rest of my meals. What soups did I simmer in the winter, what salads did I toss in the summer, what appetizers did I throw together when guests were at my doorstep? Did I bake bread? Did I have speedy pasta sauces that would wow company and quick casseroles to feed a crowd of teenagers? What did I prepare mid-week after tennis and piano lessons, soccer, school, meetings—when I was pressed for time and it felt as if every ounce of creativity had been drained from my being? I guess they thought that anyone who spent so much of the day creating desserts couldn't have a whole lot of energy left over to prepare much of anything else.

They were right. Like so many others whose days involve balancing family and career, my time is tight. While I enjoy preparing meals, I can't spend lots of time fussing over them. So, I thought, what better way to answer all those questions than to gather them up here in *The Dinner Doctor,* a collection of recipes that tackle the rest of dinner head on. Starting with appetizers and ending with those cakes and other sweets I love so much, this book brings to the whole meal the tried and true doctoring techniques I used in my baking books. It will show you how to turn supermarket convenience foods into dishes that taste so good you will think they are made totally from scratch.

You'll be able to make the most of a can of pre-seasoned tomatoes and a package of cheese tortellini, a deli-roasted chicken and a can of mush-room soup, a package of frozen corn and a bag of pre-shredded coleslaw. When doctored using the recipes I've included, these ingredients become stand-out dishes. Cans of white beans and diced tomatoes combine with fresh zucchini for a quick winter soup, while chicken and coleslaw mix join with ramen noodles for a healthy and light summer one. Boxes of couscous turn into fast salads; frozen peeled pearl onions are easily creamed for Thanksgiving; store-bought cleaned shrimp make a fuss-free skillet supper—I have found the possibilities for delicious dinner doc-toring endless, and the challenge of streamlining favorite but complicated recipes exciting.

For a dish to make it into this book, the final results had to taste fan-tastic but be simple to assemble. Take, for example, that mushroom soup and chicken combination. We have all eaten too many bland casseroles that relied on cream of mushroom soup. But mushroom soup is too handy to ignore. So I asked myself, what if that casserole also included quartered jarred artichoke hearts and used the soup, enhanced with curry powder, as a thickener? Well, the combination worked beautifully and the soup did its job, without announcing itself as canned (the Curried Chicken and Arti-choke Casserole is on page 222—do try it and see for yourself).

This book has been a joy to create, a real sharing of good food with my family that I'm pleased to be sharing with you. Ideas for family meals take precedence here, but there are plenty of recipes that double up as great for guests. Along with full recipes, each chapter contains super-quick suggestions for doctoring pantry items like canned tuna, baked beans, chicken noodle soup, pasta sauce, cream cheese, deli potato salad, frozen spinach, and much more.

The savory flavors of the lasagnas, sesame noodle salads, fun cornbread-wrapped hot dogs, warm cheesy breads, and cozy chicken casseroles you'll find in this book have made my kids more cheerful and

my husband arrive home from work relieved to know that dinner isn't going to be a slice of chocolate cake with a side of pie!

So, here's my prescription for feeding the busy, hungry family. It will relieve stress and have you feeling good in no time.

DINNER DOCTOR 101

▼▼▼

If you are familiar with my other cookbooks, you may be surprised to learn that I do not live on cake alone. I love making appetizers for impromptu get-togethers, thrive on the comfort of homemade soup, need salad to survive, feel that a meal isn't a meal without bread (the Southern girl in me, I am sure), long for those creamy casseroles of yesteryear, and turn to pasta often because everyone in our family (and that includes three children) eats it, which is a big deal! Add to this that I don't like to wait until the weekend to do my cooking; I like to eat those casseroles and soups midweek, even when I don't have all day to cook.

But, how can I do it? How can I get main dishes with bold flavor on the table most nights of the week with a minimum of fuss? What can I do for quick pre-dinner snacks when the kids are starving RIGHT NOW? And how do I create simple sides for easy main dishes that need an accompaniment? As readers of my previous books know, the answer is: doctoring. In those books, I offer up recipes for doctored cake mixes that gives them a luscious homemade flavor. Here I have expanded my techniques to doctor the rest of dinner, using the wealth of convenience foods available in the supermarket. These are dishes that can be prepared day in and day out. It is a soup-to-nuts assortment of recipes that have an impressive flavor, but are a snap to prepare.

Doctoring Dinner

▼ ▼ ▼

Just as cake mixes benefit from being doctored, so do the other convenience foods that the supermarket offers. Don't snub them; they are good starting points for preparing interesting, delicious, doable weekday dinners, and include a jar of pasta sauce, a can of soup, a bag of coleslaw, or a store-rotisseried chicken. The trick is to choose that main ingredient wisely, doctor it intelligently, and use fast but classic cooking methods to bring out flavor, letting you get dinner on the table pronto.

You can opt for convenience but still eat good food. You'll discover that when you add some fresh flavors to convenience foods it makes all the difference. Unlike other quick-cook books, this one doesn't have me hovering over you with a stopwatch. You will find estimated preparation and cooking times, but we all cook at different speeds. These recipes generally cook quickly at a high heat and have few ingredients. Many, like the sauces for pasta, are so fast they are ready before the pasta water has come to a boil!

There are also recipes that take advantage of the oven and slow cooker and need little or no attention from you as they simmer to doneness over four to eight hours.

This book features the same type of fun, casual recipes you find in my *Cake Mix Doctor* books. And the dishes here will please both your children *and* your guests. I tested them in my slightly insane kitchen with three active kids nearby doing homework, playing on the computer, or just reading me a story. To sum it up, this book is about coping. It contains a bit of speed, a bit of scratch, and it offers you strategies so you can cook well when life is abuzz around you.

Mealtime Begins at the Supermarket

▼ ▼ ▼

My friend Mindy returned from a trip to the supermarket and collapsed in the kitchen chair. Her eyes looked glazed, as if she had driven to Disney World and back. "It's not about cooking anymore. It's about shopping," she said. "Have you seen all those canned tomatoes for goodness sakes?"

All those tomatoes and all those bags of pre-shredded cheese, umpteen jars of pasta sauce, and miles and miles of salsa, I might add. The burgeoning supermarket is so overwhelming, it's almost enough to ruin your appetite. But wait a minute. . . .

While many of these convenience foods are quite tasty, they are just the taking off point, not the recipe in themselves. A bright green jar of mint sauce might be de rigueur with grilled lamb chops, but if you purée it with a handful of fresh mint and a splash of balsamic vinegar it is sweet, tangy, and memorable. And while deli-prepared olive salad scooped right from the container onto corn chips is good, it is even better when combined with tuna and served over pasta. So the trick is to select fast foods that speed your cooking process, ones you can use and improve, and keep tucked in your pantry.

To help figure out what foods are worth your purchase, look through the suggested pantry list on page 522 and trust your palate as well. I sampled Alfredo sauce after Alfredo sauce and came to the conclu-

sion that the refrigerated sauces were far fresher tasting than those sold in the pasta aisle. The same goes for pesto sauce, although the Alessi brand, sold where you buy dried pasta, is quite nice. So, when possible, taste what is out there. Even something as simple as canned beans varies from brand to brand. I found some cans of white Great Northern beans too mushy, others too salty, and some just right.

If you don't have time to taste before you cook, avoid those products with an abundance of colorings and flavor enhancers. Choose the ones that have as few ingredients as possible. For example, pasta sauces that contain only tomatoes, olive oil, herbs, spices, and garlic are a sure bet. And when making recipes in this book that call for tomato-based pasta sauce, select the plainest marinara sauce in your market. You do the doctoring.

The same goes when selecting cheese. Read the labels carefully to see if you are buying cheese with full fat, reduced-fat, or no fat. When buying refrigerated bread dough, stick with the best-known brand—Pillsbury. But keep in mind regional brands when considering frozen biscuits or pie crusts, frozen barbecued meats, or bottled pasta sauce. They usually have more local flavor than the national brands.

And, avoid frozen vegetables with sauce. When you fork into them, their bland consistency and their salty flavor will have you wishing you had just steamed some plain frozen broccoli or cauliflower and made your own quick cheese sauce instead.

Storing Food at Home

▼ ▼ ▼

Once you're home, those ready-to-go foods will need to be stored in the cupboard, refrigerator, or the freezer. Remember that many of the cupboard items, once opened, will need to be refrigerated, if there's anything leftover. Although I've tried to create recipes that use a whole container's worth, it wasn't always possible. But, if you store those small amounts of pesto and tomato sauce in glass jars in the refrigerator door,

you'll see them each time you open the fridge, and won't forget they are there! Add them to sauces and soups when the spirit moves you.

Remember that the pre-shredded cheeses and pre-washed salad greens don't have the shelf life that their cousins, the hunk of cheese or the head of lettuce do. Look at the sell-by dates on the packages before buying, and plan to use these foods within the week. Rely on your freezer to stash foods longer. Freeze foods in small portions, say a pound of ground round instead of a three-pound block, so they take less time to thaw and are just the amount you'll want to cook.

And lastly, don't overlook the bounty your garden or local produce stand offers. By adding fresh seasonal produce—local squash or tiny green beans—to your dishes, you add that fresh homemade flavor that makes quick cooking special.

Prep Time

▼ ▼ ▼

Choose your "battles" carefully so that when you must rush, you

Prepping the Oven

▼▼▼

As a reminder, when a dish you are making cooks in the oven, be sure to get the oven preheating as soon as possible. In this book, oven temperatures are considered part of the prep work, so that even if a dish takes only five minutes of actual work, if it's cooking in a 350°F oven, the time it takes to heat the oven—about ten minutes—will be listed as the total amount of prep time. Here are the oven-heating times (all are approximate):

325°F to 350°F	10 minutes
375°F	12 minutes
400°F to 425°	15 minutes
450°F	15-20 minutes

fresh basil if it is growing in your summertime herb garden and pile it on top of pasta just before you serve it. What you add will not only enhance the dish, but it also will give you the satisfaction of hands-on cooking.

But when you don't have time, learn how to cheat well. Take a bag of pre-washed salad greens, top them with heated popcorn chicken pieces you pulled out of the freezer, surround it with slices of fresh peaches, and dress it with a light vinaigrette.

It helps if you are organized. And I am not talking about cleaning out your gadget drawer or alphabetizing your spices. I am talking about cooking with common sense so that you plan ahead and freeze and stash ingredients that will save you valuable preparation time later. For example, say you are poaching chicken. Cover it with water, add salt and pepper and a bay leaf, and when the chicken is done, freeze the broth in little plastic tubs. That broth can later be thawed in the microwave to use in soups and pasta sauces.

Another effective way to organize is to look at a recipe and visualize ways to make it less laborious. Can you use

use what time you have most effectively. When you have time, by all means go ahead and sauté a little freshly minced garlic and onion in olive oil and fold them into a ready-made pasta sauce. Chop up some canned tomatoes already seasoned with onion and green pepper instead of adding the chopped vegetables? Can you use a store-bought pesto sauce instead of stirring in chopped fresh basil, garlic, and Parmesan? Can you shred a store-bought rotisserie chicken instead of cooking your own?

Look for ways to streamline the cooking process, too. While the pasta water is coming to a boil you have roughly 10 minutes to get the sauce going. While an oven preheats you have a good 10 minutes to get the cake batter assembled. Shortcuts are out there, everywhere you look.

And finally, because with this book you are already beginning with a convenience food from the supermarket, you are already on the quick and easy path. You have a great head start.

The Cooking Credo

▼ ▼ ▼

"Why bother? Why cook?" We cook because the process is fulfilling and the results rewarding. It nurtures us and fills the tummies of others. For some of us cooking is pure pleasure, for others it would be pleasurable if time wasn't a factor. But, you can rely on canned tuna for only so long. Yes it makes a great sandwich and a nice mix-in for salad, but at some point the stove must go on. And when that happens, you've got to employ the right technique to get the job done quickly and with top flavor.

In the recipes you'll find here, frequently that means cooking at a high heat so that the meat or vegetables take less time to cook but also caramelize and develop deep flavor and color. Often you'll be directed to start by stirring chopped onion in hot oil or butter to brown it and cook its natural sugars to give your dish depth. Just because you are cooking rapidly doesn't mean you need to sacrifice flavor. The little extra touch, the technique, will help give your food that fresh homemade flavor.

Get Going

▼ ▼ ▼

Here are some tips for putting together meals that will please both family and friends.

◆ Make the appetizers ahead, or if you're entertaining, ask someone to bring them.

◆ Let one dish shine and then give it a supporting cast—for example, basmati rice unadorned, some steamed broccoli with butter, or even frozen peas or carrots for that fragrant chicken curry.

◆ The starch for the main dish should complement it. So for roasted chicken, try couscous; with red meat, either pasta with parsley or interesting potatoes. When serving rice, choose basmati if there are Indian flavors, starchier Jasmine if the flavors are more Asian, and a quick brown rice if you have hearty flavors of grilled meat and roasted veggies.

◆ If you are introducing young children to a food they have never sampled before, be sure to put a food they love on the plate, too. For example, if you want them to sample the chicken curry, add a spoonful of rice to the side, if they adore rice. They'll see how the juices mingle and marry and taste wonderful together. But they'll do it on their own without your prodding, which means they'll decide for themselves that they like it.

◆ When a meal is balanced, most often the colors on the dinner plate are balanced. They should be attractive without fighting each other, and none should overwhelm. This color balance will help to keep you from serving too much meat or too much starch. Your eyes will aid in balancing your meals.

◆ When you are serving soup as the main course, pair it with a great bread and salad.

◆ Always serve good bread. Take the time to make one of the easy ones you'll find beginning on page 404, or buy good bread from the bakery. Bread tastes better when it has been warmed slightly.

◆ Serve dessert. It's your grand finale. Not everyone will eat it, or they'll just nibble at it, but it says you cared enough to plan all the way through to the end. Serve seasonal fruit desserts when each fruit is in season. Choose a

lemon-flavored dessert after a heavy meal. Serve cakes at celebratory occasions. And chocolate is always a winner.

Leftovers

▼ ▼ ▼

I know they get a bad rap, but I love leftovers. And I don't know how our busy family would have survived without them, especially on Mondays and Tuesdays. Because most of the recipes in this book feed four or six, you won't get a ton of leftovers here. There are exceptions, like soups, casseroles, and big pans of lasagna. Feel free to double-batch a recipe (cook twice as much as you need) if you want to make sure that there will be leftovers!

But if you're uncomfortable about food being leftover, here are a few words of advice for handling it so it tastes as good as the first time around:

◆ Leftover once, not twice. A wise rule of thumb is to serve food no more than twice, meaning once freshly cooked and once left over. Do not refreeze foods. They won't harm you, but they will lose moisture in the repeat freezing process, and thus lose texture.

◆ Just how long a leftover lasts really depends on its ingredients. Fish tends to be more perishable than chicken, ground beef is more perishable than cubes of beef or a roast, and meat on the bone is more perishable than boneless.

◆ Reheat the food thoroughly. It may be in the microwave, on top of the range, or in the oven. Take care to bring leftovers to a boil or until heated completely through, so that you know the food is safe to eat.

◆ Give leftovers a new look. Roast chicken on Day One can become a chicken casserole or pasta with chicken the next day. A butternut squash gratin on Day One might become butternut squash quesadillas when sandwiched between flour tortillas and lightly griddled.

And when all is done—the food is planned, bought, prepped, cooked, enjoyed, and possibly reheated for Day Two, be sure to remember your favorites—and how you doctored the ingredients. They saved you time in preparation and they satisfied you as well. So write the recipe down.

AMAZING APPETIZERS

▼▼▼

In the same appealing way that frosting on a cake both grabs your attention and tempts you with the first bite of flavor, the appetizer sets the tone for the meal, giving your guests or your family a sneak preview of all the good things that are yet to come.

But, nowadays, most of us think of the appetizer as a company-only course. If anyone in the family is hungry right before dinner, the answer is to thrust a package of popcorn into the microwave. I'd like to see that change. So, I set out to find hors d'oeuvres that not only set the right tone—are fun to eat—but also are a cinch to assemble.

Many of the recipes in this chapter can be made the day ahead. Or, they can easily be assembled in just 5 minutes. This means that if they are part of a party menu, you can confidently hand the recipe to your teenager or your spouse, leave the room, and go freshen up.

And they are just the sort of recipes you'll want to make even if company is *not* coming. For example, my sister Susan, an avid tennis player, doctors up a bag of seasoned shredded cheese to tote to tennis parties. For her Tennis Team Cheese Salsa, she adds chopped tomatoes, olives, and chiles and sets out chips to scoop it all up. When I made a batch of it recently, it wasn't for a tennis party and there was no horde of dinner guests about to arrive, but six of us sat at the kitchen counter and ate and ate until the bowl was clean! My family really bonded over that bowl of salsa.

I think all cooks need a couple of quickie bean dips in their repertoires to throw together on the spur of the moment. None is more delicious than my Baja Dip, made from black beans or from regular chickpea hummus. And everyone can use a warm dip like my Warm White Bean Spread with Cumin and Lime, which can be whipped up from a can of beans. The dips in this chapter run the gamut from cool and refreshing—Joe's Zesty Crab Dip—to the hot and hearty two-some, Baked Vidalia Onion Dip and The Famous Spinach and Artichoke Dip, made with frozen creamed spinach.

Back in the sixties, no starter was more popular than fondue. Suddenly it disappeared. In fact, fondues are tasty and simple to make. My Easy Cheese Fondue is elegant and as uncomplicated to prepare as the name implies. You combine a carton of refrigerated Alfredo-style pasta sauce with pre-shredded Swiss cheese and white wine, heat, and eat with nice crusty bread cubes.

If you're a spreader, not a dipper (and that's okay), try the New-Fashioned Pimento Cheese, the Smoked Salmon Spread, or the Beer Cheese Spread. Want to dress up a spread? Layer it! Prepare the Blue Cheese, Pesto, and Tomato Stack once and you'll make it again and again.

Crispy nibbles are big favorites. Two I love are the Aromatic Mushroom Galette, made from refrigerated crescent roll dough, and the Artichoke and Feta Puff Pastry Pizza, which uses frozen puff pastry for a crust.

While tartlets and canapés can often be time-consuming to prepare, I have streamlined mine by using readily available convenience products. Try Pat's Mini Ham Biscuits, which you stamp out of frozen biscuit dough; the Pear and Blue Cheese Tartlets, baked in those wonderful frozen miniature phyllo shells; or the Souffléed Cheese and Onion Canapés, a timeless recipe that works as well in the twenty-first century as it did when my busy mother entertained.

So there you have it, the fun first bite that whets the appetite for the meal ahead. Enjoy!

RED PEPPER AND GARLIC HUMMUS

▼ ▼ ▼

Traditional hummus is a Middle Eastern chickpea (garbanzo bean) spread, but in recent years, we've taken the same license with hummus that we have with pesto. Thus, my variation is doctored with store-bought roasted red pepper strips for color and flavor. Rest assured, garlic is still there and olive oil is present in moderation.

TO PREP:
5 MINUTES

1 cup store-bought roasted red peppers,
    cut into strips (see Tips)
2 cloves garlic, peeled
1 can (15 ounces) chickpeas,
    drained
1 to 2 tablespoons olive oil
1 teaspoon curry powder, or 1 teaspoon
    chopped fresh oregano (optional)
Salt and black pepper
Soda crackers or pita crisps,
    for serving

Place the red pepper strips and garlic in a food processor and pulse quickly 7 or 8 times until puréed. Add the chickpeas, 1 tablespoon of the olive oil, and the curry

tips You'll find roasted red peppers at your local supermarket in jars, or at the deli counter. If you don't use all the red peppers at once, you can store leftovers in the jar or another container, covered, for up to several weeks in the refrigerator. Add strips of red pepper to salads and pizzas or serve them alongside grilled chicken.

If you're really pressed for time, pick up 1 cup of hummus from the deli section of the supermarket. Place it in the processor with the pepper strips, process it until smooth, and season it with salt and pepper, to taste.

I like to add curry powder to the hummus for a more exotic flavor, or oregano for an Italian flavor.

powder, if using. Process until puréed, about 30 seconds. Midway through, stop the machine and scrape the bowl down if necessary. Season with salt and pepper to taste and add more olive oil if the purée is too dry. Using a rubber spatula, transfer the hummus to a serving bowl. Serve with crackers or pita crisps.

SERVES **6** TO **8** (MAKES **2** CUPS)

5 Fast and Fabulous Dips

—▼—

DINNER DOCTOR SAYS

1. Stir together a full jar of Thai peanut sauce, a little bit of pancake syrup, a dash of hot pepper sauce, and a squeeze of ketchup. You'll wind up with a sweet, tangy peanut sauce with a kick!

2. Mix equal parts mayonnaise and honey-flavored mustard for a great sauce to dip chicken nuggets in.

3. Begin again with mayonnaise, but this time add a dollup of ketchup, a spoonful of pickle relish, and a dash of hot pepper sauce for a speedy rémoulade. Serve with boiled shrimp or crab cakes.

4. Start with your favorite bottled Italian salad dressing and squeeze in some fresh lime juice. Add a pinch of sugar and a handful of chopped fresh cilantro. Now it'll be your favorite Mexican dip.

5. Don't forget the classic: a packet of dried onion soup mix and a container of sour cream. A chip couldn't ask for anything better.

BAJA DIP

▼ ▼ ▼

Who cares if the kitchen is torn up for remodeling? That's the perfect time to invite the neighbors over for a drink and a nibble, right? Well, that's precisely what I did recently, and when I came to my senses it was 15 minutes until show time and I needed to throw together an hors d'oeuvre. Fortunately, I had some great provisions in the refrigerator, namely, a good store-bought black bean hummus, a ripe avocado, and some fresh cilantro. This dip is yummy with tortilla chips, and the recipe can be multiplied to match your guest list.

TO PREP:
10–12 MINUTES

1 cup (8 ounces) store-bought black bean
　　　or chickpea hummus
1 medium-size avocado, cut into
　　　½-inch cubes (for 1 cup cubes)
1 tablespoon fresh lime juice
½ cup store-bought chunky tomato salsa
½ cup reduced-fat sour cream
2 tablespoons chopped fresh cilantro
Tortilla chips, for serving

1. Using a rubber spatula, spread the hummus over the bottom of a 1-quart glass or ceramic bowl. Layer the avocado cubes on top and sprinkle the lime juice over all. Top with the salsa, sour cream, and cilantro.

2. To serve, place the bowl on a large platter and surround it with tortilla chips. Make sure everyone dips in deep to get all the layers.

SERVES 4 TO 6 (MAKES 3 CUPS)

tips **You can make this dip up to 8 hours in advance. Cover it with plastic wrap and refrigerate until serving time.**

Spoon leftover dip onto flour tortillas, roll up the tortillas, wrap well in plastic wrap, and you have a delicious brown-bag lunch.

Substitute tomatillo salsa for tomato salsa if you can find it in your supermarket.

Liven up leftover salsa by adding up to ¼ cup chopped fresh cilantro.

JOE'S ZESTY CRAB DIP

▼▼▼

My cousin Joe Brady is an exceptional math teacher and a great cook who has toted this easy and refreshing dip to many family parties. I scaled back his recipe a bit to save some steps, and I think this time-saving variation is a winner. The combination of cocktail sauce and crabmeat is perfect for summertime nibbling on the patio. It's reminiscent of a

TO PREP:
4 MINUTES
TO CHILL:
1 HOUR

bloody Mary without the vodka. I like to dunk big tortilla chips into the dip but Joe prefers crisp bagel chips. Either way, you're in for some good eating!

1 jar (12 ounces) cocktail sauce
1 tablespoon fresh lemon juice
1 teaspoon Worcestershire sauce
Dash of hot pepper sauce
1 can (4.25 ounces) lump
   crabmeat, well drained
Tortilla or bagel chips, for serving

tips **If you want to serve this dip right after preparing it, keep the cocktail sauce and crabmeat in the refrigerator so they are cold when you combine them.**

If you don't like the heavy horseradish taste of cocktail sauce, use chili sauce instead.

Place the cocktail sauce, lemon juice, Worcestershire sauce, and hot pepper sauce in a small glass bowl and stir to combine. Fold in the drained crabmeat until just combined. Cover the bowl with plastic wrap and chill for 1 hour before serving. Then, place the bowl on a clean tray and surround it with tortilla or bagel chips.

SERVES 4 TO 6 (MAKES 2 CUPS)

15 WAYS TO DOCTOR A JAR OF SALSA

Most of my suggestions for doctoring salsa don't call for exact measurements. Just pour your favorite salsa into a bowl and taste as you add any of the ingredients listed below. All the variations can be scooped up with tortilla chips, but I've included a list of some other possible accompaniments on page 21 for a change of pace.

1 Add avocado cubes, chopped fresh cilantro, and a squeeze of fresh lime juice.

2 Stir in mango chunks, chopped fresh cilantro, and a squeeze of fresh lime juice.

3 Fold in a small can of drained crushed pineapple and chopped fresh cilantro.

4 Marinate chunks of Mexican white cheese in salsa. Serve on a pretty platter with toothpicks for the cheese.

5 Stir in a small can of drained yellow corn for a quick corn salsa.

6 Combine salsa with drained and rinsed canned black beans and drained canned yellow corn.

7 Add chopped jicama, shredded carrots, and chopped fresh ginger.

8 Stir in a chopped fresh, ripe tomato.

9 Mix shredded radish and a pinch of ground cumin with salsa.

10 Add chopped canned tomatillos.

11 Stir in a chopped soaked chipotle pepper for a hot and smoky taste.

12 Add 1 teaspoon of prepared horseradish, or more to taste, and fresh lemon juice. Serve this salsa alongside grilled shrimp.

13 Mix in chopped store-bought roasted red pepper, a dash of balsamic vinegar, and chopped fresh basil.

14 Add a couple of tablespoons of plain yogurt, chopped cucumber, and cumin seed. Serve this with toasted pita bread.

15 Fold in shredded carrot, a dash of Thai fish sauce, a squeeze of fresh lime juice, and chopped fresh jalapeño pepper (add ½ pepper at a time and taste the salsa before adding more). Serve this with rice crackers.

TENNIS TEAM CHEESE SALSA

▼ ▼ ▼

I have shared many of my sister Susan Anderson's recipes, and here is another goodie! Susan and her tennis pals cook as well as they serve—pardon the pun—and they like to munch on this salsa after games. Susan concocts it from a bag of shredded taco-flavored cheese. It makes you start thinking of all the other speedy cheese salsas you could make from that ocean of shredded cheese in the supermarket.

TO PREP: 8 MINUTES

tips Susan prefers to use Italian salad dressing made from a packet of Good Seasons. I like it that way, too, but you can save time by using bottled dressing.

If you are feeling creative, add a handful of cubes of avocado or cucumber to the salsa.

If there are leftovers, spoon them over hot pasta, into an omelet, or onto a hot baked potato.

1 package (8 ounces; 2 cups) pre-shredded Mexican or taco cheese blend
1 cup chopped tomatoes
1 can (4.5 ounces) chopped green chiles, drained
1 can (2.25 ounces) sliced black olives, drained
½ cup chopped scallions (from about 4), green part only
¼ cup bottled Italian salad dressing, plus more if needed
Tortilla chips, for serving

Place the cheese, tomatoes, chiles, olives, and scallions in a large glass mixing bowl and stir to combine. Pour the salad dressing over the cheese mixture and stir until all the ingredients are moistened, adding more dressing if needed. Serve at once with tortilla chips. Leftovers can be stored in the refrigerator for up to 1 week.

SERVES 12 (MAKES 4 CUPS)

BAKED VIDALIA ONION DIP

▼ ▼ ▼

TO PREP:
12 MINUTES
TO BAKE:
22–25 MINUTES

Oven baked mayo-based dips have been making the cocktail party circuit for a while, and it's no wonder. They're a cinch to prepare and contain few ingredients. You just place the dip in the oven and walk away for about 25 minutes. It comes out lightly browned and bubbling. I serve this Swiss cheese and onion dip with big, flat tortilla chips, but it's also yummy with the large corn chips that are shaped like scoops. You want them to be able to hold onto those sweet and crunchy onions.

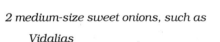

tips My friend Susan Spaulding is a master of mayonnaise dips, and she says the perfect ratio for this one is 1:1:1 of chopped onion, Swiss cheese, and mayonnaise. I also tried this dip with an extra cup of onion and it works, especially for dippers crazy about Vidalias.

Feel free to halve this recipe or to double it, and feel free to spice it up with a teaspoon of hot pepper sauce or dress it up with a couple of tablespoons of chopped fresh parsley right before you serve it.

2 medium-size sweet onions, such as
    Vidalias
1 package (8 ounces; 2 cups) pre-shredded
    Swiss cheese
2 cups mayonnaise, preferably Hellmann's
¼ teaspoon cayenne pepper or paprika
Tortilla or corn chips, for serving

1. Preheat the oven to 375°F.

2. Chop the onions; you should have about 2 cups.

3. Place the chopped onions and the Swiss cheese and mayonnaise in a large mixing bowl and stir to combine well. Transfer the onion mixture to a 2-quart glass or ceramic casserole or baking dish and sprinkle the top with the cayenne.

Bake until the dip is golden brown and bubbling throughout, 22 to 25 minutes.

4. Serve the dip warm, right from the casserole, with chips.

SERVES 12 TO 16 (MAKES 6 CUPS)

What to Dip?

—▼—

DINNER DOCTOR SAYS

When it comes to dippers, anything goes. Here is a basic list of possibilities to start you off.

- ◆ Potato chips
- ◆ Potato sticks
- ◆ Veggie chips
- ◆ Corn chips shaped like scoops
- ◆ Plain or blue tortilla chips
- ◆ Tiny rice crackers
- ◆ Puffy Cheese Twists (see page 40)

- ◆ Bagel chips
- ◆ Toasted pita triangles
- ◆ Asparagus that has been briefly steamed and then cooled
- ◆ Long cucumber slices or wedges
- ◆ Apple slices or wedges
- ◆ Carrot sticks
- ◆ Celery sticks
- ◆ Thin rounds of zucchini
- ◆ Bell pepper strips

THE FAMOUS SPINACH AND ARTICHOKE DIP

▼ ▼ ▼

Spinach and artichoke dip was such a fixture in the 1990s that if this book were put in a time capsule, anyone opening it up 1,000 years from now might date it to the wrong century. But honestly, down South, people still love this dip and serve it often. Those who don't have the recipe beg for it. So here it is. Not fancy, but incredibly delicious—perfect for the football season.

TO PREP:
15 MINUTES
TO BAKE:
12–15 MINUTES

2 microwavable bags
    (9 ounces each) frozen
    creamed spinach
3 cups (12 ounces) pre-shredded
    mozzarella cheese
1 can (14 ounces) artichoke hearts packed
    in water, drained, and each heart
    cut into 3 pieces
1 teaspoon hot pepper sauce, or 2 teaspoons
    chile-garlic sauce, or more to taste
Tortilla chips, for serving

1. Preheat the oven to 400°F.

2. Speed-thaw the creamed spinach: Place the bags in a medium-size glass bowl and pierce each once with a knife. Place the bowl in a microwave oven and cook on high power until the spinach has thawed and is warm, about 4 minutes.

3. Slit open the bags and pour the spinach into a 3-quart glass or ceramic

tips To vary this recipe:
    Mix in a handful of bacon bits or crumbled fried bacon.
    Add 2 tablespoons of fresh chopped tarragon.
    If you really want to go over the top, stir in a splash of Pernod.

casserole or oval gratin dish. Add 2 cups of the mozzarella cheese and the artichoke hearts and hot pepper sauce. Stir to combine the ingredients and smooth the top. Taste and add more hot pepper sauce, if desired. Sprinkle the remaining 1 cup of mozzarella cheese evenly over the top.

4. Bake the dip until it is bubbling throughout and the cheese has melted, 12 to 15 minutes, then serve at once with tortilla chips.

SERVES 12 TO 16

(MAKES 6 CUPS)

How to Doctor
Store-Bought Lemonade

—▼—

DINNER DOCTOR SAYS

Start with a 1-pint can of condensed frozen lemonade, mix in water following the directions on the label, then add:

◆ 1 pint fresh blueberries

◆ 1 cup crushed strawberries sweetened with 2 tablespoons sugar, or

more to taste (the sugar helps release the juice from the berries)

◆ 1 pint fresh raspberries

◆ 1 cup lemon and orange slices

◆ ½ cup seedless cucumber slices—very refreshing

NEW-FASHIONED PIMENTO CHEESE

▼ ▼ ▼

In the South we affectionately call this cheese spread pi-men-ah cheese, and ever since the 1930s, when pimiento peppers were first canned and at our fingertips, it has been a part of our food culture. We pile the cheese onto celery sticks, melt it on fat slices of ripe tomato under the broiler, or just slather it on soda crackers for a fast hors d'oeuvre. I am not going to suggest that you buy ready-made pimento cheese

TO PREP:
5–7 MINUTES

because it isn't that good; but I will advise you to save prep time by using pre-shredded Cheddar cheese.

1 package (8 ounces; 2 cups) pre-shredded
    sharp Cheddar cheese
1 jar (2 ounces) diced or sliced
    pimiento peppers, drained
1 tablespoon minced onion
Dash of Worcestershire sauce
¼ cup mayonnaise
    Black pepper
    Soda crackers or thin slices of toasted
        French bread, for serving

1. Place the Cheddar cheese, pimientos, onion, and Worcestershire sauce in a small glass bowl and stir to combine.

2. Fold in the mayonnaise and stir until everything is well blended. Season with pepper to taste.

tip   **For a Tex-Mex twist, start with a pre-shredded Mexican Cheddar and Monterey Jack cheese blend that has jalapeño peppers in it. Look for one labeled mild; add chopped and drained chiles, if you like.**

3. Place the bowl on a serving platter and surround it with soda crackers or French bread toasts. If you are making the pimento cheese ahead, cover the bowl with plastic wrap and chill until serving, then remove it from the refrigerator 30 minutes before serving to allow the flavors to develop.

SERVES 4 TO 6 (MAKES ABOUT 2 CUPS)

---

5 Great Ways to Use
A Spoonful of Pimento Cheese

—▾—

DINNER DOCTOR SAYS

1. Spread it on half an English muffin and run this under the broiler until the cheese bubbles.

2. Dollop it generously on a burger hot off the grill.

3. Tuck it inside a hot baked potato.

4. Add some pimento cheese to a toasted BLT.

5. Sandwich it between two slices of bread and sauté the sandwich in melted butter, turning once to toast both sides, for a change of pace from the usual grilled cheese.

BLUE CHEESE, PESTO, AND TOMATO STACK

▼ ▼ ▼

There are probably countless versions of this easy but elegant layered spread; this one, with blue cheese, pesto, and sun-dried tomatoes, comes from my friend Beth Meador of Nashville. Beth was coming over for dinner and offered to bring the hors d'oeuvre—one of the nicest things anyone can do. Since Beth is a purist and makes her own pesto from the basil that grows in her garden, I didn't want to offend her by calling this Beth's Blue Cheese . . .

TO PREP:
10 MINUTES
TO CHILL:
12 HOURS–OVERNIGHT

I love homemade pesto, too, but I also love the time saved by using store-bought in this dandy appetizer!

1 package (8 ounces) reduced-fat
*   cream cheese, at room temperature*
1 package (4 ounces) crumbled blue cheese
¼ teaspoon black pepper
½ cup store-bought pesto
¼ cup drained chopped oil-packed
*   sun-dried tomatoes, oil reserved*
3 large fresh basil leaves, for garnish
½ cup small oil-packed olives, such as
*   niçoise, for serving*
Soda crackers, for serving

tip Let your imagination have some fun here—use chopped fresh tomatoes instead of sun-dried and black olive paste instead of pesto or a pesto made from chopped cilantro instead of basil; sprinkle toasted pine nuts on top just before serving . . . anything goes.

1. Line a 1–quart bowl with plastic wrap so that the wrap extends over the edge of the bowl. Set the bowl aside.

2. Place the cream cheese, blue cheese, and pepper in a food processor and process until the mixture comes together and is well combined, 10 to 15 seconds. Spread a third of this mixture in the bottom of the lined bowl. Spread ¼ cup of the pesto over the cream cheese mixture, then layer on 2 tablespoons of the sun-dried tomatoes. Spread half of the remaining cream cheese mixture on top of the tomatoes, then the remaining ¼ cup of pesto, and the remaining 2 tablespoons of tomatoes. Top with the remaining cream cheese mixture. Bring the edges of the plastic wrap up over the top of the stack to cover it. Place the bowl in the refrigerator to chill for at least 2 hours, or overnight.

3. Thirty minutes before serving, remove the stack from the refrigerator, peel the plastic wrap off the top, and turn the stack out onto a serving plate. Remove the remaining plastic wrap and, if desired, drizzle a little of the oil from the tomatoes over the stack. Arrange the basil leaves down the center of the top of the stack. Place the olives around its rim and serve with crackers.

SERVES 8

How to Make a Layered Appetizer Terrine

—▼—

DINNER DOCTOR SAYS Layered terrines are easy to assemble and their multicolored slices are sure to impress. A soft cheese, like cream cheese, serves as the mortar that holds the other layers together. What you mold them in doesn't have to be fancy. A bowl will produce a rounded shape like a bombe, while using a loaf pan will result in a true terrine shape. Here's how to assemble a terrine from cream cheese, pesto, toasted pine nuts, and sun-dried tomatoes.

1. Line a bowl or loaf pan with plastic wrap so that it extends a couple of inches over the sides.

2. Spoon in a layer of softened cream cheese, spreading it evenly over the bottom of the bowl or loaf pan. Follow this with a thin layer of pesto, a layer of toasted pine nuts, another layer of cream cheese, finely sliced sun-dried tomatoes, and a top layer of more cream cheese. If you're not in a hurry, you'll get the best results by chilling the terrine for at least 30 minutes after you add each layer; this keeps each layer from blending into the layer underneath

so the terrine will look prettier when you slice it. If you're in a hurry, you can just carefully pat each layer on top of the previous one.

3. Once you have added the top layer of cream cheese, cover the terrine with the overhanging plastic wrap. Place it in the refrigerator to chill for at least 2 hours.

4. To unmold, peel the plastic wrap off the top of the terrine and turn it onto a serving platter. Gently peel the plastic wrap off the rest of the terrine while it is still cold. Let the uncovered terrine sit at room temperature for at least 30 minutes before you plan to serve it so it becomes spreadable.

Another combination of ingredients that works well is a layer of herb-flavored cream cheese, a thin layer of black olive spread, a layer of goat cheese that has been puréed with cream cheese, a thin layer of pesto, and more herb-flavored cream cheese to top it all off. Of course, these combinations are just jumping-off points; feel free to experiment with whatever other ingredients you like.

BEER CHEESE SPREAD

▼ ▼ ▼

When I think about this recipe, my mind races back to the sixties when my mother made a similar spread and packed it into crocks for Christmas gifts. Well, it's still in style today and can be made in a few minutes with the help of pre-shredded Cheddar cheese and a food processor. Keep a bowlful in your refrigerator; it's perfect to have on hand when guests drop in unexpectedly. And, since food gifts never go out of style, it will still be appreciated if you spoon it into crocks and present it to others. You choose which beer to use—pale ale, dark stout, or a light lager.

TO PREP: 5 MINUTES

1 or 2 garlic cloves, peeled

1 package (8 ounces; 2 cups) pre-shredded
    sharp Cheddar cheese

¼ cup beer of your choice

1 tablespoon Worcestershire sauce

½ teaspoon dry mustard

Dash of cayenne pepper

Soda crackers, for serving

1. Place the garlic in a food processor (the amount depends on the size of the cloves and how garlicky you want the spread to be). Pulse until the garlic is well minced, 5 seconds. Add the Cheddar cheese, beer, Worcestershire sauce, mustard, and cayenne. Process until the mixture comes together, 30 to 40 seconds.

2. Spoon the cheese spread into a small glass or ceramic serving bowl and serve it with crackers, or pack it into a small crock, cover, and chill until needed. The spread will keep for several weeks in the refrigerator.

SERVES 8 (MAKES 1 CUP)

tip **Sharp cheese is critical here, so use the best pre-shredded sharp Cheddar you can find.**

SMOKED SALMON SPREAD

▼▼▼

With just three ingredients, this spread couldn't be easier. I have made plenty of complicated smoked salmon pâtés in my day, and now I ask myself, "Why?" This speedy version is on the appetizer plate as soon as you can open two packages, snip some herbs, and whiz it into a delectable purée.

TO PREP:
3 MINUTES

1 container (5 ounces) garlic-
    and-herb-flavored cheese
    spread, such as Boursin
4 ounces sliced smoked salmon
1 tablespoon chopped fresh dill or chives
Pita triangles, crackers, and bagel chips,
    for serving

Place the cheese spread, smoked salmon, and dill in a food processor. Pulse 5 or 6 times until the mixture is well combined. Spoon the spread into a serving bowl or onto a serving plate, surround it with pita triangles, crackers, and bagel chips, and serve.

SERVES 6 TO 8 (MAKES 1¼ CUPS)

tip When the weather turns cool, heat the salmon spread in a microwave oven for 20 to 30 seconds and serve it warm with crackers.

The Salmon Spread Doctor

—▼—

DINNER DOCTOR SAYS

If you have any spread left over, though I don't predict this, here are some yummy ways to enjoy it (they might even inspire you to make a double batch).

◆ Mix a tablespoon into an omelet.

◆ Spoon a tablespoon onto a baked potato instead of butter.

◆ Spoon tiny spoonfuls into hollowed-out cherry tomatoes—this is time-consuming, but worth it.

◆ Spoon the spread into large mushroom caps and bake them at 375°F until they are bubbling, about 15 minutes.

◆ Dollop a tablespoon on a portion of cooked pasta.

◆ Spread some onto a prebaked pizza crust and top it with cooked shrimp. Bake the pizza at 400°F until the spread is bubbling, 5 to 7 minutes.

WARM WHITE BEAN SPREAD

WITH CUMIN AND LIME

▼ ▼ ▼

Don't feel guilty. No one has to know that all you did was open a can of beans, purée them with garlic and cumin, then dribble in enough olive oil to make the spread as creamy as mayonnaise. Zap this in the microwave for 30 seconds and friends will surely beg

TO PREP:
4 MINUTES

you for the recipe, for this dip is head-turning and satisfying. It is even more satisfying for the cook, because the preparation time is less than 5 minutes.

2 cloves garlic, peeled

1 can (15.5 ounces) Great Northern
   beans, drained

½ teaspoon ground cumin,
   or more to taste

1 teaspoon fresh lime juice,
   or more to taste

Pinch of salt or Creole seasoning

2 tablespoons extra-virgin olive oil

Tortilla chips, for serving

Place the garlic in a food processor and pulse until minced, 5 seconds. Add the beans, cumin, lime juice, and salt. Pulse until the

tips I serve this spread alongside salsa, but if you want to serve it on its own, get fancy with an added handful of chopped tomato or avocado, some chopped chiles, or a scattering of cilantro on top. You can also toss a tablespoon of chopped pimientos or black olives into the spread.

   If you want to serve the spread hot, heat it in the microwave oven on high power for 30 seconds.

   No lime juice? Go with lemon.

New Year's Festive Supper

▼ ▼ ▼

Celebrate the upcoming year with a sit-down dinner that tastes as if you've slaved in the kitchen since the last new year. Easy-to-prepare dishes make for the happiest of occasions.

Warm White Bean Spread with Cumin and Lime
this page

Shrimp Cocktail Four Ways
page 34

Fast-Roasted Beef Tenderloin
page 207

Mother's Party Peas and Artichokes
page 372

Angel Biscuits
page 417

Easy Italian Cream Cake
page 458

ingredients are well combined, 5 to 10 seconds. With the motor running, pour the olive oil slowly through the feed tube and process until the mixture is creamy, 20 seconds. Transfer the bean spread to a glass bowl and serve with tortilla chips.

SERVES 6 TO 8 (MAKES 1$\frac{1}{2}$ CUPS)

SHRIMP COCKTAIL FOUR WAYS

▼ ▼ ▼

Okay, I have a little confession to make: Recipe testing is really a lot of fun. It's true that much work goes into creating a cookbook, but the payoffs are many, and this recipe had such a payoff. My friends and

**TO PREP:
5 MINUTES
PER SAUCE**

I thoroughly enjoyed dunking each and every shrimp and mopping up every smidgen of sauce. Given a longer deadline, I might have come up with Shrimp Cocktail Eighteen Ways, a great excuse for a get-together, but it doesn't sound speedy, does it? The trick here is to buy already-steamed shrimp from a seafood market or to use the frozen already-cooked supermarket shrimp that you just thaw. Then, all you have to do is whip up one or all of these sauces, which are based on seasoned canned tomatoes. The prep time for each sauce is about five minutes. For an elegant presentation, spoon a couple of tablespoons of sauce into goblets and top each with four or five shrimp.

tips Hunt's makes diced tomatoes with balsamic vinegar, basil, and olive oil. Note that the common ingredient in these sauces—besides tomatoes—is lemon or lime juice. The citrus complements shrimp and peps up the tomatoes. If you are in a hurry, simply quarter limes or lemons and omit the juice in the sauce. Serve the lime or lemon quarters on the side so your guests can squeeze their own juice.

These sauces are also delicious with crab cakes.

MEXICAN COCKTAIL SAUCE:

1 can (14.5 ounces) diced tomatoes
    with mild green chiles, with
    their liquid

1 small avocado, cut into ½-inch cubes
    (for ½ cup)

2 tablespoons chopped fresh cilantro

1 tablespoon fresh lime juice

½ teaspoon ground cumin, or
    more to taste

Drop of hot pepper sauce, or
    more to taste

AMERICAN COCKTAIL SAUCE:

1 can (14.5 ounces) diced tomatoes
    with onions, with their liquid

1 tablespoon prepared horseradish

1 tablespoon fresh lemon juice

1 teaspoon Worcestershire sauce

ASIAN COCKTAIL SAUCE:

1 can (14.5 ounces) diced tomatoes,
    with their liquid

1 tablespoon hoisin sauce

1 tablespoon fresh lime juice

1 teaspoon peeled grated fresh ginger or
    pre-chopped ginger (see Tips, page 77)

½ teaspoon curry powder

ITALIAN COCKTAIL SAUCE:

1 can (14.5 ounces) diced tomatoes with
    balsamic vinegar, basil, and olive oil
    (see Tips), with their liquid

2 tablespoons chopped black olives
    (from 8 olives)

2 tablespoons chopped fresh flat-leaf parsley

1 tablespoon fresh lemon juice

1 pound store-bought, peeled, deveined,
    and steamed large shrimp, thawed if
    frozen, and chilled

1. Place the ingredients for whichever sauce you are making in a medium-size glass bowl and stir to combine. Cover the sauce with plastic wrap and refrigerate until ready to serve.

2. Place the shrimp on a pretty platter in an attractive mound. If they still have their tails attached, these can be used to pick up the shrimp. If not, set out cocktail toothpicks. Spoon the sauce(s) of your choice into a serving bowl or bowls. And don't forget to set out plenty of napkins, and forks for eating the chunkier sauces.

SERVES 6 TO 8

SOUFFLÉED CHEESE AND ONION CANAPÉS

▼▼▼

TO PREP:
10 MINUTES
TO COOK:
2 MINUTES

My husband, John, and I both have fond memories of these hot, rich cheese puffs being served at parties when our parents entertained. John recalls his mother cutting Pepperidge Farm white bread into small rounds with a biscuit cutter and then piling a teaspoonful of Parmesan and onion spread on top before heating the rounds under the broiler. I recall my mother slathering thin slices of small pumpernickel loaves with the spread. Either way, the canapés were delicious. And cutting the bread into quarters instead of stamping out rounds is a real time-saver.

This hot appetizer is a boon to the host or hostess because it contains just a few ingredients, and the mayonnaise and Parmesan combination takes on an attractive soufflélike appearance after broiling.

1 cup pre-grated Parmesan cheese
⅓ cup plus 1 tablespoon mayonnaise,
*   preferably Hellmann's*
3 tablespoons grated or finely minced onion
4 slices sturdy white sandwich bread
Cayenne pepper, for dusting (optional)

tip   **No time for piling cheese topping onto bread? Just transfer the cheese and mayonnaise mixture into a small casserole, and place it in a preheated 350°F oven for about 20 minutes while you run the vacuum and set the table. The hot and cheesy dip will be ready for tortilla chips or crackers when your guests arrive.**

1. Preheat the broiler.

2. Place the Parmesan cheese, mayonnaise, and onion in a small bowl and stir to combine. Remove the crusts from the bread, if desired, then cut each slice into quarters. With a butter knife, spread the cheese mixture on top of the bread quarters, piling it up in the center. Transfer the bread quarters to a baking sheet and dust them with cayenne if desired. Broil the canapés 4 to 6 inches from the heat until they puff up and turn deep golden brown, 1½ to 2 minutes. Carefully remove the canapés to a plate and serve warm.

SERVES 6 TO 8 (MAKES 16 CANAPÉS)

"The Green Can"

—▼—

DINNER DOCTOR SAYS Our busy family has come to rely on "The Green Can," as the cylinder of Kraft's grated Parmesan cheese is called at our house. Parmigiano-Reggiano may truly be the king of Parmesan, but it's pricey. And sometimes you just don't want to fuss with grating Parmesan, you just want to get dinner on the table. That's why we stock the green can—actually two green cans, one shredded and one grated—in our pantry. The shredded we put right on the table to top pasta, whereas the grated Parmesan is saved for garlic-cheese toast and for recipes such as the Souffléed Cheese and Onion Canapés, at left, where you want a finer-textured cheese that will blend easily.

15 WAYS TO DOCTOR CREAM CHEESE

Begin with 8 ounces of cream cheese and end up with a speedy appetizer to serve with your favorite crackers. You can easily use a food processor to blend any of the following ingredients into room-temperature cream cheese.

1 Blend ¼ cup of store-bought pesto with the cream cheese. Top it with lightly toasted pine nuts.

2 Blend ¼ cup of pitted kalamata olives into the cream cheese. Garnish it with fresh thyme leaves.

3 Blend ¼ cup of chopped, oil-packed, sun-dried tomatoes into the cream cheese. Sprinkle 1 tablespoon of chopped fresh basil over the top.

4 Blend a jar of chopped marinated artichokes into the cream cheese and spread this on pumpernickel or rye bread.

5 Drain a small can of tiny shrimp and blend them into the cream cheese. Season with a pinch of ground mace or nutmeg and sprinkle with 1 tablespoon of minced red onion. Serve with bagel chips.

6 Blend a can of drained chopped chiles, ½ cup of shredded Cheddar cheese, and a pinch of cumin into the cream cheese.

7 Blend 2 ounces of smoked trout and a squeeze of fresh lemon juice into the cream cheese. Garnish with 1 tablespoon of chopped fresh parsley.

8 Blend 1 clove of garlic that you have crushed in a garlic press, 1 teaspoon of *herbes de Provence,* and a pinch of black pepper into the cream cheese for a homemade Boursin-style cheese.

9 Blend 1 small can of deviled ham and 1 teaspoon of Dijon mustard into the cream cheese.

10 Blend ¼ cup of chopped radishes and some black pepper into the cream cheese.

11 Blend ¼ cup of finely chopped honey-roasted almonds and a dash of hot pepper sauce into the cream cheese.

12 Blend ½ cup of crumbled blue cheese into the cream cheese. Top with a spoonful of pear preserves and toasted almond slices.

13 Spread the top of the cream cheese with ½ cup of chutney. Sprinkle with toasted sliced almonds.

14 Cover the cream cheese with ½ cup of whole-berry cranberry sauce.

15 The classic: Spread the top of the cream cheese with ½ cup of top-quality pepper jelly. Let it drip down the sides.

EASY CHEESE FONDUE

▼ ▼ ▼

This is by no means an authentic Swiss recipe, but you'll love the flavor of my no-fuss fondue, which is based on store-bought Alfredo pasta sauce. The sauce works as the thickener; you just add pre-shredded Swiss cheese and a little white wine. Since most Alfredo sauces contain nutmeg, the seasoning is already in place (if the brand you buy doesn't have

TO PREP:
5 MINUTES

nutmeg in it, don't bother to add it; the fondue will taste just fine). It only takes about 5 minutes for the cheese to melt, and then you're all set to dunk cubes of French bread, apple slices—whatever you fancy. The recipe doubles easily if you want to serve more than four.

tips **If you cannot find pre-shredded Swiss cheese in your market, buy 8 ounces of sliced Swiss and cut it into thin strips.**

Make a grander presentation by serving pickled cocktail onions and tiny French pickles (cornichons) with the fondue. The Swiss often serve shots of kirschwasser, a cherry brandy, to dip the bread in before dunking it in the fondue.

1 cup refrigerated Alfredo-style pasta sauce
    (see page 277)
1 package (8 ounces; 2 cups) pre-shredded
    Swiss cheese
¼ cup dry white wine
Cubes of French bread, for dunking
Crisp apple slices, such as Gala or
    Granny Smith, for dunking

1. Place the Alfredo sauce in a 2-quart saucepan over medium heat. Add the Swiss cheese and wine and stir until

Puffy Cheese Twists

—▼—

DINNER DOCTOR SAYS

It's a snap to use frozen puff pastry to make long, slender, crunchy cheese twists. Slice unbaked, thawed puff pastry sheets into ⅓-inch-wide strips. Holding a strip at each end and working quickly, dredge it in a shallow dish of pre-grated Parmesan cheese. Turn one end of the strip clockwise to twist the strip into a gentle corkscrew. Place the strip on an ungreased baking sheet. Repeat with the remaining strips. Sprinkle a little cayenne pepper or paprika on top, then bake in a preheated 400°F oven until golden brown and aromatic, 15 minutes. Serve the cheese twists with a glass of wine, a bowl of soup, or a green salad.

the cheese melts and is bubbling, 4 to 5 minutes.

2. Pour the fondue into a fondue pot or chafing dish and light the heat source underneath to keep it warm. Serve the fondue with bowls of bread cubes and apple slices and provide long forks for dunking.

SERVES 4

tips Want a Mexican twist? Omit the white wine, use a Mexican-style pre-shredded cheese, and stir in a drained 4-ounce can of chopped green chiles. Serve tortilla chips alongside the bread cubes and quench your thirst with Margaritas.

MINI
CHEESE CALZONES

WITH HOT MARINARA SAUCE

▼ ▼ ▼

If there is any snack food that is more appealing to children than string cheese, it must be string cheese that has been wrapped in bread-stick dough and baked until golden, so it looks like a miniature calzone. My daughters love this snack, and adults like it, too, especially when it's served on a pretty ceramic platter with a bowl of hot marinara sauce for dunking. The only time-consuming part of this recipe is unwrapping individually wrapped string cheese. If you can find unwrapped cheese, the recipe will take even less time.

TO PREP:
15 MINUTES
TO BAKE:
12 MINUTES

tips **Pillsbury makes bread-stick dough, so if you have trouble finding it, a call to Pillsbury might help you locate a distributor.**

There are countless ingredients you can tuck inside a calzone, so use some creativity here. Wrap an anchovy around the cheese before wrapping it in dough, or a piece of pepperoni, which might be more kid friendly.

For a dressier look, brush the unbaked calzones with beaten egg white and sprinkle them with poppy or sesame seeds.

6 sticks (1 ounce each) string cheese

1 package (11 ounces) refrigerated bread-stick dough (see Tips)

1 cup jarred marinara sauce or pizza sauce, for serving

1. Preheat the oven to 400°F.

2. Unwrap the string cheese sticks and cut them in half crosswise. Open or unroll the bread-stick dough and separate it into 12 rectangles. Coil a rectangle of bread-stick dough around a piece of cheese stick as if you were wrapping it with yarn. Completely cover the cheese, tucking the dough ends under and pinching them to seal closed. Repeat with the remaining dough and cheese. Place the dough-covered cheese on an ungreased baking sheet.

3. Bake the mini calzones until they are golden brown, about 12 minutes. Remove them from the baking sheet and serve at once with a bowl of marinara or pizza sauce for dunking.

SERVES 6 (MAKES 12 MINI CALZONES)

Teenagers in the House

▼ ▼ ▼

When your kids' friends are over and everyone's having too good a time to go home for dinner, they don't have to. Let them help throw together a quick meal filled with favorite flavors—including plenty of cheese.

**Mini Cheese Calzones
with Hot Marinara Sauce**
page 41

Nacho Cheese Soup
page 97

Tex-Mex Layered Salad
page 139

Brownie Drops
page 516

AROMATIC MUSHROOM GALETTE

▼▼▼

TO PREP:
12 MINUTES
TO BAKE:
22–25 MINUTES

When the rest of the party is keeping you company in the kitchen, this is the fragrant appetizer to pull from the oven and serve up in slices. In fact, it's just the sort of recipe you could enlist others to help assemble while you're readying dinner. That is, if you don't mind divulging your secrets—like the refrigerated crescent rolls that make up the flaky dough, and the pre-sliced mushrooms in the filling. This appetizer is a bit more involved than some of the others in this chapter, but I love a slice of it served warm with a cold glass of white wine. It also makes a fine meal paired with a little green salad. Believe me, with the galette's heady aroma, no one will think about leaving your kitchen!

1 package (8 ounces) refrigerated
    crescent rolls
2 cups (8 ounces) pre-sliced
    mushrooms
3 cloves garlic, crushed in a garlic press
2 tablespoons olive oil, or butter, melted
½ cup pre-grated Parmesan cheese
¼ cup chopped fresh flat-leaf parsley
1 teaspoon dried oregano
Salt

tip If you prefer, instead of measuring out the garlic, olive oil, parsley, and Parmesan, you can substitute about ½ cup of store-bought pesto, stirring the mushroom slices to coat them well with it before filling the galette.

1. Preheat the oven to 375°F.

2. Unwrap the crescent rolls and unroll the dough; you will have 8 triangles. Place an ungreased baking sheet or pizza stone on a work surface. Arrange the triangles of dough so that they form an 8-pointed star. The pointed tips should face away from the center of the star. Start by placing one triangle in the 12 o'clock position, one in the 6 o'clock position, one at 3 o'clock, and one at 9 o'clock. Place the remaining 4 triangles in the remaining empty spaces. The edges of the dough triangles should overlap each other slightly, but there will be a hole in the center of the star. Using your fingertips, press down on the dough to seal the edges where they overlap. To fill the hole, press the base of each triangle toward the center until the hole is evenly covered with dough. Then, using your hand, press down on the dough so that it is flat, with no gaps.

3. Place the mushrooms, garlic, olive oil, ¼ cup of the Parmesan cheese, and the parsley and oregano in a mixing bowl, and stir to combine. Season with salt to taste. Spoon the mushroom filling into the center of the dough, then pull the tips of the dough up, and fold them over the filling to create a bundle. There will be gaps between the triangles of dough on top of the filling. Press down slightly on the bundle. Sprinkle the remaining ¼ cup of Parmesan cheese over the top of the galette.

4. Bake the galette until the crust is deeply browned and the mushroom filling bubbles, 22 to 25 minutes. Remove the galette from the oven, run a metal spatula underneath to loosen it, then slice and serve warm.

SERVES 6 TO 8

15 WAYS TO DOCTOR DELI HORS D'OEUVRES

For a spur-of-the-moment get-together, or even one planned in advance, the supermarket deli counter is a lifesaver.

1 Wrap prosciutto slices around pear slices, fresh fig halves, or chunks of melon.

2 Sprinkle olives with chopped fresh thyme or rosemary and a teaspoon of grated orange zest.

3 Arrange salad bar veggies on a pretty platter. Choose a fresh dip from the deli counter and spoon into seeded red or green bell pepper half "bowls."

4 Spread deli meats with a thin layer of cream cheese, then roll them up around lightly steamed asparagus spears or sweet baby gherkins. Secure with toothpicks.

5 Top toasted French bread rounds with chopped deli olives, sun-dried tomatoes, pesto, and an herbed cheese spread.

6 Make your own marinated mushrooms by combining salad bar mushrooms with your favorite bottled vinaigrette dressing. Serve with toothpicks and French bread rounds.

7 Spread slices of white bread with a thin layer of deli tuna or chicken salad. Cut the bread into fingers or fun shapes.

8 Arrange smoked salmon slices on a pretty platter with piles of capers and minced red onion. Accompany the salmon with lemon wedges and small slices of dark bread.

9 Set up a mustard bar, with different mustards, small knives, and slices of salami, sour pickles, and crusty bread.

10 Surround a hunk of good blue cheese with red and green grapes and mounds of toasted pecans or walnuts.

11 Spoon deli hummus into a serving bowl. Drizzle with olive oil and sprinkle with chopped fresh parsley. Serve with warm pita triangles and olives.

12 Blend a chunk of fancy pâté in a food processor with a tablespoon of brandy and a tablespoon of butter. Spoon the pâté into a bowl and surround it with French bread rounds and sour pickles.

13 Arrange heated deli Buffalo wings on a platter with celery sticks. Serve with a dip made by adding crumbled blue cheese to a blue cheese salad dressing.

14 Spear marinated mushrooms and cherry tomato halves on toothpicks to make mini kebabs.

15 Top a baked, store-bought pizza crust with olives, marinated mushrooms, and sun-dried tomatoes. Drizzle with olive oil, warm it in the oven, and cut it into small slices.

ARTICHOKE AND FETA PUFF PASTRY PIZZA

▼▼▼

Since it's elegant and simple to make, I am surprised you don't see this appetizer pizza more often at parties. Frozen puff pastry is so dependable and fast, I can't imagine taking the time to make the pastry from scratch. I have toted the fixings to a friend's house and then assembled the pizza and baked it in her kitchen. It turns out crisp and delicious whether baked on a metal baking sheet or on a pizza stone. Cut the pizza into small squares and serve it on small plates.

TO PREP:
20 MINUTES
TO BAKE:
20–25 MINUTES

1 sheet frozen puff pastry
> (half of a 17.3-ounce package;
> see box, page 48)

½ cup drained oil-packed sun-dried tomatoes

1 jar (6 ounces) marinated artichoke hearts,
> drained

1 cup (4 ounces) pre-crumbled feta cheese

⅓ cup pre-chopped pecans or pine nuts
> (optional)

1 teaspoon chopped fresh oregano, or
> ½ teaspoon dried oregano

1. Preheat the oven to 400°F.

tips Instead of plain feta, choose feta with black pepper or one with sun-dried tomatoes and basil.

For an Asian flavor, top the puff pastry with a mixture of shredded chicken, a little shredded Monterey Jack cheese, dabs of hoisin sauce, chopped scallions, and fresh cilantro.

2. Place the puff pastry on a baking sheet or pizza stone and let thaw while you prepare the toppings.

3. Chop the sun-dried tomatoes and the artichoke hearts.

4. Unfold the puff pastry and roll it out to an 8-inch square or 8-by-10-inch rectangle, using a rolling pin. Sprinkle on the feta cheese, followed by the chopped tomatoes, artichokes, nuts, if using, and oregano.

5. Bake until the pastry puffs up tall and is golden brown, 20 to 25 minutes. Remove the pan from the oven and immediately cut the pizza into squares, with a pizza cutter, and serve.

SERVES **6** TO **8**

Frozen Puff Pastry:
It's Easier Than It Looks

—▼—

DINNER DOCTOR SAYS

One of the busy cook's top convenience foods sits quietly in the frozen food case: puff pastry. Tucked away somewhere near the pie crusts and the frozen fruit, these boxes are the beginning of terrific appetizers and lofty desserts. One 17.3-ounce box contains two folded sheets of pastry. Although the sheets are packaged together, you can use them one at a time; return the second sheet to the freezer in its package. Set on a countertop or on a baking sheet, the pastry will take about 20 minutes to thaw enough to be workable, no longer. So go fold laundry or make a few phone calls, but don't go too far. Keep the sheet folded as it thaws, then unfold it to begin the recipe.

The less you handle puff pastry, the better. That's because a lot of butter has been folded into it, and the moisture in the butter turns into steam when heated, causing the pastry to bake up tall and evenly.

Handling the pastry too much causes some of the butter to melt so the pastry can't rise uniformly. Likewise, if left to thaw longer than 30 minutes in a warm kitchen, the pastry won't rise as well.

Puff pastry may be cut into rounds, sliced into strips, wrapped around ingredients, such as a small round of Brie, or topped with fruits, as in the Fresh Peach Tart on page 485. Here are a few more pointers:

♦ Preheat the oven to 400°F.

♦ Use ungreased baking sheets. Believe me, there is already enough fat in the pastry!

♦ If you glaze the exposed pastry edge with lightly beaten egg it makes the pastry turn golden brown. You can also brush the pastry with a little melted butter and sprinkle it with a little coarse herb salt, grated Parmesan cheese, or sugar—whatever goes with the other ingredients.

PEAR AND BLUE CHEESE TARTLETS

▼ ▼ ▼

TO PREP:
10 MINUTES
TO BAKE:
7–8 MINUTES

Every time I make these tiny bites of heaven— and I've been making them for six or seven years now—I prepare them differently. Sometimes the tartlets contain pears, sometimes apples; I may use a creamy blue cheese or a crumbly one. But the tartlets always start with those handy, tiny, frozen phyllo shells that you fill and quickly bake until crisp. The ones I buy come fifteen to a package. The version here is the most elegant, calling for the pears to be quickly sautéed in butter until soft. Serve the tartlets with a glass of sherry, port, or red wine, then sit back and enjoy.

2 packages (2.1 ounces each)
    frozen miniature
    phyllo shells
1 tablespoon
    butter
2 pears, peeled
    and chopped
    (for about 1½ cups)
2 teaspoons sugar
1 wedge (5 ounces) Saga blue cheese,
    or another creamy blue, trimmed of rind
    and cut into 30 small cubes

tips Instead of trimming the rind off the cheese and cutting the cheese into small cubes, you can buy a package (about 4 ounces) of crumbled blue cheese to sprinkle over the pears.

In a hurry and your pears are already soft? Don't cook the pears. Just peel them and cut them into small cubes. Pop these in the phyllo shells, top them with the creamy blue cheese, and bake.

Want to gild the lily? Sprinkle finely chopped walnuts on the tartlets just before you bake them.

1. Preheat the oven to 350°F.

2. Place the frozen phyllo shells on a rimmed baking sheet. Set the baking sheet aside.

3. Melt the butter in a small skillet over medium-high heat. Place the pears in the skillet and cook, stirring, for 1 minute to soften slightly. Sprinkle the sugar over the pears and let cook, stirring, until they are completely soft, 2 minutes longer. Remove the skillet from the heat.

4. Place 1 teaspoon of the pears and their juice in each phyllo shell. Top with a cube of blue cheese.

5. Bake the tartlets until the cheese melts and the shells are crisp and golden brown, 7 to 8 minutes. Remove the baking sheet from the oven and serve the tartlets immediately. The tartlets can be made up to 1 day in advance. Reheat them in an oven preheated to 350°F. It will take 3 to 4 minutes.

Serves 12 to 15 (makes 30 tartlets)

TOMATO, BASIL, AND PARMESAN TARTLETS

▼ ▼ ▼

I love this easy recipe that makes a ton (well, it makes sixty, not *quite* a ton) of tartlets in no time. Bake these tartlets when you have a crowd coming over for drinks, when you're baking for a wedding or baby shower, a wine and cheese party, an office party— the list could go on and on. The key to the tartlets is those small, ready-made frozen phyllo shells. You need four packages of fifteen shells each. The filling is supercheesy and supereasy, and with thirty shells to each pan, you can bake all these tartlets at once in one oven, which to me is the greatest bonus of all!

TO PREP:
15 MINUTES
TO BAKE:
8–10 MINUTES

tips **Vary this recipe as time permits, adding 2 tablespoons of dried basil instead of fresh, if you have no time to chop.**

Use a half cup of sun-dried tomatoes and a half cup of chopped black olives.

For a wonderful treat, substitute soft goat cheese for some of the cream cheese.

4 packages (2.1 ounces
    each) frozen miniature phyllo shells
12 ounces (1½ packages) reduced-fat
    cream cheese, at room temperature
1 package (8 ounces; 2 cups) pre-shredded
    mozzarella cheese
½ cup pre-grated Parmesan cheese
2 large eggs, lightly beaten
1 cup chopped drained oil-packed
    sun-dried tomatoes
1 cup chopped fresh basil
2 cloves garlic, crushed in a garlic press
Black pepper

1. Preheat the oven to 350°F.

2. Divide the frozen phyllo shells between 2 rimmed baking sheets. Set the baking sheets aside.

3. Place the cream cheese, mozzarella and Parmesan, eggs, sun-dried tomatoes, basil, and garlic in the bowl of a large mixer or a large food processor. Blend on the low speed of the mixer or pulse in the food processor until the ingredients come together and are well combined, 1 minute for the mixer, 30 seconds for the processor (stir with a rubber spatula halfway through to redistribute the ingredients). Season the cheese mixture with pepper to taste. Place a teaspoonful of the cheese mixture in each phyllo shell.

4. Bake the tartlets until the cheese mixture bubbles and the shells are crisp and golden brown, 8 to 10 minutes. Remove the baking sheets from the oven and serve the tartlets warm. The tartlets can be made earlier in the day and reheated in an oven preheated to 350°F. It will take 3 to 4 minutes.

SERVES 24 TO 30 (MAKES 60 TARTLETS)

PARMESAN AND SQUASH CUPS

▼▼▼

The Italians know how to combine flavors, and I might never have paired a purée of winter squash with Parmesan cheese had I not tasted something similar in Italy. It was a ravioli-type pasta stuffed with a squash purée, and finely grated Parmesan was piled in a delicate mound on top. These easy tartlets take off from that combination, and they begin with those fast miniature phyllo shells from the freezer case. When baked, the shells become nutty and aromatic

TO PREP:
10 MINUTES
TO BAKE:
8 MINUTES

from the Parmesan sprinkled into them, and after you spoon in the warm squash purée and take a bite they will transport you to Italy pronto!

2 packages (2.1 ounces each)
  frozen miniature phyllo shells
1 package (12 ounces) frozen
  cooked winter squash, thawed
1 clove garlic, crushed in a
  garlic press
1 tablespoon olive oil
2 teaspoons light brown sugar
Salt and black pepper
2 tablespoons heavy (whipping) cream
  or sour cream (optional)
¼ cup pre-shredded Parmesan cheese

1. Preheat the oven to 350°F.

2. Place the frozen phyllo shells on a rimmed baking sheet. Set the baking sheet aside.

> *tip* **These tiny tartlets are delicious as is, or garnish them with a grinding of black pepper or a sprinkling of minced chives or fresh thyme leaves.**

3. Place the squash, garlic, olive oil, and brown sugar in a small saucepan and cook over medium heat, stirring, until the mixture is well blended and heated through, 3 to 4 minutes. Season the squash mixture with salt and pepper to taste. Stir in the heavy cream or sour cream, if desired, and cook until heated through, 1 minute longer. Remove the pan from the heat, cover, and keep warm.

4. Spoon a little Parmesan cheese into each phyllo shell and bake until the cheese melts and the shells are crisp and golden brown, 7 to 8 minutes.

5. Remove the baking sheet from the oven and spoon enough of the squash purée into each shell to fill it to within ¼-inch of the top. Serve at once. The cheese-filled shells can be made earlier in the day and reheated in an oven preheated to 350°F. It will take 3 to 4 minutes. Fill with the squash purée after reheating the cups.

SERVES 12 TO 15 (MAKES 30 TARTLETS)

PAT'S MINI HAM BISCUITS

▼▼▼

In the South, a ham biscuit is merely a slice of ham, usually country ham, tucked inside a fresh hot biscuit. A fancier version is a cocktail-size biscuit filled with a dab of ham salad, which is simply ground ham moistened with mayonnaise and onion or pickle relish. My friend Pat Howard is a great caterer in Nashville, and these ham biscuits are one of her specialties. She explained her secret one evening—

TO PREP:
20 MINUTES
TO BAKE:
18–20 MINUTES

stamping little biscuits out of thawed frozen biscuits. She gets three small biscuits from every frozen biscuit. It saves valuable time in the home kitchen as well as in the catering kitchen, and no one will ever know you didn't make these from scratch.

1 bag (25 ounces; 12 biscuits) frozen
unbaked biscuits (see Tips, page 56)
12 ounces country ham slices, cooked
(see Tips, page 56), or 12 ounces
precooked sugar-cured ham
4 to 5 tablespoons
mayonnaise
1 tablespoon finely minced
onion or pickle relish
¼ cup all-purpose flour,
for dusting
Fresh parsley, for garnish

1. Preheat the oven to 375°F.

tip **To make these biscuits a day ahead, prepare the ham mixture and chill it. Bake the biscuits, let them cool, then wrap them in aluminum foil and store them at room temperature. The next day, place the wrapped biscuits in an oven that has been preheated to 350°F and let them warm through, about 15 minutes. Fill the biscuits and serve.**

2. Place the frozen biscuits on an ungreased baking sheet and set them aside to thaw at room temperature while you prepare the ham.

3. Tear the ham into pieces and place them in a food processor. Process until the ham is ground and crumbly, 10 seconds. Transfer the ham to a mixing bowl and stir in 4 tablespoons of the mayonnaise and either the onion or pickle relish. Add another tablespoon of mayonnaise if needed to bind the ham. Cover the bowl with plastic wrap and place it in the refrigerator while you cut out and bake the biscuits.

4. Lightly dust a work surface or cutting board with flour. When the biscuits are still cool to the touch but are soft enough to cut, place them on the lightly floured surface. Use a 1½-inch biscuit or round cookie cutter to cut each biscuit into three rounds. Place the biscuit rounds on the baking sheet. Discard the scraps of dough. Bake the biscuits until they are golden brown, 18 to 20 minutes.

5. While the biscuits bake, remove the ham salad from the refrigerator. When the biscuits are cool enough to handle, split them in half with a fork, spoon on a teaspoon of the ham mixture, and replace the tops. Place the filled biscuits on a serving tray garnished with parsley and serve at once.

SERVES 12 TO 15 (MAKES 36 BISCUITS)

tips **Pillsbury makes unbaked biscuits that they market frozen in bags.**

    The ham salad tastes best if made with country ham, but if you use it you'll need to cook it first. Simmer slices in a little water until they curl up and are cooked through, 6 to 7 minutes. Trim off the fat before using the ham.

PECAN CHEESE PATTIES

▼ ▼ ▼

TO PREP:
12 MINUTES
TO BAKE:
10–12 MINUTES

When you have small children in the kitchen it's fun to make dishes they can help prepare and serve. My son John loves to pass these crisp, cheesy snacks when guests come over and then sneak a couple in the kitchen for himself! We keep them in a tin, as you might keep cookies during the holidays, and they stay fresh for up to a week. The quick ingredient in this otherwise classic Southern cheese straw recipe is Bisquick. Drop the dough by the teaspoonful onto a baking sheet and it bakes up like little savory drop cookies. Or you can take a bit more time and form the dough into logs, then slice these and bake them. The patties are delicious in any way, shape, or form.

½ cup pecan halves

8 tablespoons (1 stick) butter, chilled
    and cut into tablespoons

1 package (8 ounces; 2 cups) pre-shredded
    sharp Cheddar cheese

1½ cups biscuit mix, such as Bisquick

Dash of cayenne pepper

1. Preheat the oven to 375°F (see Tip).

tip A convection oven is handy for baking the Pecan Cheese Patties, since it has an interior fan that circulates the hot air. The patties on the upper rack will bake at the same rate as those on the rack below, making it unnecessary to exchange them halfway through. You'll need to reduce the oven temperature by 25°F. Baked in a convection oven, the patties should be done in 8 to 10 minutes.

2. Place the pecans in a food processor and process them in short pulses until they are finely chopped, 10 seconds. Transfer the pecans to a small bowl. Place the butter, Cheddar cheese, biscuit mix, and cayenne in the food processor and pulse until the mixture comes together in a ball, 20 seconds. Add the chopped pecans and process until just combined, 5 seconds.

3. Spoon teaspoonfuls of the dough onto 2 ungreased baking sheets, positioning them about 1 inch apart and making six rows of five patties on each sheet. Or, divide the dough in half and shape each half into a log on a long sheet of waxed paper. Bring the waxed paper up around a log and roll it gently on the work surface until the log is uniform and about an inch in diameter. Repeat with the remaining log. Refrigerate the logs for 15 minutes to make slicing easier. Unwrap the logs and cut them into ¼-inch-thick slices. Arrange the slices about 1 inch apart, 30 to a baking sheet.

4. Place the baking sheets in the oven, 1 on the center rack and 1 on the upper rack (or use 2 ovens if you have them), and bake the patties until they are lightly browned, 10 to 12 minutes. Halfway through, move the top baking sheet to the center rack and the center baking sheet to the top rack.

5. Using a metal spatula, transfer the patties to a large wire rack to cool for 15 minutes. The patties can be stored between layers of waxed paper in tightly covered tins for up to 1 week. Baked patties freeze well in plastic freezer bags for up to 6 months. Thaw them overnight in the refrigerator. Let the patties return to room temperature before serving.

SERVES 25 TO 30 (MAKES 60 PATTIES)

CRAB FRITTERS

WITH CREOLE MAYONNAISE

▼ ▼ ▼

Taste one bite and you'd bet that these lovely, light fritters were fried in a swanky New Orleans restaurant kitchen, but instead, they come right from your cast-iron skillet. And the best part is that their preparation time is around five minutes because the batter is based on a biscuit mix like Bisquick. Buy the very nicest lump crabmeat you can find. You only need a cup, so indulge.

TO PREP:	
10 MINUTES	
TO COOK:	
6 MINUTES	

¼ cup Creole mustard (see Tips)

¼ cup mayonnaise

2 cups vegetable oil

½ cup biscuit mix, such as Bisquick

¼ cup milk

1 large egg, lightly beaten

¼ cup chopped scallions,
    both white and light
    green parts

Dash of hot pepper sauce

1 cup lump crabmeat,
    picked over

2 tablespoons chopped
    fresh parsley,
    for garnish

1. Make a Creole mayonnaise. Place the mustard and mayonnaise in a small glass bowl and stir to combine. Cover and refrigerate until ready to serve.

2. Pour the oil into a 10- or 11-inch cast-iron skillet and heat over medium-high heat.

3. Place the biscuit mix, milk, egg, scallions, and hot pepper sauce in a medium-size mixing bowl and stir to combine. Fold in the crabmeat. When the oil is hot, drop in teaspoonfuls of the batter, 8 to 10 at a time. Fry the fritters until deep brown, 1 minute, then turn them with a slotted spoon and fry until deep brown on the other side, 1 to 2 minutes longer. Remove the fritters with the spoon to paper towels to drain. Repeat with the remaining batter.

4. To serve, place the bowl of Creole mayonnaise in the center of a serving platter. Surround it with the crab fritters. Sprinkle the parsley over the fritters and serve.

SERVES 8 TO 12 (MAKES 16 TO 20 FRITTERS)

No Need to Starve

— ▼ —

DINNER DOCTOR SAYS

I read with a giggle a recent article in a ladies' magazine that said you should starve your guests before a proper dinner party. Oh, I think it mentioned you could pass some nuts after the second round of drinks, but that you shouldn't let your guests nibble so much that they won't eat their meal.

Who are we entertaining here? Children? Most adults I know either have the restraint to step away from the appetizer platter, saving room for dinner, or they have the social grace to eat their meal regardless of how much they have nibbled in the den. I am not for policing the intake of my dinner guests, and I think it's inhospitable not to offer food when alcohol is served.

Besides, hors d'oeuvres are fun to make and fun to eat, and they generate a lot of conversation!

CHICKEN FAJITA WRAPS

▼ ▼ ▼

The word *wrap* has the appeal of a cashmere shawl when it comes to food. Tucked in a soft flour tortilla, even pedestrian fillings like chicken, beans, and corn become exotic. The chunky wraps are quick to put together, and if you slice them into bite-size pieces, they become elegant. Of course, to feed the family midweek, leave the wraps whole and set out plenty of salsa to spoon on top.

TO PREP:
12 MINUTES

6 flour tortillas (10 inches each)

1 tablespoon olive oil

1 pound skinless, boneless chicken
*   breast halves, cut into ½-inch slices*

1 package (1.12 ounces) fajita
*   seasoning mix*

1 can (15 to 16 ounces) pinto or
*   black beans, drained*

1 can (11 ounces) yellow corn with
*   red and green peppers, drained*

1 package (8 ounces; 2 cups) pre-shredded
*   Monterey Jack cheese with*
*   jalapeño peppers (see Tips)*

1 jar of your favorite salsa or
*   Mexican Cocktail Sauce (page 35)*

tips If you want to make these fajitas ahead of time, don't heat the tortillas before filling them. Place whole filled tortillas on a baking sheet, cover them with aluminum foil, and refrigerate until needed (up to 3 hours in advance). The refrigerated tortillas will take 20 to 25 minutes to warm through in a preheated 350°F oven. Slice the tortillas just before you place them on the serving platter.

Kraft makes pre-shredded Monterey Jack cheese with jalapeño peppers.

1. Preheat the oven to 350°F.

2. Wrap the tortillas in aluminum foil so that they are completely covered and place them in the oven.

3. Place the olive oil in a large skillet over medium-high heat. While it is heating, toss the chicken and fajita seasoning together in a bowl, stirring, to coat the chicken well. Spoon the coated chicken slices into the hot oil and cook on all sides, until they are fully cooked, 4 to 5 minutes, reducing the heat to medium if the chicken is browning too fast. Add the beans and corn and cook, stirring, until heated through, 1 to 2 minutes. Add the

cheese and let simmer just until the cheese begins to melt, 1 minute longer. Turn off the heat.

4. Remove the tortillas from the oven. Place a tortilla on a work surface and spoon some of the chicken mixture evenly down the center. Roll the tortilla up tightly. Repeat with the remaining tortillas and filling. Cut each tortilla into 4 diagonal slices and arrange these on a platter around a bowl of salsa. Place some spoons near the salsa and serve at once.

**SERVES 12 AS AN APPETIZER,
6 AS A MAIN COURSE**

ZESTY TOASTED OYSTER CRACKERS

▼ ▼ ▼

I first tasted these crackers at my Aunt Elizabeth's house one evening when her neighbor Nancy Williams brought them over warm from the oven. Everyone but me seemed to know the recipe—toss oyster crackers with a package of ranch dressing mix and oil. Yet, I sensed there was more to it than this. I called Nancy and she explained that she had doctored the seasoning mix with some dill and lemon pepper and had baked the oyster crackers enough to crisp them. Like popcorn, these crackers are irresistible, and they're a breeze to throw together.

TO PREP:
10 MINUTES
TO COOK:
3–4 MINUTES

¾ cup vegetable oil

1 package (1 ounce) ranch dressing and dip mix

1 teaspoon dried dill

1 teaspoon lemon pepper seasoning

1 package (10 ounces) oyster crackers

1. Preheat the oven to 350°F.

2. Place the oil in a large mixing bowl and stir in the ranch dressing mix, dill, and lemon pepper. Add the oyster crackers and stir until they are well coated.

3. Transfer the oyster crackers to a rimmed baking sheet and bake them until they are crisp, 3 to 4 minutes. Take care not to overbake the crackers or they will burn. You just want to heat them through. Serve the crackers warm or let them cool completely and store, covered, in a tin container in a cool, dry place for up to 1 week.

SERVES 8

tip Try substituting 1 teaspoon of curry powder or cumin for the lemon pepper and 1 teaspoon of dried parsley for the dill.

SUPER SOUPS AND STEWS

▼▼▼

When there's a pot of soup or stew simmering on the stove, my children gravitate to the kitchen just like I did when I was their age. Those are fond memories for me, and I'm guessing you'll have similar ones—your mother's chicken noodle soup that staved off colds and fevers, or the hearty beef stew that was your favorite winter supper when you visited your grandparents. Catch a whiff of chili and you may be back at your best friend's house on a Saturday afternoon. A bubbling pot might make you think of the vegetable soup that seemed to always be on the stove in the house you shared with college roommates, ready to fortify you for the next day of classes. Soups and stews sum up what's best about home cooking.

But while simmering stockpots are something that memories are made of, today few of us have the time to dedicate to creating soups or stews totally from scratch. Instead, we can rely on surefire shortcuts, like I do with the canned seasoned tomatoes in my Five-Minute Gazpacho or the Tater Tots that are the basis for Sunday Night Potato Chowder. And condensed soups can be a great way to jump-start soup or stew recipes. I look to them when making Mom's Chunky Tomato Soup and Nacho Cheese Soup, to name just a couple. They're quick thickeners and provide a backdrop for whatever else you stir into the pot.

Make a huge pot of the Family-Style Vegetable Soup to serve immediately, then stash the rest in the freezer. Simmer the Pumpkin Orange Soup with Parmesan Toasts on Halloween night. Prepare Tomato and Fennel Stew with Big Shrimp when the boss is coming to dinner. Stir up Four-Bean Chili for a Crowd when there will be eight at the table. Think White Bean Soupe au Pistou when you'd rather be in southern France. Make Nancy's Popcorn Soup or Taco Soup for your kids or grandkids. And pour the Chilled Roasted Red Pepper Soup, the Creamy Cold Cantaloupe Soup, or the Ruby Borscht with Orange Cream from a cold Thermos into a goblet to sip in the park, at the beach, or in your summer garden.

This chapter contains a wealth of fast recipes for soups, stews, and chilis dressy enough to serve to company or simple enough to dish out on a Tuesday night after soccer practice. You'll find both starters and mains. Bread is an obvious go-with, and for some soups, it is enough to make them a full meal. Other soups go well with sandwiches and salads. Still others in small portions make the perfect first course to a longer meal.

Whatever soup or stew recipe you choose, rest assured that it will be a snap to prepare. And you can count on it having a homey delicious from-scratch flavor.

Soup's on!

CHILLED ROASTED RED PEPPER SOUP

▼▼▼

TO PREP:
8 MINUTES
TO CHILL:
AT LEAST 1 HOUR

Many years ago in Atlanta, I enjoyed a pimiento soup made by Kay Goldstein at her gourmet shop, Proof of the Pudding. After preparing the soup Kay's way many times, I've adapted the recipe, substituting store-bought roasted red peppers for the canned pimientos. Strips of roasted red pepper are also sold at supermarket delis, and while they are not cheap, they provide a complex flavor that is worth the price for special occasions. Serve this soup at the beach, tote it to a summer picnic along with crusty French bread, or ladle it into bowls for an elegant first course for your next dinner party.

2 jars (12 ounces each) roasted red peppers
    packed in brine, drained and cut into
    strips, or 2 generous cups store-bought
    roasted red pepper strips
1 tablespoon olive oil
1 tablespoon sugar
2 cups canned low-sodium chicken broth
½ cup reduced-fat sour cream
2 tablespoons minced fresh chives, for garnish

tips Chill the red pepper strips and chicken broth first and you can serve the soup as soon as it is made.

Feel free to lighten up this soup by omitting the olive oil, to spice it up by adding a dash of hot pepper sauce, or to make it thicker by adding ½ cup of chopped cucumber before puréeing it.

Use kitchen scissors to quickly snip chives onto the top of the soup.

Instead of garnishing the soup with chives, toss some Parmesan-flavored croutons on top.

1. Place the red pepper strips, olive oil, and sugar in a food processor. Process in short pulses until the mixture is almost smooth, 20 to 30 seconds, or purée in two batches in a blender. With the motor running, pour in the chicken broth (in two batches, if using a blender) and process until the mixture is smooth, 20 seconds longer. Remove the lid and add the sour cream (again, in batches, if using a blender). Process until smooth, 15 to 20 seconds. Chill the soup for at least 1 hour or up to 24 before serving.

2. Pour the soup into chilled serving bowls and sprinkle some of the chives on top of each serving.

SERVES 6 TO 8 AS A STARTER

Chicken Broth in a Box

— ▼ —

DINNER DOCTOR SAYS

It is perfectly okay to use canned chicken broth. However, some canned broths are salty and may overwhelm your dish. Choose a low-sodium one, especially if the recipe calls for cheese, ham, olives, or other salty ingredients. It's always easier to add a little more salt to a dish than to try to correct for too much. Chicken broth comes in 14- to 14.5-ounce cans as well as in handy quart-size boxes you can reseal and refrigerate for another use. I find the quart size handy, especially when making soup. The broth keeps in the fridge for up to three days. If you cannot use it by then, freeze it and it will keep for up to six months. Use 1¾ cups of broth for every 14-ounce can.

If you are a believer in "fresh is best," turn to page 85 for some tips on cooking up a quick chicken broth.

FIVE-MINUTE GAZPACHO

▼ ▼ ▼

No chopping here and the tomatoes come seasoned in the can. You add the crunch of cucumber and then just a bit of olive oil for smoothness and vinegar for bite. Gazpacho is the ulti- mate summer soup, so when the weather turns warm, keep a can of tomatoes in the fridge at the ready. Serve gazpacho with crusty bread or store-bought croutons.

TO PREP:
5 MINUTES

tips **If you are using tomatoes right off the pantry shelf, chill the gazpacho for at least 1 hour or up to 24 before serving it.**

    This is a master recipe, meant to serve as inspiration for quick gazpachos you can make using seasoned canned tomatoes as a soup base. For example, add some red pepper strips and chopped red onion along with the cucumber. I like canned tomatoes seasoned with balsamic vinegar as well as those with Mexican seasoning, especially with a little diced avocado and a garnish of fresh cilantro leaves.

1 can (28 ounces) diced tomatoes
    with basil, garlic, and oregano,
    with their liquid, chilled
1 large cucumber, peeled and cut into
    large pieces
2 tablespoons olive oil
1 tablespoon red wine vinegar

Place the tomatoes with their liquid and the cucumber, olive oil, and vinegar in a food processor and process in short pulses until the mixture is souplike in consistency, smooth with a few chunks, 15 to 20 seconds. Or purée the ingredients in batches in a blender, and serve.

SERVES 6 TO 8 AS A STARTER

CREAMY COLD CANTALOUPE SOUP

▼▼▼

When summertime cantaloupes roll into town you'll appreciate this delightful, fast way to serve them. Or, use the nice big chunks of cantaloupe at the supermarket salad bar. This is summer picnic fare, pure and simple. Pour the soup into a Thermos and tote it to a concert in the park or to the beach. Everyone will think you've gone to a whole lot of trouble.

TO PREP:
5–7 MINUTES

1 can (6 ounces) frozen orange
    juice concentrate, thawed
1 large ripe cantaloupe, chilled and cut
    into 1-inch cubes, or 4 cups chilled
    store-bought cantaloupe cubes
1 tablespoon heavy (whipping) cream
    (optional)
2 tablespoons fresh mint leaves,
    cut into long slivers

1. Place the orange juice concentrate and the cantaloupe in a food processor. Process in batches until the mixture is well puréed, 30 to 40 seconds. Add the cream, if using, and pulse again until the soup is blended.

2. To serve, pour the soup into serving bowls and garnish each serving with a teaspoon of fresh mint slivers. The soup can be refrigerated, covered, for up to 1 day.

SERVES 4 TO 6 AS A STARTER

tips If the cantaloupe and orange juice are not cold, you will need to chill this soup for at least 1 hour before serving it.
    To easily slice mint into slivers, stack leaves that have been rinsed and dried one on top of the other, roll them up like a cigar, then thinly slice them crosswise.

RUBY BORSCHT

WITH ORANGE CREAM

▼ ▼ ▼

I can't remember when it was I first enjoyed eating beets, but I remember they were fresh and cooked with oranges. Now, fresh beets are delicious if you have time to fool with them, but for this speedy soup, turn instead to your pantry shelf. Canned beets are flavorful and vibrantly ruby colored. They cook down much faster than fresh. Along with orange juice, add some sautéed onion and garlic, chicken broth, and a cinnamon stick and you get a wonderful soup that can be ladled hot into bowls or chilled for later. A little bit of orange cream makes the flavor of the beets sing.

TO PREP:
5 MINUTES
TO COOK:
15 MINUTES
TO CHILL:
AT LEAST 1 HOUR
(OPTIONAL)

1 tablespoon olive oil
⅓ cup chopped onion
1 clove garlic, sliced
⅓ cup fresh orange juice
    (from 1 medium-size orange)
1 can (14.5 ounces) sliced beets,
    drained
1 can (14.5 ounces) low-sodium chicken broth
1 cinnamon stick (3 inches)
¼ cup reduced-fat sour cream
½ teaspoon freshly grated orange zest

tip I prefer to use low-sodium chicken broth here because that way the amount of salt in the recipe can be controlled. Add more salt if you want to, but taste the soup first because canned vegetables are saltier than their fresh counterparts. Chilled soups need a bit more seasoning than hot ones, so you may want to add salt to the chilled version right before serving.

1. Place the olive oil in a 2-quart saucepan over medium heat. Add the onion and garlic, stir, and cook until the onion is

slightly browned, 4 minutes. Pour in the orange juice and stir to scrape up the browned bits on the bottom of the pan. Stir in the beets, chicken broth, and cinnamon stick. Cover the pan, reduce the heat to low, and let simmer for 10 minutes.

2. Meanwhile, prepare the orange cream: Place the sour cream and orange zest in a small bowl and stir to combine.

3. Remove the cinnamon stick from the soup and ladle the soup into a food processor. Process the soup in short pulses until it is nearly smooth, 30 seconds. Serve the soup hot, ladling it into serving bowls, or chill it for at least 1 hour.

The soup will keep, covered, in the refrigerator for 3 days.

4. Spoon the orange cream into a plastic squeeze bottle and pipe the cream onto each serving of soup or simply dollop the cream on top with a soupspoon.

SERVES 4 AS A STARTER

tips Feeling adventuresome? Substitute a teaspoon of prepared horseradish for the orange zest in the cream topping.

If you have leftover pork roast, add strips to the soup and serve it hot, topped with garlicky croutons.

PUMPKIN ORANGE SOUP

WITH PARMESAN TOASTS

▼ ▼ ▼

Most people think of pumpkin around Thanksgiving and the winter holidays, but this is a seasonless soup you'll surely enjoy throughout the year—the perfect way to begin any meal. The recipe is quick to make because, once mixed together, the canned pumpkin, canned chicken broth, orange juice and zest, and thyme simmer just until their flavors blend. Make crunchy little Parmesan toast rounds while the soup simmers and they'll add just the right contrast of texture and flavor when the cheese and garlic blend into the warm, fragrant soup.

TO PREP:
10 MINUTES
TO COOK:
8–10 MINUTES

1 can (15 ounces) pumpkin
(see Tips)
2 cans (14 to 14.5 ounces each)
low-sodium chicken broth
1 clove garlic, crushed in a garlic press
1 bay leaf
1 teaspoon dried thyme
1 medium-size orange, rinsed
16 slices (½ inch thick)
French bread
2 tablespoons olive oil
¼ cup grated Parmesan
cheese

1. Preheat the broiler.

2. Place the pumpkin, chicken broth, garlic, bay leaf, and thyme in a 2-quart saucepan and heat over medium-high heat, stirring just to combine. While the mixture is coming to a boil, grate enough orange zest for 1 teaspoon and add this to the soup. Cut the orange in half and juice it. You should have about ⅓ cup. Stir the orange juice into the soup. When the soup comes to a boil, cover the pan and reduce the heat to low. Let the soup simmer, stirring it occasionally, until it is thickened and the flavors blend, 8 minutes.

3. Meanwhile, make the Parmesan toasts: Place the slices of bread on a baking sheet and broil them until they are lightly browned, 1 minute. Remove the baking sheet from the broiler, turn the bread slices over, brush the untoasted side with the olive oil, and sprinkle some of the Parmesan cheese over each slice, dividing it equally among them. Return the bread slices to the broiler and broil until the Parmesan melts, 15 to 20 seconds. Remove the baking sheet from the broiler and keep the toasts warm until ready to serve.

4. To serve, remove and discard the bay leaf from the soup. Ladle the soup into serving bowls and top each with two Parmesan toasts or pass the toasts separately.

SERVES 6 TO 8 AS A STARTER

tips Be sure you use canned pumpkin, not pumpkin pie filling, when you make this soup.

If time is short, omit the toasts and top each bowl of soup with a dollop of plain yogurt and a sprinkling of cinnamon. You'll need about ½ cup of yogurt and ½ teaspoon of ground cinnamon.

If you prefer, use pulpy store-bought orange juice (the kind that comes in a carton) and leave out the zest.

Want to add a bit of panache quickly? Stir in ¼ cup of heavy cream after the soup has thickened. If you add cream, don't let it come to a boil.

CREAMY LEMON ASPARAGUS SOUP

▼ ▼ ▼

TO PREP:
5 MINUTES
TO COOK:
6 MINUTES

When I was growing up my parents were big fans of canned asparagus and they loved canned asparagus soup, too. I'll admit to turning up my nose when it came to both of them—I just preferred the color and flavor of fresh asparagus. But in testing recipes for this book I revisited canned asparagus soup and became intrigued with it because it needed so little to make it better. Lemon juice and zest are the easiest ingredients to add, and that's what I suggest. Without the expense of fresh asparagus or the need to make a complicated roux to thicken the soup, you have an elegant first course to serve to dinner party guests (the recipe can easily be doubled to serve eight). It also makes a great family supper with chicken or tuna salad sandwiches.

1 can (10.75 ounces) cream of
    asparagus soup
½ cup heavy (whipping) cream
½ cup low-sodium chicken broth
2 teaspoons grated lemon zest
    (from 1 large lemon)
2 tablespoons fresh lemon juice
    (from 1 large lemon)

1. Place the asparagus soup, cream, chicken broth, 1 teaspoon of the lemon zest, and the lemon juice in a 2-quart

tip **Want to try another fast variation of this recipe? Omit the lemon juice and zest and add ¼ cup of medium-dry sherry. Garnish the soup with fresh tarragon.**

saucepan and heat over medium-high heat, stirring to just combine. Bring to a boil, then reduce the heat to low, cover the pan, and let the soup simmer until the flavors blend, 3 to 4 minutes.

2. Ladle the soup into serving bowls and garnish each serving with some of the remaining 1 teaspoon of lemon zest.

SERVES 4 AS A STARTER

Broth or Stock?

— ▼ —

DINNER DOCTOR SAYS

The words *broth* and *stock* are often used interchangeably to describe the flavorful liquid used to make soups and sauces. According to Swanson, the broth manufacturer, stock is made by cooking bones and vegetables in liquid, while broth is more seasoned and concentrated.

In this book, when I call for chicken broth you can use either the canned kind (preferably low sodium) or any homemade version you like, whether you simply simmer boneless chicken breasts in liquid with seasonings or go all out, browning soup bones before adding such flavorful ingredients as onion, carrots, celery, parsley, and bay leaf. No recipe in this book calls for making an involved homemade stock, but on page 85 you'll find a quick way to make chicken broth.

The beef broth to use is the canned kind; it has more flavor than anything most of us have time to make at home.

WARM CURRIED CARROT SOUP

▼▼▼

My children eat a ton of those tiny carrots that come peeled in bags, and I had intended to create a soup using them. But the crunchy carrots take forever to cook down, so I turned to a speedier alternative—canned sliced carrots. They are a bril-

TO PREP:
7–8 MINUTES
TO COOK:
15 MINUTES

liant time-saver to keep on the pantry shelf, for they're tender after cooking less than ten minutes. And they marry with all sorts of flavors like curry and ginger and cinnamon. Serve this soup in cool weather, with whole-wheat bread and a salad of cubed apples, walnuts, and blue cheese tossed with a bag of your favorite greens.

tips **Don't have fresh ginger or curry powder? Just add a cinnamon stick instead, and remove it before serving.**

You don't have to sauté the onion. Finely mince it instead and cook it along with the carrots. If you do this, omit the olive oil.

If you want a sweeter soup but one with no sugar, add ½ cup of minced fresh apple with the carrots.

Should you want to serve this soup in August, chill it, then garnish the top with snipped chives and a sprinkling of finely chopped roasted peanuts.

1 tablespoon olive oil

1 cup chopped onion (from 1 medium-size onion)

2 cans (14.5 ounces each) sliced carrots, drained

1 can (14 to 14.5 ounces) low-sodium chicken broth

1 tablespoon sugar

1 teaspoon pre-chopped ginger (see opposite) or peeled chopped fresh ginger

1 teaspoon curry powder

½ cup plain yogurt

2 tablespoons minced fresh chives, for garnish

Ginger

— ▼ —

DINNER DOCTOR SAYS One of the most powerful flavorings you can add to soup is ginger, either pre-chopped or fresh. Chopped ginger in a jar is generally found where Asian ingredients are sold and is very handy to have around. A teaspoonful perks up the flavor of canned chicken broth, and the remainder can be stored in the refrigerator for several months. Fresh ginger is delicious, but it is perishable so you must use it within three weeks. A handy way to keep it stored for quick use is to place it, unpeeled, in a bag in the freezer. There's no need to thaw the ginger. Peel it, then use a coarse Microplane grater to grate the frozen root right into your dishes.

1. Place the olive oil in a 2-quart saucepan and heat over medium-high heat. Add the onion and sauté, stirring, until soft, 2 to 3 minutes. Add the carrots, chicken broth, sugar, ginger, curry powder, and ½ cup of water. Cover and bring to a boil, then reduce the heat to low and let simmer until the carrots are quite soft, 7 to 8 minutes.

2. Transfer the soup to a food processor and process until smooth or purée it in batches in a blender. Return the soup to the saucepan, stir in the yogurt, then reheat it over medium-low heat. Ladle the soup into serving bowls and sprinkle some of the chives on top of each serving.

SERVES 6 AS A STARTER, 4 AS A MAIN COURSE

MOM'S CHUNKY TOMATO SOUP

WITH GRILLED CHEESE CUBES

▼ ▼ ▼

When it comes to soups and sand-wiches there is no better combination than the tomato

TO PREP:
3 MINUTES
TO COOK:
8 MINUTES

and grilled cheese duo. Now that pair joins forces, with the sand-wich cut into croutonlike cubes for a topper. This soup is a snap to pre-pare. Unlike time-consuming from-scratch tomato soups where you have to add sugar and thicken the soup, here the celery soup is the thickener and the stewed tomatoes are already slightly sweet. Yum!

1 can (14.5 ounces) stewed tomatoes,
    with their liquid
1 can (10.75 ounces) cream of celery soup
1 can (10.75 ounces) tomato purée
1 soup can (10.75 ounces) of whole or
    skim milk
1 tablespoon butter
2 slices of mild Cheddar cheese,
    or ⅓ cup pre-shredded Cheddar cheese
2 slices of whole-wheat or white bread

tips

Ready for some variations?
    Use cream of mushroom soup instead of cream of celery.
    Instead of the stewed tomatoes, add spicy Ro-Tel tomatoes with chiles or Del Monte's diced tomatoes with green chiles or jalapeño peppers.
    Add a can of Italian-seasoned diced tomatoes instead of stewed tomatoes.
    If the kids don't like chunky, trans-fer the hot soup to a food processor and purée it until smooth.
    And if everyone is really hungry, double or triple the sandwich ingredi-ents and make lots of cubes.

1. Place the stewed tomatoes with their liquid and the celery soup, tomato purée, and milk in a 2-quart saucepan and heat over medium heat, stirring just to combine. Bring to a boil, then reduce the heat to low and let the soup simmer, uncovered, until the flavors blend, 4 to 5 minutes.

2. Meanwhile, make the grilled cheese cubes. Place half of the butter in a small nonstick skillet over medium-high heat. Place the Cheddar cheese between the bread slices and, if necessary, trim cheese slices to fit the bread.

Place the sandwich in the skillet and dot the top with the remaining butter. Cook the sandwich until the bottom is golden, 1 to 2 minutes, then flip it with a spatula. Cook the second side until the cheese is melted and the bread is crusty and golden brown, 1 to 2 minutes longer. Remove the sandwich from the skillet with a spatula and use a sharp knife to cut it into 30 small croutonlike pieces.

3. To serve, ladle the soup into serving bowls, and scatter 5 grilled cheese cubes on top of each serving.

SERVES **6** AS A LIGHT MAIN COURSE

Soup Toppers

—▼—

DINNER
DOCTOR
SAYS

French onion soup without that toasted slice of baguette blanketed in melted cheese floating on top? Never! Your favorite chili without a handful of minced onion resting on a dollop of sour cream? Unthinkable! What these two classic toppers have in common is that they provide interest—to your eyes and to your palate. Toppings shouldn't be last-minute. Fresh, flavorful, well-thought-out garnishes add another dimension to speedy soups. Here are a few suggestions.

Chopped nuts and seeds add a great flavor contrast. Finely chopped peanuts add crunch and that something extra to an Indian-inspired soup like the Warm Curried Carrot Soup on page 76, for example. And lightly salted popcorn adds fun and flavor to a creamy corn soup (see Nancy's Popcorn Soup, page 86) .

Crostini, croutons, and other crunchy things are nice in brothy soups; the bread absorbs the broth while the crunch makes a pleasing contrast with such ingredients as white beans. For a rich flavor add a little grated cheese, a bit of prepared horseradish, or a pinch of cinnamon to that topper.

Minced fresh herbs are always a last-minute winner, but take care not to get in a rut. Forgo the parsley when fresh mint or cilantro is available for tomato soup, or think chopped fresh fennel fronds for gazpacho—not just chives (you'll find Five-Minute Gazpacho on page 68). Add whole small basil leaves to a Thai-inspired chicken stew, and go with rosemary or thyme when you're serving a white bean soup.

Velvety creams add pizzazz to any soup. All you need to do is stir a bit of seasoning such as curry powder, freshly grated lemon zest, or prepared horseradish into some reduced-fat sour cream. Spoon the flavored cream into a squeeze bottle and pipe it onto a bowl of soup, making squiggles, little hearts (tiny droplets pulled down with a wooden skewer so a point forms), or cobwebs (pipe concentric circles, then using a skewer and starting at the outside circle, pull the cream in lines toward the center). Puréed soups like Ruby Borscht (page 70) benefit from a creamy topping.

LET THE KIDS MAKE BROCCOLI CHEESE SOUP

▼ ▼ ▼

My girls love broccoli cheese soup, and I concocted this four-ingredient recipe so they could make it themselves in practically no time. The key ingredient is a can of chicken soup with rice. Once the soup is puréed, the rice thickens everything beautifully. Round out the meal with soft wheat rolls or toasted biscuits and honey.

TO PREP:
5 MINUTES
TO COOK:
8 MINUTES

1 package (10 ounces) frozen
chopped broccoli
1 can (10.5 ounces) chicken
soup with rice
1¼ cups canned low-sodium chicken broth
4 ounces Velveeta or American cheese,
cubed or shredded (see Tips)

1. Place the broccoli in a 2-quart sauce-pan and add water to cover by 1 inch. Place the pan over medium-high heat, cover it, and bring to a boil. Let the broccoli boil 1 minute, then remove the pan from the heat and drain off the water.

2. Add the chicken soup and broth to the pan with the broccoli. Place the pan back over medium-high heat and bring to a boil,

tips This soup is even speedier (by about 1 minute) if you don't pre-cook the broccoli, just dump it frozen into the pan with the chicken soup and broth. But since most kids like their food a bit soft, go ahead and pre-cook that broccoli.

Don't make any extra trips to the store for the cheese. Use 4 ounces of whatever you have on hand that the children like.

I think this soup needs a grinding of black pepper, and my husband wanted to drizzle hot pepper sauce on it. So heat it up a bit when serving adults!

stirring, about 2 minutes. Remove the pan from the heat and purée the soup in a food processor or in a blender in batches. Return the puréed soup to the pan. Stir in the cheese, then place the pan over

medium heat until the cheese melts, 3 to 4 minutes longer.

3. Ladle the soup into serving bowls.

SERVES 4 AS A LIGHT MAIN COURSE

CREAMY POTATO SOUP

▼ ▼ ▼

TO PREP:
5 MINUTES
TO COOK:
10 MINUTES

I am a purist when it comes to mashed potatoes. I cook Idahos and then mash them with butter, salt, and warm milk. But I came across a super speedy way to use frozen mashed potatoes to make a warm and comforting soup, one my children are crazy about. Simmer the mashed potatoes with one part chicken broth and two parts milk for an incredibly delicious creamy soup. Then, let your creativity guide you when it comes to a topping: Add a pat of butter, a grinding of pepper, or a sprinkling of sharp Cheddar cheese, chopped scallion, snipped chives, or crumbled bacon. Ahhh . . .

4 cups frozen mashed potatoes,
  such as Ore-Ida Just Add Milk
2 cups whole milk
1 can (14 to 14.5 ounces) chicken broth
1 tablespoon butter (optional)
Pre-grated Cheddar cheese, chopped scallion,
  snipped chives, crumbled bacon, and/or
  black pepper, for garnish (optional)

1. Place the frozen mashed potatoes, milk, and chicken broth in a 2-quart saucepan and bring to a boil, stirring, over medium-high heat. Then reduce the heat to low, cover the pan, and let the soup simmer until creamy, 8 minutes, stirring frequently.

2. Remove the pan from the heat, stir in the butter, if using, and ladle the soup into serving bowls. Garnish with the topping(s) of your choice.

SERVES 4 AS A MAIN COURSE

tips **Garlic mashed potato soup? In Step 1 add 1 or 2 cloves of garlic that have been crushed in a garlic press, and cook as directed.**

  If you are garnishing the soup with cheese, scallions, or bacon, prepare the topping while the soup simmers.

SUNDAY NIGHT POTATO CHOWDER

▼ ▼ ▼

The word *chowder* may imply that what you have here is a labor-intensive old New England soup, but in reality frozen potatoes and corn kernels turn into a lightning-fast Sunday night meal that will be on the table in less than a half hour. Add some crusty bread and fresh crisp apple and pear slices and sherbet for dessert and you have a satisfying supper for the end of a busy weekend.

TO PREP:
5 MINUTES
TO COOK:
15–18 MINUTES

4 slices of bacon

4 cups (48 pieces) frozen onion-
    flavored Tater Tots

1 cup canned or frozen corn kernels,
    drained if canned

2 cups whole milk

1 can (14 to 14.5 ounces) low-sodium
    chicken broth

Black pepper

tips It takes less time to fry bacon if you cut the slices into 1-inch pieces before you cook them. Of course, you could omit the bacon altogether, but it adds just the right flavor to the potatoes and sweet corn.

If you prefer, don't simmer the bacon in the chowder, crumble it over the top as a garnish.

If you can't find onion-flavored Tater Tots, use plain ones and add ½ cup of minced onion to the chowder.

1. Cut the bacon slices into 1-inch pieces. Place the bacon pieces in a 4-quart saucepan over medium-high heat and cook, stirring, until crisp, 5 minutes. Transfer the bacon to paper towels to drain and pour off all the fat in the pan.

2. Place the Tater Tots in the saucepan and cook them over low heat, stirring constantly, until they thaw a bit, 1 to 2 minutes. Add the drained bacon pieces and the corn, milk, and chicken broth to the pan and cook, stirring, over medium-high heat until the chowder comes to a boil. Reduce the heat to low, cover the pan, and let the chowder simmer until the Tater Tots are soft, stirring and mashing them as they cook, 12 to 15 minutes. When done the chowder will still have some chunks of potato in it.

3. To serve, ladle the chowder into serving bowls and sprinkle pepper over each serving.

SERVES 4 AS A MAIN COURSE

Speedy Homemade Chicken Broth

—▼—

DINNER DOCTOR SAYS Making your own chicken broth is no trouble at all. If you're poaching two to four skinless, boneless chicken breast halves you can easily make broth at the same time. Here's how:

Place the chicken breasts in a saucepan with just enough cold water to cover them. Figure on about 3 cups of water for every two breast halves. Add whatever seasonings you have on hand—a grinding of pepper, a bay leaf, a sprig of parsley, some onion slices or scallions, a carrot, and a pinch of salt. Bring the mixture to a boil, reduce the heat to a simmer, cover the pan, and let the chicken cook until it tests done (the juices will run clear when a breast is pierced with the point of a knife) and is tender, about 20 minutes. Uncover the pan and remove the chicken breasts. Let the broth cool, then strain it. The broth can be stored in the refrigerator for up to two days or in the freezer for up to six months. You can substitute 1¾ cups homemade chicken broth for a 14-ounce can of store-bought broth.

NANCY'S POPCORN SOUP

▼ ▼ ▼

TO PREP:
2 MINUTES
TO COOK:
10–12 MINUTES

Nancy Crossman, my agent, grew up in Cleveland, Ohio, where she recalls her mother serving the family this fun soup. It is based on a mixture of canned corn kernels and canned creamed corn that's garnished with the most kid-friendly food of all—popcorn. I tinkered with her recipe, using half-and-half as a quick thickener instead of whisking in an egg as Nancy's mother used to do. Adults will love this soup, too, but they might like to spice things up with a drop or two of hot pepper sauce. A platter of sliced fruit and cheese (and some bread—maybe even corn-bread) help make this soup a terrific dinner.

tips French chefs often add butter at the end of cooking a sauce or soup to flavor it and also to thicken it slightly. I've borrowed the trick here.

To make the most of your time, pop the corn as the soup simmers. If you are using microwave popcorn, pick one that doesn't have flavorings added.

2 cans (14.75 ounces each)
    cream-style corn

1 can (11 ounces) corn kernels, drained

2 cups (1 pint) half-and-half

2 cups low-sodium chicken broth
    (from two 14- to 14.5-ounce cans)

1 chicken-flavored bouillon cube

1 teaspoon sugar

2 tablespoons butter

Black pepper

2 cups popped popcorn

Hot pepper sauce (optional)

1. Place the cream-style corn, corn kernels, half-and-half, chicken broth, and bouillon cube in a 4-quart saucepan and heat over medium heat, stirring constantly for the first few minutes. Continue cooking, stirring occasionally, until the soup thickens and is hot, but not boiling, 10 to 12 minutes total.

2. Remove the pan from the heat and stir in the sugar and butter. Season with pepper to taste. Ladle the soup into serving bowls and garnish each serving with some of the popcorn. Pass hot pepper sauce at the table, if desired.

SERVES 4 TO 6 AS A MAIN COURSE

BLACK BEAN SOUP

WITH LEMON CREAM

▼ ▼ ▼

TO PREP:
5 MINUTES
TO COOK:
10 MINUTES

One of my very favorite convenience foods is canned black beans. You can purée them for a dip, add them to impromptu quesadillas or salads, and use them to make this humble yet satisfying soup. Since the canned beans are on the salty side, either use chicken broth you make yourself or buy low-sodium broth. The soup is subtly seasoned with golden sherry and a little lemon zest. Should you want a more full-bodied flavor, omit the sherry and add a sprinkling of chopped jalapeño peppers (adults only!) and a generous teaspoon of ground cumin along with the beans in Step 1.

2 cans (15 ounces each) black beans with
    their liquid
1 cup canned low-sodium chicken broth
    (from one 14- to 14.5-ounce can)
¼ cup coarsely chopped onion
1 bay leaf
Black pepper
2 to 3 tablespoons golden or medium-dry
    sherry
½ cup sour cream
1 teaspoon freshly grated
    lemon zest

1. Place the beans with their liquid and the chicken broth, onion, and bay leaf in a 2-quart saucepan and heat over medium-high heat, stirring just to combine. Season with pepper to taste.

tips **Don't knock yourself out chopping the onion. Since there are meant to be sweet little bites of it in the puréed soup, the onion can be very coarsely chopped to begin with.**

    If you're watching fat and calories, use reduced-fat sour cream. It will work just fine in this recipe.

Cover the pan, bring the mixture to a boil, then reduce the heat to medium-low and let the soup simmer until the flavors blend, 5 to 7 minutes. Remove the pan from the heat, remove and discard the bay leaf, and stir in 2 tablespoons of the sherry. Taste, and add the remaining 1 tablespoon of sherry, if necessary.

2. Transfer the soup to a food processor and coarsely purée it or purée it in batches in a blender; you should still have little bits of onion and black beans. Return the soup to the saucepan and keep warm.

3. Prepare the lemon cream: Combine the sour cream and lemon zest in a small glass or ceramic bowl. Spoon the mixture into a plastic squeeze bottle, if desired.

4. To serve, ladle the soup into serving bowls and garnish each serving with a dollop of lemon cream or drizzle the cream on top of the soup in squiggles.

SERVES 4 TO 6 AS A MAIN COURSE

Zest in a Flash

—▼—

DINNER DOCTOR SAYS

The fastest way to zest a lemon, orange, or lime is with a Microplane, a sharp grater that resembles a wood file. Scrub the fruit under running water and pat it completely dry. Rub the Microplane over the skin and you'll have plenty of zest in 30 seconds or less. Now that's fast.

WHITE BEAN SOUPE AU PISTOU

▼▼▼

A shortcut version of the Provençal classic *soupe au pistou,* this soup is based on canned Great Northern beans and seasoned canned tomatoes, with some fresh zucchini added to the mix. *Pistou* is the French version of pesto. And, while I grow basil and make my own pesto in the summer, in the depths of winter or when I'm pressed for time I have used store-bought pesto with great success. Taste the various brands until you find the one you like best. Alessi's pesto in jars is excellent, as is the refrigerated pesto sold at warehouse stores like Costco. Voilà! With help like that, this soup's ready in 30 minutes.

TO PREP:
5 MINUTES
TO COOK:
22–25 MINUTES

1 tablespoon olive oil

1½ cups thinly sliced zucchini
    (from 1 medium-size zucchini)

2 cans (15.5 ounces each) Great Northern
    beans, drained

3 cups low-sodium chicken broth
    (from two 14- to 14.5-ounce cans)

1 can (14.5 ounces) diced tomatoes with
    garlic and onions, drained

Black pepper

1 cup 1-inch pieces of vermicelli

2 tablespoons store-bought pesto

1. Place the olive oil in a 4-quart saucepan and heat over medium-high heat.

> *tip* **In most of my other bean recipes you don't need to drain canned beans because the starch in their liquid helps thicken the soup or chili. You drain the beans for this soup because it's the starch from the pasta that serves as the thickener.**

Add the zucchini and cook, stirring constantly, until the slices are soft and begin to brown around the edges, 3 to 4 minutes. Add the beans, chicken broth, and tomatoes and stir. Season with pepper to taste. Bring to a boil, then reduce the heat to low, cover the pan, and let simmer until the flavors blend, 15 minutes. Stir in the vermicelli pieces and 1 tablespoon of the pesto. Cover the pan and let simmer until the vermicelli is al dente, 4 to 5 minutes longer.

2. Ladle the soup into serving bowls and garnish each serving with some of the remaining 1 tablespoon of pesto.

SERVES 6 AS A MAIN COURSE

Movie Night

▼▼▼

Break out the TV trays and enjoy dinner and a movie at home. This menu will serve four to six fairly comfortably, but if serving six, you might want to up the amounts of some of the salad ingredients to 1½ bags spinach, ⅓ cup cheese, and 3 tablespoons nuts. All else can remain the same.

Tomato and Garlic Focaccia
page 411

White Bean Soupe au Pistou
page 90

**Spinach and Orange Salad
with Sesame Vinaigrette**
page 122

Chocolate Fudge Ribbon Cake
page 471

Cream of Mushroom Soup: A History

— ▼ —

DINNER DOCTOR SAYS

In 1897 a young chemist named John T. Dorrance was reluctantly hired by his uncle to work for the Joseph A. Campbell Preserve Company—the family fruit and vegetable business—in Camden, New Jersey. Dorrance was so eager to do research for the company that he agreed to pay for his own lab equipment. He set out to devise condensed canned soup, which he hoped would appeal to the home cook—and to his uncle. Needless to say, Dorrance's canned soups were a hit. The company's name was eventually changed to the Campbell Soup Company, and the cans' classic bright red-and-white labels ultimately became a symbol of American pop culture.

The first condensed soup was cream of tomato (1897), but the most popular of them all—cream of mushroom—didn't appear until 1934, paving the way for what is perhaps the most-requested recipe of all time, the Green Bean Casserole (originally the Green Bean Bake). Campbell estimates some 20 million Thanksgiving holiday tables feature the casserole right alongside the roast bird.

Over the years, cream of mushroom soup has taken on different forms, including low-sodium and reduced-fat versions and, most recently, a creamier formula. It remains a favorite casserole ingredient because of its miraculous thickening power and a flavor that seems to perk up with just about any addition: a tablespoon of sherry, soy sauce, Worcestershire sauce—you name it.

Another popular recipe using cream of mushroom soup is what is known affectionately as mushroom soup chicken in home kitchens but is called Tasty 2-Step Chicken by Campbell. This calls for browning four boneless chicken breast halves, adding a can of soup and a half cup of water, and simmering the chicken until it's done. Variations abound. You can add a half cup of anything from milk to white wine to beef broth, sour cream or tomato juice, plus a half cup of sautéed vegetables and the seasoning of your choice—Dijon mustard, fresh basil, rosemary, lemon juice, or crumbled bacon. Canned soup never tasted so good.

CHEESE TORTELLINI IN A SPINACH AND GINGER BROTH

▼ ▼ ▼

TO PREP:
5 MINUTES
TO COOK:
9 MINUTES

Now, this recipe might sound fancy, but it is a simple medley of cheese tortellini, canned broth, and spinach from a bag. The secret ingredient is chopped ginger, which transforms a nice but predictable Italian soup into something more exotic. To save time, you'll find pre-chopped ginger in jars where Asian ingredients are sold. It is just as flavorful as fresh ginger, and there is no need to peel and chop. Serve a salad and bread alongside the tortellini soup and you'll have a satisfying supper for family and friends.

6 cups canned low-sodium chicken
   broth (from one 49-ounce can)
1 teaspoon pre-chopped ginger or
   peeled chopped fresh ginger
1 package (9 ounces) refrigerated cheese
   tortellini (see Tips)
1 package (7 ounces) pre-washed
   fresh spinach
Black pepper
2 scallions, green parts only, chopped
   (for ¼ cup), for garnish
¼ cup pre-grated Parmesan cheese
   (optional), for serving

tips Use refrigerated cheese tortellini; they are better than dried.

Not crazy about ginger? Add 1 teaspoon of grated lemon zest instead.

Try to time things so you serve the soup as soon as the spinach is wilted. Spinach is bright green and beautiful when not overcooked.

1. Place the chicken broth and ginger in a 4-quart saucepan and heat over medium-high heat. Cover the pan and bring to a boil, then add the tortellini. Reduce the heat to low, and let simmer until the tortellini are plump and nearly done, 5 minutes. Add the spinach and season with pepper to taste. Cover the pan and let the broth simmer until the spinach is wilted and the tortellini are soft but the cheese centers are still firm, 2 to 3 minutes longer.

2. Ladle the soup into serving bowls. Garnish each serving with some of the scallions and Parmesan cheese, if desired.

SERVES 6 AS A MAIN COURSE

TACO SOUP

▼ ▼ ▼

The bare-bones name says it all—this soup is no-frills. But when it comes to flavor, that name is deceptive. The soup is delicious. Browned lean ground beef, some pantry staples, and a 15-minute simmer is all it takes to put dinner on the table. While the flavors mingle in the pot, you can assemble the toppings: avocado cubes, sour cream, pre-shredded cheese, cilantro sprigs, and refreshing lime wedges. This soup is for those last-minute suppers, and it appeals to all ages. The recipe doubles and triples well, too, for Super Bowl crowds.

Olive oil cooking spray

½ pound ground beef round

1 cup chopped onion
    (from 1 medium-size onion)

1 can (14.5 ounces) Mexican-style diced
    tomatoes (see Tips, page 96),
    with their liquid

TO PREP:
10 MINUTES
TO COOK:
20–22 MINUTES

1 can (15.5 ounces) light red kidney
    beans, with their liquid

1 can (11 ounces) corn kernels,
    with their liquid

1 can (8 ounces) tomato sauce
    (see Tips, page 96)

1 package (1.25 ounces) reduced-sodium
    taco seasoning

1 avocado, peeled and cubed

1 cup sour cream

1 cup pre-shredded Cheddar or
    Monterey Jack cheese or a
    Mexican blend

¼ cup fresh cilantro sprigs

1 lime, halved and each
    half cut into
    4 wedges

Tortilla chips

1. Spray a 4-quart saucepan with olive oil cooking spray and place it over medium-high heat. Crumble in the ground beef and break it up with a wooden spoon, then cook, stirring, 30 seconds.

Add the onion and, continuing to stir, cook until the beef browns all over and is cooked through and the onion softens, 3 to 4 minutes. Stir in the tomatoes, beans and corn with their liquids, tomato sauce, and taco seasoning. Fill the tomato sauce can with water, add this to the pan, and stir. Bring to a boil, then reduce the heat to low, cover the pan, and let simmer 15 minutes.

2. Ladle the hot soup into serving bowls and pass the avocado cubes, sour cream, cheese, cilantro, lime wedges, and tortilla chips separately.

SERVES 4 TO 6 AS A MAIN COURSE

tips **Be creative when you select the canned tomatoes—if you haven't paid attention recently you're going to be surprised by the selection now available. I was torn between Mexican-style tomatoes (flavored with cumin), tomatoes and chiles (mild or hot), and tomatoes ready for chili (with onions, chiles, and seasonings). As long as the tomatoes are diced and it's a 14.5-ounce can, you can add any tomato combination you like.**

You can vary the beans and the corn, too. We're partial to white corn down South, but add yellow or even a combination of yellow and white if you like.

By all means purchase pre-shredded cheese, preferably a Mexican blend.

Don't throw out the tomato sauce can until everything is in the pot. It can double as a measuring cup when you add the water.

NACHO CHEESE SOUP

▼ ▼ ▼

Mention Nacho Cheese Soup to children and the line will start forming at the kitchen counter, with everyone eager for a steaming bowl topped with all sorts of lively Mexican-style garnishes. Normally, I am not a big fan of condensed cheese soups, but in this recipe the canned soup makes things thicken quickly, so there's no standing around stirring endlessly.

So, not only do my kids love this soup, but I do as well. With them happy and dinner ready in about 20 minutes, what's not to love?

tip Because of the saltiness of the canned soup, it is important for you to use canned low-sodium chicken broth or a homemade chicken broth (see box, page 85).

TO PREP:
8 MINUTES
TO COOK:
12 MINUTES

½ pound ground beef round
1 teaspoon ground cumin
¼ teaspoon black pepper
1 can (14 to 14.5 ounces) low-sodium
    chicken broth or homemade
    chicken broth (see Tip)
1½ cups mild store-bought salsa
1 can (11 ounces) Campbell's Fiesta
    Nacho Cheese soup
1 cup tortilla chips
1 avocado, peeled
    and cubed
¼ cup fresh
    cilantro sprigs

1. Crumble the ground beef into a 2-quart nonstick saucepan over medium-high heat and break it up with a wooden spoon. Add the cumin and pepper. Cook the beef, stirring, until it browns all over and is cooked through, 3 to 4 minutes. Add the chicken broth and

1 cup of the salsa and bring the mixture to a boil, stirring constantly, 2 minutes. Reduce the heat to low, cover the pan, and let simmer until the ingredients cook down a bit, 4 to 5 minutes. Stir in the cheese soup and cook only until blended but not boiling. Remove the pan from the heat.

2. Ladle the soup into serving bowls and garnish each serving with some of the tortilla chips, avocado, cilantro, and the remaining ½ cup of salsa.

SERVES 4 AS A MAIN COURSE

Don't Knock It

—▼—

"More pretentious cooks today, of course, seem to relish ridiculing and condemning Southerners' liberal use of canned soups in making certain casseroles. At one time, I did too, until I began trying to reproduce some of Mother's creations and realized that my more refined substitutes for the liquid base simply never yielded the same tasty results."

—James Villas,
My Mother's Southern Kitchen

FAMILY-STYLE VEGETABLE SOUP

▼ ▼ ▼

This vegetable soup makes regular appearances on our dinner table. My family craves it after being away from home on vacation. We pack it into quart jars and tote it to friends and family when they need a hot meal. I squirrel the soup away in the freezer for those insane days when there is no time to do anything but reheat and eat. We like the soup with sourdough bread, soda crackers,

TO PREP:
5 MINUTES
TO COOK:
35–40 MINUTES

cornbread, or grilled cheese sandwiches. You'll notice that, thanks to a package of frozen soup veggies, the ingredient list is short compared to those of other homemade vegetable soups.

1 tablespoon olive oil

1 pound ground beef round

½ teaspoon salt

¼ teaspoon black pepper

1 can (28 ounces) diced tomatoes
   with basil, garlic, and oregano (see Tips,
   page 100), with their liquid

1 can (14.5 ounces) diced tomatoes
   (see Tips, page 100)

1 can (14 to 14.5 ounces) beef broth

1 package (16 ounces) frozen mixed
   vegetables

1 bay leaf

1 cup uncooked macaroni, or 1 cup spaghetti
   broken into 1-inch pieces

tip My mother always used to say that beef, even just a little bit of beef, makes a better vegetable soup. And, I agree. Although I have made this soup both with and without meat, I prefer the heartiness that ground round adds. Why ground beef, you may ask? It cooks through more quickly than cubes.

1. Place the olive oil in a stock pot over medium-high heat. Crumble in the ground beef and break it up with a wooden spoon. Add the salt and pepper. Cook, stirring, until the beef browns all over and is cooked through, 3 to 4 minutes. Stir in the 2 cans of tomatoes with their liquid and the beef broth, frozen vegetables, and bay leaf. Fill both the larger and smaller tomato cans with water, add this to the pot, and stir. Bring the mixture to a boil, stirring, 3 to 4 minutes, then reduce the heat to medium-low, cover the pot, and let the soup simmer until the flavors blend, 20 minutes.

tips This soup has a longer cooking time than the other soups in this chapter. Vegetable soup really benefits from slow cooking. If you have the time, let it simmer for up to 1 hour and 15 minutes—it will be even better.

I call for seasoning the beef with only ½ teaspoon of salt since the tomatoes and the beef broth both contain salt.

Don't throw out the tomato cans until everything is in the pot. They can double as measuring cups when you add the water.

2. Stir in the pasta and cover the pot. Let the soup simmer until it has thickened somewhat and the pasta is al dente, 8 to 10 minutes.

3. To serve, ladle the soup into serving bowls. The soup can be frozen for up to 3 months.

SERVES 8 AS A MAIN COURSE

WINTER'S NIGHT BEEF STEW

WITH TURNIPS AND MADEIRA

▼ ▼ ▼

When the weather turns cold it's time to make this simple but elegant stew. It's quick to make because you use pre-cut beef cubes and a can of beef stew. Pick up a bag of peeled carrots and prep time is reduced even more. You can substitute parsnips or potatoes for the turnip. By all means add Madeira, sherry, or red wine if you have it on hand. The stew is delicious spooned over lightly buttered wide egg noodles and served alongside a green salad made with blue cheese and sliced red Bartlett pears. Crusty bread or Dun-Buttered Muffins (page 419) will round out the meal nicely. The noodles cook in even less time than the stew; you'll find instructions for preparing them on page 102.

TO PREP:
8 MINUTES
TO COOK:
26 MINUTES

1 tablespoon vegetable oil

1 pound pre-cut lean beef cubes
(½-inch cubes)

1 cup thinly sliced onion
(from 1 medium-size onion)

1 tablespoon all-purpose flour

¼ teaspoon black pepper

1 can (14 to 14.5 ounces) beef broth

1 can (10.75 ounces) beef stew
(see Tips, page 101)

1 cup chopped turnip
(from 1 medium-size turnip)

1 cup chopped carrots

1 bay leaf

1 tablespoon Madeira, sherry, or red wine
(optional; see Tips, page 101)

1. Heat the oil in a large pot over medium-high heat. Add the beef cubes and cook, stirring occasionally, until well browned on all sides, 3 to 4 minutes. Add the onion and cook, stirring, until the

No-Fuss Noodles

—▼—

DINNER DOCTOR SAYS Buttered noodles make a wonderful bed for stews, soups, leftover casseroles— you name it. And they're fuss free to prepare, boiling away on the back of the stove while you pull the rest of the meal together. If you boil 8 ounces of uncooked wide egg noodles, you'll have 4 cups cooked, enough for between four and six people. To prepare them, bring 3 quarts of water to a boil in a 4-quart saucepan over high heat. Add the noodles and 1 teaspoon of salt and let the noodles boil until tender, 7 to 8 minutes, stirring them occasionally. Once they're done, drain the noodles in a colander, return them to the pan, and toss them with butter. Start to finish it will take you about 13 minutes.

tips Canned beef stew isn't bad, it's just uninteresting and its texture is too mushy. In this recipe the canned stew serves as a thickener, along with the flour. If you want to omit it, add another tablespoon of flour and another can of beef broth. You'll need to let the stew cook another 30 minutes to thicken.

Madeira is a delightfully rich and dark fortified wine from Portugal. It blends beautifully into this stew, as well as into bean soups, but if you don't have any on hand, you can use sherry or red wine.

If you want to give the stew the flavor of fresh herbs, toss in 1 tablespoon of thyme leaves as the stew cooks and garnish it with more fresh thyme or chopped fresh flat-leaf parsley.

onion softens, 2 minutes longer. Add the flour and pepper and stir to coat the beef. Add the beef broth, canned beef stew, turnip, carrots, bay leaf, and Madeira, if using. Bring the mixture to a boil and cook for 2 minutes, then reduce the heat to low, cover the pot, and let simmer until the turnip and carrots are cooked through, 18 minutes more.

2. To serve, remove and discard the bay leaf from the stew. Ladle the stew into serving bowls.

SERVES 4 TO 6 AS A MAIN COURSE

SPRINGTIME LAMB STEW

WITH PEAS AND MINT

▼ ▼ ▼

TO PREP:
12 MINUTES
TO COOK:
33–37 MINUTES

Imagine the staid lamb stew of Ireland meeting an unexpected, provocative flavor. What do you get? A chunky stew filled with lamb, potatoes, and carrots, garnished with a refreshing sprinkle of chopped mint. This stew is great in the early spring, when a nip is still in the air but your palate needs reviving after a long winter's nap.

tip If no lamb cubes are available in the meat department, buy lamb on the bone and cube it. Add the bone to the pan as you brown the lamb cubes. Then, let it simmer along with the other ingredients, and remove it just before serving. Bones add flavor and their own built-in thickener to stews such as this.

Frozen diced potatoes make the stew quick to put together. Serve this meal-in-one with warmed whole-wheat tortillas or garlic bread.

2 tablespoons olive oil

1 pound pre-cut lean lamb cubes,
    or 1½ pounds untrimmed lamb
    trimmed and cubed (2 cups; see Tip)

Salt and black pepper, to taste

2 cloves garlic, crushed in a garlic press

3 cups frozen diced potatoes with onions
    and peppers, such as Ore-Ida
    Potatoes O'Brien

2 tablespoons all-purpose flour

2 cans (14 to 14.5 ounces each) beef
    broth or low-sodium chicken broth

2 tablespoons red wine (optional)

1 cup chopped carrots

½ cup frozen peas

¼ cup chopped fresh mint, for garnish

tips **If you have instant potato flakes in your pantry, omit the flour and add a couple tablespoons of flakes when you add the broth. The stew will thicken beautifully.**

Feel like something a bit more classically French? Omit the mint and add sautéed bread crumbs as a topping (see page 106 for the recipe).

Feel free to experiment with an Indian flavor by adding a bit of curry powder or ground cumin to the stew after you brown the lamb.

1. Heat the olive oil in a large pot over medium-high heat. Add the lamb cubes and cook, stirring occasionally, until well browned on all sides, 3 to 4 minutes.

Season with salt and pepper and stir in the garlic. Add the frozen potatoes, stir, and cook until the potatoes are heated through, 1 minute. Stir in the flour, making sure it is well distributed throughout. Add the beef broth, wine, if using, carrots, and peas. Bring the stew to a boil, stirring constantly to scrape up the delicious browned bits stuck to the bottom of the pot. Once the stew boils, reduce the heat to medium-low, cover the pot, and let the stew simmer until the lamb and carrots are tender, 25 to 30 minutes.

2. To serve, ladle the stew into shallow serving bowls and sprinkle some of the chopped mint on top of each serving.

SERVES 6 AS A MAIN COURSE

THAI CHICKEN NOODLE STEW

▼ ▼ ▼

TO PREP:
7 MINUTES
TO COOK:
28 MINUTES

Chicken noodle soup is the stuff mothers usually serve us when we're not feeling well. But this stew version is a little different, a little exotic, and something to serve when everyone is feeling just fine. It is light and fresh and healthy—a meal-in-one that needs only some fresh mango or cantaloupe slices on the side. Thai rice noodles are also called cellophane noodles, and you'll find them in the Asian food section of your supermarket.

1 large skinless, boneless chicken breast half
    (about 8 ounces)
1 chicken-flavored bouillon cube
2 cloves garlic, sliced
1 packet (2 ounces) Thai cellophane noodles
1 cup small fresh spinach leaves

2 scallions, green part only, chopped
    (for ¼ cup)
1 teaspoon pre-chopped ginger
    (see page 77) or peeled chopped
    fresh ginger
1 teaspoon Thai garlic-chile sauce

1. Place the chicken breast, bouillon cube, garlic, and 4 cups of water in a 4-quart saucepan and heat over medium-high heat. Bring to a boil, then reduce the heat to low, cover the pan, and let simmer, stirring occasionally, until the chicken is cooked through, 20 minutes. Remove the chicken from the broth in the

tip **By adding the bouillon cube to the simmering chicken broth you will have a fuller flavored broth.**

pan. Set aside the broth. When the chicken is cool enough to handle, shred it into strips. Set the chicken aside.

2. Place the pan of chicken broth back over medium-high heat, cover the pan, and bring to a boil. Once boiling, stir in the cellophane noodles, spinach, scallions, ginger, and garlic-chile sauce. Let the noodles boil, uncovered, until al dente, 4 minutes. Reduce the heat to medium-low, stir in the shredded chicken, and cook until the chicken heats through, 1 minute.

3. Ladle the stew into serving bowls and serve at once.

SERVES 4 AS A LIGHT LUNCH

Bread Crumb Toppers

—▼—

DINNER DOCTOR SAYS

To make those crunchy bread crumb toppings like they produce in France, crumble 1 cup of torn slices of day-old French bread or sourdough bread. Heat a tablespoon of butter in a skillet over medium heat until it's sizzling, then add the bread crumbs. Cook the bread crumbs, stirring, until they absorb the butter and take on a rich golden color. Sprinkle the toasted crumbs over a stew just before serving.

15 WAYS TO DOCTOR CANNED CHICKEN NOODLE SOUP

The old standby canned chicken noodle soup takes on a little excitement with any of these easy additions. Unless otherwise noted, the suggested ingredients should be stirred into the soup while it is heating.

1 Add a slice or two of peeled fresh ginger. Remove the ginger before serving.

2 Add a handful of tiny broccoli florets.

3 Toss in ¼ cup of mushrooms that have been lightly sautéed in butter.

4 Ladle the soup into bowls. Add a squeeze of fresh lemon juice and a tablespoon of grated Parmesan cheese to each bowl before serving.

5 Add 2 tablespoons of minced fresh parsley, snipped chives, or chervil just before serving.

6 Add a pinch of ground cumin and a chopped small tomato.

7 Mix in a small can of corn niblets and a healthy grinding of black pepper.

8 Stir in a pinch of curry powder and a handful of finely diced apple.

9 Stir in ¼ cup of drained and rinsed canned white beans and a tablespoon of store-bought pesto.

10 Add a handful of young spinach leaves. Stir; the heat will cook the spinach. Drizzle extra-virgin olive oil over the soup and serve.

11 Stir in a minced and seeded small jalapeño pepper and a squeeze of fresh lime juice.

12 Heat the soup, then purée it in a food processor or blender and ladle it into bowls. Garnish each serving with a dollop of store-bought green salsa and some tortilla chips.

13 Stir a handful of watercress leaves into the hot soup. Ladle into bowls and drizzle a little heavy cream over each serving.

14 Ladle the hot soup into bowls and shower each serving with crumbled crisp bacon and chopped scallion.

15 Add a generous handful of frozen green peas, another of fresh carrot slices, and a couple of sprigs of fresh dill. Remove the dill sprigs before serving and top each bowl with a sprinkling of snipped dill.

FOUR-BEAN CHILI FOR A CROWD

▼ ▼ ▼

Incredibly easy to make, this chili also provides a master recipe for any type of quick chili you wish to pull off at the last minute. You just need four cans of your favorite beans (hence the name). Then, toss in whatever cooked meat you have on hand: Shredded chicken, diced pork, or pieces of last night's grilled steak all work well. Or if you want to forgo the meat, add a cup and a half of your favorite chopped raw veggies—zucchini, eggplant, or carrots,

TO PREP:
5 MINUTES
TO COOK:
30–35 MINUTES

for example. Serve the chili with hot buttered corn bread, Dun-Buttered Muffins (page 419), or crusty garlic bread from the grocer's freezer.

4 cans (15 ounces each) beans of your
choice (black, pinto, white, and/or
kidney), with their liquid
3 cans (14.5 ounces each) Mexican-style
diced tomatoes, with their liquid
1½ cups shredded cooked chicken,
pork, or beef
1 teaspoon ground cumin
1 bay leaf
½ teaspoon hot pepper sauce,
or more to taste (optional)

tips The beans go into the pot with their liquid. The starch in the liquid helps the chili thicken quickly.

There is a plethora of Mexican-style diced tomatoes out there, and they are a smart addition to your pantry. Not just for this chili—you can add them to other quick soups or main dishes.

1. Place the beans and tomatoes with their liquid, chicken, cumin, bay leaf, and the hot pepper sauce, if using, in a 4-quart saucepan and heat over medium-high heat.

2. Cook, stirring, until the chili comes to a boil, 4 to 5 minutes, then reduce the heat to low and cover the pan. Let the chili simmer until it thickens and the flavors come together, 25 to 30 minutes, stirring occasionally.

3. To serve, remove and discard the bay leaf. Ladle the chili into serving bowls.

SERVES 8 AS A MAIN COURSE

tips To turn this chili into a fiesta, ladle it into shallow bowls and set out all sorts of toppings: cubes of avocado, sour cream, cilantro sprigs, crisp tortilla chips, and wedges of lime.

The chili freezes well and can be frozen for up to three months. Defrost and reheat it in a microwave oven.

CARIBBEAN CHICKEN CHILI

▼ ▼ ▼

The beguiling flavor of jerk seasoning transforms ordinary white beans and chicken in this easy-to-make chili. You simply sauté some chopped sweet onion, Vidalia if you can find it, and toss in some leftover chicken. It's up to you how much hot pepper sauce to add at the end, as well as what to use for garnish: chives, cilantro, mango. . . . I get hungry just

TO PREP:
8–10 MINUTES
TO COOK:
18 MINUTES

thinking about it! With the addition of crusty bread and a green salad, you've got dinner.

1 medium-size sweet onion

1 tablespoon olive oil

2 cups cubed, cooked chicken

1 teaspoon jerk seasoning

2 cans (15.5 ounces each; see Tips at left)
    white beans, with their liquid

1 chicken-flavored bouillon cube

Dash of hot pepper sauce, or more to taste

1 tablespoon heavy (whipping)
    cream (optional; see Tips at right)

Chopped fresh chives, chopped and whole
    fresh cilantro leaves, and/or diced
    mango and red bell pepper,
    for garnish (optional)

1. Cut the onion in half lengthwise, then cut each half crosswise into thin half-moon slices; you'll need 1 cup.

2. Place the olive oil in a 4-quart saucepan over medium heat. Add the sliced

tips **White beans are a delicious pantry staple. You can use Great Northern beans, navy beans, or cannellini beans. But do take the time to taste the various brands of beans on the market because they are all a bit different. Some brands are saltier than others. Some just taste better.**

   Set aside one of the empty bean cans to use as a handy measuring cup when you add the water to the chili.

tips I add cream to temper the heat of the chili and add a touch of richness. But I realize not everyone has heavy cream sitting around in the refrigerator. Add it if you have it, omit it if you don't.

To turn this chili into a Mexican-flavored one, substitute ground cumin for the jerk seasoning and garnish the chili with salsa and chips.

pan from the heat and stir in the beans with their liquid and the bouillon cube and hot pepper sauce. Fill one of the bean cans with water, add this to the pan, and stir. Place the pan over high heat until the liquid comes to a boil and the bouillon cube dissolves. Reduce the heat to low, cover the pan, and let the chili simmer for 10 minutes.

3. Add the cream to the chili, if desired, stir, cover, and cook for 2 minutes longer. Ladle the chili into serving bowls and serve garnished with chopped chives, cilantro, and/or diced mango and red bell pepper, if desired.

onion and cook, stirring with a wooden spoon until soft, 3 minutes. Add the chicken and jerk seasoning and cook, stirring, until the chicken is coated with the seasoning, 1 minute longer. Remove the

SERVES 6 AS A MAIN COURSE

TOMATO AND FENNEL STEW

WITH BIG SHRIMP

▼ ▼ ▼

TO PREP:
10 MINUTES
TO COOK:
7 MINUTES

Fast but fancy, this shrimp stew will bail you out when you have folks coming to dinner and have no idea what to cook. Brothy main courses like this are a great equalizer when you're entertaining. They cry out for crusty bread, and they need big soupspoons.

They're so unpretentious that even your fussiest dinner guests will give in, roll up their sleeves, and have some fun. Serve a nice hearty green salad either before or after the stew, and have ready a bottle or two of chilled sauvignon blanc.

tip **There are fennel bulbs and there are fresh fennel fronds and there are fennel seeds, familiar in Italian sausage. This recipe calls for the bulb, which can be found nearly year-round now but is typically in season during the cooler months. It has a faint licorice taste. If your fennel bulb has fronds, you can save these for garnish. Cut off and discard the stalks before chopping the bulb.**

2 tablespoons olive oil

1 cup chopped fresh fennel bulb
    (from 1 medium-size bulb; see Tip at left)

1 can (28 ounces) diced tomatoes with basil,
    garlic, and oregano, with their liquid

1 cup canned low-sodium chicken broth

½ cup dry vermouth or dry white wine

1 pound pre-cleaned jumbo shrimp

¼ cup chopped flat-leaf parsley (optional),
    for garnish

Good-quality salad croutons (optional),
    for garnish

1. Place the olive oil in a 4-quart saucepan over medium-high heat. Add the fennel and cook, stirring, until it softens, 2 minutes. Add the tomatoes with their liquid and the chicken broth and wine, cover the pan, and bring the mixture to a boil. Reduce the heat to low and let the soup simmer for 10 minutes. Add the shrimp and cook until they just turn pink, 3 minutes longer.

2. Ladle the stew into serving bowls and garnish each serving with the chopped parsley and/or croutons, if desired. Serve at once.

SERVES 4 AS A MAIN COURSE

tips Buy the very best shrimp at your supermarket, and have the fish department shell and devein it for you if you want to save time.

Looking for just the right enhancement for seafood stews and soups? Keep a bottle of dry vermouth on hand. Vermouth combines beautifully with the olive oil, fennel, and tomatoes in this shrimp stew.

It pays to keep salad croutons in your pantry if you don't have time to make your own.

CURRIED CRAB "GUMBO"

▼ ▼ ▼

Making a classic gumbo is an important life skill if you hail from Louisiana. I don't mean to insult anyone by offering up this fast alternative. But browning the ever-critical roux to a perfect mahogany takes a back seat to picking up children after school, meeting work deadlines, washing clothes, and other daily tasks! So, I've come up with a quick but unconventional alternative. I thicken my gumbo with a tablespoon of rice, which I always have in the pantry and which is a good partner for the tomatoes and okra. And I rely on sautéed onion, curry powder, and hot pepper sauce to provide depth of flavor to an otherwise unfussy dish. It isn't traditional, but it is delicious.

TO PREP:
8 MINUTES
TO COOK:
20–25 MINUTES

1 tablespoon olive oil
½ cup chopped onion
        (from 1 small onion)
1 can (14.5 ounces) diced tomatoes with
        green peppers, celery, and onions,
        with their liquid
3 cups low-sodium chicken broth
        (from two 14- to 14.5-ounce cans)
        or water
1 bay leaf
1 teaspoon curry powder
1 tablespoon rice
1 can (6 to 8 ounces) jumbo lump crabmeat
1 package (9 ounces) frozen sliced okra, or
        1 cup sliced fresh okra
1 teaspoon hot pepper sauce, or more to taste
Crusty bread, for serving

1. Place the olive oil in a large saucepan over medium-high heat. Add the onion and cook, stirring with a wooden spoon, until it softens and begins to brown, 3 minutes.

tip **Instead of making the gumbo with just crabmeat, you could mix in some shrimp. Add a half pound of peeled and deveined shrimp during the last 2 minutes of cooking.**

2. Add the tomatoes with their liquid and the chicken broth, bay leaf, and curry powder. Bring to a boil, then add the rice, crabmeat, and okra and stir. Reduce the heat to low, cover the pan, and let simmer until the rice cooks through and the flavors blend, 15 to 20 minutes.

3. Stir in the hot pepper sauce. Remove and discard the bay leaf from the gumbo. Ladle the gumbo into serving bowls and serve at once with crusty bread.

SERVES 6 TO 8 AS A MAIN COURSE

SALAD IN THE BAG

▼▼▼

A salad is fresh; it's uncomplicated; it's often uncooked; it's unassuming; and it just tastes right. When you fork into a salad that includes crisp, fresh greens, you're not only pleasing your taste buds, you're doing something good for yourself.

But while salads are not difficult to make in the first place, supermarket produce departments have made preparing them even easier. Bags of washed and dried lettuce leaves of every imaginable variety beckon even the most time-challenged salad maker. Gone are the days when a head of iceberg lettuce lay neglected and then rotted in my refrigerator drawer. I use bags of greens as a taking-off point for salads, and this gives me more time to be creative with the other ingredients in the bowl. When time is short, pre-shredded, pre-washed greens get my creative juices going, and my family enjoys eating the healthy, delicious, fast results. How can I not be a huge fan?

That miraculous word *salad* is so encompassing, it can mean a meal or the perfect side dish. And this chapter includes a selection of both. Will tonight's salad be a side dish of greens topped with strawberries, blue cheese, and walnuts? Or spinach tossed with mandarin oranges? Or a sweet-and-sour salad of broccoli, onion, and bacon? Might tonight's salad be a quick coleslaw with an Asian dressing? Or, possibly a slaw with avocado, red onion, and cumin?

If you're looking for a salad for company, there's nothing like a layered one. You can layer all the ingredients in a large bowl well in advance and let the salad wait in the refrigerator until your guests arrive. Try the Tex-Mex Layered Salad or the New Year's Layered Spinach Salad—good even when it's not New Year's.

If you are looking to make that salad a main dish, top a bag of spinach with fresh peach slices, pecans, and hot popcorn chicken pieces baked straight from the freezer. Then there's the quick-to-make chicken salad with an Asian touch—ramen noodles.

Maybe tonight's salad doesn't include a lot of greens, but instead is based on pasta or grains. Toss penne with spinach, tomatoes, and feta, or with tuna and beans. Slice some crusty bread to serve alongside, and dinner will be on the table in no time.

Sides and starters and mains made with greens, grains, and pasta are easy and fast. Enjoy making these salads in minutes.

STRAWBERRY FIELD SALAD

▼ ▼ ▼

TO PREP:
10 MINUTES

Fruit, blue cheese, crunchy nuts, and greens—it's a combination that has been making the gourmet-shop circuit for many years. But it can be frightfully expensive to buy salad for a family at these shops. Better to prepare your own at home; it takes little time. The trick is to make a sweet and tangy sesame vinaigrette from bottled salad dressing. After much sampling and adding a bit of this and a bit of that, I came up with one that's a winner!

1 bag (5 ounces) spring mix salad greens
1½ cups strawberries, halved (about 1 pint)
½ cup pre-chopped walnuts or pecans
¼ cup (2 ounces) pre-crumbled blue cheese
Sesame Vinaigrette (recipe at right)

Place the spring mix in a large serving bowl and top it with the strawberries, nuts, and blue cheese. Pour the vinaigrette over the salad, toss to coat the ingredients well, and serve.

SERVES 5 OR 6 AS A SIDE DISH

tips It's easy to double the strawberry salad, and it doesn't take any more time. Just make twice as much Sesame Vinaigrette. Buy two bags of greens. Buy 2 pints of berries. Use a cup of nuts, and the whole container (4 ounces) of crumbled blue cheese.

I used Kraft Zesty Italian dressing and found it was just the right starting point for a sesame dressing. If you want to use a bottled sesame vinaigrette, go ahead, but make sure it has a little sugar in it to balance the saltiness of the blue cheese in this salad. If necessary, add a little honey.

To Wash or Not to Wash

—▼—

DINNER DOCTOR SAYS The labels on the bags of greens read "triple washed," but what would your mother do? I sampled quite a lot of bagged lettuce while writing this chapter, and I found it to be clean and fresh, without a speck of grit. But there are purists who insist that bag salads taste better if you let the greens soak in cold water for a few minutes, then spin them dry. They say they taste perkier, and that the dressing clings to the greens better. I tested this on several varieties of greens and found soaking was most helpful with the Caesar salad kits and plain chopped romaine.

Sesame Vinaigrette

A little doctoring turns bottled Italian dressing into something any salad would be proud to wear.

¼ cup bottled Italian salad dressing
1 tablespoon honey
1 tablespoon low-sodium soy sauce
½ teaspoon Asian (dark) sesame oil

Pour the salad dressing into a small mixing bowl and whisk in the honey, soy sauce, and sesame oil. Set the vinaigrette aside until ready to use.

MAKES ABOUT ⅓ CUP

SOUTHERN CRANBERRY SALAD

▼ ▼ ▼

People tend to have strong opinions about cranberries. To please everyone at Thanksgiving, I serve fresh cranberry sauce, canned cranberry

TO PREP:
10 MINUTES
TO CHILL:
AT LEAST 3 HOURS

sauce, and this easy do-ahead gelatin salad made with cranberries, mandarin oranges, pineapple, and pecans. Of course, the cranberry sauces marry well with roast turkey, but this festive-looking salad is also perfect with ham. Gelatin salads are no trouble to put together; the refrigerator firms it up while you go on about your business. In the South these types of salads are called congealed salads and they are a mainstay of buffet tables.

1 package (3 ounces) strawberry or
　　cherry gelatin
1 cup boiling water
1 can (16 ounces) whole berry cranberry
　　sauce
2 cans (11 ounces each) mandarin oranges,
　　drained
1 can (8 ounces) crushed pineapple, drained
1 cup finely chopped toasted pecans
　　(optional; see Tips)

tips My mother knew all sorts of ingenious ways to speed up the chilling process of a congealed salad. She would add ice to them or make sure the ingredients were cold. To make this salad gel more quickly, chill the cranberry sauce, mandarin oranges, and pineapple before stirring them into the dissolved gelatin.

Toasted pecans give the cranberry salad crunch. To toast chopped pecans, spread them out on a rimmed baking sheet and bake them in a 350°F oven until they begin to take on color, 3 to 4 minutes. Make sure they have cooled completely before adding them to the salad.

1. Place the gelatin in a large heatproof glass or stainless steel bowl and pour the boiling water over it. Stir the gelatin with a fork until it has dissolved. Add the cranberry sauce, mandarin oranges, pineapple, and pecans, if using, and stir until well blended. Set the mixture aside.

2. Lightly oil a 4-cup ring mold or 2-quart glass or ceramic baking dish. Transfer the cranberry salad to the mold or baking dish and cover the top with plastic wrap. Place the salad in the refrigerator and let it chill at least 3 hours, preferably overnight. The ring mold will take longer to set than the baking dish.

3. To serve, if using a ring mold, fill the sink with 1 inch of hot water. Let the ring mold sit in the water briefly. Run a sharp knife around the edges of the mold, then gently shake it to loosen the salad. Invert the mold onto a platter lined with lettuce leaves. If using a baking dish, run a knife around the edges of the dish, cut the salad into servings, and, using a metal spatula, transfer them to a platter lined with lettuce leaves.

SERVES 8 TO 10

Let's Give Thanks Dinner

▼▼▼

Here's a selection of delicious traditional Thanksgiving dishes to serve with the turkey. They're filled with shortcuts, but no one will guess you didn't spend days in the kitchen.

Relish tray of carrot and celery sticks, black and green olives, and radishes

---

Roast turkey with dressing

Thanksgiving Souffléed Sweet Potatoes
page 384

The Green Bean Casserole Revisited
page 368

Southern Cranberry Salad
this page

Dun-Buttered Muffins
page 419

Orange Crumble Pumpkin Pie
page 493

SPINACH AND ORANGE SALAD

WITH SESAME VINAIGRETTE

▼ ▼ ▼

Like the Strawberry Field Salad (see page 118), this salad features the delicious combination of sweet, salty, and tangy. Spinach provides the green. The sweet fruit is the easy and accessible canned mandarin orange sections. The cheese can be feta or blue—you choose. Mushrooms add texture and substance. The salad goes well with grilled chicken and a baked potato or stands on its own with crusty bread for lunch or a light supper.

TO PREP:
10 MINUTES

1 bag (6 ounces) spinach, leaves
    torn into pieces
1 package (8 ounces) pre-sliced mushrooms
1 can (11 ounces) mandarin orange sections,
    drained
¼ cup pre-crumbled feta or blue cheese
2 tablespoons pre-chopped pecans
Sesame Vinaigrette (page 119)

Place the spinach leaves in a large serving bowl. Scatter the mushrooms, orange sections, cheese, and pecans on top. Pour the vinaigrette over the salad and toss to coat the ingredients well. Serve at once.

SERVES 4 AS A SIDE DISH

> **tips** Pre-sliced mushrooms are a big timesaver. If your supermarket does not carry them, simply slice an 8-ounce package of whole mushrooms. Use the slicing disc of a food processor or a stainless steel knife, as carbon steel knives tend to discolor mushrooms. And don't worry about making each slice a clone of the others.
>
> A delicious tip is to add the mushrooms to the Sesame Vinaigrette before you dress the salad. Marinating the mushrooms for 1 to 15 minutes will give them more flavor.

5-Step Something Salad

—▼—

DINNER DOCTOR SAYS

Putting together an interesting green salad isn't difficult, but you do need the right balance of ingredients. I like to make what I call the Something Salad because it contains:

1. Something green

2. Something sweet

3. Something crunchy

4. Something tangy

5. Something to dress it with

Begin with the greens of your choice: spring mix, watercress, romaine, spinach, you name it. Don't forget fresh herbs. Toss them in the salad bowl, too. And remember that too much of the same green isn't as interesting as a little of several greens.

Next, add something sweet (but not necessarily sugary): carrot slivers, pear slices, chopped tomatoes, apple slices, strawberries, halved grapes, dried cranberries or cherries, roasted red peppers, and/or raisins.

Then, add something crunchy: toasted pine nuts, sliced almonds, pecan halves, walnuts, croutons, even canned onion rings. Now for something tangy—think cheese: crumbled feta or blue cheese or a soft goat cheese. And lastly, you need something to dress the salad with. Greens taste better with oil and vinegar-based dressings. Mayonnaise-based dressings weigh down greens any lighter than iceberg or romaine. Balsamic dressings, on the other hand, are light yet can hold their own with the depth of flavor of sweet roasted vegetables. Sesame dressings are light too, but they are also sweet and tangy and marry well with bitter greens, strong cheese, and salty ingredients.

Once dressed, green salads need to be eaten pronto! If it looks like you've made too much salad for the crowd, serve undressed portions as needed, and dress individually. Store the undressed leftover salad under plastic wrap. It will keep for a day or two in the refrigerator.

SWEET SOUTHERN PERFECTION SALAD

▼ ▼ ▼

If you think Southerners sit around eating green salads day in and day out then you haven't popped into a tearoom, hit a church potluck supper, or been invited to a ladies' luncheon lately. More often you see gelatin salads, salads made from frozen fruit, and sweet salads of canned fruit. I have included this simple fruit salad because you can prepare it from easy-to-find ingredients. The marshmallows plump up nicely when mixed with the mandarin oranges and pineapple. It is "perfection" served alongside chicken salad, chicken casserole, or anything rather ladylike.

TO PREP:
3–5 MINUTES

tip You'll find sweetened flaked coconut in the baking aisle of the supermarket.

1 cup sweetened flaked coconut
    (see Tip)
1 can (11 ounces) mandarin orange sections,
    drained
1 can (8 ounces) crushed pineapple, drained
1 cup reduced-fat
    sour cream
1 cup miniature
    marshmallows

Place the coconut, mandarin oranges, pineapple, and sour cream in a medium-size mixing bowl and stir to combine. Fold in the marshmallows and mix until they are well coated. Serve the salad at once or cover the bowl with plastic wrap and refrigerate it for at least 1 hour or up to 4.

SERVES 6 AS A SIDE DISH

RIPE TOMATO PANZANELLA

▼ ▼ ▼

Croutons are not just for garnishing pea soup and salads. The Italians use croutons made from day-old bread as the starting point for *panzanella*— bread salad. Once tossed with chopped tomatoes and a vinaigrette, the bread soaks up the juice from the sweet tomatoes and the vinegar and olive oil,

TO PREP:
10 MINUTES

taking on a wonderful flavor in just 5 minutes. Fresh basil and crisp red onion pair beautifully with the softened bread. For a complete meal, serve the salad with already peeled and steamed shrimp you've picked up at the supermarket.

tips **Buy the best plain croutons you can for this salad (try to find them unseasoned). You can make the salad up to 3 hours ahead of time, but don't add the croutons and the basil until the last minute.**

You can use canned diced tomatoes if you are in a real pinch and have no wonderful ripe tomatoes, but make sure they are plain diced tomatoes that have no sugar added.

4 large ripe tomatoes, cut into 1-inch cubes
    (about 4 heaping cups)
½ cup thinly sliced red onion
½ cup halved pitted kalamata
    olives
1 or 2 cloves garlic, crushed
    in a garlic press
2 tablespoons balsamic vinegar
2 tablespoons extra-virgin olive oil
¼ teaspoon salt, or more to taste
1 box (5.5 ounces) croutons (see Tips)
1 cup torn fresh basil leaves
1 bag (10 ounces) Italian blend lettuce
    (optional), for serving

A Word on Croutons

—▼—

DINNER DOCTOR SAYS

My youngest child, John, is a fan of croutons, and I have to watch my salad or he'll pluck those crunchy squares right off the top. John is especially fond of supermarket croutons, the ones you see all lined up in the salad dressing aisle, and he has no particular favorite when it comes to flavor. They all taste good to him. They all have that crunch.

But if you, too, are a crouton fan, you'll want to make your own when you have day-old bread. Just cut slices into cubes, toss these with a little olive oil and salt, and bake them at 350°F until they are well toasted, about 15 minutes. Sprinkle the croutons with pre-shredded Parmesan cheese and cracked black pepper, or even with minced garlic and cayenne pepper. Croutons add texture; they add interest; they add substance. Just ask John.

Place the tomatoes, onion, olives, garlic, vinegar, olive oil, and salt in a large mixing bowl and stir to combine. Taste for seasoning, adding more salt if necessary. Stir in the croutons and the basil leaves. Let the salad sit at room temperature for 5 minutes, then serve on its own or on a bed of salad greens.

SERVES 4 TO 6 AS A SIDE DISH

BLUE CHEESE, WALNUT, AND APPLE SLAW

▼▼▼

A simple slaw mix meets fresh apple, toasted walnuts, and a fast blue cheese dressing. What could be better? It's delicious made with regular coleslaw mix, and I've also made it with julienned broccoli. It pairs well with grilled pork chops or roast pork loin and mashed potatoes. As with any slaw, this one gets a bit better with

TO PREP AND COOK:
10–12 MINUTES

time, so when you feel motivated, make it a day ahead, but don't sprinkle the toasted walnuts on top until just before serving. And if the pears in your fruit bowl look better than the apples, go with a pear.

⅓ cup walnut pieces (see Tips)
1 medium-size apple
½ cup bottled ranch salad dressing
¼ cup pre-crumbled blue cheese
1 bag (16 ounces) coleslaw mix
Black pepper

1. Preheat the oven to 350°F.

2. Place the walnut pieces on a rimmed baking sheet and bake them until they begin to darken, 5 to 7 minutes. Meanwhile, coarsely grate the apple using the side of a box grater

> **tips** If you buy walnut halves and pieces, or chopped walnuts, it is not only cheaper than buying all halves, but these smaller pieces take less time to toast. You'll need to keep an eye on the walnuts as they bake. Turn the oven light on if you have one.
>
> No need to salt this slaw, as the blue cheese has plenty of salt in it.

with the largest holes; you should have about 1 cup.

3. Place the ranch dressing and blue cheese in a large serving bowl. Stir to combine and mash the blue cheese a bit to incorporate it into the dressing. Add the coleslaw mix and grated apple and stir to coat it well with the dressing. Season the slaw with black pepper to taste. Just before serving, sprinkle the toasted walnuts on top of the slaw.

SERVES 6 TO 8 AS A SIDE DISH

You Say "Coleslaw," I Say "*Koolsla*"

—▼—

DINNER DOCTOR SAYS

But, let's *not* call the whole thing off. Coleslaw, the classic American salad of shredded white or red cabbage (or both), carrots, onions, and bell peppers, gets its name from the Dutch word *koolsla*— *kool* (cabbage) *sla* (salad). Coleslaws are refreshing when the weather's warm; they really do cool you off.

Look for bags of traditional coarsely sliced cabbage for slaw in the produce section of the supermarket. You'll also find finer grated slaws and slaws made from julienned broccoli, cauliflower, and carrots. All you need to do is add a sweet mayonnaise-based salad dressing or an oil and vinegar dressing.

JOHN'S SUMMERTIME SLAW

▼ ▼ ▼

My husband, John, is known far and wide for his excellent coleslaw, which he seems to assemble in no time, especially when he begins with a bag of coleslaw mix. The secret to a good slaw, he says, is sweet-pickle juice and Vidalia onions. We like to buy a big bag of these sweet onions when they come into season in the spring, then keep them in the refrigerator vegetable drawer to use all through the summer.

TO PREP:
7–8 MINUTES

1 bag (16 ounces) coleslaw mix
½ cup chopped sweet onion,
    such as Vidalia (see Tips)
½ cup chopped green bell pepper
½ cup mayonnaise
¼ cup sweet-pickle juice
3 tablespoons pickle relish
3 tablespoons sugar, or more to taste
1 teaspoon seasoned salt, or more to taste

Place the coleslaw mix, onion, and green bell pepper in a large mixing bowl and stir to combine. Make a well in the center of the slaw mixture and add the mayonnaise, pickle juice, pickle relish, sugar, and seasoned salt. Stir with a fork to mix the dressing, then stir the dressing and the slaw mixture with a wooden spoon to combine. Serve at once or cover with plastic wrap and refrigerate for up to 2 days.

SERVES 6 TO 8 AS A SIDE DISH

tips I think a secret to good slaw is to chop, not grate, the onion right before you mix it in.

In a rush? Pick up a bottle of coleslaw dressing, which is just heavily sweetened mayonnaise. Substitute it for the mayonnaise, pickle juice, and sugar in the Summertime Slaw recipe, but add the pickle relish and seasoned salt.

SOUTHWESTERN SLAW

WITH AVOCADO AND CUMIN

▼ ▼ ▼

TO PREP:
10 MINUTES

Some people get all weak in the knees when they see chocolate, taste lemon, or smell vanilla. I'll admit I succumb to these, but I also have a weakness for avocados, especially the small black-green skinned Hass avocados from California. For a memorable slaw that's quick to make, I combine creamy ranch dressing, soft avocado cubes, spicy cumin, and crunchy onion and cabbage, and shower just the right touch of cilantro on top. Serve the slaw with strips of grilled chicken, alongside barbecued pork, or with pan-seared fish and a slice of ripe tomato.

tip **Feeling fancy? Add a squirt of fresh lime juice to the dressing and top the slaw with a handful of crushed tortilla chips just before serving.**

1 package (16 ounces) coleslaw mix
½ cup thinly sliced or finely chopped
    red onion
1 teaspoon ground cumin
½ cup bottled ranch salad dressing
1 ripe avocado, peeled and cubed
    (for about 1 cup cubes)
Creole seasoning or salt
Black pepper
2 tablespoons chopped fresh cilantro

Place the coleslaw mix and onion in a serving bowl and stir to combine. Stir the cumin into the salad dressing. Pour the salad dressing over the slaw, tossing to coat it well. Fold in the avocado cubes and season with Creole seasoning and pepper to taste. Wipe the rim of the bowl clean with a paper towel and sprinkle the cilantro on top of the slaw. Serve the slaw at once or cover the bowl with plastic wrap and refrigerate it for up to 24 hours.

SERVES 6 TO 8 AS A SIDE DISH

FAST ASIAN SLAW

▼ ▼ ▼

What a welcome and easy change of pace a lighter coleslaw makes, one dressed in oil and vinegar instead of the heavier mayonnaise. You'll enjoy the unexpected Asian flavors of this salad; they marry well with roast or fried chicken, grilled grouper or snapper, and all manner of grilled pork dishes. Not having to shred the cabbage saves you a lot of preparation time!

**TO PREP:
5 MINUTES**

¼ cup rice vinegar

*2 tablespoons low-sodium
    soy sauce*

1 tablespoon sugar

2 teaspoons Asian (dark) sesame oil

Dash of hot pepper sauce

*4 scallions, both white and light green parts,
    chopped (for ½ cup)*

1 package (16 ounces) coleslaw mix

*1 teaspoon toasted sesame seeds
    (see Tips)*

tips **If you can get your hands on a good bottled sesame vinaigrette, then by all means use about ⅓ cup of it in the slaw instead of making your own.**

To toast sesame seeds, place them in a heavy skillet over medium heat and stir them until they begin to darken, 2 to 3 minutes. (Don't use a nonstick skillet for this.)

Place the vinegar, soy sauce, sugar, sesame oil, and hot pepper sauce in a large serving bowl. Whisk to combine. Add the scallions and coleslaw mix and stir to combine well. Sprinkle the sesame seeds on top. Serve the slaw at once or cover the bowl with plastic wrap and refrigerate it for up to 3 days.

SERVES 4 TO 6 AS A SIDE DISH

MOM'S POTATO SALAD

▼ ▼ ▼

Can't you just hear the mom mantra, Eat your peas, repeated over and over in your head? So, isn't it just like a mom to sneak peas into potato salad? Well, to be honest, my mom wasn't looking for a way to get us to eat our vegetables when she hit on this recipe. She just never cared for mayonnaise, so she searched for a potato salad recipe with a different type of dressing. Her salad—a family favorite—contains frozen peas for their already-shelled speed and just-steamed

TO PREP AND COOK: 25 MINUTES

potatoes for their freshness. Those peas add color and crunch. Serve the salad with fried chicken, hamburgers, or steaks from the grill, or with slices of ripe tomato.

2½ pounds new potatoes
Pinch of salt
1 package (10 ounces) frozen peas
1 cup finely chopped celery (from 1 to 2 ribs)
½ cup chopped scallions, both white and light
*   green parts (from 4 scallions)*
1 envelope (0.7 ounce) Good Seasons Italian
*   salad dressing mix*
⅓ cup olive oil

1. Rinse the potatoes well under running water, and scrub them to remove any dirt. Cut larger potatoes into eighths. Cut smaller potatoes into quarters. Place the potatoes in a 4-quart saucepan and cover them with cold water, then add the salt. Place the pan over high heat, cover it, and bring to a boil. When the water is boiling, reduce the heat to low and let the potatoes simmer, covered, until they are just tender

tip You can omit the salad dressing mix if you like and add 1 teaspoon of salt, or more to taste, ½ teaspoon of pepper, and 4 tablespoons of chopped fresh parsley. But the virtue of using a salad dressing mix is that you don't have to keep tasting and adding salt, tasting and adding salt . . . and you don't have to chop the parsley.

when tested with a fork, 10 minutes. Pour off the water and place the potatoes on a work surface to cool for 10 minutes.

2. Meanwhile, place the frozen peas, celery, scallions, and salad dressing mix in a large serving bowl and stir to combine.

3. When the potatoes are cool enough to handle (but still quite warm), remove the skins and cut each potato into about 1-inch cubes. Add the cubed potatoes to the bowl with the peas and toss (the warmth of the potatoes will thaw the frozen peas). Pour the olive oil over the salad and stir with a large spoon to combine well, making sure that all of the potatoes are coated with olive oil. Serve the salad at once or cover the bowl with plastic wrap and refrigerate it for up to 3 days.

SERVES 6 TO 8 AS A SIDE DISH

15 WAYS TO DOCTOR DELI POTATO SALAD

On its own, deli potato salad with the usual celery, onion, and mayo is pretty ho-hum. By adding a few well-chosen ingredients, however, you can make it something special. The suggestions here are for doctoring a pound of potato salad.

1 Add pitted kalamata olives that have been cut in half and 1 tablespoon of fresh oregano.

2 Fold in chopped cucumber and plenty of chopped fresh dill.

3 Stir in several slices of smoked salmon that have been cut into slivers.

4 Sprinkle crumbled cooked bacon on top of the potato salad.

5 Fold in more finely chopped celery for extra crunch.

6 Add a teaspoon of curry powder and some chopped scallions and shredded carrots. Sprinkle with fresh parsley.

7 Stir in diced pimiento peppers and a handful of shredded sharp Cheddar cheese.

8 Sprinkle crumbled blue cheese and cracked black pepper on top.

9 Top each serving with a dollop of caviar and a dusting of minced chives.

10 Season the salad with a teaspoon of ground cumin and add a tablespoon of canned or fresh chopped chile.

11 Fold a tablespoon of prepared horseradish into a pound of potato salad. Surround the salad with peppery watercress.

12 Add ¼ cup of chopped fresh parsley and a tablespoon of chopped tarragon.

13 Make an American-style salade niçoise by serving steamed green beans, chunks of tuna, and black olives alongside the potato salad.

14 Create a Greek-influenced salad by placing the potato salad in the bottom of a salad bowl and covering it with shredded iceberg lettuce, cucumber slices, bell pepper rings, tomatoes, kalamata olives, and feta cheese.

15 Squeeze the juice of a lemon over the potato salad, then sprinkle it with black pepper.

WARM ARUGULA SALAD

WITH ROASTED ASPARAGUS AND BALSAMIC VINAIGRETTE

▼ ▼ ▼

Who says a salad has to be cold? Not only does the flavor of asparagus come through once it has been roasted, but the arugula leaves are more delicious when topped with a warm medley of asparagus, roasted red peppers, and olives. This is a delicious starter or side dish, which can be turned into a main course with the addition of a can of tuna or some grilled fish

TO PREP AND COOK:
15 MINUTES

or chicken. Many super-market produce depart-ments carry bags of arugula that are already washed and dried. You save even more time by using bottled bal-samic dressing.

1 bunch of thin asparagus (about 30 stalks)
2 tablespoons olive oil
Salt, to taste
⅓ cup bottled balsamic vinaigrette
½ cup store-bought roasted
    red pepper strips
¼ cup halved pitted kalamata olives
        4 cups prewashed baby arugula,
            trimmed and leaves
            torn into pieces

1. Preheat the oven to 400°F.

2. Rinse the asparagus spears, pat dry, and snap off and discard the tough ends. Place the asparagus in a shallow baking pan, drizzle with the olive oil, and sprinkle with salt. Bake the asparagus until it just

tips **The thinner the asparagus spears are, the faster they cook. Plus, the thin spears are delicious in salads: They blend with the greens and you don't need a knife to cut them.**

Add fresh basil and good ripe tomatoes if you have them on hand.

begins to take on a roasted appearance, 5 to 6 minutes.

3. Meanwhile, warm the balsamic vinaigrette in a small saucepan over low heat. Do not let it come to a boil.

4. Remove the baking pan from the oven and toss the red pepper strips and olives with the hot asparagus. Either divide the arugula among 4 salad plates or place the arugula in a medium-size salad bowl. Top it with the asparagus mixture. Spoon the warmed dressing over the salad and serve at once.

SERVES 4 AS A STARTER OR SIDE DISH

Do-It-Yourself Balsamic Dressing

—▼—

DINNER DOCTOR SAYS I think a bottled balsamic vinaigrette, like Newman's Own, is quite good. But here's a quick homemade version that will keep in the fridge for 10 days: Into ½ cup of olive oil, whisk 2 tablespoons of balsamic vinegar, a pinch each of salt and pepper, and a crushed clove of garlic. Store, covered, in the refrigerator. The olive oil will thicken and turn cloudy. Just let the dressing come to room temperature before using.

SWEET-AND-SOUR BROCCOLI SALAD

▼ ▼ ▼

If you've ever been to a potluck supper, you've tasted a broccoli salad or two. That's because broccoli salad goes with so many different foods, including sliced ham, fried chicken, and roast turkey. It's even good all by itself with bread hot out of the oven. The sweet-and-sour combination

TO PREP AND COOK:
10–12 MINUTES

of bacon, vinegar, and sugar is a classic salad dressing, perfect for pairing with the broccoli along with onion and shredded Cheddar. If it strikes your fancy, you can also add raisins, dried cherries, or sunflower seeds to the salad.

tips **Bags of broccoli florets are available in the produce department of many supermarkets. Using these makes this recipe superfast.**

You will need about 3 cups of florets. I like raw broccoli florets—they save time. If you prefer lightly steamed florets, plunge them into boiling water until they are bright green, 1 to 2 minutes, then immerse them in a bowl of ice water to cool off.

10 slices of bacon, cut into 1-inch pieces

1 bunch of broccoli (see Tips)

½ cup mayonnaise

1 tablespoon sugar

1 tablespoon cider vinegar

½ cup chopped onion

½ cup pre-shredded sharp Cheddar cheese

1. Place the bacon in a skillet over medium heat. Cook the bacon until it is crisp on both sides, 3 to 4 minutes, then drain it on paper towels. Crumble the bacon into a small bowl and set aside.

2. Cut the florets off the broccoli stalks. Break or cut the florets into small pieces; reserve the stalks for another use.

3. Place the mayonnaise, sugar, and vinegar in a large mixing bowl. Whisk to combine. Add the broccoli florets, onion, cheese, and crumbled bacon. Stir until all of the ingredients are coated with dressing. Serve the salad at once or cover the bowl with plastic wrap and refrigerate it for up to 3 days.

SERVES 6 AS A SIDE DISH

Seaside at Home

▼▼▼

When the weather turns hot, bring a coastal feel to your backyard. Serve up crispy crab cakes with a couple of refreshing side salads and a plateful of quick-baking butter cookies.

**Jumbo Crab Cakes
with Spicy Mayonnaise**
page 191

**Stir-Fried Sweet Carrot Slivers
with Orange**
page 359

Sweet-and-Sour Broccoli Salad
page 137

Potato Chip Cookies
page 513

TEX-MEX LAYERED SALAD

▼ ▼ ▼

A layered salad is a knockout when presented in a large glass bowl so the layers of bright festive color show. And this one tastes like a knockout, too, with a stellar combination of beans, corn, tomatoes, lettuce, and corn bread—perfect for a potluck dinner. The salad stays fresh and crisp in the refrigerator for several days because the dressing soaks into the

TO PREP:
18 MINUTES

corn bread, rather than making the lettuce soggy. Enjoy!

1½ cups bottled ranch salad dressing or
    reduced-fat sour cream
½ cup chopped fresh cilantro
1 teaspoon ground cumin
2 tablespoons fresh lime juice
2 cups chopped tomatoes
    (from about 4 medium-
    size tomatoes)
8 scallions, both white and
    light green parts, chopped
    (for 1 cup)
1 package (10 ounces) iceberg lettuce salad
1 package (8 ounces; 2 cups) pre-shredded
    Mexican-style cheese
1 can (15 ounces) black beans, rinsed
    and drained
1 can (11 ounces) yellow corn kernels
    with peppers, drained
4 cups crumbled corn bread
    (see Tip)

tip You can buy corn muffins at the supermarket bakery, or you can find corn muffins and corn bread in the freezer section of supermarkets in many parts of the country. If not, you can always make your own corn bread from a packet of corn bread mix. A 6.5-ounce package of corn bread mix bakes for 20 minutes, and all you need to add is an egg and ¾ cup of milk.

1. Place the salad dressing, cilantro, cumin, and lime juice in a small mixing bowl. Whisk to combine and set the salad dressing aside.

2. Place the tomatoes and scallions in a mixing bowl and stir to combine.

3. Prepare the garnish: Set aside, in separate containers, ½ cup each of the lettuce salad and cheese and ¼ cup each of the black beans, corn kernels, and tomato and scallion mixture. You'll use these in Step 5.

4. Make the salad: Place half of the remaining lettuce salad in the bottom of a 4-quart glass serving bowl or trifle dish. Then, scatter 2 cups of the corn bread on top of the lettuce. Pour ½ cup of the salad dressing over the corn bread. Place half of the remaining black beans on top of the corn bread, then add half of the remaining corn kernels. Sprinkle ¾ cup of the remaining cheese over the layer of corn. Place the rest of the lettuce salad on top of the corn. Place the remaining 2 cups of corn bread on top of the lettuce. Pour ½ cup of the salad dressing over the corn bread. Layer the rest of the black beans on

tip Spice up this salad by adding a drained 4.5-ounce can of chopped green chiles to the dressing and selecting a pre-shredded cheese with peppers in it.

top of the corn bread, followed by a layer of the corn kernels, and then the rest of the cheese. Pour the remaining ½ cup of salad dressing over the cheese and scatter the rest of the tomato and scallion mixture on top.

5. Garnish the salad by creating an attractive pattern using the ingredients set aside in Step 3: Arrange the remaining lettuce in a ring around the outer edge of the salad. Arrange the remaining cheese in a ring inside the lettuce. Fill the center of the cheese with the remaining black beans. Place the remaining corn on top of the beans. Pile the remaining tomato and scallion mixture on top of the corn. Serve the salad at once or cover the bowl with plastic wrap and refrigerate it for up to 3 days.

SERVES 8 AS A HEARTY SIDE DISH

NEW YEAR'S LAYERED SPINACH SALAD

▼▼▼

TO PREP AND COOK:
15 MINUTES
TO CHILL:
AT LEAST 1 HOUR

The notion of cooking on New Year's Day has never seemed like a good one to me. The first day of the year ought to be a time to kick back, recuperate, spend time with family and friends, and of course, eat. But cook? No. So, I love the idea of having a salad in waiting. On the afternoon of the day before I plan to serve it, I put the salad together, cover it, and let it chill. It's yummy the next day served with sliced ham, smoked salmon, black-eyed peas and rice, a pot of chili, an omelet— you name it. Add some crusty bread and you have a perfect start for the year ahead!

1 package (10 ounces) frozen peas

8 ounces bacon, cut into 1-inch pieces

1 bag (10 ounces) spinach, torn into pieces

4 hard-cooked eggs, shelled and sliced (see Tip)

4 scallions, both white and light green parts, chopped (for ⅓ cup)

1 can (8 ounces) sliced water chestnuts, drained

1 bottle (15 ounces) ranch salad dressing

½ cup pre-grated Parmesan cheese

2 tablespoons chopped fresh parsley

tip **The best way to hard-cook eggs is to cover them with water in a saucepan, then cover the pan and bring the water to a boil over medium-high heat. When the water boils, turn off the heat and leave the eggs in the covered pan for 20 minutes. Remove the eggs from the water and rinse under cold water, then remove the shells. The eggs will be ready to slice.**

1. Remove the peas from the freezer so they begin to thaw.

2. Place the bacon in a large skillet over medium heat. Cook the bacon until it is crisp on both sides, 3 to 4 minutes, then drain it on paper towels. Crumble the bacon into a small bowl and set aside.

3. Layer the spinach, egg slices, crumbled bacon, scallions, peas, and water chestnuts in that order in a 4-quart glass serving bowl or trifle dish. Pour the salad dressing over the salad, then sprinkle the Parmesan and parsley on top. Cover the bowl with plastic wrap and place it in the refrigerator to chill for at least 1 hour, or preferably overnight.

SERVES 8 AS A SIDE DISH

BLACK-EYED PEA AND SPINACH SALAD

WITH JASMINE RICE

▼ ▼ ▼

Down South they say that if you eat a plateful of black-eyed peas on New Year's Day, you will have good luck for the entire year. They also say that if you eat some leafy greens, you'll be blessed monetarily. Once Southerners figured out they could combine the two in one dish, their bases were covered!

TO PREP AND COOK:
20–25 MINUTES

But don't save this recipe just for New Year's: Canned black-eyed peas make it quick enough to serve this salad any night of the week.

Salt (optional), for cooking the rice

1 cup jasmine rice

4 slices of bacon, cut into 1-inch pieces

2 cans (15 to 16 ounces each)
    black-eyed peas

½ cup thinly sliced red onion

½ cup bottled olive oil and vinegar
    salad dressing

¼ cup packed light brown sugar

1 bag (6 ounces) spinach

1 cup cherry tomatoes, halved

tips This salad can be made up to two days ahead of time. The black-eyed peas will taste better after they have had time to marinate. And the rice holds well, too. Just place the crumbled bacon in a plastic bag in the refrigerator and put the salad together at the last minute.

If you like, add a handful of chopped fresh mint to the spinach leaves.

1. Pour 2 cups of water and the salt, if using, in a 1-quart saucepan and bring to a boil over high heat. Stir in the rice, cover the pan, and reduce the heat to low. Let the rice simmer until done, 15 to 20 minutes.

2. Meanwhile, place the bacon in a skillet over medium heat. Cook the bacon until it is crisp on both sides, 3 to 4 minutes, then drain on paper towels and crumble. Set aside both the crumbled bacon and the skillet with the bacon fat. Drain the black-eyed peas and place them in a large mixing bowl.

3. Place the skillet with the bacon fat over medium heat. Add the onion and cook, stirring, until soft and lightly browned, 3 to 4 minutes. Add the salad dressing, brown sugar, and ¼ cup of water. Bring the mixture to a boil, scraping the bottom of the pan with a wooden spoon to loosen any bits of bacon. Let the mixture reduce a bit, 4 to 5 minutes. Pour the dressing over the black-eyed peas and toss well. Cover the bowl with plastic wrap and refrigerate it until time to serve.

4. When the rice has cooked, transfer it to a large serving platter and fluff it with a fork to separate the grains. Spoon the black-eyed pea mixture on top of the rice. Arrange the spinach and cherry tomatoes attractively around the peas and rice, then garnish the top with the reserved crumbled bacon.

SERVES 6 TO 8 AS A SIDE DISH

Rice-A-Roni

— ▼ —

DINNER DOCTOR SAYS

Rice-A-Roni, one of America's most beloved convenience foods, is rooted in the San Francisco of the 1930s. The wife of one of the DeDomenico brothers, owners of the Golden Grain Macaroni Company, served her family a rice pilaf dish she learned to make from a neighbor. Prepared by sautéing rice and macaroni in butter before stirring in the liquid, the recipe became a family favorite. Eventually another family member changed the recipe a bit by adding dry chicken soup mix to the rice and using vermicelli in place of the macaroni, and yes, the rest became history. In 1958 Rice-A-Roni was born, and thanks to television, a popular slogan of this company—"The San Francisco Treat"—and the clanging cable car featured in the advertisement both became part of baby-boomer pop culture. Quaker Oats bought the Golden Grain Macaroni Company in 1986, and today there are more than fifteen flavors of Rice-A-Roni and twenty flavors of its sister, Pasta Roni.

SUMMERTIME CURRIED RICE SALAD

▼ ▼ ▼

O ur family has been making curried rice salad for at least fifteen years, using an old favorite standby, Rice-A-Roni. Tossing Rice-A-Roni with marinated artichoke hearts, scallions, green olives, and mayonnaise laced with curry powder makes a reliable, flavorful salad that keeps well for days in the refrigerator. I like to make a batch in the summertime and, when

TO PREP AND COOK:
18 MINUTES

it's just too hot to turn on the oven, serve it on week- nights along with hamburgers or some grilled chicken or fish. It's also a per- fect salad to take on picnics.

1 package (6.9 ounces) chicken-flavor
    Rice-A-Roni
Vegetable oil, for cooking the Rice-A-Roni
2 to 3 scallions, trimmed
1 jar (6 ounces) marinated artichoke hearts
¼ cup sliced green olives or
    chopped "salad" olives
¼ cup mayonnaise
1 teaspoon curry powder
¼ cup toasted sliced almonds
    (see Tips), for garnish

tips To toast sliced almonds, preheat a toaster oven to 350°F, then bake the almonds until golden brown, 2 minutes. You can do this while the rice cooks if you are serving the salad warm.

This recipe doubles well for a crowd, and it takes no more time to prepare.

If you have a little red or green bell pepper in the refrigerator, chop ¼ cup and add it to the salad.

1. Prepare the Rice- A-Roni following the instructions on the package and using vegetable oil. Cook the rice until it just tests done and the liquid has evaporated, 15 minutes.

2. Meanwhile, chop the scallions, using both the white and light green parts. You should have ¼ cup. Place the scallions in a large serving bowl. Drain and chop the artichoke hearts and add them to the bowl. Add the green olives. Place the mayonnaise in a small bowl and stir in the curry powder. Set the curry mayonnaise aside.

3. Add the Rice-A-Roni to the bowl with the artichokes. Spoon the curry mayonnaise on top of the rice. Stir until all of the ingredients are well coated. Serve at once or cover the bowl with plastic wrap and refrigerate it for at least 1 hour if you want to serve the salad cold. The salad can be refrigerated for up to 5 days. Garnish the salad with the toasted almonds right before serving.

SERVES 4 TO 6 AS A SIDE DISH

Three Easy Dressings

—▼—

DINNER DOCTOR SAYS

If salad boredom sets in, enliven your greens with one of these quick combinations.

Cilantro and Lime Vinaigrette: Doctor store-bought Italian dressing with chopped fresh cilantro, the juice of a lime, and a dash of soy sauce.

Mindy's Lemon-Soy Dressing: Begin with ¼ cup of vegetable oil and whisk in 2 tablespoons of fresh lemon juice, a tablespoon of soy sauce, and a teaspoon of sugar. Kids will like this dressing poured over chopped iceberg or romaine lettuce.

Black-and-Blue Vinaigrette: Begin with an oil and vinegar dressing you like—it can be either store-bought or made from scratch. Add a generous handful of crumbled blue cheese and an ample grinding of black pepper. This dressing is sinful spooned over sliced ripe tomatoes!

WARM RICE SALAD

WITH GRAPE TOMATOES AND PESTO

▼ ▼ ▼

Preparing this rice salad is a snap because it calls for a foolproof standby, a jar of pesto, and you can cut the tomatoes and kalamata olives in half and toast the pine nuts while the rice is cooking. Delicious as a side dish, the salad turns into a pretty main dish if you pile it on a ceramic platter and surround it with skewers of grilled shrimp.

TO PREP AND COOK:
25 MINUTES

Salt (optional), for cooking
the rice

1½ cups jasmine or Arborio rice

1 pint grape tomatoes

½ cup pitted kalamata olives

¼ cup pine nuts

¾ cup store-bought pesto (see Tip), or
more if needed

1. Preheat the oven to 350°F.

2. Pour 3 cups of water and the salt, if using, in a 2-quart saucepan and bring to a boil over high heat. Stir in the rice, cover the pan, and reduce the heat to low. Let the rice simmer until done, 15 to 20 minutes.

3. Meanwhile, cut the tomatoes and olives in half. Toast the pine nuts: Place them in a pie pan and bake them until they are golden brown, 5 to 6 minutes.

tip **Many commercial pesto sauces are quite delicious, but others are just so-so. I like the Alessi brand of pesto found in the pasta aisle of the super-market as well as the refrigerated pestos sold both at supermarkets and at wholesale clubs. If the pesto is thick and seems like it will be difficult to mix into the rice, thin it with a little warm water.**

4. Transfer the cooked rice to a shallow bowl and fluff it with a fork to separate the grains. Let cool 5 minutes.

5. Pour the pesto over the rice and stir to combine well. Fold in the tomato and olive halves. Transfer the salad to a serving platter and top it with the toasted pine nuts. Serve warm.

SERVES **6** AS A SIDE DISH

Julia's Simple Salad

—▾—

DINNER DOCTOR SAYS

I'll never forget having lunch with Julia Child in her kitchen when she lived in Cambridge, Massachusetts. She had just celebrated her eightieth birthday, and *The Atlanta Journal-Constitution* sent me north to roast chicken and toss a green salad with her. As you can imagine, the interview was peppered with Julia's usual wisdom, including advice on how to select the right chicken for roasting. Yet when Julia made the salad, her method was surprisingly simple. She sprinkled greens that had been rinsed and dried with kosher salt, then drizzled extra-virgin olive oil over them. The salt sticks to the dry lettuce leaves, she explained, and helps the olive oil adhere to them. Julia used no vinegar or lemon juice. The chicken was crisp and juicy, but it is that salad—on the table in mere minutes—that is particularly memorable.

SESAME PEANUT NOODLES

WITH SLIVERED CARROTS

▼ ▼ ▼

My family makes a meal of this salad in the summertime, when I might serve it with a slice or two of tomato from the garden and maybe a quick sauté of squash, alongside. And it carries well into the cooler months, when it can be paired with last night's pork roast or roast chicken from the deli. The add-ins are pretty much up to you, but do

TO PREP AND COOK:
12 MINUTES

take advantage of those pre-shredded carrots in the bag, for they make adding a vegetable to salads so very easy.

Salt (optional), for cooking the pasta
8 ounces linguine, broken in half
1 cup bottled red wine vinaigrette
2 tablespoons smooth peanut butter
    2 teaspoons Asian (dark) sesame oil
    2 teaspoons low-sodium soy sauce
2 teaspoons ketchup
½ cup pre-shredded carrots
½ cup chopped red bell pepper
2 scallions, both white and light green parts,
    chopped (for ¼ cup)

1. Bring a large pot of water to a boil over high heat. Add salt, if using, and stir in the linguine. Reduce the heat to medium-high and cook the linguine, uncovered, until al dente, 7 minutes.

tip **Experiment with seasoning the dressing by using more or less peanut butter and adding a grating of fresh ginger.**

2. Meanwhile, whisk together the vinaigrette, peanut butter, sesame oil, soy sauce, and ketchup or place them in a food processor and purée until smooth, 10 seconds. Set this dressing aside.

3. Drain the linguine well in a colander, shaking it a few times to remove any water that might still cling to the pasta. Transfer the linguine to a large serving bowl and pour the dressing over it. Stir to combine. Add the carrots, red bell pepper, and scallions. Stir until all of the ingredients are coated with dressing. Serve the salad at once or cover the bowl with plastic wrap and refrigerate it for up to 24 hours.

SERVES 4 AS A MAIN DISH,
6 AS A SIDE DISH

GAZPACHO COUSCOUS SALAD

▼ ▼ ▼

Couscous is one of the world's best convenience foods. You just let it soak in boiling-hot water for 5 minutes, and it's ready. While the couscous gets its beauty rest, chop the tomato, cucumber, and parsley. Serve this refreshing salad with grilled chicken, shrimp, beef, or lamb. (For more about couscous, see page 179.)

**TO PREP:
8 MINUTES**

½ teaspoon salt

1 tablespoon olive oil

1 package (10 ounces) plain couscous

1 large ripe tomato

1 medium-size cucumber, peeled

Several sprigs of fresh parsley or mint
    (for ¼ cup chopped)

¾ cup store-bought salsa

Juice of 1 lemon (about 2 tablespoons)

1. Place the salt and olive oil and 2 cups of water in a 2-quart saucepan over high heat. Bring to a boil, then stir in the couscous. Cover the pan and remove it from the heat. Let rest for 5 minutes.

2. Chop the tomato, cucumber, and parsley and combine them with the salsa and lemon juice in a small mixing bowl.

3. Transfer the couscous to a large mixing bowl and fluff it with a fork. Add the tomato and cucumber mixture and stir to combine. Serve at once or refrigerate it, uncovered, for up to 24 hours.

SERVES 8 AS A SIDE DISH

tip **For a heartier salad, top it with crumbled feta and black olives and serve it on a bed of lettuce.**

SUSAN'S PENNE AND TOMATO SALAD

▼ ▼ ▼

Here is a delicious, totable salad from my sister Susan. It is one of those recipes that's hard to put on paper because Susan doesn't usually work from a recipe, she just dumps, tosses, and adds a bit of this and a little of that. That's how pasta salads are usually constructed. But some days, who has time to think? So here is a real recipe. Feel free to doctor it, adding an ingredient or two to make it your own. Flake in a can of tuna or sprinkle on some pre-cooked shrimp, for example. Serve the salad with a nice fresh loaf of crusty bread.

TO PREP AND COOK:
15 MINUTES

Salt (optional), for cooking the pasta

1 pound penne

1 bag (6 ounces) spinach

1 pint grape tomatoes

½ cup bottled balsamic vinaigrette, or more if needed

1 package (4 ounces) pre-crumbled basil and tomato feta cheese

½ cup fresh basil slivers

tips I have found that the amount of vinaigrette the penne salad needs depends on the temperature of the pasta. If it is warm, you will need just ½ cup, but if you place the salad in the refrigerator to chill, you will need to add another ½ cup of dressing before serving it, just to moisten the ingredients.

I like to use Newman's Own balsamic vinaigrette in this salad.

1. Bring a large pot of water to a boil over high heat. Add salt, if using, and stir in the penne. Reduce the heat to medium-high and cook the penne uncovered, until al dente, 8 to 10 minutes.

2. Meanwhile, chop the spinach and cut the tomatoes in half.

3. Drain the penne well in a colander, shaking it a few times to remove any water that might still cling to the pasta. Transfer the penne to a serving bowl and pour the vinaigrette over it. Stir to combine. Fold in the chopped spinach, tomato halves, and feta cheese. Stir until all of the ingredients are coated with vinaigrette. Add more vinaigrette if needed to moisten the salad. Sprinkle the basil over the top of the salad and serve at once or cover the bowl with plastic wrap and refrigerate it for up to 24 hours.

SERVES 6 TO 8 AS A MAIN COURSE

ASIAN CHICKEN SALAD

▼ ▼ ▼

TO PREP AND COOK:
15 MINUTES

Here's another easy recipe from my sister Susan. This one was passed along to her by her friend Veronica Young, who lives in South Carolina. I have tweaked it a bit and now pass it along to you. Based on a bag of coleslaw mix, it's a simple salad to serve for company or to take along when you're traveling to a get-together. Ramen noodle soup adds both flavor and crunch. For additional crunch, the ramen noodles and sliced almonds are toasted briefly in the oven. To keep everything tasting crisp and fresh, don't dress the salad or add the noodles and nuts until just before serving.

tips **My sister makes a homemade dressing to go with this salad, whisking together ¾ cup of vegetable oil, 6 tablespoons of red wine vinegar, 4 to 5 tablespoons of sugar, ½ teaspoon of black pepper, and the seasoning packet from the ramen noodles. But when you are in a hurry, I think the incredibly easy dressing you get by mixing a store-bought red wine vinaigrette (I use Wish-Bone) and the packet of ramen noodle seasoning is pretty flavorful.**

Use leftover chicken, if you have it, or buy a roasted bird.

1 package (3 ounces) Oriental-flavor ramen
    noodle soup mix
½ cup pre-sliced almonds
¾ cup bottled red wine vinaigrette
    (see Tips at left)
1 package (16 ounces) coleslaw mix or
    broccoli slaw mix
2 cups shredded cooked chicken
    (see Tips at left)
½ cup fresh cilantro leaves
2 scallions, both white and light green parts,
    chopped (for ¼ cup)

1. Preheat the oven to 350°F.

2. Break up the ramen noodles with your hands and place them and the almonds on a rimmed baking sheet. Bake until the noodles and almonds turn light brown, 6 to 7 minutes.

3. Meanwhile, pour the red wine vinaigrette into a measuring cup and stir in the packet of seasoning from the ramen noodle soup mix. Set the salad dressing aside.

4. Place the slaw mix, chicken, cilantro, and scallions in a large

tip You could substitute dry-roasted peanuts for the almonds if you want a more Thai-flavored salad.

serving bowl. Toss to combine the ingredients well.

5. Just before serving, pour the salad dressing over the salad and toss to coat. Scatter the toasted almonds and noodles on top and serve.

SERVES **4** TO **6** AS A MAIN COURSE

SPINACH SALAD

WITH FRESH PEACHES, PECANS, AND POPCORN CHICKEN

▼ ▼ ▼

In the South and Midwest folks toss both fruit and green salads in a sweet and tangy dressing made with crunchy little poppy seeds. In this speedy salad, the dressing is perfect for bringing together spinach, peaches, nuts, and fried chicken. If you can't find poppy seed dressing, substitute a sweet-and-sour one or make your own by sweetening Italian dressing with honey and adding a sprinkling of poppy seeds. Serve this salad as a meal with Angel Biscuits (page 417) on the side.

TO PREP:
20 MINUTES
TO BAKE:
10–12 MINUTES

tip **Popcorn chicken pieces are bits of white chicken meat that have been breaded and fried. They're sold frozen. All you need to do is reheat them in a hot oven. I like to keep some on hand in the freezer, pop them in the oven, and then add them to salads like you might croutons.**

1 package (12 ounces) frozen popcorn chicken pieces
1 bag (6 ounces) spinach
1 cup fresh peach slices (from 2 peaches)
¼ cup thinly sliced red onion
2 tablespoons pre-chopped pecans
½ cup bottled poppy seed salad dressing

1. Preheat the oven to 450°F.

2. Place the popcorn chicken pieces on a baking sheet. Bake until the chicken is heated through and crisp, 10 to 12 minutes.

3. Meanwhile, place the spinach in a large serving bowl. Scatter the peach slices on top of the spinach. Add the onion. Scatter the pecans on top and add the reheated chicken pieces when they are ready.

4. Pour the dressing over the salad, toss gently, and serve.

SERVES 4 AS A MAIN COURSE

15 WAYS TO DOCTOR A CAESAR SALAD KIT

A typical Caesar salad kit contains chopped romaine lettuce, grated Parmesan cheese, croutons, and a creamy dressing. It will serve 3 or 4. Here are some ways to make the salad a bit more interesting.

1 Add canned anchovies and a poached egg to each serving of salad.

2 Bake frozen popcorn chicken and scatter it over the top of the salad while it's still hot.

3 Top each serving of the salad with a small slice of grilled salmon.

4 Surround the salad with halved cherry or grape tomatoes and top it with a mound of slivered fresh basil.

5 Marinate chicken slices in bottled Caesar dressing. Remove the chicken and discard the dressing. Grill the chicken, and pile onto salad that is dressed with the packet that comes with the kit.

6 Serve the salad with pre-cooked shrimp and slices of fresh mango.

7 Add grated lemon zest and a tablespoon of drained capers to the salad dressing.

8 Top the salad with roasted asparagus and store-bought roasted red pepper strips.

9 Grill raw shrimp that have been wrapped with prosciutto, then arrange them on top of the salad.

10 Pick over crabmeat, then add it to the salad along with pickled pepper strips and diced cucumbers.

11 Mix a tablespoon of store-bought olive tapenade or olive paste to the dressing.

12 Add a tablespoon of Dijon mustard to the dressing.

13 Fold a drained, flaked can of tuna into the salad and garnish the top with oil-marinated green olives.

14 Toss the salad with 3 cups of hot cooked penne and pass extra grated Parmesan cheese at the table.

15 Fold cubed avocado into the salad and season the dressing with a little chili powder and fresh lime juice.

TUSCAN TUNA AND WHITE BEAN SALAD

▼ ▼ ▼

O ne of my family's favorite last-minute pantry suppers is hot pasta combined with canned white beans and flaked tuna in an olive oil and lemon vinaigrette. Add fresh basil and a ripe tomato, and you have a hearty salad that needs only crusty bread, a chilled bottle of

TO PREP AND COOK:
10 MINUTES

white wine, and a cool breeze on the porch. When it's wintertime, the salad is just as comforting made with canned diced tomatoes and, in place of the basil, chopped scallions.

Salt (optional), for cooking the pasta

1 cup (4 ounces) pasta, such as penne, radiatori, or bow ties

¼ cup olive oil

Juice of 1 lemon (about 2 tablespoons)

¼ teaspoon black pepper

1 cup rinsed and drained canned Great Northern beans (see Tips)

½ cup chopped tomato

½ cup chopped fresh basil

1 can (6 ounces) tuna, drained and broken into chunks

tips **If you're a fan of white beans, use the entire 15.5-ounce can. When using canned beans in a salad, be sure to rinse them in a colander and let them drain well.**

   Turn this salad into an even more filling pasta supper by slicing 2 cloves of garlic and sautéing them in ¼ cup olive oil with 2 cups of zucchini. Spoon the sautéed zucchini on top of the pasta salad and shower it with pre-shredded Parmesan. Delicious!

1. Bring a large pot of water to a boil over high heat. Add salt, if using, and stir in the pasta. Reduce the heat to medium-high and cook the pasta, uncovered, until al dente, 8 to 10 minutes.

2. Meanwhile, place the olive oil, lemon juice, and black pepper in a large serving bowl and whisk to combine. Set the vinaigrette aside.

3. Drain the pasta well in a colander, shaking it a few times to remove any water that might still cling to it. Transfer the pasta to the bowl with the vinaigrette and stir until it is coated. Add the Great Northern beans, tomato, and basil. Add the tuna and stir until all of the ingredients are coated with vinaigrette. Serve at once.

SERVES 2 TO 4 AS A MAIN COURSE

THE MAIN DISH

▼▼▼

*I*t used to be you'd hit the main dish chapter in a cook-book and you'd think, okay, these are the main events. But nowadays, if your family is anything like mine, you're just as likely to find a main dish in the soup or salad chapter. Just add bread, and maybe some fruit or cheese, and dinner's on. So, why am I calling this chapter "The Main Dish," when so many of the other chapters include mains as well?

This chapter gives you fresh takes on reliable and speedy standbys. It will fuel your creativity when you need a new way of preparing boneless chicken breasts. It offers great recipes for beef

and shrimp. Perhaps you have a craving for pork but can't decide what to do with it. Or you run across some mouthwatering lamb chops in the market, and you'd like to serve them Saturday but just broiling them sounds too boring. Whether it's chicken, seafood, beef, pork, or lamb, I have focused here on fast-cooking cuts. In addition to those chicken breasts, you'll find chicken tenders, salmon fillets, crabmeat, ground beef, beef and pork tenderloins, and yes, lamb chops.

The goal here is to cook fast, cook fresh, cook with little fuss—and end up with great tasting meals. (If you're in the mood for a big-boy roast, page ahead to the "Hands-Off" chapter, starting on page 316, where you'll find a recipe for a beef pot roast you can place in the oven and let cook until it's meltingly tender in about three hours while you garden or ferry the kids to and fro.) The ingredients used here are very versatile. Combine a package of chicken tenders with soy sauce, sherry, scallions, and ginger to produce a velvety Chinese Chicken. Pair chicken tenders with prunes, olives, white wine, and brown sugar and you have a quick version of the Silver Palate's signature crowd-pleasing Chicken Marbella. Or dredge the tenders in seasoned bread crumbs, pan-fry them, then pour an easy lemon sauce over them and garnish them with capers for Chicken Piccata.

If seafood, not chicken, is on your mind, a couple of my favorites include the Oven-Roasted Salmon with Spinach and Coconut that tastes far more complicated than it is to make and yummy Sunday Lunch Salmon Cakes that use leftover baked or grilled salmon. Or think, too, about wrapping shrimp in prosciutto and serving them over lemon-flavored couscous. Or, you can cook shrimp with rice and tomatoes or turn them into a fast, Thai-inspired asparagus medley.

Where's the beef? My family loves the exotic flavors of Cuban-style *picadillo,* which begins with ground beef round. You can rely on the ease of Fast-Roasted Beef Tenderloin for celebrations, when you want a blockbuster entrée but don't want to spend all evening in the kitchen. And of course, there's the old favorite, meat loaf, or I should say meat loaves—making a batch of little ones cuts cooking time; Italian seasoning makes them tasty.

Take advantage of all these great dishes. Whether you're in the mood to dress up a deli chicken or spice up a pork tenderloin, these really are all main events.

CHINESE CHICKEN

▼ ▼ ▼

Doctor chicken tenders with a little sherry, soy sauce, garlic, and fresh ginger, to turn out a flavorful meal that's just right for midweek family suppers or weekend company dinners. The chicken

TO PREP:
5 MINUTES
TO COOK:
10–11 MINUTES

is delicious spooned over jasmine rice. For a fancier presentation, garnish it with a few spears of lightly steamed asparagus or a spoonful of frozen French-cut green beans that have been briefly steamed and tossed with toasted sliced almonds. For suggestions for quicker-cooking varieties of rice, see page 354.

¼ cup reduced-sodium soy sauce
      (see Tips)
3 tablespoons sherry (see Tips)
2 tablespoons cornstarch
2 teaspoons sugar
1 pound chicken tenders (about 12),
      rinsed and patted dry
1 tablespoon vegetable oil
4 scallions, both white and light green parts,
      sliced on the diagonal (for ½ cup)
2 tablespoons chopped peeled fresh ginger
      (see Tips)
2 cloves garlic, sliced

tips I like reduced-sodium soy sauce because it is just as flavorful as regular soy sauce and is better for you.

While I prefer a medium-dry sherry for cooking, this recipe works with just about any sherry except those overly sweet dessert sherries.

Fresh ginger and garlic are key components of this dish because they scent the cooking oil. Omit the ginger if you don't care for spicy foods. Fresh ginger keeps for up to three weeks, stored in the refrigerator drawer loosely wrapped in a paper towel in a plastic bag. If you want to keep it longer than this, place it in the freezer, and peel and slice it frozen.

1. Place the soy sauce, sherry, cornstarch, and sugar in a medium-size mixing bowl with ¼ cup of water and whisk until the cornstarch is dissolved. Stir in the chicken tenders and set the bowl aside.

2. Pour the oil into a large skillet and heat over medium heat. Add the scallions, ginger, and garlic and cook, stirring, until softened, 2 minutes. Drain the marinade from the chicken; do not discard the marinade. Add the chicken to the skillet and cook for 1 minute on each side. Pour the marinade over the chicken, reduce the heat to medium-low, and stir until the chicken is cooked through, and the sauce has thickened, 6 to 7 minutes. Serve at once.

SERVES 4

CHICKEN PICCATA

▼ ▼ ▼

Tiny chicken tenders are true to their name—tender. And they cook up fast. Doctor them with garlic, lemon juice, bread crumbs, and fresh parsley for a quick weekday *piccata* that's got a special weekend dinner feel to it. If you want to use boneless chicken breasts, use ones that have not been frozen (I find that breasts that have been frozen cook up tougher). Slicing the tenders into strips before sautéing them will make them cook even faster. Serve this classic but simple recipe with rice (see page 354 for some quicker-cooking varieties of rice) or risotto.

TO PREP:
8 MINUTES
TO COOK:
9–12 MINUTES

tip **One hamburger bun, split and toasted in a toaster oven, torn into pieces, then processed into crumbs in the food processor or blender will yield 1 cup of toasted crumbs. These will be softer and fresher tasting than bread crumbs out of a can.**

1 cup toasted bread crumbs
   (see Tip)
Salt and black pepper,
   to taste
1 clove garlic, crushed in
   a garlic press
1 pound chicken tenders
   (about 12), rinsed
   and patted dry
3 tablespoons vegetable oil
2 tablespoons butter
⅓ cup canned low-sodium
   chicken broth
2 tablespoons fresh lemon juice
¼ cup chopped fresh parsley
1 tablespoon drained capers

1. Place the bread crumbs in a shallow bowl. Season them with salt and pepper and add the garlic. (If you are making your own bread crumbs by pulsing a toasted bun in a food processor, just add the salt, pepper, and a whole clove of garlic to the processor along with the bun.) Dredge the chicken tenders in the bread crumb mixture and set them aside.

2. Place 2 tablespoons of the oil and 1 tablespoon of the butter in a large skillet and heat over medium-high heat. When the butter has melted, add half of the chicken tenders and cook until they are well browned and cooked through, 2 to 3 minutes per side. Transfer the cooked tenders to a platter. Add the remaining tablespoon each of oil and butter to the skillet and, when the butter has melted, add the remaining tenders and cook them until they are well browned and cooked through, 2 to 3 minutes per side. Transfer these tenders to the platter.

3. Add the chicken broth and lemon juice to the skillet. Scrape up the browned bits from the bottom of the skillet and cook until the juices reduce to a glaze, 1 to 2 minutes. Pour the hot glaze over the chicken tenders and garnish with the parsley and capers. Serve at once.

SERVES 4

MOCK CHICKEN MARBELLA

▼▼▼

It is a testament to *The Silver Palate Cookbook* that its Chicken Marbella is one of the most loved chicken dishes, and one that is frequently served at dinner parties and buffets. The unique combination of ingredients—prunes, green olives, garlic, bay leaves, white wine, and brown sugar—creates one of the most alluring sauces for chicken. I have longed for a way to streamline the recipe so that the flavors are the same but the preparation time is shorter. Here it is, using boneless chicken tenders that cook quickly and green olives that require no chopping. The chicken is good with rice or couscous. You'll find pointers on rice on page 354. For more about couscous see page 179.

½ cup bottled balsamic or red wine vinaigrette

¼ cup store-bought olive salad (see Tip at right)

2 cloves garlic, crushed in a garlic press

1 teaspoon dried oregano

3 bay leaves

½ cup pitted prunes

1¼ pounds chicken tenders (about 16), rinsed and patted dry

¼ cup firmly packed light brown sugar

¼ cup dry white wine

tip If you have the willpower to endure the heady aroma of the chicken baking and can chill it for serving the next day, you will have a superb cold buffet dish for summertime. This recipe can also be baked ahead and frozen (it will keep for up to 2 weeks). But I cannot hold back, and I begin steaming rice as soon as I smell the garlic, wine, and brown sugar coming together.

1. Place a rack in the center of the oven and preheat the oven to 400°F.

2. Place the balsamic vinaigrette, olive salad, garlic, oregano, bay leaves, and

> **tip** Olive salad is made from chopped olives mixed with capers and sometimes pickled vegetables, along with herbs and spices. In some parts of the country it's called tapenade. If you cannot find olive salad, place ¼ cup pitted pimiento-stuffed green olives in the food processor with 1 tablespoon of drained capers and process them until fairly smooth. You will need ¼ cup of this mixture to make Mock Chicken Marbella.

prunes in a large mixing bowl and stir to combine. Fold in the chicken tenders. Transfer the mixture to a 13-by-9-inch (3-quart) glass or ceramic baking dish and arrange the tenders so they are in one layer. Sprinkle the brown sugar over the tenders and pour the wine around them.

3. Bake the chicken until the juices bubble and the chicken has caramelized on top, 25 to 30 minutes. Remove and discard the bay leaves. Serve the chicken warm or chill it and serve it cold.

SERVES **6**

CURRIED CHICKEN AND APPLE STEW

OVER BASMATI RICE

▼ ▼ ▼

I love those canned curry sauces made by Patak's, for with a little doctoring they take the work out of cooking Indian food. Add chicken and some onion, apple, and sliced almonds, and a fragrant, exotic dinner is on the table in less then 30 minutes. And by the way, my children adore this dish, probably because the apple and coconut sauce make it sweet. I like to serve the curry with the aromatic long-grain rice known as basmati. If you cannot locate it in your super-market, try a health food store or Indian

TO PREP:
10 MINUTES
TO COOK:
9–12 MINUTES

market. Not only is the rice delicious, but it cooks in just 15 minutes! (For more about rice, see page 354.) If you are looking for a vegetable, steamed fresh or frozen spinach makes a perfect side dish.

2 tablespoons vegetable oil

1 medium-size onion, sliced (for about 1 cup)

1 pound chicken tenders (about 12),
rinsed, cut into pieces, and patted dry

1 can (10 ounces) Indian coconut
cooking sauce (korma; see Tips)

1 cup diced peeled apple

1 cinnamon stick

1 tablespoon heavy (whipping) cream (optional)

2 tablespoons toasted pre-sliced almonds
(optional; see Tips)

Sweetened flaked coconut, for garnish
(optional)

Pour the oil into a large skillet and heat over medium heat. Add the onion and cook, stirring, until it browns slightly, 2 to 3 minutes. Add the chicken pieces and cook until they also brown slightly all over, 3 to 4 minutes. Add the coconut sauce, apple, cinnamon stick, and ¼ cup of water. Let simmer, uncovered, until the chicken cooks through, 2 to 3 minutes. Add the cream, if using, increase the heat to medium-high, and cook until the liquid thickens a bit, 2 minutes longer. Remove and discard the cinnamon stick. Serve the stew garnished with the almonds and flaked coconut, if desired.

SERVES 4

tips **Korma is a north Indian cooking sauce. Patak's is made with coconut and flavored with garlic, ginger, and coriander. I find Patak's brand of Indian sauces and curry pastes in my supermarkets here in Nashville. I hope you can locate them in your area.**

The curry is delicious on its own, but it is even more intriguing when you add garnishes like toasted almonds. Toast almonds in a preheated 350°F toaster oven until they start to take on color, 3 to 4 minutes. You can also top the curry with fresh cilantro sprigs, sweetened flaked coconut, and/or mango chutney.

15 WAYS TO DOCTOR A DELI ROAST CHICKEN

Store-roasted chickens are dinnertime lifesavers. Delicious to begin with, they are the jumping-off point for several of the dishes in this chapter. In addition to the complete recipes you'll find in this and other chapters in this book, here are fifteen really quick tricks for dressing up these chickens (for information on storing, see the box on page 181). Let the tips inspire you—the list could probably have run to 15,000!

1 Shred or chunk the chicken while it's warm, place it on top of a bowl of hot pasta (strands or short tubes), and add a dollop of pesto or black-olive paste.

2 Slice the chicken and pile in onto slices of bread, then put some Swiss cheese on top. Pass the sandwiches under the broiler and serve them with avocado slices and a spicy mayonnaise.

3 For delicous hot open-faced sandwiches, place slices of warm chicken on toast, add slices of crisp bacon and ripe tomato, then blanket everything with your favorite cheese sauce.

4 Serve the chicken warm on toasted bread or a bed of cooked spinach with a fruit chutney or your favorite salsa.

5 Shred the chicken and scatter it over a Caesar salad. Or any favorite salad mix, for that matter—green, garden, or pasta.

6 Top sliced chicken with mushrooms that have been sautéed in olive oil with a bit of dry sherry or dry white wine.

7 Shred the meat, layer it onto warmed flour tortillas along with black beans, pre-shredded cheese, and your favorite salsa, then roll the tortillas up. If you have a ripe avocado, add slices to the filling.

8 Spread Dijon mustard all over the chicken, sprinkle it with black pepper, then shower it with chopped fresh tarragon and bake it in a 350°F oven until warmed through.

9 Save the juices from the deli packaging to make gravy. Whisk 2 tablespoons of flour into ½ cup of cold milk in a medium-size saucepan. Whisk in the chicken juices and cook over medium heat, stirring, until bubbling, thickened, and smooth. Season the gravy with salt and black pepper, then spoon it over sliced chicken and mashed potatoes. Delicious, too, over chicken for a hot open-faced sandwich.

10 Chop the chicken into bite-size pieces and toss these with pre-chopped pecans, seedless green grapes you have cut in half, a little minced onion, fresh tarragon, and enough mayonnaise to pull the salad together. Season with salt and serve with sliced ripe red tomatoes.

11 Spread the chicken salad from No. 10 out on flour tortillas, then roll up the tortillas, slice them into pinwheels, and serve with your favorite salsa. These make wonderful company appetizers.

12 Chop the chicken, heat it along with your favorite canned curry sauce, and serve on top of basmati rice.

13 Spread a little bit of mayonnaise on slices of sourdough bread. Layer slices of chicken, followed by slices of jellied cranberry sauce, and slices of sharp Cheddar cheese on top. Top with a second slice of bread, then brush the sandwiches with olive oil. Grill or broil until the cheese melts and the bread is golden brown on both sides.

14 Place chicken slices on top of split squares of hot corn bread. Boil the juices from the deli packaging and spoon them over all.

15 Serve sliced chicken cold with a quick *gribiche* sauce made by adding chopped sour pickles, capers, parsley, and minced hard-cooked egg to your favorite salad vinaigrette.

CAESAR GRILLED CHICKEN

▼ ▼ ▼

There are only two ingredients in Caesar Grilled Chicken, and yet it tastes like a million bucks. I am a bit embarrassed to divulge its secret because it's so easy to prepare and because I have served it to many people who thought I'd gone to a lot of trouble cooking. First the chicken marinates in Caesar salad dressing. Then, just before dinnertime, or an hour or so ahead if you want to serve the chicken at room temperature, you fire up the grill. I've topped the chicken with fresh fruit salsa in the summer and with a warm chunky tomato sauce when the weather is cool. Moist and flavorful, the chicken is delicious with a salad, pasta, or vegetables from the garden.

TO PREP:
2 MINUTES
TO MARINATE:
AT LEAST 4 HOURS
TO COOK:
10–12 MINUTES

4 skinless, boneless chicken
    breast halves (about 1 pound),
    rinsed and patted dry
1 cup Caesar salad dressing
    (see Tips at right)

1. Place the chicken breasts between 2 sheets of waxed paper on a work surface and pound

tip Pounding the chicken breasts to an even ½-inch thickness makes them cook more evenly and faster. Plus, the thinner breasts are easy to cut into strips for serving. If you have any left over, you can add them to salads or pack them into lunch boxes the next day. In fact, you may want to make extra to have on hand for dishes like the One-Bowl Chicken Souvlaki on page 182. Just figure on an additional ¼ cup dressing for each ¼ pound of chicken.

them to a ½-inch thickness with a meat pounder or the bottom of a heavy skillet. Place the pounded chicken breasts in a glass or ceramic baking dish or mixing bowl and pour the dressing over them, turning them to coat on both sides. Cover the baking dish or bowl with plastic wrap and place the chicken in the refrigerator to marinate for at least 4 hours or as long as 24 hours.

2. Heat the grill to medium-high. Remove the chicken from the baking dish and shake off some of the excess marinade. Place the chicken on the hot grill, searing the first side for 2 minutes. Turn the chicken over and sear the second side for 2 minutes. Reduce the heat to low (see Tip), cover the grill, and cook the chicken until the juices run clear when a breast is

tips I'm partial to Newman's Own Caesar salad dressing. Of course, you can use whatever brand you favor or just about any kind of salad dressing instead of the Caesar, but it will not have the salty, cheesy, zesty flavor you get from a Caesar dressing.

If you're cooking on a charcoal grill, pile the lit coals on one side and leave the other side bare. Sear the breasts over the coals, then move them to the coal-free zone to finish cooking with the grill covered.

pricked with the tip of a sharp knife, 6 to 8 minutes. Cut each breast crosswise into ½-inch slices and serve.

SERVES 4

GRILLED CHICKEN TANDOORI

WITH RAITA

▼ ▼ ▼

TO PREP:
5 MINUTES
TO MARINATE:
AT LEAST 1 HOUR
TO COOK:
10–12 MINUTES

Recipe purists may argue that tandoori chicken isn't grilled and that you must have a tandoori oven to achieve true Indian-style spicy, dry tandoori chicken. But if you use a bit of culinary license here, you can apply spicy tandoori seasonings (from a jar!) to chicken breasts, then grill them to save time (heat the grill as the breasts marinate). The same yogurt and cucumber *raita* that accompanies tandoori chicken in an Indian restaurant comes into play here, too. It's easily made by doctoring plain yogurt.

tips   Tandoori paste is a flavorful mixture of ground ginger, tamarind, coriander, cumin, and garlic. Patak's makes a good one. If you can't find tandoori paste, use 2 tablespoons of hot curry paste and a cup of plain yogurt as a marinade instead.

Instead of grilling the chicken breasts, you can also bake them, uncovered, in a 375°F oven until cooked through, 25 to 30 minutes.

4 skinless, boneless chicken breast halves
    (1 pound), rinsed and patted dry
1½ cups plain low-fat yogurt
½ cup tandoori paste (see Tips)
½ cup chopped peeled cucumber
¼ cup finely chopped onion
2 tablespoons chopped fresh mint
    (optional)
Salt and black pepper
Cilantro sprigs, for garnish
Mango chutney and pita bread,
    for serving

1. Place the chicken breast halves between 2 sheets of waxed paper on a work surface and pound them to a ½-inch thickness with a meat pounder or the bottom of a heavy skillet. Score them gently with a knife in several places. Place the chicken in a 1 gallon resealable plastic bag with ½ cup of the yogurt and the tandoori paste. Seal the bag, then massage it with your fingertips so that the yogurt and tandoori paste combine and the chicken is well coated. Place the bag in the refrigerator and let the chicken marinate for at least 1 hour or as long as 24 hours.

2. Meanwhile, place the remaining 1 cup of yogurt and the cucumber, onion, and the mint, if using, in a small glass bowl. Stir to combine and season with salt and pepper to taste. Cover the bowl with plastic wrap and refrigerate the *raita* until serving time. It will keep for up to 24 hours.

3. Heat the grill to medium-high, remove the chicken from the bag and shake off some of the excess marinade. Place the chicken on the hot grill, searing the first side for 2 minutes. Turn the chicken over and sear the second side for 2 minutes. Reduce the heat to low (see Tip, page 173), cover the grill, and cook the chicken until the juices run clear when a breast is pricked with the tip of a sharp knife, 6 to 8 minutes.

4. Slice the chicken into strips and garnish it with cilantro sprigs. Serve the chicken with the *raita*, mango chutney, and pita bread.

SERVES 4

SAUTÉED CHICKEN PAILLARDS

WITH CRANBERRY-ORANGE SALSA AND BLUE CHEESE GRITS

▼ ▼ ▼

TO PREP:
10 MINUTES
TO COOK:
10 MINUTES

Oh, this recipe might sound a bit fancy since it does have the interesting flavor combinations you would expect in a trendy restaurant, but I promise it truly is a cinch to assemble. Cranberry sauce, cinnamon, and mandarin oranges take a spin in the food processor to make a tasty salsa. Quick-cooking grits are delicious seasoned with butter, crumbled blue cheese, and black pepper. And chicken paillards (breasts that have been pounded to make them thinner) sauté in less than five minutes. It's a cinch to put together, but no one needs to know that but you.

tips You can use either a Creole seasoning salt or Lawry's seasoned salt. The Creole seasoning salt is a bit spicier.

To serve the chicken with polenta instead of grits, cut a roll of pre-cooked polenta into slices and cook them in milk, mashing the slices into the milk until the mixture is creamy. Then add the blue cheese and butter.

If you'd rather grill the pounded chicken, feel free. It will take 3 to 4 minutes per side.

CRANBERRY-ORANGE SALSA

1 can (16 ounces) whole-berry cranberry
    sauce
1 can (11 ounces) mandarin orange sections,
    drained
Pinch of ground cinnamon

BLUE CHEESE GRITS

1 can (14 to 14.5 ounces) low-sodium
    chicken broth
¼ cup milk
½ cup quick (not instant) grits
½ cup pre-crumbled blue cheese
1 tablespoon butter
Black pepper

CHICKEN PAILLARDS

4 skinless, boneless chicken breast halves
    (1 pound), rinsed and patted dry
½ teaspoon seasoned salt (see Tips) or
    table salt
2 tablespoons vegetable oil
2 tablespoons butter
2 tablespoons dry white wine

1. Place the cranberry sauce, mandarin oranges, and cinnamon in a food processor or blender and pulse until well combined, 30 seconds. Set the salsa aside.

2. Make the blue cheese grits: Pour the chicken broth and milk into a 2-quart saucepan and heat over medium-high heat. When they come to a boil, stir in the grits, reduce the heat to low, and let simmer, stirring occasionally, until the grits thicken, 5 minutes. Remove the pan from the heat, and stir in the blue cheese and butter. Season with pepper to taste. Cover the pan and set aside.

3. Make the chicken paillards: Place the chicken breast halves between 2 sheets of waxed paper on a work surface and pound them to a ⅓-inch thickness with a meat pounder or the bottom of a heavy skillet. Season on both sides with the salt.

4. Place the oil and the butter in a large skillet over medium-high heat. When the butter has just melted, add the pounded chicken and cook until lightly browned, 2 minutes. Turn the chicken over and cook the second side for 1 minute. Add the wine, cover the skillet, reduce the heat to medium-low, and let the chicken simmer until cooked through, 2 to 3 minutes longer.

5. To serve, spoon the grits onto plates. Place a paillard next to the grits and garnish it with the salsa.

SERVES 4

ROTISSERIE CHICKEN

WITH FIRE AND ICE SALSA

▼ ▼ ▼

One of the greatest additions to supermarkets in the past few years is the rotisserie, providing customers with a bounty of roast chickens, ready to be taken home warm and crisp-skinned to the dinner table. I cannot tell you how many times one of these perfectly roasted birds has saved me. I just add a salad, a vegetable, some bread, and I have a healthy, substantial meal every-

**TO PREP:
7–8 MINUTES**

one loves. Here's a way to doctor one of those birds in the summertime by making a quick fire and ice salsa (so named because the jalapeño provides the fire and the sweet watermelon and strawberries are the cooling ice). Add pasta, rice salad, or Garlicky Cheese Grits Casserole (see page 265), and dinner's ready.

1 cup chopped seeded watermelon

1 cup chopped strawberries

¼ cup finely chopped red onion

*2 tablespoons finely chopped
    jalapeño pepper*

2 tablespoons chopped fresh mint

2 tablespoons olive oil

1 tablespoon fresh lime juice

*1 teaspoon sugar
    (optional)*

*1 store-bought
    rotisserie chicken
    (3 to 4 pounds)*

tips   **Vary the salsa by adding yellow watermelon, if you can find it, and mango instead of the strawberries.**

Most rotisserie chickens feed four people. If there are young children at your table, a bird will stretch and feed six.

Remember to save the carcass to make a quick chicken broth. See page 181 for instructions.

1. Place the watermelon, strawberries, onion, jalapeño, and mint in a medium-size glass bowl. Stir to combine. Pour the olive oil and lime juice over the salsa and sprinkle the sugar, if using, on top. Stir gently to combine. Cover the bowl with plastic wrap and refrigerate until serving time. The salsa can be made up to 1 day in advance.

2. Slice the chicken into serving pieces and spoon some salsa alongside. Serve more salsa at the table.

SERVES 4

Couscous

—▼—

DINNER DOCTOR SAYS

Pronounced koose-koose, this tiny pasta grain is the frantic cook's best friend, for it cooks simply by sitting for five minutes in liquid that has been brought to a boil. Yes, in five minutes! I have never tasted a food that "cooks" so deliciously just by doing nothing. You select the liquid—water, broth, coconut milk—then, once it's boiling, add the couscous and some seasonings, cover the pot, and that's it. Couscous originated in Morocco, Tunisia, and Algeria. It was first made by mixing wheat flour with water, running that through a sieve, and then steaming the tiny pieces that formed. Nowadays couscous comes pre-cooked, dried, and sifted and has a texture similar to dried pasta.

Couscous expands to roughly twice its original size after "cooking." I prefer to use plain couscous and season it myself, but there are all kinds of couscous out there, flavored with cheese, garlic, or pine nuts, to name a few. Couscous is a natural with roast chicken or grilled fish, and it is a perfect partner for lamb stew or grilled chops. Like pasta, it will keep on your pantry shelf for up to a year, although I doubt it will be around that long.

TUSCAN CHICKEN, ZUCCHINI, AND WHITE BEAN RAGOÛT

▼ ▼ ▼

A deli-roasted chicken is the lifeline to dozens of quick, tasty dinners, and this one is a favorite around my house. With white beans, fresh zucchini, a handful of crunchy chopped onion, and a healthy dose of garlic, the ragoût makes a delicious main dish that can be on the table in less than 20 minutes. That little bit of cream isn't necessary, but it does give the dish an extra-smooth finish. Serve the Tuscan chicken on a cold, rainy night in deep bowls with crusty bread and topped with lots of shredded Parmesan cheese.

TO PREP:
10 MINUTES
TO COOK:
7–8 MINUTES

2 tablespoons olive oil

½ cup chopped onion

2 cloves garlic, sliced

2 cups shredded roast chicken

2 cups zucchini, cut into 1-inch pieces
  (from 2 medium-size zucchini)

1 can (15 to 16 ounces) white beans,
  drained (see Tips)

1 tablespoon heavy (whipping)
  cream (optional)

½ teaspoon dried thyme, or
  1 tablespoon chopped
  fresh thyme

Salt and black pepper

½ cup pre-shredded Parmesan
  cheese (optional)

tips **You can use any kind of beans that you prefer. Choose from small white beans, navy beans, cannellini, or Great Northern beans.**

If you'd like the consistency of the Tuscan chicken to be more like a soup, add a cup of chicken broth (canned is fine) along with the white beans.

Roast Chicken Tips

—▼—

DINNER DOCTOR SAYS

Roast chickens are handy and delicious, but keep in mind:

♦ They will not keep for days on end in the refrigerator. Use them or freeze them within two days.

♦ Once you slice off meat for one meal, remove any leftover meat from the carcass and bag it for a second meal. Or, freeze the chicken; wrapped well it will keep for up to three months.

♦ Use the carcass to make a quick broth. Toss it into a pot, cover it with water, and simmer it for 45 minutes, then discard the carcass. If you freeze broth in one-cup containers, it will keep for up to two months.

1. Pour the olive oil into a 2-quart saucepan and heat over medium heat. Add the onion and garlic and cook, stirring, until softened but not brown, 2 minutes.

2. Add the chicken and the zucchini and continue to cook, stirring, until the zucchini softens, 3 to 4 minutes. Add the beans, cream, if using, and thyme. Season the ragoût with salt and pepper to taste. Continue cooking until the beans are heated through and the flavors are combined, 2 minutes longer.

3. Spoon the ragoût into serving bowls and serve the Parmesan cheese, if using, on the side.

SERVES 4 TO 6

ONE-BOWL CHICKEN SOUVLAKI

▼ ▼ ▼

For potluck suppers or for feeding the family, this Greek-style dish is welcome and quick to toss in the bowl. It's perfect in the summertime when tomatoes are in season and cucumbers grow freely and fast in the garden. But I like it so much I make it with sweet grape or cherry tomatoes year-round. It's great for using up leftover grilled chicken.

TO PREP:
12 MINUTES

4 cups cubed or shredded
    cooked chicken

2 large cucumbers, peeled, seeded,
    and cut into ½-inch cubes
    (about 3 cups)

2 scallions, both white and
    light green parts, chopped
    (for ¼ cup)

8 pitted kalamata olives

2 cups (1 pint) grape tomatoes, halved,
    or 2 large ripe tomatoes, chopped

½ cup plain low-fat yogurt

½ cup pre-crumbled feta cheese (see Tips)

Black pepper

¼ cup chopped fresh parsley or mint

Wedges of pita bread, for serving

tips An easy way to vary the flavor here is to use one of the seasoned feta cheeses, such as feta with basil and sun-dried tomato.

To make pita toasts, cut whole pitas into wedges, brush them with olive oil, and sprinkle them with a little coarse salt. Bake at 400°F until crisp, 5 minutes.

Place the chicken, cucumbers, scallions, olives, and tomatoes in a large serving bowl. Stir to combine. Place the yogurt and feta in a small bowl and whisk together or, if you want a creamier dressing, place them in a food processor or blender and purée until smooth, 30 seconds. Pour the yogurt dressing over the chicken mixture and stir just to coat. Sprinkle pepper and the parsley on top, then serve with wedges of pita bread.

SERVES 6

Spring Supper in the Park

▼ ▼ ▼

A beautiful, warm, long spring evening when the daffodils are in bloom and the trees have just leafed out, calls for an easy-to-tote outdoor picnic.

Smoked Salmon Spread
page 30

One-Bowl Chicken Souvlaki
this page

Crusty bread

Fresh fruit

Butterscotch Pecan Saucepan Blondies
page 518

MICRO-STEAMED HOISIN FISH AND VEGETABLES

▼ ▼ ▼

In my kitchen the microwave oven is most often used for reheating leftovers, but I'll admit that when it comes to steaming fish and veggies the microwave is fast and there's only one bowl to clean, too! You can use this recipe to prepare whatever fish you find fresh in your market. Look for nice fillets that are about 1½ inches thick.

It couldn't be easier to put this dish together. You slice the fish into strips, toss the vegetables on top, and drizzle a hoisin sauce doctored with soy sauce and rice vinegar over everything. Jasmine rice is a nice accompaniment to the fish and vegetables. (For more on rice, see page 354.)

TO PREP:
10 MINUTES
TO COOK:
6 MINUTES

You'll need 4 cups cooked rice to go along with this dish.

1 pound salmon, grouper, or other fish fillets,
    1½ inches thick
1 package (8 ounces) fresh sugar
    snap peas
1 package (3.2 ounces; 1 cup)
    sliced shiitake mushrooms,
    wiped clean and stems removed
1 tablespoon sliced peeled fresh ginger
½ cup pre-shredded carrots
4 scallions, both white and light green parts,
    thinly sliced (for ½ cup)
3 tablespoons hoisin sauce
    1 tablespoon reduced-sodium
        soy sauce
    1 tablespoon rice vinegar

1. Cut the fish into 1-inch wide strips and place these in a 2-quart microwave-safe dish. Scatter the sugar snap peas, mushrooms, ginger, carrots, and scallions evenly over the fish.

2. Pour the hoisin sauce, soy sauce, and vinegar into a small bowl and stir until well combined. Drizzle this mixture over the fish and vegetables. Cover the dish with plastic wrap, folding back one corner to allow the steam to escape.

3. Place the dish in the microwave oven and cook on high power until the fish is cooked through and the vegetables are crisp-tender, 6 minutes. Stop every 2 minutes to gently stir and reposition the fish so that the outside pieces are moved to the inside. Spoon the fish and vegetables onto plates and serve.

SERVES 4

tip **Microwave ovens vary in power, so use the timing here as a guide. You may need to add another minute for the fish and vegetables to cook through.**

15 WAYS TO DOCTOR A CAN OF TUNA

There's no end to the doctoring you can do to canned tuna, the busy cook's best friend. Figure on a 6-ounce can feeding two people—or more, depending on how far you stretch it with other ingredients. I prefer albacore tuna packed in water.

1 Combine tuna with a drained can of cannellini beans; chopped onion, celery, and fresh parsley; olive oil; and fresh lemon juice. Serve it with crusty bread.

2 Flake the tuna with a little olive oil to make it moist. Serve it over salad greens with steamed green beans, hard-cooked egg, anchovies, and an oil and vinegar dressing.

3 Make a fast tuna spread by puréeing the tuna with black olives, salt, pepper, and an oil and vinegar dressing.

4 Add chopped hard-cooked egg and fresh tarragon to tuna, using mayonnaise to bind it.

5 Fold sweet or dill pickle relish into tuna, add a dab of mayonnaise, and serve it on sturdy white bread.

6 Add a squeeze of fresh lemon juice—my mother's surefire trick for freshening up canned tuna.

7 Add a handful of any chopped fresh herb—basil or chervil, for example—and enough mayonnaise to make the tuna moist.

8 Turn leftover tuna salad into an easy tuna melt by spooning it onto slices of bread and topping it with shredded cheese. Broil until bubbling.

9 Put the tuna on slices of bread and top it with roasted red bell pepper strips. For a stupendous tuna melt, blanket everything with Monterey Jack cheese before broiling.

10 Add olives—any olives, such as stuffed green olives, chopped kalamata, or oil-cured French olives.

11 Mix in diced pickled jalapeño peppers and a dollop of mayonnaise. Sprinkle the tuna with a little cumin before serving.

12 Stir chunks of mango, mayonnaise, and a squeeze of fresh lemon or lime juice into the tuna.

13 Heat marinara sauce in a medium-size saucepan, stir in tuna, then serve it on top of pasta with drained capers.

14 Add chopped water chestnuts or diced jicama to tuna for maximum crunch. Use mayonnaise to moisten it.

15 Blend drained tuna with a little softened cream cheese, fresh lemon juice, and chopped scallions for an easy sandwich spread.

OVEN-ROASTED SALMON

WITH SPINACH AND COCONUT

▼ ▼ ▼

TO PREP:
15 MINUTES
TO BAKE:
9–12 MINUTES

What a wonderfully versatile fish salmon is. You can grill it with nothing more than soy sauce and slices of garlic and ginger. You can mix it with mashed potatoes and make salmon cakes (see page 189 for a recipe). Or you can pan roast it, as in this yummy recipe, which pairs salmon fillets with baby spinach leaves (pre-washed, of course, so there's no need to rinse) and coconut. The pan juices are so delicious you won't want to waste a spoonful—serve the salmon and spinach on top of steamed jasmine rice to sop up all the liquid. Savor it all with chopsticks and a spoon! (For tips on quicker-cooking rice see page 354.)

tips The coconut is essential to the flavor of this dish, so don't omit it. If you prefer a very intense coconut flavor, use coconut milk instead of cream.

For a lighter touch, use chicken broth rather than cream, and add 1 teaspoon of freshly grated lemon zest.

1 tablespoon olive oil

2 pounds salmon fillets, cut into 6 pieces
    (5 to 6 ounces each)

½ teaspoon seasoned salt

1 bag (5 ounces) baby spinach

¼ cup heavy (whipping) cream (see Tips)

2 to 3 tablespoons sweetened
    flaked coconut

1. Place a rack in the center of the oven and preheat the oven to 400°F.

2. Pour the olive oil into a large oven-proof skillet and heat it over medium-high heat. Season the salmon pieces with the seasoned salt on both sides. When the olive oil is hot, add the salmon and cook it until lightly browned, 1 to 2 minutes per side. Remove the salmon from the skillet and set it aside.

3. Add the spinach to the pan juices in the skillet. Pour the cream over the spinach and sprinkle the coconut on top. Place the salmon pieces back in the skillet on top of the spinach and place the skillet in the oven. Bake the salmon until it is opaque and the juices are bubbling, 7 to 8 minutes. Serve at once.

SERVES 6

Tuna Burgers

— ▼ —

DINNER DOCTOR SAYS

My mom used to turn tuna salad into tuna burgers in minutes. Unlike the grilled ahi tuna burgers that are now served at trendy restaurants, her tuna burgers resembled tuna melts. She would season canned tuna with chopped green olives, minced onion, black pepper, and shredded Cheddar cheese and add only enough mayonnaise to hold the mixture together. Then she would form patties and bake these on an aluminum foil-lined baking sheet in a toaster oven at 350°F until the patties were heated through, 8 to 10 minutes. Served on toasted English muffins with a slice of ripe tomato, those tuna burgers were heavenly when I was a girl, and they still are.

SUNDAY LUNCH SALMON CAKES

▼ ▼ ▼

If you're lucky enough to have about a half a pound of leftover cooked salmon on hand, you can put these salmon cakes together in less than 20 minutes. Fresh parsley, scallion, and Worcestershire sauce all add flavor to the crisp cakes. And if you have a cup of mashed potatoes left over, too, so much the better—mashed potatoes help bind the cakes. But don't worry if you don't; you'll find instructions for whipping mashed potatoes up quickly in the Tip below.

TO PREP:
8 MINUTES
TO COOK:
8 MINUTES

1 cup leftover mashed potatoes (see Tip)

1 large egg

¼ cup chopped fresh parsley

1 scallion, both white and light green parts, chopped

1 teaspoon Worcestershire sauce

Salt and black pepper, to taste

2 cups (8 ounces) flaked leftover baked or grilled salmon

4 to 5 slices of sturdy white bread

3 tablespoons vegetable oil, for frying

Lemon wedges, for serving

1. Place the mashed potatoes, egg, parsley, scallion, Worcestershire sauce, salt, and

tip To make 1 cup of mashed potatoes from frozen ones, heat ⅔ of a cup of milk in a saucepan until it steams, and then fold in 1⅓ cups of frozen potatoes. Cook, stirring, over medium heat until the potatoes are soft and creamy, 3 to 4 minutes. These aren't as nice as homemade mashed potatoes, but they are a whole lot better than those made from a box of potato flakes.

pepper in a large mixing bowl. Stir to distribute the egg well throughout the mixture. Fold in the salmon and stir only enough to bring the ingredients together. Place the bowl, uncovered, in the refrigerator while you prepare the bread crumbs.

2. If the bread slices are dry, crumble enough bread between your fingers to make 2 cups of crumbs. If the bread is fresh, briefly toast it, tear the toast in pieces, process them in a food processor until crumbly, then measure out 2 cups. Set the crumbs aside in a shallow bowl.

3. Place the oil in a large skillet and heat over medium-high heat. While the oil is heating, take a large spoonful of the salmon and gently pat it into a cake about 1 to 1½ inches thick. Press both sides of the cake into the bread crumbs. When the oil is hot, gently slide the cake into the pan. Repeat this with the remaining salmon mixture, making 8 cakes in all and frying no more than 4 at a time. Fry the cakes until deep brown on one side, 2 minutes. Turn the cakes with a metal spatula and fry on the other side until deep brown, 2 minutes longer. Transfer the salmon cakes to paper towels to drain.

4. To serve, place the salmon cakes on plates and garnish them with lemon wedges. Serve at once.

SERVES 4 TO 6

JUMBO CRAB CAKES

WITH SPICY MAYONNAISE

▼ ▼ ▼

The secret ingredient in these crab cakes and their sauce is a simple one—mayonnaise. Not only does mayonnaise add richness and flavor to the cakes, mix it with Creole mustard and hot pepper sauce and you have a quick sauce. A full cup of fresh parsley adds texture and a fresh flavor, so don't scrimp. Also, buy the best blue crabmeat you can find. Because these crab cakes are so deliciously rich, I often serve them on a bed of salad greens.

TO PREP:
10 MINUTES
TO COOK:
2–3 MINUTES

2 slices of sturdy white bread,
    torn into pieces
1 cup fresh parsley leaves
4 scallions, both white and light green parts,
    chopped (for ½ cup)
⅓ cup plus 2 tablespoons
    mayonnaise (see Tips)
3 teaspoons Creole mustard
1 teaspoon Worcestershire sauce
1 large egg
1 pound lump crabmeat (see Tips)
1 cup vegetable oil, for frying
Hot pepper sauce
Lemon wedges, for serving

tips I like Hellmann's mayonnaise for cooking as well as for spreading on sandwiches.

When buying crab, you will obviously get better quality crab at a lower price if you live near the Atlantic shore. Blue crab is the best crab for making crab cakes. But fear not if you are landlocked, as I am in Nashville. (We don't even have a large fish market as many cities do.) I buy blue crab at a wholesale club like Costco, where it is sold in 16-ounce cans.

1. Place the bread, parsley, and scallions in a food processor or blender and process until the mixture is fine, 30 seconds. Add 2 tablespoons of the mayonnaise, 1 teaspoon of the mustard, and the Worcestershire sauce and egg and process just until combined, 10 seconds more. Transfer this mixture to a bowl.

2. Pick over the crabmeat, then separate it carefully with a fork. Gently fold it into the parsley and mayonnaise mixture. Divide the crab mixture into 6 even portions and form these into cakes about 1-inch thick. Place the cakes on a large plate.

3. Pour the oil into a large deep skillet and heat over medium-high heat. When it is hot, gently slide the crab cakes into the oil and fry until they are deep brown on one side, 1 minute. Turn the cakes with a metal spatula and fry on the other side until deep brown, 1 minute longer. Transfer the crab cakes to paper towels to drain.

4. Meanwhile, place the remaining ⅓ cup of mayonnaise and 2 teaspoons of mustard in a small bowl and stir to combine. Stir in hot pepper sauce to taste. To serve, place the crab cakes on plates and spoon some of the mustard sauce over each. Serve with lemon wedges.

SERVES 4 TO 6

COASTAL SHRIMP AND TOMATO RICE

▼ ▼ ▼

Onions, bell peppers, and celery are the "holy trinity" of Creole cooking, but surely shrimp, rice, and tomatoes are the trinity of Lowcountry cooking down Charleston or Savannah way. That's the inspiration for this easy skillet supper, based on already cleaned (but not cooked) shrimp and pre-seasoned tomatoes that you doctor with instant rice, green olives, black pepper, and

TO PREP:
5 MINUTES
TO COOK:
15 MINUTES

feta cheese. If you buy shrimp in the shell, figure on 10 minutes more prep time to peel them. Serve the shrimp with crusty bread and a green salad.

1 can (14.5 ounces) diced tomatoes
    with green pepper and onion
1 cup instant rice
2 tablespoons sliced pimiento-stuffed
    green olives
½ pound medium-size shrimp,
    sliced lengthwise in half
½ teaspoon black pepper,
    or more to taste
½ cup pre-crumbled
    feta cheese

1. Place the tomatoes in a 2-quart saucepan or skillet. Fill the tomato can with water, add this to the pan, and stir. Bring to a boil over high heat, then stir in the rice and green olives and let come to a boil. Cover the pan, reduce the heat to

tip **This recipe is very adaptable. You can add flavored feta cheese or crumbled goat cheese. Scatter chopped fresh parsley or basil over the top. Or use a different type of canned tomatoes, such as diced tomatoes with green chiles. In that case, you might want to omit the feta and serve the shrimp with soft flour tortillas.**

low, and let simmer until the rice is half-cooked, 5 minutes.

2. Remove the lid from the pan, and stir in the shrimp and pepper. Cover the pan and let the shrimp cook until they turn pink and opaque, 4 to 5 minutes. The rice will be cooked through. Remove the pan from the heat and scatter the feta over the shrimp. Cover the pan once again and let it sit until the feta melts a bit, 1 to 2 minutes. Taste and add more pepper, if desired, then serve.

SERVES 2 TO 4

THAI SHRIMP AND ASPARAGUS

▼ ▼ ▼

TO PREP:
12 MINUTES
TO COOK:
4–5 MINUTES

Here's a no-fuss dish: Simmer shrimp in a zesty store-bought Thai chile sauce and cook asparagus in another pot. Spoon everything over jasmine rice, sprinkle cilantro and sesame seeds on top, and you have one of the most interesting combinations of sweet and hot flavors around.

½ cup Thai chile sauce
    (see Tips)
¼ cup canned
    low-sodium
    chicken broth or water
½ pound already peeled and deveined
    medium-size shrimp
16 medium-size asparagus spears
    (about ½ pound)
1 teaspoon reduced-sodium soy sauce
¼ cup fresh cilantro leaves
1 teaspoon toasted sesame seeds
    (optional)

tips I use Thai Kitchen Sweet Red Chile Sauce in this recipe; it comes in a 7-ounce bottle. The recipe uses about half a bottle. A spoonful of what was left over livened up a ho-hum chicken salad. The rest made a delicious dip for crab fritters.

Jasmine rice is starchier and stickier than long-grain converted rice and much more flavorful. You can find it at many supermarkets and at natural-food stores and Asian markets.

Toast sesame seeds in a small heavy, dry skillet over medium-high heat, stirring until the seeds turn golden brown, 2 to 3 minutes. Don't use a nonstick skillet for this.

1. Pour the chile sauce and broth into a medium-size skillet and bring to a simmer over medium-high heat. Add the shrimp, reduce the heat to medium, and cook, turning the shrimp, until they turn

pink and opaque and are cooked through and the sauce thickens somewhat, 3 to 4 minutes.

2. Meanwhile, pour water to a depth of 1 inch in a large skillet and bring to a boil over medium-high heat. Rinse the asparagus spears and snap off and discard their tough ends. When the water comes to a boil, add the asparagus and reduce the heat to medium. Let the asparagus simmer until it turns bright green, 3 minutes. Drain the water from the skillet, then add the soy sauce to the asparagus.

3. To serve, spoon the shrimp onto plates. Garnish the shrimp with the asparagus, cilantro, and sesame seeds, if using.

SERVES 2 TO 4

A Note About Rice

—▼—

DINNER DOCTOR SAYS The amount of rice you prepare for your family and guests depends, of course, on the appetites of those you are feeding and what else is being served alongside. I figure on ¾ cup to 1 cup cooked rice per adult and ⅓ to ½ cup per child. Generally raw white rice doubles in volume when cooked, so about 1 cup of raw white rice will yield 2 cups cooked. The exception is basmati rice, which has a slightly lower yield: 1 cup of raw basmati rice will give you 1½ cups once cooked. For tips on rice, see page 354.

SHRIMP CURRY IN A HURRY

▼ ▼ ▼

TO PREP:
10 MINUTES
TO COOK:
8 MINUTES

Although this recipe had been in my mother's recipe box for a long time, I had never tried it until recently. Now I know why it was there, for it's a very fast way to make shrimp curry. The prep and cooking time is further shortened if you use pre-cooked shrimp from the seafood counter. Feel free to season the curry as you like, adding more curry powder or hot pepper sauce to suit your taste. Serve the curry over steamed basmati rice.

1 can (10.75 ounces) cream of
    mushroom soup
Generous ½ cup milk
3 tablespoons sweetened flaked
    coconut
2 tablespoons barbecue sauce
1½ teaspoons curry powder
1 teaspoon hot pepper sauce
½ pound already peeled and deveined
    medium-size shrimp (see Tips)
1 cup frozen peas
1 teaspoon capers, drained (optional)

tips If you are using pre-cooked shrimp, add the frozen peas first and let them cook for 2 minutes before adding the shrimp. Let the shrimp cook until they are heated through, 2 minutes more.

Since the curry takes less than 20 minutes to prepare and cook, you'll want to get water boiling for rice before you begin the shrimp. Most rice takes 20 minutes to cook, but basmati cooks in just 15.

Instead of capers, you could garnish the shrimp with 2 tablespoons of toasted sliced almonds. You'll find toasting instructions in the Tips on page 145.

Place the mushroom soup, milk, coconut, barbecue sauce, curry powder, and hot pepper sauce in a 2-quart saucepan over medium heat. Cook, stirring, until the sauce comes to a boil and is well combined, 2 to 3 minutes. Add the shrimp and frozen peas and continue to cook the curry, stirring, only until the shrimp turn pink and opaque and are cooked through, 4 to 5 minutes longer. To serve, spoon the curry onto plates and garnish it with the capers, if using.

SERVES 2 TO 4

Curry in a Flash

—▼—

DINNER DOCTOR SAYS

They're as reliable as a chocolate cake mix, which means they hardly need doctoring. I am talking about the curry pastes and curry sauces in cans that can be found at many supermarkets as well as at Indian markets and some health food stores. They range in spiciness from mild to hot, so read the labels carefully. The curry pastes are highly concentrated, and adding only one tablespoon to marinades and sauces will give you a powerful curry flavor.

Canned curry sauces, on the other hand, are sort of like concentrated soups. Use them in quick-cooking dishes with tender cuts of meat: Chicken tenders, fillet of beef, and lamb chops are all good choices. Shrimp are also good curried. To start with, brown the meat or sauté the shrimp in a little oil. Adding sliced onion and/or garlic will give you more flavor. Then add a can of curry sauce, the amount of liquid called for on the can (use coconut milk, if you like it), and vegetables or fruit like diced eggplant, frozen peas, tiny green beans, lima beans, or chopped apple. The curry only needs to simmer long enough to cook the meat and veggies through. Serve it over rice, topped with chopped cilantro, sweetened flaked coconut, toasted almond slices, fresh mango or mango chutney, and/or golden raisins or currants.

SHRIMP AND CORN MAQUE CHOUX

▼ ▼ ▼

This is a variation on the Creole corn dish maque choux. I used to make it with oysters when you could get really good ones from the Florida or the Carolina coast, but those days are dwindling. However, the dish is still memorable made with shrimp from the supermarket. And, it is especially easy when you buy shrimp that are already peeled and

TO PREP:
10–15 MINUTES
TO COOK:
13 MINUTES

deveined! The secret ingredient is frozen creamed corn. Season the dish as you like, adding black pepper for a bit more heat. Serve it in shallow bowls with crusty bread for dipping and a green salad on the side.

1 tablespoon olive oil

1 cup chopped onion (from 1 medium-size
 onion)

1 green bell pepper, stemmed, seeded,
 and chopped

3 cloves garlic, sliced

20 ounces frozen creamed corn (see Tip),
 thawed

1 can (28 ounces) diced tomatoes

¼ teaspoon cayenne pepper

2 bay leaves

¼ teaspoon Creole seasoning, or more to taste

1 pound already peeled and deveined large
 shrimp

¼ cup chopped fresh parsley (optional)

tip **Frozen creamed corn is sold in 20-ounce logs in the South, and you even get to choose between white or yellow kernels. I prefer white. I have also found frozen corn in 10-ounce packages from Green Giant. Frozen creamed corn is preferable to canned, and if you cannot find it, substitute 2½ cups of corn kernels. The recipe won't be as thick and creamy, but it will still be delicious.**

1. Pour the olive oil into a heavy Dutch oven or 4-quart saucepan and heat over medium heat. Add the onion, bell pepper, and garlic and cook, stirring, until the onion is translucent, 3 minutes. Add the creamed corn, tomatoes, cayenne, bay leaves, and Creole seasoning. Taste for seasoning, adding more Creole seasoning if necessary. Continue to cook, stirring, until the mixture bubbles, 3 to 4 minutes longer.

2. Add the shrimp, stir, then cover the pan and turn off the heat. After 5 minutes, stir the mixture, checking to see if the shrimp have turned pink and opaque and are cooked through. If not, place the pan over low heat and let the shrimp cook gently until done, 1 minute. Spoon the maque choux into bowls, garnish it with parsley, if using, and serve at once.

SERVES 4

GRILLED PROSCIUTTO-WRAPPED SHRIMP

ON A BED OF LEMON COUSCOUS

▼ ▼ ▼

I have served these grilled shrimp kebabs for many, many years, making them for picnics at Chastain Park in Atlanta or as quick finger food for guests before dinner. The idea, I think, came from *The Silver Palate Good Times Cookbook* by Sheila Lukins and Julee Rosso, and hats off to them for another classic recipe. Over time, I have streamlined the recipe, sticking with the tails-on shrimp, prosciutto, and large basil leaves, but shortening the prep time. Heat your grill toward the end of the marination time. I like to serve these shrimp on a bed of lemon-scented couscous (for more about couscous see page 179).

TO PREP:
10 MINUTES
TO MARINATE:
AT LEAST 1 HOUR
TO COOK:
9–11 MINUTES

SHRIMP

1 cup bottled balsamic vinaigrette

1 tablespoon Dijon mustard

Black pepper

16 already peeled and deveined jumbo shrimp, tails left on

LEMON COUSCOUS

¾ cup couscous

2 tablespoons chopped fresh parsley

1 teaspoon grated lemon zest

1 tablespoon fresh lemon juice

1 tablespoon olive oil, or as needed

16 large basil leaves

16 thin slices of prosciutto (4 ounces)

1. To make the shrimp, place the balsamic vinaigrette and mustard in a medium-size glass bowl and whisk to combine. Season with pepper to taste. Add the shrimp and stir to coat them

with the marinade. Cover the bowl with plastic wrap and refrigerate it for at least 1 hour, or for up to 6 hours.

2. One hour before serving, make the lemon couscous. Pour 1½ cups of water into a 2-quart saucepan and bring to a boil over high heat. Stir in the couscous, remove the pan from the heat, and cover it. Let the couscous sit for 5 minutes. Fluff the couscous with a fork, then stir in the parsley, lemon zest and juice, and enough olive oil to moisten the mixture (start with 1 tablespoon). Set the couscous aside.

3. Heat the grill to medium. Remove the shrimp from the marinade, setting aside the marinade. Wrap each shrimp first with a basil leaf and then with a slice of prosciutto. Thread 4 shrimp onto each of 4 metal skewers. Grill the shrimp, basting them with a little of the marinade, until they turn pink and opaque and are cooked through, 2 to 3 minutes per side. Serve the grilled shrimp on or off the skewers on top of the couscous.

SERVES 2 TO 4

> **tip** Prosciutto is an Italian ham that should be bought thinly sliced. There isn't really a substitute for it here, for it has a sweet, smoky, and salty flavor that is very compatible with shrimp. Plus, it is pliable, enabling you to wrap the shrimp well before grilling. When grilled, prosciutto is crisp and sweet, and much of the fat around its edge will have melted away. If you are watching your fat intake and you have a few spare minutes, remove the fat from the prosciutto before wrapping the shrimp.

EASY BEEF STROGANOFF

WITH PARSLEY NOODLES

▼ ▼ ▼

Retro recipes are the ones you remember fondly from childhood but don't see on tables much anymore, so you re-create them. I did this with beef Stroganoff. While the dish was named after the nineteenth-century Russian Count Paul Stroganoff, my sisters and I knew it best as our mother's party food. It was what she prepared for her most special dinner guests. She served it over buttered egg noodles, with a green salad or green vegetable, hot rolls, and some wonderful frozen dessert she had stashed away in the depths of her cavernous Frigidaire freezer. Today this recipe is a snap to make, thanks to onion soup mix and pre-sliced fresh mushrooms. The sour cream goes in at the last minute so it just heats through. If you have any leftovers, serve them the next night spooned over split loaves of French bread.

TO PREP: *8 MINUTES*
TO COOK: *30 MINUTES*

1 pound beef tenderloin or top sirloin,
*   cut into 1-inch cubes*
Salt
½ teaspoon paprika
4 tablespoons (½ stick) butter
1 can (14.5 ounces) low-sodium beef broth
1 can (8 ounces) tomato sauce
1 package (1.3 ounces) onion soup mix
1 package (8 ounces) pre-sliced fresh
*   mushrooms*
Black pepper
1 pound egg noodles
¼ cup chopped fresh parsley
1 tablespoon all-purpose flour
1 cup sour cream

1. Season the beef cubes all over with salt and the paprika. Melt 2 tablespoons of the butter in a 4-quart saucepan over medium-high heat. Add the beef cubes and cook, stirring, until browned on all sides, 2 to 3 minutes. Reduce the heat to medium. Pour ¼ cup of the broth into a measuring cup and set it aside. Add the remaining broth to the beef, along with the tomato sauce, onion soup mix, and mushrooms. Season with pepper to taste.

tips Use the tenderest beef you can find for the Stroganoff; tenderloin and top sirloin both work well. My mother always cubed the beef for this dish, but traditionally it is sliced. If you would rather serve it that way, cut the beef into thin slices and sauté them for 1 to 2 minutes per side in Step 1. The simmering time will be reduced to 15 minutes.

By whisking the sour cream into some of the hot beef, you raise the temperature of the sour cream so that when it is added to the hot pan it does not curdle.

There are countless ways to season this dish: Add a bit of sherry at the end; use a tablespoon of spicy mustard instead of seasoning the meat with paprika; or add a dash of hot pepper sauce.

Let the mixture come to a boil, stirring, then reduce the heat to low and let simmer, uncovered, until the Stroganoff thickens and the beef and mushrooms are cooked through 20 to 25 minutes.

2. Meanwhile, bring a large pot of water to a boil over high heat. Add salt, if using, and stir in the egg noodles. Reduce the heat to medium and cook the noodles, uncovered, until al dente, 7 to 8 minutes. Drain the noodles well in a colander, shaking it a few times to remove any water that might still cling to them. Toss the noodles with the remaining 2 tablespoons of butter and the parsley. Cover to keep warm and set aside.

3. Place the flour in the reserved ¼ cup of beef broth and whisk until free of lumps. Pour the broth slowly into the hot beef, stirring constantly. Spoon ½ cup of the hot beef mixture into a small bowl. Add the sour cream and stir until blended. Pour the sour cream mixture into the Stroganoff and stir to combine. Raise the heat to medium and cook until the liquid almost boils. Serve the Stroganoff spooned over the buttered noodles.

SERVES 4 TO 6

CUBAN PICADILLO

WITH CHILES AND RAISINS

▼ ▼ ▼

The Cuban equivalent of a sloppy joe, *picadillo* is a dish that's quick to throw together, beginning with two cans of tomatoes with green chiles and a pound of ground beef round. Chances are you have the rest of the ingredients on hand—the onion, garlic, red wine, oregano, tomato paste,

TO PREP:
10 MINUTES
TO COOK:
20–25 MINUTES

and raisins. To be festive, serve the *picadillo* over yellow rice, garnished with green olives and capers; to be more down-home, pile it into pita rounds. The sweet, the savory, the salty, it's all here.

1 tablespoon olive oil

1 pound ground beef round

½ cup chopped onion

5 cloves garlic, sliced

2 cans (14.5 ounces each) diced tomatoes with green chiles

1 can (6 ounces) tomato paste

¼ cup dry red wine or water

¼ cup raisins

2 teaspoons dried oregano

Salt and black pepper

¼ cup sliced pimiento-stuffed green olives (optional)

2 teaspoons capers (optional), drained

tips The green olives and capers can be cooked with the beef and tomatoes but I find that children don't care for them. I use them as a garnish instead.

If you keep 1 pound packages of ground beef round in the freezer, you can reach for one when you feel like making spaghetti, chili, or the **picadillo.** Turn to the microwave for quick thawing.

1. Pour the olive oil into a large deep skillet or 4-quart saucepan and heat it over medium-high heat. Crumble in the ground beef and add the onion and garlic. Cook, stirring and breaking up the lumps of beef, until the beef browns all over, about 3 minutes. Add the tomatoes, tomato paste, wine, raisins, and oregano. Season to taste with salt and pepper. Reduce the heat to low, cover the pan, and let the *picadillo* simmer until it thickens, 15 to 20 minutes.

2. Spoon the *picadillo* onto plates and garnish it with the green olives and capers, if desired.

SERVES 4 TO 6

FAST-ROASTED BEEF TENDERLOIN

▼ ▼ ▼

No matter its elegant simplicity, beef tenderloin can cause a cook a lot of anxiety because of the fear of winding up with a gray and overcooked expensive cut of meat. Fear be gone. Years ago my mother found this recipe a bit avant-garde, I think because the meat cooks in a turned-off oven. But it turns out perfectly each time. I will warn you that if your smoke alarm is close to the kitchen, the 475°F needed to crank up the heat to start with might create enough smoke to set off that alarm. It does occasionally at our house, but usually when I am cooking a tenderloin it is Christmas or New Year's, and the house is already pretty noisy. Serve the beef with its horseradish sauce and mashed potatoes, steamed broccoli, and soft rolls.

TO PREP:
20 MINUTES
TO BAKE:
30 MINUTES
TO REST:
30 MINUTES

4 tablespoons (½ stick) butter,
    at room temperature
1 trimmed beef tenderloin (about 5 pounds)
2 teaspoons garlic salt
1 cup sour cream
2 tablespoons prepared horseradish

tip Beef tenderloins range in size, so use the same method but adjust the cooking time if you find a slightly smaller or larger one. The ends will cook more quickly than the thicker part in the middle. I find this works out well, for some people will want their beef more well done than others.

1. Place a rack in the center of the oven and preheat the oven to 475°F.

2. Massage the butter into the beef and sprinkle it on all sides with the garlic salt. Place the beef in an aluminum foil–lined shallow roasting pan.

> **tips** If you are hosting a party and need to roast two tenderloins at once, you can double the recipe and roast them both in the same pan—leave three or four inches between them. The cooking time will be the same.
>
> If you can only find untrimmed tenderloins, have the butcher trim one for you, and use those trimmings for beef stew (see page 101) or beef Stroganoff (see page 203).

3. Bake the beef for 15 minutes, then turn the oven off. Let the beef sit in the turned-off oven for 15 minutes. Remove the pan from the oven, tent it with aluminum foil, and let the beef rest for 30 minutes before carving. The interior will be a perfect medium-rare.

4. Meanwhile, place the sour cream and horseradish in a small glass bowl and stir. Slice the beef and serve it with the horseradish cream.

SERVES 8 TO 10

ITALIAN-STYLE MINI MEAT LOAVES

▼ ▼ ▼

TO PREP:
12 MINUTES
TO BAKE:
15–20 MINUTES

By adding packaged bread crumbs or stuffing mix to a favorite meat loaf recipe and by making small loaves, you not only speed up the preparation but shorten the baking time by as much as 20 minutes—these little loaves need just 15 to 20 minutes to cook through. Season them as you wish; I like to add fresh garlic and chopped parsley and often a dash of Italian seasoning. Begin with ground round and you will have little fat drain out of the loaf and into the pan. What to serve alongside the meat loaves? Mashed potatoes—naturally!

tips **Using a food processor to chop the onion and parsley saves time here, especially since the pieces don't have to be perfect and uniform, just chopped.**

Be careful not to overwork the ground beef. You want to mix it only enough to combine the ingredients so that the loaves stay light and moist when baked.

I am not a fan of sage-flavored stuffing mixes, so I like to use a plain stuffing mix or the coarse bread crumbs that come in bags.

2 large eggs

1 cup plain bread crumbs or stuffing mix (see Tips)

1 can (8 ounces) tomato sauce

½ medium-size onion

2 cloves garlic, minced

¼ cup fresh parsley leaves

1 teaspoon Italian seasoning

1 pound ground beef round

1. Place a rack in the center of the oven and preheat the oven to 375°F.

2. Crack the eggs into a large mixing bowl and beat with a fork until lemon colored. Stir in the bread crumbs and tomato sauce. Cut the onion half in half. Place the onion halves, garlic, and parsley in a food processor. Pulse several times until finely chopped. Add the onion mixture to the bread crumb mixture along with the Italian seasoning and stir to combine. Add the ground round to the bread crumb mixture and mash it with a fork to combine.

3. Divide the ground round mixture into 6 even portions and form these into loaves. Place the meat loaves in a 13-by-9-inch glass or ceramic baking dish. Bake until the tops brown and the meat loaves have cooked through, 15 to 20 minutes. Remove the meat loaves from the oven, serve at once, or let cool, wrap in aluminum foil, and freeze for a later meal. The meat loaves will keep in the freezer for up to 3 months.

SERVES 4 TO 6

BARBECUE QUESADILLAS

WITH CILANTRO LIME CREAM

▼ ▼ ▼

TO PREP:
15 MINUTES
TO COOK:
8 MINUTES

Yum. That's what you'll say when you bite into quesadillas that pair the Mexican classic with Southern barbecue. These are a particular favorite of my children, who have gravitated toward spicier dishes, and like to eat these foods when entertaining their friends. I dress up the quesadillas with a cilantro and lime cream. If you want more heat, you can season it with canned chipotle peppers (see Tips). A slaw you assemble in minutes gives the quesadillas some crunch. And by all means use the best local barbecue you can find. If your area is not barbecue territory, you can use frozen barbecued pork or beef from the supermarket. Hormel is one popular brand. Pull out the pancake griddle for this recipe; it's faster than cooking the quesadillas one at a time in a skillet.

tips Use any type of coleslaw mix you can find. I like rainbow slaw, which contains shredded cabbage, carrots, broccoli, and cauliflower.

If you want to increase the heat of the cilantro and sour cream topping, add 1 tablespoon, or more, of canned chipotle chiles in adobo sauce to it before puréeing.

If you are using frozen barbecue, thaw it in the microwave oven on high power for 7 to 8 minutes.

1 package (16 ounces) coleslaw mix or
    broccoli slaw (see Tips, page 211)

½ cup mayonnaise

¼ cup sweet pickle juice

¼ cup bottled Italian salad dressing or
    sesame salad dressing

1 tablespoon sugar, or more to taste

1 cup sour cream

½ cup fresh cilantro leaves

1 tablespoon fresh lime juice

1 tablespoon vegetable oil

1 package (18 ounces frozen or 16 ounces
    fresh) shredded pork or beef barbecue,
    thawed if frozen (see Tips, page 211), or
    2 cups shredded cooked chicken mixed
    with ½ cup store-bought barbecue sauce

1 package (8 ounces; 2 cups) pre-shredded
    Cheddar or Monterey Jack cheese or
    a Mexican blend

16 flour tortillas (10 inches each)

1. Place the coleslaw mix, mayonnaise, pickle juice, salad dressing, and sugar in a medium-size bowl, and stir to combine. Taste for sweetness, adding more sugar if necessary. Cover the bowl with plastic wrap and place the slaw in the refrigerator to chill. It will keep for up to 2 days.

2. Place the sour cream, cilantro leaves, and lime juice in a food processor or blender and purée until smooth, 30 seconds. Set the cilantro cream aside.

3. Place a rack in the center of the oven and preheat the oven to 300°F.

4. Heat a griddle or large, heavy skillet over medium-high heat. Brush the griddle or skillet with the oil. Scatter an eighth of the barbecue, ¼ cup of the slaw, and about ¼ cup of the cheese evenly over each of 8 tortillas and top with the remaining tortillas. Place 4 quesadillas on the griddle or cook them one at a time in the skillet. Cook on one side until crisp, 2 minutes. Carefully turn the quesadillas over and cook on the other side until cooked through and crisp, 2 minutes longer. Place the quesadilla(s) on a baking sheet in the oven to keep warm until serving. Repeat the cooking process until all the quesadillas are cooked. Slice the hot quesadillas into wedges and serve with the cilantro cream drizzled over them or on the side.

**Serves 4 as a main course,
8 as an appetizer**

15 WAYS TO DOCTOR A CAN OF BAKED BEANS

Canned baked beans, whether vegetarian or smoky and laced with pork, make a great candidate for doctoring. Use these ideas as a jumping-off point, and season the results to suit your taste.

1 Add pan-fried smoked sausage or slices of kielbasa to the beans and then heat them through.

2 Heat the beans and spoon them over hot dogs served in toasted buns.

3 Spoon the beans into a baking dish, then stir in ketchup, brown sugar or maple syrup, and a dash of yellow mustard. Top this with bacon slices and bake in a 375°F oven until heated through.

4 Brown some ground beef and chopped onion in a skillet. Stir this into the beans, then heat them through for what I call "cowboy beans."

5 Stir enough smoky barbecue sauce to suit your taste into the beans and cook them until they are heated through.

6 Combine baked beans with a can of black beans for a bean medley and bake this at 375°F until bubbling.

7 Fold shredded cooked pork into the beans, heat them in a saucepan, and serve with dill pickle wedges.

8 Add as much chili powder as you like and a can of Tex-Mex flavored chili beans to the baked beans, heat through, and serve.

9 Add a chipotle or dried chile pepper to the beans while they are heating up. Remove the pepper before serving.

10 Season the beans with diced country ham and a handful of chopped sweet onion, then heat them through and serve.

11 Spoon warmed beans into pita pockets along with coleslaw and pickle relish.

12 Spoon warmed beans over toast as they do in England and serve them with a spicy English mustard.

13 Add a smidgen of ground cinnamon and a spoonful of Dijon mustard to the beans, then heat them through and serve.

14 Create a fast casserole by layering the beans with browned pork sausage, chopped tomatoes, and pre-shredded Cheddar cheese, then bake them at 375°F until bubbling.

15 Add a dab of curry powder, some crushed pineapple, and a handful of chopped scallions to the beans before heating them in a saucepan.

ROAST PORK TENDERLOIN

WITH A FIG AND CHIPOTLE JAM

▼ ▼ ▼

TO PREP:
15–20 MINUTES
TO BAKE:
20–25 MINUTES
TO REST:
10 MINUTES

Fruit and spices marry very well with pork, and this combination of sweet fig jam and smoky, spicy chipotles is particularly delicious. Serve the pork with mashed white potatoes or sweet potatoes and sautéed spinach, or with cheese grits and slaw. Leftovers are delicious sliced and served cold—that is if the pork's not all gone!

½ cup fig jam or preserves
1 to 2 tablespoons canned chipotle peppers
in adobo sauce (see Tips)
1 pound pork tenderloin
Salt and black pepper
1 lime, cut into quarters

tips Go easy on the chipotle peppers if you like milder foods. If you cannot find chipotle peppers, you can use slices of pickled jalapeño peppers instead.

Pork tenderloins are perfect for quick cooking because they remain tender, while tougher cuts of pork and beef need to be slowly cooked to become tender. If you can find a pork tenderloin already coated in black pepper, it will make an incredibly delicious variation on this recipe.

Two more variations: Combine ½ cup of apricot preserves with 2 tablespoons of balsamic vinegar or mix ½ cup of mango chutney and 2 tablespoons of balsamic vinegar for quick and flavorful toppings.

1. Place a rack in the center of the oven and preheat the oven to 450°F.

2. Place the fig preserves and the chipotle peppers in a food processor or blender and pulse until the mixture is smooth, 30 seconds. Set aside.

3. Place the pork tenderloin in a 13-by-9-inch (3 quart) glass or ceramic baking dish. Season the pork with salt and pepper. Spoon the jam mixture evenly over the top.

4. Roast the pork until it browns, the juices run clear when pierced with a knife, and the meat is still barely pink, 20 to 25 minutes. Remove the baking dish from the oven, cover the meat with aluminum foil, and let it rest for 10 minutes.

5. Slice the tenderloin and serve with the lime quarters.

SERVES 4

Fast Tips from the Grill
—▼—

DINNER DOCTOR SAYS

◆ To keep cooking times short, it's best to grill food in small pieces.

◆ Flatten chicken breasts to a ⅓- to ½-inch thickness by placing them between two sheets of waxed paper and pounding them with a meat pounder or the bottom of a heavy skillet.

◆ Make burgers flatter rather than thicker, for quicker and more even cooking.

◆ Cut meat into kebab-size pieces and slice pork tenderloins in half the long way for ultrafast cooking.

◆ Cut a whole fillet of fish into individual serving pieces before cooking.

ITALIAN SAUSAGE AND SPINACH SCRAMBLE

▼ ▼ ▼

Since mild and hot Italian sausage are already seasoned with fennel seeds and pepper, adding them is an easy way to doctor eggs, turning out an enjoyable brunch dish that's good just about any time of the day. Serve these eggs with biscuits, grits or roasted potatoes, and fresh fruit.

TO PREP:
15 MINUTES
TO COOK:
6–7 MINUTES

1 tablespoon olive oil

1 pound mild or hot Italian sausage links,
     cut into ½-inch pieces

½ cup chopped red bell pepper

¼ cup chopped onion

1 bag (5 ounces) baby spinach

8 large eggs, lightly beaten

Black pepper

½ cup pre-crumbled feta cheese

Place the olive oil in a large skillet and heat over medium-high heat. Add the sausage pieces, bell pepper, and onion, and cook, stirring, until the sausage has browned and the pepper and onion are soft, 3 to 4 minutes. Stir in the spinach and cook it until it wilts, 1 minute. Pour in the eggs and season with pepper. Reduce the heat to medium-low, sprinkle the feta cheese on top, and cook, stirring, until the eggs have just set, 2 minutes more. Serve the scrambled eggs at once.

SERVES 4 TO 6

tip To reduce the fat in this dish, omit the olive oil, use a nonstick pan, and choose reduced-fat sausage. You can also use an egg substitute, like Egg Beaters.

SWIRLY DOGS

▼ ▼ ▼

TO PREP:
12 MINUTES
TO COOK:
16–18 MINUTES

My kids ask me to make this recipe again and again, and it makes you wonder—there are only two ingredients, not rocket science here, what's the attraction? Well, kids don't like fussy food. They like food they can pick up with their fingers and dunk into ketchup and mustard. And this delicious variation on the old favorite pigs in blankets speedily fits the bill. Serve the hot dogs with baked beans, grape tomatoes, and something green.

1 package (11 ounces) refrigerated
    corn bread twist dough
8 beef hot dogs
Ketchup and yellow mustard,
    for serving

1. Place a rack in the center of the oven and preheat the oven to 375°F.

2. Unroll the package of dough and separate it to form 16 strips. Depending on the size of the hot dogs, you'll need up to 2 strips of dough for each hot dog. Start wrapping at one end of a hot dog using 1 strip of dough, and when it runs out, overlap it with a second piece of dough so that the pieces stick together. The dough will spiral around the hot dog and not completely cover it. Place the wrapped hot dog on an ungreased baking sheet. Repeat with the remaining hot dogs and dough.

3. Bake the hot dogs until they sizzle and the dough is light golden brown, 16 to 18 minutes. Remove the pan from the oven and, using a metal spatula, transfer the hot dogs to plates. Serve the hot dogs at once with ketchup and yellow mustard.

SERVES 4 TO 8

tip For a fast nibble, cut the hot dogs in half crosswise and wrap just one strip of dough around each half. Pile the baked Little Swirly Dogs on a platter around bowls of ketchup and mustard.

GRILLED LAMB CHOPS

WITH BRUISED TOMATO SALAD AND TABBOULEH

▼ ▼ ▼

The lively combination of grilled lamb, fragrant tomatoes, and tabbouleh salad is perfect once the weather warms up enough to cook outdoors. Not only do loin lamb chops cook quickly, they go well with all sorts of side dishes. One of the easiest is made with tabbouleh salad mix. The mixes, which contain bulgur—cracked wheat—are so easy to prepare and tasty, it is a mystery to me why anyone would want to make tabbouleh from scratch. To dress up the lamb, I add a salad of smashed cherry tomatoes, red wine vinegar, olive oil, and a handful of fresh mint leaves. You can include a quarter cup of those wonderful pitted kalamata olives if you like. Mint pairs well with the tabbouleh, the tabbouleh soaks up the lamb juices, and the result is incredibly fine eating.

TO SOAK THE TABBOULEH: *30 MINUTES*
TO PREP: *10 MINUTES*
TO COOK: *12–16 MINUTES*

1 package (5.25 ounces) tabbouleh
   salad mix (see Tips)

1 cup boiling water

2 tablespoons fresh lemon juice

2 to 3 tablespoons olive oil, plus olive oil for
   brushing the lamb chops

12 loin lamb chops (1 to 1½ inches thick;
   about 3 pounds total)

Garlic salt and black pepper

1 pint (2 cups) grape or cherry tomatoes

1 tablespoon red wine vinegar

1 cup torn fresh mint or basil leaves

tips You can prepare the tabbouleh as described in Steps 1 and 5 the day or night before, adding the lemon juice and olive oil mixture and refrigerating it covered with plastic wrap. Or use the soaking time to heat the grill and prep the rest of the dish.

The tomato salad can be made several hours in advance, but it should not be refrigerated.

1. Place the tabbouleh salad mix with its seasonings and the boiling water in a large heatproof mixing bowl. Stir to combine, then let the tabbouleh soak in the refrigerator, uncovered for 30 minutes. Whisk together the lemon juice and 1 tablespoon of the olive oil in a small bowl and set aside.

2. Meanwhile, heat the grill to medium-high.

3. Brush the lamb chops with olive oil, season them with garlic salt and pepper, and set aside.

4. Place the tomatoes in a large bowl and mash them with a potato masher until they are flattened. Add the vinegar, 1 to 2 tablespoons of olive oil, and the mint and stir to mix. Set the tomato salad aside.

5. Remove the tabbouleh from the refrigerator and stir it. If the water hasn't been completely absorbed, drain off the excess. Stir in the reserved lemon juice and olive oil mixture. Set the tabbouleh aside.

6. Place the lamb chops on the grill and cook until medium-rare, about 6 minutes per side if they are 1-inch thick, 8 minutes per side if they are thicker. Transfer the grilled chops to a platter.

7. To serve, divide the tabbouleh among 6 serving plates. Top each serving with 2 lamb chops and spoon some of the tomato salad on the top and to the side. Serve at once.

SERVES 6

ONE-DISH COMFORT FOOD

▼ ▼ ▼

Turn to Webster's dictionary and you'll find that the word *comfort* has a variety of meanings, but surely it's "a satisfying or enjoyable experience" that's the comfort in comfort food. The classic I-gotta-have-seconds dishes—the smooth and creamy macaroni and cheese, chicken and rice, and tuna and noodles, the potpies, spaghetti, "impossible" pies, even grits with cheese—have made for decades of contented family dining. And comfort foods tend to be inexpensive. They're indispensable when you want to feed the whole neighborhood.

Since casseroles first appeared in cookbooks at the turn of the twentieth century, they have helped frugal cooks stretch food budgets without cutting back on flavor. They really came into their own with the invention of casserole-friendly condensed soups. It was John T. Dorrance, a nephew of the president of the Joseph A. Campbell Preserve Company, who first came up with the idea. The soups became so popular that the company changed its name to Campbell Soup. It wasn't until 1934, however, that cream of mushroom, the king of casserole soups, made its debut. This red-and-white can liberated home cooks, making it no longer necessary to prepare a white sauce of flour, butter, and milk to bind casserole ingredients. With the help of cream of mushroom soup, chicken and rice casserole, tuna noodle casserole, and the ubiquitous green bean casserole became mainstays of the dinner table.

The challenge in putting together this chapter was how to present cherished dishes in such a way that they retained their identity while becoming a snap to prepare. Many of the original casseroles now taste more bland than flavorful. So, I revisited a number of familiar recipes and lightened some of them up. I streamlined them and used lower-fat and fresher ingredients whenever possible. I shortened the cooking times by baking at a higher temperature. You'll also find a batch of new family-friendly dishes to try. Chili Dog Pie, Mock Cassoulet, Pork Fried Rice, Turkey Hash in a Flash—dig into these casseroles, pies, and "bakes" anytime. You can always use a little more comfort.

CURRIED CHICKEN AND ARTICHOKE CASSEROLE

▼ ▼ ▼

Plucked from my mother's recipe box, this casserole brings back so many fond memories of dinner parties in the 1960s. My sisters and I anticipated my parents' parties as much as their guests did, for my mother was an accomplished cook and hostess. But with three little children under foot, I am amazed she actually pulled dinner parties off! We ogled the "grown-up" food as it was prepared, then were fed our own meal and rushed upstairs out of sight before the guests arrived. Of course, we managed to sneak back down to the kitchen after dinner was served and enjoy the leftovers. This chicken and artichoke casserole was a mainstay, and I'll bet it gave me my first taste of curry. Serve it with basmati or jasmine rice (you'll find

TO PREP:
15 MINUTES
TO BAKE:
32–35 MINUTES

tips for cooking rice quickly on page 354), a green salad, and a chocolate dessert. Add good friends and conversation and you'll have a memorable evening.

4 cups shredded cooked chicken
    (see box, page 226)
1 can (14 ounces) artichoke hearts,
    drained and quartered
1 can (8 ounces) sliced water chestnuts,
    drained
1 can (7 ounces) mushroom pieces, drained
1 can (10.75 ounces) cream of chicken soup
    (see Tips)
1 cup sour cream (see Tips)
½ cup mayonnaise (see Tips)
1 teaspoon curry powder
¼ cup pre-chopped pecans or slivered
    almonds

1. Preheat the oven to 400°F.

2. Place the chicken, artichoke hearts, water chestnuts, mushrooms, chicken

soup, sour cream, mayonnaise, and curry powder in a large mixing bowl and stir until well blended. Transfer the mixture to a 13-by-9-inch (3-quart) glass or ceramic baking dish and scatter the nuts over the top.

tips Unlike the casserole recipes of the sixties, this one is baked uncovered and at a higher heat (400°F instead of 350°F). But although it's been sped up, the flavors still have enough time to mingle and cook down.

To reduce the amount of fat in the casserole, use reduced-fat cream of chicken soup, sour cream, and mayonnaise.

3. Bake the casserole until it is bubbling throughout and the nuts are toasted, 32 to 35 minutes. Remove the casserole from the oven and serve at once.

SERVES 8

Casserole Toppers

—▼—

DINNER DOCTOR SAYS Casseroles tend to be smooth and creamy, so the topper— the brooch on the lapel, the icing on the cake, the crunch, the fun—provides the contrast needed to make a dish memorable. Here are some traditional toppers. They should always be added just before baking, so they stay crisp. If you are planning on assembling and then freezing a casserole, leave off the topping until baking time.

◆ Canned French-fried onions

◆ Crumbled crackers, such as Ritz or soda crackers

◆ Toasted white bread crumbs

◆ Crumbled potato chips or crushed tortilla chips

◆ Nuts, such as sliced almonds or finely chopped pecans (you don't have to toast these; they'll toast as they bake)

CHICKEN TETRAZZINI

▼▼▼

When I was growing up, chicken tetrazzini for dinner meant that company was coming. Making this fancy fare was a time-consuming process and only worth the trouble for special occasions. My shortcut version is every bit as good as one made from scratch; my husband thinks it's even better. Combining Alfredo sauce from the supermarket with a can of cream of mushroom soup provides a creamy backdrop for pieces of chicken, thin noodles, crunchy pecans, and salty olives. Not only is it easy to double the amounts, if you're feeding a crowd, but the dish freezes well, too, so you can cook it ahead of time.

TO PREP:
20 MINUTES
TO BAKE:
25–30 MINUTES

tips **The preparation time here includes cooking the vermicelli, so you can shorten the time it takes to assemble this casserole if you boil the pasta the day before (see the box on page 286).**
  If you make this dish well in advance and wish to freeze it before baking, leave off the pecans. Sprinkle on the nuts after defrosting the casserole and right before you put it in the oven.

Salt (optional) for cooking the pasta

8 ounces vermicelli, broken into thirds

1 container (10 ounces) refrigerated
    Alfredo-style pasta sauce
    (see page 277)

1 can (10.75 ounces) cream of mushroom
    soup

3 cups shredded or chopped cooked chicken
    (see box, page 226)

1 cup pre-shredded Parmesan cheese

¼ cup drained pre-sliced pimiento-stuffed
    green olives

2 tablespoons golden or dry sherry

¼ cup pre-chopped pecans

1. Preheat the oven to 375°F.

2. Bring a medium-size pot of water to a boil over high heat. Add salt, if using, and stir in the vermicelli. Reduce the heat to medium-high and cook the vermicelli, uncovered, until al dente, 5 to 7 minutes, stirring once or twice. Reserve ½ cup of the pasta cooking water, then drain the vermicelli well in a colander, shaking it a few times to remove any water that might still cling to the pasta.

3. Transfer the pasta to a large mixing bowl. Add the Alfredo sauce, mushroom soup, reserved cooking water, chicken, Parmesan cheese, olives, and sherry and stir until well combined. Scoop the mixture into a 13-by-9-inch (3-quart) glass or ceramic baking dish. Scatter the pecans over the top.

4. Bake the casserole until it is bubbling throughout, 25 to 30 minutes. Remove the casserole from the oven and serve at once or cover it with aluminum foil to keep it warm. Serve within 30 minutes.

SERVES 6 TO 8

How Much Chicken?

—▾—

Many of the recipes in this book call for shredded or chopped chicken in cup measures. Here's a quick chart of chicken equivalents.

1 CUP = 1 small boneless half breast (about 4 ounces)
One quarter of a whole chicken

2 CUPS = 2 small boneless half breasts
1 large boneless half breast (about 8 ounces)
Half of a whole chicken

3 CUPS = 3 small or 1½ large boneless half breasts (about 12 ounces)
Three quarters of a whole chicken

4 CUPS = 4 small or 2 large boneless half breasts (about 1 pound)
1 whole chicken

Something to Cluck About

— ▼ —

DINNER DOCTOR SAYS

What (besides, maybe, canned tuna) is the hurried cook's lifesaver? Pre-cooked chicken. So, we cook a lot of chicken dishes at our house. Chicken adds protein and substance to casseroles, soups, and salads but doesn't add a lot of fat. I prefer the less fatty breast meat to the fattier, darker leg and thigh meat. Having a whole roast chicken or boiled or grilled chicken breasts on hand—whether home cooked or store bought—is the first step for getting dinner on the table in no time flat. When I'm really busy, I buy rotisserie-cooked chicken from the supermarket. When not quite so pressed for time, I simmer chicken breasts. Either way the chicken is superior to what comes in a can. A lot of my recipes call for the pre-cooked chicken to be shredded, and you can shred the chicken ahead of time.

To cook chicken breasts: Place skinless, boneless chicken breast halves in a skillet that has a lid and cover them with water. The number of breasts you can cook at one time will depend upon the size of your skillet. You don't want to stack the chicken breasts. Add a pinch of salt and a bay leaf, if you like. Place the skillet over medium-high heat and bring the water to a boil. Reduce the heat to low, cover the skillet, and let the breasts simmer until they are tender and cooked through, 15 to 20 minutes. Remove the cooked breasts from the water, let them cool on a plate until you can handle them, about 20 minutes, then shred the meat.

You can use the shredded chicken right away or refrigerate it for up to three days. You can also freeze shredded chicken; see page 233 for instructions. Although not deeply flavored, the chicken cooking liquid makes a nice base for soups, stews, gravies, or almost any recipe that calls for liquid. It keeps for two days, covered, in the fridge, or for up to three months in the freezer.

CHICKEN LAREDO

▼▼▼

TO PREP AND COOK:
15 MINUTES
TO BAKE:
28–32 MINUTES

A very dear friend of my mother used to make Chicken Laredo for her ladies' bridge lunches. My mother copied the recipe and passed it on to me. I have tinkered with it, lightening it up and using more beans and less chili and Velveeta. But you need *some* Velveeta, the retro cheese product of my youth. It melts into a wonderful and creamy goo—perfect for this dish. Of course times have changed and so has Velveeta. Now there are both mild varieties and hot ones with jalapeño peppers, which is what I call for here. Serve the chicken with crisp tortilla chips and a green salad, and let the card playing begin!

tip **Velveeta is a pasteurized cheese product that has long been used in grilled cheese sandwiches and dips because it melts so well. When it is flavored with jalapeño peppers, it saves you the step of adding a lot of seasoning. You can decide whether you want to use the mild or the hot kind. I tried this recipe using shredded mild Cheddar and shredded cheese with taco seasoning added, but the recipe just did not taste as good as when made with Velveeta.**

3 cups cooked shredded chicken
  (see box, page 226)
2 tablespoons vegetable oil
1 cup chopped onion
  (from 1 medium-size onion)
1 cup chopped green bell pepper
1 can (15 ounces) chili with beans
1 can (15.5 ounces) pinto beans, drained
¼ cup diced canned tomatoes with green chiles
  (see Tips, page 228), drained
8 ounces (half of a 16-ounce package)
  Mexican-flavor Velveeta
  (see Tip at left)

Draining Beans

—▼—

DINNER DOCTOR SAYS

Canned beans are a busy cook's friend, and most of the time they taste better after they have been drained of their starchy and often salty liquid. (Many people find them easier to digest drained, too.) The exception is when you are assembling a bean dish or a fast soup with just a few minutes of cooking time. The bean liquid serves as a natural thickener and the beans won't need as much time to cook down.

1. Preheat the oven to 375°F.

2. Scatter the chicken evenly over the bottom of a 13-by-9-inch (3-quart) glass or ceramic baking dish and set aside.

3. Heat the oil in a 7-inch skillet over medium heat and add the onion and bell pepper. Cook, stirring, until the vegetables are soft, 3 to 4 minutes. Scatter the onion and bell pepper mixture evenly over the chicken. Top with the chili, then the pinto beans, and the tomatoes, spreading each evenly into a layer before adding the next. Cut the Velveeta into thick slices and arrange them over the tomatoes.

4. Bake the casserole until it bubbles around the edges and the Velveeta has melted, 28 to 32 minutes. Serve at once.

SERVES 8

tips I used the Ro-Tel brand of tomatoes with chiles. It is a bit spicier than other brands, and it comes in a 10-ounce can. I know Ro-Tel tomatoes are not available everywhere. If you can't find them, substitute the spiciest canned tomato and chile combination you can find.

Want more heat? Scatter sliced jalapeño peppers over the casserole before baking it.

KENTUCKY CHICKEN AND WILD RICE CASSEROLE

▼ ▼ ▼

You have to come up with something good when you cook for a crowd. When asked to feed some fifty volunteers a hot lunch at a fundraiser, I knew it was going to be a casserole that I'd pull out of my hat. I don't remember how I ended up making this chicken and wild rice casserole, but I did, and luckily I made plenty of it because everyone came around for seconds. After the lunch, my friend Katy Varney Goetz, who's a good cook, asked if that casserole went by the name Mulberry Garden, for the Mulberry Garden casserole of Kentucky, she said, was quite famous and was much like mine. I later asked Katy to share that recipe. She did, and I think her recipe is tastier, so here it is.

TO PREP:
15 MINUTES
TO BAKE:
25–30 MINUTES

4 cups shredded cooked chicken
    (see box, page 226)
1 package (6 ounces) Uncle Ben's
    Long Grain and Wild Rice
    Original Recipe
1 can (10.75 ounces) cream of celery soup
    (see Tips, page 230)
⅔ cup Miracle Whip
    salad dressing
    (see Tips, page 230)
1 can (8 ounces) sliced water
    chestnuts, drained
1 jar (2 ounces) sliced
    pimiento peppers, drained
1 package (9 ounces) frozen French-cut
    green beans, thawed and drained
    (see Tips, page 230)
1½ cups low-sodium chicken broth
    (from one 14- to 14.5-ounce can)
    or water
2 tablespoons pre-grated Parmesan cheese

1. Preheat the oven to 400 °F.

2. Combine the chicken, rice with its seasonings, celery soup, salad dressing, water chestnuts, pimientos, green beans, and chicken broth in a large bowl. Transfer the mixture to a 13-by-9-inch (3-quart) glass or ceramic baking dish and top with the Parmesan cheese. Cover the baking dish with aluminum foil.

3. Bake the casserole until it is bubbling and the rice has cooked, 25 to 30 minutes. Let cool 5 minutes, then serve.

SERVES 8

tips **It is important for the flavor of the casserole not to substitute another type of soup for the cream of celery or mayonnaise for the sweeter Miracle Whip.**

To quickly thaw the green beans, follow the microwave directions on the package, then drain them well. Or substitute a drained can of French-cut green beans for the frozen ones.

This casserole freezes well, either baked or unbaked, and it can be doubled or tripled for feeding a crowd. If you freeze it unbaked, don't add the Parmesan cheese. Sprinkle it on before baking.

POPPY SEED CHICKEN CASSEROLE

▼ ▼ ▼

I first tasted this easy casserole at a school fund-raiser in Nashville and knew I had to have the recipe: It was a natural to add to my repertoire of dinner dishes. The casserole is buttery and rich, so a little goes a long way. It doubles, triples, and quadruples well, should you want to prepare a few ahead of time and stash them unbaked in your freezer (hold off on adding the cracker topping until right before baking). Serve it with a fruit salad or steamed asparagus.

TO PREP:
12 MINUTES
TO BAKE:
25–30 MINUTES

1 package (6.2 ounces) fried-rice–flavor
    Rice-A-Roni, cooked (see Tip)
4 cups shredded cooked chicken
    (see box, page 226)
1 cup reduced-fat sour cream

tip **Cook the Rice-A-Roni ahead of time, using just 1 tablespoon of vegetable oil.**

1 can (10.75 ounces) reduced-fat
    cream of chicken soup
36 buttery round crackers,
    such as Ritz, crushed
    (for 4 ounces)
6 tablespoons (¾ stick) unsalted butter or
    margarine, melted
1 tablespoon poppy seeds

1. Preheat the oven to 375°F.

2. Spoon the rice in an even layer over the bottom of an 11-by-7-inch (2-quart) glass or ceramic baking dish. Combine the chicken, sour cream, and chicken soup in a medium-size bowl. Spoon this evenly over the rice. In the same bowl, combine the crackers and butter. Scatter this over the chicken mixture. Sprinkle the poppy seeds evenly on top.

3. Bake the casserole until it is bubbling and the crackers have lightly browned, 25 to 30 minutes. Serve at once.

SERVES 8

PARMESAN CHICKEN AND BISCUIT PIE

▼ ▼ ▼

TO PREP:
15 MINUTES
TO BAKE:
20–25 MINUTES

When I was a child, I always hoped for a whole biscuit from the top of the chicken and biscuit pie and so I counted the biscuits, then counted how many people were at the table to find out if my mother had made enough—just another way math came in handy! These days, I don't have the time to whip up biscuits from scratch, so I top this delicious pie with enough frozen biscuits to keep everyone happy. The cream and Parmesan give a real lift to canned soup.

2 cups shredded cooked chicken
(see box, page 226)
2 cups frozen mixed vegetables
1 can (10.75 ounces) cream of
chicken soup
Half a soup can (about 5½ ounces)
of heavy cream or
half-and-half
¼ teaspoon black pepper
6 unbaked frozen biscuits (each 2 inches in
diameter)
3 tablespoons pre-grated Parmesan cheese

1. Preheat the oven to 425°F.

2. Combine the chicken, frozen vegetables, chicken soup, and cream in a large mixing bowl. Season with black pepper. Transfer the filling to an 11-by-7-inch

tips Want to fancy up this dish? Add a tablespoon of medium-dry sherry to the chicken mixture or 1 tablespoon of fresh lemon juice and 1 teaspoon of grated lemon zest.

For simple creamed chicken when you are craving comfort but not a heavy meal, omit the biscuits, sprinkle 1½ tablespoons of pre-grated Parmesan on top, and bake the casserole at 425°F until it is bubbling, 15 to 20 minutes.

(2-quart) glass or ceramic baking dish and smooth the top with a rubber spatula. Arrange the frozen biscuits on top of the filling in 2 rows of 3. Sprinkle the tops of the biscuits with the Parmesan cheese.

3. Bake the pie until the biscuits are golden brown and the filling is bubbling, 20 to 25 minutes. Serve at once.

SERVES 6

Freezing Shredded Cooked Chicken

—▼—

DINNER DOCTOR SAYS

What's the best way to make sure you have shredded chicken on hand, ready to turn into a quick dinner? Cook it in advance following the tips in the box on page 226, then freeze it.

To freeze shredded cooked chicken: Place 1-cup portions in plastic freezer bags and label and date them. This works for both chicken you've cooked yourself and for supermarket rotisserie chicken. The shredded chicken can be frozen for up to three months.

To thaw frozen shredded chicken: If you can plan ahead, place as many bags of frozen chicken as the recipe calls for in the refrigerator to thaw overnight (remember one bag equals one cup). If you are in a hurry, place the bags in the sink under warm running water until the chicken thaws enough that you can break it up, 4 to 5 minutes. Or transfer the frozen chicken to a microwave-safe bowl and thaw it in a microwave oven.

When not to freeze cooked chicken: If you have cooked and shredded or chopped chicken breasts that have been frozen and then thawed, don't refreeze them. Refreezing chicken makes it dry and tasteless.

SUSAN'S CHICKEN POTPIE

▼ ▼ ▼

My sister Susan bakes this speedy chicken potpie for her friends and family. It has become her signature food gift, and she keeps the recipe interesting by varying the vegetables in it. She relies on frozen veggies but also tosses in sliced fresh summer squash, carrots, or asparagus tips. The pie has a double crust, so no one has to fight to get a piece of it. Use either frozen deep-dish pie shells or refrigerated pie pastry. If the filling is bubbling but the pie hasn't browned enough on top for you, simply place it under the broiler until it gets deeply golden (do keep a close watch).

TO PREP:
15–20 MINUTES
TO BAKE:
27–34 MINUTES
TO REST:
10 MINUTES

tips **Look in your vegetable bin or in the freezer and fridge to see what vegetables are available. Frozen peas, carrots, or lima beans or leftover green beans, summer squash slices, or asparagus tips all work. If only raw vegetables are available, cut them into small pieces. They'll cook up fine during the baking time.**

Make two pot pies, one for you and one for a friend.

1 package (12 ounces) frozen deep-dish
  pie crusts (2 crusts), or 1 package
  (15 ounces) refrigerated pastry rounds
  (2 rounds)
2 tablespoons butter
1½ cups cooked vegetables of
  your choice (see Tips)
2 cups (packed) shredded
  cooked chicken
  (see box, page 226)
3 tablespoons all-purpose flour
Salt and black pepper
2 cups low-sodium chicken broth

1. Place a rack in the center of the oven and preheat the oven to 450°F.

2. Remove the packaging from the frozen crusts or pastry rounds and set one crust aside. Place a crust or refrigerated pastry round in a 9-inch pie pan that is 2 inches deep. If using pastry rounds, press 1 into the pie pan and crimp the edge with a fork. Prick the bottom of the crust a few times with a fork. Bake the crust until it is well browned, 7 to 8 minutes. Remove the pie pan from the oven and set it aside. Reduce the oven temperature to 350°F.

3. While the pie crust bakes, melt the butter in a large skillet over medium heat. Add the vegetables and cook, stirring, for 1 minute. Add the chicken and cook, stirring for 1 minute longer. Sprinkle the flour over the vegetables and chicken, then season with salt and pepper to taste. Cook, stirring, until the flour is incorporated, 1 minute longer. Add the broth to the skillet, increase the heat to medium-high, and cook, stirring constantly, until the mixture thickens slightly, 1 to 2 minutes.

4. Pour the chicken mixture into the baked pie crust. Cover the top with the remaining pie crust. (If you are using a frozen deep-dish crust, it will have thawed by now and will be easy to lay over the top of your pie.) Turn the edge of the top crust under the crimped edge of the bottom crust with your fingertips. Press around the edge with a fork to seal the two crusts together. Make several vents in the top crust with a sharp knife.

5. Bake the pie on top of a baking sheet until the pie crust is golden brown and the juices are bubbling, 20 to 25 minutes. Remove the pie from the oven, let it rest for 10 minutes, then slice it and serve.

SERVES 6

If the Dish Fits, Bake in It!

— ▼ —

DINNER DOCTOR SAYS

I don't know about you, but I seldom look at what size baking dish a recipe calls for. I check the number of servings instead, then rummage through my cupboards to find the right baking dish for the job. I have a ton of rectangular glass and ceramic ones. They're inexpensive and a must for toting food to potlucks. And somehow, they've managed to accumulate over the years. When I started testing the dishes for this chapter, I realized I needed to find out just how much my baking dishes held so I could fill readers in on how to determine what size baking dishes to use. I measured both the dimensions and volume.

So how do you figure out how your baking dishes correspond to the ones called for here? For the dimensions of a dish, first take the length and width by measuring across the top from one inside edge to the other in both directions. Then measure the depth: Stand the ruler upright and measure the distance from the bottom of the dish to the rim. If your baking dish has slanted sides, don't lean the ruler against one of them; hold it perpendicular to the bottom of the dish.

You may find that the dimensions of your baking dishes don't correspond exactly to mine. Or your baking dishes may be oval (many beautiful ones are). For that reason, volume is a more dependable way of determining capacity. To find out how much a dish holds, using a measuring cup, keep pouring water into the dish until it's full. Keep track of how many cups it takes to fill the dish to the top—that's its volume. Divide the number of cups by four and you have the volume in quarts. (Don't pour the water down the drain; use it to water your plants.)

HEAD COUNT

Here's how my baking dish sizes correspond to the number of people I plan on serving.

Dimensions	Volume	Serves
8 by 8 by 1½ inches	1½ quarts	4 to 6 people
11 by 7 by 1½ inches	2 quarts	6 to 8 people
13 by 9 by 2 inches	3 quarts	8 to 12 people

CHICKEN BURRITO BAKE

▼ ▼ ▼

TO PREP:
15 MINUTES
TO BAKE:
20–25 MINUTES

There are a gazillion southwestern-style chicken casseroles out there, many of them wannabes of the pretty famous King Ranch chicken, a time-consuming powerhouse of a casserole with roots that are said to be found in Texas. What will make this version appealing to the busy cook is that it contains just five ingredients and does not call for sautéed bell peppers and onions or a cream sauce made from scratch. A good store-bought tomatillo salsa plus a convenient refrigerated Alfredo-style pasta sauce add just the right flavor. You can assemble this crowd pleaser in just fifteen minutes.

The prep time assumes you've cooked and shredded the chicken

in advance. If you haven't, a chicken from the supermarket rotisserie is a quick substitute. Shred enough meat to make four cups. Shredding the chicken will add about five minutes to the prep time.

4 cups shredded cooked chicken
   (see box, page 226)
1 cup store-bought medium-hot green
   tomatillo salsa, plus more for serving
1 package (8 ounces; 2 cups) pre-shredded
   cheese blend for tacos
8 to 10 flour tortillas (8 inches each)
2 containers (10 ounces each) refrigerated
   Alfredo-style pasta sauce (see page 277)
Shredded lettuce, avocado cubes, and
   chopped fresh cilantro leaves, for serving

1. Preheat the oven to 375°F.

2. Place the chicken, tomatillo salsa, and ½ cup of the cheese in a large mixing bowl. Stir until the ingredients are well combined.

3. Spoon ½ to ¾ cup of the chicken mixture down the center of a tortilla. Fold 1 edge of the tortilla over the filling, then roll the tortilla to the other edge, creating a filled log. Carefully place the filled tortilla, seam side down, in a 13-by-9-inch

tips The unbaked burrito bake will keep in the refrigerator, covered with plastic wrap, for a day.

The Mexican seasonings in the cheese make it a time-saver, but feel free to use any Cheddar, Monterey Jack, or other mild cheese you have on hand, instead. Season it with a pinch of cumin and chili powder.

You can substitute an equal amount of shredded pork or drained black beans for the chicken in the burritos.

(3-quart) glass or ceramic baking dish. Repeat with the remaining tortillas and filling, placing the burritos snugly side by side in the baking dish. Place the pasta sauce and the remaining 1½ cups of cheese in the mixing bowl and stir to combine. Pour this mixture over the burritos.

4. Bake the burritos until the sauce bubbles, 20 to 25 minutes. Remove the baking dish from the oven and let cool 10 minutes, then serve. You can either serve the burritos whole with sauce or you can cut them into pieces. Serve the burritos with more tomatillo salsa, shredded lettuce, cubes of avocado, and fresh cilantro leaves.

SERVES 8

TURKEY HASH IN A FLASH

▼ ▼ ▼

My memories of our Christmas brunch at my Aunt Elizabeth's house in Nashville are wonderful. The children were allowed to feast on decorated sugar cookies before noon, while the adults served themselves copious spoonfuls of turkey hash and cheese grits. That satisfying hash, simmered with bits of onion and potatoes, made good use of the leftover Christmas Eve turkey and took on a reputation all its own. I often make hash the morning

TO PREP:
10 MINUTES
TO COOK:
15–18 MINUTES

after roasting a turkey, but what about those times when no bird is around? No problem. Begin with a turkey leg or roast chicken from the supermarket deli, combine that with frozen potatoes with onions and bell peppers, and you have a mighty delicious, speedy dish. Serve the hash alongside the Garlicky Cheese Grits Casserole (page 265) on a holiday morning—or just anytime.

2 tablespoons butter

Half of a 28-ounce bag of frozen diced potatoes with onions and bell peppers, such as Ore-Ida Potatoes O'Brien

2 cups finely chopped roast turkey or chicken (see box, page 226)

1½ cups low-sodium chicken broth (from one 14- to 14.5-ounce can; see Tips)

1 clove garlic, crushed in a garlic press

Salt

Cayenne pepper or hot pepper sauce

tips If you are using canned chicken broth that is not low in sodium, don't add any salt to this recipe.

By all means use another ½ cup of turkey if you have it on hand.

The frozen chopped potatoes with onions and bell peppers not only taste great but they are a real time-saver in recipes such as this.

1. Melt the butter in a large skillet over medium heat. Add the frozen potatoes and cook, stirring, until the onions brown slightly, 2 to 3 minutes. Add the turkey, chicken broth, and garlic. Stir to combine, then season with salt and cayenne to taste. Let the hash simmer, stirring occasionally, until all of the liquid is absorbed, 10 to 15 minutes.

2. Taste the hash and add more salt and cayenne as needed. Serve at once.

SERVES 6 TO 8

The Hot Brown

—▼—

DINNER DOCTOR SAYS

No, it's not another Derby-winning racehorse: The Hot Brown is the legendary open-faced turkey sandwich that's smothered in cheese sauce and topped with crisp bacon. It originated in 1923 at The Brown Hotel in Louisville, and it makes an incredibly tasty Sunday-night supper. To prepare a Hot Brown, put slices of cooked turkey breast on toasted white bread, pour a hot cheese sauce over the top, and broil the sandwich until the cheese sauce is bubbling. Right before serving, top the sandwich with sliced tomato and fried bacon. For the cheese sauce, use your favorite recipe for one made with Parmesan or substitute a store-bought Alfredo pasta sauce (the refrigerated kind), adding 2 tablespoons of pre-grated Parmesan for every cup of sauce. Other variations on the classic dish include one made with biscuits: Bake frozen ones, split them, and use the biscuits in place of the toast. And, should you want your Hot Brown hotter, drain a 4.5-ounce can of chopped green chiles and fold them into the cheese sauce.

SPAGHETTI CASSEROLE

▼ ▼ ▼

You can't have enough satisfying recipes like this one that can be whipped up in no time and will feed a lot of people. The spaghetti has a tomato and meat sauce but with the

TO PREP AND COOK:
15 MINUTES
TO BAKE:
18–20 MINUTES

addition of cream of mushroom soup, there is no edge, no roughness, not too much garlic. It's very middle of the road, predictable, and comforting. The recipe doubles and triples well. Serve the spaghetti with a green salad and crusty bread.

tips Much of the flavor of this dish depends on the pasta sauce you choose to use. I found one with fire-roasted tomatoes that was lovely, adding a bit of spice to the otherwise mild flavoring.

You can also spice up this casserole with a pinch of hot pepper flakes or make it more substantial by adding a small can of drained sliced mushrooms.

Cooking the pasta takes anywhere from 7 to 10 minutes after the water comes to a boil. Do this the night before, if possible. Drain and toss the cooked spaghetti with 1 tablespoon of olive oil, then cover and refrigerate it.

1 tablespoon olive oil
1 pound ground beef
    round
½ cup chopped onion (from 1 small onion)
1 clove garlic, peeled and cut into slices
1 can (10.75 ounces) cream of
    mushroom soup
1½ cups of your favorite tomato-based
    pasta sauce (see Tips)
1 cup pre-shredded sharp Cheddar cheese
4 cups cooked spaghetti
    (8 ounces uncooked; see Tips)
2 tablespoons pre-shredded Parmesan cheese

1. Preheat the oven to 400°F.

2. Place the olive oil in a large skillet over medium-high heat. Crumble in the ground beef and add the onion and the garlic. Cook, stirring and breaking up the lumps of meat, until the beef is brown all over and cooked through, 4 to 5 minutes. Remove the skillet from the heat and transfer the beef to a large mixing bowl. (If there is a lot of fat in the pan, drain the mixture in a strainer before transferring it.) Add the mushroom soup, pasta sauce, ½ cup of the Cheddar cheese, the cooked spaghetti, and ½ cup of water and stir to mix. Transfer the spaghetti to a 13-by-9-inch (3-quart) glass or ceramic baking dish and sprinkle all but 1 tablespoon of the remaining Cheddar and 1 tablespoon of the Parmesan over the top.

3. Bake the spaghetti until it bubbles throughout and the cheese has melted, 18 to 20 minutes. Sprinkle on the remaining tablespoon of each cheese and serve at once.

SERVES 8

MEXICAN "LASAGNA"

▼ ▼ ▼

TO PREP AND COOK:
15 MINUTES
TO BAKE:
20–25 MINUTES

Now, here's one clever and down-right simple dish. I wish I could take credit for it, but this recipe has made the circuit. The only trick is to find corn tortillas the same size as your glass pie pan. And actually, that's no trick either—you can always cut to fit. I use a 10-inch pie pan, but a 9-incher works well, too. With it's Mexican flavors, the "lasagna" is comforting and that is why it is in this chapter! I discovered that substituting reduced-fat sour cream and fat-free refried beans does not reduce the flavor, so I'm all for using them.

tip **I enjoy cooking with lean ground beef because for most recipes it isn't necessary to fuss with draining off the fat. But should you have a fattier beef, brown it, then rinse it in a colander under running hot water. Return it to the skillet, stir in the salsa, and continue with the recipe.**

Vegetable oil cooking spray for misting the skillet

1 pound ground beef round (see Tip)

1 jar (12 ounces) chunky salsa

6 corn tortillas (10 inches each)

1 can (16 ounces) refried beans, fat free if possible

1 cup reduced-fat sour cream

1 package (8 ounces; 2 cups) pre-shredded Mexican-style four-cheese blend

Chopped fresh tomato and chopped scallions, for garnish (optional)

1. Preheat the oven to 400°F.

2. Mist a large skillet with vegetable oil cooking spray, and place over medium-high heat. Crumble in the ground beef and cook, stirring and breaking up the lumps with a wooden spoon, until the beef browns all over and is cooked through, 4 to 5 minutes. Stir in ½ cup of the salsa. Set the beef mixture aside.

3. Spread the remaining salsa in the bottom of a 10-inch glass pie pan. Top it with 3 of the tortillas. Spread half of the beans over the tortillas, then half of the meat mixture, then ½ cup of the sour cream, then 1 cup of the cheese. Top with the remaining 3 tortillas and repeat the layers, ending with all but ¼ cup of the remaining cheese. Cover the pie pan loosely with aluminum foil.

4. Bake the "lasagna" until it is hot throughout and the cheese has melted, 20 to 25 minutes. Remove the "lasagna" from the oven, let it rest for 5 minutes, then cut it into wedges or spoon servings onto plates, garnished with the remaining ¼ cup cheese and the chopped tomato and scallions, if desired.

SERVES 6 TO 8

Feeding Friends

—▼—

DINNER DOCTOR SAYS Any of these easy recipes can be made for others—family, friends feeling a little under the weather, new parents, new neighbors. Simply bake the casserole in a clean disposable aluminum pan, cover it, and include instructions on how to reheat it.

I buy aluminum pans at the supermarket or restaurant supply store. Since many casseroles freeze well in aluminum pans, you can fill your freezer with goodies ready to deliver when the occasion arises. Frozen, most will keep for up to three months.

NOT-SO-IMPOSSIBLE MOUSSAKA PIE

▼▼▼

Some recipes come about by accident—and boy, do we enjoy a lot of those at our house! I arrived at this one when I was meaning to make something else entirely. I was testing a Bisquick "impossible" pie. After I added some crumbled ground beef, my husband, John, declared it was almost like Greek moussaka, except that it didn't have eggplant or oregano in it. So I added oregano and a little onion and, instead of the eggplant, the quicker cooking zucchini. We both loved the results. There was no need for the mashed potatoes or the béchamel sauce you find in moussaka, since the pie was creamy and velvety on its own. It's perfect served with a crisp salad of greens and cucumbers.

TO PREP:
15 MINUTES
TO BAKE:
20–25 MINUTES

Vegetable oil cooking spray,
  for misting the pie pan
1 tablespoon olive oil
8 ounces ground beef round
  (see Tips, page 246)
2 tablespoons minced onion
2 tablespoons minced green bell pepper
1 cup thinly sliced zucchini
  (from 1 small zucchini;
  see Tips, page 246)
1 to 1½ teaspoons dried oregano,
  or 1 tablespoon chopped fresh
  oregano leaves
Salt and black pepper
1 cup pre-crumbled feta cheese
½ cup biscuit mix, such as Bisquick
1 cup milk
2 large eggs

1. Place a rack in the center of the oven and preheat the oven to 400°F.

2. Mist a 9-inch glass pie pan with vegetable oil cooking spray.

3. Heat the olive oil in a large skillet over medium-high heat. Crumble in the ground beef and cook, stirring and

> **tips**   **I like to cook with the leanest beef possible because it is healthier and because you don't have to go through the process of draining off the fat. A little bit of olive oil keeps the beef from sticking to the pan, and in this recipe it adds flavor, too.**
>
> **If the zucchini is small, cut it cross-wise into thin slices. If you have a fatter zucchini, slice it in half lengthwise, then cut the halves into thin half-moon slices.**
>
> **For a fun twist, use a flavored feta, such as one with sun-dried tomatoes or peppercorns.**

breaking up the lumps of meat, until the beef is browned all over, 2 to 3 minutes. Add the onion, bell pepper, zucchini, oregano, salt, and pepper. Reduce the heat to medium and cook, stirring, until the zucchini softens, 4 minutes.

4. Transfer the beef mixture to a 9-inch glass pie pan. Sprinkle the feta cheese evenly over the top. Whisk together the biscuit mix, milk, and eggs in a small bowl, then pour this evenly over the feta.

5. Bake the pie until it is golden brown and firm to the touch, 20 to 25 minutes. Remove the pie from the oven and let it cool for 5 minutes, then cut it into wedges and serve.

SERVES 4

HAM AND CHEDDAR NOT-SO-IMPOSSIBLE PIE

▼▼▼

An adaptation of the classic ham and cheese "impossible" pie from Bisquick, this easy recipe uses Cheddar instead of Swiss cheese. Bisquick is the only thickener needed to turn ordinary ingredients into a wonderfully velvety quichelike pie. It's

TO PREP:
15 MINUTES
TO BAKE:
20–25 MINUTES

so easy your children can make it. In fact, before one of my out-of-town trips, I left the recipe and the ingredients in the kitchen so my twelve-year-old daughter Kathleen could fix supper for everyone. She called me later, thrilled at how well the pie turned out and at her new-found prowess in the kitchen! You'll find some more tasty ideas for "impossible" pies on page 249.

tips I love to bake a small ham on the weekend so we have leftovers during the week, and I place little bags of chopped ham or ham "scraps" as we call them in the freezer for recipes just like this. They will keep for up to one month. But if you don't have ham on hand, buy slices of a good smoked ham from the supermarket and cut it into strips for this recipe.

You can reheat slices of the pie in the microwave on high for 1 to 2 minutes.

Vegetable oil cooking spray,
    for misting the pan
1½ cups chopped ham
1 cup pre-shredded sharp
    Cheddar cheese
½ cup biscuit mix,
    such as Bisquick
1 cup milk
2 large eggs

1. Preheat the oven to 400°F.

2. Mist a 9-inch glass pie pan with vegetable oil cooking spray. Sprinkle the ham, then the Cheddar cheese over the bottom of the pie pan.

3. Whisk together the biscuit mix, milk, and eggs in a small bowl, then pour this evenly over the ham and cheese.

4. Bake the pie until it is golden brown and firm to the touch, 20 to 25 minutes. Remove the pie from the oven and let it cool for 5 minutes, then cut it into wedges and serve.

SERVES 6

Impossibly Easy "Impossible" Pies

— ▼ —

DINNER DOCTOR SAYS

Chances are you've forked into the infamous "impossible" pie. Whether sweet and made with coconut or bananas or savory and containing cheese and broccoli, the pies have become a mainstay of the American kitchen. They turned up thirty years ago in a church cookbook, according to the Betty Crocker test kitchen. So named because these pies don't have a pie crust and are therefore virtually foolproof, the pies do contain at least a half cup of Bisquick that bakes into a faux crust. According to Betty Crocker, the first "impossible" pie was coconut.

The variations below use ingredients in addition to or in place of the ham and Cheddar in Ham and Cheddar Not-So-Impossible Pie on page 247. To make the pie, follow the instructions on the opposite page.

◆ **Ham, Cheese, and Broccoli Pie:** Add 1 cup of chopped cooked broccoli, or thawed and drained frozen broccoli pieces, to the ham and cheese in Step 2, adding a dash of nutmeg, if desired, then proceed with Step 3.

◆ **Mexican Tomato and Chile Pie:** Substitute 1 can (14.5 ounces) Mexican-style diced tomatoes (the kind with garlic, cumin and jalapeños) for the ham. Drain the tomatoes before placing them in the pie pan. Use Mexican-style shredded cheese instead of Cheddar, then proceed with Step 3. It will take 10 minutes longer for the pie to bake since the tomatoes make it more liquid.

◆ **Smoked Salmon and Chive Pie:** Substitute 1 cup of chopped smoked salmon for the ham and use a milder cheese, such as Monterey Jack, instead of the Cheddar. Sprinkle 1 tablespoon of minced fresh chives or scallion over the cheese, then proceed with Step 3.

◆ **Asparagus and Tarragon Pie:** In place of the ham, arrange 1 cup of lightly steamed thin asparagus tips on the bottom of the misted pie pan. Scatter 1 cup of Swiss cheese, ¼ cup of chopped scallions, and 1 tablespoon of minced fresh tarragon or 1 teaspoon of dried tarragon over the asparagus, then proceed with Step 3.

CHILI CORN DOG PIE

▼ ▼ ▼

TO PREP:
15 MINUTES
TO COOK:
25–30 MINUTES

Kids are wonderful and funny, and watching all that energy and creativity may make you feel old, but in the end, the silliness that takes over the household really makes you younger at heart. Your children will silly up your diet, too, if you're not careful, letting things like corn dogs, hot dogs, chicken fingers, fish fingers, Tater Tots, and Popsicles creep into your meal plan. This casserole is for kids of all ages to enjoy with ballpark mustard and creamy coleslaw.

2 cans (15 ounces each) chili with beans

6 to 8 hot dogs, sliced in half lengthwise

1 cup self-rising cornmeal mix (see Tips)

½ cup milk

1 large egg

2 tablespoons vegetable oil

1 cup pre-shredded sharp Cheddar cheese

tips Of course, the best chili is your homemade chili, and by all means use it in this recipe if you have it on hand (you'll need 4 cups). But in a pinch, canned chili works just fine. Buy the best brand at your supermarket.

If you can't find self-rising cornmeal mix, use 1 cup of regular cornmeal mixed with 1 teaspoon of baking powder.

Adjust the number of hot dogs based on who will be enjoying this pie. You can leave them out entirely, if you like, but remember that that's what makes this casserole a corn dog pie. Without them it is just corn bread with chili and cheese.

1. Preheat the oven to 400°F.

2. Pour the chili into an 11-by-7-inch (2-quart) glass or ceramic baking dish. Arrange the hot dog slices on top of the chili.

3. Whisk together the cornmeal mix, milk, egg, and oil in a small bowl and pour it evenly over the hot dogs. Sprinkle the Cheddar cheese on top.

4. Bake the casserole until the corn bread topping is lightly browned and firm and the chili bubbles around the edges, 25 to 30 minutes. Remove the baking dish from the oven and set it aside to cool for 5 minutes before spooning the chili corn dogs onto plates.

SERVES **6** TO **8**

PORK FRIED RICE

▼▼▼

Nothing's quite like comforting Chinese fried rice, and there's nothing like this recipe to get that rice to the table quickly. The recipe gets its start from Rice-A-Roni, "that San Francisco treat." I add some strips of seared lean pork chops, toss in frozen

TO PREP:
10 MINUTES
TO COOK:
21–24 MINUTES

peas straight from the freezer, and shower the rice with thinly sliced scallions. Dinner's on the table in no time flat.

5 to 6 (about 12 ounces) thin lean bone-in
   pork chops, or 3 to 4 (8 to 10 ounces)
   thin lean boneless pork chops
2 teaspoons olive oil
1 package (6.2 ounces) fried rice–flavor
   Rice-A-Roni (see Tips)
½ cup frozen green peas
2 scallions, both white and light green parts,
   thinly sliced (optional)
Soy sauce, for serving (optional)

1. Remove any bones and fat from the pork chops. Slice the meat crosswise into ¼-inch strips. You should have about 1½ cups of pork strips.

2. Place the olive oil in a large skillet and heat it over medium-high heat. Add the pork strips and cook, stirring, until the pork is

tips There are a couple of different fried rice mixes in the stores, but I like the Rice-A-Roni version best. It is the most straightforward and includes the brand's signature pasta–rice combination. The only problem with using a rice mix is that it serves so few, but this recipe doubles well should you need to feed more.

You can vary the vegetables. Try a pea and carrot combination, French-cut green beans, or broccoli florets.

No pork? Use 1½ cups chicken strips or peeled and deveined raw shrimp.

If you have the time, scramble an egg and mix it into the fried rice.

browned and cooked through, 2 to 3 minutes. Add the Rice-A-Roni and the contents of its seasoning packet and stir. Pour in 2 cups of water and stir to loosen the brown bits from the bottom of the skillet. Let the mixture come to a boil, then reduce the heat to medium-low and cover the skillet. Let simmer for 15 minutes.

3. Stir in the frozen peas and let the mixture continue to cook until the peas and the rice mixture are cooked through, 3 to 5 minutes longer. Serve at once in shallow bowls with the scallions and soy sauce, if desired.

SERVES 4

COUNTRY SAUSAGE, CHEDDAR, AND APPLE BAKE

▼ ▼ ▼

TO PREP:
15 MINUTES
TO BAKE:
25–28 MINUTES

Brunches in the South usually include this wonderful sausage casserole in some version or another. The beauty of the recipe is that it can be assembled and refrigerated a day in advance, then baked up hot on the morning of a breakfast or brunch. Don't be shy about doctoring it up, adding your own creative touches. Vary the sausage, sauté the apples before adding them to the casserole, or sprinkle in a half cup of uncooked coarse grits. But do always use sharp Cheddar. So take a look at my version, then let your creativity be your guide and design your own "bake."

tips I cook sausage patties because they are quick to fry and drain, but if you prefer, use 12 ounces of bulk country sausage; crumble it, then fry and drain it.

You could give this casserole a Mexican touch by omitting the apples and adding a drained 4-ounce can of chopped chiles. Substitute a Mexican blend cheese, and add 1 teaspoon of ground cumin to the egg and milk mixture.

1 tablespoon butter, melted

6 slices soft white bread, crusts removed

9 sausage patties (12 ounces total)

5 to 6 fresh thyme sprigs, or 1 teaspoon dried
    thyme (optional)

1 medium-size apple, peeled, cored, and
    thinly sliced

1 package (12 ounces; 3 cups) pre-shredded
    sharp Cheddar cheese

6 large eggs

2 cups milk

1. Preheat the oven to 400°F.

2. Brush the melted butter on the bread slices and place them side by side in the bottom of a 13-by-9-inch (3-quart) glass or ceramic baking dish. Set aside.

3. Place the sausage patties in a skillet over medium heat and cook until browned and cooked through, 2 to 3 minutes per

> **tip** The unbaked casserole can be covered with plastic wrap and refrigerated for 24 hours. Remove the plastic wrap and let it sit on the kitchen counter while the oven preheats to 400°F. It will take about 30 minutes to puff up and turn golden brown.

side. Drain on paper towels. Cut the patties in half and randomly place them on top of the bread. Scatter the thyme and the apple slices on top of the sausage. Sprinkle the Cheddar cheese evenly over the sausage and apples, so that it completely covers the top of the casserole. Whisk together the eggs and milk in a small bowl. Pour this mixture on top of the cheese.

4. Bake the casserole until it puffs up and is deeply golden brown, 25 to 28 minutes. Serve at once.

SERVES 8 TO 10

MOCK CASSOULET

▼ ▼ ▼

I will never forget my first taste of cassoulet in south-western France. It was a blazing hot day in mid-July, the cassoulet was brought hot from the oven, and the red wine was nearly hot, too. If only a swimming pool had been nearby!

When made following the classic method, cassoulet is a delicious but time-consuming stew of dried white beans and all sorts of smoked sausages and pork or lamb, buried under a bread-crumb crust. But I have streamlined that recipe for those of you in a hurry. The combination of a tablespoon of wine, some fresh thyme, and smoked sausage takes on a life of its own, elevating a simple white-bean supper to lofty fare. Canned beans only need to simmer a little while, and for the crust, you simply sauté bread crumbs and parsley in olive

TO PREP:
15 MINUTES
TO COOK:
20–25 MINUTES

oil and sprinkle them over the stew. Serve the cassoulet with a green salad and crusty bread.

1 pound lightly smoked sausage,
　　such as kielbasa, cut on the
　　diagonal into 1-inch slices
1 cup chopped onion (from 1 medium-size
　　onion)
2 cloves garlic, peeled and halved
2 cans (15.5 ounces each) Great Northern
　　beans, with their liquid
1 can (14.5 ounces) diced tomatoes with
　　onions, celery, and green peppers
1 tablespoon dry red wine (optional; see Tips)
1 bay leaf
5 to 6 fresh thyme sprigs, or 1 teaspoon
　　dried thyme (see Tips)
2 tablespoons olive oil
　　1½ cups coarse homemade bread
　　　　crumbs (see Tips)
2 tablespoons chopped fresh parsley

1. Place the sausage, onion, and garlic in a 7-quart pot over medium heat. Cook, stirring, until

the sausage browns slightly, 3 minutes. Pour in the beans with their liquid and the tomatoes, wine, if using, bay leaf, and thyme. Bring to a boil, then cover the pot, reduce the heat to medium-low, and let simmer for 15 to 20 minutes, stirring occasionally.

2. Meanwhile, heat the olive oil in a small skillet over medium heat. Add the bread crumbs and parsley and cook, stirring, until the bread crumbs turn golden brown, 3 to 4 minutes. Set aside.

3. Remove the bay leaf and thyme sprigs, if any, from the pot. Ladle the cassoulet into bowls, sprinkle some of the parsleyed bread crumbs on top, and serve.

SERVES 8

tips If you have a tablespoon of red or, for that matter, white wine around, use it. If not, don't worry; the cassoulet will still be memorable.

Fresh thyme is better than dried, but use what you have on hand.

Bread crumbs are easy to make from bread that's slightly stale. Tear it into chunks and toss these in the food processor. A few pulses and you have bread crumbs.

Browning the sausage, onion, and garlic first is important because it gives the cassoulet much more depth and dimension than if you just dumped these ingredients into the pot with the beans.

EAST COAST OYSTER AND SPINACH CASSEROLE

▼ ▼ ▼

Whoever says comfort food must be plain-Jane has obviously never forked into this elegant casserole that stars fresh briny oysters, a hint of vermouth, and that healthy time-saver, frozen chopped spinach. It's perfect for holiday brunches, pre-game lunches, and post-opera dinner buffets. Take care to assemble the casserole ahead of time and refrigerate it, then bake it right before serving so the oysters don't overcook.

TO PREP AND COOK:
15 MINUTES
TO BAKE:
15–18 MINUTES

4 tablespoons (½ stick) butter

1 cup finely chopped onion
(from 1 medium-size onion)

2 tablespoons all-purpose flour

1 quart fresh oysters, drained
with their liquor reserved

1 cup whole milk

¼ cup dry vermouth or
dry white wine

¼ teaspoon ground nutmeg

Salt and black pepper

2 packages (10 ounces each) frozen
chopped spinach, thawed and
drained well (see Tips)

1 cup coarse bread crumbs
(see Tips, page 257)

Chopped fresh tarragon or parsley,
for garnish

1. Preheat the oven to 400°F.

2. Melt the butter in a large skillet over medium heat. Tip the pan, spoon out 2 tablespoons of the melted butter into a small bowl, and set aside. Add the onion to the butter remaining in the skillet and cook, stirring,

until the onion is soft, 2 to 3 minutes. Sprinkle the flour over the onion and cook, stirring, 1 minute longer. Pour ½ cup of the reserved oyster liquor and the milk and vermouth over the onion. Cook the sauce, stirring constantly, until it thickens, 2 to 3 minutes. Add the nutmeg and season with salt and pepper to taste. Remove the pan from the heat and set it aside.

3. Spoon the spinach evenly into the bottom of a 13-by-9-inch (3-quart) glass or ceramic baking dish. Place the oysters on top of the spinach. Ladle the warm sauce over the oysters. Toss the bread crumbs with the reserved melted butter and sprinkle them on top of the sauce.

4. Bake the casserole until it is bubbling and the crumbs are browned, 15 to 18 minutes. Serve at once, garnished with fresh tarragon.

SERVES 8

tips This may seem like a lot of ingredients, but the casserole goes together quickly. You need to make this dish when oysters are in season—preferably in cold weather. Buy the freshest oysters you can, ones that have just been shucked if possible.

Try to plan ahead and thaw the frozen spinach overnight in the refrigerator, then drain it well. But if you forget, just unwrap the spinach, place the frozen blocks in a microwave-safe dish, and thaw them in a microwave oven on high power for 2 minutes. Then break them up and drain well.

The unbaked casserole can be covered with plastic wrap and refrigerated for up to 24 hours. Don't prepare the crumb topping until right before you are ready to bake. This means melting only 2 tablespoons of the butter in Step 2. Remove the plastic wrap and let the casserole sit on the kitchen counter while the oven preheats to 400°F. Add the crumb topping right before baking. It will take about 25 minutes for the casserole to bubble and the crumbs to brown.

So Easy Tuna Noodle Casserole

▼▼▼

TO PREP AND COOK:
15 MINUTES
TO BAKE:
20–25 MINUTES

Many creamy casseroles originally began with a white sauce made from scratch with butter, flour, and milk. But once moms like mine got pressed for time, they found canned cream of mushroom soup was a handy substitute. The soup is the base for the classic tuna noodle casserole. I revisited the recipe, lightening up the mushroom soup with fresh lemon juice and crowning the casserole with just enough crushed potato chips to add salt and crunch without being overwhelming. This dish will make you smile.

tips If you have a box of frozen peas, you can add the entire box (10 ounces)—the more vegetables, the better.

I like albacore tuna, but you can add the same size can of any kind of tuna as long as you drain it well.

Because of the potato chips and the salt in the tuna, there is no need to add salt to the casserole.

Should you have no potato chips on hand (you healthy soul), mix together 1/3 cup of dry bread crumbs and 2 tablespoons of pre-grated Parmesan cheese for a topping.

Salt (optional), for cooking the noodles

1½ cups egg noodles, macaroni, fusilli,
    or penne

1 tablespoon olive oil

½ cup chopped onion (from 1 small onion)

1 can (10.75 ounces) cream of
    mushroom soup

1 cup milk (whole, reduced fat, or skim)

1 tablespoon fresh lemon juice

Black pepper

1 cup frozen peas (see Tips)

1 can (6 ounces) water-packed albacore
    tuna (see Tips), drained and flaked

1 cup potato chips, crushed

1. Preheat the oven to 425°F.

2. Bring a large pot of water to a boil over high heat. Add salt, if using, and stir in the noodles. Reduce the heat to medium-high and cook the noodles, uncovered, until al dente, 8 minutes.

3. Meanwhile, heat the olive oil in a large saucepan over medium heat. Add the onion and cook, stirring, until soft, 2 to 3 minutes. Whisk in the mushroom soup, milk, and lemon juice. Season with pepper, to taste. Stir until the sauce is smooth, thickened slightly, and bubbling, 4 minutes. Remove the pan from the heat.

4. Drain the noodles well in a colander, shaking it a few times to remove any water that might still cling to them. Fold the noodles, frozen peas, and tuna into the mushroom sauce. Transfer the tuna mixture to a 1½- or 2-quart casserole and smooth the top with a rubber spatula. Scatter the crushed potato chips evenly over the top.

5. Bake the casserole until it bubbles throughout and the potato chips turn golden brown, 20 to 25 minutes.
Serve at once.

SERVES 4

15 WAYS TO DOCTOR MACARONI AND CHEESE

A perennial kids' favorite and a life-saving dinner dish for parents, mac and cheese—whether from a box, from the deli carryout, or made from scratch—is an easy-to-doctor main dish. Most of the ingredients you'll find here can be stirred into the macaroni and cheese before you heat it in the oven. If you are making the boxed kind that doesn't bake, stir the add-ins directly into the pot: Macaroni and cheese from the stovetop is just as comforting as it is from the oven. The amounts below will doctor three to four servings; they can be doubled as needed.

1 Stir in 1 cup of chopped ham.

2 Add ½ cup of frozen peas or chopped broccoli (and ½ cup chopped ham, too, if it's in the fridge).

3 Drain a small can of sliced mushrooms and fold them into the macaroni and cheese.

4 Add 1 cup of chopped fresh, ripe tomatoes and 1 tablespoon of minced fresh basil.

5 Stir in ½ cup of drained flaked tuna plus 1 teaspoon of drained capers.

6 Fold in ½ cup of smoked salmon strips.

7 Add ½ cup of cooked cauliflower florets and a dash of ground nutmeg.

8 Top each serving with a spoonful of fresh spinach that has been briefly sautéed.

9 Add 1 cup of browned ground beef that you have lightly seasoned with salt and black pepper.

10 Sauté 2 sliced garlic cloves briefly in melted butter and fold these into the macaroni and cheese.

11 Stir in 1 cup of drained canned white beans, then season the macaroni and cheese with a little dried thyme.

12 Spoon the macaroni and cheese into a serving bowl and top it with strips of grilled sausage.

13 Toss a cup of toasted bread crumbs in olive oil, run these under the broiler, then shower them on top of the macaroni and cheese.

14 Stir in ½ cup of sautéed shrimp and a dash of Cajun seasoning.

15 Sauté some thin slices of red bell pepper briefly in olive oil, then stir them into the macaroni and cheese.

HOME-STYLE MACARONI AND CHEESE

▼ ▼ ▼

For years I fretted because my children preferred the orange or blue boxes of macaroni and cheese to my homemade. How could they resist the made-from-scratch white sauce, the melted aged Vermont Cheddar cheese, the al dente penne pasta? The answer is that they were kids, and kids like the creamy, often blander stuff. When I started creating recipes for this chapter, macaroni and cheese was the first recipe idea I jotted down. I was determined to create a creamy, cheesy, fast casserole that my whole family would adore. This definitely is it!

TO PREP AND COOK:
12 MINUTES
TO BAKE:
25–30 MINUTES

tips **Alfredo-style pasta sauces differ, and after tasting many brands, I discovered I preferred the refrigerated sauces (especially the DiGiorno brand) over those found on the shelf. I tried making this recipe with Cheddar cheese soup and with Velveeta, but nothing short of a homemade cream sauce has the preferred consistency— except the Alfredo sauce (see also the box on page 277).**

If you like, you can add a pinch of dried mustard or a little Worcestershire sauce when you add the Alfredo sauce.

Vegetable oil cooking spray, for misting the baking dish

8 ounces elbow macaroni

Salt (optional), for cooking the macaroni

1 container (10 ounces) refrigerated Alfredo-style pasta sauce (see Tips)

1 package (12 ounces; 3 cups) pre-shredded sharp Cheddar cheese

1 tablespoon olive oil

1 cup coarse bread crumbs (see Tips, page 257)

1. Preheat the oven to 375°F.

2. Lightly mist an 11-by-7-inch (2-quart) glass or ceramic baking dish with vegetable oil cooking spray and set it aside.

3. Bring a large pot of water to a boil over high heat. Add salt, if using, and stir in the macaroni. Reduce the heat to medium-high and cook the macaroni uncovered, until al dente, about 8 minutes. Reserve 1 cup of the pasta cooking water, then drain the macaroni well in a colander, shaking it a few times to remove any water that might still cling to the pasta.

4. Transfer the macaroni to the prepared baking dish. Add the pasta sauce, 2 cups of the cheese, and the reserved pasta cooking water, and stir until the ingredients are well combined. Scatter the remaining 1 cup of cheese over the top.

5. In a small bowl, toss the olive oil with the bread crumbs, and then scatter them on top of the cheese.

6. Bake until the macaroni and cheese is bubbly and the bread crumbs are lightly browned, 25 to 30 minutes. Serve at once.

SERVES 8

GARLICKY CHEESE GRITS CASSEROLE

▼ ▼ ▼

TO PREP AND COOK:
15 MINUTES
TO BAKE:
35–40 MINUTES

Grits are a mainstay of the Southern diet. They are our mashed potatoes, even though they are most often served at breakfast. This recipe has been around a long time. It was a favorite of my mother—and of all of us—because it was so cheesy and garlicky. The secret speedy ingredient is Velveeta processed cheese—not exactly a gourmet product, but you won't knock it once you've tried it in this recipe! Serve these grits alongside Turkey Hash in a Flash (page 239), baked ham, grilled fish, you name it. The grits reheat well the next day.

Vegetable oil cooking spray, for misting the baking dish
1 cup quick (not instant) grits
1 package (8 ounces; 2 cups) pre-shredded sharp Cheddar cheese
6 ounces Velveeta (see Tips), cut into pieces
3 large cloves garlic, squeezed through a garlic press
4 tablespoons (½ stick) butter, cut into pieces
3 large eggs, lightly beaten
1 teaspoon Worcestershire sauce

1. Preheat the oven to 400°F.

tips It is easy to slice 6 ounces off a log of Velveeta because the package is conveniently marked in 4-ounce increments. So, you need 1½ "sections."

No Velveeta? Add 1½ cups more shredded Cheddar cheese, but be forewarned that the grits won't be as creamy.

If you are really short on time, eliminate the baking. Simply omit the eggs, spoon the warm grits onto plates, and serve.

2. Lightly mist an 11-by-7-inch (2-quart) glass or ceramic baking dish with vegetable oil cooking spray and set it aside.

3. Pour 4 cups of water into a large saucepan over medium-high heat. When the water comes to a boil, stir in the grits, then cover the pan, reduce the heat to low, and let simmer for 5 minutes, stirring occasionally. Remove the pan from the heat, add the cheeses, the garlic, and the butter, and stir until they are melted. Add the eggs and the Worcestershire sauce and stir until well combined. Pour the grits mixture into the prepared baking dish.

4. Bake the grits until they are golden brown and bubbling, 35 to 40 minutes. Let them rest for 10 minutes before serving.

SERVES 6 TO 8

A Spring Fling

▼▼▼

Here's another spring menu, this one good for a Saturday night dinner for eight (just double the recipe for the chicken and the succotash). It even has Mother's Day possibilities. The Garlicky Cheese Grits Casserole is meant to substitute for the basmati rice called for in the chicken recipe. If you prefer making the rice, then it's not necessary to serve grits, too. The dessert recipe makes two Angel Food Loaves. Keep one frozen to enjoy a little later in the season.

Artichoke and Feta Puff Pastry Pizza
page 46

Curried Chicken and Apple Stew
page 168

Garlicky Cheese Grits Casserole
page 265

So Fast Succotash
page 363

Three-Berry Angel Food Loaves
page 502

TAMALE PIE

▼ ▼ ▼

Growing up in the middle of Tennessee, we didn't eat a lot of tamales. So, when my friend Mindy passed along this ultracomfort recipe, I had no idea it was a shortcut version of something more authentic. Tamale pie is an old recipe; John Mariani writes in *The Dictionary of American Food & Drink* that it was first cited in print in 1911. Made both with and without beef, it was a good way for wartime cooks to use cornmeal to feed more with less. My modern version uses both corn chips and white hominy. With this recipe, you'll have south-of-the-border flavor in roughly half an hour.

TO PREP:
15 MINUTES
TO BAKE:
25 MINUTES

tips **Prepare the pie in a 13-by-9-inch glass or ceramic baking dish, bake it for 12 to 15 minutes, and you have a tasty appetizer to serve with crisp tortilla chips for dipping.**

This is a substantial dish, just right for football parties in the fall and winter.

3 cups corn chips, such as
    Fritos, lightly crushed
1 can (15.5 ounces) white hominy
    with its liquid
2 cans (15 ounces each) chili with beans
1 cup pre-shredded Cheddar cheese
Pre-shredded iceberg lettuce, chopped onion,
    avocado cubes, tomato salsa, chopped
    fresh cilantro leaves, and sour cream,
    for serving

1. Preheat the oven to 400°F.

2. Place the corn chips and the hominy with its liquid in an 11-by-7-inch (2-quart) glass or ceramic baking dish. Stir to combine. Pour the chili on top.

3. Bake the pie until hot throughout, 20 minutes. Sprinkle the cheese on top and bake until it melts, 5 minutes. Serve immediately with lettuce, onion, avocado, salsa, cilantro, and sour cream.

SERVES 8

BLENDER CHEESE SOUFFLÉS

▼ ▼ ▼

These cheese soufflés taste as great as fussy homemade ones, and you save a lot of time when you substitute slices of bread for the standard thick white sauce. In fact, the preparation time is so short you'll still have time to set the table, unload the dishwasher, and open mail while the oven preheats. The soufflés puff up golden and gorgeous, and you look gorgeous, too, since you didn't slave all day in the kitchen. Serve the soufflés with Warm Curried Carrot Soup (page 76), Five-Minute Gazpacho (page 68), Chilled Roasted Red Pepper Soup (page 66), or a green salad.

TO PREP:
15 MINUTES
TO BAKE:
30–35 MINUTES

tips It is important to use 6 ounces of bread in this recipe, so if you have a kitchen scale, be sure to weigh the bread. If your bread is lighter, you'll need more slices.

Please feel free to doctor the recipe with any seasoning you like. A pinch of dry mustard, a dash of hot pepper sauce, a tablespoon of a chopped fresh herb, a dash of black pepper—you get the idea.

2 teaspoons butter, at room temperature

1 large clove garlic, peeled

1 package (8 ounces; 2 cups) pre-shredded
    sharp Cheddar cheese

4 slices (6 ounces) sourdough bread,
    each slice torn into 3 or 4 pieces
    (see Tips)

4 large eggs

2 cups milk

1. Preheat the oven to 400°F.

2. Rub 8 ramekins (4 inches in diameter and 2 inches deep) with the butter. Place the ramekins on a baking sheet and set aside.

3. With the food processor running, drop the peeled garlic clove down the feed tube and process until minced, 5 to 10 seconds. Stop the machine. Add the cheese and bread and process until the bread has become crumbs, 30 seconds. Stop the machine and add the eggs and the milk and process until well combined, 15 seconds. Pour the cheese mixture into the prepared ramekins, filling them three-quarters full. Carefully place the baking sheet with the ramekins in the oven.

4. Bake the soufflés until they puff up and are golden brown, 30 to 35 minutes. Serve at once.

SERVES 8

PASTA PRESTO

▼ ▼ ▼

From bow ties to spaghetti, from no-boil lasagna to orzo, a generous supply of pasta is a must for the busy cook. Stock your pantry well, and you'll always have a fallback plan for dinner. Thin pasta cooks in no time: Angel hair takes just four minutes when dry and only one minute when fresh! Most pastas cook in six to eight minutes, boiling right alongside the simmering sauce. But don't forget pasta casseroles like baked ziti or lasagna. They may take a little longer to bake to bubbling doneness, but they're a breeze to assemble.

Doctoring a jar of red pasta sauce from the supermarket is almost second nature. Add a little olive oil or red wine, a bit more garlic, or some mushrooms and green bell pepper and who can tell it's not homemade? It's easy to dress up white pasta sauces, too. If you begin with a store-bought Alfredo-style sauce, you can build on that rich flavor by folding in crabmeat and a little sherry. You can also combine that handy Alfredo sauce with a package of frozen creamed spinach before you toss in fettuccine.

Canned tuna mixed with lemon juice and olives becomes a sauce for pasta shells. Leftovers from last night's baked ham combined with a package of sliced mushrooms and a bit of cream turn into a velvety sauce for linguine. Jazz up a commercial marinara sauce with black-olive paste, red pepper flakes, and capers and you have Saturday Night Fever Pasta. Make a sauce from a jar of roasted red peppers and top angel hair pasta with it, or combine artichoke hearts and fresh tomatoes and spoon this over cheese tortellini. Crumbled blue cheese, toasted walnuts, and thin asparagus are good with penne. Asparagus—as well as many other vegetables—can be added to the cooking water during the last few minutes the pasta cooks and drained in the colander right along with the pasta.

The same great sauces that are so tasty with pasta are delicious poured over pasta's country cousin, polenta. A yellow cornmeal mush popular in northern Italy, polenta is sold ready to heat in supermarket produce departments. You can slice it and bake, fry, or microwave it or mix it with milk and seasonings and serve it as you would mashed potatoes.

See an interesting shape of pasta on the supermarket shelf that you've never tried? Buy it, boil it, sauce it, serve it! Pasta is the time-starved cook's best friend.

ANGEL HAIR

WITH ROASTED RED PEPPER SAUCE

▼ ▼ ▼

You can make an incredibly versatile pasta sauce by doctoring a jar of roasted red peppers. It doesn't take much, just some onion, garlic, half-and-half, and a touch of cayenne pepper. When I want a delicate dish, I pair the sauce with angel hair pasta. For a more robust version, serve the sauce with plain or whole-wheat fettuccine. If you'd prefer a less rich dish, substitute evaporated skim milk for the half-and-half.

TO PREP:
8 MINUTES
TO COOK:
4 MINUTES

Salt (optional), for cooking
the pasta
8 ounces angel hair pasta
2 tablespoons olive oil
1 cup finely chopped onion
(from 1 medium-size onion)
2 cloves garlic, sliced
1 jar (12 to 13 ounces; about 1½ cups)
roasted red peppers, drained
½ cup half-and-half
Pinch of cayenne pepper
Basil leaves, or 2 tablespoons
store-bought pesto, for garnish

(tip) This recipe makes a little more than 2 cups of sauce. Depending on how much sauce you like on your pasta, this will be just about right for 8 ounces of angel hair. If you have leftover sauce, you can refrigerate it and boil more pasta the next day. Or, if you prefer lightly sauced dishes, cook an entire pound of angel hair; this will serve eight. The more lightly sauced pasta is particularly good served with skewers of grilled chicken or shrimp alongside.

1. Bring a large pot of water to a boil over high heat. Add salt, if using, and stir in the angel hair pasta. Reduce the heat to medium-high and cook the angel hair, uncovered, until al dente, 4 minutes. Drain the angel hair well in a colander, shaking it a few times to remove any water that might still cling to the pasta. Return the angel hair to the pot, toss it with 1 tablespoon of the olive oil, and cover the pot to keep the pasta warm.

2. Heat the remaining 1 tablespoon of olive oil in a large skillet over medium-high heat. Add the onion and garlic, reduce the heat to medium-low, and cook, stirring, until the onion softens, 3 minutes.

3. Place the onion and garlic mixture and the red peppers, half-and-half, and cayenne in a food processor or blender and purée until smooth, 30 seconds. Spoon the sauce over the angel hair and stir to coat it well. Serve at once, garnished with basil leaves.

SERVES 4

A Pasta Prep Note

—▼—

DINNER DOCTOR SAYS The prep times in this chapter include the time it takes for a pot of water to come to a boil over high heat.

SATURDAY NIGHT FEVER PASTA

▼ ▼ ▼

Don't you just love angel hair pasta? The dry kind cooks in just four minutes! A full-bodied Italian *puttanesca* sauce is a perfect accompaniment for the delicate pasta. The version here is based on a jar of marinara that you doctor with store-bought black-olive paste, capers, and hot

TO PREP:
8 MINUTES
TO COOK:
4 MINUTES

red pepper flakes. Its bite is tempered by fresh parsley—the sauce goes great with a big red wine. It's just what you need for a Saturday night. Serve the pasta with crusty bread.

Salt (optional), for cooking the pasta
8 ounces angel hair pasta
2 cups store-bought marinara sauce
        (from one 26-ounce jar)
3 tablespoons black-olive paste
        (see box at right)
2 tablespoons capers, drained
½ teaspoon hot red pepper flakes or
        more to taste
¼ cup chopped fresh parsley, for garnish

1. Bring a large pot of water to a boil over high heat. Add salt, if using, and

tips If getting angel hair pasta to stay on the fork gives you trouble, breaking the pasta in half before you add it to the pot will make it easier to eat. The difference is like combing out tangles in short versus long hair.

Vary the sauce as you please, using an Asian chile sauce instead of hot red pepper, chopped black olives instead of black-olive paste, and/or chopped fresh cilantro or basil instead of parsley.

stir in the angel hair pasta. Reduce the heat to medium-high and cook the angel hair, uncovered, until al dente, 4 minutes.

2. Meanwhile, place the marinara sauce, olive paste, capers, and red pepper flakes in a small saucepan over medium-high heat. Bring to a boil, stirring, then remove the pan from the heat. Cover the pan to keep the sauce warm.

3. Drain the angel hair well in a colander, shaking it a few times to remove any water that might still cling to the pasta. Return the angel hair to the pot. Spoon the sauce over it and stir to coat the pasta well. Serve at once, garnished with the parsley.

SERVES 4

Olive Paste vs. Tapenade

—▼—

DINNER DOCTOR SAYS

Olive pastes contain only olives—black or green—olive oil, and perhaps some herbs. The classic tapenade, a flavorful olive spread, originated in the south of France. It is traditionally made with capers, black olives, anchovies, olive oil, and lemon juice. Today you can buy olive salads, sometimes referred to as tapenades and made with such ingredients as green olives, artichokes, or sun-dried tomatoes. While a traditional tapenade is smooth, these commercial ones are often chunky.

SPINACH FETTUCCINE ALFREDO

▼ ▼ ▼

If you love the creaminess of classic fettuccine Alfredo as well as the texture of creamed spinach, then you'll enjoy this easy recipe that combines them both. The Alfredo sauce contains nutmeg, which is a perfect complement to the spinach. Wine or lemon juice brighten the flavor and cut the saltiness of the commercial pasta sauce.

TO PREP:
10 MINUTES
TO COOK:
3 MINUTES

tips **Fresh fettuccine cooks in just 3 minutes, but dried fettuccine takes up to 12 minutes. Use 8 ounces dried fettuccine, if you prefer.**

For a lighter dish, substitute a 10-ounce package of frozen chopped spinach for the creamed spinach. Drain the chopped spinach after it thaws, then add it to the pasta sauce.

Salt (optional), for cooking the
    pasta
1 package (9 ounces) refrigerated
    fresh fettuccine (see Tips)
1 container (10 ounces) refrigerated
    Alfredo-style pasta sauce
    (see the box on the facing page)
1 package (10 ounces) frozen creamed
    spinach, thawed
1 tablespoon dry white wine or
    fresh lemon juice
¼ teaspoon black pepper
½ cup pre-shredded Parmesan cheese
2 tablespoons chopped fresh basil, parsley,
    or scallions, for garnish

1. Bring a large pot of water to a boil over high heat. Add salt, if using, and stir in the fettuccine. Reduce the heat to medium-high and cook the fettuccine, uncovered, until al dente, 3 minutes (for instructions on cooking pasta ahead of time see page 286).

2. Meanwhile, place the pasta sauce, spinach, wine, and pepper in a 2-quart saucepan and stir to combine. Bring the mixture to a boil over medium-high heat and let boil, stirring, to reduce the liquid slightly, 2 minutes. Remove the pan from the heat and cover to keep warm.

3. Drain the fettuccine well in a colander, shaking it a few times to remove any water that might still cling to the pasta. Return the fettuccine to the pot. Spoon the spinach sauce over it. Add the Parmesan cheese and stir to coat the pasta well with the sauce. Spoon onto serving plates and garnish with the basil.

SERVES 4

Fettuccine Alfredo

— ▼ —

DINNER DOCTOR SAYS

Ubiquitous fettuccine Alfredo is named for an Italian restaurateur in Rome. Alfredo di Lelio created the classic recipe in the 1920s by coating fettuccine noodles in a sauce made from butter and Parmesan. Later on black pepper and grated nutmeg became part of the recipe. Today's supermarket Alfredo-style sauces have little in common with the original recipe. Monterey Pasta Company makes an excellent refrigerated Alfredo sauce with herbs; you'll find it at warehouse stores. And as I noted elsewhere, I am also partial to the DiGiorno brand found in supermarkets. As a rule, the refrigerated versions are better than the ones that come in jars. Add freshly shredded Parmesan cheese, a grinding of pepper, or a spoonful of crabmeat, and these fast alternatives to the renowned sauce can create memorable meals.

CRABMEAT AND SHERRY FETTUCCINE ALFREDO

▼ ▼ ▼

Fantastic flavor alert! Crab, sherry, cream, and Parmesan all meld so well together in this dish that you will pat yourself on the back for putting together such a fancy but easy recipe. And since the crab is already cooked and the Alfredo sauce just needs heat-ing, the time you invest in preparing this dish is minimal.

TO PREP:
8 MINUTES
TO COOK:
12 MINUTES

Salt (optional), for cooking the pasta

8 ounces fettuccine

1 tablespoon olive oil

1 cup finely chopped red bell pepper
    (from 1 large bell pepper)

1 container (10 ounces) refrigerated
    Alfredo-style pasta sauce
    (see the box on page 277)

2 tablespoons medium-dry
    sherry

Cayenne pepper

2 cans (6 ounces each) lump
    crabmeat (see Tips),
    drained and picked over

2 tablespoons chopped fresh
    parsley, for garnish

¼ cup pre-shredded Parmesan
    cheese, for garnish

tips   **The better the crabmeat, the better the dish. Lump crabmeat is the most desirable, preferably from the claws. The meat from the body comes in smaller, stringier pieces, but it is less expensive and will work in this recipe. You'll need to pick over the crabmeat to remove any little pieces of cartilage.**

If you have fresh fettuccine in the fridge, by all means use it. It will be ready after cooking for only 3 minutes.

1. Bring a large pot of water to a boil over high heat. Add salt, if using, and stir in the fettuccine. Reduce the heat to medium-high, and cook the fettuccine, uncovered, until al dente, 12 minutes (for instructions on cooking pasta ahead of time see page 286).

2. Meanwhile, heat the olive oil in a large skillet over medium-high heat. Add the bell pepper, reduce the heat to medium, and cook, stirring, until the bell pepper softens, 2 minutes. Stir in the pasta sauce and sherry and season with cayenne to taste. Bring the mixture to a boil, stirring. Remove the skillet from the heat and fold in the crabmeat.

3. Drain the fettuccine well in a colander, shaking it a few times to remove any water that might still cling to the pasta. Return the fettuccine to the pot. Spoon the crab sauce over it and stir to coat the pasta well. Serve at once, garnished with the parsley and Parmesan cheese.

SERVES 4

THAI SPAGHETTI

▼ ▼ ▼

TO PREP: 8 MINUTES
TO COOK: 9 MINUTES

Yum. That is about all I could say when I tasted this dish, which starts with a jar of Thai peanut sauce. Thai ingredients are commonplace in supermarkets today, and when you squeeze fresh lime juice over the spaghetti and add a few cilantro sprigs, you have an easy dish with complex flavors. Serve this to friends at home, or tote it to a potluck.

Salt (optional), for cooking the pasta

8 ounces spaghetti

1 tablespoon vegetable oil

1 package (8 ounces) pre-sliced mushrooms

2 cups pre-shredded carrots

½ pound already peeled and deveined medium-size shrimp

4 ounces (1 cup) fresh snow peas

1 jar (8 ounces) Thai peanut sauce

¼ cup fresh cilantro sprigs, for garnish

4 lime wedges, for garnish

1. Bring a large pot of water to a boil over high heat. Add salt, if using, and stir in the spaghetti. Reduce the heat to medium-high and cook the spaghetti, partially covered, until al dente, 9 minutes (for instructions on cooking pasta ahead of time, see page 286).

2. Meanwhile, heat the oil in a large skillet over medium-high heat. Add the mushrooms and carrots and cook, stirring, until the mushrooms begin to yield their liquid, 3 minutes. Add the shrimp and cook, stirring, until they turn pink and opaque and are cooked through, 3 minutes longer.

tip **Don't care for shrimp? Substitute baked popcorn chicken pieces instead. These come frozen and can be baked while the spaghetti is boiling.**

3. During the last 2 minutes of the spaghetti cooking time add the snow peas to the pot and cook them until they turn bright green and are crisp-tender.

4. Add the peanut sauce to the shrimp in the skillet, stir to mix, then cook until the peanut sauce is just heated through. Drain the spaghetti and snow peas well in a colander, shaking it a few times to remove any water that might still cling to the pasta. Ladle the spaghetti and snow peas into a serving bowl, spoon the sauce over them, and garnish with the cilantro sprigs. Squeeze some lime juice over the top of each serving.

SERVES 4

MUSHROOM AND HAM LINGUINE

▼ ▼ ▼

Have some good left-over ham on hand, like Bebe's Coca-Cola Ham, on page 344. Combine it with sliced mushrooms, onion, cream, Parmesan, and some thyme and you'll have a simple pasta supper. It is perfect midweek fare—pre-sliced mushrooms speed the recipe along. Serve the linguine with a green salad or steamed broccoli.

TO PREP:
12 MINUTES
TO COOK:
9 MINUTES

Salt (optional), for cooking
    the linguine
8 ounces linguine
2 tablespoons olive oil
½ cup finely chopped onion
1 package (8 ounces) pre-sliced
    mushrooms
1 cup diced ham or thin strips of sliced
    smoked ham (see Tips)
2 tablespoons all-purpose flour
1 cup heavy (whipping) cream
    (see Tips)
1 tablespoon fresh thyme leaves,
    or 1 teaspoon dried thyme
1 cup pre-shredded Parmesan cheese

tip **Sliced ham from the deli can be easily turned into this gourmet fare by rolling the slices into a tight cigar shape and then cutting them crosswise into ¼-inch slices.**

　　To make the pasta more manageable for children, break the linguine into three pieces before adding them to the pot.

　　You can use milk instead of cream, but you don't need me to tell you the results won't be as creamy.

1. Bring a large pot of water to a boil over high heat. Add salt, if using, and stir in the linguine. Reduce the heat to medium-high and cook the linguine, uncovered, until al dente, 9 minutes (for instructions on cooking pasta ahead of time see page 286).

2. Meanwhile, heat the olive oil in a large skillet over medium-high heat. Add the onion and reduce the heat to medium. Cook, stirring, until the onion is soft, 3 minutes. Add the mushrooms and ham and cook, stirring constantly, until the mushrooms begin to yield their liquid, 3 minutes. Sprinkle the flour over the ham and mushrooms and stir to coat well. Pour in the cream and stir until thickened, 2 minutes. Spoon in some

water from the c
to thin the sau
and stir in the P
the skillet from
keep the sauce v

3. Drain the lir shaking it a few times to remove any water that might still cling to the pasta. Return the linguine to the pot. Spoon the mushroom and ham sauce over it and stir to coat the pasta well. Serve at once.

SERVES 4

ROTINI

WITH PROSCIUTTO AND SUGAR SNAP PEAS

▼ ▼ ▼

The sweet crunch of sugar snap peas balances the salt of the prosciutto in this easy-to-make yet elegant dish that is bound to please your family and dinner guests alike. Sugar snaps are sold frozen, but they are better fresh and can be found ready to use in handy 8-ounce bags. They cook for a few minutes in the same pot as the pasta, which I love because sharing pans reduces cleanup. Pass the pepper mill and the Parmesan cheese at the table, and be prepared for the compliments.

TO PREP:
8 MINUTES
TO COOK:
8 MINUTES

Salt (optional), for cooking the pasta
8 ounces rotini
1 tablespoon olive oil
4 ounces prosciutto, diced (see Tip)
½ cup chopped red onion
1 cup heavy (whipping) cream
1 package (8 ounces; 1 cup) fresh
*   sugar snap peas*
Pre-grated Parmesan cheese, for serving
Black pepper, for serving

1. Bring a large pot of water to a boil over high heat. Add salt, if using, and stir in the rotini. Reduce the heat to medium-high and cook the rotini, uncovered, until al dente, 8 minutes (for instructions on cooking pasta ahead of time see page 286).

tip **Prosciutto, the distinctive uncured bacon of Italy, is easier to dice if you buy it from the deli in one piece. But if all you find is a 4-ounce package of sliced prosciutto, slice it into thin strips. If there is no prosciutto at your supermarket, you can substitute thin strips of a good baked ham.**

2. Meanwhile, heat the olive oil in a large skillet over medium-high heat. Add the prosciutto and onion, reduce the heat to medium, and cook, stirring, until the onion is soft, 3 minutes. Pour in the cream, increase the heat to medium-high, and bring to a boil. Lower the heat to medium-low and let the mixture simmer, stirring often, until it has reduced slightly, 2 to 3 minutes.

3. After the rotini has cooked for 5 minutes, add the sugar snap peas to the pot and cook them until they turn bright green and are crisp-tender. Drain the rotini and sugar snaps well in a colander, shaking it a few times to remove any water that might still cling to the pasta. Return the rotini and sugar snaps to the pot. Spoon the sauce over them and stir to coat the pasta well. Serve at once with Parmesan cheese and pepper on the side.

SERVES 4

Summer Supper al Fresco

▼▼▼

When the weather turns summery and the back porch is where you want to be at dinnertime, serve up a gorgeous chilled red pepper soup and an easy-to-prepare pasta (if you're serving eight, the recipe can be doubled). For dessert? A peach tart is perfect.

Chilled Roasted Red Pepper Soup
page 66

Rotini with Prosciutto and Sugar Snap Peas
this page

Fresh Peach Tart
page 485

To Cook Pasta Fast

—▼—

◆ **Get going:** On days when you are really pressed for time, put a pot of water on to boil as soon as you walk in the door. It will be bubbling away once you've taken off your coat and kissed the kids.

◆ **The right amount of water:** Italian cooks recommend using 4 to 6 quarts of water to cook 1 pound of pasta and 3 quarts of water for 8 ounces.

◆ **Boil water quickly:** Cover the pot and place it over high heat. It doesn't matter whether the water is cold, warm, or hot to start with.

◆ **When to salt:** I have clocked how much time it takes to bring a pot of water to a boil both with and without salt in it and have found no difference. So if you use salt to cook your pasta, add it whenever you please.

◆ **To cover the pot or not:** If you are using a pot smaller than 7 quarts, cook the pasta uncovered to avoid boil-overs. But if your pot is larger, you may cook the pasta partially covered. Be sure the water remains at a rapid rolling boil while the pasta cooks.

◆ **Watch the clock:** Fresh pasta cooks faster than dried. It takes only about 3 to 4 minutes, so be sure the sauce will be ready when the pasta's cooked. Asian rice pastas also cook quickly, and thin pastas, like angel hair, cook faster than thicker ones.

◆ **Shake but don't rinse pasta:** Many of the recipes in this chapter have sauces, and these will cling better to the pasta if you don't rinse off the starch when you drain it. Just dump the pasta in a colander, shake out any clinging water, then put the pasta back into the pot or onto plates to await the sauce.

◆ **Cook extra:** If you have a busy week ahead of you, cook twice as much pasta as you need for dinner. If the recipe calls for 8 ounces of pasta, cook a pound and leave half of it unsauced for another meal. Toss the extra pasta with a little olive oil and refrigerate it in a tightly covered container or heavy resealable plastic bag. It will keep for up to five days. To reheat the pasta, remove it from the container or plastic bag and put it in a pot of boiling water. You can also reheat pasta in a microwave oven; place it in a microwave-safe bowl, cover the bowl, and microwave it on high power for a minute or two, or until it is heated through. Stir the pasta once or twice while it is heating.

PASTA SHELLS

WITH TUNA, LEMON, AND OLIVES

▼ ▼ ▼

The flavors of an olive salad are earthy and wonderful, especially when mixed with pasta shells and garnished with capers and basil. The result is a sophisticated dish that will appeal to grownups. You can frequently buy ready-made olive salad in the supermarket (sometimes you'll find it in the deli section; it may be labeled tapenade). This recipe doctors that store-bought olive salad by adding a can of tuna and some lemon juice and zest.

TO PREP:
8 MINUTES
TO COOK:
8 MINUTES

Salt (optional), for cooking
    the pasta
8 ounces medium-size pasta shells
1 can (6 ounces) solid white albacore tuna,
    packed in water (see Tips), drained
1 cup store-bought olive salad
    (see the box on page 275)
1 teaspoon grated lemon zest
1 tablespoon fresh lemon juice
2 teaspoons capers, drained, for garnish
¼ cup chopped fresh basil or parsley,
    for garnish
Lemon wedges (optional), for garnish

1. Bring a large pot of water to a boil over high heat. Add salt, if using, and stir in the pasta shells. Reduce the heat to medium-high and cook the shells, uncovered, until al dente, 8 minutes (for instructions on cooking pasta ahead of time see the facing page).

tips I prefer solid tuna packed in water, but you can use any kind you have in the pantry with good results.
    The pasta sauce here is also delicious spread on toasted rounds of French bread. Packed into a ramekin, it can be refrigerated, covered, for up to 4 days.

2. Meanwhile, place the tuna, olive salad, and lemon zest and juice in a food processor or blender, and purée until smooth, 30 seconds.

3. Drain the pasta shells well in a colander, shaking it a few times to remove any water that still clings to the pasta. Return the shells to the pot. Fold in the tuna sauce and stir to coat the pasta well. Serve at once, garnished with the capers, basil, and lemon wedges, if using.

SERVES 4

10 Fast Pasta Sauces

— ▼ —

DINNER DOCTOR SAYS

No time to simmer a sauce? Here are some ingredients to toss with hot pasta.

1. Pressed garlic, a dribble of olive oil, a pinch of red pepper flakes

2. Chopped fresh tomato, pressed garlic, and olive oil

3. Grated lemon zest, a squeeze of fresh lemon juice, and a little cream

4. Butter, Parmesan cheese, black pepper, and a touch of cream

5. Thawed frozen green peas, strips of smoked ham, and a little cream

6. Chopped anchovies, a drizzle of olive oil, chopped black olives, and bread crumbs

7. Pesto, ricotta cheese, and olive oil

8. Chopped fresh herbs, such as parsley, tarragon, chevril, or basil, a little pepper, and olive oil

9. A drained can of tuna, a few capers, a grinding of black pepper, and chopped fresh parsley

10. A splash of commercial pasta sauce, a splash of cream, and a splash of vodka

BLACK-EYED PEAS AND PASTA

▼ ▼ ▼

When a Southerner mentions peas, it is usually not the sweet green variety he or she is talking about. More likely it's black-eyed peas, crowder peas, or lady peas. Use a can of any of those in this easy and satisfying dish that combines peas with tomatoes, garlic, feta, and pasta, with crumbled bacon on top.

TO PREP:
8 MINUTES
TO COOK:
8 MINUTES

tips You can substitute any kind of canned tomatoes, seasoned or plain, for the ones in this recipe.

It takes about 8 slices of fried bacon to make ½ cup of crumbled bacon. To save time, purchase already-cooked bacon and heat it in the microwave oven or substitute thin slices of smoked ham. Canned tuna flaked over the top of the pasta is also as delicious as the bacon and turns this dish into a nice luncheon do-ahead served at room temperature.

Salt (optional), for cooking the pasta
8 ounces medium-size pasta
    shells or bow ties
1 can (28 ounces) diced tomatoes with
    green pepper and onion, drained
1 can (15.5 to 16 ounces) black-eyed peas,
    drained
2 tablespoons olive oil
2 cloves garlic, crushed in
    a garlic press
Pinch of cayenne pepper
½ cup pre-crumbled
    feta cheese
½ cup crumbled already-cooked
    bacon (about 8 slices, optional; see Tips)
3 tablespoons chopped fresh parsley

1. Bring a large pot of water to a boil over high heat. Add salt, if using, and stir in the pasta shells. Reduce the heat to medium-high and cook the shells, uncovered, until al dente, 8 minutes (for instructions on cooking pasta ahead of time see page 286).

2. Meanwhile, place the tomatoes, black-eyed peas, olive oil, garlic, and cayenne in a large mixing or serving bowl and stir to combine.

3. Drain the pasta shells well in a colander, shaking it a few times to remove any water that might still cling to the pasta. Transfer the shells to the mixing bowl and stir to combine well. Serve topped with the feta cheese, bacon, if using, and parsley.

SERVES 4

15 WAYS TO DOCTOR MARINARA SAUCE

Start with a 26-ounce jar of basic marinara sauce. Here are some easy ways to doctor the sauce so it tastes more homemade. Simmer these add-in ingredients along with the sauce, then pour it over hot pasta. You'll have enough sauce for 8 ounces of pasta.

1 Add some good, dry hearty red wine—a zinfandel, cabernet, or merlot will all work well. You can add anywhere from 2 tablespoons to ½ cup.

2 Spoon in a generous tablespoon of pesto.

3 Sauté 1 cup of sliced zucchini in olive oil for 2 minutes. Season it with salt and pepper to taste, then add it to the sauce.

4 Stir in a handful of roasted red pepper strips and a pinch of hot pepper flakes.

5 Crush 3 or 4 cloves of garlic in a garlic press directly over the pot of sauce.

6 Sauté an 8-ounce package of sliced mushrooms in 2 tablespoons of olive oil until they are soft and then fold the mushrooms into the sauce.

7 Add 1 pound sliced, cooked Italian sausage.

8 Stir in 1 can of drained tuna, a squeeze of lemon, and 1 to 2 tablespoons of drained capers.

9 Add a can of clams, a tablespoon or two of dry white wine, and a handful of chopped fresh parsley.

10 Fold in ½ cup of olive salad (see page 275) or chopped kalamata olives.

11 Sauté chopped green bell pepper and onion in a little olive oil until soft. Add this and 2 cups of cooked shrimp to the sauce. Serve the sauce over rice.

12 Add a handful of pre-shredded carrots and a pinch of sugar, for a sweeter marinara sauce.

13 Purée a cup of parsley leaves and several cloves of garlic in a food processor until chunky, then fold them into the sauce.

14 Add ¼ cup of dry vermouth and chopped green olives.

15 Stir in a can of chopped green chiles and 1 tablespoon of ground cumin for a Southwestern flavor.

MEATY ZITI

▼ ▼ ▼

No need to pre-boil pasta when it's going in the oven. The ziti goes into the casserole raw and bakes to perfection blanketed by a meaty tomato sauce and creamed spinach. My children love this recipe, and they didn't even fuss over the spinach! Serve the ziti at potlucks or family gatherings, and assemble it in advance to save precious last-minute time.

1 pound ground beef round

1 can (28 ounces) crushed tomatoes,
*   or 1 jar (26 ounces) marinara sauce*

1 clove garlic, crushed in
*   a garlic press*

1 teaspoon dried oregano

1 teaspoon dried basil

8 ounces ziti

1 package (9 ounces) frozen creamed
*   spinach, thawed (see Tips)*

1 package (8 ounces; 2 cups) pre-shredded
*   mozzarella cheese*

TO PREP AND COOK:
15 MINUTES
TO BAKE:
30 MINUTES
TO REST:
10 MINUTES

1. Place a rack in the center of the oven and preheat the oven to 375°F.

2. Crumble the ground beef into a large skillet over medium-high heat. Cook, stirring and breaking up the lumps with a wooden spoon, until the beef browns all over and is cooked through, 4 to 5 minutes. Stir in the tomatoes, garlic, oregano, and basil.

3. Spoon 1 cup of the meat sauce on the bottom of a 3-quart glass or ceramic

tips To thaw the creamed spinach in a microwave oven, place the pouch on a microwave-safe plate, cut a slit in the pouch so the steam can escape, and microwave it on high power until the spinach is thawed, 45 seconds to 1 minute.

    Feel free to jazz up the meat sauce with a little red wine, pesto, olive paste, garlic—you name it.

casserole. Arrange the ziti in an even layer on top of the sauce. Pour the remaining meat sauce over the ziti. Spread the creamed spinach evenly over the top with a knife. Cover the baking dish with aluminum foil. (The dish can be made up to 1 day in advance to this point. Refrigerate until baking time.)

4. Bake the ziti until bubbling, 30 minutes. Remove the baking dish from the oven and carefully remove the aluminum foil and set aside. Scatter the mozzarella evenly over the top and re-cover the dish with the foil. Let the ziti rest until the cheese melts, 10 minutes. Serve at once.

SERVES 6 TO 8

Which Pasta Is Fasta?

—▼—

DINNER DOCTOR SAYS I timed some favorite shapes and strands, and here is how long they took to cook once the water came to a rolling boil.

DRIED PASTA

Angel hair	4 minutes	Rotini	8 minutes
Penne	6 to 7 minutes	Linguine	9 minutes
Ziti	6 to 7 minutes	Spaghetti	9 minutes
Gemelli	8 minutes	Farfalle (bow ties)	11 minutes
Medium-size shells	8 minutes	Fettuccine	12 minutes
Orzo	8 minutes	Dried tortellini	15 minutes

FRESH PASTA

Angel hair	1 minute	Fettuccine	3 minutes
Linguine	2 minutes	Tortellini	5 minutes

SMOKED SALMON ZITI

WITH CAPERS AND LEMON

▼ ▼ ▼

Even when the cupboard is practically bare, most of us still have pasta on the shelf. And if you buy a package of smoked salmon at the warehouse store, it keeps beautifully for weeks. There always seems to be an onion, some capers, a lemon, parsley, and some sour cream on hand. So after a quick sauté, smoked salmon turns ziti into a regal dish, one that pairs well with a full-bodied chardonnay and good bread.

TO PREP:
10 MINUTES
TO COOK:
6–7 MINUTES

Salt (optional), for cooking
    the pasta
8 ounces ziti
1 tablespoon olive oil
½ cup thinly sliced onion
4 ounces smoked salmon
    (see Tips), cut into slivers
1 tablespoon fresh lemon juice
1 tablespoon capers, drained
¼ cup chopped fresh parsley
¼ cup reduced-fat sour cream
    (see Tips)
Black pepper

tips Any smoked fish will work here. Try mesquite-smoked salmon, if you live in Texas, or oak-smoked trout, if you live in trout country.
    For a richer dish, substitute ½ cup of heavy cream for the sour cream.

1. Bring a large pot of water to a boil over high heat. Add salt, if using, and stir in the ziti. Reduce the heat to medium-high and cook the ziti, uncovered, until al dente, 6 to 7 minutes (for instructions on cooking pasta ahead of time see page 286).

2. Meanwhile, place the olive oil in a large skillet over medium-high heat. Add the onion and reduce the heat to medium. Cook, stirring, until the onion begins to soften, 2 minutes. Add the salmon and cook, stirring, for 1 minute. Add the lemon juice, capers, parsley, and sour cream. Cook the sauce, stirring, until it just thickens, 30 seconds. Do not let the sauce come to a boil. Turn off the heat.

3. Drain the ziti well in a colander, shaking it a few times to remove any water that might still cling to the pasta. Spoon the ziti onto serving plates. Top each with a big spoonful of smoked salmon sauce, then grind some black pepper on top.

SERVES 4

Valentine's Dinner for Two (or Four)

▼▼▼

It's the day of love and this is a menu meant for romance—even if you're sharing it with the kids. Although it's not the season for asparagus and raspberries, they are usually not too hard to find, even in February.

**Smoked Salmon Ziti
with Capers and Lemons**
this page

**Warm Arugula Salad with Roasted
Asparagus and Balsamic Vinaigrette**
page 135

Very Raspberry Cake
page 481

CHEESE TORTELLINI

WITH A FRESH TOMATO AND ARTICHOKE SLAW

▼ ▼ ▼

TO PREP:
3 MINUTES
TO COOK:
5–6 MINUTES

One of my favorite ways to make a meal is to boil pasta, and while it is cooking, look in the pantry to see what I have on hand to put together a sauce. It might be roasted red peppers, it might be a jar of marinara sauce and a little olive paste. Or, it might be artichoke hearts with some fresh tomatoes, as in this recipe. This dish has a summer freshness because the sauce is light and does not smother the tortellini, and for that reason I think it goes nicely with grilled fish, garnished with fresh basil, of course.

Salt (optional), for cooking the pasta

1 package (9 ounces) refrigerated
*   fresh cheese tortellini*

1 jar (6 ounces) marinated artichoke
*   hearts with their liquid*

1 tablespoon chopped fresh basil, or
*   1 teaspoon store-bought pesto*

1 pint (2 cups) grape or cherry tomatoes,
*   or 2 cups chopped tomatoes*
*   (from 2 medium-size tomatoes)*

1 teaspoon capers, drained

¼ cup pre-shredded
*   Parmesan cheese*

1. Bring a large pot of water to a boil over high heat. Add

tips **For a beautiful yellow color, use yellow tomatoes in the slaw. Add a little chopped yellow bell pepper for bite, and substitute another herb for the basil, if you like.**

    The tomato and artichoke slaw goes well with cheese ravioli, too.

salt, if using, and stir in the tortellini. Reduce the heat to medium-high and cook the tortellini, uncovered, until al dente, 5 to 6 minutes.

2. Meanwhile, place the artichoke hearts with their liquid, basil, and tomatoes in a food processor. Pulse 10 times, or until the mixture has a slaw-like consistency. Stir in the capers.

3. Drain the tortellini well in a colander, shaking it a few times to remove any water that might still cling to the pasta. Transfer the tortellini to a serving bowl or serving plates. Pour the slaw over the tortellini and sprinkle the Parmesan cheese on top. Serve at once.

SERVES 4

Who Is Al Dente Anyway?

—▼—

DINNER DOCTOR SAYS

I'll never forget seeing the words *al dente* in an Italian cookbook and not having a clue what they meant. I was raised on soft American elbow macaroni, so if you boiled it to mush it didn't matter because it was going to become macaroni and cheese anyway. But cooking pasta just the right amount of time really does make a difference. Pasta needs to be cooked through yet still have some resistance when you bite into it. And that is what al dente means in Italian—to the tooth.

MONDAY NIGHT PENNE MARINARA

▼ ▼ ▼

TO PREP:
8 MINUTES
TO COOK:
12 MINUTES

If you're inspired to cook but have less than 30 minutes, when you crave marinara but want to make your own, try this recipe. It has a homemade flavor, plus it's quick because you use basil, red wine, and tomato paste to doctor cans of already-seasoned diced tomatoes.

Salt (optional), for cooking the pasta

8 ounces penne or other medium-size
    chunky pasta, such as ziti

2 cans (14.5 ounces each) diced tomatoes
    with green pepper and onion (see Tips)

1 can (14.5 ounces) diced tomatoes with
    basil, garlic, and oregano

3 tablespoons tomato paste

2 tablespoons olive oil

2 tablespoons dry red wine (see Tips)

1 cup chopped fresh basil

½ cup pre-crumbled feta cheese,
    for serving

1. Bring a large pot of water to a boil over high heat. Add salt, if using, and stir in the penne. Reduce the heat to medium-high and cook the penne, uncovered, until al dente, 6 to 7 minutes (for instructions on cooking pasta ahead of time see page 286).

2. Meanwhile, place all of the canned tomatoes and the tomato paste, olive oil, and red wine in a 2-quart saucepan over

tips **Any combination of seasoned diced tomatoes will do for this sauce, as long as you have a total of three 14.5-ounce cans.**

    You can substitute 2 tablespoons of balsamic vinegar for the red wine, if you like.

    You can also add those wonderful pitted kalamata olives to the sauce.

medium-high heat. Bring the mixture to a boil, stirring, then reduce the heat to medium and let it simmer, uncovered, until it has thickened somewhat, 10 minutes. Stir in the basil after 8 minutes of simmering.

3. Drain the penne well in a colander, shaking it a few times to remove any water that might still cling to the pasta. Spoon the penne into serving bowls. Spoon the sauce over the penne and sprinkle each serving with about 2 tablespoons of the feta cheese.

SERVES 4

PENNE

WITH BLUE CHEESE PESTO, WALNUTS, AND ASPARAGUS

▼ ▼ ▼

TO PREP:
10 MINUTES
TO COOK:
6–7 MINUTES

As the Cake Mix Doctor I have been asked many times, "What is the one cake from your books you would bake for yourself?" If you asked me this question as the Dinner Doctor, I would answer this penne. It requires little effort but delivers a big impact, the result of doctoring a good commercial pesto sauce with blue cheese. Toss the sauce with cooked penne, toasted walnuts, and tiny asparagus spears that cook in the same water as the pasta, and dinner is ready in about ten minutes. And, by the way, the cake I'd bake for myself? Butternut Squash Layer Cake with Maple Cream Cheese Frosting (page 456).

Salt (optional), for cooking the pasta
8 ounces penne
1 cup walnut pieces
1 jar (3.5 ounces) pesto (about ½ cup; see Tip)
¼ cup pre-crumbled blue cheese, or to taste
½ pound thin asparagus spears

1. Preheat the oven to 350°F.

2. Bring a large pot of water to a boil over high heat. Add salt, if using, and stir in the penne. Reduce the heat to medium-high and

tip Not all commercial pesto sauces may be to your taste, so it's a good idea to sample a few until you find your favorite. I particularly like the refrigerated kind, and your local specialty food store may make a tasty one. Wholesale clubs also carry surprisingly good pestos. When it comes to supermarket pesto in a jar, I like Alessi, a brand you'll find in the pasta aisle.

cook the penne, uncovered, until al dente, 6 to 7 minutes (for instructions on cooking pasta ahead of time see page 286).

3. Meanwhile, place the walnuts on a rimmed baking sheet and bake them until lightly toasted, 4 to 5 minutes.

4. Place the pesto and blue cheese in a large serving bowl and, using a fork, mash the blue cheese into the pesto.

5. Rinse the asparagus spears and snap off and discard their tough ends. Break the spears into 1½-inch long pieces.

6. During the last 3 minutes of the penne cooking time, add the asparagus to the pot and cook until they turn bright green and are crisp-tender. Drain the penne and asparagus well in a colander, shaking it a few times to remove any water that might still cling to the pasta. Add the penne and asparagus to the bowl with the pesto and stir to coat them well. Top with the toasted walnuts and serve at once.

SERVES 4

FAST FOUR-STEP LASAGNA

▼ ▼ ▼

Few recipes are as simple as this one, so the creative aspects are up to you. Choose the best pasta sauce you can find in a large jar. I like fire-roasted tomato sauces. You might also want to try one with basil and garlic. And look for an interesting blend of pre-shredded

TO PREP AND COOK:
12 MINUTES
TO BAKE:
38–40 MINUTES
TO REST:
10 MINUTES

cheeses, such as Parmesan, mozzarella, and smoked Provolone. This recipe is a no-brainer, but sometimes that is about all my busy mind can handle!

1 pound ground beef round

1 jar (3 pounds) tomato-based
    pasta sauce (see Tip at right)

9 no-boil lasagna noodles
    (see Tip at left)

1 container (15 ounces) ricotta
    cheese

3 cups pre-shredded Italian cheese blend

> **tip** No-boil lasagna noodles have ruffled edges and can be used in lasagna dry or after being soaked in water to flatten them. Either way, no lengthy, messy pre-boiling is required. No-boil lasagna noodles come in ounce boxes of 12. I always use dry noodles because I find that the extra ⬭h they contain helps prevent ⬭ from being watery. Tightly ⬭ed unused no-boil lasagna noo⬭ be stored in an airtight con⬭ at least six months.

1. Place a rack in the center of the oven and preheat the oven to 375°F.

2. Crumble the ground beef into a large skillet over medium-high heat. Cook, stirring and breaking up the beef with a wooden spoon, until it browns all over and is cooked through, 4 to 5 minutes. Stir in the pasta sauce.

3. Spoon enough of the meat mixture into the bottom of a 13-by-9-inch (3-quart) glass or ceramic baking dish to just cover the bottom evenly. Arrange 3 of the lasagna noodles side by side the long way on top of the meat mixture. Top the noodles with one third of the ricotta cheese, followed by 1 cup of the Italian cheese blend. Then, starting with half of the remaining meat mixture, repeat the layering two more times. Cover the baking dish with aluminum foil.

4. Bake the lasagna until bubbling, about 40 minutes. Remove the baking dish from the oven and let the lasagna rest for 10 minutes, covered, then serve (see Tips, page 306).

SERVES 8

tip If you can't find a 3-pound jar of pasta sauce, two 26-ounce jars will do. The slight difference in amount won't matter to the lasagna.

CREAMY LASAGNA FOR THE KIDS

▼ ▼ ▼

Any time I add cream of mushroom soup to a dish, my kids love it. There is something about its creamy texture that children really appreciate—and adults do, too! This recipe could not be simpler; it's dinner doctoring at its most basic and successful, relying on store-bought tomato pasta sauce, pre-shredded mozzarella, some ground beef, and Italian seasoning, as well as the mushroom soup. Be sure to use lasagna noodles that don't have to be cooked first.

1 pound ground beef round

1 jar (26 ounces) tomato-based
*   pasta sauce (see Tips)*

1 can (10.75 ounces) cream of
*   mushroom soup*

¼ cup milk

TO PREP AND COOK:
15 MINUTES
TO BAKE:
40–45 MINUTES
TO REST:
10 MINUTES

1 package (8 ounces; 2 cups)
pre-shredded mozzarella cheese
6 no-boil lasagna noodles
*   (see Tip, page 302)*
½ teaspoon Italian seasoning
¼ teaspoon black pepper

1. Place a rack in the center of the oven and preheat the oven to 400°F.

2. Crumble the ground beef into a large skillet over medium-high heat. Cook, stirring and breaking up the beef with a wooden spoon, until it browns all over and is cooked through, 4 to 5 minutes. Stir in the pasta sauce and set the skillet aside.

3. Pour the mushroom soup and milk into a medium-size mixing bowl and stir to combine. Fold in ½ cup of the mozzarella and set aside.

4. Spoon half of the meat mixture into a 11-by-7-inch (2-quart) glass or ceramic baking dish, spreading it evenly over the bottom. Arrange 3 of the lasagna noodles side by side the long way on top of the meat. Spoon all of the mushroom soup mixture on top of the noodles, spreading it out evenly. Sprinkle the Italian seasoning and black pepper over the soup mixture. Arrange the remaining 3 lasagna noodles side by side the long way on top of the soup mixture. Cover the noodles with the remaining meat mixture. Cover the baking dish with aluminum foil.

5. Bake the lasagna until bubbling, 40 to 45 minutes. Remove the baking dish from the oven and carefully remove the aluminum foil and set it aside. Scatter the remaining 1½ cups of mozzarella evenly over the lasagna and re-cover the dish with the foil. Let the lasagna rest until the cheese melts, 10 minutes, then serve (see Tips, page 306).

SERVES 6 TO 8

tips You have your pick of the pasta sauces here, and boy, are there plenty from which to choose! Try to keep it pretty basic, such as a tomato and basil sauce. I used the Classico Fire-Roasted Tomato and Garlic sauce for this recipe, and it was a winner.

The casserole can be made in advance and can be refrigerated, unbaked, for up to 1 day. Or, you can go ahead and cook the ground beef and refrigerate it (also for up to 1 day) until you are ready to assemble the lasagna.

If you want to cut back on the beef, use ½ pound plus 1 cup of drained canned black beans.

To enhance the flavor a bit for adults, add 2 tablespoons of red wine to the pasta sauce.

SPINACH AND BLACK BEAN LASAGNA

▼ ▼ ▼

What a winner! My husband loved this lasagna, my kids asked for seconds, and I felt smug because it contained not only black beans but spinach. This is a great make-ahead or do-at-the-last-minute dish for family gatherings and it uses those wonderful no-boil lasagna noodles. Both vegetarians and meat eaters will heartily approve of its Italian-Mexican flavor combination.

TO PREP:
12 MINUTES
TO BAKE:
40–45 MINUTES
TO REST:
10 MINUTES

2 cans (15 ounces each) black beans, drained

1 jar (26 ounces) tomato-based pasta sauce

½ teaspoon ground cumin

1 container (15 ounces) ricotta cheese

1 package (10 ounces) frozen chopped spinach, thawed and well drained (see Tips)

2 large eggs, lightly beaten

½ cup chopped fresh cilantro

9 no-boil lasagna noodles (see Tip, page 302)

1 package (8 ounces; 2 cups) pre-shredded Monterey Jack cheese with jalapeño peppers

tips Zap the spinach in a microwave oven for 45 seconds to 1 minute on high power to thaw it, then place the spinach in a sieve and squeeze out the water.

As the lasagna rests, not only will the cheese melt but the lasagna will set so that it will be easier to cut.

1. Place a rack in the center of the oven and preheat the oven to 375°F.

2. Place the beans in a medium-size bowl and mash them with a potato masher until smooth. Stir in the pasta sauce and cumin and set aside. Place the ricotta, spinach, eggs, and cilantro in another bowl and stir until just combined.

3. Spoon one third of the bean mixture evenly over the bottom of a 13-by-9-inch (3-quart) glass or ceramic baking dish. Arrange 3 of the lasagna noodles side by side the long way on top of the bean mixture. Spoon half of the spinach mixture on top of the noodles and spread it out evenly. Scatter 1 cup of the cheese evenly over the spinach mixture. Spread the remaining spinach mixture over the cheese, then arrange 3 of the lasagna noodles side by side the long way on top. Spread half of the remaining bean mixture on top

of the noodles. Arrange the remaining 3 lasagna noodles side by side the long way on top of the bean mixture, then top with the remaining bean mixture. Cover the baking dish with aluminum foil.

4. Bake the lasagna until bubbling, 40 to 45 minutes. Remove the baking dish from the oven and carefully remove the aluminum foil and set it aside. Scatter the remaining 1 cup of cheese evenly over the lasagna and cover the dish again with the foil. Let the lasagna rest until the cheese melts, 10 minutes, then serve (see Tips).

SERVES 8

BLUE CHEESE POLENTA

WITH WILTED SPINACH AND TOASTED PINE NUTS

▼ ▼ ▼

TO PREP:
10 MINUTES
TO COOK:
10 MINUTES

Wondering what to serve your vegetarian friends? Polenta with spinach and pine nuts pairs perfectly with grilled portobello mushrooms. And if you're entertaining folks who are keen on meat, you can't find a better side dish for a juicy steak right off the grill. The secret ingredient is that log of cooked polenta found in the supermarket alongside the fresh pasta. Polenta comes in a variety of flavors, but here plain will do just fine. This is a spoonable polenta, cooked down with milk; think of it as the cornmeal equivalent of mashed potatoes.

1 package (1 pound) refrigerated cooked polenta, cut into 1-inch-thick slices

½ cup milk, or more as needed

1 package (4 ounces; 1 cup) pre-crumbled blue cheese

1 tablespoon olive oil

2 tablespoons pine nuts

1 package (10 ounces) fresh spinach, rinsed and shaken of excess water

Salt

1 to 2 tablespoons fresh lemon juice

tips Spinach, kale, mustard, or turnip greens are all good in this dish. Spinach is the fastest to prepare, however, as the other greens usually need to be chopped first and take a little longer to cook.

You can use any cheese you like in this polenta, so toss in a cup of pre-shredded sharp Cheddar if you don't care for blue cheese.

1. Place the polenta and milk in a 2-quart saucepan over medium-high heat. Bring to a boil, stirring, then reduce the heat to medium and mash out the lumps in the polenta with the back of a wooden spoon until smooth. This will take 5 minutes. Add the blue cheese and stir until it is melted, about 1 minute longer. Remove the pan from the heat and cover it to keep the polenta warm.

2. Heat the olive oil in a large skillet over medium-high heat. Add the pine nuts and cook until lightly browned, 1 minute (be careful not to let the pine nuts burn). Leaving the olive oil in the skillet, transfer the pine nuts to a bowl and set aside. Add the spinach with the water clinging to its leaves to the skillet. Cook, stirring, until the spinach is just wilted and bright green, 1 to 2 minutes. Remove the skillet from the heat and add salt and lemon juice to taste.

3. To serve, spoon the polenta onto plates, spoon the spinach and its pan juices over it, and sprinkle the toasted pine nuts on top.

SERVES **4** TO **6**

SANTA FE POLENTA

▼ ▼ ▼

Polenta may be the Italian cousin of Southern grits, but who's to say it can't travel farther west—Southwest, that is. Adding some pre-cooked chicken (available from the deli or refrigerator case), tomatillo salsa, and all the familiar Southwestern toppings to polenta makes this dish a Santa Fe breeze to assemble.

TO PREP:
10 MINUTES
TO COOK:
3 MINUTES

1 package (1 pound) refrigerated cooked polenta with cilantro and green chiles

2 pre-cooked, skinless, boneless chicken breasts (about 8 ounces each; see box, page 226)

1 cup store-bought tomatillo salsa

½ cup reduced-fat sour cream

½ cup pre-shredded Mexican blend cheese

½ cup fresh cilantro sprigs

Lime wedges (optional), for serving

tips Using a microwave is not the only way to heat polenta. You can bake slices in a 400°F oven until heated through, about 10 minutes. Or you can panfry them in a little olive oil over medium-high heat until crisp on both sides, 2 minutes per side.

You can also prepare this recipe with shredded cooked pork, sautéed sausages, or steamed shrimp in place of the chicken.

1. Cut the polenta into 12 even slices and place them in a glass pie pan, overlapping as needed. Cover the pie pan with waxed paper. Heat in a microwave oven on high power until heated through, 1 to 2 minutes. Set the polenta aside, covering it to keep warm.

2. Slice the chicken breasts diagonally across the grain. Place the sliced chicken and the salsa in a large skillet over medium heat and simmer until the sauce bubbles and the chicken is heated through, 1 to 2 minutes.

3. To serve, place 3 slices of warm polenta on each of 4 plates. Top with the sliced chicken and salsa, then garnish with a dollop of sour cream and a sprinkling of cheese and cilantro. Serve a lime wedge alongside, if desired.

SERVES 4

Polenta

—▼—

DINNER DOCTOR SAYS

Polenta is a fancier name for yellow cornmeal mush. In northern Italy polenta is as much a staple on the dinner table as rice is in the United States. Most often polenta is served hot with butter or, like Southern grits, it can be poured into a pan, cooled, cut into squares, and fried in butter. Polenta takes on a whole new personality when crumbled blue cheese or good shredded Parmesan cheese is folded into it. And cooked polenta logs, available plain and seasoned with cilantro and chiles, make serving polenta a snap. Look for them in the produce section of the supermarket.

PORK BARBECUE AND POLENTA

WITH SLAW

▼ ▼ ▼

I seriously doubt that there is a smidgen of Southern barbecue in Italy, but since polenta and grits are kissing cousins, I took a bit of creative license here and topped polenta with barbecued pork and slaw—sort of like we would down South with corn cakes. The

TO PREP:
2 MINUTES
TO COOK:
8 MINUTES

result is an extremely easy and satisfying supper that will be on your table in ten minutes. Although the recipe calls for plain polenta, I am partial to polenta flavored with cilantro and green chiles and find it gives this recipe zip. If you like zip, too, use flavored polenta instead.

1 package (16 ounces) coleslaw mix
¼ cup bottled coleslaw dressing
1 tablespoon cider vinegar (optional)
1 package (1.25 pound) frozen or
    refrigerated shredded barbecued
    pork (see Tip)
1 package (1 pound) refrigerated cooked
    polenta
1 tablespoon vegetable oil

1. Place the coleslaw mix, dressing, and vinegar, if using, in a large mixing bowl

tip | I've found that brands of barbecue vary greatly not only in quality but also in availability. If you live in an area of the country known for its barbecue then you'll have a nice selection. For those of you not in barbecue country, your best bet may be the refrigerated barbecue found where bacon, ham, and hot dogs are sold. You don't need to limit yourself to serving the polenta with pork; you can use barbecued beef or even chicken.

and stir until just combined. Place the slaw in the refrigerator to chill while you prepare the rest of the dish.

2. Place the barbecued pork in a 2-quart saucepan over medium heat. Cover the pan and let the pork thaw, if frozen, and come to a simmer. Cook until warmed through, 4 minutes, stirring often and adding a little water if the barbecue sauce seems too thick.

3. Meanwhile, cut the polenta into 12 even slices. Place the oil in a large skillet and heat over medium-high heat. Add the polenta slices and cook until lightly browned and crisp on both sides, 3 minutes per side.

4. To serve, place 3 slices of polenta on each of 4 plates, spoon the barbecued pork over them, then top with the slaw.

SERVES 4

CREOLE SHRIMP WITH POLENTA

AND SO FAST SUCCOTASH

▼ ▼ ▼

TO PREP:
15 MINUTES
TO COOK:
5 MINUTES

Down South, we add shrimp to as many dishes as we possibly can. And if we're talking Louisiana or South Carolina, chances are a little Creole seasoning or hot pepper sauce gets added to that dish as well. Slices of pre-cooked polenta topped with a flavorful succotash benefit in taste and texture from the garnish of jumbo shrimp. But, if a garnishing of shrimp just isn't enough for you, by all means, increase the amount.

So Fast Succotash (page 363)
1 package (1 pound) refrigerated cooked
    polenta with green chiles and cilantro
2 tablespoons butter
8 already peeled and deveined jumbo
    shrimp, cut in half horizontally
½ teaspoon Creole seasoning, or
    ½ teaspoon hot pepper sauce
¼ cup dry white wine
2 scallions, both white and light green parts,
    chopped (for ¼ cup)

1. Prepare the So Fast Succotash and set it aside, covered to keep warm.

2. Cut the polenta into 12 even slices and place them in a glass pie pan, over-lapping as needed. Cover the pie pan

tips For a richer version of this dish, cook the succotash in chicken broth and garnish it with crumbled fried bacon along with the chopped scallions.

with waxed paper. Heat the polenta in a microwave oven on high power until heated through, 1 to 2 minutes. Set the polenta aside, covering it to keep warm.

3. Melt the butter in a large skillet over medium-high heat. Add the shrimp, sprinkle the Creole seasoning over them, and cook, stirring, until the shrimp turn pink and opaque and are cooked through, 2 minutes. Pour in the white wine and stir well to combine.

4. To serve, place 3 slices of warm polenta on each of 4 plates and spoon the succotash over the polenta. Top each serving with 4 shrimp halves and spoon the pan juices over all. Garnish with the scallions and serve at once.

SERVES 4

HANDS-OFF COOKING

▼▼▼

So much in our lives is hands-on. Our jobs, helping with the children's homework, sewing on Scout badges, the laundry, driving, attending meetings—the list could go on and on. It's refreshing to know that there are recipes that do not require our undivided attention. We can put these dishes together in minutes, then stash them in the slow cooker or the oven, where they will cook over time, gently, and without our supervision.

Even before I planned to write this cookbook, recipes for these kinds of dishes were a mainstay of my life.

Since I would be out of the house all day, first thing in the morning I assembled chili or a stew in the slow cooker, knowing it would be ready to eat late in the afternoon. As my family grew and my work schedule changed, I spent a bit more time at home in the afternoon, but I couldn't necessarily be fussing with supper. I was picking up children from school and taking them to piano, soccer, or tennis lessons, the tutor, and occasionally, to the doctor. That's when I rediscovered those great braising recipes I loved as a child—beef cubes smothered in onion gravy, chicken breasts swimming in a creamy sauce, flavorful pot roasts, hams so delicious everyone at the table clamored for the first slice.

If you've got a large family, have company coming, or just want a delicious dinner that will provide versatile leftovers, bake Bebe's Coca-Cola Ham, a treasured recipe from my mother that turns a boneless supermarket ham into a rich and delicious country-style ham. Equally hands-off and tasty are the Roast Turkey Breast in a Bag and Steak and Gravy for the Kids (the cube steak recipe I've already mentioned). I've updated a classic mushroom soup recipe for Litton's Favorite Chicken with Mushroom Gravy, and included Shirley's Braised Beef—a winner served over warm noodles—and Mom's Pot Roast with Vidalia Onion Gravy to make when those big sweet southern Georgia onions are in season. When they're not, it's equally wonderful made with any sweet onions you have on hand, even red ones.

I have tested innumerable recipes in the slow cooker and share my favorites here. Slow-Cooker Macaroni and Cheese couldn't be easier to prepare; it makes a perfect side dish for baked ham. I also particularly like Hearty Lentil and Sausage Stew, Slow-Cooker White Chili, All-Day Beef Bourguignon, and Savory Pork Carnitas.

Pull out the slow cooker and dust off the Dutch oven. You are about to make dishes your whole family will savor, using recipes generous enough that you're likely to have leftovers for the next day. Not fancy, just delicious and memorable.

ROAST TURKEY BREAST IN A BAG

▼ ▼ ▼

One of the easiest and most delicious ways to cook a turkey breast is to tuck it into an oven bag and roast it until it's golden brown. You season the turkey breast, rub it with butter to help it brown, and then nestle bay leaves and an aromatic onion on top of it. Pop the turkey breast in the oven, walk away, and when you return 1½ to 2 hours later it will be beautiful and moist, thanks to the oven bag. It keeps the turkey from drying out, and should you want to make gravy or save the cooking juices for soup, they're right in the bag! Steamed asparagus and sugar snap peas will round out the meal nicely.

TO PREP:
10 MINUTES
TO BAKE:
1½–2 HOURS
TO REST:
15 MINUTES

1 tablespoon all-purpose flour

1 bone-in turkey breast (about 5 pounds)

Salt and black pepper

2 tablespoons butter, at room temperature

1 medium-size onion, peeled and quartered

3 bay leaves

1. Place a rack in the center of the oven and preheat the oven to 350°F.

2. Dust the inside of a large-size (14 by 20 inch) oven bag with the flour.

3. Rinse the turkey breast under cold running water and pat dry with paper towels. Season it, skin side and bone side, with salt and pepper. Rub the butter all over the skin side, then place the breast skin side down. Place the

> **tip**　You can also roast a whole turkey this way. Begin with a turkey-size oven bag, which is 19 by 23.5 inches. Bake the turkey at 350°F for 2 to 2½ hours for a 12-pound turkey, or 3 to 3½ hours for a 24-pound turkey.

onion quarters and bay leaves in the breast cavity. Place the turkey breast in the oven bag, gather the bag loosely around the turkey, allowing room for heat circulation. Secure the bag with its nylon tie. Cut six 1-inch slits in the top of the bag. Place the bag in a 13-by-9-inch (3-quart) baking dish.

4. Bake the turkey until it is deep golden brown and the meat is cooked through, 1½ to 2 hours. Let the turkey breast rest in the bag for 15 minutes, then transfer it to a platter to slice. Remove and discard the bay leaves and onion quarters. Reserve the pan juices and strain them for making gravy, if desired, or freeze them for making turkey soup.

SERVES 12 TO 16

LITTON'S FAVORITE CHICKEN

WITH MUSHROOM GRAVY

▼ ▼ ▼

TO PREP:
10 MINUTES
TO COOK:
10–12 MINUTES
TO BAKE:
2½–3 HOURS

Adding chicken must be one of the most popular ways to doctor a can of cream of mushroom soup, and my daughter Litton requests this dish often. It was a mainstay at our house while I was growing up, except there wasn't any sherry in it. I think a little bit of sherry picks up the flavor. I begin with bone-in chicken breasts instead of boneless ones because they can take the longer braising time, plus the bones add flavor to the dish.

This recipe produces chicken that is really tender. It's easy to remove the bones before serving. I like to spoon the chicken over steamed rice (for tips on quick-cooking varieties of rice, see page 354). The chicken is even more delicious if you use wild mushrooms instead of sliced button mushrooms and if you add cream instead of milk—but you could have guessed that, right?

4 bone-in chicken breast halves
(about 1½ pounds)
Salt and black pepper
2 tablespoons vegetable oil
1¼ cups thinly sliced onion
(from 1 large onion)
1 package (8 ounces)
pre-sliced mushrooms
2 cans (10.75 ounces each)
cream of mushroom soup
1 soup can (10.75 ounces) of milk
2 to 3 tablespoons dry sherry or
amontillado sherry

1. Place a rack in the center of the oven and preheat the oven to 300°F.

2. Rinse the chicken breasts under cold running water, remove and discard the skin, and pat the breasts dry with paper towels. Season the chicken all over with salt and pepper.

3. Heat the oil in a 5- to 6-quart heavy covered flameproof casserole or Dutch oven over medium-high heat. Add the chicken, bone side up. Cook the chicken until it browns slightly, 3 to 4 minutes, then using a metal spatula, turn the chicken over. Cook it on the other side until it browns slightly, 3 to 4 minutes longer. Transfer the chicken breasts to a plate. Add the onion and mushrooms to the casserole and cook, stirring, until they begin to soften, 2 minutes. Pour in the mushroom soup, milk, sherry, and 1 soup can of water and cook, stirring, until the ingredients are combined and the sauce comes to a boil, 2 minutes. Remove the casserole from the heat and place the chicken in it. Spoon the sauce over the chicken, then cover the casserole.

4. Bake the chicken breasts until they are fork-tender and the liquid thickens into a gravy, 2½ to 3 hours. Remove and discard the bones, then serve the chicken with the gravy.

SERVES 4

tips **When you return home to this wonderful dinner, remove the casserole from the oven and let the chicken rest, covered, while you cook rice and steam broccoli.**

You can adjust the seasoning as you like, adding more black pepper at the end, adding chopped parsley before baking, and/or a tad more sherry.

CHILI MOLE CINCINNATI-STYLE

▼ ▼ ▼

TO PREP:
15 MINUTES
TO COOK:
8–10 HOURS

Chili fans in Cincinnati say it isn't chili if it isn't served atop pasta. You're dubious? Give it a try! This recipe is a twist on that town's favorite, which is made not only with cocoa but also contains chili powder, cinnamon, and allspice. It's an unusual and delicious dish that has a robust flavor and aroma. The chili is a breeze to prepare, since it simmers in the slow cooker and it's made with those wonderful Mexican-seasoned canned tomatoes. Add the toppings they do in Cincinnati—chopped white onions, shredded Cheddar cheese, and kidney beans.

1 pound ground beef round

1 cup finely chopped onion
    (from 1 medium-size onion)

3 cloves garlic, sliced

2 cans (14.5 ounces each) Mexican-style
    stewed tomatoes, with their liquid

1 can (8 ounces) tomato sauce

2 tablespoons chili powder

1 tablespoon unsweetened cocoa powder

½ teaspoon ground cinnamon

¼ teaspoon ground allspice

8 ounces cooked and drained spaghetti
    (see box, page 286)

Chopped white onion, pre-shredded Cheddar
    cheese, and canned kidney beans
    (see Tips), for serving

tips To heat the kidney beans, first drain them, rinse them, and drain them again—this will make them less salty. Then place them in a microwave-safe bowl and heat on high for about 1 minute.

This chili will be done after 8 hours, but if you are late getting home, don't worry. The chili can cook for up to 10 hours without being over cooked.

Add ground turkey instead of beef if you like, and use any Mexican-style tomatoes, stewed or just seasoned and diced.

1. Place the beef, onion, and garlic in a large skillet over medium-high heat. Cook, stirring with a wooden spoon to break up the lumps, until the beef browns all over and the onions and garlic are softened, 4 to 5 minutes. Drain the beef mixture and place it in a 4½- to 5-quart slow cooker. Add the tomatoes with their liquid, and the tomato sauce, chili powder, cocoa, cinnamon, and allspice and stir to combine.

2. Cover the cooker and cook the chili until it thickens, 8 to 10 hours on low heat. To serve, spoon the spaghetti into serving bowls, top it with the chili, followed by some onion, Cheddar cheese, and kidney beans.

SERVES 8

15 WAYS TO PUT YOUR SLOW COOKER TO BEST USE

There was a time not so long ago when the slow cooker was the bridal shower gift of choice. But like so many pieces of kitchen equipment, once newer things came on the market, many of us relegated ours to the back of the cupboard—alongside the electric frying pans and fondue sets. However, busy schedules and time pressure has made this old favorite new again. Here are some tips for choosing a cooker and using it to its best advantage.

1 Buy the right size. Slow cookers range from 1 to 6 quarts, and while smaller cookers are best for smaller families, the larger ones are good for cooking stews and big batches of soup. A cooker should be at least half full, but no more than two thirds full, when cooking.

2 Use less-tender (a.k.a. less expensive!) cuts of meat (see box, page 332).

3 Cut vegetables into small, uniform pieces so that they all cook at the same rate.

4 For easier cleanup when making a casserole or cake, mist the cooker with vegetable oil cooking spray before adding the ingredients.

5 Add ingredients in the proper order. Aromatic veggies, like onions, garlic, and carrots should go on the bottom of the cooker. Place meat or chicken on top of them.

6 For the best color and flavor, brown meat and chicken in a skillet before placing it in the cooker.

7 Use whole, rather than ground, herbs and spices. Their flavors hold up better during the slow cooking process.

8 Use less liquid if you are converting stovetop soup and stew recipes to the slow cooker. The cooker conserves liquid (little boils away), so you don't need as much. You'll have to experiment on the first go-around, then keep adjusting the amount until you arrive at the optimal one. Try cutting the liquid by a quarter, and if that's not enough, a third. When the dish is fully cooked, if there is still too much liquid, remove the lid and let the mixture boil on high until it reduces to your liking.

9 Cook at the right temperature. The high temperature cooks foods twice as fast as the low. If a recipe calls for cooking on low all day (8 to 10 hours), it's a good idea to turn the cooker on high first to heat the ingredients through, then turn it down to low before you leave the house. To help you convert conventional recipes, remember that high in a slow cooker is about 300°F and low is about 200°F.

10 Peek, but don't lift the lid. Each time you remove it the temperature drops 10 to 15 degrees, significantly lengthening the cooking time. The steam condensing on the lid lets you know the food is cooking evenly.

11 Dried beans should be soaked for 10 minutes and pre-cooked for about 1½ hours before being added to a slow cooker. Therefore, I prefer using canned beans in slow-cooker dishes; I don't care for how dried beans cook in them. Dried lentils, on the other hand, do not need pre-cooking and work well in the cooker.

12 Pasta should be pre-cooked before being added to a slow cooker, but you can do that up to five days ahead (see the box on page 286). Stir it into soups or stews during the last hour of cooking.

13 If you decide to add raw rice as an ingredient, increase the liquid in the dish by 1 cup for each cup of uncooked rice.

14 Dairy products, such as milk, cream, and sour cream, should not be added until the last hour of cooking so that they don't curdle.

15 Remember to use your slow cooker for hot party drinks like mulled cider and wassail. Pour the ingredients into the cooker and heat them on low for 3 to 4 hours before serving, holding the temperature on low. Or, bring the drink to a boil on top of the stove, transfer it to the cooker, and let it cook on high for 1 hour before serving. Turn the cooker down when you serve.

SLOW-COOKER WITE CHILI

▼ ▼ ▼

Today a chili supper isn't complete without two types of chili—what I think of as the traditional one, made with beef and pinto beans, and this fragrant and colorful version, made with white beans and chicken. Thanks to the supermarket rotisserie, freshly cooked chicken is readily available. This is an easy dish for a party; serve it in the slow cooker, surrounded by decorative little bowls of toppings. Steamed rice would make a good accompaniment (for tips on quick-cooking varieties of rice, see page 354).

TO PREP:
15 MINUTES
TO COOK ON HIGH:
4–5 HOURS
TO COOK ON LOW:
8–10 HOURS

3 cans (15 ounces each) Great
Northern beans, drained
2 cups shredded cooked chicken
(see the box on page 226)
1 cup chopped red bell pepper
(from 1 medium-size bell
pepper; see Tips)
1 cup finely chopped onion
(from 1 medium-size onion)
4 cloves garlic, sliced
1 can (4 ounces) chopped green
chiles, with their liquid (see Tips)
1 tablespoon ground cumin
1 teaspoon dried oregano
½ teaspoon salt, or 1 chicken-flavored
bouillon cube
2 cans (14.5 ounces each) low-sodium
chicken broth
2 cups tortilla chips
Lime wedges, fresh cilantro sprigs,
and reduced-fat sour cream, for serving

1. Place the beans, chicken, bell pepper, onion, garlic, chiles, cumin, oregano, salt, and broth in a 4½- to 6-quart slow cooker. Stir to combine.

2. Cover the cooker and cook the chili until bubbling, the ingredients have cooked down, and the liquid has thickened, 4 to 5 hours on high heat or 8 to 10 hours on low heat. If desired, just before serving, crush the tortilla chips into roughly ½-inch pieces, add them to the chili, and stir until they soften (or garnish the chili with them). Spoon the chili into bowls and serve it with bowls of lime wedges, cilantro, and sour cream on the side for toppings.

SERVES 8

tips If you prefer, you can use a yellow or green bell pepper.

I have stopped trying to drain canned green chiles because the liquid seems to cling to them. Instead, I just dump the entire can, liquid and all, into the pot.

If you like a hotter chili, add 2 seeded and sliced fresh jalapeño peppers.

Slow Cooker on the Go

—▼—

DINNER DOCTOR SAYS Even if you didn't cook your casserole or stew in a slow cooker, you can still make good use of it. It comes in really handy if you are taking your dish to a gathering of any kind—potluck, picnic, church or school event. Transfer the food, hot, to the cooker, set the temperature on low, and the slow cooker will keep the food warm throughout the gathering.

STEAK AND GRAVY FOR THE KIDS

▼ ▼ ▼

First off let me say that this isn't *really* a doctored dish. But, I was raised on these easy steaks, which my mother would brown on the stove, then simmer with onions in a big electric skillet until they were done. We kids loved them, and your kids will, too. So, how could I not share the recipe? As the Dinner Doctor, I prescribe it as a cure for the dinner doldrums.

TO PREP:
10 MINUTES
TO COOK:
5 MINUTES
TO BAKE:
1 HOUR 15 MINUTES

Forget the electric skillet. (Does anyone own one anymore?) Instead, brown the cube steaks in a heavy, covered flameproof casserole, then let them simmer in the oven. You can walk away, and those steaks will bake to the fork-tender stage in a little over an hour. Mashed potatoes are the perfect accompaniment for the flavorful gravy. And a side of steamed broccoli rounds out the meal.

tips Cube steaks are cut from beef round and are run through a machine to tenderize the meat.

If you need to be away from the house for 2 hours rather than 1¼, bake the steaks in a 250°F oven.

4 beef cube steaks
  (about 1¼ pounds total; see Tips)
Salt and black pepper
¼ cup all-purpose flour
2 tablespoons vegetable oil
1¼ cups thinly sliced onion
  (from 1 large onion)

1. Place a rack in the center of the oven and preheat the oven to 300°F.

2. Pat the steaks dry with paper towels and season them on both sides with salt and pepper. Place the flour in a shallow bowl. Dredge both sides of the steaks in the flour, then shake off the excess.

3. Heat the oil in a 5- to 6-quart heavy, covered flameproof casserole or Dutch oven over medium-high heat. Add the steaks and brown them on both sides, 1 minute per side. Transfer the steaks to a plate. Add the onion to the casserole. Reduce the heat to medium and cook the onion, stirring with a wooden spoon, until it softens slightly, 1 minute. Pour in ⅔ cup of water and stir to loosen up any brown bits stuck to the bottom of the casserole. Bring the mixture to a boil, then turn off the heat. Place the steaks on top of the liquid and onions and cover the casserole.

4. Bake the steaks until they are fork-tender and the liquid has thickened into a gravy, about 1 hour and 15 minutes. Serve the steaks topped with the onions.

SERVES 4

Braising

—▼—

DINNER DOCTOR SAYS

Only after I had attended cooking school in France did I realize that my mother and grandmother were classic cooks. They browned chicken or a beef roast in a little fat until it had a rich color, then added onions, garlic, carrots, seasoning, and a modest amount of liquid, covered the pan, and placed it in an oven at a low temperature or on a back burner at a bare simmer for several hours. What resulted was the succulent, fall-off-the-bone sort of food we savored as children. This method of cooking is braising, and it's crucial there be just enough liquid to merely moisten the meat. (Covering the meat completely with liquid, essentially cooking the meat in liquid, is stewing, not braising.)

During the slow cooking process the meat and veggies produce liquid of their own, and the pan juices cook down. Over the years, and influenced by my children, I have streamlined and perfected the braising process to meet the need of my family. I often use cream of mushroom soup when braising chicken breasts or pork chops or add a package of fresh sliced mushrooms and a shot of sherry. A marvelous gravy results. I frequently rely on packaged pre-cubed beef, lightly flouring and seasoning them, then browning them in oil so the flour has a chance to thicken the juices into a spoonable gravy, which my kids adore.

To braise in the oven, you need the right vessel—a heavy, flameproof casserole with a tight-fitting lid. It can be an old, worn, but much-loved cast-iron Dutch oven. Or, it can be a bright and beautiful enameled cast-iron pot like a Le Creuset. It should ideally be between 6 and 8 quarts in size. I like to braise at between 250° and 300°F, which means that with some recipes I have nearly four hours for other things—even to leave the house. When I return to the kitchen, all I need to do is to remove the casserole from the oven. If I have the time I let it rest, covered, for 20 minutes while I steam rice or boil pasta. Then dinner is ready to serve!

SHIRLEY'S BRAISED BEEF

▼ ▼ ▼

TO PREP:
8 MINUTES
TO BAKE:
4½ HOURS

My friend Martha Bowden's mom is known for a recipe that's just perfect for the packages of stew beef cubes that you see in the supermarket. That beef is so lean you have to cook it slowly to tenderize it. And her recipe is perfect for busy nights when you want to get dinner on the table quickly but you'll be out of the house for the entire afternoon.

> **tip** Vary this recipe as you like, adding a dash of dried oregano or basil, a couple of cloves of fresh garlic, or even carrot cubes. And if you don't think you'll have time to cook noodles to go with the beef, add small cubes of potatoes, too. Prep time will increase, but not by very much.

When you get home, boil some egg noodles, toss a green salad, and you'll have a filling and satisfying meal. I serve the beef tips in wide bowls atop those boiled noodles.

Vegetable oil cooking spray
1 package (1.3 ounces)
  onion soup mix
1 can (10.75 ounces) tomato soup
1 can (10.75 ounces) cream of
  mushroom soup
¾ cup dry red wine
2 pounds pre-cubed lean beef stew meat
1 package (8 ounces) pre-sliced
  mushrooms

1. Place a rack in the center of the oven and preheat the oven to 250°F.

2. Mist a 6- to 8-quart covered casserole with vegetable oil cooking spray. Place the onion soup mix, tomato soup, mushroom soup, and wine in the casserole and stir to combine. Stir in the beef and mushrooms. Cover the casserole.

3. Bake the beef until it is very tender and the sauce has cooked down and thickened, about 4½ hours. Serve at once.

SERVES 6 TO 8

When Less Tender Is Better

—▼—

DINNER DOCTOR SAYS

Tougher cuts of meat call out for slow cooking. When given plenty of time, they have a chance to cook down and become tender. For example, an inexpensive beef chuck roast (about 3 pounds) can be browned in a skillet in a little oil, then placed in a slow cooker with garlic, sliced onions and bell papers, a jar of salsa, and about 3 cups of Mexican-seasoned canned tomatoes. Let the roast cook on low for 8 to 10 hours, and you'll have tender and delicious beef to shred and wrap in warm flour tortillas.

ALL-DAY
BEEF BOURGUIGNON

▼ ▼ ▼

Beef Bourguignon is a classic French beef stew enhanced with red wine. This one has been streamlined by using pre-sliced fresh mushrooms and already-peeled baby carrots. I like to cook potatoes in the microwave, slice them in half lengthwise, place them in the bottom of a serving bowl, and ladle the stew on top. Or, you can serve it as you would beef Stroganoff, over egg noodles. Either way, the stew is rib sticking and memorable.

TO PREP:	
15 MINUTES	
TO COOK ON HIGH:	
6 HOURS	
TO COOK ON LOW:	
10 HOURS	

tip **Red wine greatly elevates the flavor of humble beef stew. And the beef benefits from the acid in the wine, which tenderizes the meat as it simmers.**

2 cups thinly sliced onion
   (from 1 extra-large onion
   or 2 medium-size ones)
1 cup thinly sliced pre-peeled
   baby carrots
4 cloves garlic, sliced
2 pounds pre-cubed lean beef stew meat
Salt and black pepper
¼ cup all-purpose flour
1 package (8 ounces)
   pre-sliced
   mushrooms
1 teaspoon dried
   oregano
2 bay leaves
1 can (14 ounces)
   low-sodium beef broth
1 cup dry red wine
2 scallions, both white and light green parts,
   chopped (for ¼ cup), for garnish

1. Place the onion, carrots, and garlic in the bottom of a 4½- to 6-quart slow cooker and stir to mix.

2. Pat the beef dry with paper towels and season with salt and pepper. Place the flour in a shallow bowl. Dredge the beef in the flour, then shake off the excess. Place the beef on top of the onion mixture, then scatter the mushrooms, oregano, and bay leaves on top of the beef. Pour the beef broth and red wine over the beef.

3. Cover the cooker and cook the beef until it is quite tender and the liquid has cooked down and thickened, 6 hours on high heat or 10 hours on low heat.

4. To serve, remove and discard the bay leaves. Spoon the stew into bowls and garnish with the chopped scallions.

SERVES 8

A Meal for a Winter Weekend

▼ ▼ ▼

When company's coming for a winter's Saturday night dinner party, get the beef started early in the morning. A hassle-free main course will be ready by the time they arrive and you'll have had a whole day free to do other things.

All-Day Beef Bourguignon
page 333

Egg noodles

Parmesan and Pepper Cornmeal Twists
page 408

Green salad

Banoffee Tart
page 487

Mom's Pot Roast

WITH VIDALIA ONION GRAVY

▼▼▼

TO PREP:
10 MINUTES
TO COOK:
7–9 MINUTES
TO BAKE:
3–3½ HOURS

The secret to this slowly cooked pot roast is that you add no liquid to the pan. The big sweet onions cook down, and this provides all the juices you need for the beef to simmer. If you're around an hour before the pot roast is done, pull the casserole from the oven and add some pre-peeled baby carrots from the produce department and some chunks of potato.

Return the casserole to the oven, and they will steam on top of the roast, becoming tender and flavorful.

1 boneless beef chuck roast (about 4 pounds)

Salt and black pepper

¼ cup all-purpose flour

2 tablespoons vegetable oil

3 large sweet onions, such as Vidalias, peeled and cut in half crosswise

4 cups pre-peeled baby carrots (optional)

4 cups quartered peeled potatoes (optional)

1. Place a rack in the center of the oven and preheat the oven to 300°F.

2. Pat the roast dry with paper towels and season it with salt and pepper. Place the flour in a shallow bowl. Dredge the roast in the flour, then shake off the excess.

tips The beef will slice better if you let it rest for 10 minutes in the casserole with the lid on to keep the pot roast warm.

You can vary the root vegetables here, adding parsnips, rutabagas, and/or turnips instead of the carrots and potatoes.

Doctor the pot roast by adding garlic, a bay leaf, or a dash—but only a dash—of red wine.

3. Heat the oil in a 5- to 6-quart heavy, covered flameproof casserole or Dutch oven over medium-high heat. Add the roast and brown it on both sides, 3 to 4 minutes per side. Remove the casserole from the heat, and transfer the roast to a plate. Place the onion halves, cut-side down, in the bottom of the casserole. Place the roast on top of the onions and cover the casserole.

4. Bake the beef until it is quite tender and the juices have thickened, 3 to 3½ hours. One hour before the beef is done, add the carrots and potatoes, if using, to the casserole. Spoon the juices over the vegetables to baste them, replace the casserole lid, and return the casserole to the oven.

5. To serve, carefully remove the roast from the casserole and slice it. Arrange the slices of beef on plates with the carrots, onions, and potatoes, if using, and spoon the pan juices on top.

SERVES 8

SWEET-AND-SOUR BRISKET OF BEEF

▼ ▼ ▼

This nostalgic beef brisket recipe has been in my file for years. Onion soup mix and tomato soup tenderize and flavor the beef. The brisket is easy to prepare, and although the sauce is nothing more than brown sugar and red wine vinegar stirred into the pan juices, the result is delicious. Sliced and served with mashed potatoes (you can smother those with the sauce, too), stir-fried spinach, coleslaw, and hot corn bread, the brisket makes a hearty dinner.

TO PREP:
10 MINUTES
TO COOK:
6 HOURS

tips Feel free to tinker with this recipe. For an extra spot of flavor, slice several cloves of garlic and add them along with the tomato soup. Or use balsamic vinegar and honey in place of (and in the same amounts as) the red wine vinegar and brown sugar.

If you have the time, place the gravy in the freezer to let the fat separate to the top. This makes it very easy to remove all the fat.

1 beef brisket (4 to 5 pounds),
    trimmed of fat
¼ cup all-purpose flour
1 packet (1.25 ounces) onion
    soup mix
1 can (10.75 ounces) tomato soup
¼ teaspoon black pepper
2 tablespoons light brown sugar
2 tablespoons red wine vinegar

1. Pat the brisket dry with paper towels. Place the flour in a shallow bowl. Dredge the brisket in the flour, then shake off the excess. Place the brisket in a 4½- to 6-quart slow cooker.

2. Place the onion soup mix, tomato soup, and pepper in a small bowl with ¼ cup of water and stir to combine. Pour this mixture over the brisket.

3. Cover the cooker and cook the beef on high heat until it is quite tender, 6 hours. Remove the brisket from the cooker and place it on a platter. Cover

tip For an attractive presentation, arrange slices of brisket on a platter, pour some of the sauce on top, then sprinkle the brisket with chopped parsley and spoon mashed potatoes around the meat.

it loosely with aluminum foil to keep it warm.

4. Strain the liquid that is left in the cooker. Spoon off as much fat as possible or use a gravy separator to remove the fat from the liquid (see Tips, page 337). Pour the strained and defatted liquid into a 2-quart saucepan and heat over medium heat. Add the brown sugar and vinegar and stir until the sauce heats through and the brown sugar melts. Slice the brisket, pour enough sauce over it to moisten it, then serve the remaining sauce on the side.

SERVES 12

CORNED BEEF AND CABBAGE

▼▼▼

I used to cook corned beef once or twice a year and always on St. Patrick's Day—naturally. When I saw how beautiful the corned beef looked sliced on a platter, how everyone gobbled it up, and how delicious the leftovers were in sandwiches, I wondered why I didn't

TO PREP:
10 MINUTES
TO COOK ON HIGH:
4–4½ HOURS
TO COOK ON LOW:
8 HOURS

cook it more often. Now I do, no special occasion necessary. The constant low temperature of a slow cooker is perfect for simmering corned beef, making it delectably tender.

1 small onion, quartered

2 cloves garlic, sliced

1 corned beef brisket (about 3½ pounds)

2 cups sliced carrots (from 3 to 4 carrots)

Black pepper

1 head green cabbage (about 2 pounds),
*   cored and quartered*

Salt

Butter

Dark bread and
*   coarse mustard,*
*   for serving*

tips If there's no seasoning packet with the brisket, add 2 bay leaves, black pepper to taste, and ½ teaspoon mustard seeds.

You can add the cabbage quarters to the slow cooker after 1 hour if you are cooking the brisket on low heat. They take a long time to cook, and this is why I prefer to cook them on top of the stove.

1. Place the onion and garlic on the bottom of a 4½- to 6-quart slow cooker. Place the corned beef and carrots on top. Add the seasoning packet if one comes with the brisket (see Tips, page 339) and the ¼ teaspoon of pepper. Pour enough water over the beef to just cover it. Cover the cooker. Cook the corned beef until it is tender and just cooked through, 4 to 4½ hours on high heat or 8 hours on low heat.

2. During the last 30 minutes of cooking, place the cabbage in a pot of boiling water and cook it until it is tender, 20 to 25 minutes. Drain the cabbage and season it with salt, pepper, and butter.

3. Transfer the corned beef to a cutting board and let rest 10 minutes, if you have the time, then slice it. Serve the corned beef with the cabbage and carrots, being sure to spoon the cooking juices over the meat and vegetables. Serve dark bread and coarse mustard alongside.

SERVES 6 TO 8

SAVORY PORK CARNITAS

▼ ▼ ▼

There is nothing more delectable than a pork roast that has cooked down to fork-tender shreds along with aromatic seasonings. I guess it was growing up in barbecue country that made me such a fan of pork roast, and this recipe lends a Mexican flavor to Southern barbecue. You simmer the pork for a long time, doctoring it with taco seasoning, garlic, onion, and chiles, then once it's cooked shred it and pile it onto flour tortillas with all sorts of tasty garnishes. It's perfect party food and can be cooked ahead and frozen for up to one month.

TO PREP:
15 MINUTES
TO COOK ON HIGH:
6 HOURS
TO COOK ON LOW:
10 HOURS

1 Boston butt pork roast (3 to 4 pounds),
*   trimmed of visible fat*
1 package (1.25 ounces) reduced-sodium
*   taco seasoning*
3 cloves garlic, sliced
1 large onion, quartered
1 can (4 ounces) whole green chiles, drained
6 to 8 flour tortillas
*   (10-inches each)*
Shredded lettuce
Chopped tomatoes
Sliced avocados
Sour cream
Lime wedges
Chopped scallions and
*   fresh cilantro sprigs, for garnish*

tips The trick to slow cooking is arriving at the right amount of moisture, enough so that the food does not burn, but not so much that the flavors are diluted. If the pork roast is nearer 3 pounds, use slightly less than 1 cup of water. If it is closer to 4 pounds, use a full cup.

You could also serve the pork with steamed rice and spoon the pan juices over it. See page 354 for tips on quick-cooking varieties of rice.

1. Place the pork roast, taco seasoning, garlic, onion, and chiles in a 4½- to 6-quart slow cooker and add about 1 cup of water (see Tips, page 341). Stir to combine. Cover the cooker and cook the pork until it is tender enough to shred, 6 hours on high heat or 10 hours on low heat.

2. Remove the pork from the cooker and shred the meat with a fork. Spoon some of the shredded pork evenly down the center of a tortilla and roll it up. Repeat with the remaining pork and tortillas. Serve the filled tortillas with shredded lettuce, chopped tomato, sliced avocado, sour cream, and lime wedges. Garnish them with the chopped scallions and cilantro sprigs.

SERVES 6 TO 8

15 WAYS TO DOCTOR COOKED RICE

Make a scoop of rice more inviting with any of the easy ideas you'll find here. Unless otherwise noted, in each case you're starting with 2 cups of cooked rice.

1 Stir a handful of finely chopped fresh parsley into the rice.

2 Add 1 tablespoon of fresh lemon juice and 1 teaspoon of grated lemon zest.

3 Pour in ¼ cup of heavy cream, add ½ cup of grated Parmesan cheese, then stir the rice slowly over low heat for a time-pressed person's risotto.

4 Sauté sliced fresh mushrooms in butter and toss them with the rice.

5 Toss some melted butter, a squeeze of fresh lemon juice, and a spoonful or so of drained capers with the rice.

6 Add sautéed minced onion and cooked peas to the rice.

7 Stir in chicken stock to moisten the rice, then add currants and sliced toasted almonds. Reheat the rice before serving.

8 Toss the rice with garlic slices you have browned in butter.

9 Mince a scallion and some fresh parsley. Reheat the rice with butter and salt, then fold in the minced scallion and parsley.

10 Toss the rice with drained canned corn kernels, the kind that come with diced red and green peppers, then reheat it.

11 Warm 2 teaspoons of curry powder in 1 tablespoon of butter in a small skillet for 1 minute, then transfer the rice to the skillet and reheat it.

12 Reheat the rice, then fold in toasted sesame seeds, a dash each of soy sauce and Asian sesame oil, and minced scallion.

13 Add minced onion and chopped tomato that have been lightly sautéed in olive oil with a dash of saffron or turmeric.

14 Brown some mild Italian sausage, toss in some fennel seeds, and stir in the rice. Add enough stock to make the rice moist.

15 Sauté a ¼ cup each of chopped onion and bell pepper in 1 tablespoon of olive oil, and stir in 1 cup of rice. Season the rice with salt and black pepper, then pour in 4 lightly beaten eggs. Stir and cook, adding ½ cup shredded Monterey Jack cheese at the last minute so it melts.

BEBE'S COCA-COLA HAM

▼▼▼

Today's supermarket ham tastes little like the country-style smoked hams of yesteryear. But my mother came up with a way of baking a good-quality store-bought ham so that the excess water that was pumped into it when it was cured slowly cooks out. The result is a sweet, yet rich, faintly salty, faintly smoky ham that is equally delicious hot or sliced for sandwiches. Why Coca-Cola? It's acidic, it's usually in the fridge, and the flavors work well with the ham. Easy Sweet and Hot Pickles (page 364) and Angel Biscuits (page 417) make perfect accompaniments.

TO PREP:
10 MINUTES
TO BAKE:
4½–5 HOURS
TO REST:
15 MINUTES

tips Buy a pre-cooked boneless ham, but if you cannot find one that weighs the 3 to 3½ pounds I call for, use my recipe as a guide, increasing or decreasing the cooking time depending on whether the ham is larger or smaller.

Both light and dark brown sugar will work in this recipe.

If you don't have Coca-Cola, you can use apple juice or pineapple juice.

You'll probably have leftovers. At our house, we have the ham with fresh vegetables and hot biscuits on day one, then use it for sandwiches and/or any of myriad salads and/or casseroles on the following day.

1 pre-cooked boneless ham (3 to 3½ pounds), unsliced (see Tips)
½ cup firmly packed brown sugar (see Tips)
1 cup Coca-Cola (see Tips)

1. Place a rack in the center of the oven and preheat the oven to 300°F.

2. Tear off two 24-inch-long sheets of aluminum foil. Place one on top of the other, with the shiny sides facing each other. Starting at one of the long edges, double over the pieces of foil ½ inch, then fold them over again ½ inch to form a seam. Open up the foil and place it shiny side down in a 13-by-9-inch (3-quart) glass or ceramic baking dish. Place the ham on top of the foil so that it is in the center of the baking dish. Pat the brown sugar onto the top of the ham, then pour the Coca-Cola over the brown sugar. It is okay if the cola drips onto the foil. Bring the edges of the foil up to meet and double fold them to seal the foil well on all sides.

3. Bake the ham until much of the liquid has cooked out of it, 4½ to 5 hours. Remove the pan from the oven, carefully tear open the foil at the top to let the steam escape, then let the ham rest in the foil for 15 minutes. Transfer the ham to a serving platter or carving board, then slice it and serve.

SERVES 12 TO 16

HEARTY LENTIL AND SAUSAGE STEW

▼ ▼ ▼

TO PREP:
10 MINUTES
TO COOK:
8 HOURS

Lentils take less time to cook than other dried beans and therefore make a fine candidate for the slow cooker. They are, however, bland, so it is your job to doctor them up with smoked sausage, cumin, a cinnamon stick, and so on. Then, when this heady stew emerges from the cooker, the lentils will have taken on an exotic new flavor. An added benefit of the slow cooker is that you arrive home from a long day to find dinner waiting and your kitchen fragrant. That's something you will never get from a zapped frozen dinner. Serve the stew with crusty bread and Spinach and Orange Salad with Sesame Vinaigrette (page 122).

2 cups dry lentils, picked over and rinsed

1 medium-size onion, finely chopped

3 garlic cloves, sliced

1 can (14.5 ounces) diced tomatoes
*   (see Tips)*

½ cup chopped pre-peeled baby carrots

4 cups canned low-sodium chicken broth
*   or water (one 32-ounce container)*

1 teaspoon ground cumin

1 bay leaf

1 cinnamon stick (about 3 inches)

½ pound reduced-fat smoked pork or
*   beef sausage (see Tips),*
*   cut into 2-inch pieces*

tips **Add pre-seasoned diced tomatoes if you like.**

Chicken broth gives this recipe more body than mere water, so even if you don't have the full four cups, add as much as you can and make up the difference with water.

You can omit the sausage or add a cup of chopped cooked ham instead.

Place the lentils, onion, garlic, tomatoes, carrots, chicken broth, cumin, bay leaf, and cinnamon stick in a 4½- to 6-quart slow cooker. Stir to combine. Place the sausage pieces on top. Cover the cooker and cook the lentils on low heat until they have absorbed all the liquid and are tender, 8 hours. If possible, check during the last hour of cooking to see if the lentils need more liquid. Add up to 1 cup more, if they seem too dry. To serve, remove and discard the bay leaf and cinnamon stick and spoon the stew into deep bowls.

SERVES 6

SLOW-COOKER MACARONI AND CHEESE

▼▼▼

TO PREP:
5 MINUTES
TO COOK:
2½–3 HOURS

I'll admit to being skeptical about this recipe when it was passed along to me. I have mentioned elsewhere in this book that preparing macaroni and cheese for kids that they will think is better than the kind that comes from the orange freezer package or in the blue box is a feat in itself. But I discovered that there is something very appealing about having macaroni and cheese baking away so that when you or your teenager arrive home hungry, you can heap it on a plate and dig in. I think you'll agree.

Vegetable oil cooking spray

2 cups milk (see Tips)

1 can (12 ounces) evaporated milk

1 teaspoon Worcestershire sauce

¼ teaspoon salt

¼ teaspoon black pepper

Pinch of dry mustard

1 package (8 ounces; 2 cups)
     pre-shredded sharp
     Cheddar cheese

8 ounces (2 cups)
     uncooked macaroni

tips You can use whatever milk you have in your refrigerator—whole, skim, or reduced fat—but you must also use a can of evaporated milk. The evaporated milk is critical, since it keeps the macaroni and cheese from curdling or separating.

You can change the amount or type of cheese you add depending on the tastes of your household.

Be sure to cook the macaroni on low; you need a slow, gentle heat.

Mist the bottom and side of a 4½- to 6-quart slow cooker with vegetable oil cooking spray. Place

the milks, Worcestershire sauce, salt, pepper, mustard, Cheddar cheese and macaroni in a large mixing bowl and stir to combine, then pour into the slow cooker. Cover and cook the macaroni on low heat until it is bubbling around the edges and has cooked through, 2½ to 3 hours. Spoon onto serving plates.

SERVES 6

Slow-Cooker Quirks

—▼—

DINNER DOCTOR SAYS

I love the slow cooker, but just as I don't expect the food processor or blender to perform all tasks, I prefer to save my cooker for what it does best. Like all-day braising of tough cuts of beef. Or cooking chicken gently while I am out of the house. Or simmering a pot of white bean chili on Saturday afternoon so I can get some chores done and still have a delicious dish to feed my dinner guests.

However, after working with my slow cooker over the years, I have found that there are some ingredients that it doesn't cook as well as I thought it would. For instance, at this point, I don't expect the slow cooker to turn out perfectly cooked dried beans or steamed rice. I find dried beans turn out creamier if left to simmer in a big heavy pot at the back of the stove. If I want to cook rice, I also do this on the stovetop.

These are my slow-cooker quirks; you may have yours. Work your way through my recipes, read my suggestions, then go off on your own and find what you like best about it. I keep my cooker on the top of my pantry shelf, pull it down, and find I may use it·two or three nights in a row, then not at all for a week or two. And don't just think of the slow cooker as a casserole or stew maker. I use mine to prepare a knockout Chocolate Chip Pudding Cake (see page 504). If you adore chocolate, you will, too.

VEGGIE HEAVEN

▼ ▼ ▼

I cook broccoli as if I were a scientist. When it turns a vivid green and a jab with a fork reveals a texture a bit past al dente, I immediately pull the pan from the heat, drain off the water, and toss in butter and salt. My children gobble up the stuff, but only when it's been cooked to this precise stage. They don't like their broccoli crunchy, and they won't eat it when it has languished in the water too long and turns olive drab. Cooking other vegetables doesn't pose a problem, but that's because the kids flat out won't touch most. Kathleen, Litton, and John will dutifully eat peas, but with the same gusto they show when making their beds. Not a one enjoys spinach, all three go for carrots as long as they are raw. One likes green beans, one favors white beans, one prefers black-eyed peas. However, potatoes? In our house they're so beloved they're not counted as a vegetable, just a reward for eating your beans!

So, with that off my chest, it's pretty obvious that this chapter was not created for my kids, but for those folks who do not have to be cajoled, bribed, or threatened into eating their veggies. It is for people who find themselves eating more meatless meals by choice (like my husband and myself). It is for folks who adore all kinds of beans, wait eagerly for nice firm eggplants to arrive at the market, and munch on carrots because they're sweet (*and* they're good for you). People who love all the rabbit foods sautéed, braised, grilled, steamed, even raw. But because time is ever short, we vegetable lovers don't always get all the veggies we need. So this chapter is filled with plenty of quick ways to help you get some great vegetable recipes onto your table, both as main dishes and sides.

For a summer supper, with a green salad on the side, you can enjoy the Caramelized Onion and Garlic Tart, and in midwinter, when only the cherry tomatoes look good in the market, try the Cherry Tomato and Basil Tart. Both are quick to put together because their buttery crusts are made from refrigerated crescent roll dough. If you're craving tomato sauce, pair it with gargantuan mushrooms to make Portobellos Braised in Red Sauce. You'll also find tomatoes in Our Favorite Eggplant Parmesan and in the Butternut Squash and Tomato Gratin. For a healthy and hands-off method for making ratatouille, try One-Bowl Ratatouille, which is cooked in the microwave oven.

If your sister is coming to supper and she does not eat meat, serve her Black Bean and Vegetable Stack, a light lasagna-style dish that tastes like you went to a lot more trouble than you did. Fried Green Tomatoes with Herbed Goat Cheese and Tortilla Española with Sweet Peppers make great nibbles before dinner or a light meal along with a salad. To accompany shrimp and polenta, pork tenderloin, or crab cakes, try So Fast Succotash. And for a holiday gathering, there's Thanksgiving Souffléed Sweet Potatoes, which can be put together in a flash.

Your kids may actually like the dishes in this chapter. Although, as I mentioned, I didn't develop them with children in mind, my eight-year-old loved the tomato tart; everyone licked their spoons after they tried the yummy Coconut-and-Curry-Scented Peas and Rice. They all sampled the Mediterranean Roast Potatoes and Asparagus, and two even ate the asparagus (but then, that recipe includes potatoes). And when I served Family-Style Broccoli and Cheddar Soufflé the plates were cleaned. As for Down Home Corn, my pickiest child could have eaten the entire pan.

SIDE DISHES

LEMON-PARMESAN STEAMED BROCCOLI AND FRIENDS

▼ ▼ ▼

My mother taught me that a colorful plate was a healthy plate. Thank goodness that combinations of fresh broccoli and cauliflower florets and baby carrots now come in bags, so colorful nutrients are at our fingertips with no effort. The veggies are easily steamed. Toss them with lemon

TO PREP:
3 MINUTES
TO COOK:
3–4 MINUTES

zest and Parmesan cheese, and you have a medley that's perfect to spoon alongside roast chicken and mashed potatoes.

1 package (16 ounces) broccoli florets,
     carrots, and cauliflower florets
Pinch of salt (see Tips)
2 tablespoons pre-shredded
     Parmesan cheese
1 teaspoon freshly grated lemon zest
     (see Tips)
Black pepper

1. Place a medium-size saucepan filled with water to a depth of 1 inch over high heat. Cover the pan and bring the water to a boil, then add the vegetables and salt. Reduce the heat to low, re-cover the pan, and

tips I find that with the addition of lemon zest, little if any salt is needed in this dish, but suit yourself. I also feel that olive oil and butter aren't necessary, but if you must, add just a smidgen so as not to overwhelm the fresh, clean flavor of this dish.

It takes a whole medium-size lemon to produce a teaspoon of grated zest. No lemons in the house? Use lemon pepper seasoning instead.

let the vegetables steam until they are bright in color and just tender, 3 to 4 minutes.

2. Remove the pan from the heat, drain off the water, and sprinkle the Parmesan cheese and lemon zest over the top. Season with pepper to taste. Toss the vegetables and serve at once.

SERVES 4 TO 6

A Few Vegetable Handling Tips

—▼—

DINNER DOCTOR SAYS

1. In the depths of winter, cherry tomatoes are sweeter and more flavorful than regular tomatoes. They also hold their juices well, making them a good choice when you are making tarts and pies and you don't want a lot of moisture to escape and make the crust soggy.

2. Don't cut eggplant with a carbon-steel knife or it will discolor. Use only a stainless steel blade.

3. Frozen veggies rarely need all the cooking time recommended on the package. Don't overcook them. Some, like frozen spinach, don't need to be cooked at all.

4. When preparing asparagus, rinse it well, then snap off the tough end of the spears (the spears will break where the tender part meets the tough part). Slender asparagus spears take less time to cook than thick ones.

5. You can buy frozen onions if you like, but it is more economical and just as easy to use fresh. To quickly slice a fresh onion, cut off both ends, remove the skin, and cut the onion in half lengthwise. Place the onion halves cut side down and slice them crosswise into half-moons. These sauté well and will add crunch to any number of dishes.

Tips for
Cooking and Doctoring Rice

—▼—

DINNER DOCTOR SAYS

I learned from my mother to measure twice as much liquid as rice when cooking the grain and to allow a 20-minute cooking time. For the most part, this rule of thumb still works, but here are some exceptions.

- Fragrant, elegant basmati rice cooks in just 15 minutes.

- Instant brown rice is done in 10 minutes.

- Instant rice needs only 5 minutes to cook.

Rice is perfect for doctoring. The suggestions here all start with 1 cup of uncooked rice, which will make 3 cups when cooked and serve about 4 people.

- Any kind of rice is good with butter and salt.

- Stir ¼ cup of chopped scallions, 1 teaspoon of chopped fresh ginger, and 2 teaspoons of rice vinegar into basmati rice.

- When cooking brown rice, add ¼ cup of finely chopped pecans and 1 teaspoon of soy sauce.

- To dress up instant rice, add a bit of butter, some salt, a squeeze of lemon juice, and a tiny bit of grated lemon zest.

- Basmati and instant brown or white rice can all be cooked in a liquid other than water—canned beef broth, chicken broth, coconut milk, or a blend of chicken broth and coconut milk. Add a cinnamon stick or a piece of lemongrass to the boiling liquid.

MOM'S BROCCOLI AND RICE CASSEROLE

▼ ▼ ▼

TO PREP:
15 MINUTES
TO BAKE:
25–30 MINUTES

For many people, the memorable casserole of childhood is green bean or tuna noodle. But for my sisters and me, it is this simple combination of rice, cheese, and broccoli. How clever of our mother to concoct something delicious enough to seduce us into eating broccoli. I will admit to serving this casserole to my children for that reason and also because I can assemble it on those frantic days when even chopping an onion seems laborious. Serve the casserole with roast or fried chicken from the deli and a green salad or sliced tomatoes ripe from the garden.

tip Mushroom soup casseroles used to be de rigueur, and I still cook with cans of mushroom soup today. The soup adds a welcome creaminess, and by minimizing the number of ingredients, it saves time, allowing you to put together a salad while the casserole bakes. You can use either regular mushroom soup or the reduced-fat and low-sodium kind.

*2 packages (10 ounces each) frozen
    chopped broccoli*

1 cup instant rice

*1 can (10.75 ounces) cream of
    mushroom soup (see Tip)*

*½ cup processed cheese spread,
    such as Cheez Whiz*

⅓ cup milk (see Tips, page 356)

*Pinch of black pepper, or
    dash of hot pepper sauce
    (optional)*

*½ cup pre-shredded sharp
    Cheddar cheese*

1. Place a rack in the center of the oven and preheat the oven to 375°F.

2. Place the frozen broccoli in a microwave-safe dish and microwave on high power until the broccoli thaws enough to be broken up, 2 minutes. Transfer the broccoli and its liquid to a 13-by-9-inch (3-quart) glass or ceramic baking dish and place in the oven to continue thawing while you complete Step 3.

3. Place the rice, mushroom soup, cheese spread, milk, and pepper, if using, in a large mixing bowl. Stir until well combined. The mixture will be thick.

4. Remove the baking dish from the oven and, using a wooden spoon, spread the broccoli evenly over the bottom of the dish. It is fine if the broccoli is still a little

tips **Both whole and skim milk work equally well in this recipe.**

For added crunch, drain a small can of sliced water chestnuts and add them to the rice mixture, then bake the casserole as directed.

frozen. Spoon the rice mixture over the broccoli in an even layer. Sprinkle the Cheddar cheese on top.

5. Return the baking dish to the oven and bake the casserole until it is bubbling throughout and lightly browned around the edges, 25 to 30 minutes. Serve the casserole at once or cover it with aluminum foil and let it rest for up to 20 minutes before serving.

SERVES 8 TO 10

FAMILY-STYLE BROCCOLI AND CHEDDAR SOUFFLÉ

▼ ▼ ▼

Many classic French soufflé recipes call for a homemade white sauce, but here is a streamlined broccoli and Cheddar one that uses refrigerated Alfredo-style pasta sauce instead. It's great for both family dinners and festive occasions. Most soufflés are so fragile they deflate like a popped balloon once out of the oven, but this one stands tall—until it's all gone. Accompanied by a salad or some fruit the soufflé will make a light meal, or pair it with roast chicken, grilled pork, or sautéed shrimp.

TO PREP:	
20 MINUTES	
TO BAKE:	
15–17 MINUTES	

tips To thaw frozen broccoli, unwrap it and place the frozen block on a microwave-safe plate. Microwave the broccoli on high power until it thaws enough that you can squeeze the moisture out of it with a fork, about 2 minutes.

The nutmeg in the Alfredo-style sauce complements the broccoli, so no extra seasoning is needed in this recipe.

1 teaspoon butter, at room temperature

1 package (10 ounces) frozen chopped broccoli, thawed (see Tips)

1 container (10 ounces) refrigerated Alfredo-style pasta sauce (see page 277)

3 large eggs, separated, yolks lightly beaten, plus 2 large egg whites

1 cup pre-shredded Cheddar cheese

1. Place a rack in the center of the oven and preheat the oven to 425°F.

2. Rub the bottom and sides of a 11-by-7-inch (2-quart) glass or ceramic baking dish with the butter, then set the dish aside.

3. Drain the broccoli well, then place it and the pasta sauce, egg yolks, and Cheddar cheese in a large bowl and stir to combine. Set the bowl aside.

4. In another large bowl, beat all the egg whites on high speed with an electric mixer until stiff peaks form, 2 minutes. Scrape the egg whites into the broccoli mixture and fold together using a rubber spatula, taking care not to overmix. Transfer the broccoli mixture to the prepared baking dish.

5. Bake the soufflé until it puffs up and is deep golden brown, 15 to 17 minutes. Spoon the soufflé onto serving plates and serve at once.

SERVES 6

Broccoli Revisited

—▼—

DINNER DOCTOR SAYS

Most of us cook broccoli on top of the stove, but leftovers often go into the microwave to be reheated the next night. I have found a great way to get the kids to eat broccoli the second time around. Microwave it on high power in a small casserole until it is hot. Sprinkle some finely shredded cheese over the broccoli—you can use any kind you like. Cover the casserole with a lid or aluminum foil and let it rest until it's time to serve dinner. After about ten minutes the cheese will melt into an instant sauce.

STIR-FRIED SWEET CARROT SLIVERS

WITH ORANGE

▼ ▼ ▼

TO PREP:
3 MINUTES
TO COOK:
4–5 MINUTES

Somewhat like a relish, much like a crunchy stir-fry, this dish can be assembled and on the table in less than 10 minutes thanks to those handy packages of shredded carrots in the produce section. I have long bought carrots this way because they are a healthy and fast addition to salads, soups, and pasta combinations. But only recently did it occur to me to let the shredded carrots be the star instead of a contributing actor. With just the right balance of tang and sweetness, the carrots are delicious hot on the first day and equally tasty piled onto turkey sandwiches the next.

tips Add a tablespoon of minced fresh ginger or a pinch of ground ginger along with the orange juice.

Instead of orange juice, sugar, and scallions, add 2 tablespoons rice vinegar, 1 teaspoon Asian (dark) sesame oil, and 1 tablespoon chopped fresh cilantro or parsley.

If you want a more substantial side dish, steam a package of sugar snap peas and toss them with the carrots.

1 tablespoon olive oil
1 package (8 ounces)
    pre-shredded carrots
¼ cup store-bought orange juice
2 teaspoons light brown sugar
    or granulated sugar
Salt
1 scallion, green part only,
    minced

Heat the olive oil in a large skillet over medium heat. Stir in the carrots and cook, stirring constantly, until they soften, 2 to 3 minutes. Be careful that the carrots do not stick to the bottom of the skillet. Add the orange juice and brown sugar and season with salt to taste. Cover the skillet, reduce the heat to low, and let the carrots simmer until they soften a bit more, 2 minutes longer. Sprinkle the scallions over the top and serve the carrots at once.

SERVES 4 TO 6

The Shelf Life of Pre-Shredded Veggies

—▼—

DINNER DOCTOR SAYS It's incredibly convenient to buy carrots that have already been shredded and coleslaw that's ready for tossing, but remember that these products don't last as long as whole carrots and cabbage. Because they have been shredded and bagged, they need to be used within a couple of days of purchase.

DOWN HOME CORN

▼▼▼

TO PREP:
5 MINUTES
TO COOK:
8–10 MINUTES

What a beautiful recipe this is—not only because it makes the most creamy and hard-to-resist creamed corn you can imagine but also because it originated as a comforting food gift for grieving families. Nancy Bradshaw of Nashville is known for the recipe, which she calls Bereavement Corn. She likes to make it with fresh Silver Queen corn, but when that corn is not in season, she turns to the freezer for tiny white shoepeg kernels. The results are equally delicious, and taste as if you had carefully scraped fresh corn from the ears. Serve the corn with sliced ripe tomatoes, fried chicken, skewered grilled shrimp—most anything!

1 package (16 ounces; 3 generous cups)
    frozen white shoepeg corn
    (see Tips)
4 tablespoons (½ stick) butter
½ cup heavy (whipping) cream
    (see Tips)
2 teaspoons
    cornstarch
1 teaspoon sugar
Salt and black
    pepper

tips **If you can't find frozen shoepeg corn, you can use a package of frozen yellow corn. In this case you will definitely need to pulse the corn in a food processor.**

Don't have heavy cream? Use 1 cup of half-and-half instead of the cream and ½ cup of water, or use a 5-ounce can of evaporated milk, then fill the can two thirds full with water and add this to the corn.

Place the corn, butter, cream, corn-starch, sugar, salt, and pepper in a large skillet or 2-quart saucepan over medium heat. Add ½ cup of water and stir until the mixture just comes to a boil, making sure that the cornstarch dissolves completely. Reduce the heat to medium-low and let the mixture simmer, uncovered, stirring occasionally, until it thickens, 6 to 7 minutes longer. If you want a creamier consistency, transfer the corn mixture to a food processor and pulse several times to break up the corn kernels. If you do this, reheat the corn briefly, then serve it at once.

SERVES 6

tips **Feeling creative? Add a pinch of curry powder and a dash of hot pepper sauce after the cornstarch is dissolved.**

A handful of chopped scallions or a spoonful of crumbled cooked bacon makes a tasty garnish.

So Fast Succotash

▼ ▼ ▼

Succotash, popular in the South, is a wonderful vegetable medley of lima beans and corn. It's delicious topped with crab cakes, shrimp, or pork tenderloin and with polenta (see Creole Shrimp with Polenta and So Fast Succotash, on page 314). My version includes tomatoes. Although most Southern vegetable dishes are cooked to death, don't overcook this one. You don't want mushy succotash. Thank goodness frozen vegetables allow us to enjoy succotash year-round!

TO PREP:
5 MINUTES
TO COOK:
12 MINUTES

tips **Small lima beans go by the names tiny and baby, and when inspecting them I found the tiny were a bit smaller than baby and needed slightly less cooking time.**

   This dish is also delicious when you cook the vegetables in chicken broth and garnish it with crumbled bacon.

1 package (10 ounces) frozen baby lima beans
1 package (10 ounces) frozen white shoepeg corn
1 cup chopped tomato (from 2 medium-size tomatoes)
½ cup chopped onion (from 1 small onion)
Salt and black pepper
1 tablespoon butter

Place the lima beans in a 2-quart saucepan with water to cover by 1 inch. Bring to a boil over medium-high heat, then reduce the heat to medium-low, cover the pan, and let the beans simmer until they are just tender, 9 minutes. Add the corn, tomato, and onion and season with salt and pepper to taste. Cook until the tomato just softens, 3 minutes. Remove from the heat, drain, add the butter, and stir until it melts. Serve at once.

SERVES 4

EASY SWEET AND HOT PICKLES

▼ ▼ ▼

TO PREP:
30 MINUTES
TO MARINATE:
2 TO 3 DAYS

My mother-in-law, Flowerree Oakes, passed along this recipe years ago. She and her sister Janet Moon made the pickles every holiday season to give as gifts at Christmas. I had tried without success to make great pickles from my garden cucumbers. Flowerree's pickles were superb; what was her secret? Doctoring supermarket pickles! Well, you will be amazed, too, but don't wait too long to try making them. You'll need to allow two to three days for the pickles to marinate in the refrigerator (the ultimate hands-off recipe!) before you can pile them onto sandwiches or pack them into clean jars to give as presents. I have tweaked the original recipe, adding garlic and a serrano pepper.

1 quart whole dill pickles, drained (see Tips)
1 quart whole sour pickles, drained
4 cups sugar (see Tips)
4 cloves garlic, thinly sliced
1 fresh serrano pepper,
*   thinly sliced*

tips **Regardless of how the pickles are sold—in 8 ounce-jars, 16-ounce jars, or 32-ounce jars—you'll need a quart, or 32 ounces each, of both the dill and sour pickles.**

You must use only granulated sugar in this recipe.

You can omit the garlic and/or the serrano pepper if you want simple bread-and-butter pickles like the ones Flowerree and Janet make.

1. Cut off the ends of the pickles and discard them. Cut the pickles into ¼-inch slices. Place a layer of the dill and sour pickle slices in the bottom of a very large glass, stainless steel,

or ceramic bowl (do not use an aluminum one). Sprinkle some of the sugar over them, then scatter some of the slices of garlic and serrano pepper on top. Continue layering until all of the ingredients have been used. Cover the bowl with plastic wrap and place it in the refrigerator. Let the pickles marinate for 2 to 3 days, stirring them several times each day. They are best if they marinate for 3 days. The sugar will dissolve as the pickles marinate.

2. Pack the pickles into 4 or 5 clean half-pint jars and pour their liquid over them, dividing it equally among the jars. The pickles can be stored in the refrigerator for up to 4 months.

MAKES 4 TO 5 CUPS

Sweet-and-Sour Pickles Between the Bread

—▼—

DINNER DOCTOR SAYS

Pickles are a favorite condiment to serve alongside a sandwich, but they taste great layered between the slices of bread as well. Set out your favorite meat and/or cheese on a slice of bread and before you complete the sandwich, add some pickles to:

1. Slices of Bebe's Coca-Cola Ham (page 344) with mayonnaise on white bread.

2. Thin slices of Roast Turkey Breast in a Bag (page 318), tomato, and avocado, with mustard and mayonnaise on fresh whole-wheat toast.

3. Thick slices of one of the Italian-Style Mini Meat Loaves (page 208), topped with lettuce, tomato, and mustard or mayonnaise on sourdough.

4. Slices of Fast-Roasted Beef Tenderloin (page 206), smeared with mayonnaise, a dab of horseradish, and a grinding of black pepper, on a crusty roll.

5. A scoop of New-Fashioned Pimento Cheese (page 24), a slice of tomato, and a handful of alfalfa sprouts on fresh whole-wheat bread.

FRENCH GREEN BEANS TOSSED WITH FRIED GARLIC

▼ ▼ ▼

I love to string fresh green beans in the kitchen with the help of my daughter Litton, but let's face it, we don't always have the time to prepare fresh beans. For that matter, those at the market are not always that fresh. Thank goodness for the slivered frozen green beans known as French cut. We've been eating them in cold marinated salads and casseroles for as long as I can recall, and they can make an easy side dish that you can dress up quickly. Try mixing them with slices of garlic that have been briefly fried until fragrant, golden, and yummy.

TO PREP:
4 MINUTES
TO COOK:
8 MINUTES

1 tablespoon olive oil

1 tablespoon butter

4 cloves garlic, thinly sliced

1 package (9 ounces) frozen
    French-cut green beans

Salt

1 tablespoon chopped
    fresh parsley

1. Place the olive oil and butter in a small saucepan and heat over medium heat until the butter melts. Add the garlic and cook, stirring, until it browns, 3 to 4 minutes. Turn off the heat and set the pan aside.

tips If you have leftover green beans, add them to chicken soup, tuck them into an omelet with a little shredded Parmesan cheese, or reheat them with some frozen hash brown potatoes.

The green beans are nice seasoned with pepper—black pepper or hot pepper sauce.

2. Place the green beans in a medium-size glass bowl and heat in the microwave oven on high power until the beans are hot, 4 minutes. Season the green beans with salt to taste and pour the garlic and oil mixture over them. Stir to combine. Garnish with the parsley and serve.

SERVES 4

Just Gotta Have Garlic

—▼—

DINNER DOCTOR SAYS

When you crave garlic but are short on time, don't reach for a jar of minced cloves. Use the real thing! It takes almost no time to crush a clove of garlic with the flat side of a heavy knife or cleaver and slip off the papery skin. Then, using a sharp knife, cut the clove into halves, quarters or long slices, or squeeze it through a garlic press. The taste of fresh garlic is worth a few extra seconds. Once a garlic clove is cut, its pungent flavor will perfume your stews, soups, and sauces. Whole peeled cloves take on a sweeter flavor when added to a pan of roasting meat; serve them alongside slices of the roast. And if you only want a touch of garlic, sprinkle garlic salt on meat, poultry, fish, or veggies, or add a drop of Thai hot pepper and garlic sauce to a soup or sauce.

THE GREEN BEAN CASSEROLE REVISITED

▼ ▼ ▼

TO PREP AND COOK:
12 MINUTES
TO BAKE:
20–25 MINUTES

The classic green bean casserole is beloved by millions, especially around Thanksgiving when it appears alongside the roast turkey and sweet potatoes. But just about any recipe needs an update from time to time as our tastes and the ingredients in the marketplace change, and the green bean casserole benefits from a slight facelift. I've added a little onion and red bell pepper for crunch and color and kept the cream of mushroom soup but opted for the reduced-fat kind. I've also used frozen green beans instead of canned, added a bit of sherry to liven things up, and included some sliced almonds along with those wonderfully crunchy French-fried onions on top. Serve it with a quickly broiled ham steak. Or if the casserole didn't make it to the Thanksgiving table, it's a perfect dish to serve with leftover turkey.

1 tablespoon butter

1 cup thinly sliced onion
    (from 1 medium-size onion)

1 cup thinly sliced red bell pepper
    (from 1 medium-size bell pepper)

1 can (10.75 ounces) reduced-fat cream of
    mushroom soup

½ cup milk

¼ cup golden sherry or medium-dry sherry
    (see Tips, right)

1 package (16 ounces) frozen French-cut
    green beans

1 can (2.8 ounces; 1⅓ cups) French-fried
    onions

¼ cup pre-sliced almonds

tip Mushrooms are delicious in the green bean casserole. You can substitute a cup of sliced fresh mushrooms for the red bell pepper.

1. Place a rack in the center of the oven and preheat the oven to 375°F.

2. Melt the butter in a large skillet over medium heat. If you use a 10-inch (3-quart) ovenproof skillet you will also be able to bake the casserole in it. Add the onion and bell pepper and cook, stirring, until soft, 3 minutes. Add the mushroom soup, milk, and sherry, and continue cooking, stirring, until the mixture comes to a boil, 2 minutes. Stir in the frozen green beans. Turn off the heat and stir until the beans begin to thaw. If you are not baking the casserole in the skillet, transfer it to a 13-by-9-inch (3-quart) glass or ceramic baking dish. Top with the French-fried onions and almonds.

3. Bake the casserole until it is bubbling throughout and the French-fried onions and almonds are browned, 20 to 25 minutes. Serve at once.

SERVES 8

tips **Frozen green beans are crunchier than canned. They take a little more time to cook because they need to thaw in the sauce, but I think they are fresher tasting. If you like canned green beans, by all means use those.**

If you don't cook with sherry, just omit it and add ¼ cup more milk.

It's Easy Being Green

— ▼ —

DINNER DOCTOR SAYS Campbell's test kitchen manager Dorcas Reilly developed what was first called the Green Bean Bake in 1955. She used two ingredients she always had on hand—canned green beans and cream of mushroom soup—for the casserole. Seasoned with soy sauce and topped with those irresistible canned fried onion rings, this perennial potluck favorite is now requested from the Campbell Soup Company 10,000 times each holiday season.

CREAMED PEARL ONIONS

▼ ▼ ▼

When I brought these creamed onions to the table, you would have thought I was serving a six-course French dinner. My husband's face brightened, and he launched into stories of Thanksgivings past. It seems his family alternated menus each year, with recipes from his mother's family one year and his father's the next. The creamed onions he loved were from his father's family, and he only got to savor them every other year. Considering this

TO PREP:
10 MINUTES
TO COOK:
8 MINUTES

was the first time I had cooked them for him, the poor man hadn't eaten creamed onions in quite a while! Understandably, in years past cooks shied away from the lengthy process of peeling tiny pearl onions one at a time. Today there's a faster alternative—pearl onions may be found peeled and ready to go in the grocer's freezer case. I know what we're serving alongside turkey this Thanksgiving!

1 package (16 ounces) frozen
    small whole pearl onions
2 tablespoons butter
2 tablespoons all-purpose flour
1 can (5 ounces) evaporated milk,
    or a generous ½ cup heavy
    (whipping) cream
Salt and black pepper
1 tablespoon pre-shredded Parmesan
    cheese
Paprika

tip My husband's family transferred the onions directly from the saucepan to a warm serving dish. I think the added step of running them under the broiler finishes them off nicely. But, if you are pressed for time, omit it. The onions will still be delicious.

1. Preheat the broiler.

2. Place the frozen onions and ½ cup of water in a small saucepan and bring to a boil over medium-high heat. Reduce the heat to medium-low and break the onions apart with a fork. Cover the pan and cook the onions until just tender, 4 minutes. Remove the pan from the heat, drain the onions, transfer them to a bowl, and set aside.

3. Melt the butter in the small saucepan over medium heat. When the butter has melted, whisk in the flour and cook it until it begins to turn golden, about 30 seconds. Pour in the evaporated milk and cook, whisking, until the mixture thickens, 2 minutes. Remove the pan from the heat, season the sauce with salt and pepper to taste, and fold in the boiled onions. Transfer the onion mixture to a shallow heatproof 2-quart baking dish, spreading it out evenly. Sprinkle the top with the Parmesan cheese and some paprika.

4. Broil the onions until the sauce is bubbling and the Parmesan cheese begins to brown, 2 minutes. Serve the onions at once.

SERVES 6

Easy, Creamy Veggie Purée

—▼—

DINNER DOCTOR SAYS

Place a 10-ounce package of frozen cauliflower, carrots, or broccoli in a medium-size saucepan and pour in enough milk to cover it. Add a cup of unreconstituted frozen mashed potatoes (such as Ore-Ida Just Add Milk). Season with salt and pepper. Cover and cook over medium heat until the veggies are tender, 10 to 15 minutes, then purée them in a food processor until smooth. Return the purée to the saucepan, thin it with a little more milk, if necessary, and add anywhere from 1 to 4 tablespoons of butter (you decide how much). Adding a pinch of grated nutmeg or cayenne pepper is a nice touch.

MOTHER'S PARTY PEAS AND ARTICHOKES

▼ ▼ ▼

TO PREP:
5 MINUTES
TO COOK
5–6 MINUTES

Thank my mother for this superfast dish, which is ready to eat in less than 15 minutes. It was a staple for her dinner parties. If you have frozen peas in the freezer and a can of artichoke hearts and an onion on hand, all you have to do is raid the pantry and toss them together. Seasoned just so with salt and butter and garnished with chopped parsley, you end up with a delicious side dish that goes with just about anything— grilled fish, roast chicken, steaks, meat loaf—you name it.

2 packages (10 ounces each)
    frozen peas
1 can (14 ounces) artichoke hearts
    packed in water, drained and
    quartered
½ cup chopped onion
2 tablespoons butter
2 tablespoons chopped fresh parsley
Salt and black pepper

Place the peas, artichoke hearts, and onion in a 2-quart saucepan and add 1 cup of water. Cover and bring to a boil over medium-high heat. Reduce the heat to low and let simmer, stirring once, until the peas and onion have softened, 4 to 5 minutes. Drain, then stir in the butter and parsley and season with salt and pepper to taste. Serve at once.

SERVES 8

tip   Use whatever kind of onion you have in the house—white, yellow, red, scallions—you can even use chives!

15 WAYS TO DOCTOR FROZEN PEAS

Stand-alone frozen peas are good; dressed up they are great. These suggestions for doctoring all start with a 10-ounce package.

1 Sauté ¼ cup of minced onion or shallots in 1 tablespoon of butter until soft, then fold this into cooked peas.

2 Sauté 1 diced small red bell pepper in 1 tablespoon of butter until it is soft. Fold into cooked peas. This tastes delicious and looks festive.

3 Cook a package of your favorite rice blend and stir it into cooked peas for a quick take-off on Italian *risi e bisi.*

4 Combine cooked peas, a 10-ounce package of cooked, drained, frozen spinach and ¼ cup of butter-sautéed minced onion.

5 Add thawed uncooked peas to a salad of baby lettuces. Dress the salad with a mustardy vinaigrette and top it with shavings of Parmesan cheese.

6 Add a little salt, butter, and 2 tablespoons of chopped fresh mint to drained cooked peas.

7 Add some chopped ham or crumbled cooked bacon to cooked peas to hearty them up.

8 Toast a handful of sliced almonds or pine nuts, then fold them into cooked peas.

9 Cook a package of peas in 2 cups of chicken stock; do not drain. Season them with salt and 2 tablespoons of chopped fresh tarragon or chervil. Purée in a food processor, adding ¼ cup of heavy cream at the end to make a rich soup.

10 Mix thawed peas with a 10-ounce container of refrigerated Alfredo-style pasta sauce and a handful of chopped ham. Fold into a pound of cooked fettuccine, and toss to coat.

11 Make a two-pea salad by combining thawed peas with 1 cup of lightly steamed sugar-snap peas. Add a handful of red bell pepper strips and chopped scallions and stir in some store-bought blue cheese dressing.

12 Fold thawed peas into your favorite potato salad.

13 Add thawed peas to egg salad. Spread on thin slices of wheat bread and cut into canapés or tea sandwiches. Garnish with fresh watercress sprigs.

14 Purée thawed peas, 1½ cups of chicken stock, a little minced onion and chopped cucumber, and 2 tablespoons of plain nonfat yogurt in a food processor. Season with salt and pepper and serve as a cold soup with a dollop of yogurt.

15 Make a pea salad using thawed peas, ¼ cup of minced onion, ½ cup of cucumber cubes, 2 tablespoons of chopped fresh cilantro, and ½ cup plain nonfat yogurt seasoned with a pinch of ground cumin.

COCONUT-AND-CURRY-SCENTED PEAS AND RICE

▼ ▼ ▼

I will go to any length to have my children fall in love with green peas, and they adore this dish. Yet it's just a dump-everything-in-the-pan dish; it simmers while you set the table and carve a chicken from the supermarket deli. Add some sliced mango or melon, and you have a fresh, exotic, and extremely satisfying supper.

TO PREP:
5 MINUTES
TO COOK:
16–19 MINUTES

1 cup long-grain white rice
    (basmati or jasmine)

1 package (10 ounces) frozen peas

1 can (13.5 ounces) light unsweetened
    coconut milk

¾ cup canned low-sodium chicken broth
    or water

3 scallions, both white and light green parts,
    chopped (for ⅓ cup)

1 teaspoon curry powder

½ teaspoon salt

Place the rice, peas, coconut milk, chicken broth, scallions, curry powder, and salt in a 2-quart saucepan. Stir to combine, then cover the pan and bring to a boil over medium heat. Reduce the heat to low and let simmer, covered, until the rice is tender and most of the liquid has evaporated, 15 to 17 minutes. Spoon the peas and rice onto plates and serve at once.

SERVES 6

tip For a fancier dish, garnish the peas and rice with lightly toasted coconut and more chopped scallions.

MEDITERRANEAN ROAST POTATOES AND ASPARAGUS

▼▼▼

Asparagus spears elevate the humble potato to dinner party status. Begin with a bag of frozen potato wedges, top them with feta cheese and rosemary, then add the asparagus at the end, and voilà—a vibrant no-fuss side dish that cozies right up to grilled steaks, or chops, or any roasted meat.

TO PREP:
15 MINUTES
TO BAKE:
12 MINUTES

2 tablespoons olive oil

1 package (24 ounces) frozen
    potato wedges

Coarse salt

¼ cup pre-crumbled feta cheese

1 teaspoon fresh whole rosemary leaves

1 bunch thin asparagus stalks
    (16 to 20 spears)

1. Place a rack in the center of the oven and preheat the oven to 425°F.

2. Drizzle 1 tablespoon of the olive oil on a rimmed baking sheet. Arrange the potatoes on the baking sheet, season them with salt, and drizzle the remaining 1 tablespoon of oil over them. Toss the potatoes with a large spoon or spatula to

tips You can make this recipe as simple or as complicated as you like. Use one of the coarse herb salts, omit the feta, and add red pepper strips instead of asparagus. Or, try tarragon instead of rosemary. Add some onion quarters and baby carrots sliced in half lengthwise with the potatoes in Step 1. The possibilities are endless—roasting at a high temperature brings out the flavor of all kinds of veggies.

coat them well, then arrange them in a single layer. Scatter the feta cheese and rosemary over the potatoes.

3. Bake the potatoes until softened, 7 minutes.

4. Meanwhile, rinse the asparagus and pat dry. Snap off and discard their tough ends. Place the asparagus spears on top of the potatoes and return the baking sheet to the oven. Bake until the potatoes are crisp and the asparagus has cooked through, 5 minutes longer. Remove the baking sheet from the oven, toss the potatoes with the asparagus, and serve at once.

SERVES 6 TO 8

CREAMY SCALLOPED POTATOES

▼ ▼ ▼

TO PREP:
15 MINUTES
TO BAKE:
30–35 MINUTES

As far as I'm concerned, well made scalloped potatoes are right up there with foie gras when it comes to being decadently rich— definitely something to be savored, but not every day. For years I have prepared them by peeling lots of potatoes and slicing them very thin, but as of late I have found a simpler method. I pop frozen hash browns in a baking dish along with pre-shredded Parmesan and slices of garlic, and pour in enough heavy cream to thoroughly coat the potatoes. These scalloped potatoes bake in half the time of ones made from scratch.

1 package (32 ounces) frozen hash brown potatoes, slightly thawed
½ cup pre-shredded Parmesan cheese
2 to 3 cloves garlic, sliced
Salt and pepper
2 cups heavy (whipping) cream
Paprika

1. Place a rack in the center of the oven and preheat the oven to 400°F.

2. Place half of the hash browns in an even layer in a 13-by-9-inch (3-quart) glass or ceramic baking dish. Break the hash browns apart with your hands if they are still mostly frozen. Sprinkle the Parmesan cheese and garlic slices evenly over the top.

tip **If you want a more colorful but equally easy dish, use frozen hash browns made with onions and peppers. Instead of paprika, dust the top with cayenne pepper.**

You can substitute whatever kind of cheese you like for the Parmesan.

Season with salt and pepper. Place the remaining hash browns in an even layer on top of the Parmesan. Pour the cream over the potatoes, then dust the cream with paprika. Cover the baking dish with aluminum foil.

3. Bake the potatoes until the cream bubbles and the potatoes are tender, 30 to 35 minutes. Remove the baking dish from the oven, let the potatoes rest for 5 minutes, then serve.

SERVES 8 TO 10

About Heating the Oven

—▼—

DINNER DOCTOR SAYS

Here, as elsewhere, the oven-heating time is figured into the prep time. For an oven to heat to between 375° and 400°F takes from 12 to 15 minutes. If you're arriving home with little time to prepare dinner and you're planning on roasting or baking, turn the oven on as soon as you walk in the door. That way, it will be preheated by the time you are ready to bake.

SAUTÉED SPINACH

WITH LEMON

▼ ▼ ▼

O ne of my favorite ways to eat spinach is a snap to prepare if you use those big bags of pre-washed leaves. I love to serve this lemony spinach alongside juicy steaks hot off the grill and with Garlicky Cheese Grits Casserole (page 263), pasta, or polenta. Don't be deceived into thinking a large bag of greens will feed a crowd—it cooks down considerably and will feed just four.

TO PREP:
3–4 MINUTES
TO COOK:
3–5 MINUTES

1 small lemon

2 tablespoons olive oil

2 cloves garlic, sliced

1 bag (10 ounces) spinach

Salt and black pepper

1. Grate the zest of the lemon, then squeeze the juice from it. Set the lemon zest and juice aside.

2. Heat the olive oil in a large skillet over medium heat. Add the garlic and cook it until it deepens in color, 1 to 2 minutes. Add the spinach to the skillet, and carefully pack it down with your hand. Cook, stirring, until the spinach wilts and is tender, 2 to 3 minutes. Season the spinach with salt and pepper to taste. Add the lemon zest and juice to the spinach, stir well to mix, then serve.

SERVES 4

tips **This dish can be made in the microwave oven by placing the olive oil, garlic, and spinach in a large glass mixing bowl. Cook on high power for 2 minutes, stirring halfway through the cooking. Add the lemon juice and zest to the spinach then season it with salt and pepper.**

To dress up either pan-cooked spinach or microwaved, add a sprinkling of toasted pine nuts at the end.

15 WAYS TO DOCTOR FROZEN SPINACH

Frozen spinach is tasty, convenient, and good for you. And here's some more good news: Despite what you read in the directions on the package, it's not necessary to cook frozen spinach before combining it with other ingredients. All you need to do is thaw it, either by leaving the package at room temperature overnight or by removing the spinach from the package, placing it on a microwave-safe plate, and microwaving it on high power until it thaws and breaks apart, 1 to 2 minutes.

Once the spinach is thawed, be sure to drain off the liquid. Place the spinach in a strainer and use a fork or wooden spoon to squeeze all of the water from it—or use your hands to do this. What you'll end up with is blanched spinach ready to doctor. With the exception of the casserole (no. 5), all of the variations that follow here use a 10-ounce package of chopped spinach that has been thawed and drained. Each will serve four people.

1 Cut a 3-ounce package of cream cheese into cubes. Place the spinach in a small glass bowl and top with the cream cheese, a sprinkling of Parmesan cheese, and if you like, a drained 6-ounce jar of marinated artichoke hearts. Microwave the spinach on high power until the cream cheese melts, 1 minute. Stir, season with salt and pepper to taste, and serve.

2 Stir a softened 3-ounce block of cream cheese and 1 cup of pre-shredded Swiss cheese into the spinach. Spoon this onto English muffin halves and bake at 350°F until the Swiss cheese melts.

3 Microwave the spinach on high with ¼ cup of Parmesan cheese shavings.

4 Sauté the spinach in 1 tablespoon of butter over medium heat for 1 minute. For an elegant dish, stir in 1 tablespoon of heavy cream, ¼ teaspoon of nutmeg, and 2 teaspoons of sherry and cook 1 minute longer.

5 Make a creamed spinach casserole: Place 2 packages of spinach in a 2-quart casserole with ½ cup of sour cream and half of a 10.75 ounce can of cream of mushroom soup. Add 1 tablespoon of sherry and season with salt and pepper. Stir and bake in a preheated 375°F oven until bubbling, 25 to 30 minutes.

6 Warm the spinach, then serve slices of any grilled or broiled boneless meat, chicken, or fish you like on a bed of it. The meat or chicken juices will mingle nicely with the spinach.

7 Stir the spinach into 4 beaten eggs, add slices of sautéed Italian sausage, and scramble in a skillet in 1 tablespoon of melted butter. Or sauté omelet style, turning to cook the top once the eggs have set.

8 Sauté the spinach in olive oil, and add a good squeeze of fresh lemon juice. Scatter pine nuts and raisins over the top to garnish, if desired.

9 Combine the spinach with a drained 15-ounce can of chickpeas, a 14.5-ounce can of diced tomatoes with green pepper and onion, 1 teaspoon of curry powder, and ½ teaspoon of cumin. Heat through and serve with roast chicken.

10 Stir a 14.5-ounce can of plain diced tomatoes into the spinach. Season it with 1 teaspoon of minced garlic, a pinch of sugar, and a pinch of ground allspice. Heat through and serve with jerk chicken.

11 Fold the spinach into a combination of ¼ cup each of sour cream and mayonnaise. Season well (a little ground cumin is good here). Open a bag of chips and start dipping!

12 Fold 1 cup of refrigerated Alfredo-style pasta sauce and some chipped beef into the spinach and serve over toast.

13 Arrange spoonfuls of spinach on top of a large frozen pizza, sprinkle it with Parmesan cheese and a little garlic powder (if desired), and bake it according to the directions on the pizza package.

14 Sprinkle hot spinach with chopped hard-cooked eggs and ½ cup of crumbled bacon for an easy main dish.

15 Add spoonfuls of spinach to your favorite pasta sauce before you heat it through. This is delicious over pasta, but is also great as a bed for poached eggs—an easy brunch or light dinner dish.

BUTTERNUT SQUASH AND TOMATO GRATIN

▼ ▼ ▼

My mother used to make this easy gratin, but not as often as I wanted her to because the butternut squash took so long to boil and then it had to cool down before

TO PREP:
15 MINUTES
TO BAKE:
18–20 MINUTES

she could continue with the recipe. I have found a faster way—steam the squash in the microwave. I love the dish with pork or roast chicken. With couscous and a salad it makes a hearty vegetarian meal. And you can use whatever cheese you like to top the squash.

1 medium-size butternut squash
   (about 2 pounds)
1 tablespoon olive oil
1 can (14.5 ounces) diced tomatoes with
   basil, garlic,and oregano, drained
1 cup pre-shredded Cheddar cheese

1. Place a rack in the center of the oven and preheat the oven to 400°F.

2. With a sharp knife, trim off and discard the ends of the squash, then slice it

tip For a delicious way to use up leftovers (if there are any), purée them in a blender or food processor. Spread the purée onto flour tortillas, sprinkle a little cheese (whatever kind you've got on hand) over the purée, then top it with another tortilla. Heat a little oil on a griddle or in a nonstick skillet, and cook the quesadillas until lightly browned, 3 minutes per side. Cut into wedges and serve at once.

in half lengthwise. Scoop out the seeds with a spoon and discard them. Place the squash halves, cut side up, in a microwave oven and cover them with a piece of waxed paper. Cook on high power until soft, yet still firm enough to cut into cubes, 8 minutes.

3. Carefully remove the squash halves from the microwave and place them on a cutting board. Discard the waxed paper and let the squash cool off enough to handle it. Peel the squash and cut it into 1-inch cubes. Place the cubes of squash in an 11-by-7-inch (2-quart) glass or ceramic baking dish and drizzle the olive oil over them. Scatter the tomatoes on top of the squash and sprinkle the Cheddar cheese evenly over the top.

4. Bake the gratin until the cheese melts and the squash and tomatoes are heated through, 18 to 20 minutes. Serve at once.

SERVES 6

A Birthday Dinner

▼ ▼ ▼

Birthday meals are meant to be special, but special doesn't mean you can't incorporate some time-saving tricks. This menu, as is, comfortably serves four, but if you're serving six to eight, prepare two pork loins. You'll have too many muffins, but they'll keep for a day or two in an airtight container.

Strawberry Field Salad
page 118

Dun-Buttered Muffins
page 419

Roast Pork Tenderloin with a Fig and Chipotle Jam
page 213

Basmati rice

Butternut Squash and Tomato Gratin
this page

Lemon Poppy Seed Layer Cake with Creamy Lemon Frosting
page 450

THANKSGIVING SOUFFLÉED SWEET POTATOES

▼ ▼ ▼

TO PREP:
15 MINUTES
TO BAKE:
25–30 MINUTES

Don't get me wrong, I adore fresh sweet potatoes. I love to see them in the produce markets in the fall, freshly dug, ready for me to roast them in cubes seasoned with garlic and lime juice or to bake whole and serve with butter and brown sugar. But cooking fresh sweet potatoes takes time. That time may not be part of your schedule at Thanksgiving, especially if you are preparing the whole meal and expect to feed a houseful of family and friends. So here is how to dress up canned sweet potatoes quickly. Orange juice perks up the potatoes, and the crunchy pecan topping is a favorite of all ages.

2 tablespoons (¼ stick) butter, plus ½ cup
(8 tablespoons), melted

2 cans (29 ounces each) sweet potatoes
in syrup, drained

¾ cup sugar

⅔ cup all-purpose flour

¼ cup milk

2 large eggs

1 teaspoon grated orange zest (see Tip at left)

3 tablespoons fresh orange juice
(from 1 large orange)

1 cup pre-chopped
pecans

1 cup firmly packed
light brown sugar

tip **If you are squeezing fresh orange juice, grate the zest of the orange. But of course you can use orange juice from a carton. Pick the pulpy kind and forget about the zest.**

1. Place a rack in the center of the oven and preheat the oven to 400°F.

2. Place the 2 tablespoons of butter in a 13-by-9-inch (3-quart) glass or ceramic baking dish and place the baking dish in the oven while it preheats.

3. Meanwhile, place the sweet potatoes in a large mixing bowl and mash them with a potato masher or fork until smooth. There should be about 4 cups. Add the sugar, ⅓ cup of the flour and the milk,

eggs, and orange zest and juice to the mashed sweet potatoes. Mix with an electric mixer on low speed or with a wooden spoon until the ingredients are well combined and the mixture is smooth.

4. Remove the baking dish from the oven. Tilt the baking dish back and forth until the melted butter coats the bottom. Transfer the sweet potato mixture to the baking dish and spread it out evenly. Set it aside.

5. Place the pecans, brown sugar, the ½ cup of melted butter, and the remaining ⅓ cup of flour in a small mixing bowl and, using a fork, stir until a crumbly mixture forms. Using the fork or your fingers, scatter the pecan topping evenly over the top of the sweet potatoes.

6. Bake the sweet potatoes until they bubble around the edges and the pecans have turned golden brown, 25 to 30 minutes. Serve at once.

SERVES 6

tips **A fast way to prepare the topping is to place pecan halves in a food processor and pulse them just a bit. Add the brown sugar, melted butter, and flour and pulse a few more times until it's crumbly.**

You can cut this recipe in half; use just one can of sweet potatoes and half of each of the other ingredients. Bake the sweet potatoes in an 11-by-7-inch (2-quart) glass or ceramic baking dish for about 25 minutes.

FRIED GREEN TOMATOES

WITH HERBED GOAT CHEESE

▼ ▼ ▼

TO PREP:
10 MINUTES
TO COOK:
10–15 MINUTES

Tomatoes grow well in our garden, and although we adore the ripe red Bradleys in August, we also look forward to October's hard green ones. They're quick to fry up and delicious. I arrange them on a big platter and dab them with a quick-to-mix goat cheese spread. If you doctor soft goat cheese with an herbed cheese like Boursin, you don't need to add anything else. Red tomatoes may be sensational, but these green tomatoes are sublime.

Salt
4 to 5 large green tomatoes
2 cups vegetable oil, for frying
1 cup white or yellow cornmeal
Black pepper
1 package (5.3 ounces) soft
    goat cheese
½ package (5 ounces whole) garlic-and-herb
    flavored cheese spread, such as Boursin
2 tablespoons chopped fresh parsley

1. Fill a large bowl half-full of water and ice cubes and stir in ½ teaspoon of salt.

2. Cut the tomatoes into ⅓-inch-thick slices and place them in the bowl of salted ice water as they are cut. You should get about 20 slices. Set aside.

> **tip** Small fried green tomatoes make unusual and tasty canapés. Fry them as directed on the opposite page and dab them with the goat cheese mixture. Place the tomatoes on an attractive platter and serve warm.

3. Pour the oil into a 10-inch cast-iron skillet or other heavy frying pan and heat over medium-high heat.

4. Meanwhile, place the cornmeal in a small bowl and season it with salt and pepper. Place the goat cheese and cheese spread in a food processor or a blender and purée until smooth, 30 seconds. Transfer the goat cheese mixture to another small bowl and set it aside.

5. Drain the tomatoes. Arrange a double thickness of paper towels on a counter near the skillet. Dredge the tomato slices on both sides in the seasoned cornmeal. Cook the tomato slices, a few at a time, until they are golden brown all over, 3 to 5 minutes per batch, turning them once. Using tongs, transfer the fried tomatoes to the paper towels to drain. Repeat with the remaining tomato slices.

6. To serve, place the warm tomato slices around the outside of a pretty platter. Either place the small bowl of goat cheese in the center of the platter or place dabs of the cheese mixture on every other tomato. Sprinkle the chopped parsley over the tomatoes and serve at once.

SERVES 5 OR 6

How to Fry Green Tomatoes

—▼—

DINNER DOCTOR SAYS When I know that the weather won't be warm enough to turn the tomatoes in our garden a rosy red, I pluck them from the vine, while they're still green. After rinsing and slicing them, I place them in a bowl of salted ice water. This is an old trick I learned many years ago from a good Georgia cook who was an expert at frying green tomatoes. Frying green tomatoes is easy: First get those slices good and cold, pull out your favorite heavy skillet, and follow the recipe on this page. Delicious! You may even start picking still-green tomatoes mid-summer.

ONE-BOWL RATATOUILLE

▼ ▼ ▼

When I learned to make ratatouille, I was taught to sauté each and every vegetable separately and then add them back to the pan to simmer together. It was a perfectly lovely way to prepare it, and maybe someday life will slow down enough for me to do that again. For now, here is a lightning fast and healthy alternative. I zap the vegetables in a microwave. The seasoning comes with the canned tomatoes. And, it takes just a touch of olive oil to add a little more flavor and body.

TO PREP:
10 MINUTES
TO COOK:
13–14 MINUTES

This dish can be made up to two days ahead of time, chilled, and served cold or reheated just before serving.

3 medium-size zucchini, diced
(4½ to 5 cups; see Tip at left)
1 medium-size onion, sliced
(for 1 cup)
1 small green bell pepper, stemmed,
seeded, and cut into strips
1 can (28 ounces) diced tomatoes
with basil, garlic, and
oregano
2 tablespoons
olive oil
Salt and black pepper
½ cup pitted kalamata olives
(optional)
¼ cup pre-shredded Parmesan
cheese (optional)

tip   **To quickly dice the zucchini, trim the ends, halve the zucchini lengthwise, then cut each half lengthwise into three strips and cut the strips into dice.**

1. Place the zucchini, onion, bell pepper, and tomatoes in a large glass bowl. Cover the bowl with plastic wrap, pulling back one corner to vent it. Place the bowl in a microwave oven and cook on high power for 6 minutes. Carefully remove the bowl from the microwave, peel back the plastic wrap, and stir to combine the vegetables.

2. Place the plastic wrap back over the top of the bowl, pulling back one corner to vent it, and return the bowl to the microwave. Cook on high power until the zucchini is soft, 7 to 8 minutes longer. Carefully remove the bowl from the microwave, remove the plastic wrap, stir in the olive oil and season with salt and pepper to taste. Serve the ratatouille at once or refrigerate it, covered, until serving time. Top each serving with some of the olives and Parmesan cheese, if desired.

SERVES 6 TO 8

tips This recipe is only a starting place; you can use just about any vegetable you have at your fingertips. However, do stick with traditional summer vegetables and avoid members of the cabbage family, such as broccoli and cauliflower. A small eggplant, peeled and diced, would be a delicious substitute for some of the zucchini. Try a red bell pepper instead of the green. Add some chopped fresh herbs at the end, such as basil, oregano, or parsley, if they are growing in your garden.

CHERRY TOMATO AND BASIL TART

▼ ▼ ▼

TO PREP:
15 MINUTES
TO BAKE:
26–28 MINUTES

Okay, the sweet, home-grown tomatoes of August are only a memory, but you can still make a fresh tomato tart using cherry or grape tomatoes. Arrange them on a crust made from refrigerated crescent roll dough and garnish them with slivers of fresh basil. Add a simple green salad, some good bread, and fruit, and you have a light but filling meatless meal. The tart is also perfect as an appetizer; serve slim wedges with glasses of white wine. To make it easy to slice, use a tart pan with a removable bottom. If you don't have one, a pie pan will do just fine.

1 package (8 ounces) refrigerated
    crescent rolls

1 pint cherry or grape tomatoes

2 tablespoons olive oil

Coarse salt

½ cup finely sliced fresh basil
    or parsley (see Tips)

2 large eggs

½ cup heavy (whipping) cream or
    whole milk

1 cup pre-shredded mozzarella cheese

1. Place a rack in the center of the oven and preheat the oven to 375°F.

tips The most efficient way to slice basil leaves is to stack them, roll them into a cigar shape, then slice them crosswise. This creates basil slivers, or a chiffonade, as it is called in French.

You can add slices of garlic to the tomatoes if the mood hits you.

If you use half Parmesan and half mozzarella cheese, the tart will have a richer flavor and the top will be browner.

2. Open the package of crescent roll dough and separate it into 8 triangles. Arrange the triangles in a 10-inch tart pan or pie pan with the long points toward the center so that the bottom and side of the pan are covered with dough. Press the edges of the dough triangles firmly together to seal them. Bake the crust until it is lightly browned and puffed, 8 minutes.

3. Meanwhile, cut the tomatoes in half (slice cherry tomatoes crosswise and grape tomatoes lengthwise).

4. Remove the tart pan from the oven; leave the oven on. Press down on the crust with the back of a spoon to flatten it. Arrange the tomatoes, cut side up, on the bottom of the crust, completely covering it. Drizzle the olive oil over the tomatoes, sprinkle them with salt, then scatter the basil evenly over the top. Crack the eggs into a small bowl, add the cream and mozzarella cheese, and whisk to combine. Pour the egg mixture over the tomatoes.

5. Bake the tart until the custard has set and the crust is a deep golden brown, 18 to 20 minutes. Remove the tart from the oven and place it on a wire rack to cool, 5 minutes, then slice the tart and serve it.

SERVES **6** TO **8**

CARAMELIZED ONION AND GARLIC TART

▼ ▼ ▼

It took a lot of willpower to get the sweet, fragrant onions and garlic out of the skillet and into the crust of this easy to make tart. I wanted to eat them all up right then and there. Still, baked in a Parmesan-scented custard, the onions are even better. This tart rewards a little discipline and patience.

1 package (8 ounces) refrigerated
    crescent rolls

2 tablespoons butter

2 packed cups thinly sliced onions
    (from 2 medium-size onions)

4 to 5 cloves garlic, sliced or crushed
    in a garlic press

1 tablespoon sugar

1 tablespoon fresh thyme leaves
    (optional; see Tip)

2 large eggs

½ cup heavy (whipping) cream or whole milk

½ cup pre-shredded Parmesan cheese

TO PREP AND COOK:
15 MINUTES
TO BAKE:
26–28 MINUTES

1. Place a rack in the center of the oven and preheat the oven to 375°F.

2. Open the package of crescent roll dough and separate it into 8 triangles. Arrange the triangles in a 10-inch tart pan or pie pan with the long points toward the center so that the bottom and side of the pan are covered with dough. Press the edges of the dough triangles firmly together to seal them. Bake the crust until it is lightly browned and puffed, 8 minutes.

tip If you have fresh thyme in the garden, it makes a wonderful addition to the tart. If not, don't go out and buy a bunch, just dust the tart with grated nutmeg, paprika, or cayenne pepper before baking it.

3. Meanwhile, melt the butter in a large skillet over medium heat. Add the onions and garlic, reduce the heat to medium-low, and cook, stirring, until the onions begin to brown and take on a deep color, 8 minutes. Add the sugar and thyme, if using. Cook, stirring, until the sugar dissolves, another minute or two. Remove the skillet from the heat.

4. Remove the tart crust from the oven; leave the oven on. Press down on the crust with the back of a spoon to flatten it. Arrange the onions on the bottom of the tart, using a fork to spread them out so that they completely cover it. Crack the eggs into a small bowl, add the cream and Parmesan cheese, and whisk to combine. Pour the egg mixture over the onions.

5. Bake the tart until the custard has set and the crust is a deep golden brown, 18 to 20 minutes. Remove the tart from the oven and place it on a wire rack to cool 5 minutes, then slice the tart and serve it.

SERVES **6** TO **8**

TORTILLA ESPAÑOLA

WITH SWEET PEPPERS

▼ ▼ ▼

TO PREP AND COOK:
15 MINUTES
TO BAKE:
3–4 MINUTES

One of the most elegant meatless meals I've prepared is one with the simplest ingredients—eggs, olive oil, potatoes, and salt and pepper, the classic Spanish *tortilla española.* In Spain a *tortilla* is a type of omelet, not the familiar Mexican flat bread. It's an example of peasant cooking at its finest. Moist and dense, the potato omelet can be served hot, warm, or at room temperature. I've taken the basic recipe but substituted frozen diced potatoes with onions and bell peppers to save valuable time yet not sacrifice flavor. I also cook the omelet first on the stove, then transfer it to the oven. While it bakes I toss the salad and set the table.

4 tablespoons olive oil

2 cups frozen diced potatoes with onions
    and red and green bell peppers,
    such as Ore-Ida Potatoes O'Brien

6 large eggs

Salt and black pepper

Fresh rosemary sprigs, for garnish
    (optional)

tip Have some fun with this basic recipe: Add crumbled cooked bacon along with the potatoes. Place some tiny asparagus spears on the potatoes before you add the eggs. Season the eggs with an herb salt instead of plain salt. Add a sprinkling of cayenne pepper before the omelet goes into the oven.

1. Place a rack in the center of the oven and preheat the oven to 400°F.

2. Heat the olive oil in an ovenproof skillet over medium-high heat. Add the frozen potatoes, stirring, and cook until they break apart, are coated with olive oil, and begin to brown, 2 minutes. Crack the eggs into a bowl and beat them with a fork or a whisk until they are lemon-colored. Season the eggs with salt and pepper. Pour the eggs over the potatoes and cook until they begin to set around the edge, 3 to 4 minutes.

3. Carefully place the hot skillet in the oven and bake the omelet until it just sets in the center, 3 to 4 minutes. Remove the skillet from the oven, run a sharp knife around the edge of the omelet, and invert it onto a serving plate. Garnish the omelet with fresh rosemary sprigs, if desired. Slice into wedges and serve the omelet at once, or allow it to cool to room temperature before serving.

SERVES 6

BLACK BEAN AND VEGETABLE STACK

▼ ▼ ▼

Quick and satisfying, this tasty black bean dish could just as easily have been placed in the main dish chapter, or the comfort food chapter, or even the pasta chapter, since it's like a lasagna made with tortillas instead of noodles. But this stack, made with tomatoes, supermarket salsa, spicy cheese, and a touch of cumin, joins the veggies because it's perfect for vegetarian meals. I like it because it goes together effortlessly and because I always have its ingredients in the pantry or refrigerator. Making dinner has never been easier. Serve the stack with coleslaw or a green salad.

TO PREP AND COOK:
15 MINUTES
TO BAKE:
22–23 MINUTES
TO REST:
10 MINUTES

2 cans (15 ounces each) black beans, drained

1 can (14.5 ounces) diced tomatoes, with their liquid

1 package (10 ounces) frozen white or yellow corn kernels

1 cup store-bought salsa

½ cup chopped green bell pepper (from 1 medium-size bell pepper)

2 cloves garlic, crushed in a garlic press

2 teaspoons ground cumin

10 flour tortillas (7 inches each)

1 package (8 ounces; 2 cups) pre-shredded Cheddar cheese for tacos (see Tips)

1. Place a rack in the center of the oven and preheat the oven to 400°F.

tips You can use plain shredded Cheddar or Monterey Jack cheese in place of the taco cheese.

You can shorten your prep time by using "chili-ready" tomatoes—the ones that are already seasoned—so there's no need to add the cumin.

2. Place the beans, tomatoes with their liquid and the corn, salsa, bell pepper, garlic, and cumin in a 2-quart saucepan. Stir and bring to a boil over medium-high heat, then reduce the heat to medium-low and let simmer, uncovered, until thickened, 4 to 5 minutes.

3. Spoon a third of the bean mixture over the bottom of a 13-by-9-inch (3-quart) glass or ceramic baking dish. Top it with 5 of the tortillas, overlapping them as needed. Scatter 1 cup of the cheese over the tortillas. Spoon half of the remaining bean mixture over the cheese and top it with the remaining tortillas. Spoon the remaining bean mixture over the tortillas, spreading it out to completely cover them. Cover the baking dish with aluminum foil.

4. Bake the stack until hot, 15 minutes, then remove the baking dish from the oven and uncover it. Sprinkle the remaining 1 cup of cheese on top and return the uncovered baking dish to the oven. Bake the stack until the cheese melts, 7 to 8 minutes longer. Let the casserole rest 10 minutes before slicing and serving.

SERVES 6

TUESDAY NIGHT WHITE BEANS

▼ ▼ ▼

A can of white beans in the pantry means a dinner dish is only minutes away on any busy weeknight (in my house, invariably it's Tuesday when I reach for the beans). After quickly sautéing onion and garlic, it takes no time for the beans to simmer with a little chicken broth until they are thickened. A dab of store-bought basil or cilantro pesto, some flaked tuna, and pre-shredded Parmesan finish things off, but are not essential.

TO PREP:
5 MINUTES
TO COOK:
7–8 MINUTES

If you want a more substantial dish, you can serve the beans over a bed of pasta or polenta.

2 tablespoons olive oil

1 cup chopped onion
    (from 1 medium-size onion)

2 cloves garlic, sliced

1 bay leaf

1 can (15 to 16 ounces) Great Northern
    or navy beans, drained

½ cup canned low-sodium chicken broth
    or water

Salt and black pepper

2 tablespoons store-bought pesto (optional)

1 can (6 ounces) tuna packed in water
    (optional), drained

2 tablespoons pre-shredded Parmesan
    cheese, for garnish (optional)

2 tablespoons chopped fresh parsley,
    for garnish (optional)

tips This side dish makes a hearty sauce for pasta. Before you begin sautéing the onion, start the water boiling for the pasta. When the pasta has cooked, spoon some of the bean stew alongside.
   The Tuesday Night White Bean recipe can be easily doubled.

1. Heat the olive oil in a 2-quart saucepan over medium heat. Add the onion and garlic, stirring, and cook until soft, 3 minutes. Add the bay leaf, beans, and broth. Season the beans with salt and pepper to taste. Stir the beans, then cook them, uncovered, until they are heated through and the liquid reduces a bit, 4 to 5 minutes.

2. To serve, remove and discard the bay leaf, dab the beans with pesto and flake

tip To make a dip from this bean dish, purée it in a blender or food processor and serve it warm with tortilla chips.

the tuna over it, if desired. Garnish the beans with Parmesan cheese and parsley, if desired. Serve at once.

SERVES 4

OUR FAVORITE EGGPLANT PARMESAN

▼ ▼ ▼

I have been making this easy one-dish meal for many years, and I arrived at it out of sheer necessity. My husband and I love the flavor of sautéed eggplant, but I knew that if I was going to spend my time at the stove carefully tending the eggplant until it was fried to a perfect golden brown, I was going

TO PREP AND COOK:
22 MINUTES
TO BAKE:
25–30 MINUTES

to have to save time on the sauce. So I decided to cheat and use a store-bought one—with a little doctoring, of course. I dump the sauce into a pan, add a glug of red wine, some garlic (and some black olives or basil if I have them), and let the mixture simmer to concentrate its flavor, while I fuss with the eggplant. Since the eggplant and sauce are warm before they go into the oven, the baking time is shortened. I know you will love this one.

tips Depending on what else you serve with eggplant Parmesan, there is a good chance you'll have leftovers. Don't think it will go to waste. It will keep for two days. I reheat it, covered, in an oven preheated to 300°F, cut it into squares, and serve it on top of toasted crusty bread.

Choose eggplants that are firm and shiny. Smaller eggplants tend to have fewer bitter seeds; you can use three or four small eggplants in place of one larger one.

1 jar (26 ounces) tomato-based pasta sauce

2 tablespoons dry red wine

2 cloves garlic, crushed in a garlic press

½ cup vegetable oil, or more as necessary

2 large eggs

Salt and black pepper

1 large eggplant (1½ to 1¾ pounds), peeled and sliced ¼ inch thick (see Tips)

1 package (8 ounces; 2 cups) pre-shredded mozzarella and Parmesan cheese

1. Place a rack in the center of the oven and preheat the oven to 375°F.

2. Place the pasta sauce, wine, and garlic in a 2-quart saucepan. Bring the sauce to a simmer over medium heat stirring occasionally. Let simmer while you prepare the eggplant.

3. Heat the oil in a heavy skillet over medium-high heat. Crack the eggs into a wide shallow bowl, season them with salt and pepper, and beat lightly with a fork. Arrange a double thickness of paper towels on a counter near the skillet. Place the eggplant slices in the beaten egg, 2 to 3 at a time; turn them to coat, then using a fork, transfer them to the hot oil. Cook the eggplant slices until they are golden brown and puffy but not cooked through, 1 minute per side. Drain the cooked eggplant on the paper towels and repeat with the remaining eggplant slices, adding more oil if necessary.

4. When all of the slices of eggplant are cooked, remove the pasta sauce from the heat. Place half of the eggplant slices in the bottom of an 11-by-7 inch (2-quart) glass or ceramic baking dish. Pour half of the pasta sauce over the eggplant, spreading it out evenly with a spatula. Scatter 1 cup of the cheese over the sauce. Repeat with the remaining eggplant, pasta sauce, and cheese. Cover the baking dish with aluminum foil and bake the casserole until it is bubbling and the cheese has melted, 25 to 30 minutes. Remove the baking dish from the oven, take off the foil, and let the eggplant rest for 5 minutes, then slice and serve.

SERVES 4 TO 6

PORTOBELLOS BRAISED IN RED SAUCE

▼▼▼

If you're in the mood for a flavorful meal that's no trouble to put together, pick up a package of the hefty and delicious portobello mushrooms. They satisfy like steaks, and when braised in a pasta sauce, are the heart of a hands-off recipe that's perfect for busy winter nights. Add garlic bread,

TO PREP:
12 MINUTES
TO BAKE:
18–20 MINUTES

a green vegetable or a salad, and you'll have dinner on the table in less than 30 minutes.

2 cups store-bought chunky
       tomato-based pasta sauce
1 package (6 ounces) whole
       portobello mushrooms
       (4 large or 6 small mushrooms)
½ cup pre-shredded mozzarella cheese
½ cup pre-shredded Parmesan cheese

1. Place a rack in the center of the oven and preheat the oven to 375°F.

2. Spoon ½ cup of the pasta sauce into the bottom of a 9-inch glass or ceramic pie pan. Wipe the mushrooms clean with a damp paper towel. Place the mushrooms in the pie pan, rounded side up, trimming the caps as needed so that they fit into the pie pan. Place all of the mushroom

tip **Portobellos are also delicious grilled. Brush the mushrooms with olive oil and grill them over a medium fire on both sides until they are soft and start to give off their juices. Then transfer them to a flameproof baking dish, add the pasta sauce, sprinkle the cheeses over the top, and broil the mushrooms until the sauce is bubbling and the cheese melts, 3 to 4 minutes.**

trimmings in the pie pan as well. Pour the remaining 1½ cups of pasta sauce on top of the mushrooms. Sprinkle the mozzarella and Parmesan cheeses on top, then cover the pie pan with aluminum foil.

3. Bake the mushrooms until they are tender and the pasta sauce has heated through, 18 to 20 minutes. Remove the pie pan from the oven and take off the foil. With a spatula, place the mushrooms in shallow bowls or on serving plates. Spoon the pasta sauce and cheeses over the top and serve at once.

SERVES 4

SAVORY & SWEET LIGHTNING FAST BREADS

▼▼▼

When I was a girl and the bread basket was passed at the dinner table, hot biscuits just plucked from my mother's oven were usually tucked inside. We could not slather butter on those biscuits quickly enough. We topped that with a little honey, sorghum, molasses, or if we were lucky, peach preserves put up the summer before. I still get a warm and fuzzy feeling thinking about bread.

It's always been one of the high points of our family meals. Perhaps as a reflection of the hardship of raising and educating five daughters as a widow, I remember my grandmother often saying that as long as there was bread on the table at supper, then there was supper. Just think of the word *breadwinner;* it means the one who earns the money to buy bread—and all else the family needs.

Bread baked at home has changed since my grandmother's day. It's become much more eclectic, multicultural, exotic. Our busy schedules don't permit us to stamp out biscuits or punch down dough in the afternoon. So we have come to rely on shortcuts—bread ready to heat from the deli, ready to bake from the supermarket freezer and refrigerator or ready to mix from a box.

And my message here is the same as in my *Cake Mix Doctor* books—the fact that you're baking is more important than the convenience foods you choose.

Now, while my mother's biscuits may not be in my bread basket, it's likely there will be warm and crusty French bread, garlicky focaccia topped with fresh tomato slices, bread sticks made with Cheddar and chives, a soft scallion and Cheddar quick bread, tiny cinnamon rolls, slices of lemon and poppy seed loaf, or maybe sweet yet tangy orange-cranberry scones.

My children don't care that the bread dough I season with cheese and bake into those golden bread sticks began in a blue refrigerated can. They only know that a sweet and yeasty fragrance permeates the house, summoning them to dinner better than any intercom system. They could care less

that the Sour Cream Cinnamon Loaf started with a cinnamon muffin mix I've doctored with a full cup of sour cream and a handful of finely chopped pecans. This loaf is so luscious we declare it better than its made-from-scratch counterpart and worthy of a satin ribbon for gift giving during the holidays. Your dinner guests will never know that the Provençal Olive Bread they savor with a sip of wine began with Bisquick. Or that the warm Crisp Cornmeal Waffles draped with smoked salmon started as a combination of Bisquick and a self-rising cornmeal mix.

Don't let yourself feel guilty about taking shortcuts. What really matters is that we are putting hot breads on our family dinner tables. As we do, bread rounds out the meal, making a simple roast chicken or an impromptu spaghetti supper seem more satisfying. So pass the bread basket, share, eat, and give thanks.

BREAD STICKS THREE WAYS

▼ ▼ ▼

TO PREP:
12 MINUTES
TO BAKE:
15–20 MINUTES

One of the fastest ways to put fresh bread on your table is to bake bread sticks. If you use refrigerated dough, they'll be done in 15 to 20 minutes. I think refrigerated bread stick dough is one of the best quick doughs available, but it's up to you to make it interesting. In my family there are differing opinions as to what's best, so I am used to making bread sticks with an array of toppings to please everyone. You can bake the bread sticks straight or twist them like a corkscrew—any way they are shaped, they'll be aromatic and irresistible when they come hot out of your oven.

1 package (11 ounces) refrigerated plain
    bread stick dough

TOPPING 1: GARLIC AND FENNEL

1 tablespoon olive oil

2 cloves garlic, crushed in a garlic press

1 teaspoon fennel seeds

Coarse salt

TOPPING 2: POPPY SEED AND PAPRIKA

1 tablespoon olive oil

1 teaspoon poppy seeds

Paprika

Seasoned salt

TOPPING 3: CHEDDAR AND CHIVE

¼ cup pre-shredded sharp Cheddar cheese

1 tablespoon minced fresh chives

tips **Instead of making three different kinds of bread sticks, triple the ingredients of one of the toppings so they're all the same flavor.**

Purists might prefer bread sticks brushed with nothing but melted butter before they're baked.

1. Place a rack in the center of the oven and preheat the oven to 375°F.

2. Unroll the bread stick dough and separate it into 12 pieces. Place the strips of dough on an ungreased baking sheet.

3. For Topping 1: Brush 4 strips of dough with 1 tablespoon of olive oil. Sprinkle the garlic and fennel seeds over these strips of dough, dividing them

> **tip** Other possible toppings include tapenade or black olive paste (see box on page 275), crumbled blue cheese and black pepper, or chopped sun-dried tomatoes and fresh basil.

evenly among them. Season these bread sticks with coarse salt.

For Topping 2: Brush 4 more strips of dough with 1 tablespoon of olive oil. Sprinkle the poppy seeds over these strips of dough, dividing them evenly among them. Season these bread sticks with paprika and seasoned salt.

For Topping 3: Sprinkle the remaining 4 strips of dough with the Cheddar cheese and chives, dividing them evenly among them.

4. Bake the bread sticks until they are golden brown, 15 to 20 minutes. Using a metal spatula, transfer the bread sticks to a serving plate and serve at once.

MAKES 12 BREAD STICKS

PARMESAN AND PEPPER CORNMEAL TWISTS

▼ ▼ ▼

TO PREP:
12 MINUTES
TO BAKE:
8–10 MINUTES

I highly recommend refrigerated corn bread twist dough, for it bakes up sweet and golden, resulting in a complement to any soup or salad. The dough needs a little doctoring, so I added some Parmesan cheese and black pepper. I can't imagine how much time it would take to match these twists from scratch.

1 package (11 ounces) refrigerated
    corn bread twist dough
2 tablespoons pre-shredded
    Parmesan cheese
½ teaspoon black pepper

1. Place a rack in the center of the oven and preheat the oven to 375°F.

2. Unroll the dough and separate it into 16 strips. Holding a strip at one end, twist the other end to form a corkscrew. Place the twists an inch apart on an ungreased baking sheet. Sprinkle them with the Parmesan cheese and pepper, dividing them evenly among the twists.

3. Bake the twists until they are a light golden brown, 8 to 10 minutes. Using a metal spatula, transfer the twists to a serving plate and serve at once.

MAKES 16 TWISTS

> *tip* You can make eight larger twists by twisting two strips of dough together. Pinch the ends of dough under to seal them. These will take a little longer to bake, 12 to 13 minutes.

PROVENÇAL OLIVE BREAD

▼ ▼ ▼

Several years ago I tasted this speedy yet sophisticated bread at a gathering of gardeners who discussed their basil while lunching on green salads full of the herbs they had grown. The bread, flavored with olive oil, white wine, ham, green olives, and Gruyère cheese, is also delicious sliced into small pieces and served as an hors d'oeuvre. It freezes well, too.

Vegetable oil cooking spray,
　for misting the loaf pans
1½ cups biscuit mix, such as
　Bisquick, plus more
　for dusting the pans
2 to 3 slices ham (for ½ cup chopped)
½ cup pre-sliced green olives
1 large egg, lightly beaten
4 tablespoons olive oil
⅓ cup dry white wine
½ cup pre-shredded Gruyère or Swiss cheese

TO PREP:
15 MINUTES
TO BAKE:
22–25 MINUTES

1. Place a rack in the center of the oven and preheat the oven to 400°F.

2. Lightly mist 3 miniature loaf pans (5½ by 3 by 2 inches) with vegetable oil cooking spray, then dust them with biscuit mix. Shake out the excess.

3. Place the ham and olives in a food processor and pulse until finely chopped. Place 1½ cups of the biscuit mix and the egg, olive oil, and wine in a large mixing bowl. Fold in the chopped ham and olives and the cheese and stir until the ingredients are just

tip　Freeze the loaves for up to 3 months, well wrapped in aluminum foil and placed in a zipper-lock bag. Thaw in the refrigerator over night.

incorporated. Divide the batter evenly among the prepared pans.

4. Bake the loaves until they are golden brown and spring back when lightly pressed with a finger, 22 to 25 minutes. Remove the pans from the oven and place them on a wire rack to cool for 5 minutes. Run a long, sharp knife around the edges of the loaves, invert them onto your hand, then invert them again onto the rack so they are right side up. Allow the loaves to cool another 15 minutes, then slice and serve.

MAKES 3 SMALL LOAVES

5 Fast Ways to Doctor French Bread

— ▼ —

DINNER DOCTOR SAYS

Here's a quick way to make garlic toast with Parmesan, plus four more easy toppings. To use these pastes with a loaf of French bread, cut it in half lengthwise and spread both halves with one of the pastes, then place the bread under the broiler until the topping is bubbling. Or, make slits in the top of a loaf of unbaked refrigerated French bread dough, spoon one of the pastes into the slits, and bake the bread following the instructions on the package.

1. Parmesan cheese and garlic paste: Mix ½ cup of pre-shredded Parmesan cheese, 1 clove of garlic that has been crushed in a garlic press, and 3 tablespoons of olive oil.

2. Spanish paste: Mix 1 tablespoon of thinly sliced garlic, ½ cup chopped ripe tomato, and 2 tablespoons of olive oil, then season the paste to your taste with coarse salt.

3. Herb paste: Mix ¼ cup chopped fresh tarragon, rosemary, chives, or parsley and 1 tablespoon melted butter.

4. Herb and Parmesan cheese paste: Mix ¼ cup chopped fresh tarragon, rosemary, chives, or parsley, ¼ cup pre-shredded Parmesan cheese, and 2 to 3 tablespoons of olive oil.

5. Cheddar cheese and chile paste: Mix ½ cup of pre-shredded sharp Cheddar cheese and a 4.5 ounce can of chopped green chiles.

TOMATO AND GARLIC FOCACCIA

▼ ▼ ▼

Focaccia is an Italian flat bread with dimples that are perfect for collecting ingredients like olive oil and garlic. The first time I baked this recipe I used frozen bread dough, and I loved the big, thick, almost cakey, focaccia that resulted. Yet it took far too long. While waiting for the frozen dough to thaw, I could have sampled my way through the focaccia in every bakery

TO PREP:
15 MINUTES
TO BAKE:
15–18 MINUTES

in town! So when I tried the recipe again, I used refrigerated pizza crust dough and was thrilled. I ended up with an easy flat bread, not quite as thick and cakey as the first version, but dimpled and chewy nevertheless and ready in less than 30 minutes. The focaccia makes a light meal with a green salad and a glass of red wine.

1 package (10 ounces) refrigerated pizza
   crust dough
2 tablespoons olive oil
3 cloves garlic, crushed in a garlic press
⅓ cup pre-crumbled feta cheese (optional)
½ cup thinly sliced tomato
   (from 1 medium-size tomato)
Coarse salt

tips Once you start using refrigerated pizza crust dough, you will be making all kinds of fabulous flat breads. Here are some more ideas for toppings. The baking time remains the same.

Combine ¼ cup of pre-shredded Parmesan cheese, 2 sliced cloves of garlic, and a little herb salt.

Spread ⅓ cup of store-bought tapenade on the dough and sprinkle a little chopped fresh oregano over it.

1. Place a rack in the center of the oven and preheat the oven to 400°F.

2. Unroll the dough onto an ungreased rimmed baking sheet. Using your hands, form the dough into an 11-by-7-inch rectangle. With your fingertips, make indentations all over the dough. Drizzle the olive oil evenly over the dough. Scatter the garlic and feta cheese, if using, over the dough. Arrange the tomato slices evenly on top of the dough. Sprinkle salt over the tomatoes.

3. Bake the focaccia until it is golden brown, 15 to 18 minutes. Remove the pan from the oven and, when the focaccia is cool enough to handle, cut it into squares, using a pizza cutter. Serve the focaccia with dinner or drinks.

MAKES 1 FOCACCIA

tip For a variation on the BLT, drizzle 2 tablespoons of olive oil evenly over the dough, scatter a couple of tablespoons of crumbled cooked bacon on top, then arrange ½ cup of thin tomato slices over the dough. Bake the focaccia as described in Step 3 at right, then just before serving, shower the top with shredded iceberg lettuce.

MEXICAN SKILLET CORN BREAD

▼ ▼ ▼

To me, nothing makes a more comforting or suitable accompaniment to a pot of chili or a thick soup than just baked corn bread. This easy recipe streamlines the process of making it by using two packages of corn bread mix and adding eggs, buttermilk, green chiles, and cheese. It is delicious served right from the skillet, dabbed with soft butter.

TO PREP:
15–20 MINUTES
TO BAKE:
18–20 MINUTES

1 tablespoon vegetable oil

2 packages (6.5 ounces each)
     corn bread mix

2 large eggs

1½ cups buttermilk

1 can (4.5 ounces) chopped green
     chiles, with their liquid

1 cup pre-shredded Mexican-style cheese

Butter, for serving

1. Place a rack in the center of the oven and preheat the oven to 450°F. Pour the oil into a 10- or 10½-inch cast-iron skillet and place the skillet in the oven while it preheats.

2. Place the corn bread mix, eggs, buttermilk, chiles with their liquid, and cheese in a large mixing bowl and stir just to combine. When the oven temperature reaches 375°F (if you don't have an oven thermometer, that should take 10 to 15 minutes) carefully remove the hot skillet. Pour the batter into the skillet and

tip **If you don't own a cast-iron skillet, place the oil in a 9- or 10-inch square or round cake pan, making sure the sides are oiled, and heat it in the oven before adding the batter.**

smooth the top. Return the skillet to the oven immediately. Keep the oven set to 450°F.

3. Bake the corn bread until it is golden brown and springs back when lightly pressed with a finger, 18 to 20 minutes. Carefully remove the corn bread from the oven and run a knife around the edge of the corn bread to loosen it, then invert it onto a plate. Invert the corn bread again on a cutting board so that it is right side up. Slice the corn bread into wedges while hot and serve with butter.

MAKES 1 CORN BREAD

An Autumn Meal with Friends

▼▼▼

What could be nicer when the weather turns a little cool, then to gather with friends over dinner and rehash the summer just past and the winter activities to come. Bake the corn bread first, then lower the oven to bake the lasagna. The corn bread will still be nice and warm when you serve it.

Pumpkin Orange Soup with Parmesan Toasts
page 72

Spinach and Black Bean Lasagna
page 306

Green salad

Mexican Skillet Corn Bread
page 413

Butternut Squash Layer Cake with Maple Cream Cheese Frosting
page 456

SCALLION AND CHEDDAR SUPPER BREAD

▼ ▼ ▼

This is a batter bread—the leavening is in the biscuit mix—which makes it a lot faster to prepare than a yeast bread. Batter, or quick, breads are a snap to assemble; often they can be mixed in just 5 minutes, and they are usually ready for baking before the oven has pre-heated! They are soft and delicious.

TO PREP:
15 MINUTES
TO BAKE:
16–18 MINUTES

served warm from the pan. I like this bread with grilled steak or pork chops or with a bowl of chili.

Vegetable oil cooking spray, for misting the pan

1½ cups biscuit mix, such as Bisquick

½ cup milk

1 large egg

1 cup pre-shredded sharp Cheddar cheese

4 scallions, both white and light green parts, chopped (for ½ cup)

¼ teaspoon black pepper

1 tablespoon olive oil

1. Place a rack in the center of the oven and preheat the oven to 400°F.

2. Lightly mist an 8-inch round or square cake pan with vegetable oil cooking spray. Set the cake pan aside.

> *tip* **Vary this recipe as you like, adding ½ cup chopped of whatever fresh herbs you have on hand instead of the scallions. You can also use a different pre-shredded cheese.**

3. Place the biscuit mix, milk, and egg in a large mixing bowl and stir to just combine. Add the Cheddar cheese, scallions, and pepper and stir until all the ingredients are just incorporated. Scrape the dough into the prepared cake pan. Press it lightly with a spatula so that it reaches the sides of the pan. Drizzle the olive oil over the top.

4. Bake the bread until it is golden brown and springs back when lightly pressed with a finger, 16 to 18 minutes. Remove the pan from the oven and place it on a wire rack to cool for 5 minutes, then slice the bread into squares and serve at once.

MAKES 1 LOAF

Biscuits, an Informal Taste Test

— ▼ —

DINNER DOCTOR SAYS
Here's how some of the various types of supermarket biscuits and biscuit mixes compare with homemade biscuits.

Unbaked frozen biscuits sold in bags: These are delicious and bake up pretty. If brushed with melted butter before baking, they have a homemade look. Large and perfect for filling with sliced sausage, they can also be cut into miniatures and baked for hors d'oeuvres. I like a variety of brands of frozen biscuits.

Unbaked refrigerated biscuits available in "cans": Not my first choice, and in fact, I don't keep these on hand. I do, however, buy refrigerated crescent roll dough, pizza crust dough, bread stick dough, corn bread twist dough, just not the *biscuit* dough. The signature trait of biscuits made from refrigerated cans is those layers you peel off. They taste nothing like homemade biscuits.

Biscuits made from Bisquick, or other biscuit mixes: These make excellent fast biscuits for supper, for strawberry shortcake, for—you name it. Add milk or buttermilk and the results are soft and crumbly. The only drawback is that the biscuits can be salty. Spread them with unsalted butter.

ANGEL BISCUITS

▼ ▼ ▼

Flaky like a biscuit, soft and doughy like a roll, sweet like a scone, these biscuits encompass the best of all worlds according to my children, who split them and fill them with sausage patties, peach preserves, or honey. In the summer, we like them with a simple meal of vegetables and sliced tomatoes from the garden. The biscuits reheat nicely for breakfast the next morning. Thanks to biscuit mix, you can assemble them in 10 minutes or less. By the way, the added yeast is for texture and flavor, not to give height, so no rising time is required.

TO PREP:
18 MINUTES
TO BAKE:
8–10 MINUTES

2 tablespoons very warm water
1 envelope (.25 ounce) rapid-rise
    dry yeast
3 tablespoons sugar
5 cups biscuit mix, such as Bisquick,
    plus more for dusting
½ cup solid vegetable shortening
1 cup buttermilk
2 tablespoons butter, melted
Butter, preserves, and cooked sausages,
    for serving (optional)

1. Place a rack in the center of the oven and preheat the oven to 425°F.

2. Place the very warm water in a large mixing bowl, sprinkle the yeast over it, and stir until it dissolves. Add the sugar and stir until it dissolves. Add the 5 cups of baking mix and stir to combine well. Add the shortening and, using 2 dinner knives or a pastry cutter, cut the shortening into the mixture until well distributed and the mixture resembles peas. Pour in the buttermilk and stir with a fork until the ingredients come together.

tip **Easily turn this biscuit recipe into delightful scones by increasing the sugar to 4 tablespoons and cutting the dough into triangles instead of rounds. Dust the top of the scones with another tablespoon of sugar, then bake as in Step 4.**

3. Dust a clean work surface or large cutting board with biscuit mix. Turn the dough out onto the surface, dust your fingers with biscuit mix, and pat the dough out to flatten it. Flip the dough so that the floured side is up, then continue patting it with your fingertips until it is ¾ inch thick. With a lightly dusted 2-inch round biscuit cutter, stamp out biscuits and line them up closely on an ungreased baking sheet. As needed, collect the scraps of dough into a ball, knead it a few times, and press it out to a ¾-inch thickness, then stamp out more biscuits. Repeat until all of the dough has been used. Brush the tops of the biscuits with the melted butter.

4. Bake the biscuits until they are light brown, 8 to 10 minutes. Remove the biscuits from the baking sheet and serve at once with butter and/or preserves, if desired.

MAKES 3 DOZEN BISCUITS

Dun-Buttered Muffins

▼▼▼

TO PREP:
10 MINUTES
TO BAKE:
15–18 MINUTES

Browsing through my mother's recipe box, I found these wonderful quick muffins that she and I used to bake and that now my daughters can make on their own. These are fast to prepare, having only three ingredients, and yet the result is incredibly flaky and buttery muffins. Don't scrimp and substitute the fat-free stuff for reduced-fat sour cream—the muffins won't be the same. We have a large muffin pan that can hold twenty-four small muffins, which means I can bake all of the batter at one time. Yes!

2 cups biscuit mix,
    such as Bisquick
8 tablespoons (1 stick) butter,
    melted
1 cup reduced-fat sour cream

1. Place a rack in the center of the oven and preheat the oven to 350°F. Set aside a miniature muffin tin with 24 cups or two 12-cup tins.

2. Place the biscuit mix, butter, and sour cream in a large mixing bowl and stir with a wooden spoon until the ingredients come together. Spoon the batter by the tablespoonful into the ungreased muffin tin(s), filling the cups two-thirds full.

tip **What's for dessert? Mini strawberry shortcakes. When local strawberries are in season, slice a quart of them and toss with ¼ cup or more of sugar. Whip 1 cup of heavy (whipping) cream with a little sugar. Place two or three muffins on a plate. Top the muffins with the strawberries and their juice, then generously dollop on the sweetened whipped cream. Yum.**

3. Bake the muffins until they are light brown, 15 to 18 minutes. Remove the muffin tins from the oven and place them on a wire rack to cool for 10 minutes. Then, run a sharp knife around the edges of the muffins and invert them onto the rack. Transfer them to a platter and serve at once.

MAKES **2** DOZEN SMALL MUFFINS

Bisquick, the First Baking Mix

—▼—

DINNER DOCTOR SAYS

The most famous biscuit mix, Bisquick, was born on a late-night trip from Portland, Oregon, to San Francisco in 1930. Carl Smith, a sales executive for General Mills, sat down in the dining car and was served hot biscuits, something that amazed him, given the late hour and the fact that he was traveling on a train. The chef explained that, before the train had pulled out of Portland, he had put together a baking mix of flour, baking powder, salt, and lard. Smith was elated and could not wait to pass along the idea to the company chemist, and you know the rest of the story.

But, creating Bisquick didn't happen overnight. The research department had to find an oil that would not turn rancid en route to the home kitchen and it had to find the right packaging material. Researchers discovered that if the ingredients were not perfectly blended, with lumps of oil mixed with layers of flour, the biscuit mix would not produce consistent results when baked. Bisquick was unveiled in 1931 and has been a pantry staple ever since.

SWEET ORANGE CORN MUFFINS

▼ ▼ ▼

TO PREP:
12 MINUTES
TO BAKE:
15–20 MINUTES

I write a bi-monthly on-line newsletter for my Cake Mix Doctor Web site, and early on a reader requested a recipe for a corn bread that was made with both yellow cake mix and corn bread mix. Well, that recipe was so widely circulated that any number of readers e-mailed it in. I love the sweet flavor of the corn bread, even though in the South I was raised on the kind that didn't have a speck of sugar. I've played up that sweetness by adding a little orange to the mix and turning the corn bread into muffins. They're delicious with pork chops, fried chicken, a supper of summer vegetables, or a bowl of soup.

Vegetable oil cooking spray, for misting
the muffin cups (optional)
2 medium-size oranges
1 package (9 ounces) Jiffy yellow cake mix
(see Tips)
2 large eggs
1 package (8.5 ounces) Jiffy
corn muffin mix (see Tips)
⅓ cup milk

1. Place a rack in the center of the oven and preheat the oven to 375°F.

2. Lightly mist 18 muffin cups (you'll need 2 muffin tins) with vegetable oil cooking spray or line them with paper muffin cups. Set the muffin tins aside.

tips For this recipe, you must use the small boxes of Jiffy cake and corn muffin mix.
　You can speed up the prep time by using orange juice from a carton and omitting the zest, but be forewarned that orange zest adds a more distinctive orange flavor to the muffins.

3. Rinse the oranges and pat them dry. Using a grater, remove and set aside about 1 tablespoon of zest. Juice the oranges and set aside ½ cup of orange juice.

4. Place the cake mix in a large mixing bowl with 1 of the eggs and the ½ cup of orange juice. Beat with an electric mixer on low speed for 30 seconds. Stop the machine and scrape down the side of the bowl with a rubber spatula. Increase the mixer speed to medium and beat 2 minutes longer, scraping down the side again if necessary. The batter should look well combined. Set the cake batter aside.

5. Place the muffin mix, the remaining egg, and the milk in a medium-size mixing bowl and whisk until the ingredients are just combined. Add the corn muffin batter and the orange zest to the cake mix batter and, using a rubber spatula, mix the two batters until just blended. Spoon the batter into the prepared muffin cups, filling them two-thirds full. Fill the empty muffin cups halfway with water, to prevent them from warping. Place the muffin tins side by side in the oven.

6. Bake the muffins until they just turn golden brown and a toothpick inserted in the center of one comes out clean, 15 to 20 minutes. Remove the muffin tins from the oven and place them on a wire rack to cool for 10 minutes. Invert the muffins onto the rack (if the muffins baked directly in the tins, run a sharp knife around the edges of the muffins first), then transfer them to a platter and serve at once.

Makes 15 to 18 muffins

BANANA AND CINNAMON SWIRL MUFFINS

▼ ▼ ▼

How can any recipe with banana, sour cream, and cinnamon in it go wrong, you wonder? It can't. One of my favorite doctoring tricks is adding mashed banana to a cake mix to boost the flavor and make the cake more moist. Another trick I like is to use sour cream as some of the liquid and some of the fat, which makes the cake richer. It works for muffins, too. These cinnamon ones are not only delicious, they're pretty, what with the streusel topping; don't let on that it came right out of the box!

tip **You can make these muffins without bananas by increasing the sour cream to 1 cup and adding 3 tablespoons of water.**

TO PREP:
15 MINUTES
TO BAKE:
18–22 MINUTES

Vegetable oil cooking spray,
   for misting the muffin cups
   (optional)

1 package (19.1 ounces) cinnamon swirl
   muffin mix (see Tips, page 438)
½ cup reduced-fat sour cream
1 large egg
¾ cup mashed banana (from 2 ripe medium-
   size bananas)
¼ cup pre-chopped pecans (optional)

1. Place a rack in the center of the oven and preheat the oven to 400°F.

2. Lightly mist 12 muffin cups with vegetable oil cooking spray (you'll need one 12-muffin tin or two 6-muffin tins) or line them with paper muffin cups. Set the muffin tins aside.

3. Set aside the packets of cinnamon swirl and of topping mix from the muffin mix. Place the muffin mix, sour cream, egg, and banana in a large mixing bowl. Stir with a wooden spoon, until the ingredients are moistened, about 50 strokes. Knead the packet of cinnamon swirl with your fingers a few times, then open it and squeeze the contents over the batter, swirling it in with a rubber spatula. Spoon the batter into the prepared muffin cups, filling them two-thirds full. Place the pecans, if using, in a small mixing bowl and stir in the topping mix. Sprinkle the topping evenly over the muffin batter.

4. Bake the muffins until a toothpick inserted in the center of one comes out clean, 18 to 22 minutes. Remove the muffin tins from the oven and place them on a wire rack to cool for 10 minutes. Invert the muffins onto the rack (if the muffins baked in the tin, run a sharp knife around the edges of the muffins first), then transfer them to a platter and serve at once.

MAKES 1 DOZEN MUFFINS

To Line or Not to Line Muffin Tins

— ▼ —

DINNER DOCTOR SAYS

Want to give your muffins a more interesting texture? Forgo paper muffin cups, and bake the batter directly in the unlined tins. Yes, there will be a little more cleanup. You'll need to soak the tins in the sink to loosen any bits that cling to them. But you get a nice, almost crunchy, crust around the edges of the muffins, a pleasing contrast to the soft interior. Just lightly grease the muffin tins by brushing or swabbing solid vegetable shortening on the sides and bottoms of the cups or mist them with vegetable oil cooking spray. You can also dust the muffin cups with a little flour after greasing them. This contributes to a crunchy exterior. After baking, run a small, sharp knife around the edges of the cooled muffins, turn the muffin tin upside down, and the muffins should all come out at once.

LEMON BLUEBERRY MUFFINS

WITH A LEMON DRIZZLE

▼ ▼ ▼

Blueberry muffins hot from the oven are hard to resist, and from the looks of supermarket baking aisles, shoppers obviously give into this temptation! There are countless blueberry muffin mixes out there, but I felt these mixes left something to be desired when I sampled them. So I added a touch of lemon, both to the batter and to the glaze, and the result is quite nice, perfect for serving at home or packaging for bake sales at school.

TO PREP:
15 MINUTES
TO BAKE:
18–22 MINUTES

Vegetable oil cooking spray, for misting the muffin cups (optional)

1 package (18.9 ounces) blueberry muffin mix

¾ cup whole milk

1 large egg

1 teaspoon grated lemon zest (see Tip)

⅔ cup confectioners' sugar

1 tablespoon fresh lemon juice (see Tip)

1. Place a rack in the center of the oven and preheat the oven to 400°F.

2. Lightly mist 12 muffin cups with vegetable oil cooking spray (you'll need one 12-muffin tin or two 6-muffin tins) or line them with paper muffin cups. Set the muffin tins aside.

3. Rinse the blueberries from the muffin mix with cold water, then drain them well and set them aside. Place the muffin mix, milk, egg, and

tip You will need 1 large lemon for this recipe. It will easily give you the 1 teaspoon of grated zest and 1 tablespoon of juice you need.

lemon zest in a large mixing bowl and stir with a wooden spoon until the ingredients are moistened, about 50 strokes. Fold the blueberries into the batter until they are just incorporated. Spoon the batter into the prepared muffin cups, filling them two-thirds full.

4. Bake the muffins until they are golden brown and a toothpick inserted in the center of one comes out clean, 18 to 22 minutes. Remove the muffin tins from the oven and place them on a wire rack to cool for 10 minutes. Invert the muffins onto the rack (if the muffins baked directly in the tin, run a sharp knife around the edges of the muffins first) and let continue to cool while you prepare the lemon drizzle.

5. Place the confectioners' sugar and lemon juice in a small bowl and stir to combine. Drizzle this glaze over the muffins, then transfer them to a platter and serve.

MAKES 1 DOZEN MUFFINS

15 WAYS TO DOCTOR BLUEBERRY MUFFIN MIX

If you add just a little something extra to a package of blueberry muffin mix, you'll end up with far better muffins. Here are fifteen ways to doctor the box. Follow the directions on the package for making the batter, then add any of the following. The amounts given are for mixes that are between 18.25 and 18.9 ounces. These will make a dozen delicious muffins.

1 Mash a ripe banana and stir it into the muffin batter.

2 Add ½ teaspoon of almond extract to the batter. After the muffins have cooled, glaze the tops with ½ cup of confectioners' sugar moistened with 2 tablespoons of milk and press sliced toasted almonds into the glaze.

3 Fold 1 cup of chopped dried cherries into the muffin batter.

4 Add 1 cup or more of fresh blueberries to the muffin batter.

5 Stir the juice and zest of an orange into the muffin batter.

6 Mix 1 tablespoon of softened butter, 2 tablespoons of oatmeal (quick or old-fashioned), 1 tablespoon of brown sugar, and 1 tablespoon of chopped nuts together and sprinkle the mixture over the unbaked muffins, patting it onto them lightly, for a streusel topping.

7 Stir 1 tablespoon of poppy seeds and a dash of lemon extract into the batter.

8 Mix a pinch of ground nutmeg into the muffin batter.

9 Substitute sour cream for part of the liquid to make the muffins more moist.

10 Bake the batter in an 8-inch-square baking pan, then glaze the blueberry bread with ½ cup of confectioners' sugar moistened with 2 to 3 tablespoons of milk, for a quick coffee cake.

11 Fold about 1 cup of dried cranberries into the batter for double-berry muffins.

12 Add a pinch of cardamom to the batter.

13 Mix 1 teaspoon of pure vanilla extract into the muffin batter.

14 Add 1 teaspoon of grated lemon zest and 2 tablespoons of finely chopped walnuts to the batter.

15 Use eggnog in place of the liquid called for and add a little grated nutmeg.

APPLE-CINNAMON BRAN MUFFINS

WITH OATMEAL STREUSEL TOPPING

▼ ▼ ▼

It's nice to have an easy bran muffin in your reper-toire. This recipe is a tried-and-true standby and very easy to put together. Sprinkling a simple streusel topping of brown sugar, pecans, and oatmeal on top of the muffins right before baking gives them a homemade touch.

TO PREP:
15 MINUTES
TO BAKE:
18–22 MINUTES

Vegetable oil cooking spray,
   for misting the muffin cups
   (optional)
1 package (17.4 ounces) apple-cinnamon
   bran muffin mix
1¼ cups milk
1 large egg
3 tablespoons vegetable oil
3 tablespoons light brown sugar
2 tablespoons oatmeal (see Tips)
2 tablespoons pre-chopped pecans
Dash of cinnamon

1. Place a rack in the center of the oven and preheat the oven to 400°F.

2. Lightly mist 12 muffin cups with vegetable oil cooking spray (you'll need one 12-muffin tin or two 6-muffin tins) or line them with paper muffin cups. Set the muffin tins aside.

tips Doctoring up a bran muffin mix with the apple packet from the box is all too easy. If you like, omit the apple packet and fold in ½ cup of raisins instead.

I used a Duncan Hines bran muffin mix in testing this recipe.

You can use either Old Fashioned Quaker Oats or Quick Oats in this recipe.

3. Set aside the packet of apple filling from the muffin mix. Place the muffin mix, milk, egg, and oil in a large mixing bowl and stir with a wooden spoon, until the ingredients are moistened, about 50 strokes. The batter will be lumpy. Fold the apple filling into the batter until it is incorporated. Spoon the batter into the prepared muffin cups, filling them two-thirds full.

4. Place the brown sugar, oatmeal, pecans, and cinnamon in a small mixing bowl and stir to mix. Sprinkle this topping evenly over the muffin batter.

5. Bake the muffins until a toothpick inserted in the center of one comes out clean, 18 to 22 minutes. Remove the muffin tins from the oven and place them on a wire rack to cool for 10 minutes. Invert the muffins onto the rack (if the muffins baked directly in the tin, run a sharp knife around the edges of the muffins first), then transfer them to a platter and serve.

MAKES 1 DOZEN MUFFINS

ORANGE AND CRANBERRY SCONES

▼ ▼ ▼

I'll never forget the first time I traveled to England. The plane was an hour or two from landing when breakfast was served—scones, clotted cream, and strawberry jam. Even though those scones were stone cold and the presentation on an in-flight tray left a lot to be desired, I fell in love with them. Here is a dandy of a fast recipe concocted using a biscuit mix, such as Bisquick. The orange and cranberry combination is a natural, but of course you can omit one or even both ingredients if you prefer plain scones. You can cut these sweet cousins of the Southern biscuit into large or small triangles or even rounds, diamonds, or squares.

TO PREP:
12 MINUTES
TO BAKE:
10–16 MINUTES

3 cups plus 2 tablespoons biscuit mix, such as Bisquick

4 tablespoons (½ stick) cold unsalted butter, cut into pieces, plus more for serving

⅓ cup plus 1 tablespoon sugar

1 heaping teaspoon grated orange zest (from 1 medium-size orange)

⅓ cup dried cranberries, chopped

1 large egg, lightly beaten

½ cup buttermilk

Butter and jam, for serving

1. Place a rack in the center of the oven and preheat the oven to 375°F.

2. Place the 3 cups of biscuit mix and the butter in a large mixing bowl. With a pastry blender or two knives, cut the butter into the biscuit mix until the mixture resembles

tip To make the scones even more quickly, place 3 cups of the biscuit mix and the butter in a food processor. Pulse the machine several times until the cold butter is cut in well. Add the sugar, orange zest, cranberries, egg, and buttermilk and process only until the mixture just comes together, then proceed with Step 3.

peas. Stir in the ⅓ cup of sugar and the orange zest and cranberries. Add the egg and buttermilk and stir until the dough is well blended. It should be sticky but not wet.

3. Dust a clean work surface with 1 tablespoon of the biscuit mix. Turn the dough out on the surface and knead it 6 to 8 times on the floured surface. Sprinkle the remaining 1 tablespoon of biscuit mix over the dough and press it into a 10-inch round about ⅝ inch thick. Using a sharp knife, cut the dough into 8 large or 16 small wedges.

Place the wedges on an ungreased baking sheet, slightly apart for a crusty edge or just touching for a softer scone. Sprinkle the tops with the remaining tablespoon of sugar.

4. Bake the scones until they are light brown, 13 to 16 minutes for large scones or 10 to 12 minutes for small scones. Remove the baking sheet from the oven and, using a metal spatula, transfer the scones to a serving plate. Serve at once with butter and jam.

MAKES 8 LARGE SCONES OR 16 SMALL SCONES

When Is a Biscuit Not a Scone?

—▼—

DINNER DOCTOR SAYS

When you are in England, where the word *biscuit* refers to a cookie. End of riddle. In the United States, however, biscuits and scones have a lot in common. They both are made from batters of leavened flour, shortening (once lard, now butter), and enough liquid to just hold the dough together. Both require little or no kneading, for the less the dough is worked the more tender the biscuit—or scone. And they are at their best hot from the oven. Serve them wrapped in a linen or cotton towel and tucked in a bread basket.

There are some differences: There's never any sugar in biscuits; scones are usually slightly sweet. Only scones contain eggs. And if they don't all disappear right after you've baked them, you should not serve biscuits cold. Instead, split them, spread them with soft butter, and run the biscuits under the broiler until they sizzle. You may serve cold scones, preferably the way they are served at high tea—smothered with clotted cream and strawberries.

LITTLE CINNAMON SWEET ROLLS

▼ ▼ ▼

My daughter Kathleen will eat anything wrapped in crescent roll dough, so I expected her to enjoy these buttery little rolls, but the irresistible cinnamon aroma wafting around the house drew the entire family to sample them. What a success! They take little time to put together and bake, and it makes four dozen, so there's enough for your family and your neighbors.

Vegetable oil cooking spray,
    for misting the cake pans
2 packages (8 ounces each)
    refrigerated crescent rolls
5 tablespoons butter, at room temperature
⅓ cup packed light brown sugar
1 tablespoon granulated sugar
1 teaspoon ground cinnamon
⅔ cup confectioners' sugar
1 to 2 tablespoons milk

TO PREP:
15 MINUTES
TO BAKE:
18–20 MINUTES

1. Place a rack in the center of the oven and preheat the oven to 375°F.

2. Lightly mist two 9-inch round cake pans with vegetable oil cooking spray and set them aside.

3. Open the packages of crescent roll dough and divide each log of dough in half at the middle perforated seam. Unroll each of the 4 pieces of dough. Firmly press the

tips If you like, add ¼ cup of finely chopped raisins or pecans to the sugar and cinnamon filling.

For the Christmas holidays, decorate the glazed sweet rolls with red and green candied cherries.

These rolls freeze well, either glazed or unglazed, for up to six months. Wrap well in aluminum foil before freezing.

diagonal perforations within each rectangle together to seal them.

4. Place the butter, brown sugar, granulated sugar, and cinnamon in a small mixing bowl and stir to combine. With a small rubber spatula, spread this mixture evenly over the 4 rectangles of dough, dividing it evenly among them. Starting at one of the long ends, roll up each of the rectangles like a jelly roll. Pinch the long edge of each to seal it. Using a serrated knife, cut each roll into twelve ½-inch slices. Arrange the sweet rolls with cut sides down in the prepared pans so that they are nearly touching. Place the pans side by side in the oven.

5. Bake the rolls until they are golden brown, 18 to 20 minutes. Remove the baking pans from the oven and place them on a wire rack to cool for 10 to 15 minutes.

6. Meanwhile, place the confectioners' sugar in a small bowl and stir in enough milk to make a smooth glaze. Spread or drizzle this over the baked rolls with a dinner knife or small metal spatula. Serve the rolls right from the pans.

MAKES 4 DOZEN SWEET ROLLS

APRICOT-ALMOND COFFEE CAKE

▼ ▼ ▼

Biting into this flaky coffee cake flavored with apricots and almonds, you would never guess it was so simple to prepare. Or that the base is a layer of crescent roll dough, the apricots come from a can of pastry filling, and the glaze is nothing more than confectioners' sugar and milk dribbled on at the end. My friends and I love this coffee cake, especially served warm, with a cup of coffee.

TO PREP:
12 MINUTES
TO BAKE:
15–20 MINUTES

2 packages (8 ounces each)
refrigerated crescent rolls
1 can (12 ounces) apricot filling
1 package (2.25 ounces; ½ cup) pre-sliced almonds
1 cup confectioners' sugar
1 to 2 tablespoons milk

1. Place a rack in the center of the oven and preheat the oven to 375°F.

2. Open the packages of crescent roll dough and divide each log of dough in half at the middle perforated seam. Unroll the 4 pieces of dough on a 15½-by-10½-by-1-inch rimmed baking sheet so that they are side by side and extend the width of the sheet and 1 inch up the sides. Firmly press the seams and the diagonal perforations within each rectangle together to seal them. Spread the apricot filling evenly over the dough with a rubber spatula. Sprinkle the almonds over the filling.

tips If you are in a hurry, go ahead and glaze the coffee cake before it cools completely. The glaze will run a bit and not keep its shape, but the coffee cake will be just as delicious.

Add ¼ teaspoon of almond extract to the glaze to intensify the almond flavor.

Transfer any leftover coffee cake to a plastic container with a lid. It will keep for up to 2 days.

3. Bake the coffee cake until the edges are golden brown, 15 to 20 minutes. Remove the baking sheet from the oven and place it on a wire rack to cool completely, 20 minutes.

4. Meanwhile, place the confectioners' sugar in a small bowl and stir in the milk to make a smooth glaze. With a spoon, drizzle the glaze over the top of the cooled coffee cake. Serve the cake directly from the pan.

Makes 1 coffee cake

LEMON-POPPY SEED LOAF

▼ ▼ ▼

While I love the taste of lemon, I don't always care for lemon-flavored cake and bread mixes because the flavor can be overpowering. Yet, when lemon yogurt is folded into a lemon and poppy seed muffin mix, it seems to tone down the intensity. And if you bake the mix as a loaf and spoon a delicately lemony glaze on top, you have an attractive and moist bread that's perfect for slicing for a weekend brunch or giving to friends.

Vegetable oil cooking spray, for misting
the loaf pan
Flour, for dusting the pan
1 package (15.8 ounces) lemon–poppy seed
muffin mix (see Tips)
1 cup lemon yogurt
2 large eggs
¼ cup vegetable oil
1 cup confectioners' sugar
1 tablespoon fresh lemon juice

TO PREP:
10 MINUTES
TO BAKE:
43–47 MINUTES

1. Place a rack in the center of the oven and preheat the oven to 350°F.

2. Lightly mist a 9-by-5-inch loaf pan with vegetable oil cooking spray, then dust it with flour. Shake out the excess flour. Set the loaf pan aside.

3. Place the muffin mix, yogurt, eggs, and oil in a large mixing bowl. Beat with an electric mixer on low speed for 20 seconds. Stop the machine and scrape down the side of the bowl with a rubber spatula. Increase the mixer speed to medium and beat 1 minute longer, scraping the

tips I used a Betty Crocker lemon and poppy seed muffin mix in testing this recipe.
  This loaf is delicious unglazed if you are running short on time. Just dust it with a little confectioners' sugar.

side down again if necessary. The batter should be well combined. Scrape the batter into the prepared loaf pan.

4. Bake the loaf until it springs back when lightly pressed with a finger, 43 to 47 minutes. Remove the loaf pan from the oven and place it on a wire rack to cool for 15 minutes. Run a long, sharp knife around the edges of the loaf and remove it from the pan. Place the loaf on its side on the rack to cool completely, 20 minutes longer.

5. Meanwhile, place the confectioners' sugar and lemon juice in a small mixing bowl. Add 1 teaspoon of water and stir to combine. The glaze should be thick but spreadable. If necessary, add up to 2 teaspoons more water to the glaze to get the proper consistency. When the loaf has cooled, spoon the glaze over the top, allowing it to dribble down the sides, then slice the loaf and serve.

MAKES 1 LOAF

SOUR CREAM CINNAMON LOAF

▼ ▼ ▼

Chances are that when you flipped to this recipe, your eyes fixed on the words *sour cream* and *cinnamon*. I was trying to imitate a much beloved from-scratch sour cream and cinnamon bread with this recipe, and boy, did it ever turn out delicious. It's better than the more time-consuming original! The secret is combining a cinnamon muffin mix with a hefty addition of sour cream. Bake the loaf for a dinner buffet, for brunch, or to give as a present to a teacher.

TO PREP:
10 MINUTES
TO BAKE:
43–47 MINUTES

tips I used a Duncan Hines cinnamon swirl muffin mix to test this recipe. Feel free to go full-fat here and use regular sour cream.

Vegetable oil cooking spray,
    for misting the loaf pan
Flour, *for dusting the loaf pan*
1 package (19.1 ounces) cinnamon swirl
    muffin mix (see Tips)
1 cup reduced-fat sour cream (see Tips)
1 large egg
¼ cup pre-chopped pecans (optional)

1. Place a rack in the center of the oven and preheat the oven to 350°F.

2. Lightly mist a 9-by-5-inch loaf pan with vegetable oil cooking spray, then dust it with flour. Shake out the excess flour. Set the loaf pan aside.

3. Set aside the packets of cinnamon swirl and of topping mix from the muffin mix. Place the muffin mix, sour cream, egg, and 3 tablespoons of water in a large mixing bowl. Beat with an electric mixer on low speed for 20 seconds. Stop the machine and scrape down the side of the bowl with a rubber spatula. Increase the mixer speed to medium and beat 1 minute longer, scraping the side down again if necessary. The batter should be well combined and thick. Pour half to two-thirds of the batter into the prepared loaf pan.

4. Knead the packet of cinnamon swirl with your fingers a few times, then open it and squeeze the contents evenly over the batter. With a rubber spatula, spread the remaining batter over the top.

Place the pecans, if using, in a small bowl and stir in the topping mix. Sprinkle the topping over the loaf.

5. Bake the loaf until it springs back when lightly pressed with a finger, 43 to 47 minutes. Remove the loaf pan from the oven and place it on a wire rack to cool for 15 minutes. Dust with confectioners' sugar. Then, run a long, sharp knife around the edges of the loaf and serve warm slices right from the pan, if you wish.

MAKES 1 LOAF

PUMPKIN GINGERBREAD

▼ ▼ ▼

Martha Bowden, a wonderful cook and friend who does a lot of recipe testing for me, just flipped over this delicious gingerbread loaf. Martha is from New England and is partial to gingerbread. And, as a runner, she is always on the lookout for baked goods that aren't loaded down with fat. The gingerbread is particularly good in autumn, when a nip has returned to the air. The fragrant loaf can be on the table in less than an hour.

TO PREP:
10 MINUTES
TO BAKE:
45–47 MINUTES

Vegetable oil cooking spray,
*   for misting the loaf pan*
Flour, for dusting the loaf pan

1 package (14.5 ounces) gingerbread mix
*   (see Tips)*
1 cup canned pumpkin purée (about half
*   of a 15-ounce can)*
2 large eggs
¼ cup warm water
½ cup golden raisins

1. Place a rack in the center of the oven and preheat the oven to 325°F.

2. Lightly mist a 9-by-5-inch loaf pan with vegetable oil cooking spray, then dust it with flour. Shake out the excess flour. Set the loaf pan aside.

3. Place the gingerbread mix, pumpkin, eggs, and water in a large mixing bowl. Beat with an electric mixer on low speed for 30 seconds. Stop the machine and scrape down the side of the bowl with a

tips I used a Betty Crocker gingerbread mix when I tested this recipe.

You can shorten the baking time of this recipe—cook it in a 9-inch-square pan at 350°F for about 30 minutes.

Feel free to use other dried fruit, such as currants or cranberries, instead of the golden raisins.

rubber spatula. Increase the mixer speed to medium and beat 1 minute longer, scraping the side down again if necessary. The batter should be well combined. Fold in the raisins, making sure they are well incorporated. Pour the batter into the prepared loaf pan.

4. Bake the loaf until it springs back when lightly pressed with a finger, 45 to 4_ Remove the loaf pan from the o_ place it on a wire rack to cool for 15 _ utes. Run a long, sharp knife around t_ edges of the gingerbread and remove it from the pan. Place the loaf on its side on the rack to cool completely, 20 minutes longer. Slice and serve.

MAKES 1 LOAF

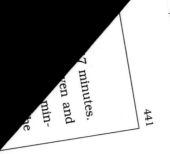

;P CORNMEAL WAFFLES

▼ ▼ ▼

A cross between corn muffins and regular waffles, these delightful and easy cornmeal waffles can be made morning, noon, or night at a moment's notice. They are perfect for those families where some like savory and some like sweet. You can top them with slices of smoked salmon and salty capers or dribble melted butter and maple syrup over them.

tips **If you can't find self-rising cornmeal, substitute 1 cup of regular cornmeal.**

Both biscuit mix and self-rising cornmeal mix have baking soda and salt added. For this reason you might want to use unsalted butter on the waffles.

TO PREP:
5 MINUTES
TO COOK:
12–18 MINUTES

Vegetable oil cooking spray,
for misting the waffle iron
1 cup biscuit mix, such as Bisquick
1 cup self-rising cornmeal mix (see Tips)
1¼ cups buttermilk
2 large eggs
2 tablespoons vegetable oil
Toppings of your choice
(see opposite page)

1. Preheat an electric waffle iron (see box, page 445). Mist the top and bottom of the interior with vegetable oil cooking spray. Preheat the oven to 250°F (you'll use it to keep the waffles warm until they are all ready to serve).

2. Place the biscuit mix, cornmeal mix, buttermilk, eggs, and oil in a large mixing bowl and stir until the eggs are well incorporated. Ladle about ½ cup of the batter onto the hot waffle iron, spreading it out so that it almost but not entirely covers the bottom. Close the lid and cook the waffle for 2 to 3 minutes or until the light comes on to indicate that the waffle is done. The waffle is fully cooked when it does not stick to the top or bottom of the iron and has a light brown color. Using a fork, transfer the waffle to a heatproof plate and place it in the oven to keep warm. Repeat with the remaining waffle batter.

3. Serve the waffles with your choice of sweet or savory toppings.

MAKES 6 WAFFLES (6 INCHES EACH)

What to Do with Waffles?

—▼—

DINNER DOCTOR SAYS

Waffles are quick and easy to stir together—even on a weekday (you'll find recipes on pages 442 through 449)—but for a fun brunch or supper the children or grandchildren will never forget, put together a "waffle bar" by setting out an assortment of toppings. In addition to the traditional maple syrup, the following are favorites at our house:

SWEET TOPPINGS
Blueberry syrup
Fresh blueberries and sour cream
Bananas and a sprinkling of light brown sugar
Sliced strawberries that have been tossed with sugar

Lemon curd and fresh strawberries
Chocolate syrup and fresh raspberries
Sliced peaches mixed with sugar (particularly good served along with crisp sausage patties)
And, who needs to make a cobbler? Spoon fresh blackberries you've tossed with sugar onto waffles and top them with whipped cream.

SAVORY TOPPINGS
Smoked salmon or smoked trout and chopped onions, capers, and/or chopped fresh dill
Caviar
Smoked ham and chopped scallions
Poached eggs and cracked black pepper
Pan-fried sausages and chopped tomato

SCHOOL MORNING WAFFLES

▼ ▼ ▼

Mornings are frantic at our house when school is in session. Luring the children from their warm beds, getting breakfast on the table, and locating missing shoes and math homework is exhausting. All the more reason to have a routine in place, and a breakfast routine that is not boring. My children love these waffles, which I make twice a week. They're fast, they're satisfying, and they're every bit as good as those made totally from scratch. Serve them with the customary butter and

TO PREP:
5 MINUTES
TO COOK:
18–40 MINUTES

syrup or jam or see the box on page 443 for some other toppings.

Vegetable oil cooking spray,
for misting the waffle iron
2 cups biscuit mix such as
Bisquick (see Tip)
1½ cups buttermilk
1 large egg
2 tablespoons vegetable oil
Butter and pancake syrup or jam,
for serving
Crisp bacon, for serving (optional)

1. Preheat an electric waffle iron (see box). Mist the top and bottom of the interior with vegetable oil cooking spray. Preheat the oven to 250°F (you'll use it to keep the waffles warm until they are all ready to serve).

2. Place the biscuit mix, buttermilk, egg, and oil in a large mixing bowl and stir until the egg is well incorporated. Ladle about ⅓ cup of the batter onto the hot

tip **I have tried this recipe with three or four of the biscuit mixes on the market, and all of them work reasonably well for making waffles.**

waffle iron, spreading it out so that it almost but not entirely covers the bottom. Close the lid and cook the waffle for 3 to 5 minutes or until the light comes on to indicate that the waffle is done. The waffle is fully cooked when it does not stick to the top or bottom of the iron and has a light brown color. Using a fork, transfer the waffle to a heatproof plate and place it in the oven to keep warm. Repeat with the remaining waffle batter.

3. Serve the waffles with butter and jam or a pitcher of pancake syrup. If desired, serve with slices of crisp bacon, too.

MAKES 6 TO 8 WAFFLES (6 INCHES EACH)

The Other Iron

—▼—

DINNER DOCTOR SAYS Waffle irons come in a variety of sizes and they make waffles in a variety of shapes. Depending on the type of iron you own, you may need slightly more or less batter per waffle. Cooking time also depends on the type of waffle iron you have. Although I have given a normal range, it's best to follow your manufacturer's directions.

CHOCOLATE CHIP CINNAMON WAFFLES

▼ ▼ ▼

There are some people who believe that I add chocolate to most everything, and that is very nearly correct! I adore chocolate. So when I whip up these fast waffles I toss in a spoonful of cocoa and a handful of chocolate chips. I adore waffles almost as much as chocolate, and I love them together. Serve these for supper or breakfast with crisp bacon on the side and, if you're feeling really indulgent, banana slices and maple syrup on top.

TO PREP:
5 MINUTES
TO COOK:
18–24 MINUTES

Vegetable oil cooking spray,
    for misting the waffle iron
1¾ cups biscuit mix,
    such as Bisquick
2 tablespoons unsweetened cocoa
1¼ cups milk
1 large egg
2 tablespoons vegetable oil
Pinch of ground cinnamon
¼ cup miniature semisweet
    chocolate chips (see Tip)

1. Preheat an electric waffle iron (see box, page 445). Mist the top and bottom of the interior with vegetable oil cooking spray. Preheat the oven to 250°F (you'll use it to keep the waffles warm until they are all ready to serve).

2. Place the biscuit mix, cocoa, milk, egg, oil, and cinnamon in a large mixing bowl and stir to combine well. Fold in the chocolate chips and mix until they are just

tip If you don't have any miniature chocolate chips, simply place a small chunk of semisweet chocolate in a food processor and pulse a few times to create chocolate shavings.

incorporated. Ladle about ⅓ cup of the batter onto the hot waffle iron, spreading it out so that it almost but not entirely covers the bottom. Close the lid and cook the waffle for 3 to 4 minutes or until the light comes on to indicate that the waffle is done. The waffle is fully cooked when it does not stick to the top or bottom of the iron. Using a fork, transfer the waffle to a heatproof plate and place it in the oven to keep warm. Repeat with the remaining waffle batter.

MAKES 6 WAFFLES (6 INCHES EACH)

In the Mix

—▼—

DINNER DOCTOR SAYS

Don't stop with toppings. Adding a little something to the batter can make good waffles special. It doesn't need to take a lot of time. Here are ten quick waffle add-ins. All go with any of the waffles in this book, except for the last two suggestions, which go with the School Morning Waffles (page 444) or Crisp Cornmeal Waffles (page 442):

- ½ cup fresh blueberries
- ¼ teaspoon ground cinnamon; these waffles are tasty served topped with cut up plums that have been tossed with sugar
- ½ cup mashed banana
- 2 tablespoons crunchy peanut butter; serve these waffles topped with sliced bananas
- ½ teaspoon maple flavoring; for a very intense maple flavor, serve these waffles topped with melted butter and pure maple syrup
- ½ cup miniature chocolate chips
- ½ cup butterscotch chips and ¼ cup chopped pecans
- ½ cup white chocolate chips
- ½ cup pre-shredded Cheddar cheese and ¼ cup crumbled cooked bacon
- ½ cup pre-shredded Cheddar cheese and 2 tablespoons chopped scallions; top these waffles with sour cream and salsa

DESSERTS FROM THE DOCTOR

▼▼▼

Long before I wrote the first *Cake Mix Doctor* cookbook, I was frequently the person asked to bake the cake for family get-togethers. Okay, not only the cake—the pie, the brownies, the cookies . . . anything that required turning on the oven, mixing a batter, baking, and frosting. That was my department. I never complained because ever since I became tall enough to open the oven door without standing on a chair, I've enjoyed making desserts. I've learned that once you start baking, you just don't stop. Just ask anyone who contributes to the cakemixdoctor.com's message board. The more you bake, the more people eagerly anticipate your delectable layer cakes and sumptuous pies. And of course, with practice the results get better and better.

If you have never considered yourself much of a baker then you are in for a treat. These recipes all rely on doctoring cake mixes and are easy to prepare, with great results. If you turned to this chapter before you looked at anything else in the book because you, too, are a happy designated dessert maker, you'll find lots of goodies to add to your repertoire.

This chapter offers delicious doctored cake mixes that are my new favorites, desserts I just had to include, not only because they taste terrific but because I strongly believe everyone should occasionally set aside some time for baking. So when it's a rainy Saturday afternoon, stir up a luscious Easy Italian Cream Cake, Triple-Decker Peanut Butter Cake, or Orange Dreamsicle Layer Cake, to name just a few of the layer cakes you'll find here. But don't stop with layer cakes. Try some of my beloved Bundts, the Apple Spice Cake or The Best Pound Cake, for example. Or whip up a sheet cake like the Coconut Tres Leches Cake or the Fruit Cocktail Cake.

Do you want to break out of the cake mold? Use a frozen pie crust to prepare Bebe's Chocolate Cream Pie. Turn refrigerated crescent roll dough into Spiced Plum Pastries or bake a Fresh Peach Tart using frozen puff pastry. Both are elegant enough for a dinner party but simple enough for a weeknight dessert.

A brownie mix is the starting point for chewy chocolaty Brownie Drops, perfect for gift giving or the school bake sale. Finally, there's the venerable biscuit mix, Bisquick, at the heart of Wintertime Blackberry Cobbler and Butterscotch Pecan Saucepan Blondies. All the shortcuts in these recipes are no-brainers, and yet they provide subtle and easy ways to bake interesting and delectable desserts.

And, if you're looking for a fantastic, quick dessert you can throw together even on a hectic Monday or Tuesday evening, see the Weekday Wonders box on page 512.

Doctoring mixes to turn them into something special has been a favorite pastime of many for the last few decades. Whether you are new to the practice or eager for a fresh batch of recipes to try, be my guest.

LEMON POPPY SEED LAYER CAKE

WITH CREAMY LEMON FROSTING

▼ ▼ ▼

Few things are prettier than a bright yellow lemon cake, and there's no lemon cake more scrumptious than this one. The cake is loaded with lemon, since it's made with both lemon yogurt and lemon pudding. And it has another plus, the crunch of poppy seeds.

TO PREP:
10 MINUTES
TO BAKE:
25–30 MINUTES
TO COOL:
30 MINUTES
TO ASSEMBLE:
10 MINUTES

Its big, dense layers cry out for a substantial frosting—one made with cream cheese and full of fresh lemon juice and zest. You'll want to bake this cake for birthdays, luncheons, and anniversaries. It's truly cause for celebration.

CAKE:

Solid vegetable shortening,
for greasing the pans
All-purpose flour, for dusting the pans
1 package (18.25 ounces) plain lemon
cake mix (see Tips at right)
1 package (3.4 ounces) lemon instant
pudding mix
1 container (8 ounces) low-fat lemon
yogurt
½ cup vegetable oil
4 large eggs
2 tablespoons poppy seeds

tip **A medium-size lemon will give you about 2 tablespoons of juice and 2 teaspoons of grated zest so you will use about half the zest and some of the juice of the lemon. You'll get more juice from the lemon if it is at room temperature, not chilled.**

FROSTING:

1 package (8 ounces) reduced-fat
cream cheese, at room temperature
8 tablespoons (1 stick) butter,
at room temperature
About 4 cups confectioners' sugar, sifted
1 teaspoon grated lemon zest (see Tip at left)
2 teaspoons fresh lemon juice
(see Tip at left)

1. Place a rack in the center of the oven and preheat the oven to 350°F.

2. Lightly grease two 9-inch round cake pans with vegetable shortening, then dust them with flour. Shake out the excess flour. Set the pans aside.

3. Place the lemon cake mix, pudding mix, yogurt, oil, eggs, and poppy seeds in a large mixing bowl. Add ¾ cup of water, then beat with an electric mixer on low speed until the ingredients are moistened, 30 seconds. Stop the machine and scrape down the side of the bowl with a rubber spatula. Increase the mixer speed to medium and beat 2 minutes longer, scraping down the side again if necessary. The batter should be thick and well blended. Divide the batter evenly between the prepared pans, smoothing it

tips If you cannot find a lemon cake mix, you can use a yellow cake mix and add the leftover lemon juice to the cake batter.

When baking with cream cheese, remember that it must be soft in order for it to be beaten to make a fluffy frosting. If the cream cheese is straight out of the refrigerator, unwrap it and place it on a small microwave-safe plate. Microwave it on high power for 20 seconds and it will become soft.

Make sure that the other ingredients for the frosting—the butter and the lemon juice—are also at room temperature.

out with a rubber spatula. Place the pans in the oven side by side.

4. Bake the cakes until they are golden brown and spring back when lightly pressed with a finger, 25 to 30 minutes. Remove the cakes from the oven and place them on wire racks to cool for 10 minutes. Run a dinner knife around the edge of each cake and invert each one onto a rack, then invert them again onto another rack so that the cakes are right side up. Allow the cakes to cool completely, 20 minutes longer.

5. Meanwhile, make the frosting: Place the cream cheese and butter in a large mixing bowl and beat them with an electric mixer on low speed until creamy, 30 seconds. Add 2 cups of the confectioners' sugar and the lemon zest and juice, then beat on low until the mixture is combined, 30 seconds. Add 1½ cups of the remaining confectioners' sugar and beat until smooth and spreadable, 30 seconds. Then, increase the mixer speed to high and beat, adding the remaining ½ cup of sugar a little at a time if necessary to make the frosting thickened and fluffy, 1 minute longer.

6. To assemble the cake, place one cake layer, right side up, on a cake plate and spread some of the frosting over the top. Place the second layer, right side up, on top of the first, then frost the top and side with the remaining frosting, using smooth, clean strokes.

SERVES 12

Store this cake, in a cake saver or under a glass dome, at room temperature for up to 3 days or in the refrigerator for up to 1 week. Or freeze it, in a cake saver, for up to 6 months. Thaw the cake overnight in the refrigerator before serving.

What You Need to Know to Bake Great Cakes

— ▼ —

That your oven thermostat is accurate: You need to be sure that the temperature you are setting your oven to will in fact be the temperature inside the oven. It may be off by as much as 50 degrees or more. To find out how accurate your oven thermostat is, buy an inexpensive oven thermometer; you'll find one at a kitchen shop or hardware store. Place the thermometer in your oven and set the temperature for 350°F. Check inside the oven after 10 minutes to see what temperature the thermometer registers (it should take about 10 minutes for the oven to reach 350°F). If the temperature inside the oven is not 350°F, the oven thermostat is not correctly calibrated. Contact an appliance specialist to have the thermostat recalibrated.

How to prepare a baking pan: For cakes that come out of the pan easily each and every time, grease your baking pans with vegetable shortening or spray them with cooking oil, then dust them with flour. It is especially important to use vegetable shortening when using those decorative Bundt pans that have lots of crevices.

How to tell when a cake is done: I have learned to rely on my senses when baking cakes in ovens I am not familiar with. If the oven has a window (and the window is clean enough), I keep the light on to watch for any early browning that may indicate the cake is baking faster than it should. When that happens, I reduce the oven's temperature by 25 degrees to slow the baking down. I use my nose to tell me when the eggs in the cake have cooked and it is almost done. And I use my sense of touch, pressing the top of the cake ever so lightly with a finger to see if it springs back. If it does, it's time to take the cake out of the oven. If the cake gives a bit, I give it another two to three minutes, then test it again.

FARMHOUSE CHOCOLATE POTATO CAKE

▼ ▼ ▼

Mashed potatoes can add depth and richness to a cake mix cake. But what if you don't have any mashed potatoes on hand? Use frozen ones plumped up with buttermilk. Devil's food cake never tasted so great.

TO PREP:
20 MINUTES
TO BAKE:
25–30 MINUTES
TO COOL:
30 MINUTES
TO ASSEMBLE:
10 MINUTES

CAKE:

Solid vegetable shortening, for greasing
the pans
All-purpose flour, for dusting the pans
1 cup firmly packed frozen mashed
potatoes, such as Ore-Ida
Just Add Milk (see Tips)
1⅓ cups buttermilk
1 package (18.25 ounces)
plain devil's food cake mix
½ cup vegetable oil
3 large eggs
1 teaspoon pure vanilla
extract

FROSTING:

12 tablespoons (1½ sticks) butter
½ cup unsweetened cocoa powder
½ cup whole milk
About 5½ cups confectioners' sugar,
sifted

1. Place a rack in the center of the oven and preheat the oven to 350°F.

2. Lightly grease two 9-inch round cake pans with vegetable shortening, then dust with flour. Shake out the excess flour.

3. Place the frozen mashed potatoes in a small glass mixing bowl. Stir in ⅔ of a cup of buttermilk and microwave on high power until the potatoes are hot, 2 minutes. Stir and set aside until cool, 5 minutes.

4. Place the remaining ⅔ cup of buttermilk in a large mixing bowl with the cake mix, oil,

eggs, vanilla, and the cooled mashed potatoes. Beat with an electric mixer on low speed until the ingredients are moistened, 30 seconds. Stop the machine and scrape down the side of the bowl with a rubber spatula. Increase the mixer speed to medium and beat for 2 minutes longer, scraping down the side of the bowl again if necessary. The batter should be smooth. Divide the batter evenly between the prepared pans, smoothing it out with a rubber spatula. Place the pans in the oven side by side.

5. Bake the cakes until they spring back when lightly pressed with a finger, 25 to 30 minutes. Remove the cakes from the oven and place them on wire racks to cool for 10 minutes. Run a dinner knife around the edge of each cake and invert them onto a rack, then invert them again onto another rack so that the cakes are right side up. Allow the cakes to cool completely, 20 minutes longer.

6. Meanwhile, make the frosting: Melt the butter in a medium-size saucepan over low heat, 2 to 3 minutes. Stir in the cocoa and milk. Cook 1 minute, stirring, until thickened and just beginning to boil. Remove from the heat. Stir in 5 cups of the confectioners' sugar, adding more if necessary, until the frosting is the consistency of a hot fudge sauce.

7. To assemble the cake, place one cake layer, right side up, on a cake plate and, working quickly so that the frosting does not harden, ladle frosting over the cake to coat it smoothly. Place the second layer, right side up, on top of the first. Ladle frosting over the second layer to coat it smoothly. Using a long metal spatula, spread the warm frosting around the edge of the cake smoothly and evenly.

SERVES 12

Store this cake, in a cake saver or under a glass dome, at room temperature for up to 5 days. Or freeze it, in a cake saver, for up to 6 months. Thaw the cake overnight in the refrigerator before serving.

tips **To substitute homemade mashed potatoes, use 1 cup that has been warmed slightly so that the potatoes are soft enough to mix into the batter.**

Adding a pinch of cinnamon will bring out the chocolate flavor.

BUTTERNUT SQUASH LAYER CAKE

WITH MAPLE CREAM CHEESE FROSTING

▼ ▼ ▼

TO PREP: 10 MINUTES
TO BAKE: 20–30 MINUTES
TO COOL: 30 MINUTES
TO ASSEMBLE: 10 MINUTES

What the flavor of maple does to spice cake mix is sheer magic. And when you fold in puréed butternut squash the cake no longer resembles a mix. It turns into an earthy, moist layer cake with the flavors and colors of fall. Sprinkle toasted pecans over it and you have the perfect contrast of crunchy, salty, sweet, creamy, and spicy. I get hungry just thinking about it!

tip Chilling a cake with a cream cheese frosting until the frosting hardens slightly makes it easier to slice.

CAKE:

Solid vegetable shortening,
     for greasing the pans
All-purpose flour, for dusting the pans
1 package (18.25 ounces) plain
     spice cake mix
1 package (12 ounces; 1⅓ cups)
     frozen butternut squash purée,
     thawed but not drained
¼ cup vegetable oil
3 large eggs
1 teaspoon maple flavoring

FROSTING:

1 package (8 ounces) reduced-fat
     cream cheese, at room temperature
8 tablespoons (1 stick) butter,
     at room temperature
4 cups confectioners' sugar, sifted
½ teaspoon maple flavoring
½ teaspoon pure vanilla extract
½ cup chopped toasted pecans, for garnish

1. Place a rack in the center of the oven and preheat the oven to 350°F.

2. Lightly grease two 9-inch round cake pans with vegetable shortening, then dust them with flour. Shake out the excess flour. Set the pans aside.

3. Place the cake mix, squash purée, oil, eggs, and maple flavoring in a large mixing bowl. Beat with an electric mixer on low speed until the ingredients are moistened, 30 seconds. Stop the machine and scrape down the side of the bowl with a rubber spatula. Increase the mixer speed to medium and beat 2 minutes longer, scraping down the side again if necessary. The batter should be well blended. Divide the batter evenly between the prepared pans, smoothing it out with a rubber spatula. Place the pans in the oven side by side.

4. Bake the cakes until they are golden brown and spring back when lightly pressed with a finger, 25 to 30 minutes. Remove the cakes from the oven, and place them on wire racks to cool for 10 minutes. Run a dinner knife around the edge of each layer and invert each cake onto a rack, then invert them again onto another rack so that the cakes are right side up. Allow the cakes to cool completely, 20 minutes more.

5. Meanwhile, make the frosting: Place the cream cheese and butter in a large mixing bowl and beat with an electric mixer on low speed until creamy, 30 seconds. Add the confectioners' sugar, maple flavoring, and vanilla and beat on low until combined, 30 to 45 seconds. Increase the mixer speed to high and beat until the frosting is fluffy, 30 seconds longer.

6. To assemble the cake, place one cake layer, right side up, on a cake plate and spread some frosting over the top. Place the second layer, right side up, on the first, then frost the top and side of the cake with the remaining frosting, using smooth, clean strokes. Sprinkle the pecans over it. Refrigerate the cake, uncovered, until the frosting sets, 20 minutes, before serving.

SERVES 12

Store this cake, covered with waxed paper, in the refrigerator for up to 1 week. Or freeze it, in a cake saver, for up to 6 months. Thaw the cake overnight in the refrigerator before serving.

EASY ITALIAN CREAM CAKE

▼ ▼ ▼

Italian cream cake has been a favorite cake in the South for years and yet no one seems to know where the recipe came from. It seems more Southern than Italian to me, what with the pecans and coconut. Name aside, the three-layer cake is a knockout. To stream-line it, I began with a white cake mix and added buttermilk and all sorts of other good things. I covered it with a cream cheese frosting that's fla-vored with a tad of coconut flavoring to mirror the coconut in the cake. The result is delicious.

TO PREP:
20 MINUTES
TO BAKE:
22–27 MINUTES
TO COOL:
25 MINUTES
TO ASSEMBLE:
10 MINUTES

CAKE:

Solid vegetable shortening,
    for greasing the pans

All-purpose flour,
    for dusting the pans

3 large eggs, separated,
    plus 2 large egg whites

½ teaspoon cream of tartar

1 package (18.25 ounces) plain
    white cake mix

1 cup buttermilk

½ cup vegetable oil

1 teaspoon pure vanilla extract

1 cup sweetened flaked coconut

1 cup finely chopped pecans

FROSTING:

1 package (8 ounces) cream cheese,
    at room temperature

8 tablespoons (1 stick) butter,
    at room temperature

4 cups confectioners' sugar, sifted

½ teaspoon coconut flavoring

1. Place a rack in the center of the oven and preheat the oven to 350°F.

2. Lightly grease three 9-inch round cake pans with vegetable shortening, then dust them with flour. Shake out the excess flour. Set the pans aside.

3. Place the 5 egg whites and the cream of tartar in a medium-size mixing bowl. Beat with an electric mixer on high speed until stiff peaks form, 2 to 3 minutes. Set the egg whites aside.

4. Place the cake mix, 3 egg yolks, buttermilk, oil, and vanilla in a large mixing bowl and beat on low speed until blended, 1 minute. Stop the machine and scrape down the side of the bowl with a rubber spatula. Increase the mixer speed to medium and beat for 2 minutes longer, scraping down the side again if necessary. The batter should be well blended. Spoon the beaten egg whites onto the cake batter and, using a rubber spatula, fold them into the batter until the mixture is light but well blended. Gently fold in the coconut and pecans. Divide the batter evenly among the prepared pans, smoothing it out with a rubber spatula. Place the pans in the oven side by side or, if your oven is not large enough, place two on the center rack and the third pan in the center of the highest rack.

5. Bake the cakes until they spring back when lightly pressed with a finger, 22 to 27 minutes. Check the pan on the highest rack first, as it will bake the quickest and may need to be rotated to a lower rack while it bakes.

6. Remove the cakes from the oven and place them on wire racks to cool for 10 minutes. Run a dinner knife around the edge of each layer and invert each cake onto a rack, then invert them again onto another rack, so that the cakes are right side up. Allow the cakes to cool completely, 15 minutes longer.

7. Meanwhile, make the frosting: Place the cream cheese and butter in a large

tips **Not a coconut fan? Omit the coconut in the cake batter and the coconut flavoring in the frosting.**

A coconut devotee? After frosting the cake, sprinkle more sweetened flaked coconut over the top.

mixing bowl and beat with an electric mixer on low speed until creamy, 30 seconds. Add the confectioners' sugar and coconut flavoring and beat on low speed until the sugar is incorporated. Increase the mixer speed to high and beat until the frosting is fluffy, 1 minute longer.

8. To assemble the cake, place one cake layer, right side up, on a serving plate and spread some of the frosting over the top. Place a second layer, right side up, on top of the first. Spread some of the frosting over the top. Place the third layer, right side up, on top of the second layer, then frost the top smoothly and generously. Frost the side with smooth, clean strokes.

SERVES 12 TO 16

Store this cake, in a cake saver or under a glass dome, at room temperature for 1 day or in the refrigerator for up to 1 week. Or freeze it, in a cake saver, for up to 6 months. Thaw the cake overnight in the refrigerator before serving.

Trim the Tree Buffet

▼ ▼ ▼

Share the fun of trimming the Christmas tree with a group of friends, then admire the beautiful results as you nibble a selection of easy to prepare dishes. This menu will serve sixteen nibblers. Prepare two recipes of the Stack, if you wish, and serve the soup in demitasse cups.

Crab Fritters with Creole Mayonnaise
page 59

Soufléed Cheese and Onion Canapés
page 36

Blue Cheese, Pesto, and Tomato Stack
page 26

Pat's Mini Ham Biscuits
page 55

Black Bean Soup with Lemon Cream
page 88

Easy Italian Cream Cake
page 458

TRIPLE-DECKER PEANUT BUTTER CAKE

▼ ▼ ▼

L ucille Osborn is the talented chef behind the great-looking cakes I present on television's QVC. She takes my recipes and makes them look stupendous in front of the camera. Lucille had the clever idea to chop up Reese's peanut butter cups and sandwich them between the layers of my peanut butter cake, scattering a few more pieces on top. I have taken things a step further, covering the triple layer cake with a creamy peanut butter frosting, then garnishing it with whole peanut butter cups. Careful—the cake is addictive!

TO PREP:	**10 MINUTES**
TO BAKE:	**18–20 MINUTES**
TO COOL:	**25 MINUTES**
TO ASSEMBLE:	**10 MINUTES**

tip **You can also use chunky peanut butter or peanut butter with chocolate in it in place of the smooth.**

CAKE:

Vegetable oil cooking spray,
* for misting the pans*
All-purpose flour, for dusting
* the pans*
1 package (18.25 ounces) plain
* yellow cake mix*
⅓ cup smooth peanut butter (see Tip)
⅓ cup vegetable oil
3 large eggs
1 teaspoon pure vanilla extract

FROSTING:

38 bite-size Reese's peanut butter cups
4 tablespoons (½ stick) butter,
* at room temperature*
¼ cup smooth peanut butter
About 4 cups confectioners' sugar,
* sifted*
About ½ cup warm milk
2 teaspoons pure vanilla extract

1. Place a rack in the center of the oven and preheat the oven to 350°F.

2. Lightly mist three 9-inch round cake pans with vegetable oil cooking spray, then dust them with flour. Shake out the excess flour. Set the pans aside.

3. Place the cake mix, peanut butter, oil, eggs, and vanilla in a large mixing bowl. Add 1⅓ cups of water, then beat with an electric mixer on low speed until blended, 30 seconds. Stop the machine and scrape down the side of the bowl with a rubber spatula. Increase the mixer speed to medium and beat for 2 minutes longer, scraping down the side again if necessary. The batter should be well blended. Divide the batter evenly among the prepared pans, smoothing it out with a rubber spatula. Place the pans in the oven side by side or, if your oven is not large enough, place two on the center rack and the third pan in the center of the highest rack.

4. Bake the cakes until they spring back when lightly pressed with a finger, 18 to 20 minutes. Check the pan on the highest rack first, as it will bake the quickest and may need to be rotated to a lower rack while it bakes. Remove the cakes from the oven, and place them on wire racks to cool for 10 minutes. Run a dinner knife around the edge of each layer and invert each onto a rack, then invert them again onto another rack so that the cakes are right side up. Allow the cakes to cool completely, 15 minutes longer.

5. Meanwhile, place 28 of the peanut butter cups in the freezer for 15 to 20 minutes so that they will be easier to chop, then finely chop them and set aside with the whole peanut butter cups.

6. Make the frosting: Place the butter and peanut butter in a large mixing bowl and beat with an electric mixer on low speed until creamy, 30 seconds. Add 2 cups of the confectioners' sugar, ¼ cup of the milk, and the vanilla and beat on low until the mixture is combined, 30 seconds. Add 1½ cups of the remaining confectioners' sugar and the remaining ¼ cup milk and beat the frosting until it is smooth and spreadable, 30 seconds. Then, increase the mixer speed to high and beat, adding the remaining ½ cup of sugar a little at a time until the frosting is thickened and fluffy, 1 minute longer.

7. To assemble the cake, place one cake layer, right side up, on a serving plate and spread some of the frosting over the top. Press half of the chopped peanut butter cups into this frosting, distributing them evenly. Place a second cake layer, right side up, on top of the first. Spread some of the frosting over the top. Press the remaining chopped peanut butter cups into this frosting. Place the third cake layer, right side up, on top of the second layer, then frost the top smoothly and generously. Frost the side of the cake with smooth, clean strokes. Place the remaining whole peanut butter cups decoratively around the edge of the cake.

SERVES 12

Store this cake, in a cake saver or under a cake dome, at room temperature for up to 1 day or in the refrigerator for up to 4 days.

9 Ways to Become Known as the Dessert Diva

— ▼ —

DINNER DOCTOR SAYS

1. Butter is better. Bake with it whenever possible. If you have no butter, find a recipe that calls for oil. Use margarine when baking only if the recipe specifically calls for it.

2. Be a seasonal shopper. Buy fresh fruit when it's at its peak: peaches in the summer, pears and apples in the fall, cranberries and citrus fruits in the winter, strawberries in the spring. If you can get local fruit, all the better.

3. Choose chocolate, and mix different kinds. For example, drizzling a white or milk chocolate glaze over a decadent dark chocolate cake both looks and tastes great.

4. Go for lemon and other citrus flavors. A lemon cake or lime pie will chase away the blues on a gray day in no time.

5. Don't knock yourself out. If your Bundt cake is unadorned but delicious, people will line up for seconds.

6. Neatness counts. When you are frosting a cake, spread the frosting on with a long metal spatula, making it nice and sleek. Your cake will look positively elegant.

7. Don't be afraid to improvise. If the cobbler turned out to be tasty but unsightly, spoon it warm into bowls and top it with a lot of good ice cream. It will be all gone in no time.

8. Think portable: Invest in a cake saver with a handle so you can easily take cakes to friends and neighbors, to school, to work. Baking for others makes everyone feel good.

9. Share your recipes. Be generous and gracious.

ORANGE DREAMSICLE LAYER CAKE

▼▼▼

Bright orange inside, this tasty cake is a colossal three-tier showstopper. Dreamily moist, it pairs the delightful flavor of oranges with sweet coconut. A tube cake with this name appeared in my *Cake Mix Doctor,* but the one here uses an orange cake mix, giving it a more intense orange taste.

TO PREP:	
15 MINUTES	
TO BAKE:	
18–22 MINUTES	
TO CHILL:	
3 HOURS	
TO ASSEMBLE:	
10 MINUTES	

CAKE:

Vegetable oil cooking spray,
for misting the pans
All-purpose flour, for dusting
the pans
1 package (18.25 ounces) plain
orange cake mix
1 package (3 ounces) orange gelatin
⅓ cup vegetable oil
3 large eggs
1 teaspoon pure orange extract

FROSTING:

1 package (8 ounces) sour cream
1 cup sweetened flaked coconut
1¼ cups confectioners' sugar, sifted
½ cup fresh orange juice
1 container (8 ounces) frozen
whipped topping, thawed

1. Place a rack in the center of the oven and preheat the oven to 350°F.

2. Lightly mist three 9-inch round cake pans with vegetable oil cooking spray, then dust them with flour. Shake out the excess flour. Set the pans aside.

3. Place the cake mix, orange gelatin, oil, eggs, and orange extract in a large mixing bowl. Add 1¼ cups of water, then beat with an electric mixer on low speed until the ingredients are moistened, 30 seconds. Stop the machine and scrape down the side of the bowl with a rubber spatula. Increase the mixer speed to medium and beat, scraping down the side again if necessary, until the batter is well blended and smooth, 2 minutes longer. Divide the batter evenly among the prepared pans, smoothing it out with a rubber spatula. Place the pans in the oven side by side or, if your oven is not large enough, place two on the center rack and the third pan in the center of the highest rack.

4. Bake the cakes until they spring back when lightly pressed with a finger, 18 to 22 minutes. Check the pan on the highest rack first; it will bake the quickest and may need to be rotated to a lower rack while it bakes. Remove the pans from the oven and place them on wire racks to cool for 10 minutes. Run a knife around the edge of each and invert them onto a rack, then again onto another rack so that they are right side up. Allow the cakes to cool completely, 15 to 20 minutes longer.

tip **This cake is best made a day ahead of serving.**

5. Meanwhile, start making the frosting: Place the sour cream and coconut in a large bowl, stir to combine, and place in the refrigerator, uncovered, for 1 hour.

6. Remove the bowl with the sour cream from the refrigerator, add the confectioners' sugar and orange juice, and beat with an electric mixer on medium speed until well combined, 30 seconds. Fold the whipped topping into the frosting until just combined.

7. To assemble the cake, place one cake layer, right side up, on a cake plate and spread some of the frosting over the top. Place a second layer, right side up, on top of the first. Spread some of the frosting over the top. Place the third layer, right side up, on top of the second layer, then frost the top and side of the cake smoothly and generously. Place the cake in a cake saver and refrigerate it until well chilled, 2 hours.

SERVES 12

Store this cake, in a cake saver or under a glass dome, in the refrigerator for up to 1 week.

APPLE SPICE CAKE

▼▼▼

I dearly love this Bundt cake recipe from Diana Crawford. She submitted it to the on-line recipe contest of my newsletter, and it was the grand-prize winner. Her cake is moist and memorable. Bake it when Golden Delicious—or whatever your favorite—apples come to the market in the early fall. The apples sink down into the cake as it bakes. When you turn the cake out onto a plate, they form a soft and tempting crown. A bit of cinnamon and maple flavoring add just the pick-me-up the spice cake mix needs. Dust the cake with confectioners' sugar or, do as Diana does, and drizzle your favorite caramel ice cream topping on top.

TO PREP:
10 MINUTES
TO BAKE:
43–47 MINUTES
TO COOL:
20 MINUTES

Solid vegetable shortening,
for misting the pan
All-purpose flour, for dusting the pan
1 package (18.25 ounces) plain
spice cake mix
1 cup whole milk
10 tablespoons (1¼ sticks) butter, melted
⅓ cup vegetable oil
3 large eggs
2 teaspoons maple flavoring
1 large apple, peeled and sliced
(1 heaping cup)
¼ cup firmly packed light brown sugar
½ teaspoon ground cinnamon
1 tablespoon confectioners' sugar,
for dusting the cake, or your favorite
caramel syrup or icing, for serving

1. Place a rack in the center of the oven and preheat the oven to 350°F.

tip **Substitute 1 heaping cup of ripe but slightly firm pears for the apples and you'll have an equally delicious pear spice cake.**

2. Lightly grease a 12-cup Bundt pan with vegetable shortening, then dust it with flour. Shake out the excess flour. Set the Bundt pan aside.

3. Place the cake mix, milk, 8 tablespoons of the melted butter, oil, eggs, and maple flavoring in a large mixing bowl. Beat with an electric mixer on low speed until just combined, 30 seconds. Stop the machine and scrape down the side of the bowl with a rubber spatula. Increase the mixer speed to medium and beat 1 to 1½ minutes longer, scraping down the side again if necessary. The cake batter should be smooth and well blended. Pour half of the batter into the prepared Bundt pan and set the pan aside.

4. Place the apple, brown sugar, cinnamon, and the remaining 2 tablespoons of melted butter in a small mixing bowl and stir to combine. Spoon the apple mixture on top of the batter in the Bundt pan. Pour the remaining cake batter on top of the apple mixture, smoothing it out with a rubber spatula.

5. Bake the cake until it springs back when lightly pressed with a finger, 43 to 47 minutes. Remove the cake from the oven and place it on a wire rack to cool for 20 minutes. As the cake cools in the pan it will fall about 1 inch.

6. Carefully run a long, sharp knife around the edge of the cake, shake it gently to loosen it from the Bundt pan, then invert it onto a cake plate. Dust the top with confectioners' sugar or drizzle your favorite caramel syrup or icing on top. Slice and serve the cake while it's still a little warm.

SERVES 12

Store this cake, wrapped in aluminum foil or plastic wrap or in a cake saver, at room temperature for up to 1 week. Or freeze it, wrapped in aluminum foil, for up to 6 months. Thaw the cake overnight in the refrigerator before serving.

BLACKBERRY WINE CAKE

▼ ▼ ▼

Avery close friend of my mother used to make this cake for her, and I know many more people who are fond of the cake's moist texture; sweet, fruity flavor; and distinctive purplish color. You will find sweet blackberry wine in the kosher section of the liquor store, but blackberry gelatin is a bit more difficult to locate. I can't always find it in Nashville, so I tested the recipe with black raspberry and black cherry gelatin as well. They turned out to be good substitutes. Enjoy!

TO PREP:
10 MINUTES
TO BAKE:
43–48 MINUTES
TO REST:
20 TO 25 MINUTES
TO ASSEMBLE:
2 MINUTES

tip **Yes, you can bake this in a Bundt pan, too. It may bake a little faster as Bundts have more surface area than tube (angel food cake) pans.**

CAKE:

Solid vegetable shortening,
*   for greasing the pan*
All-purpose flour,
*   for dusting the pan*
½ cup finely chopped pecans

1 package (18.25 ounces) plain
*   white cake mix*
1 package (3 ounces) blackberry,
*   black raspberry, or black cherry gelatin*
1 cup blackberry wine
½ cup vegetable oil
4 large eggs

GLAZE:

1 cup confectioners' sugar, sifted
½ cup blackberry wine
8 tablespoons (1 stick) butter, melted

1. Place a rack in the center of the oven and preheat the oven to 325°F.

2. Lightly grease a 10-inch tube pan with vegetable shortening, then dust it with flour. Shake out the excess flour. Sprinkle the pecans evenly over the bottom of the tube pan. Set the tube pan aside.

3. Place the cake mix, gelatin, blackberry wine, oil, and eggs in a large mixing bowl. Beat with an electric mixer on low speed until just combined, 30 seconds. Stop the machine and scrape down the side of the bowl with a rubber spatula. Increase the mixer speed to medium and beat 2 minutes more, scraping down the side again if necessary. The batter should be thick and well blended. Pour the batter into the prepared tube pan, smoothing the top with a rubber spatula.

4. Bake the cake until it is light brown and springs back when lightly pressed with a finger, 43 to 48 minutes.

5. Meanwhile, prepare the glaze: Place the confectioners' sugar, blackberry wine, and butter in a small bowl and whisk to combine. Set the glaze aside.

6. Remove the Bundt pan from the oven and place it on a wire rack. Immediately pour half the glaze over the cake while it is still in the pan. The top of the cake will look quite wet. Let the cake rest in the pan 20 to 25 minutes so the glaze is absorbed by the cake. Run a long, sharp knife around the edge of the cake, give the pan a gentle shake, and invert the cake onto a rack, then invert it again onto a serving plate so that the cake is right side up. Pour the remaining glaze over the cake so that it drizzles down the sides, then slice and serve.

SERVES 12

Store this cake, covered in plastic wrap or in a cake saver, at room temperature for up to 1 week. Or freeze it, wrapped in aluminum foil, for up to 6 months. Thaw the cake overnight in the refrigerator before serving.

CHOCOLATE FUDGE RIBBON CAKE

▼ ▼ ▼

H ere's a rich Bundt cake for anyone who loves chocolate. The recipe has been a real hit on my Web site. It involves some pretty amazing—yet so easy— kitchen alchemy. You start out with a devil's food cake mix and spoon a mixture of cream cheese, butter, and sweetened condensed milk over it. When the cake comes out of the oven and is flipped out of the pan, a wonderful flanlike custard will be at the top. The final touch? A graceful chocolate glaze.

TO PREP:
15 MINUTES
TO BAKE:
48–52 MINUTES
TO COOL:
20 MINUTES
TO ASSEMBLE:
5 MINUTES

tip This cake with its custardy top is delicious without the glaze, too. A quick dusting with some confectioners' sugar and a small amount of cocoa makes a pretty topping.

CAKE:

Solid vegetable shortening,
*   for misting the pan*
All-purpose flour, for dusting the pan
1 package (8 ounces) cream cheese,
*   at room temperature*

2 tablespoons butter, at room temperature

1 tablespoon cornstarch

1 can (14 ounces) sweetened condensed milk

1 teaspoon pure vanilla extract

4 large eggs

1 package (18.25 ounces) plain devil's food
*   cake mix*

1⅓ cups buttermilk or water

½ cup vegetable oil

GLAZE:

½ cup semisweet chocolate chips

2 tablespoons butter

1 tablespoon light corn syrup

1. Place a rack in the center of the oven and preheat the oven to 350°F.

2. Lightly grease a 12-cup Bundt pan with vegetable shortening, then dust it with flour. Shake out the excess flour. Set the Bundt pan aside.

3. Place the cream cheese, butter, and cornstarch in a medium-size mixing bowl. Beat with an electric mixer on low speed until creamy, 30 seconds. Add the sweetened condensed milk, vanilla, and 1 of the eggs, and beat until smooth. Set the cream cheese mixture aside.

4. Place the cake mix, buttermilk, oil, and the remaining 3 eggs in a large mixing bowl and beat with an electric mixer on low speed until blended, 1 minute. Stop the machine and scrape down the side of the bowl with a rubber spatula. Increase the mixer speed to medium and beat 2 minutes longer, scraping down the side again if necessary. The batter should be well blended. Pour the batter into the prepared Bundt pan, smoothing it out with a rubber spatula. Spoon the cream cheese mixture evenly over the top of the batter but do not stir it in.

5. Bake the cake until it springs back when lightly pressed with a finger, 48 to 52 minutes. Remove the cake from the oven and place it on a wire rack to cool for 20 minutes.

6. Meanwhile, make the glaze: Place the chocolate chips, butter, and corn syrup in a small saucepan over low heat and stir until the chocolate and butter are melted and the glaze is smooth, 1 to 2 minutes.

7. Run a long, sharp knife carefully around the edge of the cake, shake it gently to loosen it from the Bundt pan, then invert it onto a cake plate. Pour or spoon the glaze over the top, then slice and serve.

SERVES 12

Store this cake, wrapped in plastic wrap or in a cake saver, at room temperature for up to 1 day or in the refrigerator for up to 1 week.

THE BEST POUND CAKE

▼ ▼ ▼

One of the things I remember most vividly from my childhood is a buttery, fragrant made-from-scratch pound cake cooling on the kitchen counter. My mother was a prolific baker and I thought about baking a lot—especially my mother's pound cake. So you will understand my skepticism when Carol McMillion said she had a pound cake recipe to share, one that began with a box of yellow cake mix. And one, she added, that had replaced the cake she made from scratch. I was intrigued, so I baked her cake for a family gathering and brought along a container of sweetened sliced fresh peaches to spoon on top. Let me tell you that my cousins liked the pound cake so well that they ate every crumb and didn't touch the peaches!

TO PREP:
15 MINUTES
TO COOL:
40 MINUTES
TO BAKE:
60–65 MINUTES

Solid vegetable shortening,
    for greasing the pan
1 cup all-purpose flour, plus more
    for dusting the pan
8 tablespoons (1 stick) butter,
    at room temperature
½ cup vegetable oil
1 cup sugar
5 large eggs
1 package (18.25 ounces) plain
    yellow cake mix
1 container (8 ounces) sour cream,
    at room temperature
1 cup evaporated milk
1 tablespoon pure vanilla extract

1. Place a rack in the center of the oven and preheat the oven to 350°F.

2. Lightly grease a 10-inch tube pan with vegetable shortening, then dust it with flour. Shake out the excess flour. Set the tube pan aside.

3. Place the butter and oil in a large mixing bowl and beat with an electric mixer on medium-low speed until **creamy, 1 minute. Add the sugar and** beat until creamy, 1 to 2 minutes longer. Add the eggs, 1 at a time, beating each until the yolks of the eggs have just been incorporated. Stop the machine and scrape down the side of the bowl with a rubber spatula. Add the cake mix, the 1 cup of flour, and the sour cream, evaporated milk, and vanilla. Increase the

Pound Cake Terrine

— ▼ —

DINNER DOCTOR SAYS

Let me introduce you to an old standby, a quickie dessert I make with just three ingredients—frozen pound cake, two pints of great ice cream that have been softened slightly, and store-bought chocolate sauce. I call it pound cake terrine, and it's a year-round sure-fire winner. To make a pound cake terrine, remove a frozen pound cake from its aluminum pan, cut it horizontally into thirds, and place the bottom piece back in the pan. Then spread one pint of the softened ice cream over the cake in the pan. Place a second piece of cake on top and spread the remaining pint of ice cream over it. Place the remaining piece of cake on top. Wrap the pound cake and ice cream well in aluminum foil. You'll need to allow at least an hour for the ice cream to freeze solid. To serve, cut the pound cake and ice cream into slices and drizzle warm chocolate sauce over them. The terrine will serve eight people. Since pound cake terrines can be frozen for up to one month, it's a great idea to keep one on hand for spur-of-the-moment entertaining.

There's no end to the ice cream possibilities you can use to make this treat. In the summer, blueberry and strawberry ice cream make a pretty combination, especially when topped with fresh berries. Or, go for butter pecan and peach ice cream and garnish the cake with sweetened peach slices. In the winter I like to make the terrine with chocolate and peppermint or with chocolate chip and mocha ice cream. Have fun experimenting.

mixer speed to medium and beat until the batter is thick and well blended, 1½ to 2 minutes longer, scraping down the side of the bowl again if necessary. Pour the batter into the prepared tube pan, smoothing it out with a rubber spatula.

4. Bake the cake until it is golden brown and springs back when lightly pressed with a finger, 60 to 65 minutes.

> *tip* **Both tube pans and Bundt pans have holes in the center. Bundt pans have fluted curving sides. The sides of a tube pan, sometimes referred to as an angel food cake pan, are straight. Tube pans sometimes come with removable bottoms.**

Remove the tube pan from the oven and place it on a wire rack to cool for 20 minutes. Run a dinner knife around the edge of the cake, shake it gently to loosen it, and invert it onto a rack, then invert it again onto another rack so that the cake is right side up. Allow the cake to cool completely, 20 minutes longer.

SERVES 12

Store this cake, loosely covered with plastic wrap or in a cake saver, at room temperature for up to 1 week. Or freeze it, wrapped in aluminum foil, for up to 6 months. Thaw the cake overnight in the refrigerator before serving.

COCONUT TRES LECHES CAKE

▼▼▼

During my frequent book tours to Texas I thought about *tres leches* cakes a lot. Texan Laura Teague got me started when she sent me her favorite recipe for the moist rich cake and asked if I could create a quicker version. I came up with a sturdy yellow cake that soaks up the ocean of liquid you pour over it. My version is drenched in evaporated milk, cream of coconut, and heavy cream. Incredibly flavorful, it's ideal for toting to potlucks and other gatherings, as it feeds a multitude. Don't skimp on the time required for cooling and chilling the cake—it's essential that the cake absorb all the liquid. *Tres leches* cakes are not traditionally made with coconut; you'll find instructions for a plain one in the Tips on the opposite page.

TO PREP:
15 MINUTES
TO BAKE:
32–34 MINUTES
TO COOL:
1 HOUR
TO CHILL:
2 HOURS

CAKE:

Vegetable oil cooking spray,
   for misting the baking dish
1 package (18.25 ounces) plain
   yellow cake mix
1 package (3.4 ounces) vanilla
   instant pudding mix
1 cup milk
1 cup vegetable oil
4 large eggs

MILK SYRUP:

1 can (15 ounces) cream of coconut
1 can (12 ounces) evaporated milk (see Tips)
1 cup heavy (whipping) cream
1 teaspoon pure vanilla extract
1 tablespoon rum (optional)

GARNISHES (OPTIONAL):

2 medium-size bananas
2 cups Sweetened Cream
   (see the box on page 478)
1 cup sweetened flaked coconut, toasted
   (see Tips)

1. Place a rack in the center of the oven and preheat the oven to 350°F.

2. Lightly mist a 13-by-9-inch baking dish with vegetable oil cooking spray. Set the baking dish aside.

3. Place the cake mix, pudding mix, milk, oil, and eggs in a large mixing bowl. Beat with an electric mixer on low speed until combined, 1 minute. Stop the machine and scrape down the side of the bowl with a rubber spatula. Increase the mixer speed to medium and beat 2 minutes longer, scraping the side

tips Once the cake is baked, you can toast the coconut: Spread it out on a rimmed baking sheet and bake it at 350°F until golden brown, 7 minutes.

For a plain, unadulterated *tres leches* cake, use one can (14 ounces) sweetened condensed milk instead of the cream of coconut. Omit the bananas and toasted coconut and serve the cake with whipped cream. (If you have access to a Latin market, substitute *cajeta,* which is sweetened caramelized goat's milk, for the cream of coconut.)

down again if necessary. The batter should be well blended. Pour the batter into the prepared baking dish, smoothing it out with a rubber spatula.

4. Bake the cake until it is golden brown and springs back when lightly pressed with a finger, 32 to 34 minutes. Remove the cake from the oven and place it on a wire rack to cool completely, 1 hour. (If you are toasting the coconut, don't turn off the oven.)

5. Meanwhile, make the milk syrup: Whisk together the cream of coconut, evaporated milk, cream, vanilla, and rum, if using, in a medium-size bowl.

6. Pierce the cooled cake all over the top with the tines of a fork or a thin wooden skewer. Using a large spoon or ladle, spoon some of the milk syrup over the cake. Let the syrup soak into the cake, then continue spooning the syrup on top until all of it has been used up. When you have finished, not all of the syrup will be completely absorbed but that's okay. Cover the cake loosely with plastic wrap and refrigerate it until all of the syrup is absorbed, 2 hours.

7. Cut the bananas, if using, crosswise into ¼-inch slices. Slice the cake and serve it with the sliced bananas, Sweetened Cream, and toasted coconut, if desired.

SERVES 16 TO 20

Store this cake, loosely covered with plastic wrap, in the refrigerator for up to 1 week.

Sweetened Cream

—▼—

DINNER DOCTOR SAYS Chill a large mixing bowl and a pair of electric mixer beaters for 15 minutes. Pour 1 cup of heavy (whipping) cream into the chilled bowl and, using the chilled beaters, beat it on high speed until thickened, 1½ minutes. Stop the machine and add ¼ cup of confectioners' sugar and ½ teaspoon of pure vanilla extract. Beat on high speed until stiff peaks form, 1 to 2 minutes longer.

Makes 2 cups of Sweetened Cream

FRUIT COCKTAIL CAKE

▼ ▼ ▼

Mary Hill proudly shared this recipe with me; she has successfully simplified a popular made-from-scratch cake, so that now it's a snap to put together. The cake is moist because the coconut topping seeps down into it after it is baked. And your eyes are not deceiving you—there is no oil in this recipe. The fruit cocktail is a dandy substitute.

TO PREP:
10 MINUTES
TO BAKE:
35–40 MINUTES
TO ASSEMBLE:
2 MINUTES

CAKE:

Vegetable oil cooking spray,
*   for misting the baking dish*
1 can (15.25 ounces) fruit cocktail

> **tip** This cake is most delicious served warm. When it has cooled down, you can reheat squares in the microwave oven on high power for 15 seconds.

1 package (18.25 ounces)
*   plain white cake mix*
2 large eggs
½ cup firmly packed
*   light brown sugar*
½ cup finely chopped pecans or walnuts

TOPPING:

¾ cup granulated sugar
8 tablespoons (1 stick) butter
1 can (5 ounces) evaporated milk
1 package (7 ounces; about 1 cup)
*   sweetened flaked coconut*
Vanilla ice cream, for serving (optional)

1. Place a rack in the center of the oven and preheat the oven to 350°F.

2. Lightly mist a 13-by-9-inch baking dish with vegetable oil cooking spray. Set the baking dish aside.

3. Drain the fruit cocktail and place the juice in a large mixing bowl with the cake mix and eggs. Set aside the fruit cocktail.

Beat the cake mix with an electric mixer on low speed until moistened, 30 seconds. Stop the machine and scrape down the side of the bowl with a rubber spatula. Increase the mixer speed to medium and beat until the batter is well combined, 1 minute longer. Stir in the fruit cocktail. The batter will be quite thick. Turn the batter into the prepared baking dish, smoothing it out with a rubber spatula. Sprinkle the brown sugar and chopped nuts on top.

4. Bake the cake until it springs back when lightly pressed with a finger, 35 to 40 minutes.

5. Meanwhile, prepare the topping: Place the sugar, butter, and evaporated milk in a 2-quart saucepan. Bring to a boil over medium-high heat, stirring, 2 to 3 minutes. Remove the pan from the heat and stir in the coconut. Cover the pan to keep the topping warm.

6. As soon as the cake is removed from the oven, poke holes in it with the tines of a fork or a thin wooden skewer. Spoon the warm topping over the cake, allowing it to seep into the holes. Cut the warm cake into squares and serve with vanilla ice cream, if desired, or allow the cake to cool, then slice and serve.

SERVES 16 TO 20

Store this cake, covered in plastic wrap, at room temperature for up to 4 days.

VERY RASPBERRY CAKE

▼ ▼ ▼

My friend Elizabeth Rogers passed this recipe along to me, promising a cake that would be shockingly hot pink, beautiful, and brimming with raspberry flavor. And that it was. I have tinkered with her sheet cake recipe, including fresh raspberries in the frosting. The result is luscious, a salute to spring and summer or something to bake in midwinter to beat the blahs. More fresh raspberries make a pretty garnish. I suggest soaking them first in a little of the black raspberry liqueur Chambord.

TO PREP:
15 MINUTES
TO BAKE:
30–35 MINUTES
TO COOL:
20 MINUTES
TO ASSEMBLE:
10 MINUTES

CAKE:

Solid vegetable shortening,
    for greasing the baking dish
All-purpose flour, for dusting
    the pan
1 package (18.25 ounces) white cake mix
    with pudding
1 package (12 ounces) frozen unsweetened
    raspberries, thawed, with their juices
½ cup vegetable oil
¼ cup sugar
4 large eggs
1 teaspoon pure vanilla extract

RASPBERRY WHIPPED CREAM:

2 cups heavy (whipping) cream
4 to 5 tablespoons confectioners' sugar
1½ cups (6 ounces) fresh raspberries, mashed
1½ cups (6 ounces) fresh raspberries soaked
    in 1 tablespoon Chambord for
    20 minutes, for garnish (optional)

tips **You don't have to remove this cake from the baking dish. If you frost the top you can serve it right from the dish.**

If fresh raspberries are not in season in your area, frost the cake with sweetened whipped cream instead and garnish it with chocolate shavings.

1. Place a rack in the center of the oven and preheat the oven to 350°F.

2. Lightly grease a 13-by-9-inch baking dish with vegetable shortening, then dust it with flour. Shake out the excess flour. Set the baking dish aside.

3. Place the cake mix, raspberries with their juices, oil, sugar, eggs, and vanilla in a large mixing bowl. Add ¼ cup of water, then beat with an electric mixer on low speed until the ingredients are moistened, 30 seconds. Stop the machine and scrape down the side of the bowl with a rubber spatula. Increase the mixer speed to medium and beat until the batter is well blended, scraping down the side again if necessary, 2 minutes longer. Pour the batter into the prepared baking dish, smoothing it out with a rubber spatula.

4. Bake the cake until it springs back when lightly pressed with a finger, 30 to 35 minutes. Remove the cake from the oven and place it on a wire rack to cool completely, 20 minutes.

5. Meanwhile, prepare the raspberry whipped cream: Chill a large mixing bowl and a pair of electric mixer beaters for 15 minutes. Pour the cream into the chilled bowl and, using the chilled beaters, beat on high speed until soft peaks form, 2 to 3 minutes. Add the confectioners' sugar. Continue beating on high until stiff peaks form, 1 minute longer. Fold in the mashed raspberries, cover the bowl with plastic wrap, and place it in the refrigerator to chill, until the cake has cooled.

6. Run a dinner knife around the edges of the cake and invert it onto a rack. Invert the cake again onto a serving platter so that it is right side up. Frost the top and sides with the raspberry whipped cream, then garnish the cake with the fresh raspberries, if desired.

SERVES 16 TO 20

Store this cake, loosely covered with waxed paper, in the refrigerator for up to 4 days.

TARTS AND PIES

LULA'S COCONUT TARTS

▼ ▼ ▼

When I was a small child we lived on this idyllic street that we called a dead end but which I realize today is more eloquently called a cul-de-sac. It was a parents' dream

TO PREP:
15 MINUTES
TO BAKE:
24–27 MINUTES

because children could roam between yards and there was no cut-through traffic. Lula Estes, a gifted portrait artist and a generous person, still lives on the curve of the cul-de-sac, up on the hill. I continue to visit her even though I have moved many times since I lived nearby. Lula entertained my husband and me for dinner not too long ago, and she served these marvelous tarts, which she freezes and reheats in a toaster oven just before serving.

tips In the South you can buy unsweet-ened coconut, which you find in the freezer case. You can use sweetened flaked coconut from the baking aisle instead; cut the sugar back to 1¼ cups.

For an even more pronounced coco-nut flavor, use 3 tablespoons of cream of coconut instead of the heavy cream.

You can also substitute 1 table-spoon of fresh lemon juice for the vanilla extract. If you do, add the grated zest of 1 lemon, too.

Lula likes to bake her tarts very slowly, at 325°F, on the bottom rack of the oven, but I don't have the patience for this, so I've called for a faster, higher heat.

10 frozen 3½-inch tart shells

3 large eggs

1½ cups sugar

2 teaspoons pure vanilla extract

3 tablespoons heavy (whipping) cream

1½ cups flaked coconut (one 6-ounce bag),
*   preferably unsweetened (see Tips),*
*   thawed if frozen*

Vanilla or banana ice cream, for serving

1. Place a rack in the center of the oven and preheat the oven to 400°F.

2. Place the frozen tart shells, still in their aluminum foil pans, on a baking sheet and set aside.

3. Place the eggs, sugar, vanilla, and cream in a medium-size mixing bowl. Beat with a fork or a whisk until the mixture is lemon-colored and smooth. Fold in the coconut. Ladle the coconut mixture into the 10 tart shells, dividing it evenly among them and filling them two thirds full.

4. Bake the tarts until they are puffed and golden and the crusts have browned, 24 to 27 minutes. Remove the tarts from the oven and let them rest 2 to 3 minutes. Slide the tarts out of their foil pans and serve at once with ice cream or let cool and serve at room temperature.

MAKES 10 TARTS

Store these tarts, in a resealable plastic bag or plastic container, at room temperature for up to 3 days or in the refrigerator for up to 1 week. To freeze the tarts, leave them in their foil pans and wrap them well in aluminum foil, then place them in an airtight plastic container. They can be frozen for up to 3 months. To reheat the frozen tarts, place them in their foil pans in a toaster oven at 350°F and reheat until warmed through, 10 minutes.

FRESH PEACH TART

▼ ▼ ▼

TO PREP:
15 MINUTES
TO BAKE:
28–32 MINUTES

Who can pass up an incredibly easy to prepare dessert that brings ripe peaches and a sheet of frozen puff pastry together in a sublime summertime union? There's no fuss, no rolling out pastry here. Just unfold the frozen rectangle of puff pastry on a baking sheet, top it with peaches, sugar, and a touch of cinnamon if you like, and then bake the tart until the pastry puffs up beautifully. My family was wowed by this speedy dessert. I took a bow, then quickly sat down and joined them for a warm slab smothered in vanilla ice cream.

1 sheet frozen puff pastry dough
      (half of a 17.3-ounce package; see Tip),
      thawed for 20 minutes
2 cups sliced peaches (from 6 to 8 medium-
      size peaches)
⅓ cup sugar, reserve 1 tablespoon of the
      sugar for the topping
¼ teaspoon ground cinnamon (optional)
2 tablespoons butter (optional)
Vanilla ice cream or heavy (whipping) cream,
      for serving

1. Place a rack in the center of the oven and preheat the oven to 400°F.

2. Place the puff pastry sheet on an ungreased baking sheet and set aside.

3. Peel and slice the peaches. Place the sliced peaches, sugar, and cinnamon, if using, in a small bowl and stir to combine. Spoon the peaches into the center

tip   Frozen puff pastry is found in supermarket cases along with frozen pie pastry. Pepperidge Farm is the most common brand. Packages contain two sheets. You can use one sheet and return the other to the freezer, or you can simply double this recipe and enjoy the leftovers.

of the puff pastry, leaving a 1-inch border around the edges. Dot the top of the peaches with butter, if using. Gently fold the edges of the puff pastry up around the peaches. Sprinkle the pastry and peaches with the reserved 1 tablespoon of sugar.

4. Bake the tart until the pastry puffs up around the edges and is well browned, 28 to 32 minutes. Remove the tart from the oven and let cool slightly, about 5 minutes. Slice the tart into rectangular pieces. Serve the tart in shallow bowls, topped with vanilla ice cream or a drizzling of heavy cream.

SERVES 6 TO 8

Store this tart, lightly covered with plastic wrap, at room temperature for up to 4 days.

Tart Variations

—▼—

DINNER DOCTOR SAYS

Try substituting 1 cup of fresh blueberries for 1 cup of the peaches.

Sprinkle ¼ cup of finely chopped pecans on top of the tart before baking it.

Omit the cinnamon and add nutmeg—or nothing at all.

Sprinkle ¼ cup of fresh raspberries and another 1 tablespoon of sugar on top of the peaches before baking the tart.

Drain the peaches and sugar mixture well. Spread the pastry with lemon curd, then top it with the peaches.

BANOFFEE TART

▼ ▼ ▼

When my family and I lived in England, Pat Banks, a dear friend, used to invite us for dinner. The conversation was always lively, the oven-baked salmon was memorable, and her signature banoffee pie became one of my husband's favorite desserts. Beloved by the British, the pie is made with caramelized sweetened condensed milk that's layered in a pie shell with sliced bananas and topped with whipped cream (banana

TO PREP:
35–40 MINUTES
TO BAKE:
10–12 MINUTES

plus toffee equals *banoffee*). But while the method for caramelizing canned milk is far too time-consuming, my method of microwaving the milk in a bowl ensures perfect results and fits my busy timetable. So does starting with a frozen pie crust. The results are fantastic; even Pat would approve.

1 frozen or refrigerated 9-inch
  pie crust
1 can (14 ounces) sweetened
  condensed milk
1 container (18 ounces) frozen
  whipped topping, thawed
½ cup sour cream
½ teaspoon pure vanilla extract
5 small ripe bananas
Ground cinnamon, for dusting the tart

1. Place a rack in the center of the oven and preheat the oven to 400°F.

2. Unwrap the pie crust and let it thaw, if frozen, 10 to 15 minutes, while the oven preheats. Carefully lift the crust out of its

tips If you want to use real whipped cream, by all means go ahead and use it instead of whipped topping. You won't need to add the sour cream in this case. See the recipe for Sweetened Cream, page 478.

This recipe was tested in a 650-watt microwave oven. Depending upon the power of your oven, you may have to decrease or increase the cooking times. Consult the manufacturer's instructions.

aluminum foil pan and transfer it to a 9-inch tart or pie pan that is about 1 inch deep. Gently press the crust into the side of the pan. The crust will not quite reach the top edge. Prick the bottom and side of the crust with a fork. Bake the crust until it is golden brown, 10 to 12 minutes. Remove the crust from the oven and place on a wire rack to cool, 10 to 15 minutes.

3. Meanwhile, pour the sweetened condensed milk into a 2-quart microwave-safe bowl. Microwave it on medium (50 percent) power for 4 minutes, stopping the microwave and stirring halfway through. Decrease the power to medium-low (30 percent) and microwave the milk for 14 minutes, stirring it well every 2 minutes. As it cooks the milk will become thick and light brown; when done it will be puddinglike in consistency. Remove the bowl from the microwave and let the milk cool at room temperature for 5 minutes. Use a rubber spatula or a big metal spoon to spread the caramelized milk over the bottom of the cooled crust and set aside. Don't wait too long to do this or the milk will stiffen and become hard to work with.

4. Place the whipped topping, sour cream, and vanilla in a medium-size mixing bowl and gently stir to combine. Peel the bananas and slice them in half lengthwise. Starting at the outer edge of the tart pan, arrange as many banana halves as will fit around the perimeter. The halves should be as close together as possible and the curve of the bananas should follow the curve of the pan. Arrange a second ring of banana halves next to the first, cutting them if necessary to make them fit. Cut the remaining banana halves into pieces and use these to fill the center of the tart pan (you may have a few pieces left over). Spread the whipped topping mixture on top of the bananas and dust the top of the tart with cinnamon.

5. Slice and serve the tart within 2 hours of preparation, if possible. If not serving the tart within 1 hour, refrigerate it loosely covered with plastic wrap. The bananas will darken slightly the longer the tart keeps.

SERVES 8

Caramel

—▼—

DINNER DOCTOR SAYS

Caramel has long been a popular flavor for desserts—in pies, cheesecakes, cookies, and frostings. When you caramelize sweetened condensed milk, a reaction takes place between the milk protein and the sugar, and the liquid cooks out. As the milk cooks down it becomes thicker and more golden in color, and the flavor deepens, taking on a more buttery taste. The caramel makes a delicious sandwich cookie filling or you can add dollops of it to the batter of your next batch of chocolate chip cookies.

The people at Eagle Brand condensed milk warned me to never heat an unopened can of milk in the oven or in a pan of boiling water because the can could explode. But there are safe ways to caramelize sweetened condensed milk. Here are two. Once made, use the caramel immediately.

In the oven: Pour a can of sweetened condensed milk into a 9-inch pie pan. Cover the pan with aluminum foil and place this in a larger shallow pan. Fill the larger pan with hot water to a depth of 1 inch, and bake at 425°F until the milk is thick and caramel colored, about 1½ hours.

On the stovetop: Pour a can of sweetened condensed milk into the top of a double boiler placed over simmering water. Let the milk simmer, uncovered, for 1 to 1½ hours, until thick and caramel colored.

BANANA BREAD PIE

▼ ▼ ▼

After forking into this custardy banana pie one evening, my family agreed that it was like a cross between banana bread and pie. And that's how it got it's name. It's really a takeoff on one of those marvelous Bisquick "impossible" pies (for savory "impossible" pies, see pages 245 through 249). Although the crustless pie is delicious cold, my family likes it best warm from the oven, with a spoonful of vanilla ice cream melting over the top.

TO PREP:
15 MINUTES
TO BAKE:
25–30 MINUTES
TO REST:
30 MINUTES

Vegetable oil cooking spray,
    for misting the pan
2 very ripe medium-size bananas
    (see Tip), sliced
½ cup biscuit mix, such as Bisquick
2 large eggs
1 can (14 ounces) sweetened
    condensed milk
1 tablespoon butter,
    melted
1 teaspoon pure vanilla
    extract

Vanilla ice cream or Sweetened Cream
    (page 478), for serving

1. Place a rack in the center of the oven and preheat the oven to 400°F.

2. Mist a 9-by-1¼-inch pie pan with vegetable oil cooking spray. Set the pie pan aside.

3. Place the bananas in a large mixing bowl and beat them with an electric

> **tip** As with most baked goods made with bananas, the riper the fruit, the better the flavor. Use bananas that are too soft to eat out of hand.

mixer on low speed until they are smooth, 1 minute. You should have 1 cup of banana purée. Stop the machine and add the biscuit mix, eggs, condensed milk, butter, and vanilla. Beat on low speed until the ingredients are well blended, 1 to 1½ minutes longer. Using a rubber spatula, scrape the batter into the prepared pie pan and smooth the top.

4. Bake the pie until it is well caramelized on top and firm around the edge but still a little soft in the center, 25 to 30 minutes. Remove the pie from the oven and let it rest 30 minutes before slicing. Serve it warm with vanilla ice cream or chilled with Sweetened Cream.

SERVES 8

Store this pie, covered in plastic wrap, at room temperature for a day or in the refrigerator for up to 4 days.

15 Items to Stock in Your Emergency Baking Pantry

—▼—

DINNER DOCTOR SAYS

1. Bisquick baking mix

2. Devil's food cake mixes, both with and without pudding

3. Plain German chocolate cake mix

4. Plain brownie mix

5. Plain yellow cake mix

6. Plain white cake mix

7. Plain lemon cake mix

8. Plain spice cake mix

9. Bran muffin mix

10. Quick-cooking oatmeal

11. Sweetened flaked coconut

12. Instant pudding mix, vanilla and chocolate

13. Chocolate chips

14. Evaporated milk

15. Sweetened condensed milk

Doctoring
Frozen Pumpkin Pies

— ▼ —

DINNER DOCTOR SAYS

My friend Beth Meador, who is a purist about many recipes, confessed to me one night that she doesn't bake her own pumpkin pies. "Why bother when the frozen pies are so good?" she said. So, I watched as she prepared a frozen pie for the oven—she sprinkled the top with cinnamon and sugar before baking it—and that was that. Doctoring pumpkin pies couldn't be easier and the results are delicious. Here are some toppings that are quick to put together.

Streusel topping: While the pie is baking, combine 2 tablespoons of flour, 2 tablespoons of light brown sugar, 2 tablespoons of room temperature butter, and ½ cup of chopped pecans. About 10 minutes before the pie will be done, remove it from the oven and sprinkle the streusel evenly over the top. Return the pie to the oven and bake it until the streusel has browned, another 10 to 15 minutes.

Orange streusel topping: Follow the directions for the streusel topping above and add 1 teaspoon of grated orange zest to the streusel mixture.

Maple walnut streusel topping: Follow the directions above for plain streusel topping but substitute chopped walnuts for the pecans and add ½ teaspoon of maple flavoring.

Cream cheese cinnamon swirl topping: Unwrap a 3-ounce package of cream cheese and place it on a microwave-safe plate. Microwave the cream cheese on high power until it is soft, 10 seconds. Fold in 2 tablespoons of light brown sugar and ½ teaspoon of ground cinnamon. About 20 minutes before the pie is done, remove it from the oven and dollop the cream cheese mixture on top. Using a fork, gently swirl the cream cheese into the pie. Return the pie to the oven and bake it until done.

Apple and pecan topping: Open a can of apple pie filling and measure out ½ cup. Reserve the remaining filling for another use. About 20 minutes before the pie is done, remove it from the oven and spoon the apple filling around the edges. Scatter 2 tablespoons of chopped pecans over the apple filling. Return the pie to the oven and bake it until done.

ORANGE CRUMBLE PUMPKIN PIE

▼ ▼ ▼

Creamy, crunchy, and no fuss, this pie brings together flavors you might not have expected, but canned pumpkin and orange zest turn out to be a natural combination. Sweeten and spice them and add a handful of nuts and you have a cross between a pumpkin and a pecan pie with just a hint of orange. I speed up this recipe by using a refrigerated pie crust, which I place in my own pie pan. No one will ever know the crust isn't homemade.

| TO PREP: |
| 12 MINUTES |
| TO BAKE: |
| 57–63 MINUTES |

PIE:

1 refrigerated 9-inch pie crust

1 can (15 ounces) solid pack pumpkin

1 cup milk

2 large eggs

⅔ cup firmly packed light brown sugar

1 tablespoon all-purpose flour

1 teaspoon pumpkin pie spice

½ teaspoon salt

TOPPING:

⅔ cup pre-chopped pecans

½ cup firmly packed light brown sugar

1 teaspoon grated orange zest

1 teaspoon light corn syrup

Whipped cream, for serving (optional)

1. Place a rack in the center of the oven and preheat the oven to 375°F.

2. Carefully place the pie crust in a 9-inch pie pan and press it in place. Fold the edge under and crimp it or press down along the top edge with a fork. Prick the bottom

tip To make the topping in a food processor, add the pecans first and pulse, then add the brown sugar, orange zest, and corn syrup and pulse until combined.

and side of the crust with a fork. Bake the crust until it just begins to brown, 7 to 8 minutes. Remove the crust from the oven and place it on a wire rack to cool. Leave the oven on.

3. Meanwhile, place the pumpkin, milk, eggs, brown sugar, flour, pumpkin pie spice, and salt in a large mixing bowl. Beat with a fork or with an electric mixer on low speed until just combined. Pour the pumpkin filling into the cooled crust and return the pie to the oven. Bake the pie until it has nearly set, 40 minutes.

4. Meanwhile, make the topping: Place the pecans, brown sugar, orange zest, and corn syrup in a small bowl and beat with a fork to combine. After the pie has baked for 40 minutes sprinkle the pecan mixture evenly over the top. If the crust looks too brown, cover the crust edge with strips of aluminum foil. Then, return the pie to the oven to bake until set, 10 to 15 minutes longer. Remove the pie from the oven and place it on a wire rack to cool completely. Slice the pie and serve it with whipped cream, if desired.

SERVES 8

Store this pie, covered with plastic wrap or aluminum foil, in the refrigerator for up to 1 week.

BEBE'S CHOCOLATE CREAM PIE

▼ ▼ ▼

The South is famous for its "meat-and-three" restaurants where you order meat and three vegetables and try to save some room for a piece of cream pie for dessert. The triumvirate of cream pies consists of chocolate, coconut, and banana. Each has a filling of pudding that's piled on a flaky crust and topped with a tall meringue. My mother was such a fan of chocolate cream pie that she made her own. I fondly recall her standing at the stove slowly stirring chocolate filling so

TO PREP:
25 MINUTES
TO BAKE:
22–27 MINUTES
TO REST:
30 MINUTES

that it wouldn't form lumps or scorch. As her life grew more hectic we noticed that she stopped making the pudding from scratch, reaching instead for the chocolate pudding mix and doctoring it with more chocolate, butter, and a little vanilla. Here is her wonderful and fast recipe, sure to please the cream pie lovers at your house.

1 frozen deep-dish 9-inch pie crust

1 package (3.4 ounces) cook-and-serve chocolate pudding mix

2 cups milk

½ cup semisweet chocolate chips

2 tablespoons unsalted butter

1 teaspoon pure vanilla extract

3 large egg whites

¼ teaspoon cream of tartar

6 tablespoons sugar

> *tip* Before baking the crust, you can transfer it to your own deep-dish pie pan if you like. Once the crust has thawed, carefully lift it out of its aluminum foil pan, then press it into place in your pie pan with your fingers; press down all along the top edge with a fork.

tips **It is important when making a meringue pie to work quickly so that the meringue is spread on top of a warm filling. And you need to be sure the filling reaches all the way to the crust so that the meringue has something to hold onto and does not shrink away from the edge as it cools.**

Of course, if you'd rather "cream" it up, top the pie with Sweetened Cream (page 478).

1. Place a rack in the center of the oven and preheat the oven to 400°F.

2. Unwrap the frozen pie crust and let it thaw for 10 to 15 minutes while the oven preheats. Prick the bottom and side of the thawed crust with a fork. Bake the crust until it is lightly browned all over, 10 to 12 minutes. Remove the pie crust from the oven and place it on a wire rack to cool, 10 to 15 minutes. Lower the oven temperature to 350°F.

3. Meanwhile, place the pudding mix and the milk in a 2-quart saucepan over medium-high heat.

Whisk constantly until the mixture comes to a boil and thickens, 4 to 5 minutes. Turn off the heat. Add the chocolate chips, butter, and vanilla and stir until the butter and chocolate chips melt, 2 minutes. Spread the filling in the cooled pie crust and smooth the top with a rubber spatula. Set the filled pie crust aside.

4. Place the egg whites and cream of tartar in a large mixing bowl. Beat with an electric mixer on high speed until soft peaks form, 2 to 3 minutes. Add the sugar, 1 tablespoon at a time, beating on high, until stiff peaks form, 3 minutes longer. Spoon the meringue onto the warm filling. With a spatula, smooth the meringue, making sure it touches the crust to seal the pie and prevent it from shrinking.

5. Bake the pie until the meringue is lightly browned, 12 to 15 minutes. Remove the pie from the oven, let it rest for at least 30 minutes, then slice and serve.

SERVES 8

Store this pie, in a pie saver or covered loosely with wax paper, in the refrigerator for up to 1 week.

BLUEBERRY LEMON YOGURT NO-BAKE PIE

▼ ▼ ▼

If the mercury is rising and you can't bear to turn on the oven, try this no-bake blueberry pie. It starts with lemon yogurt and sweetened condensed milk thickened with a little gelatin, and it's covered with loads of fresh blueberries. Piled into a graham cracker crust from the supermarket and sprinkled with confectioners' sugar, the pie is bright, fresh and easy—exactly what summertime is all about.

TO PREP:
10 MINUTES
TO CHILL:
1¼ HOURS

1 can (14 ounces) sweetened condensed milk

1 cup low-fat lemon yogurt

1 teaspoon grated lemon zest (see Tips)

2 tablespoons fresh lemon juice (see Tips)

1 envelope (.4 ounce) unflavored gelatin

1 store-bought graham cracker crust
 (9 ounces; see Tips)

1 pint fresh blueberries, rinsed and drained

1 tablespoon confectioners' sugar

tips One medium-size lemon will give you what you need for this pie—2 tablespoons of juice and more than enough grated zest. For perfect zest with no bitter white pith, grate a rinsed lemon with a Microplane grater.
  Be sure you buy a 9-ounce graham cracker crumb crust, not a 6-ounce one.

1. Place the condensed milk, yogurt, and lemon zest and juice in a large mixing bowl and stir to combine. Set the filling aside.

2. Place 2 tablespoons of water in a small heatproof bowl and sprinkle the gelatin over it. Without stirring, let the gelatin soften 1 minute. Meanwhile, pour water to a depth of 1 inch into a skillet and bring to a simmer over medium-high heat. When the water is quite hot, turn off the heat and place the bowl of gelatin in the skillet. Stir the gelatin until it dissolves. Whisk the dissolved gelatin into the lemon yogurt filling. Cover the bowl with plastic wrap and place it in the refrigerator to chill for 15 minutes.

3. When the filling has chilled and has begun to set, using a rubber spatula, scrape it into the graham cracker crust and smooth the top. Arrange the blueberries evenly over the top. Lightly cover the pie with plastic wrap and chill until set, 1 hour. Just before serving, sift the confectioners' sugar over the top.

SERVES 8

Store this pie, covered with plastic wrap, in the refrigerator for up to 1 week.

The History of Sweetened Condensed Milk

— ▼ —

DINNER DOCTOR SAYS

What do lemon icebox pie and the Alamo have in common? Well, you can't make the classic pie without sweetened condensed milk, and the man who wrote the immortal words "Remember the Alamo!" was also the inventor of condensed milk.

Gail Borden Jr. was a man of many interests. He penned that famous motto when he was a newspaperman reporting about the attack on the Alamo (he also helped write the constitution for the state of Texas). But, at a time when there was no refrigeration, it was Borden's interest in food preservation that would make his name a household word. After witnessing the deaths of children who drank raw milk from diseased cows during the long voyage across the Atlantic, Borden was determined to figure out how to make milk safer. He came up with a way to remove the water based on a method the Shakers had used for extracting water from fruit juice. He then added sugar to milk to retard spoilage and received the first patent for sweetened condensed milk in 1856.

Borden's milk fed Union troops during the Civil War. Hoping to convey an image of wholesomeness, Borden named his sweetened condensed milk Eagle Brand, after the national bird. When refrigeration became more common, pasteurized fresh milk replaced the canned kind. However, during World War II, when sugar was scarce on the home front, Eagle Brand milk was frequently used in desserts, such as lemon icebox pie. And Borden's name is now firmly linked with the American icon, Elsie the Cow.

FROZEN MUD PIE

▼ ▼ ▼

One of the very easiest pies to make, this "mud pie" takes only eight minutes to throw together. It's a freezer pie and will surely become a favorite of your children . . . and you, too, of course. And it's great when company is coming, since just about everyone loves an ice cream pie. The crust is made of crushed Oreos, filling and all. The flavor of the ice cream that you use is up to you (I've listed some of my favorites). And you choose the topping, too—whipped cream, hot fudge, or fresh berries are all scrumptious.

TO PREP:
8 MINUTES
TO CHILL:
30 MINUTES
TO FREEZE:
ABOUT 45 MINUTES

tip **To crush the cookies, pulse them in a food processor or buy already-crushed chocolate sandwich cookies.**

1½ cups crushed chocolate
    sandwich cookies, such as
    Oreos (15 cookies; see Tip)
4 tablespoons (½ stick) butter,
    melted

2 pints mint chocolate chip, mocha,
    chocolate almond, or Moose Tracks
    ice cream
¼ cup chocolate syrup
1 cup Sweetened Cream
    (½ recipe, page 478; optional)
Hot fudge sauce (optional)
Fresh berries (optional)

1. Place the cookie crumbs and butter in a small mixing bowl and stir to combine. Press the crust mixture into the bottom of an ungreased 9-inch glass or ceramic pie pan, taking care to distribute it evenly so there is crust all the way up the side of the

pie pan. Chill the crust, uncovered, in the refrigerator for 30 minutes.

2. About 15 minutes before the crust has finished chilling, remove the ice cream from the freezer to soften it slightly.

3. Spoon 1 pint of the ice cream into the crust, smoothing the top evenly. Drizzle 2 tablespoons of the chocolate syrup over the ice cream. Spoon the second pint of ice cream on top of the syrup, smoothing the top evenly. Drizzle the remaining 2 tablespoons of chocolate syrup over the top. Loosely cover the pie pan with plastic wrap and freeze until the ice cream is firm, 45 minutes to 1 hour.

4. Remove the pie from the freezer 10 minutes before serving. Garnish each serving with a dollop of Sweetened Cream, hot fudge sauce, or berries, if desired.

SERVES 8

Store this pie, covered in plastic wrap or aluminum foil, in the freezer for up to 2 weeks.

THREE BERRY ANGEL FOOD LOAVES

▼ ▼ ▼

Judi Bowen's frozen strawberry angel food cake was so good she was named one of four finalists in my first on-line newsletter recipe contest. A recipe of her mother's, it calls for baking an angel food cake from a mix, then tearing the cake into pieces and freezing it with ice cream and berries. The cake easily feeds a crowd. But what if you don't need to serve that many at once? I've played a bit with the recipe, dividing it into two loaves instead of making one big cake. And I've taken advantage of fresh summer fruit and added raspberries and blueberries to the mix.

TO PREP:
20 MINUTES
TO FREEZE:
4 HOURS
OR OVERNIGHT

1 package (3 ounces) strawberry
  gelatin
1 cup hot water
1 cup finely chopped fresh strawberries
  (from 8 very large berries; see Tip)
1 cup chopped fresh raspberries
  (6 ounces; see Tip)
1 heaping cup fresh blueberries
1 angel food cake, made from 1 package
  (16 ounces) angel food cake mix,
  torn into bite-size pieces
½ gallon vanilla ice cream,
  softened at room temperature
  for 10 minutes
Fresh mint sprigs, for garnish

1. Line two 9-by-5-inch loaf pans with plastic wrap, leaving 4 inches overhanging each long side so you can wrap the loaves before freezing them.

tip To speed up chopping the strawberries and raspberries, place them in batches in a food processor fitted with the steel blade. Pulse gently until chopped.

2. Place the strawberry gelatin and the hot water in a very large mixing bowl and stir until the gelatin dissolves. Fold in the strawberries, raspberries, and blueberries and stir to combine. Fold in the pieces of angel food cake.

3. Remove the ice cream from the container and cut it into chunks. Fold the chunks of ice cream into the berry mixture until they are just combined. Divide the mixture evenly between the 2 prepared loaf pans. Pull the ends of the plastic wrap up and over the top to seal the ice cream mixture in each pan.

4. Freeze the loaves until they are firm, at least 4 hours or overnight. When you are ready to serve, let the loaves sit at room temperature for 5 minutes, then turn them onto a serving plate. Slice and serve garnished with mint springs.

MAKES 2 LOAVES; SERVES 16 TO 20

Store these loaves, wrapped in aluminum foil, in the freezer for up to 1 month.

Slow-Cooker Chocolate Chip Pudding Cake

▼▼▼

A country cousin of those sophisticated warm cakes that exude molten chocolate when you fork into them, this pudding cake is rich and no trouble to prepare. It "bakes" in a Crock-Pot. The first time I made the big, moist, spoonable chocolate brownie, my kids came back for seconds, then thirds, then fourths. . . . It's now become my standby dessert for gatherings. At informal ones, my guests serve themselves right from the slow cooker, adding as much ice cream as they like. For more formal dinner parties, I spoon out daintier portions in the kitchen. With just a few additional ingredients, cake mix triumphs again. And since the cake takes its leisurely time in the slow cooker, you can leave home knowing you'll come back to a kitchen filled with the scent of chocolate and have dessert at your fingertips.

TO PREP:
8 MINUTES
TO COOK ON HIGH:
3½ HOURS
TO COOK ON LOW:
6½–7 HOURS

1 package (18.25 ounces)
    plain devil's food cake mix
1 package (3.9 ounces) milk chocolate
    or chocolate instant pudding mix
1 container (16 ounces; 2 cups) sour cream
4 large eggs
¾ cup vegetable oil
2 teaspoons pure vanilla extract
1 package (6 ounces; 1 cup) semisweet
    chocolate chips
Vegetable oil cooking spray,
    for misting the slow cooker
Ice cream of your choice, for serving

1. Place the cake mix, pudding mix, sour cream, eggs, oil, and vanilla in a large

mixing bowl. Add 1 cup of water. Beat with an electric mixer on low speed until blended, 30 seconds. Stop the machine and scrape down the side of the bowl. Increase the mixer speed to medium and beat until the ingredients come together and are well blended, 2 minutes longer, scraping down the side of the bowl again if necessary. Fold in the chocolate chips.

2. Mist the bottom and side of a 4½- to 6-quart slow cooker with vegetable oil cooking spray. Transfer the batter to the cooker and cover it. Cook the cake until it is quite puffed in the center and begins to pull away from the side of the cooker, 3½ hours on high heat or 6½ to 7 hours on low heat. Spoon the warm cake into serving bowls. Serve with your favorite ice cream.

SERVES 12

> **tips** Although this cake is at its very best warm on day one, it is still scrumptious on day two and three if there is any left. Reheat leftover servings in the microwave oven for 20 seconds, then serve them with ice cream.
>
> You can use different flavors of pudding mix and vary the kind of chips, too, if you feel like doctoring this recipe.

WINTERTIME BLACKBERRY COBBLER

▼ ▼ ▼

Who says we can't enjoy cobblers when it's cold outside? It has never seemed quite fair to me that at the time of the year when the fruit is finest for making cobblers, I don't want to turn on the oven in my already steaming kitchen. When it's mid-January and there are

TO PREP:
12 MINUTES
TO BAKE:
35–40 MINUTES

six inches of snow outside, *that's* when I crave a cobbler. And if I use frozen blackberries, I can have it. I spoon the cobbler warm from the oven into my family's favorite soup bowls and crown it with vanilla ice cream. A sweet drop batter based on Bisquick makes this cobbler a breeze to assemble.

tip **You can buy frozen blackberries but why not freeze your own during the summer when they're at their peak? It's no trouble. To freeze enough berries for one cobbler, place 8 cups (4 pints) on a rimmed baking sheet in one layer, if possible and put it in the freezer until the berries are frozen solid, 8 hours. Transfer the frozen berries to a resealable plastic bag. The blackberries will keep frozen for up to 6 months.**

Butter, for greasing the baking dish

2 cups plus 2 tablespoons biscuit mix,
    such as Bisquick

1½ cups sugar

1 large egg

½ cup milk

4 tablespoons (½ stick)
    unsalted butter, melted

½ teaspoon pure vanilla extract

½ teaspoon ground cinnamon

2 packages (16 ounces each; 8 cups total;
    see Tip), frozen blackberries, thawed

Vanilla ice cream, for serving

1. Place a rack in the center of the oven and preheat the oven to 375°F.

2. Lightly grease the bottom and sides of a 9-inch square glass or ceramic baking dish with butter. Set the baking dish aside.

3. Place 2 cups of the biscuit mix, ½ cup of the sugar, and the egg, milk, butter, vanilla, and cinnamon in a large mixing bowl and stir with a fork until blended, 20 to 30 seconds. Set the cobbler topping aside.

4. Place the blackberries with their juice, the remaining 2 tablespoons of biscuit mix, and all but a heaping 1 tablespoon of the remaining sugar in a large mixing bowl and stir to combine. Spoon the berry mixture into the prepared baking dish and smooth the top. Spoon the cobbler topping over the blackberries in 9 large dollops. Sprinkle the remaining tablespoon of sugar over the cobbler.

5. Bake the cobbler until the filling is bubbling and the topping has browned, 35 to 40 minutes. Remove the cobbler from the oven and serve it at once with vanilla ice cream.

SERVES 9

Store this cobbler, covered with plastic wrap, in the refrigerator for up to 4 days.

BUTTERSCOTCH PECAN FOCACCIA

▼ ▼ ▼

Bread for dessert? Why not? This is a sweet and enticing focaccia, perfect to bake during the holidays or any time, for that matter. It is pretty set out whole on a wooden cutting board, surrounded by cheeses and fruit, and it is even better cut into squares and served warm with a cozy cup of tea.

TO PREP:
15–20 MINUTES
TO BAKE:
15–18 MINUTES

1 package (10 ounces) refrigerated
    pizza crust dough
2 tablespoons melted butter
½ cup butterscotch chips
¼ cup firmly packed light brown sugar
¼ cup finely chopped pecans

1. Place a rack in the center of the oven and preheat the oven to 400°F.

2. Unroll the dough onto an ungreased rimmed baking sheet. Using your hands, form the dough into an 11-by-7-inch rectangle. With your fingertips, make indentations all over the dough. Drizzle the melted butter evenly over the dough. Scatter the butterscotch chips, brown sugar, and pecans on top.

3. Bake the focaccia until it is golden brown, 15 to 18 minutes. Remove the pan from the oven and, when the focaccia is cool enough to handle, cut it into squares, using a pizza cutter, and serve.

MAKES 1 FOCACCIA

Store the focaccia, covered in aluminum foil or plastic wrap, at room temperature for up to 2 days.

tips **Want to serve this focaccia for dinner? Substitute ¼ cup of golden raisins for the butterscotch chips.**

You can also make a variation with cherries and chocolate. Brush the dough with the melted butter, then sprinkle ¼ cup of chopped dried cherries and ¼ cup of semisweet chocolate chips on top.

CINNAMON PALMIERS

▼ ▼ ▼

TO PREP AND THAW:
28 MINUTES
TO BAKE:
10–12 MINUTES

The sweet pastries called *palmiers,* also known as elephant's ears, take their name from their resemblance to palm leaves (*palmier* is French for palm). Envision sugar layered between sheets of puff pastry that have been folded, cut into strips, and baked until crisp. And these pastries can be made more quickly than you can dig your heirloom teacups out of the cupboard. That's because they begin with frozen puff pastry, one of my favorite convenience foods. I've added a touch of cinnamon to the classic *palmier.*

tip To make savory palmiers, substitute grated Parmesan cheese and minced fresh rosemary for the sugar and cinnamon.

1 sheet frozen puff pastry dough (half of a 17.3-ounce package), thawed for 20 minutes
8 tablespoons sugar
1 teaspoon ground cinnamon

1. Place 1 rack in the center and 1 rack in the top third of the oven and preheat the oven to 425°F.

2. Unfold the thawed sheet of puff pastry and cut it in half lengthwise. On a clean work surface, roll each piece out to an 11-by-7-inch rectangle. Sprinkle each piece with 2 tablespoons of the sugar and ¼ teaspoon of the cinnamon. Working with 1 piece of pastry dough at a time, fold both short edges toward the center so that the edges just meet in the middle. Sprinkle the top of the folded piece with 2 tablespoons of the sugar and ¼ teaspoon of the cinnamon.

Fold each side in half again so that the edges just meet in the middle, then fold the piece of dough in half again and press down on it gently. You will have 8 layers. Repeat the process with the remaining piece of pastry dough and the sugar and cinnamon.

3. With a sharp knife, cut the folded pieces of puff pastry crosswise into ½-inch slices. Place them, with a cut side up, on 2 ungreased baking sheets. Place the baking sheets in the oven, positioning 1 sheet on the center rack and the other on the top rack.

4. Bake the *palmiers* until they are golden brown and crisp, 10 to 12 minutes. Rotate the baking sheets after the *palmiers* have baked for 5 minutes. Remove the baking sheets from the oven and, with a metal spatula, immediately transfer the *palmiers* to a wire rack to cool for 5 minutes, then serve.

MAKES 32 TO 34 PALMIERS

Store these palmiers, *in a container with a tight-fitting cover, at room temperature for up to 2 days.*

SPICED PLUM PASTRIES

▼ ▼ ▼

I like having a pie all to myself. That's why I favor these marvelous miniature pastries that fill refrigerated crescent roll dough with a mix of plums, sugar, and cinnamon. They bake up crusty and brown and are delicious served in a bowl with vanilla ice cream or eaten plain right out of your hand. Cleanup is a breeze because the pastries pop out of the muffin tin so easily.

TO PREP:
15 MINUTES
TO BAKE:
12–15 MINUTES

1 package (8 ounces) refrigerated
    crescent rolls
4 fresh ripe medium-size red plums,
    halved, pitted, and chopped
4 tablespoons sugar
¼ teaspoon ground cinnamon
3 tablespoons butter, diced
Vanilla ice cream, for serving
    (optional)

1. Place a rack in the center of the oven and preheat the oven to 400°F.

2. Open the package of crescent roll dough and separate it into 8 triangles along the perforated lines. Into each cup of an 8-cup (3-inch) muffin tin place 1 triangle of dough, letting the corners hang over the edge of the cup. Place a generous tablespoon of chopped plum on top of each piece of dough, then add a teaspoon of sugar to each. Dust the plums with the cinnamon and dot them with the butter. Pull the corners of each piece of dough up and fold them over on top of each other. Loosely tuck

tip Instead of plums, use 2 large sliced bananas or 4 chopped peaches. For that matter, any soft fruit will work well and cook down in these quick-cooking pastries.

the edges down into the muffin cups. Sprinkle the top of each pastry with some of the remaining 4 teaspoons of sugar.

3. Bake the pastries until they are well browned and the plums are bubbling, 12 to 15 minutes. The bottom of the pastry will still be soft. Remove the muffin tin from the oven and let the pastries rest 2 to 3 minutes. Slide a fork underneath each pastry to remove it and transfer it to a bowl or plate. Serve vanilla ice cream on the side, if desired.

SERVES 8

Store these little pastries, in a cake saver or under a cake dome, at room temperature for up to 3 days.

Weekday Wonders

—▼—

DINNER DOCTOR SAYS Just because it's Tuesday, just because time is short, just because some nights getting dinner on the table is hard enough, does not mean dessert is out of the question. These quick yummy finales can fit into the tightest of schedules. After all, if you've survived an especially long Tuesday, don't you deserve a treat?

POTATO CHIP COOKIES

▼ ▼ ▼

After noticing the crowd hovering over these cookies at a recent gathering, I wormed my way through to the table and found a plate of what appeared to be plain old butter cookies. I took one, nevertheless, and found the cookie dissolved deliciously in my mouth, with a teasing interplay of sweet and salty. These were no ordinary butter cookies, I concluded, and I knew I had to find the recipe. Well, I must admit I was aghast at first when I learned they were butter cookies to which crushed potato chips had been added! Then I stopped and thought. Remember what crushed chips do for a bland tuna noodle casserole? They're even better in cookies.

TO PREP:
10 MINUTES
TO BAKE:
10–12 MINUTES
TO COOL:
30 MINUTES

1 cup (2 sticks) unsalted butter,
     at room temperature

1 cup granulated sugar

3 cups all-purpose flour

2 teaspoons pure vanilla extract

1½ cups crushed potato chips
     (see Tip)

1 cup confectioners' sugar

1. Place a rack in the center of the oven and preheat the oven to 350°F.

2. Place the butter and granulated sugar in a large mixing bowl and beat with an electric mixer on low speed until the mixture is well blended, 30 seconds. Increase the speed to medium and beat until fluffy, 30 seconds longer. Add the flour and the

tip Use your favorite plain potato chips here—but no barbecued or green onion, just plain chips, smooth or ridged!

vanilla and beat on low speed until the flour is just incorporated. There's no need to scrape down the side of the bowl. Add the potato chips and beat on low until the batter just comes together and the potato chips are incorporated, 30 to 45 seconds.

3. Drop the batter by teaspoonfuls onto ungreased baking sheets (you'll need 2), leaving an inch between the cookies. Bake the cookies until they are lightly browned around the edges but still soft in the center, 10 to 12 minutes. Remove the baking sheets from the oven and let the cookies rest on them for 1 minute.

4. Transfer the cookies to a wire rack to cool, then immediately generously sprinkle half of the confectioners' sugar over them. Let the cookies cool completely, 30 minutes. Sprinkle the cookies with the remaining confectioners' sugar before serving.

MAKES 48 COOKIES

Store these cookies, in a plastic container or cookie jar, at room temperature for up to 1 week. Or, after they are cool but before you sprinkle them with the confectioners' sugar, freeze them in a resealable plastic bag for up to 6 months. Thaw the cookies overnight in the refrigerator before serving.

15 WAYS TO DOCTOR A BROWNIE MIX

Let me make this clear: Brownie mixes beg you to add your magic to them. Here are a few suggestions for how to take a plain 18 to 21 ounces brownie mix and make it better.

1 Sprinkle tiny M&M candies over the top before baking.

2 Spread cinnamon, white chocolate, peanut butter, or milk chocolate chips over the brownies right after you take them out of the oven. The chips will melt into a thin glaze.

3 Add 1 tablespoon of pure vanilla extract to the brownie batter.

4 Bake the brownies for 10 to 15 minutes less than called for instead of following the baking time on the box. They should still be fudgy in the center when you remove the pan from the oven. Spread the cooled under-baked brownies with a quick ganache made by adding ¾ cup heavy (whipping) cream that has been brought just to the boil to a cup of semisweet chocolate chips and stirring until the chips are melted and smooth.

5 Add ¼ teaspoon of mint extract to the batter. Or go one step further and fold chopped peppermint patties into the batter.

6 Stir a handful of roughly chopped caramels into the batter.

7 Add 1 tablespoon of powdered instant coffee and a pinch of cinnamon to the batter.

8 Top the baked brownies with caramel topping, sweetened flaked coconut, and chopped toasted pecans.

9 Swirl softened cream cheese into the batter before baking the brownies. For an unusual twist, use orange- or strawberry-flavored cream cheese.

10 Stir sliced almonds, chopped dried cherries, and a dash of almond extract into the batter.

11 Make triple chocolate brownies by stirring white, milk, and semisweet chocolate chips into the batter.

12 Add chopped macadamia nuts and white chocolate chips to the batter and drop spoonfuls onto a lightly greased cookie sheet for easy brownie cookies. Bake until crisp at the edges, but soft in the center, 8 to 10 minutes.

13 Fold a mashed ripe banana into the batter just before baking.

14 Swab hot baked brownies with Kahlúa when they come out of the oven.

15 For a nostalgic version, fold chopped black walnuts and a big handful of chocolate chips into the batter.

BROWNIE DROPS

▼ ▼ ▼

Brownies meet the cookie jar here in the form of chewy, chocolaty, fudgy cookies that won't be around for long. I love how brownie mix makes these cookies a snap to prepare, and the goodies you add to the batter add crunch and extra chocolate flavor. For kids, add milk-chocolate chips, but you might want to leave out the nuts. For adults, I'd go with semisweet chips or chopped bittersweet chocolate and walnuts or pecans—whatever you have on hand. To really dress up the cookies, drizzle melted white chocolate over them.

TO PREP:
15 MINUTES
TO BAKE:
8–10 MINUTES

1 package (21.2 ounces) brownie mix
    with chocolate added
8 tablespoons (1 stick) unsalted butter,
    melted
2 large eggs
1 teaspoon pure vanilla extract
1 package (6 ounces; 1 cup) semisweet or
    milk-chocolate chips
1 cup pre-chopped walnuts or pecans
    (optional)

1. Place a rack in the center of the oven and preheat the oven to 350°F.

2. Place the brownie mix, butter, eggs, and vanilla in a large mixing bowl. Beat with an electric mixer on low speed until the ingredients come together, 30 seconds. Stop the machine and scrape down the side of the bowl with a rubber spatula. Add the chocolate chips and nuts, if

tip This is a fast recipe, but you can make it even faster by using Silpat baking mats. These mats create a non-stick surface for the cookies, and you can bake batch after batch on the mats without having to let them cool down. (You'll need one mat for each baking sheet.) When the baking is over, wash the mats in warm soapy water, then wash and rinse your baking sheets. You can purchase Silpat mats at kitchen shops.

using. Beat on low until the batter is thick and well blended, 30 seconds longer.

3. Drop the batter by generous tablespoons onto ungreased baking sheets (you'll need 2), leaving an inch between the cookies. Bake the cookies until they are crisp around the edges and puffed up but still a little soft in the center, 8 to 10 minutes. Remove the baking sheets from the oven and immediately transfer the cookies to wire racks to cool for 5 minutes.

MAKES 50 COOKIES

Store these cookies, in a plastic container or cookie jar, at room temperature for up to 1 week. Or freeze them in a resealable plastic bag for up to 6 months. Thaw the cookies overnight in the refrigerator before serving.

It's How You Slice a Brownie That Counts

—▼—

DINNER DOCTOR SAYS Who says a brownie has to be square? Add some pizzazz.

1. Bake brownies 20 to 25 minutes in a pie pan, then cut them into wedges instead of squares.

2. Use a smaller, deeper pan for thicker brownies. They'll bake in about 40 minutes, then cut them extra large for the greatest appeal or smaller for tea parties.

3. Cut brownies into rounds with a biscuit cutter and sandwich two together with raspberry jam. Dust the top with confectioners' sugar.

4. Dust brownie triangles, squares, or rectangles with confectioners' sugar.

5. Crumble up brownies and serve them over ice cream.

BUTTERSCOTCH PECAN SAUCEPAN BLONDIES

▼ ▼ ▼

I dream about these bars. Maybe I'm so obsessed with them because they are delightfully chewy and loaded with flavor. Or is it the combination of butterscotch chips and pecans? They're no trouble at all to whip together, and they use ingredients I just about always have in my pantry or refrigerator. The blondies are perfect for gift giving, sharing at the office—even serving with some highbrow ice cream when company comes.

TO PREP:
10 MINUTES
TO BAKE:
30–35 MINUTES
TO COOL:
20 MINUTES

Vegetable oil cooking spray,
    for misting the baking dish
All-purpose flour, for dusting
    the baking dish
12 tablespoons (1½ sticks)
    butter
1⅓ cups firmly packed light
    brown sugar
⅔ cup granulated sugar
3 cups biscuit mix, such as Bisquick
1 teaspoon pure vanilla extract
3 large eggs
1 cup butterscotch chips
1 cup pre-chopped pecans

tip To turn this recipe into Chocolate, Oat, and Walnut Saucepan Blondies, substitute semisweet chocolate chips for the butterscotch chips and use walnuts instead of pecans. Reduce the biscuit mix to 2 cups and add 1 cup of quick-cooking oatmeal.

1. Place a rack in the center of the oven and preheat the oven to 350°F.

2. Lightly mist a 13-by-9-inch baking dish with vegetable oil cooking spray, then dust it with flour. Shake out the excess flour. Set the baking dish aside.

3. Place the butter in a 2-quart saucepan over medium heat. Using a wooden spoon, stir the butter until it melts. Add the brown sugar and cook, stirring, until it darkens and dissolves, 3 minutes. Remove the pan from the heat and add the granulated sugar, biscuit mix, vanilla, and eggs, stirring until the eggs are incorporated, 1 minute. Fold in the butterscotch chips and pecans. Scrape the batter into the prepared baking dish.

4. Bake the blondies until the center is glossy brown and a little soft but the edges rise up and are crusty, 30 to 35 minutes. Remove the baking dish from the oven and place it on a wire rack to cool for 20 minutes. Cut the blondies into roughly 1½-inch squares.

MAKES 48 SQUARES

Store these blondies, covered with plastic wrap or aluminum foil, at room temperature for up to 4 days or in the refrigerator for up to 1 week. Or freeze them, in a resealable plastic bag, for up to 6 months. Thaw the blondies overnight in the refrigerator before serving.

EASY LEMON CHEESECAKE BARS

▼ ▼ ▼

My children love these cheesecake bars so much they willingly squeeze lemon juice for me when I make them. You'll find packages of graham cracker crumbs in the baking aisle at the supermarket. If you have some graham crackers on hand and want to make your own crumbs, you'll need one sleeve of crackers to make one and a half cups of crumbs.

1½ cups graham cracker crumbs

⅓ cup pecans

⅓ cup sugar

4 tablespoons (½ stick) butter, melted

2 packages (8 ounces each) reduced-fat cream cheese, at room temperature

1 can (14 ounces) sweetened condensed milk

2 large eggs

1 teaspoon grated lemon zest

½ cup fresh lemon juice

TO PREP:
10 MINUTES
TO BAKE:
28–32 MINUTES
TO COOL:
1 HOUR

1. Place a rack in the center of the oven and preheat the oven to 325°F.

2. Place the graham cracker crumbs, pecans, sugar, and butter in a food processor and process in pulses until well combined. Set aside ⅓ cup of the crumb mixture for a topping. Press the remaining crumb mixture evenly into the bottom of a 13-by-9-inch glass or ceramic baking dish. Bake the crumb crust until browned and firm, 6 to 7 minutes. Remove the baking dish from the oven and place it on a wire rack to cool. Leave the oven on.

3. Place the cream cheese in a large mixing bowl and beat it with an electric mixer on low speed until fluffy, 1 minute. Add the sweetened condensed milk and beat for 1 minute, then add the eggs and lemon zest and juice. Stop the machine and scrape down the side of the bowl with a rubber spatula. Increase the mixer speed to medium and beat until the filling is well combined, 1 minute longer. Pour the filling over the cooled crust, smoothing it out with a rubber spatula. Scatter the reserved crumb mixture over the top.

4. Bake the bars until they are firm around the edges and a toothpick inserted in the center comes out clean, 28 to 32 minutes. Remove the baking dish from the oven and place it on a wire rack to cool for 1 hour. Cut into roughly 3-by-2-inch bars.

tip Make sure the cream cheese is very soft. And the sweetened condensed milk shouldn't be cold when you add it to the cream cheese or it will create lumps in the cream cheese.

MAKES 18 BARS

Store these bars, loosely covered with plastic wrap, in the refrigerator for up to 1 week. They can be served either at room temperature or chilled.

THE DINNER DOCTOR PANTRY

▼ ▼ ▼

To be a dinner doctor you need a collection of ingredients you can call on to doctor ho-hum dishes. There's a wealth of foods on supermarket shelves to help you do this—everything from the familiar hot pepper sauce to the more exotic Thai peanut sauce; from canned sliced green olives to store-bought pesto. And, of course, the now indispensable seasoned canned tomatoes and pre-shredded cheeses. Here, you'll find a list of ingredients that are particularly useful to keep on hand and that in most cases store well—not the usual staples like eggs, butter, flour, sugar, or onions that are likely to be in your kitchen, but some reliable items that turn up in many of the recipes in this book.

If your pantry is well stocked with ingredients to doctor, such as frozen pre-cleaned shrimp, pastas, canned tuna, frozen ground beef round and chicken breasts, pre-washed salad greens, refrigerated crescent rolls, chicken noodle soup, and cake mixes, you'll always have at your fingertips everything you need to prepare a meal quickly.

Of course, you don't need to stock everything at once. After looking in your cupboards, refrigerator, and freezer, consult the lists here. See what strikes your fancy, then make a shopping list. It will be a prescription for no-fuss dinner doctoring.

In the cupboard

Once open, some of these items should be stored in the refrigerator. Check the manufacturer's label for storing instructions.

spices

ground allspice
dried basil
bay leaves
cayenne pepper
chili powder
cinnamon sticks and
    ground cinnamon
Creole seasoning
cumin seed and ground
    cumin
curry powder
fennel seeds
hot red pepper flakes
Italian seasoning
jerk seasoning
ground nutmeg
dried oregano
paprika
poppy seeds
seasoned salts
taco seasoning
dried thyme

nuts

pine nuts
pre-chopped pecans and
    walnuts
pre-sliced almonds

spirits

dry red wine
dry white wine
sherry
vermouth

ready-made baking essentials

CAKE & SWEET MUFFIN MIXES

blueberry muffin mix*
brownie mix*
semisweet chocolate chips
chocolate instant pudding
    mix
cinnamon swirl muffin mix
unsweetened cocoa powder
Devil's food cake mix, both
    with and without
    pudding
German chocolate cake mix
lemon cake mix
lemon instant pudding mix
lemon–poppy seed muffin
    mix
orange cake mix
spice cake mix
vanilla instant pudding mix
yellow cake mix
white cake mix

SAVORY BREAD MIXES

biscuit mix, such as Bisquick
bran muffin mix
corn bread mix
corn muffin mix
self-rising cornmeal mix

canned soups & broths

cream of asparagus
beef broth
cream of celery
cream of chicken
low-sodium chicken broth
chicken noodle soup*
cream of mushroom
tomato soup

canned tomatoes & tomato sauces

marinara sauce*
canned crushed tomatoes
canned/ diced tomatoes,
    plain and your favorite
    seasoned ones, such as
    with green chiles; with
    basil, garlic, and
    oregano; or with
    balsamic vinegar, basil,
    and olive oil
canned stewed tomatoes
tomato paste
tomato purée
tomato sauce

vegetables in cans or jars

BEANS

baked beans*
black beans
black-eye peas
cannellini beans
chickpeas
Great Northern beans
kidney beans
navy beans
pinto beans
refried beans

OTHER VEGETABLES

artichokes and artichoke
    hearts
beets
carrots
corn—kernels both plain
    and with red and green
    peppers, and cream-
    style corn
mushroom pieces

other canned goods

chili with beans
lump crabmeat
cranberry sauce
crushed pineapple
evaporated milk

*Check the index for a box containing "15 Ways to Doctor" this ingredient.

mandarin orange sections
pumpkin
sweetened condensed milk
tuna*

crackers & chips

bagel chips
corn chips
pita crisps
potato chips
soda crackers
tortilla chips

pastas & noodles

angel hair
couscous
egg noodles
fettuccine
macaroni and macaroni
    and cheese mix*
no-boil lasagna noodles
pasta shells
penne
rotini
spaghetti
vermicelli
ziti

rice*

arborio
basmati
jasmine
rice mixes, such as
    Rice-A-Roni

bottled salad dressings

balsamic vinaigrette
Caesar salad dressing
Italian dressing
olive oil and vinegar
    dressing
poppy seed dressing
ranch dressing
red wine vinaigrette
sesame salad dressing

miscellaneous

Asian (dark) sesame oil
barbecue sauce
bread crumbs
canned chopped green
    chiles
capers
chipotle peppers in
    adobo sauce
cocktail sauce
croutons
prepared curry pastes
garlic
pre-chopped ginger
Good Seasons Italian salad
    dressing mix
hoisin sauce
hot pepper sauce,
    such as Tabasco
hummus, both regular
    and black bean
honey
jalapeño peppers
mustards, including
    Creole, Dijon, and
    honey-mustard
olives, including kalamata
    and pre-sliced green
    olives
olive salad (tapenade)
    and olive paste
peanut butter
pickle relish
pimiento peppers in cans
prepared pesto
prepared roasted red
    peppers
prepared salsas*, including
    tomatillo
sun-dried tomatoes
Thai fish sauce
Thai garlic and chile
    sauce
Thai peanut sauce
vinegars—balsamic, cider,
    red wine, and rice
Worcestershire sauce

In the refrigerator

cheeses

PRE-CRUMBLED

blue cheese
feta, both plain and
    tomato-basil

PRE-SHREDDED

Cheddar
Italian cheese blend
Mexican blend
Monterey Jack, both plain
    and with jalapeños
mozzarella
Parmesan and pre-grated
    Parmesan
Swiss cheese

breads and rolls

refrigerated bread-stick
    dough
refrigerated corn bread
    twist dough
refrigerated crescent rolls
refrigerated pizza crust
    dough
refrigerated unbaked
    French bread*
tortillas, both corn and
    flour

dairy products

buttermilk
cream cheese*
plain low-fat yogurt
reduced-fat sour cream

fresh herbs

basil
chives
cilantro
dill
mint

parsley
oregano
tarragon
thyme

salad fixings

Caesar salad kit*
pre-shredded carrots
pre-shredded coleslaw
   and broccoli slaw
pre-shredded iceberg
   lettuce
pre-washed Italian blend
   lettuce*
deli potato salad*
pre-washed spinach
pre-washed spring mix
   salad greens*

miscellaneous

Alfredo-style pasta sauce
bacon
deli-roast chicken*
fresh ginger
prepared horseradish

pre-sliced mushrooms
refrigerated cooked
   polenta, both plain
   and with cilantro
   and green chiles
smoked salmon
sweetened flaked
   coconut
cheese-filled tortellini

In the freezer

breads and pastries

unbaked biscuits
phyllo shells
pound cake*
puff pastry
pumpkin pie*

frozen vegetables

chopped broccoli
corn, both kernels and
   creamed

French cut green beans
mixed vegetables
peas*
potatoes—including with
   onions, with onions
   and bell peppers,
   and mashed
spinach, both chopped*
   and creamed
winter squash

miscellaneous

chicken—shredded
   chicken, chicken
   breasts, and popcorn
   chicken
ground beef round,
   frozen in one-pound
   packages
ice cream—your favorite
   flavors
macaroni and cheese*
orange juice concentrate
pie crusts
pre-cleaned shrimp

CONVERSION TABLES

Approximate Equivalents

1 stick butter = 8 tbs = 4 oz = ½ cup

1 cup all-purpose presifted flour or
dried bread crumbs = 5 oz

1 cup granulated sugar = 8 oz

1 cup (packed) brown sugar = 6 oz

1 cup confectioners' sugar = 4½ oz

1 cup honey or syrup = 12 oz

1 cup grated cheese = 4 oz

1 cup dried beans = 6 oz

1 large egg = about 2 oz = about 3 tbs

1 egg yolk = about 1 tbs

1 egg white = about 2 tbs

Weight Conversions

U.S.	METRIC	U.S.	METRIC
½ oz	15 g	7 oz	200 g
1 oz	30 g	8 oz	250 g
1½ oz	45 g	9 oz	275 g
2 oz	60 g	10 oz	300 g
2½ oz	75 g	11 oz	325 g
3 oz	90 g	12 oz	350 g
3½ oz	100 g	13 oz	375 g
4 oz	125 g	14 oz	400 g
5 oz	150 g	15 oz	450 g
6 oz	175 g	1 lb	500 g

Please note that all conversions are approximate but close enough to be useful when converting from one system to another.

Liquid Conversions

U.S.	IMPERIAL	METRIC
2 tbs	1 fl oz	30 ml
3 tbs	1½ fl oz	45 ml
¼ cup	2 fl oz	60 ml
⅓ cup	2½ fl oz	75 ml
⅓ cup + 1 tbs	3 fl oz	90 ml
⅓ cup + 2 tbs	3½ fl oz	100 ml
½ cup	4 fl oz	125 ml
⅔ cup	5 fl oz	150 ml
¾ cup	6 fl oz	175 ml
¾ cup + 2 tbs	7 fl oz	200 ml
1 cup	8 fl oz	250 ml
1 cup + 2 tbs	9 fl oz	275 ml
1¼ cups	10 fl oz	300 ml
1⅓ cups	11 fl oz	325 ml
1½ cups	12 fl oz	350 ml
1⅔ cups	13 fl oz	375 ml
1¾ cups	14 fl oz	400 ml
1¾ cups + 2 tbs	15 fl oz	450 ml
2 cups (1 pint)	16 fl oz	500 ml
2½ cups	20 fl oz (1 pint)	600 ml
3¾ cups	1½ pints	900 ml
4 cups	1¾ pints	1 liter

Oven Temperatures

°F	Gas	°C	°F	Gas	°C
250	½	120	400	6	200
275	1	140	425	7	220
300	2	150	450	8	230
325	3	160			
350	4	180	475	9	240
375	5	190	500	10	260

Note: Reduce the temperature by 20°C (68°F) for fan-assisted ovens.

BIBLIOGRAPHY

▼ ▼ ▼

My thanks to the following good books and their authors for giving me food for thought:

Anderson, Jean. *The American Century Cookbook: The Most Popular Recipes of the 20th Century.* New York: Clarkson Potter, 1997.

———, and Elaine Hanna. *The New Doubleday Cookbook.* New York: Bantam Doubleday Dell, 1985.

General Mills, Inc. *Betty Crocker's Bisquick Cookbook.* Minneapolis: IDG Books Worldwide, 2000.

Child, Julia, Louisette Bertholle, and Simone Beck. *Mastering the Art of French Cooking,* Vol. 1. New York: Knopf, 2001.

Campbell Soup Company. *Cooking with Soup,* 14th ed. Camden, NJ: Campbell Soup Company, 1977.

Herbst, Sharon Tyler. *The New Food Lover's Companion: Comprehensive Definitions of Over 4,000 Food, Wine and Culinary Terms,* 2nd ed. Hauppauge, NY: Barron's Educational Services, Inc., 1995.

Krohn, Norman Odya. *Menu Mystique: The Diner's Guide to Fine Food & Drink.* Middle Village, NY: Jonathan David, 1983.

Martha White Foods, Inc. *Martha White's Southern Sampler,* Nashville: Rutledge Hill Press, 1989.

Rosso, Julie, and Sheila Lukins. *The Silver Palate Cookbook.* New York: Workman, 1979.

———, with Sarah Leah Chase. *The Silver Palate Good Times Cookbook.* New York: Workman, 1984.

Villas, James, with Martha Pearl Villas. *My Mother's Southern Kitchen.* New York: Macmillan, 1994.

INDEX

▼▼▼